Myth in American History

Myth in American History

PATRICK GERSTER & NICHOLAS CORDS

Lakewood State Junior College
White Bear Lake, Minnesota

GLENCOE PRESS

A division of Benziger Bruce & Glencoe, Inc.
Encino, California
Collier Macmillan Publishers
London

Extensive quotes from Dixon Wecter, The Hero in America: A Chronicle of Hero-Worship reprinted courtesy of the publisher, Charles Scribner's Sons.

Glencoe Press
A division of Benziger Bruce & Glencoe, Inc.
17337 Ventura Boulevard
Encino, California 91316
Collier Macmillan Canada, Ltd.

Library of Congress catalog card number: 76-4061

2 3 4 5 6 7 8 9   80 79 78

ISBN 0-02-473290-7

We wish to express our thanks to
　　Carole
　　Maggie
　　Mark, Jennifer, and Jason
　　James, John, Nicholas, and Daniel
　　Ms. Loving
　　and Van

Mundus vult decipi
(The world wants to be deceived.)

CONTENTS

ix

PREFACE

Myth in American History is a narrative text which explores the entire span of the nation's history. It touches on traditional topics as well as those that are less traditional, including the historical experience of minorities. Particular attention has been given to those events and personalities which, because of their usual emphasis in American history, have become objects of the greatest number of myths. The authors have also attempted to demonstrate the day-to-day tyranny which mythically based ideas and policies can have. In linking our commentary to the compelling theme of myth we have sought to reflect the very latest in scholarly research in a lively writing style.

The book is organized into ten chapters, within each of which are four sections. Historical events are examined in chronological order. Each chapter begins with a preview—a brief comment that establishes the background and themes, and sets the stage for the reading that follows. In most instances, the preview is a sort of precis of the subject matter of the chapter. In other instances, however, the preview examines topics that are not looked at further in the chapter. The previews therefore serve a dual function: as an introduction and as a supplement. The illustrations in *Myth in American History* are rather special. Unlike many textbooks, they were not selected simply to offer the reader a respite. They were chosen, instead, because they highlight the role that illustrators, cartoonists, photographers, and artists have played in visualizing the nation's past. Art in its many forms has made a significant contribution to the mythmaking process in America.

Before one embarks on reading *Myth in American History*, one should keep this thought in mind: There are no absolutes in history. It is not possible to categorize history into what is false on the one hand and what is true on the other. Rather, most events of the past involve an intricate blend of what might be called "history as actuality" and "history as perceived"; that is, they represent both what happened and what has come to be believed as what happened.

American history, in short, is a combination of facts, cultural prejudices, stereotypes, romantic images, nostalgia, distortions in the name of patriotism, rationalizations, the good and bad scholarship of historians as well as national hopes, dreams, and ideals. Therein, perhaps, lies the continued fascination and usefulness of their history for succeeding generations of Americans. We trust that *Myth in American History* will illuminate that fascination and usefulness in a meaningful way.

Patrick Gerster
Nicholas Cords

INTRODUCTION

The average student gathers a knowledge of American history from several sources. Most students first study the nation's history in about the seventh grade. Later, in senior high school, they devote another year to this subject. In college, when supposedly introduced to the latest scholarship, the student is expected to obtain a solid grasp of the truth of the past. These formal stages of study, however, also tend to be the time when one is introduced to the nation's rather elaborate collection of historical myths. For despite the illusion of accuracy associated with such academic experiences, it is significant that historians themselves, and the textbooks they write, have been proven to contribute substantially to both the origins and survival of American mythology.

In addition to the academic experience, a vast array of informational sources constantly assault the average citizen with a barrage of historical "facts." Radio, television, and the movies, for example, offer recreations of the past in sight and sound to eager audiences, more often with an eye on drama than on solid research. Similarly, novels, poetry, political rhetoric, paintings, jokes, anecdotes, ballads, oral traditions and folklore, political cartoons, and culturally created stereotypes also contribute their share to one's impression of the past. And for the mobile twentieth-century American, vacation pilgrimages to historical "shrines" can be added to the list. The attractiveness of a tourist area, apparently, is in direct proportion to the number of myths and legends which have come to surround it. Such places as Independence Hall in Philadelphia, the battlefield at Gettysburg, and the Mt. Rushmore Memorial in South Dakota add dimension and understanding to their perceptions of America's historical saga. Unfortunately, what tends to happen in such encounters is not an increase in historical understanding but a further distortion of the heroic reputations of the events and characters involved.

Any one of these experiences of itself holds, no doubt, the potential for only minor deceptions about the past. But taken collectively, they create impressions which very often bear only a remote resemblance to historical reality. Together they form a body of false beliefs which greatly influence the way a person thinks and feels about the past, and thus the present and the future. It is precisely because of these artificially created and emotionally charged mental pictures, or *images*, that false beliefs about history, accepted as valid, begin to form in peoples' minds, somewhat like a colorful mosaic. Small, brightly colored "pieces" of the past held together by an individual's emotional attachment to the nation, become the raw materials from which historical myths are created and later reinforced by song, story, nostalgia, and the media.

The selected historical myths discussed and analyzed in this book can best be understood as a series of *false beliefs* about America's past. They are false beliefs, however, which have traditionally been accepted as "true" and taken to be "real." Thus, one must come to see that myths remain both true and false simultaneously. They are true in the sense that they are believed; they are false in the sense that they often enjoy only a remote relationship to what most informed historians have judged actually happened in the past. It is therefore well to remember that there is a point at which myth and reality intersect; at that given point, they become one and the same. Myth becomes reality precisely when people act as if the myth were true and their beliefs and attitudes are based upon it. In fact, the making of myths is a twofold process by which a culture orders its world and by which it serves to perpetuate its grandest illusions.

Myth as a *false belief* will be our definition of myth in this book. But the reader must recognize that equal emphasis must be given to *both* words. It would be a mistake to assume that one need only identify misconceptions about the past and then discard them as without significance, cast on the dustheap of useless mythical nonsense no longer accepted as true. A far more useful approach to the problem of myth in American history is to realize that myths have a real existence in the minds of their believers and thus are psychologically true even though factually false. Once one understands the ways in which certain commonly held beliefs about the past are deficient, romanticized, and inaccurate, it is essential that one go further and consider how these errors in understanding came to be accepted and inspired the actions of individuals and the American nation.

Viewed in this way, on two levels, the use of mythology as a tool for analyzing America's past brings a better understanding of the complex, and at times contradictory, affairs of the nation. Hopefully, this selective study of myths in American history will launch the reader on an endlessly fascinating journey through the usable past of the United States.

Myth in American History

1 Myths of Early America

PREVIEW

The Native Americans: Beyond the Stereotypes

In the beginning were the Native Americans. Yet only recently has anyone become aware of the glaring omission of these peoples from American history. Up to the present, any measure of understanding has seldom transcended the level of myth. As a result, Native Americans have been the victims of both neglect and distortion. Since the Native Americans shaped the fundamental outlines and directions of American history, greater effort must be made to correct the historical record. In attempting to restore balance to American history by taking into account the Indians and their accomplishments, however, one is immediately confronted with the problem that Indians more often than not have been treated as stereotypes.

Convinced that the Indians have always been vastly inferior to whites in their customs, technology, and government, many Americans have been quick to conclude that all Indians were savages, stereotyped as the Bloodthirsty Savage. Indians as Bloodthirsty Savages are portrayed as ruthless, treacherous killers. They were a menace and a peril to the settlers whose destiny was to subdue and eradicate barbarism on the advancing frontier. According to this myth, whites forged westward in search of adventure while Indians were aimless nomads. The white communities, one is told, lived in settlements while the natives were content with simple huts. A second stereotype, however, portrays the Indian as a child of nature and a Noble Red Man. The child-of-nature Indian is a precious reminder of a time when people loved the land and lived a simpler, more natural existence. Based on this myth, famous individuals such as Pontiac, Joseph Brant, Tecumseh, and Chief Joseph become instant heroes. Neither extreme, however, does justice to Native Americans, a justice they seek and deserve.

A sensitive balance must be found somewhere between the Indian as either bloodthirsty or noble. Both myths fundamentally deny the versatility of the Indian legacy. The caricature of the Indian as a Bloodthirsty Savage must be rejected not only because not all Indians were warlike, but also because of the obvious contributions which American Indians have consistently made in the areas of language, oral literature, medicine, art, religion, agriculture, and ecology. The Noble Red Man image must not be overemphasized, however, because it only serves to create a new kind of imbalance, the reverse of that which has plagued traditional histories for so long.

To arrive at a historically valid appreciation of the role of the American Indian in the nation's history, one must recognize the many ways in which historians themselves have helped preserve the stereotypes of the past. Even such a reputable scholar-historian as Frederick Jackson Turner has influenced historical understanding against Native Americans. The famous "Turner Thesis," first put forward in 1893, monopolized historical debate for decades, and emphasized the importance of the frontier to the development of American institutions and traditions. In the process of exposing this neglected area to research and study, Turner stated that "the existence of an area of free land, its continuous recession, and the advance of American settlement westward, explain American development."[1] Thus the concept that Indian-occupied land was "free" was given academic respectability. In this way the assumption could easily be made that the Indian was more a victim of the impersonal forces of history than of the expansion of whites. And indeed if placed on an impersonal level, the governmental policies of removal, treaty violations, and racism seem not to carry the stigma of responsibility. Although historians have come to question many of Turner's major ideas, those ideas continue to find their way into textbooks and the classroom.

Perhaps the day will dawn when White America will move toward a better understanding of the Native Americans by recognizing that a mythology exists concerning them. A good starting point would be to study Indian ways. Indian peoples have long known that their mythology reveals much about their most basic feelings, values, and beliefs. White America, on the other hand, continually attempts to deny its own mythology. As a starting point, then, toward recognizing

"The Discovery of America by Christopher Columbus" by Salvador Dali, from the collection of Mr. and Mrs. Reynolds Morse, Salvador Dali Museum, Cleveland (Beachwood), Ohio. © by ADAGP, Paris 1977.

3

American mythology, Americans might begin by reexamining the myths that surround and obscure the natives who first occupied the land.

America As Europe's Paradise: Columbus' Brave New World

Any attempt to explain why Europeans pursued exploration and settlement in the New World must begin with the knowledge that, for Europeans, America was a mythical land from the very beginning. A predisposition for myth was as much a part of what European explorers, soldiers, and colonists brought with them as were the practical things needed to meet life's basic needs in a frontier environment. For centuries, even as early as Ancient Greece, Europeans had been fond of believing that the lands and islands to the west of Europe were paradise. The new land so captured their imaginations, in fact, that they were convinced that it was utopia. Christopher Columbus was representative of this point of view. On one of his voyages to America, he enthusiastically confided in his journal that he had arrived at the "nipple" of the earth and the biblical garden of Eden surely lay nearby.

The enthusiastic belief in the New World as utopia was gradually accepted, however. It no doubt began with intellectuals, writers, and philosophers. In time, the idea of America as utopia captivated almost everyone who was of imaginative and venturesome spirit. The expansion of Europe and the conquest of America turned out to be the combined effort of scholars, seamen, and settlers. From the fact and fancy of dreamers the utopian concept of the New World spread to the politicians at court, the merchants in the counting houses, the seafarers at the wharf, and eventually to the homes and villages in the countryside. Once the idea took hold, it motivated one of the most significant migrations in human history.

Slavery in the New World Paradise

Early in the process of establishing utopia in the New World the problem of slavery arose and there was trouble in paradise. Both America and Black Africa had been discovered by Europeans almost simultaneously. Because historians most often talk only about the affairs and accomplishments of elite groups in history and because Americans have tried to forget slavery as an embarrassing feature of an otherwise remarkable experience, the beginnings and development of slavery in America are shrouded in myth. Little is generally known, for example, about the origins of the slave trade in Africa, or about the supposedly primitive and uncivilized background from which the blacks came.

Much of our historical understanding of these early years of slavery is built on conjecture, lack of information, and half-truth. It is clear, however, that both students and scholars have largely neglected the study of slavery in its formative stages. To even begin to understand the importance of slavery in the development of America as utopia, one must understand that slavery had taken root in America long before tobacco and cotton agriculture was established. Slavery began long before the early Virginia plantations of the Beverleys, the Byrds, and the Washingtons. It can be traced back to 1607, and in fact even earlier.

While it is important to recall that black slavery had its origins well before the American Revolution and that the slave trade continued until the very eve of the Civil War, it must be remembered that slavery was not the only form of involuntary labor in early America. The demand for labor was first solved by the use of indentured servants, and only later, on a larger scale, by African slaves. Despite the strangeness of the land and its hardships and dangers, many poor Europeans sold themselves temporarily into bondage in the form of indentured servitude in return for passage to America. Indentured servants in fact were a large part of the population of early America. They most certainly made up the greatest proportion of the labor force. One historian has estimated that:

> If we leave out of account the substantial Puritan migration of 1630-40, not less than half, and perhaps considerably more, of all the white immigrants to the colonies were indentured servants, redemptioners, or convicts. Certainly a good many more than half of all persons who went to the colonies south of New

England were servants in bondage to planters, farmers, speculators, and proprietors.[2]

So, even though African slavery most definitely was important in the colonies, one should not overlook the fact that indentured servants numbered between one half to three fourths of the immigrants in the seventeenth century. Just as there were cargoes of blacks brought to the American utopia, so also were there cargoes of whites—particularly Scots and Irish. All immigrants came in search of what the New World might mean for them, but an important minority had less than free choice in selecting where they would settle once here. Not only was this true, but their voyage to America was in many respects nearly as bad as the horrors which black slaves suffered during the Middle Passage. As one historian has noted, the Atlantic crossing was "one of the terrors of the age." The tyranny of the sea was hardly less severe than the tyranny of the land. In contending with both, colonists faced at least discomfort and at most death.

Contrary to America's cherished belief, in the New Land not everyone raised himself or herself to material and financial success. Few indentured servants became colonial Horatio Algers. Having completed their specified term of service—usually from five to seven years—very few of them achieved economic success and middle-class respectability as yeomen farmers. Indeed, hard work and death took a heavy toll. Only two out of every ten finally achieved what could be called moderate comfort. One historian writes:

> The Horatio Alger mythology has long since been torn to bits by students of American social mobility, and it will surprise no one to learn that the chance of emergence from indentured servitude to a position of wealth or renown was statistically negligible. A few cases to the contrary are treasured by historians, handed down from one to another like heirlooms. . . .[3]

The ancestors of Benjamin Franklin are often cited in books as the typical success story. But more often than not the path from rags to riches in early America led nowhere. Even though colonial society and its economy were very much in flux, it was quickly realized that the promises of the New World could not be guaranteed. The realities of the New World quickly worked to modify Old World mythology.

Myths of Colonial Development

A considerable body of myths has obscured colonial development in the years from the first settlements to the Revolution. Many of these myths are concerned with Puritan America. Historical perspective has too long focused on the gloomy, somber, mythical Puritan. Sensational episodes such as the Salem witchcraft trials of 1692 have given us the impression that the average Puritan was a bigot inclined toward persecution and morbid introspection. The witch trials were a form of religious hysteria and were far more common in Europe during this period than in America. One should not therefore assume that all Puritans were religious zealots. Life in colonial America was serious business, but not all Puritans were "old sobersides." A balanced picture of Puritan life is needed. As the historian Thomas Bailey concludes, "it would be false to write off the Puritan as a joyless bore, [but] it would be even more false to picture him as spending his days with one arm around Priscilla and with the other hoisting aloft a tankard of ale."[4] The Puritans were, after all, representative of the religion-oriented societies of the seventeenth century.

As to other colonial settlers, the Catholics of Maryland were not universally committed to the idea of establishing freedom of religion. As one historian explains:

> while Catholics did go to Maryland, there existed from the beginning a large Protestant majority. Lord Baltimore solved this problem by 'accepting' a Toleration Act (1649) that guaranteed freedom of religion to anyone 'professing to believe in Jesus Christ.' Because the Calverts adjusted their pretensions to American realities, they made a fortune out of Maryland and maintained an influence in the colony until the Revolution.[5]

Colonial Maryland can be said to have shown the way in pursuing religious tolerance because its leadership sought practical solutions to issues. The democratic tradition of freedom of religion—which men like Thomas Jefferson advanced in later years—took hold in colonial times largely because practical considerations demanded it, not because of some deep and abiding philosophical commitment to liberal democratic principles.

Another popular myth relates to the southern colonies. It concerns the question of democratic theory and practice. Colonial Virginia is often thought of as a hotbed of republicanism or a conservative, plantation-based aristocracy ruled with an iron fist. Contrary to legend, however, neither extreme was true. While many famous liberals, republicans, and revolutionaries such as George Washington, George Mason, Patrick Henry, and Thomas Jefferson came from the plantation class, it is also clear that the Virginia gentry (relatively wealthy and well-born land owners) dominated Virginia's political, economic, and social life. The case of Virginia, then, presents many contradictions. The colony was not a cavalier society in the English sense, but neither was it yet committed to complete democracy. Nonetheless, legendary accounts still maintain that the golden age of the Virginia Commonwealth witnessed the beginnings of a deep commitment to self-government. The highly publicized rebellion of Nathaniel Bacon in 1676 against the policies of Governor William Berkeley is usually given as evidence. Some historians have gone so far as to say that this was something of a rehearsal for the Revolution. Though the date 1676 is convenient for drawing parallels with the upheaval a century later, the episode only vaguely fits the Revolutionary pattern. It was not a class war between frontier settlers and eastern aristocratic planters. It was not a short story with a simple plot—liberty versus tyranny. Rather, the major issues of the conflict seem to have hinged on the essentially friendly policies of Berkeley toward the Indians and demands by rural pioneers for stern actions against them. As one historian has said, "Some have contended that the revolutionary generation, eager to find precedents for its own rebellion, created a myth out of a minor incident little different from numerous rural disturbances in North Carolina, New Jersey, Maryland, and in England itself."[6] Colonial politics, at the time, were very much in flux. Colonists were developing political systems and practices which only later would bring them to revolution against England.

SECTION I. THE NATIVE AMERICANS: BEYOND THE STEREOTYPES

Even though historians continue to preach and students to believe the myth that Europeans "discovered" America, it should be obvious that the first Americans were not Europeans at all. While no one can be sure of the earliest dates of the first discovery and exploration of the New World, scholars agree that the slow process toward civilization began between 25,000 and 40,000 years ago, if not earlier. The ancestors of today's Indians migrated southward over the continent after crossing from Asia. They began permanently to inhabit what is today North and South America many centuries before the birth of Christ.

Certainly one of the longest-standing historical errors of the Western world is the cherished belief—presented in many history textbooks—that the course of American development began with the discovery of the New World by Christopher Columbus. Not only is such a view historically untrue, but it implies that the first discoverers, the Native Americans, made initial contact with North America only by accident. Yet, it is reasonable to assume that the Native Americans were as much explorers in search of a New World as were many of the European states and visionary explorers centuries later. History does not record either the names or the deeds of these early discoverers and explorers. Without their efforts, however, the estimated one million natives who inhabited the land in 1492 would never have achieved the varied levels of culture which we know existed by that time.

Myth of the Bloodthirsty Savage

It is highly inaccurate to believe that Columbus discovered a primitive land uniformly inhabited by humans barely out of the Stone

Age. It is extremely difficult in fact to make any type of generalization about the level of civilization existing in the America Columbus found. There were numerous kinds of native societies, from the most highly developed to the most primitive. It is well known, for example, that the Mayas of Central America, the Aztecs of Mexico, and the Incas of Peru had attained a level of cultural development easily rivaling many in Europe. Less widely known or accepted, however, is the fact that Native Americans in what was to become the United States were, in most respects, hardly primitive, certainly not heathens, and in most cases not deserving of the name "barbarian." As the anthropologist Oliver La Farge has written, "When the white men first landed there were three major centers of high culture: the Southeast-Mississippi Valley, the Southwest, and the Northwest Coast. None of the peoples of these regions, incidentally, knew about war bonnets or lived in tepees."[7] And contrary to the stereotypes, the cultures of the Native Americans were as varied as the land they occupied.

In the Southeast and the Mississippi Valley, Indian peoples known as Mound Builders represented a high level of civilization. Subject to invasions even prior to those by Europeans, it was through their mixture with other native groups that the Five Civilized Tribes eventually developed. The Cherokees, Chickasaws, Creeks, Choctaws, and the Seminoles were hunters and farmers, developed sophisticated social and political systems, and succeeded in establishing a stage of civilized development unexcelled east of the Rocky Mountains. Other Indian cultures, especially those of the Southeast, the Natchez, and the related Iroquois, can justly be described as "warlike." In this respect they were much like the Navahos and Apaches of the Southwest. From these groups and from incidences like the Pequot War with the Puritans in 1637 came the popular notion of the Native American as Bloodthirsty Savage. But one must quickly add that the Europeans who discovered them could hardly be described as "unwarlike" themselves. For centuries, European civilization had settled disputes by the sword. Europe's bloody Thirty Years' War (1618-1648) was contemporary to the first English settlements in North America.

In addition, students studying the initial period of American development often believe that the natives were barbarians because the vast majority were illiterate. What they don't know is that the vast majority of conquering Europeans were likewise illiterate. By emphasizing the barbarism of the Native Americans, history has created a bias in favor of America's "civilized" European origins and a bias against the many accomplishments and contributions of the Native Americans. For example, the famous Iroquois League of the Five Nations—the Mohawks, Oneidas, Onondagas, Cayugas, and Senecas—was a model of political organization which drew the attention of those who wrote the Constitution. This fact indicates that the Indians were not completely lacking in civilized habits. Moreover, by the 1830s the Cherokee had established a political system with a written constitution and a bicameral (two-house) legislature. A model of a civilized culture, they enjoyed the benefits of an alphabet, printing presses, a newspaper, churches, and schools. And among the Plains Indians, the Cheyenne established a system of law which deserves admiration. In short, one must completely ignore the Iroquois, the Cherokee, and a great many other Indian groups to feel comfortable with the myth of the Bloodthirsty Savage.

The first contact between Europeans and Native Americans foreshadowed the difficulty which whites would have in understanding the truth about the natives. Christopher Columbus immortalized his own and Europe's misconceptions and misunderstandings when he called the Native Americans "Indians." Believing that he had come upon the Asian subcontinent of India, Columbus became the first mythmaker.

The Indians seemed both a curse and a blessing to the Europeans. Those who followed Columbus saw the Indians as a threat to white settlement and also as an ally if only their friendship could be won. Early white settlements, particularly those of the Spanish and the English, in South and Central America and along the Atlantic coast, experienced good and bad relations with the natives. The image of the Indian as Bloodthirsty Savage gained credence because of the many occasions when they fought to retain the lands which they had occupied for centuries. Convinced that the

Bloodthirsty Savage or Noble Red Man?
Courtesy of Kennedy Galleries, Inc., New York

Indian was a barbarian nomad without roots, colonial governments acted to "legally" justify white occupation of Indian land. After all, was not the Indian nomadic by nature? Legally, Indians were without status. They were a part of the landscape, an aspect of the land, more like the mountains, trees, and animals than flesh-and-blood human beings. The fact that the European settlers were nomads of a sort themselves did not seem to matter. History simply has reported that when Europeans followed their roving instincts they were visionaries, pathfinders, and adventurers. Native Americans who had discovered the continent, established its paths, and explored its natural wonders were dismissed as primitives awaiting the civilization which Europeans would eventually offer them.

The view of the Indian as a barbaric Red Devil (similar to the Bloodthirsty Savage idea) became firmly established in American mythology because of the belief that all na-

tives engaged, to one degree or another, in scalping. One respected Indian historian, however, credits Governor Kieft of New Netherland with the idea of paying fees for Indian scalps. Other historians suggest that the custom grew out of the period when both the French and British were attempting to gain control of the North American continent, during the late seventeenth to the mid-eighteenth century. In this instance, not only did the Indian hold a balance of power between the contending European states, but the French and the British paid bounties for each other's scalps. One student of Indian history has traced the origins of scalping to an even earlier period:

until 1637 scalping was unknown among the New England Indians. The Puritans began by offering cash for the heads of their enemies, and later accepting scalps if both ears were attached. The French

8

were the first to offer bounties for the scalps of white people, with the English quickly following suit, and such vast sums were expended that scores of white men took up the lucrative business of hunting scalps.[8]

Since Indians also found the payments for scalps a reasonably good source of income, in some instances more rewarding than the sale of animal furs and pelts, the belief grew that the Indians had "invented" the practice of removing portions of hair and skin from the head. Two centuries later, during the 1820s and 1830s, American adventurers in the Southwest were being paid bounties for the scalps of Apaches and Comanches by the Mexican states of Sonora, Coahuila, and Chihuahua. Commenting on this practice, one historian has called the years 1835 to 1850 "the boom years of the scalp industry" in the American Southwest. Not only was this practice less widespread than legend would have it and shared by whites as well as Indians, but belief in its indiscriminate use was appealing because it fit perfectly the preconceived notion that the Indian was a base and bloodthirsty creature.

In histories of the encounters and battles between Indians and frontier colonists and settlers, one will often find that in those cases in which the Indians succeeded in protecting their land, the outcome is described as a "massacre" of whites. Even the highly respected historian Francis Parkman contributed to the mythical process by consistently describing the Indians as "man, wolf, and devil, all in one."[9] From incomplete and biased information, the Indian began to emerge in song, story, and historical legend as a creature bent on the murder and rape of whites and the destruction of their advancing civilization. Today, Indian savagery is seen as a reaction to white savagery.

Myth of the Noble Red Man

While the concept of the Indian as Bloodthirsty Savage developed during the colonial period and was reinforced during America's frontier experience, another Indian stereotype was developing simultaneously. While many had come to see the Indian as hostile and barbaric, others saw him as a Noble Red Man.

The early relationships between whites and Indians symbolized by the first Thanksgiving, for example, did much to set the myth of the Noble Red Man in motion. Two Indian leaders, Squanto and Massasoit, perhaps the first of the Noble Red Men, did indeed greatly assist the Pilgrims during their first harsh winter of settlement. It is a fact that the Indians knew a great deal about local agriculture and assisted the first colonists in growing and harvesting tobacco, corn, sweet potatoes, tomatoes, melons, beans, maple sugar, pumpkins, and squash. The Indians also provided the indispensable knowledge needed for woodcraft, hunting, and trapping. If it had not been for the friendship and practical help of the Native Americans, the early Pilgrim settlers might not have survived the terrors of the first American frontier.

Since relations between Indians and whites were often friendly, stories reaching Europe of the simplicity, honesty, and virtue of the natives led many Europeans to believe that they had at last found a true child of nature. European intellectuals, particularly in France, began to write romantic descriptions of what they imagined Indian life to be like. Convinced that the affairs of Europe had become corrupt and too complex, writers such as Montaigne began to applaud the nobility, innocence, and naturalness of the "primitive" peoples across the Atlantic. In many ways their morals, life-styles, and political relations seemed superior to those of Europeans. The Indian cultures which the Europeans had encountered thus became an exotic ideal which many saw as worthy of being followed. In important respects the Native Americans were worthy subjects for such praise, but the romantic picture of the Indians which many Europeans had—particularly in intellectual circles—was much more exotic than the harsh realities of the New World allowed. The idea that all Indians were great poets, profound philosophers, or fair maidens simply did not square with the facts. Still, this misty-eyed view of the Indians saw every native as a "king" or a "chief." This is one myth, however, which some scholars have attempted to dismiss:

another error, which has been refuted time and again both by Indian historians as well as scholars, is the use of the term

9

'king' in connection with native leadership. There were no kings, no nobility, no queens, and no princesses. This was a figment of the imagination of a few French, English and Spanish aristocrats, who used such propaganda to obtain support for their expeditions. The use of the word 'chief' is also a white man's invention.[10]

As is so often the case, the mythmakers who saw all Indians as nobles were usually those who had little or no real contact with the New World. They based their beliefs on tales, hearsay, and rumor. As a result, they generalized on a grand scale and wrote what they wanted to believe. Many early histories and "true accounts" also presented Europeans with the one-sided romantic view of the Indian way of life. Just as most Indians were not savages, neither were most nobles.

The myth of the Indian as either savage or noble was a product not only of French philosophers and romantic histories of early discovery and settlement but of American literature as well. The well-known American poet Henry Wadsworth Longfellow, for example, wrote an imaginary story of the great Indian leader Hiawatha, founder of the League of the Five Nations. Longfellow's poetic portrait errs to the point that "any resemblance between the fictional hero of Longfellow's poem and this real, dead person is purely coincidental."[11] Even today, however, school children are still taught to believe the myth of the Noble Red Man through Longfellow's highly sentimental and fictional account.

The opposite view of the Indian as a primitive savage came, in part, from writers such as James Fenimore Cooper. Cooper was born in 1789, the year in which the American Constitution was adopted and George Washington became the nation's first president. He died just one decade before the beginning of the Civil War (1851). His generation took part in the early expansion of the American people across the continent. In that age of Manifest Destiny, he knew of the many encounters which pioneers had with the Indians who fought for their land. In various novels such as *The Last of the Mohicans* and *The Prairie*, Cooper wrote about Indians and whites, and the many ways in which their cultures

clashed. Unfortunately, Cooper's writings gave the impression that all "redskins" were born with a tomahawk in hand. Years later, in commenting upon what he called "Fenimore Cooper's Literary Offenses," Mark Twain said that Cooper "was almost always in error about his Indians. There was seldom a sane one among them. . . . In the matter of intellect, the difference between a Cooper Indian and the Indian that stands in front of the cigar-shop is not spacious."[12] According to Twain, the trouble with Cooper's novels was that they were more fictitious than any good fiction should be. The Indians which Americans came to know through literature were more often than not cardboard imitations of the Indians who had once ruled the land.

There are, of course, many other reasons why Native Americans have come to be seen as mythical stereotypes rather than real human beings. In addition to the ways in which literature has distorted Indian life and culture, frontier artists such as George Catlin have portrayed Indians in an almost totally romantic manner. If one believes that Catlin's Indian portraits were authentic, one can see why many students and scholars in the past had little more than a sentimental notion of how the American Indian actually lived. In addition, toward the end of the nineteenth century, the cowboy became a popular figure in American fiction. The cowboy was always virtuous and heroic. A foil was needed for this hero, one whose sinister behavior would make the cowboy saintlike by comparison. The already accepted view of the Indian as savage fit perfectly with the new stereotype of the Indian as a villain. The cowboy versus the Indian represented the classic confrontation of good and evil. In dime novels during the nineteenth century, and again in movies and television in the twentieth century, a stirring tale of "good guys" (cowboys) versus "bad guys" (Indians) flourished. One stereotype could not exist without the other.

The best way to understand the American Indian is to set aside the stereotypes. One scholar has advised: "Some Indians may still live in tepees, wear at times their traditional clothing, maintain here and there their arts and some of their rituals, but these are little more than fringe survivals."[13] In other words, forget what you have seen in movies and begin to examine their historical role as discoverers, explorers, and settlers of the continent. From this point of view one begins to see that their civilizations were enormously varied, and that they have made important contributions in everything from artistic craftsmanship to political theory. Their agricultural contributions in tilling, planting, irrigation, and harvesting have never been fully appreciated. Their contributions in medicine—medicinal uses of cocaine, arnica, and quinine—were cultural contributions of the first order. Their expertise in textiles and weaving rivals that of almost any other civilized people. Indian sensitivity to and appreciation of nature and the land, though legendary and perhaps sentimentalized, have certainly been more profound than that of the white community. Not to be forgotten is the fact that the political ideals of young America owed much to a rich Indian democratic tradition. The pattern of states within a nation—what we call federalism—and the habit of treating leaders as servants of the people instead of masters were all part of the American way of life even before 1492 or 1787.

One must be careful, however, in the interest of good and unbiased history, not to overstate Indian accomplishments in attempting to compensate for past abuses and distortions. It was, after all, overemphasis of the accomplishments of whites which did much to create the myths about the American Indian. Fictitious heroes are as harmful as fictitious villains. Indians would only become less human were this to happen. One mythology replacing another never makes good history. With this proviso, it can be said that the Native Americans have too often not been remembered for the many historical contributions which they *have* made.

SECTION II. AMERICA AS EUROPE'S PARADISE: COLUMBUS' BRAVE NEW WORLD

Columbus' voyage of 1492 and his discovery of the New World for Europeans is one of history's most fascinating tales. An Italian by birth, sailing under the flag of Spain, Columbus has remained a hero almost without equal.

The significance of his deeds deserve much of the praise which historians have bestowed upon them. What must be recognized, however, is the fact that much of Columbus' reputation rests on myth and legend.

A most unlikely source of the mythology concerning Columbus is the American writer Washington Irving, who captured Columbus' sense of destiny and heroic personality and created a man of mythical stature. Irving is known to school children and to the general public as the author of "Rip Van Winkle" and "The Legend of Sleepy Hollow." Less widely known is his work *The Life and Voyages of Christopher Columbus,* written in 1828. Though some of his historical works are trustworthy and accurate, Irving's biography of Columbus clearly shows that "The Legend of Sleepy Hollow" is not the only legend with which he is associated. For Irving, it has been claimed, "is responsible for perpetuating the legend that Columbus proved the earth is round."[14] Irving portrayed Columbus as a visionary adventurer. An adventurer Columbus surely was, but was he a visionary prophet who alone understood that the world was not flat? Hardly. Yet in Irving's largely fictitious account, Columbus argues with a sense of vision and destiny that the world is round. It is a scene remindful of visionaries at other times in history who endured ridicule and insult. To quote from Irving's book, Columbus is "a simple mariner standing forth in the midst of an imposing array of professors, friars, and dignitaries of the church; maintaining his theory with natural eloquence, and as it were, pleading the cause of the new world."[15] While this "historical" reproduction appeals to the emotions, it disregards the facts.

Irving's portrait of the Genovese sailor displays an ignorance ofthe degree of learning in Columbus' time. Both the astronomer Ptolemy (2nd century A.D.) in his *Geography* (rediscovered and republished in 1411) and the Italian writer Dante in his work *The Divine Comedy* (written between 1302 and 1321) described the earth as round. It can be assumed that among educated people the idea of a spherical earth was an accepted belief in Columbus' time. According to one source, "all the educated men of Columbus' time thought the earth was round; the only dispute was about its size, and the location of Asia with respect to Europe."[16]

Contrary to Irving's story, the "professors, friars, and dignitaries of the church" would not have had to be convinced of Columbus' supposedly progressive ideas. Contrary to Irving's story, the reason Columbus encountered so much difficulty in persuading the Spanish to underwrite his voyage was that the voyage would be expensive in terms of aid and support. The theory that the earth was round had nothing to do with these difficulties. It seems clear that Washington Irving gave his story of Columbus an epic significance which it most certainly never deserved.

Stripped of legend, Columbus' reputation owes more to his errors of judgment than to his vision. In calculating the distance from the Canary Islands to China to be 3,550 nautical miles (actually it was 11,700 nautical miles or four times as far), he thought Asia to be much closer to Europe than it actually was. Yet, the legend created by Irving survives to this day. The Irving myth concerning Columbus enjoys such popularity in fact that it has even influenced the graffiti of the 1970s:

> The Earth is flat.
> THE CLASS OF 1491

Even before Columbus sailed westward and proclaimed America as part of an expanding Europe, the New World was already an enchanting dream in the mind of the Old World. As far back as the Greeks, the unknown regions to the west of Europe were thought to include not only legendary ferocious beasts but mythical lands. The Greeks, for example, were convinced that paradisiacal islands beyond the Pillars of Hercules were yet to be discovered, and that when found, they would be perfect. Similarly, the Romans had spoken of the so-called Fortunate Islands somewhere to the west where a paradise of lush land and ideal weather could be found. The legend of Atlantis as an earthly paradise, which goes back to Plato, had never been lost. Long after ancient times, Europeans continued to believe that magic islands lay somewhere in the misty vastness of the Atlantic. Filled with wonder and terror, Europeans had come to think that paradise, Eden, and utopia could all be discovered somewhere in the New World.

America's discovery and colonization, therefore, climaxed a period of European thinking and feeling which had long anticipated a golden utopian age. Utopia, from the Greek word meaning "nowhere" or "no place," is also a pun on the word for "good place." The term first came into modern usage in 1516, a quarter century after Columbus sighted the Bahamas. Sir Thomas More, Chancellor to King Henry VIII of England, used it as the title of one of his literary works. The word "utopia" as first used by More meant both an entirely imaginary place ("no place at all")—a pure fantasy world—and at the same time an ideal country, a "good place." Both meanings of the word have found their way into subsequent usage.[17] The importance of Sir Thomas More's work lies in the fact that it was set in the New World and reflected the idyllic nature of that world. America would provide all Europeans an escape into an ideal world like that of Sir Thomas More's in which social, political, and religious problems could be solved. Poverty and tyranny could be left behind. Religious freedom could at last be realized.

To completely understand the motives which brought Europeans to the New World, one must realize that they came not only to escape religious persecution, to express their missionary zeal, and to accumulate economic wealth. They also came because of a European belief, of long standing, that the New World in the west could be utopia. Both the oppressed and the idealistic of the Old World had become convinced that ease, abundance, and well-being were much more possible in the New World than in the Old.

Viewed within the context of this European tradition, it can be seen that "Columbus merely confirmed long-standing legend, which had been credited all along. People had known in good reason that paradisiacal states lay over the western ocean, including the Earthly Paradise, which, if located in the vicinity of Cathay [China], might be reached across the Atlantic."[18] In the vast open spaces of the New World Europeans saw the age-old dreams of the Fortunate Islands and Atlantis. The natives and the land which early explorers encountered reinforced even more deeply the idea that something like the biblical Garden of Eden might be discovered. If not Eden, at least a golden age waited beyond the horizon. It is little wonder that those who followed Columbus believed they would find cities of gold and fountains of youth in the New World.

The Spanish and French

As much as any other Europeans the Spaniards were motivated by utopian dreams. For the Spanish, the sixteenth century—the years of their encounters with the mythical New World—was golden. Historians unanimously agree that Spain experienced its greatest age, an age of supreme confidence, heroism, and romantic adventure. Spain, by almost any measure, was at the height of world leadership and power. It is difficult now to imagine the grandeur and glory of Spain at that time. Its present poverty and lack of power in international affairs are a far cry from the wealthy and powerful empire which Spain once enjoyed.

Indeed Spain's robust success in political, economic, and cultural matters during the 1500s fits perfectly with the established and growing fascination with the New World. Spain's mythical dreams had a way of becoming heroic deeds. The Spanish explorers and colonizers combined practical affairs with a vision of destiny in the age of exploration. In short, the spirit and success of Spain's imperial age went hand in hand. Spaniards explored the Caribbean islands and the mainland of North and South America with a sense of mission. Led by an adventurous impulse, conquistadors such as Cortez and Pizzarro conquered the Aztecs of Mexico and the Incas of Peru. To the east, Ponce de Leon cruised the shores of the Florida peninsula in search of the fountain of youth, while Hernando de Soto explored the Gulf Coast. In search of the legendary Seven Cities of Cibola, Francisco Coronado explored present-day Arizona, New Mexico, Texas, Oklahoma, and Kansas in the early 1540s. Though fountains of youth and cities of gold were never found, belief in their existence led the Spanish to their remarkable accomplishments. As one scholar has said, "The entire enterprise of the Spanish Conquest seems shrouded in a curious air of unreality."[19] But one must remember that even if Spanish endeavors in the New World were in many ways based on myths, to them the myths were very real.

As map-making improved and the first settlements were founded, Spain seemed to lose little of its original romantic enthusiasm for the New World. We find, for example, that early Spanish "histories" of their encounters with the new land reflect the same kind of utopian feelings. Observation had a way of confirming romantic preconception. Expectations of finding an earthly paradise influenced what the Spaniards thought they saw. One such history spoke of the "perpetual spring" to be found in the New World, and how "the flowers bloom, the trees are green, the rivers wind, the mountains are high, and the inhabitants are innocent and happy."[20] These early histories reported that Indians were gods and goddesses and that the land was paradise. Hearing reports such as this, how could Spaniards back home think anything else but that utopia had been found. They, too, could pursue fulfillment of their dreams and achieve heroic stature for themselves and for Spain. All of this was in many ways a majestic misconception, but for Spaniards at the time, such dreams did not seem to conflict with the real world. Rather, the real world was being shaped by romantic ideals. Spain, however, did not hold a monopoly on the utopian pleasures of empire-building.

France was as prepared as Spain for the mythical enchantment which America seemed to offer. Following Spanish example and hoping to be a rival in success, France also thought that America would prove to be an El Dorado, rich in souls and gold. According to one historian, America, to the French, was a "mirage in the West":

> The elements of the eighteenth-century mirage were various nostalgia for the Golden Age and the Lost Paradise, tropical or semitropical dreams and exoticism, the myth of the Good Savage, an imaginary locus for the utopian constructions of philosophers and critics of society, the well-established tradition that 'America' was a place where men could live 'free and happy' in the midst of bounteous prosperity.[21]

With its emphasis on the golden age, the lost paradise, and utopia, France viewed America through rose-tinted glasses as a paradise to be regained. America symbolized the exotic dream of perfection. For France as well as Spain, America was a bountiful and brave new world. Only here could one find the prosperity, naturalness, and leisure of which Europeans had dreamed for centuries. The world to the west was sprinkled with green islands, spices, tropical fruits, and, of course, silver and gold. America was Eden.

The English

The idea of the New World as utopia was also found in England. It is said that Sir Humphrey Gilbert, one of the first English to voyage to the New World, was sitting on the deck of his ship reading a copy of Sir Thomas More's *Utopia* just before he was lost at sea somewhere in the North Atlantic in 1583. Whether or not the account is true is unimportant. The point is that Gilbert was representative of the breed of Renaissance English who foresaw the possibilities of the New World and then attempted to realize them. In England, writers such as Edmund Spenser, Francis Bacon, and Michael Drayton all shared this vision of America as fairyland. Writing in 1606 Drayton, for example, declared that Virginia was "Earth's only Paradise." Just like the Spanish and the French, the English had "paradise on the mind." According to one colonial historian, "in pamphlets, plays, and poems Englishmen read of the New World; more importantly, they talked of the Americas, passing facts and fancies by word of mouth."[22]

It is not at all surprising, therefore, that when the Puritans set sail for America, they fully intended to establish a religious paradise—a New Jerusalem. They fervently thought that their emigration from Old England to New England was a journey of epic proportions and that they had arrived at a sacred place. Idealism, romance, and myth led these early New Englanders to believe that they had at last escaped the vices of the Old World. Holiness, peace, and happiness were now a distinct possibility. The utopian dreams of earlier generations could be realized. The perfect Commonwealth lay before them. Believing that they were on a journey to utopia, the seventeenth-century Puritans provided a sense of sacred destiny to the American experience in its formative stages.

As for the southern colonies, the pattern was basically similar. Early settlers on Roanoke Island off the coast of present-day North Carolina, for example, claimed to find "the soil richer, the trees taller, the ground firmer and

the topsoil deeper." Various exotic tales and "true reports" predicted that a golden age, paradise, and Eden were all at hand. The participants believed that their glories and great deeds would be a drama far surpassing any that Europeans had ever witnessed. Some went so far as to declare that Eden was to be found between 35° and 37° north latitude (on a line connecting present-day Fayetteville, North Carolina, and Memphis, Tennessee) where Sir Walter Raleigh in his famous book *Marrow of History* had specifically located the ideal climate of perpetual spring, "a garden shaded by palm trees."[23] Others who attempted colonization and settlement, such as Lieutenant Governor Alexander Spotswood of Virginia, allowed their dreams of utopia to color what they saw around them. Crossing the Blue Ridge Mountains in 1716, Spotswood, apparently an incurably romantic dreamer, "discovered a river which we now call the Shenandoah but which Spotswood and his company named Euphrates, after one of the four rivers of Eden, because the country looked to them like paradise."[24] Other discoverers and explorers such as William Byrd II, Sir Robert Montgomery, and Aaron Hill followed suit. They, too, envisioned a paradise in which the climate was perfect, the air was pure, and the sun shone in perpetual splendor. They and other "promoters" carried exaggerated tales back to Europe to an anxious clientele. If their objective was to dispel any lingering doubt about America as Eden, they succeeded magnificently. Since America began as an exotic, alluring, and romantic country, it could reasonably be expected that its history would be a tantalizing mixture of half-truths, hopes, and legends.

The major impact of the New World on the Old was psychological. In modern literature this psychological impact has been captured by the American writer F. Scott Fitzgerald in the closing passages of his novel *The Great Gatsby*. Trying to imagine how the "fresh, green breast" of the New World must have looked to those who first saw it, Fitzgerald muses that it "had once pandered in whispers to the last and greatest of all human dreams; for a transitory enchanted moment man must have held his breath in the presence of this continent, compelled into an aesthetic contemplation he neither understood nor desired, face to face for the last time in history with something commensurate to his capacity for wonder."[25] Inspired by the romantic utopian dreams of Europeans, then, America began as a mixture of myth and reality. Born of a tradition of glory and heroism, America was well on its way to becoming a land at ease with myth and legend. Old World utopianism blended into a New World mythology.

SECTION III. SLAVERY IN A NEW WORLD PARADISE

When the first mainland English colony was established at Jamestown in 1607, it seemed more certain than ever that Europe's utopian dreams would be realized. Though aware of the difficulties and the hardships which awaited them, the colonists' hopes overcame their doubts. These ancient dreams of a more perfect society, however, were the very things which began to blight the promise of the Promised Land. Land was plentiful and so were natural resources, but what about labor? A most important element was needed to fulfill the dream. Indentured servants temporarily solved the labor problem, but the West African slave trade appeared to be the best long-range solution. This was particularly true in the South where the tobacco boom of the 1620s in Virginia and the successful rice and indigo crops in the Carolinas created a demand for cheap, abundant labor.

Ironically, then, the tremendous ambition and enterprise of the colonists, which played such an important part in their success, also led them to establish slavery. Utopianism spawned both liberty and bondage—a serpent had entered the New World Garden of Eden.

But the problems which slavery would pose for later generations had actually taken shape long before colonists and settlers began to arrive. Christopher Columbus' first encounter with the Americas had shown what problems would eventually arise. He left a legacy, one historian has discovered, committed to both freedom *and* slavery:

The same Columbus who identified the Gulf of Paria as the gateway to the Garden of Eden had no compunction

about sending hundreds of Indians to be sold in the slave marts of Seville, although some two hundred died on the first voyage and had to be thrown into the sea. It was thus the discoverer of America who initiated the transatlantic trade, which moved originally from west to east.[26]

The West African slave trade which would satisfy the demands for labor in the South came much later. However, the basic contradiction between American ideals and the reality of slavery was already evident as the seed of an American dilemma.

One of the principle myths about slavery in America is the popular notion that it only began to play an important role in the nation's history in the years preceding the Civil War. In looking at the early colonial period, many students and scholars have been more concerned with the importance of Puritanism, the growth of democracy, and the roots of the American Revolution. While all these factors are of fundamental importance, almost no attention has been given to the fact that blacks were among the earliest arrivals and that slavery as an institution began in colonial America.

At best, Americans have only a hazy and legendary understanding of the origins of slavery. Most people's knowledge is based on traditional accounts of how blacks arrived at Jamestown on a Dutch ship in the late summer of 1619. But what is known of the experience of these blacks and their ancestors before 1619? The period before 1619 remains clouded by what one scholar has called "the myth of the Negro past."

African Sources of Slavery

Contrary to popular mythology, the ancestors of blacks who came to the New World were neither primitive nor savage. They were certainly not "natural slaves." The great majority of those transported to America on slave ships came from the coastal regions of West Africa. With few exceptions, blacks brought to port for sale to European slavers came from less than 300 miles into the interior. Seldom were they from the vast and exotic inland regions of the Dark Continent made popular centuries later by Stanley and Livingston. In most cases they came from the forested and grassland areas to the south and west of the great Sahara desert. More specifically, they were drawn from what Muslims in the Middle Ages had known as the Beled es-Sudan, or "Land of the Blacks." The Sudan was a culturally advanced area by almost any standard. The agriculture of the region was based on growing sesame, cotton, okra, and sorghum. Along the coast yams were the staple crop. The political structure consisted of large-scale and complex kingdoms with origins before the birth of Christ. The peoples of the Sudan had developed trade routes and urban societies, handling salt mined in the Sahara, gold, and luxury cloth from the Mediterranean. The affairs of the region were administered from the city of Timbuktu on the edge of the desert to the north. This fabled city on the Niger River was at once the commercial and intellectual center of West Africa at the time. It was the point of exchange for goods being sent south from northern Africa. Though the vital center of the Sudanese civilization was to the north, the southwestern Sudan—the area from which most New World blacks came—shared in its success.

Based on the studies of archaeologists, sociologists, and historians it seems clear that the civilizations of the Sudan area of Western Africa were nearly as varied as those of the Indian Americans during the same period. Some of these peoples were still developing weaving and basketry, others had advanced to ironworking and bronze casting. A few West African economic systems were in fact comparable to the Aztec and Inca empires of the New World. Some scholars have suggested that the social structure in certain regions, Dahomey, for example, was as involved as that of Western Europe. The Dahomeans had developed an elaborate social and political hierarchy including a European-style monarchy and a system of tax collection and royal officials throughout the empire. In addition, there were well-developed religious and family structures which were different from, but not necessarily more primitive than, those of Europe. In written language, technology, and mathematics Europeans were, of course, more advanced. Accordingly, they considered themselves superior. Because of European cultural

attitudes and the general lack of written histories of the African peoples, misconceptions have served in lieu of facts, and the myth of the black past has persisted.

The Slave Trade and the Nature of American Slavery

The development of the European slave trade with the African areas south of the Sahara was part of a larger economic process known as the commercial revolution. At an earlier time economic prosperity and power in Europe had been centered in the countries that bordered the Mediterranean Sea. Now it was shifting to the countries of northwestern Europe. The buying and selling of slaves, first by the Portuguese and later by the Spanish, Dutch, French, and English, was one of the factors in bringing about this shift in power. The exchange of slaves between West African and Western European traders arose without serious opposition because slave traffic soon proved profitable for both buyers and sellers. Not only was the slave trade lucrative to all concerned, but both regions were already familiar with it by the time of the commercial revolution.

Slavery, in the sense of lifetime bondage, had been known to European civilization at least since the time of Ancient Greece. The philosopher Aristotle had condoned the institution in his writings. The heritage of the Bible, classical philosophy, and Roman law all provided a rationale for the institution, even as slavery was being established in the New World at a time when its practice had virtually disappeared in Western Europe.

Among Africans, slavery was relatively common, though it differed from the system developed on plantations in the American colonial South in many important respects. In West African societies such as the Dahomean and Ashanti the enslavement of blacks by other blacks was widely practiced, but it was less restrictive, harsh, and demeaning than slavery in North America. In African societies, slaves were usually found in the households of their masters, not in the fields, and they enjoyed the right to marry free people and legally own property. While the African slave systems were no doubt discriminatory, they allowed considerable freedom. As one noted

Slavery: An American Dilemma Begins
Library of Congress

historian of both West African and North American slavery has indicated:

> In the kingdom of Benin in coastal Nigeria, slaves or their children were permitted to earn enough to purchase their freedom. Slaves of the Dahomeans, the Ashanti, and the Ibo of the Niger Delta commonly achieved free status through adoption into the families of the masters. Rulers among the Yoruba and the Muslim Hausa states of northern Nigeria frequently chose slaves for high official position, and among the Dahomeans, kings sometimes selected the son of a favorite slave wife to succeed to the throne.[27]

Though West Africans had first-hand knowledge of slavery and were a link in selling slaves into New World bondage, they could scarcely have predicted how oppressive slavery would be on the other side of the Atlantic.

Spurred on by the thought of vast new markets in the New World and favorable trade winds, Europeans began to frequent the Guinea Coast from the Senegal and Gambia Rivers to Angola. At first, gold, slaves, pepper, and ivory were the most sought-after items. But with the recognition that labor was in such short supply in the New World, slaves soon became the most lucrative commodity. Dealing through African rulers and merchants, Europeans were provided with blacks forced into slavery for debts and crimes. Most often, however, slaves were prisoners of war. Later, kidnapping of victims to meet the increased demand for slaves was common. Judging from personal accounts and barracoons (prisons), some of which still exist along the coastal areas, it is clear that most slaves accepted their fate reluctantly. One can surmise from their forced internment that they were not docile, submissive, or "natural" slaves. Contrary to prevailing myth, records show that mutinies were not uncommon, though they occurred more frequently while vessels were still at anchor off the African coast than at sea. Most mutinies did not succeed. As for the voyage, the blacks endured six to eight weeks of horrendous hardship. The infamous Middle Passage, from the coast of Africa to the American mainland or the islands of the West Indies, cost the lives of about 16 percent of the slaves who over a period of some 350 years were taken to the New World.

The impact of the slave trade on Africa was significant, but did not result in a total collapse of the tribal structure. A loss of peoples in such numbers undoubtedly caused much trauma and retarded cultural and political growth. In the opinion of one widely respected historian, however, "contrary to popular impression and despite the social disruption it caused, the transatlantic trade did not generally lead to a breakdown in West African social and political organization."[28] Indeed the trade and fortunes built on slave commerce encouraged economic growth, stimulated the rise of a trading class of African merchants, and strengthened the political power of kingdoms such as Dahomey and Ashanti. By the time the slave trade was legally abolished in the United States (1808), West Africa was no more "primitive" than it had been over three centuries earlier when Europeans first darkened the continent.

Slavery in British America was different from earlier varieties of slavery because it had a racial basis. Where older forms of slavery most often occurred for social, economic, religious, or political reasons, in the English colonies *color* became the determining factor. From the arrival of the first blacks at Jamestown in 1619 to the period of the American Civil War, the sense of difference which grew between blacks and whites seems to have been based on the most obvious difference of all— the color of skin. Interestingly enough, mythology played a part in this process as well.

The West African slave who was a "negro" to the Portuguese and Spanish, a "noir" to the French, and a "black" to the English, fell victim to an ancient cultural belief that blackness symbolized savageness and evil. More than one historian has pointed out that the alleged "power of blackness" as a force for wretchedness and gloom is to be found in many

cultures and mythologies.[29] Europeans simply assumed that one who was black was not only different but wretchedly inferior because of color. In Western mythology:

> Black was the color of death, of the River Styx, of the devil; it was the color of bad magic and melancholy, of poison, mourning, forsaken love, and the lowest pit of hell. There were black arts and black humors, blackmail and blacklists, blackguards and black knights, the Black Death . . . and there were countless legends of men turning black from sin and of black races sprung from hell.[30]

Prejudice, therefore, was present even before slavery became institutionalized in the English colonies. Mythology and superstition were not enough in themselves, however, to bring about an oppressive slave labor system in the New World. Three factors gave American slavery its peculiar character. They were the need for a large labor force, the example of slavery already established in the West Indies, and the belief that the blacks were "heathen." As a result of these factors, blacks were given a separate status in colonial America.

Contrary to popular history, however, it would be a mistake to think that the *institution* of slavery, as Americans would later know it, was established by, say, 1630. At that time racial prejudice was firmly entrenched, but neither social practice nor legal codes were yet completely relegating blacks to a separate caste. However, it is known that the earliest census reports in Virginia listed whites in separate categories from blacks. What is true is that the status of blacks began to decline at a very early date. In the 1640s, fairly solid evidence can be found that social inferiority, discrimination, and permanent slavery had become the black's lot. Court records of the 1640s reveal that in the colonies of Maryland and Virginia forms of slavery were not only being practiced, but that the condition of bondage was considered to be hereditary. By the 1660s, the law began to institutionalize the practice of slavery. At that time southern colonies began to decree that henceforth all blacks imported to their region would be slaves. By 1690 blacks in South Carolina were legally defined as real estate. And by 1750 their status before the law had declined even more. They were, by legal definition, chattel—like cattle, the personal property of their owner.

Prejudice and slavery were never restricted to any one particular region of America. There were of course many differences in the ways prejudice and slavery developed in the various colonies. But racial prejudice and hostility existed north of the Mason-Dixon line as well as south of it. All Americans shared in the development of the peculiar institution. Prejudice, unequal social and political status, and segregation made life in the North nearly as difficult as life in the South. For centuries blacks have had to confront the reality that democracy, economic opportunity, and social acceptance have not been extended from any direction. The black experience in America has been a journey which began in prejudice and has led to the urban ghettos.

SECTION IV. MYTHS OF COLONIAL DEVELOPMENT

The early years of British colonization were an interesting mixture of novelty and tradition. America was an exhilarating new frontier, but the English immigrants brought much of their past with them. Differences in life-style, political philosophy, religious persuasion and social status there surely were. Rich, middle class, and poor; gentlemen adventurers, convicts, and pious clergy, among others, all must be included in any composite picture of the "typical" colonist. Despite their individual interests and activities and the dissimilarity of their backgrounds, nearly all were convinced to a greater or lesser degree that they were an important part of God's special project for humanity: to shape a better world according to His designs. They shared a commitment to Protestantism. While it is true that the northern colonies were predominantly Puritan and the southern colonies predominantly Anglican (the Church of England), the religious differences between the two were more apparent than real. Puritans and Anglicans disagreed over questions of church doctrine and politics, but they were united in the belief that the institutional church should be a fundamental

force in their daily lives. The church was the chief agency whose legitimate function was to restrain humanity's evil nature. Despite the differences which were supposed to have existed between Puritan New England and Anglican Virginia, in reality both groups of colonists sought to answer questions of salvation and damnation.

Not only is the myth that New Englanders and Virginians were of fundamentally different religious character untrue, but it is now understood that colonial religion was more practical and less stern than formerly thought. According to the traditional and mythical view, the Puritans in particular have been seen as narrowminded, bigoted, and excessively strict in matters of morals and sexuality. The word "puritan" has in fact come to imply attitudes of hypocrisy and repression. If any group has undeservedly suffered a "bad press," however, it is they. For the Puritans, as recent historical study has rather clearly shown, do not conform to their conventional stereotype as early-day Victorians.

New England Colonies

Many forces have contributed to the Puritan myth. Historians of the late nineteenth century were among those who pictured Puritan New England as a dour and drab society populated by prigs and "moral athletes." But they were only applying a veneer of academic respectability to a portrait that had already been painted. In 1850 Nathaniel Hawthorne published his famous novel, *The Scarlet Letter*, depicting the gloom of early colonial Boston. In the novel, a young heroine, Hester Prynne, becomes intimately involved with a prominent young minister, Arthur Dimsdale. After becoming pregnant and giving birth to the minister's child, Hester is marked as an outcast in the Puritan society by being forced to wear the scarlet letter "A" (for adultress) upon her breast. Both she and the young minister, whom she refuses to betray, bear their guilt and undergo much agony and remorse as they are secretly tormented by Hester's husband who has returned from Europe. The psychological atmosphere of the novel is one of repression and guilt. As a study of repressed guilt feelings and the relationship these have to the pressures of society, the book is masterful. But as a realistic portrayal of Puritan life in the early colonial period, which it is often thought to be, it clearly fails. It much more reflects Hawthorne's creative imagination and contemporary views than the actual facts of the Puritan experience.

Later, another important Puritan mythmaker was the acid-penned Baltimore newspaperman H. L. Mencken. Writing in the 1920s, Mencken blamed Puritanism for everything from the passage of the Eighteenth Amendment (Prohibition) to the famous Scopes "Monkey" Trial. The Puritan tradition, Mencken claimed, had made Americans neurotic and bigoted kill-joys. How New England Puritanism influenced the thinking of the Kansas-born Prohibition leader Carrie Nation, or how it caused William Jennings Bryan to argue the case against evolutionist theories, Mencken never fully explained. Puritanism became a convenient and believable target for Mencken in his denunciation of those features of American life with which he disagreed. The Hawthorne-Mencken image of the Puritans as snooping busybodies has been rather widely accepted in our time largely because of the popularity of psychoanalysis. Freudian emphasis on repressed human sexuality as the root cause of all psychic problems seemed to verify Mencken's "believed reality" about the Puritans.

In addition to the mythical image established by Hawthorne, Mencken, and others, academic scholars have also contributed to and helped perpetuate misconceptions about the Puritans and their supposedly grim way of life. For example, in many literature courses, one would get the impression that Puritan ministers consistently preached "hell fire and damnation" in emotional sermons delivered to quivering congregations. The perfect representative of those who practiced this religious style is supposed to be the minister-writer Jonathan Edwards. In 1739, at Enfield, Connecticut, Edwards delivered a famous sermon entitled "Sinners in the Hands of an Angry God," which "threatened the vengeance of God on the wicked." Not only was this sermon extreme for Edwards himself, but it was delivered during the period of the Great Awakening, a reaction to a declining religious spirit among the people. Such emotionally charged sermons were not usual fare even for

Puritan congregations during the seventeenth century. Edwards was born and died in the eighteenth century. In other words, he had little to do with early Puritanism and is therefore not representative of that time. Edwards' importance lies in the fact that he was a transitional figure between early Puritanism and the religious revivalism of the Great Awakening. Nonetheless, for some Jonathan Edwards represents the "typical" Puritan, and his sermon at Enfield is a classic example of the Puritans' neurotic preoccupation with faith and morals.

Historical understanding of the Puritans has been further obscured by those who have claimed that they were antisexual, anti-intellectual, and antidemocratic. To cite H. L. Mencken again, he defined Puritanism as "the haunting fear that someone, somewhere, may be happy." Of the three negative images of the Puritans the idea that they were antisexual is perhaps the one which has been most widely accepted. While it is true that Puritans were deeply committed to discipline and self-denial, they were not fanatics who prohibited all earthly pleasures. Specifically, the view that the Puritans were squeamish about sex is largely unfounded. Samuel Willard, a Puritan clergyman of the late seventeenth century, for example, often expressed his doubts about "the Excellency of Virginity." Similarly, the minister John Cotton spoke of those who would ignore the pleasures of the "Nuptial Bed" as victims of "blind zeal" and "a blind mind." The Puritans were very sensitive to the basic drives of human nature. They believed that "the Use of the Marriage Bed" was "founded in man's Nature." Thus, if the Puritan clergy consistently spoke of sex as a human necessity, it can be concluded that the Puritan community, in general, was less "puritanical" than legend suggests. This is not simply an assumption; documents of the period support such a conclusion. The legal records of the Massachusetts Bay Colony, for example, indicate the many instances in which cases of fornication and adultery came before the courts. The records also show that early Puritan communities were troubled by problems of illegitimacy. While it is very clear that the Puritan attitude toward human sexuality was tempered by a profound awareness of the laws of church and morality, it is equally clear that

Puritans are not deserving of their antisexual reputation.

It is also mythical to believe that the Puritans were intolerant of new ideas, engaged in censorship, and were anti-intellectual. The primary architects of this portion of the Puritan myth were the historians Charles Francis Adams and James Truslow Adams (no relation). Charles Francis Adams coined the phrase "glacial period," and James Truslow Adams later elaborated on the theme. The phrase described the cultural void which the historians thought they found in the early history of New England. The lack of creativity, however, was more apparent in the Adamses' writings on this subject. Examining the record with an anti-Puritan bias, they simply concluded that the Puritans had produced very little in the way of literature during New England's early years. They ignored the fact that the focal point of Puritan creativity was theology. In addition, they overlooked the Puritan commitment to "freedom of the mind" and secular art which can be found in the poetry of Anne Bradstreet and Edward Taylor, among others.

Recent scholarly research in Puritan intellectual activity indicates that the "glacial period" is not an accurate assessment. Scholars—especially Perry Miller and Samuel Eliot Morison—have shown the many ways in which Puritan New England was not at all closed-minded. The Puritans were in fact very much committed to the classics, literature, poetry, music, and scientific research. The establishment of Harvard College in 1636 indicates Puritan attitudes toward learning. (Interestingly, the celebrated banishment of Mistress Anne Hutchinson from the Bay Colony in the 1630s seems to have come about because she had taken a firm stand against university education and not because she was being persecuted as a "free thinker.") While it is true that Harvard College prepared students for the ministry, it was more than a theological seminary. Similarly, elementary schools were "free schools" under the control of the community and not the church. In addition, the literacy level among Puritans was extraordinarily high, and leading citizens were well versed in the classics. For the Puritans, only the best learning at all educational levels would do. The theories of Copernicus, Galileo, and Kepler—the radical scientific thinkers of the age—were taught among the Puritans with little controversy. Increase Mather, an "arch-Puritan" to some, was the founder of the American branch of the prestigious Royal Society of London, an organization whose membership was comprised of the best scientific minds of the day. Cotton Mather personally demonstrated the coloney's openness to new ideas by championing the need for smallpox inoculations during the Boston epidemic of 1721. The belief that the Puritans were anti-intellectual can be easily disproved, and there is scant evidence to substantiate an attitude that they were closed-minded, religious bigots who had no use for knowledge.

The mythical Puritan has also often been characterized as antidemocratic. In this regard, students have been led to believe that a Puritan elite controlled the religious, social, and political life of the Massachusetts Bay colony. According to this viewpoint, an oligarchy (a select few) managed Puritan affairs in a strict law-and-order fashion. According to the standard view, not only was the average member of the Puritan community uninvolved in political decisions, but the Puritan clergy manipulated public opinion and conduct. Having left England in search of religious freedom and the separation of church and state, the Puritans—according to myth—almost immediately denied both within their own colony. Such a view of course fits very nicely with the idea that the Puritans were antisexual and anti-intellectual. It is easy to believe that a group of men and women who were prudes and closed-minded would also be inclined to establish an antidemocratic society. At first glance one can find evidence that *some* Puritans were not in favor of a democratic form of government. John Winthrop, the first governor of the Massachusetts Bay Colony, for example, commented in his "Speech on Liberty" in July, 1645, that democracy was "the meanest and worst of all forms of government." John Cotton, a Puritan minister, asked: "If the people shall be governors, who shall be governed?" Nonetheless, to believe that law and authority in the Bay Colony were antidemocratic is to ignore many important features of Puritan political life.

To begin with, the political influence of the Puritan clergy has been overemphasized.

Early historians, in piecing together the history of the Puritans, tended to concentrate their attention only on the elite—those who in every society leave the most durable records behind and who are the most inclined to be concerned with authority. Furthermore, it must be remembered that there was never an established church in complete control of all political and religious functions in Massachusetts during the colonial period. The Bay Colony was home to Anglicans, Quakers, and Baptists as well as Puritans. Therefore the so-called Puritan oligarchy could never have controlled the reins of power nearly as much as legend holds. In addition, the New England town meeting, which according to traditional historical accounts did not function in a truly democratic way until the later years of the colonial period, was in fact an open forum with the passage of Liberty 12 of the Massachusetts Code of 1648, a sort of early Bill of Rights.

Indeed the structures of both church and state government fostered and cultivated local and individual involvement in the making of decisions. While it would be erroneous to portray the Puritans as rabid democrats during this time, they never were a society controlled by a church-dominated elite. Shortly after the colony began to develop, it became clear that no one group, religious or otherwise, had sufficient power to force others to conform. The Puritans did much to cultivate a colonial commitment to a freedom of the mind which would be fundamental to the later growth of democracy. They established a society in which authority rested on the conscience of the individual, in so far as was practical for the time.

To support the idea that the Puritans were antidemocratic, critics point to their harsh treatment of Roger Williams. According to legend, Williams challenged the Puritan Establishment with his ideas of religious freedom and the separation of church and state. He thereby set the wheels of democracy in motion. Nearly every student of American history has seen the picture of Williams, the Puritan "heretic," trudging through the snows of a New England winter to establish the colony of Rhode Island. As an outcast from the Bay Colony, Williams is heralded as the first great hero of the American democratic tradition and a Puritan forerunner of the Founding Fathers. Williams, in short, has enjoyed a secure niche in the American Hall of Fame as a prophet of democracy, a lonely figure wandering in the wilderness struggling in noble silence for social and political democracy. Actually, the Great Democrat is in many ways undeserving of the praise he has received from generations of Americans.

In trying to explain why Williams did what he did, one important fact must be kept in mind: Williams was a religious enthusiast. He was neither the freethinker nor the political philosopher of folklore. The real reason Williams found himself unwanted in Massachusetts was that he was more puritan than the Puritans themselves. While his disputes with the leaders of the Bay Colony did indeed center on the question of the separation of church and state, Williams did not seek to enhance the power of the state. Rather, he demanded the separation so that the purity of the church might be maintained. In regard to religious tolerance, Williams favored a limited sort of toleration, consistent with his religious enthusiasms. He did not favor freedom of religion as Americans have come to understand the term. He stood for old religious ideas, not for ideas which were politically new. Despite the reputation he has acquired, Williams was neither a spiritual Robinson Crusoe nor an advance man for the New Deal.

Middle Colonies

South of New England in the Middle colonies, a different kind of myth and legend took hold. Colonial outposts such as New York and Pennsylvania produced their share of folk heroes and false traditions. The artists, writers, and historians of later generations made much of the rough materials produced on the colonial frontier. Impressed by the power and prestige of New York today, one forgets that the province did not begin to play a strategic role in the development of colonial America until the mid-eighteenth century. As to the legends, it is often believed that Dutch settlers of the New York region were liberal people of good will, especially since the Netherlands had been a refuge for religious nonconformists from England. This viewpoint comes in part from Washington Irving's popular *Knickerbocker History*. Irving's work has not really shed any light on this early period of Dutch New York. According to one reliable historical source:

> 'Diedrich Knickerbocker' (Washington Irving) created a myth of New Netherland that will never die; the jolly community of tipplers and topers, of waterfront taverns, broad-beamed fraus, and well-stocked farms. The actual New Netherland was a frustrated community. The successive governors, Wouter van Twiller, William Kieft, and Peter Stuyvesant, of whom Irving drew comic pictures, were, in reality, petty autocrats and grafters who ruled New Amsterdam with a rod of iron, used torture to extract confessions, and mismanaged almost everything, especially Indian relations.[31]

Governor William Kieft in particular was a scourge to the Indians. He attempted to collect taxes from them and succeeded only in incurring their wrath. So poor were the relations of the "liberal" Dutch with the Native Americans, in fact, that the Dutch constructed a formidable barricade to protect themselves from the natives. The original Wall Street drew its name from that barricade.

As for New York's colonial development after the English seized it in 1664, the colony was not exclusively controlled by urban Knickerbockers and upstate landed aristocrats from estates, or "patroonships," along the Hudson River. Contrary to popular history, democratic ideas began to influence New York politics even before 1765. Old-line Dutch and English families such as the Livingstons, De Lanceys, Clintons, Schuylers, and Van Rensselaers carried considerable political clout in New York during this era and even later; but like Massachusetts Bay Colony, voter participation and lower-class involvement in political decisions were well established long before the Revolution. In New York, as in most colonies, the people neither believed in nor practiced democracy as we understand it today. Politics was, however, gradually moving in that direction. While New York was perhaps the most aristocratically controlled of the colonies, voting rights were already widely held well before the democratic movement prior to American independence.

A similar point can be made concerning William Penn's "Holy Experiment" in the colony of Pennsylvania, but in a reverse sense. Like most other colonists, the Quakers of Penn's colony established political structures and procedures which were relatively responsive to the people. But to see them as full-fledged democrats marking time until the Revolution is to misunderstand their life and times. Political participation guided by a Quaker elite comprised of landowners and the well-born, with the support of the other social and economic groups, characterized Pennsylvanian politics. Contrary to legend, then, New York aristocrats were more "democratic" and Pennsylvania democrats were more "aristocratic" than usually supposed.

There is also misunderstanding about the general population of Pennsylvania. The texture of colonial life in Pennsylvania was very diversified. There were Germans—the so-called Pennsylvania Dutch—Scotch-Irish, and many others. Pennsylvania had become so cosmopolitan before the American Revolution that Benjamin Franklin, in a lapse of his usual liberalism, asked whether the "boors," as he called the Germans, should be allowed further entry to the province. Thus, ironically, among the Society of Friends and in the "City of Brotherly Love" one of the first expressions of anxiety about immigration policies was made.

Relations between Pennsylvanians and Indians were not completely harmonious. In a famous painting, Benjamin West depicted a colorful scene of Indians and Quakers signing Penn's Treaty, but the details of the event cannot be documented.[32] In pre-Revolutionary Pennsylvania relations between Indians and whites were quite strained. This was particularly true in the frontier regions where whites were pushing into Indian territory.

In religious and economic affairs the Quakers were the equal of those paragons of industriousness—the Puritans. The Quakers sought a simple life, one free from the temptations and follies of the world. Indeed, as one historian has noted, "so concerned were the Friends over the vices of ostentation and vanity that they would not permit portraits to be painted of themselves. The only concessions to the ego were black silhouettes."[33] The Quakers, like the Puritans, shared convictions and values drawn from a religiously conscious

Penn's Treaty With the Indians: An Artistic View
Courtesy of the Pennsylvania Academy of Fine Arts

age. Like the Puritans, the Quakers became noted for their business prowess and commercial energy. So true was this that the so-called Puritan Ethic was as evident in Pennsylvania as it was in Massachusetts. The relationship of God and gold in Penn's colony is explained thus:

> As early as the seventeenth century, the 'legend of the Quaker as Businessman' was widely accepted. This view, which was very close to the truth, pictured the Friends as shrewd, canny traders, 'singularly industrious, sparing no Labor or Pains to increase their Wealth,' as one seventeenth-century observer put it. Much like the Puritans, the Quakers were eminently successful in the countinghouse, preaching and practicing that doctrine of the calling which united religion and bourgeois economic virtues in happy and fruitful marriage.[34]

And so conservative, Puritan New England and liberal, Quaker Pennsylvania were not all that different in many ways. The similarities of the peoples of these two colonies are as striking as their differences.

Southern Colonies

To the south of Pennsylvania and the Susquehanna River lay the southern colonies. The southern colonies—Maryland, North Carolina, South Carolina, Georgia, and Virginia—were overwhelmingly rural. Their economies were based on tobacco, rice, indigo, and mixed farming. Their people were of varied colors and origins. Indians, blacks, English, Scotch, Scotch-Irish, Germans, and Swiss settled in the region before 1776. Even though one is tempted to imagine that the South had a regional character even during the colonial period, it should be understood that the "Old South" was actually the "Old Souths."[35] By the eve of the Revolution, distinct societies had developed in the backcountry regions, the Carolinas, and in the area of Chesapeake Bay. Differences in soil type, ethnic patterns, staple crops, political structures, and closeness to urban markets all played a role in making various sections of the southern colonies different from one another. Cotton, which supposedly made the South, was not grown in any important quantities in the southern colonies—except on the sea islands off the Carolina coast—in the years before the Revolution. Economically, socially, and politically the colonial South was not one. The myth of a unified and distinct South prior to 1776 totally ignores the variety of frontier conditions with which the early Southern settler had to contend.

The first southern colonial society to develop was that in the area of Chesapeake Bay. In this wilderness, named Virginia by Sir Walter Raleigh, the English founded their first colony in the New World in May, 1607. From the nucleus of the Jamestown settlement the colonial Commonwealth of Virginia had its origins. The leader of the colonizing expedition was Captain Christopher Newport, but Captain John Smith is justly remembered as the most famous of Jamestown's early leaders. Smith's importance, however, comes not only from his accomplishments at Jamestown, but also from the fabulous legends about him which had already become well known by the time of his death in 1631. Historians ever since have debated his merits and shortcomings as a colonial leader and a historian. Smith undoubtedly was a valiant soldier and he undoubtedly was responsible for saving the Jamestown settlement in its early years from starvation and warfare with the Indians. According to his supporters, he was the "real" founder of the English overseas empire. Further, he perfectly epitomized America's romantic utopian beginnings. Adventurer, fighter, colonist, lover, and writer—John Smith was everything one could hope for in an American hero. As one historical admirer has put it:

> John Smith provides the link between European and American folk cultures. He brings medieval chivalry to the frontier and naturalizes it with us. He stands with one mailed fist extended toward the European past, but with a moccasined foot planted in the American forest. Half knight and half resourceful woodsman, he points the way to the pioneer, the frontiersman—even to the cowboy. . . .[36]

Whereas for some people John Smith has been the ideal hero, for others he scarcely measures up to his mythical reputation.

Captain John Smith's lustrous legend was first questioned in the late nineteenth century when skeptical historians such as Henry Adams began a merciless attack on both his deeds and writings. These critics claimed that in his *Generall Historie of Virginia, New England and the Summer Isles*, Smith had taken liberties with the facts and had distorted the role which he had actually played in the early years of the colonies. He was apt to boast and exaggerate; he was an imposter, a braggart, a liar, and a distorter of facts, especially as they applied to him. Despite the criticism, however, recent historians have found evidence to rehabilitate Smith's legendary image. For even though he may on occasion have embroidered his tales with romance—for example, his celebrated relationship with Pocahantas—the greater portion of what he claimed about himself and his generation has been found to be true. Documentation has never quite caught up with all of Smith's claims, but it is clear that his achievements were not those of an impostor and a liar. One should keep in mind that the standards for writing good history in Smith's day demanded a good story and a liberal dash of adventure. His heroics can thus be put in proper perspective. Smith's *Generall Historie*, like all good history written at the time, was a piece of imaginative literature. Even so, the legend of Captain John Smith is true in that he personified the spirit of the formative years of the American experience. And after all, this faith in the promise of American life *was* real. Captain Smith was a man of courage, imagination, and strength; furthermore, "he understood well that America was destiny and possibility—that America's history lay in the future."[37]

STUDY QUESTIONS

1. What are the dominant stereotypes which have tended to obscure the cultural variety and humanity of the Native Americans? What forces have worked to reinforce and perpetuate these myths?

2. How did the longstanding belief of Europeans in the idea of utopia come to affect the

discovery and settlement of America in both theoretical and practical ways?

3. Explain the process whereby race prejudice evolved into the institution of slavery in the New World.

4. Analyze and discuss the three principle myths which have come to surround the New England Puritans. When did they originate? Why have Americans found them so appealing? In what ways, and to what degree, are they historically inaccurate?

REFERENCES

1. Quoted in Jeannette Henry, "The American Indian in American History," in *Indian Voices: The First Convocation of American Indian Scholars* (San Francisco: Indian Historian Press, 1970), p. 109.
2. Richard Hofstadter, "White Servitude," in Thomas R. Frazier, ed., *The Underside of American History: Other Readings* (New York: Harcourt Brace Jovanovich, 1974), pp. 82-83.
3. Ibid., p. 98.
4. Thomas A. Bailey, *Probing America's Past: A Critical Examination of Major Myths and Misconceptions*, I (Lexington, Mass.: D. C. Heath & Co., 1973), p. 27.
5. John A. Garraty, *The American Nation: A History of the United States to 1877*, I (New York: Harper & Row, Publishers, 1975), pp. 24-25.
6. D. Alan Williams, "The Virginia Gentry and the Democratic Myth," in H. H. Quint et al., ed.: *Main Problems of American History* (Homewood, Ill.: The Dorsey Press, 1972), p. 23.
7. Oliver La Farge, "Myths That Hide the American Indian," *American Heritage* 7 (October, 1956): 7.
8. Jeannette Henry, *Textbooks and the American Indian* (San Francisco: Indian Historian Press, 1970), p. 4.
9. William Brandon, "American Indians and American History," in Roger L. Nichols and George R. Adams, eds., *The American Indian: Past and Present* (Waltham, Mass.: Xerox College Publishing, 1971), p. 18.
10. Henry, *Textbooks*, p. 155.
11. La Farge, "Myths," p. 9.
12. Mark Twain, "Fenimore Cooper's Literary Offenses," in Charles Neider, ed., *The Complete Humorous Sketches and Tales of Mark Twain* (Garden City, N.Y.: Doubleday & Co., 1961), pp. 636-637.
13. La Farge, "Myths," p. 107.
14. Harvey Einbinder, *The Myth of the Britannica* (New York: Grove Press, 1964), p. 171.
15. Washington Irving, *The Life and Voyages of Christopher Columbus*, III (New York: G. P. Putnam's Sons, 1863), p. 88.

16. Einbinder, *Myth*, p. 170.
17. Robert C. Elliott, "Columbus Discovers America," in *Search of the American Dream Series, Minneapolis Star*, September 30, 1974, p. 7A.
18. Arthur K. Moore, *The Frontier Mind: Cultural Forces That Shaped the West* (New York: McGraw-Hill Book Co., 1963), p. 33.
19. Eric Wolf, *Sons of the Shaking Earth* (Chicago: University of Chicago Press, 1959), p. 152.
20. Howard Mumford Jones, *O Strange New World, American Culture: The Formative Years* (New York: Viking Press, 1965), p. 14.
21. Durand Echeverria, *Mirage in the West: A History of the French Image of American Society to 1815* (Princeton, N.J.: Princeton University Press, 1957), p. vii.
22. Darrett B. Rutman, *The Morning of America, 1603-1789* (Boston: Houghton Mifflin Co., 1971), p. 19.
23. Louis Wright, *The Colonial Search for a Southern Eden* (University, Ala.: University of Alabama Press, 1953), p. 42.
24. Ibid.
25. F. Scott Fitzgerald, *The Great Gatsby* (New York: Charles Scribner's Sons, 1953), p. 182.
26. David Brion Davis, *The Problem of Slavery in Western Culture* (Ithaca, N. Y.: Cornell University Press, 1969), p. 8.
27. August Meier and Elliott Rudwick, *From Plantation to Ghetto* (New York: Hill & Wang, 1970), p. 27.
28. Ibid., p. 36.
29. Davis, *Problem*, p. 447.
30. Ibid., p. 448.
31. Samuel Eliot Morison, Henry Steele Commager, and William E. Leuchtenburg, *The Growth of the American Republic*, I (New York: Oxford University Press, Inc., 1969), p. 61.
32. Thomas A. Bailey, "The Mythmakers of American History," *Journal of American History* LV (June, 1968): 9.
33. Carl Degler, *Out of Our Past: The Forces That Shaped Modern America* (New York: Harper & Row, Publishers, 1970), p. 8.
34. Ibid.
35. Carl Bridenbaugh, *Myths and Realities: Societies of the Colonial South* (New York: Atheneum Publishers, 1963), p. viii.
36. Bradford Smith, *Captain John Smith: His Life and Legend* (Philadelphia: J. B. Lippincott Co., 1953), p. 307.
37. Edwin C. Rozwenc, "Captain John Smith's Image of America," *William and Mary Quarterly* Ser. 3, XVI (January, 1959): 36.

SOURCES FOR FURTHER STUDY

THE NATIVE AMERICANS
BERKHOFER, ROBERT F., JR. "Native Americans and United States History." In *The Reinterpretation of American History and Culture*. Washington,

D.C.: National Council for the Social Studies, 1973.

HENRY, JEANNETTE. *Indian Voices: The First Convocation of American Indian Scholars.* San Francisco: Indian Historian Press, 1970.

——. *Textbooks and the American Indian.* San Francisco: Indian Historian Press, 1970.

HENRY, JEANNETTE, ed. *The American Indian Reader.* San Francisco: Indian Historian Press, 1972.

NICHOLS, ROGER, AND ADAMS, GEORGE, eds. *The American Indian: Past and Present.* Waltham, Mass.: Xerox College Publishing, 1971.

AMERICA AS EUROPE'S PARADISE

JONES, HOWARD MUMFORD. *O Strange New World, American Culture: The Formative Years.* New York: Viking Press, 1965.

MOORE, ARTHUR K. *The Frontier Mind.* New York: McGraw-Hill Book Co., 1963.

RUTMAN, DARRETT B. *The Morning of America, 1603-1789.* Boston: Houghton Mifflin Co., 1971.

TEPASKE, JOHN J., ed. *Three American Empires.* New York: Harper & Row, Publishers, 1967.

WRIGHT, LOUIS. *The Colonial Search for a Southern Eden.* University, Ala.: University of Alabama Press, 1953.

SLAVERY IN A NEW WORLD PARADISE

BLASSINGAME, JOHN W. "The Afro-Americans: From Mythology to Reality." In *The Reinterpretation of American History and Culture.* Washington,

D.C.: National Council for the Social Studies, 1973.

DAVIS, DAVID BRION. *The Problem of Slavery in Western Culture.* Ithaca, N. Y.: Cornell University Press, 1969.

DEGLER, CARL. "Black Men in a White Men's Country." In *Out of Our Past: The Forces That Shaped Modern America.* New York: Harper & Row, Publishers, 1970.

JORDAN, WINTHROP D. *White over Black: American Attitudes Toward the Negro, 1550-1812.* Chapel Hill: University of North Carolina Press, 1968.

MEIER, AUGUST, AND RUDWICK, ELLIOTT. *From Plantation to Ghetto.* New York: Hill & Wang, 1970.

MYTHS OF COLONIAL DEVELOPMENT

BRIDENBAUGH, CARL. *Myths & Realities: Societies of the Colonial South.* New York: Atheneum Publishers, 1963.

DEGLER, CARL. "Were the Puritans Puritanical?" In *Out of Our Past: The Forces That Shaped Modern America.* New York: Harper & Row, Publishers, 1970.

MORGAN, EDMUND S. "The Puritans and Sex," *New England Quarterly* XV (1942): 591–607.

MORISON, SAMUEL ELIOT. *The Intellectual Life of Colonial New England.* Ithaca, N. Y.: Cornell University Press, 1963.

SMITH, BRADFORD. *Captain John Smith: His Life & Legend.* Philadelphia: J. B. Lippincott Co., 1953.

2 Myths of the Revolutionary Era

PREVIEW

Causes of the War for Independence: Myths and Realities

Before 1763 the word "American" was used almost exclusively in referring to the Indians. But as the colonists gradually acquired an identity separate from England, they saw themselves less as British subjects and more as American citizens and the word came to be used much more widely. The question of why these new Americans came to see themselves as something other than English and to establish a separate identity has never been completely answered. At first glance, the traditional explanation would seem to be adequate. That is, the force of liberty in America created a new spirit unwilling to tolerate the tyranny of the British government. Though the issues of liberty and tyranny no doubt played a role in bringing about the first successful revolt of a colony against the mother country, the causes of the American Revolution are much more complex. In fact, they are still being debated. To better understand the myth and reality of the War for Independence, one must examine the causes which historians have identified.

Despite what tradition, patriotic groups, the media, and vast numbers of textbooks tell us, excessive taxation was not the critical issue which eventually brought the colonies into open rebellion against Great Britain. Prior to 1763, colonists voiced very few objections to the various revenue-producing English Navigation Laws. Even after the Tea Act of 1773, for example, Americans generally did not view themselves as an oppressed people who sought independence because of tyrannical tax measures enacted in London. The Revolution was not caused by the English picking the colonists' pockets without their consent, despite the occasional rhetoric to that effect at the time. For example, the tea tax of 1773 was very unpopular, but even so, the same tea which cost the English six shillings per pound cost Americans only three shillings per pound. "Despite the tradition of oppressive taxation which the myth of the Revolution has

spawned," says one historian, "the actual tax burden of the colonies was much heavier in the seventeenth century than in the years immediately before the conflict. On a per capita basis, taxes were five times greater in 1698 than they were in 1773."[1] The burden of taxation on the American colonies did not even begin to compare with that which the English in the home country carried.

Slogans like "No taxation without representation" are too simple to explain the causes of war. Significant causes are usually more subtle. In the period before the American Revolution, many colonials were becoming *Americans* because they were convinced that the English government was conspiring against them. The conviction grew stronger with each new act of Parliament. The Sugar Act, the Stamp Act, the so-called Coercive Acts all seemed to fit a pattern designed to subvert American liberties. Actually, there was no deliberate conspiracy by King George III or his ministers or Parliament, but that didn't matter. What did matter was that many Americans believed there was a conspiracy. A myth of British tyranny, fed by the illusion of conspiracy and the tendency to overdramatize the harshness of the empire's policies, began to develop in the colonies. Even more important, the notion of conspiracy was believed and acted upon as though a conspiracy actually existed. No other episode in the American experience better demonstrates the force which myths can have once they are accepted as reality.

Collected Myths of the War Years

The American Revolution produced an interesting array of events and personalities, made durable particularly because of the legends and myths which have become associated with them. Independence Day, for example, has certainly had as much of a mythical hold on the American mind as Bastille Day (July 14) has had for the French, or the October Revolution (November 7) for Russians. The Declaration of Independence, especially, is given a position as a venerated American document. For many, it is celebrated and esteemed rather than read and understood. As for the seemingly endless list of heroes and villains which the circumstances of revolution produced—from Crispus Attucks and John Paul Jones on the side of the "good guys" to Benedict Arnold and General Charles Cornwallis on the side of the "bad guys"—all have been distorted by legend. None of these luminaries was as good or as bad as the legends suggest. As a case in point, Crispus Attucks has of late been magnified out of due proportion. Even though historical records reveal almost nothing about him, a good many historians of the black experience in America have attempted to make him a black martyr of the Revolution. However, the only indisputable fact is that a man of that name was one of those slain by Captain Preston's Redcoats at the so-called Boston Massacre in 1770. But whether Attucks was black is unclear; he may have been a Natick Indian or a mulatto seaman. In any event, too little indisputable evidence exists to substantiate who he was.

The legend of John Paul Jones has followed a pattern similar to that of Attucks. Captain Jones' historical reputation has been built on two things: the famous words spoken in the heat of battle, "Sir, I have not yet begun to fight," and his defeat of the British frigate *Serapis*. As to the first, historians have no way of knowing whether or not he ever uttered this now-famous statement. It is known, however, that his illustrious defeat of the *Serapis* was of no particular military significance. In fact, Jones' ship, the *Bonhomme Richard*, was so badly damaged in the fray that it sank two days later. Even though Jones was no doubt a colorful and brave supporter of the patriot cause, he has come down through the ages more as a figure on a pedestal than a flesh-and-blood human being. As a social climber, rake, and brawler, he is a somewhat curious candidate for a mantle of immortality. Along with Crispus Attucks, he played a role in history, an even somewhat significant role, as a historical hero, but pedestals are made for statues, not for real people.

On the other side of the ledger, history has been too harsh on Benedict Arnold and General Cornwallis, making one a symbolic figure of disloyalty, the other of failure. At one time, General Arnold was second only to Washington as a military leader. He displayed great heroism, for example, during the capture of Fort Ticonderoga and at the strategic battle of Saratoga, which is considered to be the turning point of the war and convinced the French government that support of the American cause would be worthwhile. Precisely because of his early successes, Arnold lost much of his enthusiasm for the war effort. Consistently overlooked in military promotions, he made contact with the British to surrender West Point because he was convinced that he had been intolerably abused and neglected. While his actions were indeed treasonous, an understanding of why he chose to do what he did tempers our judgment of him. His many important contributions to the success of the Revolution have been too quickly forgotten or ignored.

In a similar way, the case of Lord Cornwallis—the British general who surrendered to George Washington at Yorktown, Virginia, in 1781—also proves that history is hard on losers. One will never be able to say, of course, that Cornwallis' leadership of the British forces in the American Revolution was particularly noteworthy, much less heroic; but it should be stated that he was not as inept as later generations of Americans have believed. Prior to Yorktown he had routed General Horatio Gates at Camden, South Carolina, and defeated the Revolutionary hero Nathanael Greene at the battle of Guilford Courthouse in North Carolina. Later he went on to prove himself a sound and capable military leader in both Ireland and India, where he died in 1805.

One of the more secure members of the hall of fame of the American Revolution is Benjamin Franklin. While many of Dr. Franklin's exploits are worthy of praise and even adulation, a thick gloss of legend has tended to distort our understanding of his contributions. Renowned for his experiments in practical science and for his part in the drafting of the Declaration of Independence, Franklin is perhaps best remembered for his role in securing an alliance with France during the war years. The Treaty of Friendship and Commerce of 1778, and Franklin's role in arranging it, have been subject to misconception and myth. Textbooks, for example, have often implied that French assistance was not critical to the final outcome of the war. Besides, to applaud French efforts might detract from the glorious actions of the patriots. In support of this view, it can be argued that French military support was less than completely successful in naval engagements at Savannah, Newport, and New York, and that America's alliance with the French may have hardened the British resolve to carry on the war despite growing public disapproval. Nevertheless, the treaty is usually seen as a generous move on the part of the French, and Benjamin Franklin's personal diplomacy is acknowledged as the most important factor in securing it. Neither the so-called Franklin Legend (i.e., that the author of *Poor Richard's Almanac* set down his pen long enough to personally negotiate a treaty with France favorable to America) nor the Lafayette Myth (i.e., that France came to the assistance of the colonies for sentimental reasons) find complete support in the facts.

When General Pershing brought the first American troops into France in 1917, during the First World War, he is supposed to have said: "Lafayette, we are here." Pershing's words (which were actually spoken by his military aide, Colonel Charles Stanton) express the common belief that America was repaying a debt which it had owed the French people since the American Revolution. For almost 140 years, the legend had endured that France had aided the rebel cause in 1778 either because of a philosophical commitment to America's becoming a democratic nation or because of some premonition of America's future greatness and power. While it is true that some French citizens, in particular the Marquis de Lafayette, responded to the ideals proclaimed in the Declaration of Independence, it is equally clear that the French government pursued its policy of friendship with the rebelling colonies primarily because France had recently suffered a strategic defeat at the hands of the English. In 1763, France had lost the Great Wars for Empire (which had begun in 1688) to the British, and in the process had been forced to give up most of its colonial holdings in North America. By forming an alliance with the United States, France was simply pursuing national self-interest. The French government sought to restore French prestige in Europe, regain some control over former overseas possessions, and simultaneously challenge England's solid reputation as the world's strongest military power.

Thus for these foreign policy considerations, France was inclined to support the American cause even before the first diplomatic overtures for aid had been received from America.

Diplomatic representatives from the colonies—Arthur Lee and Silas Deane—had made contact and engaged in preliminary conversations with French representatives many months before Benjamin Franklin's arrival. By the time he reached Paris, his reputation had of course preceded him; and he was warmly received as an American folk hero—beaver hat and all. One must give him credit for capitalizing on his mystique in order to bring the negotiations to a successful conclusion. But to see him as exclusively responsible for the French Alliance, or to believe that France placed sentiment before self-interest, is to misread an important part of the history of the War for Independence and Franklin's role in it. With surprising insight into what the myths and legends of the future might hold, the patriot and later president John Adams wrote to Dr. Benjamin Rush in the year of Franklin's death (1790):

> The history of our Revolution will be one continued lie from one end to the other. The essence of the whole will be that Dr. Franklin's electrical rod smote the earth and out sprang General Washington. That Franklin electrified him with his rod—and thence forward these two conducted all the policy, negotiations, legislatures, and war.

Though to some degree Adams' remarks may have been prompted by envy of the reputations which Washington and Franklin had achieved, he has been proven right in his predictions.

The Illusion of Unity: The American Loyalists

The French did not join forces with Revolutionary America in the belief that it was on a crusade to preserve freedom, and neither did a good many colonists who were not inspired by the prospect of freedom from Britain. Since Americans prefer to extol the virtues of winning, the Loyalists, or Tories—those who actively or passively opposed America's exit from the British Empire—have been buried beneath an avalanche of vituperation. Minorities have traditionally had a difficult time making it to the pages of American history textbooks. The Loyalists have suffered a similar fate. Though the Tories have received a more complete and sympathetic treatment of late, there are still many who continue to show disdain and to view them as did many early historians of the Revolution. A textbook designed for schools in mid-nineteenth-century America, for example, makes this exaggerated claim:

> And 'when the people saw that the king would not hearken unto them, they took council among themselves, and a shout went up from every hill and valley, city and hamlet, mountain and plain, from the rock of Plymouth to the lagoons of Florida, To our tents, O Israel!'[2]

This quote, with its biblical imagery, shows how the role of George III was misrepresented. But it also mistakenly implies that every ablebodied person in the colonies left the plow or the apprentice's bench or the kitchen to fight for freedom's cause. The fact is that the Tories represented an important minority of colonial society during the Revolutionary era; indeed, so did the Patriots. Neither point of view, Tory or Patriot, represented the majority opinion on the eve of rebellion. The supporters of revolution won and the Tories lost, mainly because the Patriots had better organization and leadership. A major problem among those professing loyalty to the Crown was that they relied too much on the mother country for leadership, and thus never became effectively organized as a political force. Faced with the inevitability of the success of the Revolution, many left for the more hospitable environments of Great Britain, Canada, Florida, and the British West Indies. Some of those who fled to the north are now considered to be founders of British Canada.

Myths of the Founding Fathers

The makers of the American Constitution, the so-called Founding Fathers, are so well remembered that the problem of myth concerning them is particularly acute. The true accomplishments of this illustrious group of statesmen have been lost in legend precisely because Americans have long presumed that they were the most noble representatives of the nation's golden age of politics. Supposedly,

no group of people before or since are as deserving of admiration. Historians, however, have been somewhat less inclined than the public to give unending praise to the fifty-five men who gathered to write what is now the world's oldest national constitution. Over fifty years ago, the historian Charles A. Beard wrote a study of the Constitution which was unique because it questioned the motives of those who wrote the famous document. Arguing that the Constitution was essentially economic in nature, and that the makers had been fortune-hunters, Professor Beard launched a prolonged debate on the question of what really happened at Philadelphia in 1787. While Beard's economic interpretation of the Constitution—which viewed the entire constitutional process as flawed by the selfishness and hypocrisy of economic exploiters—is no longer accepted as a valid thesis, it had an iconoclastic effect. The work reinstituted scholarly discussion on a formerly sacrosanct subject. Even so, the results of new research have not fundamentally altered pre-Beardian views. The proceedings of the Philadelphia Convention are now seen as having been shaped by the energy of like-minded individuals who were attempting to preserve the benefits of liberty and stability that had been won by the Revolution. Even though many older leaders of the Revolutionary generation did not participate in the Constitutional Convention and did not support its passage, the younger generation were convinced that the Constitution would bring the earlier rebellion to a logical and fitting conclusion.

Another legend concerns the way the Constitution was received. The common belief is that the American public greeted the Constitution with nearly universal applause. But its reception won less than universal approval, far less in fact. The historical evidence indicates that numerous well-intentioned Americans, such as Patrick Henry, George Clinton, and Richard Henry Lee, argued that the Constitution should not be ratified. This nearly forgotten group of men, who, according to their critics, were "misguided opponents who could not see the light of liberty behind the new Constitution," sought to retain local governmental rule rather than a strong national government. As with almost every political debate of any historical significance, the ratification of the American Constitution generated a lot of heated controversy. The legend that all Americans accepted the Constitution without debate greatly detracts from an episode which, even stripped of myth, remains one of the most exciting in American history.

SECTION I. CAUSES OF THE WAR FOR INDEPENDENCE: MYTHS AND REALITIES

Revolutions appeal to deep human emotions and hold special meaning for humanity in general. Because each event in a revolution is seen as crucial and because the leaders of a revolution are portrayed as heroes, most revolutions are vividly etched into the national consciousness of the countries in which they occur. Thus Russians today find much of the meaning of their existence as a nation locked within the events of the revolution against the czar in 1917. The French still debate the meaning their revolution has had for them. The American Revolution is, of course, no exception. It is important not only because it was ours, but also because it was the first of the great modern revolutions and did much to set patterns for those which followed. The French Revolution of 1789, for example, was profoundly influenced by the precepts and spirit of the American Revolution that occurred thirteen years earlier. In our own time, Ho Chi Minh consciously attempted to pattern his Vietnamese revolution after the American example. In proclaiming the new Republic of Vietnam in September, 1945, Ho said that the Vietnamese declaration should read: "All men are created equal. They are endowed by their Creator with certain inalienable rights, among these are life, Liberty and the Pursuit of Happiness...." The Vietnamese sense of kinship with the American Revolution went so far, in fact, that a group of Vietnamese women attempted to establish contact with the Daughters of the American Revolution as a way of symbolizing what the "old revolution" meant to the new. Though we might well see this Vietnamese attempt to relate to the American War for Independence as somewhat bizarre, it does make clear that the spirit of

our revolution continues to be felt throughout the world. As much as any single event in history the American Revolution holds a noble and secure place in people's memories.

Quite naturally, Americans regard the Revolution as the touchstone of their history. It was, it seems, both the nation's finest hour and the true beginning of the national experience. But it was not the true birthdate of the country, for almost 170 years had elapsed from the founding of the first mainland colony to Jefferson's Declaration of Independence. Thus if American history "began" with the Revolution, it would be necessary to ignore a span of time equal to the period from Jefferson's presidency to that of Harry S. Truman.

Still, in a sense the American Revolution did mark the birth of the nation, for it was only after its revolutionary experience that America became a community of states and finally a nation. Because the Revolution is so central to what we are as a nation, and because it is so revered, one must be more sensitive than ever to the problem of myth-making about the Revolution. The first impulse in dealing with the Revolution is to fall victim to myth by reading history backwards. The great political and economic success which the United States has enjoyed since its break with England may lead one to discover, as one historian says:

> more signs and portents of a splendid future than were at that time apparent. This provides admirable material for July Fourth oratory, but stretches at places the fabric of history. After all, history is more than an ornamental garden, laid out with hindsight by teachers and historians; it is rather a jungle where living forces were once at work, and the reconstruction of this jungle is our real business if we wish to understand the past.[3]

A typical example of reading history backwards is the conventional picture of the Revolution as a bloody contest between liberty-loving colonists and a system of tyranny. A nonbiased and nonmythical understanding of the Revolution is possible only if one seeks the meaning of the events of the Revolution for all those who lived them.

In seeking to uncover the economic, social, and political realities of the America of 1776, historians have had difficulty in detaching themselves from the age in which their own works were written. Nearly every generation of American historians has tried to revise what previous generations have said about America's revolutionary experience. By reflecting their own times, they have been unable to agree on either causes of or changes produced by the Revolution.

One of the first historians who attempted to find answers to the causes of the Revolution was George Bancroft. Writing at the time of the Civil War, Bancroft discerned in the Revolutionary War much the same pattern as was evident in the civil conflict to which he was a witness. The War for Independence, Bancroft concluded, was a contest between liberty and equality on the one hand and tyranny and despotism on the other.

Historians of the late nineteenth and early twentieth centuries have also reflected the views of their times as much as the causes of the Revolution by overemphasizing economics as the major reason for the split between the colonies and Britain. Arguing that the colonists had been forced into rebellion by harsh fiscal measures and taxing policies of England, they concluded that the war resulted from a clash of economic philosophies and interests. But this group of historians, too, were essentially reflecting their own times, creating myths in the process. As these economic histories were being written, America was going through a period of great change brought on by the industrial revolution. Historians thus became convinced that the causes of the American Revolution were economic because of the economic revolution which surrounded them in late nineteenth-century America. Both groups of scholars—those of Bancroft's age and the later economic historians—helped create a mythology about the Revolution because they were reading history backwards.

Since the Second World War, another group of historians has challenged what had formerly been thought to be real causes of the American Revolution. Their thesis is that the war was not revolutionary at all. For them, it was conservative. That is, the colonists were attempting to conserve the democracy and economic prosperity which they enjoyed before British imperialism began to pose a threat. In emphasizing triumphant democracy and economic prosperity, these historians are drawing upon the American experience following the Second World War. In line with the times in which they were writing, they were reflecting a renewed faith in democracy as a system of government which had recently defeated totalitarianism in Europe. As an explanation of the causes of the American Revolution, they were also projecting the present into the past rather than understanding the past on its own terms.

Tyranny and Taxation

The most misleading and inaccurate—as well as persistent—of the causes of the American Revolution is the one first endorsed by George Bancroft. He argued that the war came because the colonists concluded that they had suffered long enough from the tyranny of the British government. Although the idea that England systematically attempted to subvert and destroy the growing flower of freedom in America by means of despotic policies is a very fetching explanation of the events surrounding 1776, it is mostly myth. Historians interested in exploring this question, for example, have compared the English colonial system with others in operation at the same time (e.g., France and Spain) and have concluded that the British Empire was the least oppressive of all. Also, the "infamous" Navigation Acts passed in the British Parliament prior to 1763 seldom, if ever, imposed serious economic hardships upon the colonists. Various English laws controlling the trading of commodities such as wool, hats, and iron were at times inconvenient, but it would be a gross overstatement to say that they were oppressive. Some colonists felt the pinch of regulation, but the various Navigation Acts were certainly not, in themselves, ample cause for revolution. Rather, what should be emphasized is the fact that colonial America benefited and prospered from its privileged place within the British Empire. In return for the slight restrictions imposed by the Navigation Acts, the American colonies had a guaranteed market for many of their goods both in England and in other British colonies. The Royal Navy, for example, bought considerable amounts of naval stores —ship masts, turpentine, pitch, tar, and hemp for rope—not only to equip the fleet, but also to better protect the colonies from continued threats to colonial trade by France and Spain. Trade of this type helped to make the protective shield of the British navy strong while also contributing to colonial prosperity. Far from being heavily burdened by their attachments to England, the colonies owed much of their prosperity to the fact that they were junior partners in the world's strongest empire.

And relationships between the colonies and England were relatively harmonious in the years before 1763. Contrary to popular belief, the Navigation Acts had not as yet caused the colonists to believe that a break with the mother country was either necessary or advisable. The year 1763, however, proved pivotal, for it marked the conclusion of the Great Wars for Empire between England and France. Though the British emerged from the extended conflict in control of much of North America, they also possessed a national debt of some £130 million. Since the series of wars with France had been fought not only to enhance the power and prestige of the British Empire but also to protect the colonies from the French, to the British it seemed only logical that the colonies should pay a fair share of the conflicts' cost. To accomplish this, Sugar and Currency Acts were passed in 1764, a Stamp Act in 1765, and the Townshend Acts two years later. These were meant to be revenue-producing, more than regulatory, but even so, the financial burden the colonies were being asked to bear was anything but oppressive. Taxes collected in America were designed to meet only one third of England's total expenditures for protecting the colonies. "It was not injustice or the economic incidence of the taxes which prompted the colonial protests," one historian has concluded, "it was rather the novelty of the British demands."[4] The American colonies had come to enjoy a period of "salutary neglect" while England had been preoccupied with fighting the series of wars with France. Now, when England tried to reestablish closer control over its colonies, a time of trouble began. But despite what has been said, tyranny had little to do with the revolution which was to come.

Americans have long cherished the belief that the failure to resolve such issues as "internal versus external taxation" and "taxation without representation" caused the colonists finally to cut the ties that bound them to the British Empire. Much misunderstanding and myth surround these issues. Actually, "the argument that the colonists should allow England to impose external taxation, but not internal taxation was never a dominant colonial position."[5] The Americans surely protested when England attempted to impose control over the colonies it had long held on a loose leash. This protest, however, was not based on the internal-external taxation question. Faced with the Sugar Act, for example, only two colonies—North Carolina and New York—made any claim at all that Parliament did not have the legal right to tax them, either internally or externally. When the Stamp Act was passed, colonial spokesmen began to argue that the British could only regulate trade as they had done in the past, but could not tax the colonies for purposes of raising revenue. The Stamp Act crisis brought a greater sense of unity to the colonies because its effects were more immediate (i.e., it levied a tax on such regularly used items as newspapers and marriage licenses) and because it thus more directly symbolized a dramatic change in policy by the English toward the colonies. Colonists now began to perceive a grand conspiracy against their basic freedoms. Despite these new colonial claims, however, the British government did in fact hold the legal right to tax a colony, but it had never made consistent use of this power. What the colonists opposed most was not internal taxation but additional taxation in any form.

The idea that the colonists went to war with England because they objected to "taxation without representation" is also mythical. This popular slogan had actually come from England; it was not coined in America as a weapon against British tyranny. But even if the phrase had been American in origin, evidence clearly shows that the colonists had little desire to be represented in Parliament. In the first place, owing to suffrage qualifications, taxation without representation was common political practice within the individual American colonies. Second, it was well known that several districts in England—the industrial and slave trade center of Liverpool for example—were not directly represented in the British Parliament. In addition, Benjamin Franklin had gone on record against Parliamentary representation for the colonies shortly after the passage of the Stamp Act, and even earlier, Virginia and South Carolina had opposed such a solution to the crisis. The expense involved in sending colonial delegates to Parliament, plus the fact that once they were seated they would surely be outvoted on all important colonial matters, made it abundantly clear that taxation would continue even *with* representation. What the colonists seem to have wanted most of all was a return, somehow, to the "good old days" before 1763 when they enjoyed most of the advantages of membership in the British Empire while unburdened by responsibilities.

In connection with the taxation issue, one might note another mythological item: Patrick Henry's "liberty or death" speech before the Second Virginia Convention in Richmond's St. John's Episcopal Church in 1775. Indeed, the famous oration has spanned both time and place. The English poet Lord Byron, for example, was so enchanted with Henry's speech that he called him "The Forest-born Demosthenes"—the ancient Greek orator who tried to rally Athenians to victory over the Macedonians at the battle of Chaeronea. More recently, a "Gallup poll on quotations from our history," one historian has noted, "revealed that 48 percent of Americans know [Henry] as the author of those ever-inspiring words, 'Give me Liberty or give me Death!' Though topped by the 61 percent who know that Mae West said, 'Come up and see me some time,' he fared better than Lincoln, Wilson, and the two Roosevelts."[6] Even though many people have long believed that Henry's speech in itself did much to "cause" the Revolution, there is strong reason to doubt that the so-called Trumpet of the Revolution even uttered the famous words.

No record of the time contains "the speech." Rather, it is a product of the collected reminiscences of those who forty years before had heard Henry give it. The speech did not in fact appear in print until 1817 when William Wirt wrote an admiring biography of his fellow Virginian. Using imagination to overcome the problem of meager source materials, Wirt reconstructed Henry's speech according to what he thought was said back in 1775. The phrase "I know not what course others may take, but as for me, give me liberty or give me death" seems considerably more concise and polished than one might expect from an extemporaneous speech given in the heat of emotion. William Wirt's version of Patrick Henry's Liberty Speech, of course, is probably not a complete fabrication. In tone and spirit the actual speech no doubt resembled that which Wirt recorded, even though he undoubtedly injected into it considerable melodrama. Still, there is no record of the actual speech, and consequently, doubt that Henry used the words Wirt attributed to him must remain.

To substantiate the mythical belief that the British government harshly abused American colonists, it is often said that the English king—George III—brought about the separation of the American colonies from Britain because he was tyrannical. The Declaration of Independence condemned the king and many history textbooks have been equally harsh in judging him. Recent evidence, however, indicates that not until early in 1776 did the colonists see the English monarch as a tyrant who wished to take away their liberties. Indeed, almost to the very end, colonials expressed a deep loyalty and fondness for George III. The king symbolized the attachment which the colonists felt toward the empire. Believing, as British citizens, that ultimate authority within the empire rested with Parliament and not with the king, colonial leaders up to the final break directed their attention to that body and its ministers. In the years before rebellion the colonials consistently spoke of their "rights as Englishmen" and of their desire to achieve "Home rule under the King." They retained their loyalty to the Crown and sought a redress of grievances, not independence, from Parliament. Even as the Second Continental Congress began to seek the aid of foreign allies in the event of war, that group issued the "Olive Branch Petition" in which the delegates fervently requested King George to assist them in their continuing problems with ministers and Parliament. Still hoping for liberty *within* the empire, delegates at the congress considered this move their last best hope for reconciliation.

Paul Revere's Personal View of the Boston Massacre
Library of Congress

The tide of opinion against George III began to shift only when he bluntly rejected the Olive Branch Petition late in 1775 and then hired German mercenaries to fight in America. The image of George III as a tyrant truly began to take hold early in 1776, six months before the Declaration of Independence. Early in January Thomas Paine's famous pamphlet *Common Sense* "burst from the press" (as one of Paine's fellow colonists said at the time) and crystallized people's negative attitudes toward their king. At the moment when the loyalty of reluctant revolutionists was wavering, Paine leveled a direct attack not only at King George but at the institution of monarchy itself. "Government by kings," Paine declared, "was first introduced into the world by the heathens." Suggesting that the English monarch was descended from the "French bastard" William the Conqueror, Paine went on to wonder why "the title of sacred majesty" had been "applied to a worm." More than any other commentary, Thomas Paine's little pamphlet kindled the myth that King George III was a "royal brute," for Paine's words were read or heard by thousands. Six months later Thomas Jefferson reinforced the tyranny myth when he proposed to show in the Declaration of Independence that "the history of the present King of Great Britain is a history of repeated injuries and usurpations, all having in direct object the establishment of an absolute tyranny over these States." Thus, the combination of *Common Sense* and the Declaration of Independence caused the "candid world," to whom Jefferson addressed his work, to unthinkingly accept the legend of George III as a tyrannical king. While it is true that America's last king was of modest intelligence, and left much to be desired as an administrator, in his dealings with the colonists he was never the "tyrant of tyrants" portrayed by the myth.

SECTION II. COLLECTED MYTHS OF THE WAR YEARS

The idea that "independency" from Mother England was an appropriate course of action

37

in the face of Great Britain's "conspiracy" against American liberties had taken hold. But even as the fateful step toward an independent course was being made, the fighting had already begun. In fact, the English decision to use force against the colonists—and particularly against those in and around Boston who were judged to be the most radical—had been made in January, 1775, a full year before Thomas Paine's *Common Sense*. A common impression is that Thomas Jefferson brought about the actual fighting of the Revolution by writing the Declaration of Independence. Did he not write the document in the wilderness environment of his beloved Monticello and then inform an expectant America of his courageous stand?

The "shot heard round the world" actually occurred in April, 1775—nearly fifteen months before the Declaration. And six months before independence was actually declared, Jefferson had written that he remained "sincerely one of those who still wishes for union . . . and would rather be in dependence on Great Britain, properly limited, than on any other nation on earth." Yet our understanding of the early stages of the Revolution is clouded by misunderstanding and deserves much closer attention. One is forced to agree with the view

expressed by a historian who more than thirty years ago said:

> It is a singular fact that the greatest event in American history—the Declaration of Independence—has been the subject of more incorrect popular belief, more bad memory on the part of the participants, and more false history than any other occurrence in our national life.[7]

One might expect that the critical events surrounding the occasion of American independence would be clearly known because of their fundamental importance to the beginnings of the nation. But this is not the case. It is precisely because of its central importance that legends abound. Many of the basic facts surrounding Independence Day, the signing of the Declaration of Independence, the Liberty Bell, and the Fourth of July stand as monuments to America's dependency on myth.

Contrary to accepted belief, Independence Day is not July 4. Congress actually passed the resolution establishing American independence on July 2, not July 4, 1776. In addition, individuals such as John and Samuel Adams and Richard Henry Lee were probably as important as Thomas Jefferson in shaping the idea of independence. Throughout the early months of 1776, it was they who had taken the lead in urging the colonials to think seriously about separation from Great Britain. Further leadership in the direction of separation came on a practical level from the state of South Carolina, which had set up its own independent government in late March of that fateful year. With Lexington and Concord, the emergence of a revolutionary leadership, and the example of South Carolina behind him, Richard Henry Lee, on May 10, 1776, introduced a resolution in the Second Continental Congress urging that each colony "adopt such government as shall in the opinions of the representatives of the people best conduce to the happiness and safety of their constituents in particular and America in general." From this point on, events began to move rapidly and the participants themselves helped contribute to the growth of legend surrounding them.

Patriots of Valley Forge
Commonwealth of Pennsylvania

38

Lee's leadership provided the first step toward formalizing independence. Further action did not come until June 7 when he introduced his now-famous resolution of independence:

> RESOLVED: That these United Colonies are, and of right ought to be, free and independent States, that they are absolved from all allegiance to the British Crown, and that all political connection between them and the State of Great Britain is, and ought to be, totally dissolved.

The momentous resolution was not accepted immediately, though there was at this point little real doubt as to its eventual passage. After the Declaration was drafted by Thomas Jefferson, assisted by Benjamin Franklin and John Adams, the Continental Congress adopted it on July 2. Thus, despite the significant roles played by Richard Henry Lee, who had first proposed the Declaration, and John Adams, who had seconded the resolution and served as a member of the drafting committee, legend has glorified only the role of Thomas Jefferson. To emphasize the importance of Lee and Adams, however, is not at all to detract from the key role played by Jefferson. He was by far the most accomplished writer of the group, and for his abilities in giving expression to the Declaration's revolutionary ideas his contributions must never be forgotten. The fact remains, however, that the document was adopted on July 2, not July 4, and that Richard Henry Lee and John Adams were as instrumental to its development and acceptance as was "The Sage of Monticello."

Even among those who know that the Declaration was adopted on July 2, the notion remains that it was actually signed on July 4—hence the national celebration on that day. In fact, however, signatures were added to the document periodically over the remaining months of 1776. When the Declaration was publicly announced on July 8 of that year people knew only that John Hancock and Charles Thompson had officially signed it. The names of the remaining signers were not disclosed until it was better known how the document would be received. "It was not until

six months later, and after the Battle of Trenton had been fought," as the historian Charles Warren has shown, "that the people knew who the signers were."[8] Complete disclosure of the names of the signers did not occur until January 18, 1777, when Congress decided that "an authenticated copy of the declaration of independency, with the names of the members of Congress subscribing the same, be sent to each of the United States and they be desired to have the same put on record." Despite the persistent idea that the Declaration was warmly received by masses of Revolutionary patriots, the fact is that those associated with it moved very cautiously. It was only after the idea of independence became more widely accepted that the *Congressional Journal* was made to read—on a blank page left precisely for this purpose—that the signing had occurred on July 4. Looking back at the record decades later, most Americans—including John Adams and Thomas Jefferson—simply assumed that the entry in the *Congressional Journal* was "official." The July 4 date seems to have imbedded itself in the nation's consciousness and mythology simply because it was on that day that John Hancock symbolically thrust the nation closer to independence with the flamboyant flourish of his pen.

In similar ways the Liberty Bell and its connection with the Declaration of Independence have also been associated with fictitious history. Contrary to the legend, the Liberty Bell may well not have chimed the good tidings of the signing of the Declaration across the land. The Liberty Bell, one has often been told, was the "Voice of Independence." This idea, and the legend that the Liberty Bell was cracked during the first celebration, are untrue. Records make absolutely no mention of the fact that any special ringing of the bell hanging in the State House in Philadelphia took place, and the State House bell was cracked in 1835 while tolling for Chief Justice John Marshall's funeral. Further, the bell received its name as a result of debates over the slavery issue in 1839. Thus, it must be emphasized that the idea of freedom which the bell symbolized, and the word "liberty" attached to it, first referred to the hopes held by some for the freedom of the slaves. The notion that the bell was named in honor of the revolutionists of 1776 is erroneous. The mythical tale of the Liberty Bell first appeared in 1847 when a Philadelphian named George Lippard published his *Washington and His Generals or Legends of the American Revolution*. In a burst of pure youthful imagination, Lippard created an enduring legend which most Americans have ever since accepted as historically true.

Along with the myths surrounding Thomas Jefferson, the signing of the Declaration of Independence, and the Liberty Bell, the elaborate mythology of the Fourth of July evolved gradually. While it is generally believed that the Fourth immediately became an "official" date for national celebration, as already implied, the nationalization of the holiday as the nation now knows it did not occur until 1826. In the years immediately after the Declaration some communities did hold festivities and commemorations. Recognition of the Fourth of July as the "Anniversary of the United States of America" was made in 1781 by the state of Massachusetts, followed two years later by official municipal celebrations in Boston. Rather quickly, however, such celebrations became the focal point in the struggle between those who favored the new Constitution and those who opposed it. As supporters of the proposed Constitution, the Federalists declared that they were the guardians of patriotism and thus held exclusive rights to the celebration of the Fourth. Claiming that the anti-Federalists had forsaken "Americanism" and the true spirit of the original Declaration, pro-Constitution forces began to use Independence Day as an occasion on which to criticize and denounce their opponents. With the development of political parties—Federalists and Republicans—there was little unified celebration of the nation's birth. Debate, for example, centered on who among the drafters of the Declaration had been the most important—John Adams (who was now a Federalist party standardbearer) or Thomas Jefferson (leader of the Republicans). Political tensions over the Fourth of July reached such a point by 1806 that the son of a prominent Republican was murdered in Boston by an overzealous Federalist. It was not until after the "Second War for Independence," the War of 1812, that political tempers began to cool. "And finally the deaths of both Jefferson and Adams on July 4, 1826," says the historian Charles Warren, "apparently symbolized the end of an era of partisanship and also marked the nationalization of the holiday."[9] With the deaths of the pivotal figures in the controversy over the Fourth of July, the nation was finally able to agree that Independence Day was for all Americans. Unfortunately for history's sake, political emotions had already fostered the growth of multiple myths about the birth of the nation which lived well beyond 1826.

Heroes of the Revolution

Nearly every revolution has given birth to heroes and legends concerning them. The Russian Revolution produced Nicolai Lenin and Leon Trotsky, and the French Revolution Maximilien Robespierre and Napoleon Bonaparte. With respect to the American Revolution, one is forced to contend with the inevitable array of legendary heroes and heroines, among them George Washington, Paul Revere, Betsy Ross, and Francis Marion.

The war years did of course produce many outstanding examples of noteworthy sacrifice and commendable valor. Some rebels, however, have been romanticized beyond the point of believable achievement. Paul Revere is a case in point. The events surrounding Revere's now-famous "midnight ride" are mostly mythical, thanks to the historical legend created by the poet Henry Wadsworth Longfellow. "The stirring tale of Paul Revere's ride was a legend in search of a poet," one scholar has said, "and it found Henry Wadsworth Longfellow, who put the resolute rider on the wrong side of the river and had him thunder into Concord, which he failed to reach."[10] It is understandable that poets such as Longfellow would resort to imagination for detail. Their exaggeration and error, often accepted as history, however, make the serious student's job of sorting fact from fiction that much more difficult.

Other falsifiers of the historical record have taken liberties with the facts and helped create a pseudopast out of the reality of Revolutionary America. Tradition holds, for example, that General Washington knelt in the snow and bitter cold of Valley Forge, even though not a shred of evidence exists to verify that he ever did so. And the painting "Washington Crossing the Delaware" (1851) by the German-American painter Emanuel Leutze is almost entirely based on the artist's imagination. Aside from the fact that Leutze's work perfectly matched the mid-nineteenth-century mythical image of the Father of our Country, "among the various errors, he has the statuesque general standing precariously in the wrong kind of boat in broad daylight beneath an American flag that had not yet been devised by Francis Hopkinson. The stars and stripes were not adopted by Congress until June 14, 1777, nearly six months after the Delaware crossing."[11]

But Leutze is certainly not the only one who has mythologized the historical picture of General Washington. Another story based on myth is that Washington asked Betsy Ross to make the first American flag. Actually, there is no historical proof that such a request ever came from Washington or that she made any flag at all. As one might expect, the Betsy Ross legend seems to have been created and circulated by her descendants sometime in the 1860s. And it was mostly due to the imagination of later generations that the flag with a circle of thirteen stars came to be thought of as *the* flag of the Revolution.

Mythmakers have also tampered with the historical reputation of Francis Marion—the legendary Swamp Fox. In a biography of Marion, the author, Parson Weems, an early nineteenth-century preacher and biographer of George Washington, molded Marion's character more in line with what he hoped heroes would be like than with what one might reasonably expect of a flesh-and-blood human being. Weems obtained the materials for the Marion biography from the general's old fighting comrade and friend, Gerald P. Horry. Horry had wanted to write the book himself but a lack of writing ability forced him to seek another author. Although Weems was given the material under the stipulation that it would in no way be embellished or changed, he wrote to Horry on August 3, 1808: "I beg you to indulge no fears that Marion will ever die; while I can say or write anything to immortalize him." Ten months later Weems again wrote:

> It gives me great pleasure to inform you, by our mutual friend Dr. Blythe, that your ever honored and beloved Marion lives in History. . . . I have endeavored to

throw your ideas and facts about General Marion into the garb and dress of a military romance.

Horry then felt compelled to reply to Weems:

> You have carved and mutilated it [the book] with so many erroneous statements, and your embellishments, observations, and remarks must necessarily be erroneous as proceeding from false grounds. Most certainly 'tis not my history, but your romance.

The Marion of Parson's biography could scarcely be recognized by those who had known the man. Later readers of American history have also had difficulty finding the real Francis Marion behind the myth.[12]

SECTION III. THE ILLUSION OF UNITY: THE AMERICAN LOYALISTS

The names James Rivington, Samuel Curwen, Benjamin Thompson, and Catherine Byles hold no special meaning for Americans today. They are "missing persons"—part of the long list of characters who played a role in shaping American history but who have been lost to memory. They were Loyalists.

The effort to remove the Loyalists completely from American history has been almost totally successful. Most students have scarcely heard of them much less studied their history in any detail. In one sense the effort to erase a significant part of the nation's past is somewhat surprising, for in comparable historical circumstances no such obliteration has been attempted. Comparing this example of historical amnesia with instances in which it has not occurred, one historian has observed:

> George Washington's statue stands in Trafalgar Square, London; Lord Chatham's (William Pitt's), in Charleston, South Carolina. The South is dotted with statues of Civil War heroes. One searches the United States almost in vain, however, for memorials to the vanquished of the first civil war.[13]

While those who have been defeated in politics and war have very often gone on in history to be honored and respected for their commitments to their cause, this has not been the fate of the Loyalists. Unlike the Confederate rebels at the time of the second Civil War who could hold on to the mythical memory of a "Lost Cause," the Tories' was a cause both lost and forgotten. The Loyalists—or Tories as they are often called—are truly the forgotten Americans of the War for Independence, even though on the eve of the conflict with England the majority of Americans could justly be described, at best, as reluctant revolutionists. Initially, the Loyalists differed with other Americans mainly in that they remained more reluctant to support rebellion than others. If for no other reason than their numbers, however, they deserve closer attention, for according to the Patriot leader John Adams, the Tories accounted for nearly one third of all colonials. Loyalists did fail, but their position was understandable. Mainly because the historical record emphasizes the triumphs and achievements of the victors, few scholars have attended to the Loyalists. Nonetheless, the era of the War for Independence remains incomplete and mythical if the Tories are not taken into account.

The "King's Friends"—as one scholar calls them—have been overlooked and de-emphasized in the records of American history not only because they lost their cause, but also because the nation and its historians have always wanted to believe that there was wholesale agreement and little internal conflict among the colonists. Somehow, the American Revolution seems more glorious when it is believed that all "right-thinking" people supported it. This desire to believe in an illusion of unity, however, is not unique to America and its revolutionary experience. Many societies have similarly modified their past. And nearly every revolution, once it is over, has cultivated a similar type of mythology. In Russia, France, and even the American South one has witnessed history being "managed" in much the same way. Russian mythology, for example, has led the Soviet people to believe that the revolution against Czar Nicholas II in 1917 was a broadly based uprising of the proletariat, or workers, unwilling to accept tyranny. The facts of history suggest, however, that as few as 800 committed Bolsheviks may have brought the October Revolution to Russia and ushered in the Soviet regime. Though probably a conservative estimate, it nonetheless indicates that a small clique of intellectuals and politicians engineered the overthrow of a Russian government which dated back to 1613. While others have estimated a more realistic figure—that some thirty thousand Bolshevik activists took control of a country of 140 million people during the revolution—the fact remains that a decided minority ultimately caused the Romanov Dynasty to fall.

The French Revolution against King Louis XVI in 1789 offers a similar example of an implied unity among "the people" which never in fact existed. In France, the monarchy was no more despotic than others that existed in Europe at the same time, nor were the French lower classes socially, politically, or economically less fortunate than others. Yet the desire for "Liberty, Equality, and Fraternity" brought the Old Regime to an end. Here, it was a relatively small group of individuals committed to change who spearheaded the revolution. Legend aside, it was not the lower classes who were at the cutting edge of revolutionary events. Revolutionary leadership was concentrated in Paris, where organization and communication for such a movement could more easily be mobilized. The fever of revolution eventually did spread to other areas of the country, but many members of French society, particularly the clergy and nobility, remained loyal to the king or at least to the idea of monarchy. In the end, an important minority of French society, some five per thousand, became emigrés—that is, emigrated from France because of the revolution. As in Russia, however, the French have often advertised their revolution as one in which nearly all participated. It is a belief which allows succeeding generations to more readily accept both the changes which the revolution brought and the status quo.

An appreciation of the American Loyalists and their role in the War for Independence might best begin by observing that loyalty was the normal condition in the colonies until the critical early months of 1776. Before the publication of *Common Sense* and the Declaration of Independence, colonials had consistently spoken of their "rights as Englishmen" and of their desire for "Home rule under the

King." Even then, certainly not all, or even the majority, were willing to pledge their "Lives, Fortunes, and sacred Honor"—as Jefferson expressed it in the Declaration—to the Revolutionary cause. Many good Americans, for reasons of class, tradition, law, religion, and economics, neither became involved nor worked actively in favor of an independent status for the American provinces. More specifically, according to the contemporary estimate of Pennsylvania Loyalist Phineas Bond, approximately one hundred thousand people out of a total population of some 2.5 million became Tory exiles from the rebellious colonies. Using other methods of calculation, other scholars have found that twenty-four people out of every thousand actually left America during the Revolutionary era. While this figure is impressive in itself—totaling nearly five times as many as those who emigrated from France at the time of its revolution—it does not take into account those Loyalists who remained within the colonies. Although John Adams' estimate that one third of colonial society joined the revolutionary cause, one third remained neutral, and one third were Loyalists has been accepted as reasonably accurate, a more recent study has gauged Loyalist support to have included 7.6 to 18 percent of the total white population. But whether it was 7 or 33 percent of the colonials who remained loyal, the major difficulty in making an assessment of Tory strength is that Tories were not likely to advertise their loyalty. The shifting fortunes of war also had a way of altering attitudes; the precise number of Loyalists at any given time might have changed significantly from what it had been a short time before. It is known that from 1775 to 1783 between thirty to fifty thousand Tories directly opposed the Revolution by joining the king's army. In 1780, approximately eight thousand Loyalists were serving with the British army. And this was at a time, moreover, when General Washington's Continental Army numbered only about nine thousand soldiers. Precise numbers aside, however, one cannot minimize the fact that Tories everywhere in the colonies were a force to be reckoned with.

Among the few reasonably reliable sources of information concerning Loyalist strength are the legal claims made after the war by

Tories trying to obtain compensation for war damages and confiscated property. This data allows one to construct a Loyalist profile. Figures seem to suggest that Toryism was strongest in the colonies of Georgia, New York, and South Carolina; somewhat weaker in New Jersey and Massachusetts; with Virginia, Maryland, and Delaware the least inclined to the Tory point of view. Mainly

Loyalists Flee to Canada
Historical Picture Service

43

because those who had the most to lose by a revolution were concentrated in the cities, loyalty was predominantly an urban phenomenon. Political office-holders, royal administrators, professionals (teachers, lawyers, doctors), and merchants—all city dwellers—were heavily represented in Tory ranks. Recent immigrants from England as well were more likely to be Loyalists than were colonists born in America. While notable exceptions to these generalizations exist—for example, Tory sentiment was strong in some rural areas of the colonies of New York and in North Carolina—loyalty was most often to be found among those who stood to lose wealth and status, those who were newly arrived immigrants, and those who populated the urban areas along the Atlantic seaboard. In short, the Loyalists represented nearly every race, religion, occupation, class, and geographical area of Revolutionary America.

While the Tories did not enjoy the same quality of leadership as the Patriots—they had no equivalent of Washington, Adams, Jefferson, or Paine—their numbers did include men and women of considerable stature, talent, and experience.

If one were to take a representative sampling, it would be discovered that numerous motives influenced Tories to reject revolution in favor of loyalty to king and empire. Thomas Hutchinson, for example, the last royal governor of the colony of Massachusetts, spoke for many Loyalists when he offered his arguments against independence on the bases of class and tradition. A Harvard graduate and descendant of Anne Hutchinson, he believed that government should rest in the hands of "men of principle and property." Hutchinson, in short, was a true conservative. He wished to conserve and protect the political status quo from the threat of "the mob" and from "rabble-rousers" like Samuel Adams. Hutchinson had an abiding love for his native Massachusetts, which is clear from his famous *History of the Colony and Province of Massachusetts Bay*, but he was profoundly disturbed by the thought that the unity of the British Empire would be lost through colonial separation. Despite the fact that he had amassed a considerable fortune in land, and therefore had much to lose in any revolutionary upheaval, Hutchinson did op-

pose the Stamp, Sugar, and Townshend Acts. He went on to argue, however, that Parliament had the right, according to tradition, to pass such laws. Hutchinson's thinking was shared by many prior to January, 1776. His difficulty was simply that he sustained old political ideas as American thinking was shifting in a revolutionary direction. Faced with this predicament, and feeling that his reverence for the English political system was definitely worth preserving, Thomas Hutchinson left for England in 1774 and died there in 1780.

The Massachusetts lawyer Daniel Leonard was another who did not agree that separation was wise. Leonard insisted that the colonists already enjoyed the fruits of freedom and popular government by virtue of their position within the British Empire. Perhaps the most articulate and persuasive of the Tories, Leonard based his arguments on English law and the British constitution. These institutions reflected, in Leonard's view, "the most perfect system that the wisdom of the ages has produced." Using his *Letters Addressed to the Inhabitants of the Province of Massachusetts Bay* as a medium to express his ideas, Leonard did much to give credibility to the Tory position. Under the pen name "Massachusettensis," he established a dialogue on the Revolution with John Adams and others sympathetic to the idea of independence. Leonard maintained in his *Letters*, published in the *Massachusetts Gazette*, that governments had been established in the first place to save humanity from fraud, violence, murder, rape, and riot. It was the task of government to protect citizens from their own baser instincts. Because English law rested on this philosophy, and because revolution if it came would lead to abuses, Leonard urged the colonists to accept the enlightened leadership of London in their affairs. In addition, Leonard argued, colonial radicals such as Samuel Adams were "playing with the gallows." Reasonable laws protected the English state against disloyal conduct and treason. If for no other reason than the legalities involved, it was good judgment to reject the imprudent move toward revolution. Leonard's arguments emphasizing the sanctity of law and the constitution were, of course, in vain. When the revolution came, he became an exile in Halifax, Nova Scotia, along with many other colonial Loyalist refugees. After the war, however, a grateful King George, wishing to reward his loyalty, appointed Leonard Chief Justice of Bermuda. Daniel Leonard died in London in 1829, among the last surviving Tories.

Whereas some based their loyalty to Crown and empire on arguments involving class, tradition, or law, the so-called Tory Priest, Jonathan Boucher, found the most compelling reason for continued colonial ties to the mother country in religion. A leading spokesman for the Anglican Church of America, which he called "the mother of loyalty," Boucher argued that revolutionaries were tantamount to being traitors and heretics at one and the same time. Because Anglicanism was the official religion of the English nation, and George III the official head of both church and state, revolution would be a sin and a crime against both religious and secular authority. A close friend of George Washington until the Revolution strained their relationship, Boucher disagreed with the basic philosophy of democracy—that all power and authority held by a government comes ultimately from the people. Rather, he was a true believer in what is called the divine right of kings. The ultimate source of all political power, Boucher claimed, was God. Monarchy had been established by the Supreme Being who alone could bring an end to such a political arrangement. Monarchs such as George III, in short, governed by divine right, and Boucher considered government a divinely created instrument for stability and order. The American colonists could never make the king of England, or any monarch, politically responsible to them. To engage in revolution would be to disrupt God's master plan for the political well-being of a nation. Boucher's loyalty was not necessarily typical of all Anglicans—many in the southern colonies, for example, sided with the Patriot cause. Nonetheless, religious ties provided yet another reason why many could never come to accept the idea of independent and united colonies.

Samuel Seabury, who ultimately became the first American Episcopal bishop, was also much concerned with what he called "the controversy between Great Britain and her colonies." In his famous *View of the Controversy*, published in 1774, Seabury noted that the demand for representation in Parliament was "nonsense." Many people in England, he observed, were not represented in that body; in fact they could not even vote. Hence, the colonists by flirting with revolution were asking for preferential treatment, not for their rights as British citizens. But the most compelling reason for America to remain within the British Empire, Seabury pointed out, was economic. Americans simply could not maintain their current standard of living without trade with the mother country. In all fairness, Seabury went on, it had to be conceded that prevailing economic ties with the British Empire placed the colonies in a highly advantageous position relative to the rest of the world. Colonial planters and merchants, for instance, enjoyed a guaranteed market for the tobacco they produced and shipped to England. In addition, if separation of America from England occurred, trading privileges with other English colonies such as the West Indies would be lost. In a more indirect way, successful revolution would mean conducting foreign affairs and maintaining an army and navy. America's removal from the empire, Seabury concluded, would bring about serious economic dislocation. These earnest pleadings that America's prosperity depended on its connections with England were ignored. Sentiment in favor of revolution overcame such "pocketbook" arguments. As for Samuel Seabury, though he left the colonies for a time to lead the Loyalist exodus to Nova Scotia, he later returned to help organize a nationwide Protestant Episcopal Church.

There were many other notable Loyalists—Joseph Galloway, the artist John Singleton Copley, and William Franklin, illegitimate son of the illustrious Benjamin. And any representative sampling of Loyalist numbers reflects the fact that they were a significant body of people with reasonable motives for their decision in favor of loyalty. Once the myth is stripped away and they are looked at objectively, moreover, it becomes obvious that they were not arrogant and corrupt simply because they held beliefs different from those of Patriots. Their ranks included many colonists of talent and experience.

SECTION IV. LEGENDS OF THE FOUNDING FATHERS

The founding period of every organized community nearly always comes to be seen idealistically later. Societies and groups seem to identify with antiquity and their origins because these things give them roots and mold their destiny. The children of Greece, for example, grew to maturity nurtured on the stories of Olympian gods and goddesses who were said to have been responsible for the religious, social, and political concepts in their land. In like manner, Romans were enchanted with the origins of their empire and with the role that Romulus and Remus were supposed to have played in the founding of the Eternal City. Rome was named in honor of Romulus. In a more contemporary setting, one is intrigued by the patterns of a Chinese mythology which has already begun to obscure Chairman Mao Tse-Tung and the beginnings of Communism in mainland China. And in the religious sector, Jesus Christ, Mohammed, and Joseph Smith—to mention only a few—serve as legendary figures from the early years of Christianity, Islam, and Mormonism. In all of these instances, personalities and episodes critical to the beginnings of a political or religious movement have emerged in the eyes of later generations as larger than life. Events and achievements allegedly far beyond ordinary experience have propelled these figures and occurrences into the realm of myth and legend. Understandably, what one scholar calls the "magic and prestige of origins" has attached itself to the beginnings of the American nation as well. Following a pattern rather well established by other nations, societies, and groups, Americans have long viewed the founding figures and events which followed the War for Independence in mythical ways.

With respect to the origins of the American nation, misunderstanding and myth have obscured the fact that the founding documents of the republic—the Declaration of Independence and the Constitution—were written at different times and reflected different political philosophies. These keystones of the American system have become so enshrined in patriotic mythology, and so misrepresented by Fourth of July orators, that most Americans fail to recognize their differences and that they were written eleven years apart.

The Declaration of Independence was written in the heat of revolution in 1776. It boldly declares "the right of the people to alter or to abolish" a government which attempts to destroy humanity's "unalienable rights" to "life, liberty, and the pursuit of happiness." While the Declaration warns very clearly that revolution is never to be engaged in for "light and transient causes," it just as clearly argues that people have not only the right but the duty to throw off a government which does not attempt to honor the needs and wishes of the people. The Constitution of the United States, on the other hand, written in 1787, outlines and describes a specific form of government. In tone and intent it fundamentally differs from the Declaration which had sought to dissolve political ties and end political allegiances. The Constitution was designed to be a political instrument which would work "to form a more perfect Union, establish Justice, insure domestic Tranquility, provide for the common defence, promote the general Welfare, and secure the Blessings of Liberty to ourselves and our Posterity." In very important ways, then, the two documents together focused attention on the tensions between freedom and authority which have always existed in America. Within a relatively short period of time, Americans had stated a philosophical and practical commitment to both revolution and a rational system of law and order. Since the term "Founding Fathers" includes the architects of both the Declaration and the Constitution, fundamental differences between the two documents as to tone, philosophy, and the circumstances in which they were written must be noted at the outset.

The Articles of Confederation

American reverence for the Declaration of Independence and the Constitution, however, has not only caused many to ignore the documents' important differences, but it has also caused them to overlook the document which served as America's first constitution—the Articles of Confederation. It is often forgotten that in the late Revolutionary era a confederated government, which had developed during the war itself, served the nation's political needs from 1781 through 1789. Though by 1781 America was independent, its form of government was not yet permanently settled, and a union among the states which would serve as a "firm league of friendship" was deemed desirable by political leaders who might profitably be seen as Founding Fathers. While the Articles essentially provided a legal basis for the authority which the Continental Congress had been exercising, they strongly reflected the major fears of Revolutionary America. For when finally established in March, 1781, the new central government possessed a minimum of power. Fresh from their experience with Britain, colonial Americans were unwilling to create a political system in any way similar to that from which they had only recently separated. Looking back on the immediate past, colonists wanted neither big government nor a strong "executive" like George III. Understandably, the Articles represented ways in which to limit rather than expand the powers of government. Accordingly, a political system was established by America's earlier Founding Fathers without an executive branch or a court system, which at the time of the Revolution served as arms of the British government. Allowing for no king, president, or prime minister, the Articles placed all power and authority in a single-house legislature composed of delegates from each of the states. Each state delegation voted as a unit with a two thirds majority needed for passage of legislation. Most important, the power to tax and the power to regulate commerce between states and with foreign powers was reserved to each state government. Under this "united nations" type of arrangement, bound together to solve mutual problems, the states retained all powers not specifically granted the federal government. Under this system authority was primarily vested in the states.

When compared to the power of the national government after 1789, and with the powers currently exercised in Washington, it would appear that the Articles of Confederation guaranteed a helpless central government, and some students of this portion of the American past have accordingly judged the years from 1781 to 1789 to be the "critical period" of the nation's history. Aware that decay and chaos gripped the country in the years after the war, they have concluded that the national government was so weak that it was unable to respond to the growing needs of the infant nation. They suggest that the later

Founding Fathers saved America from an early death by establishing the Constitution as a new basis for national government. Such a view, however, tends to overdramatize the situation.

These conclusions concerning the 1780s are based on John Fiske's book *The Critical Period of American History*, published in 1888. "Without fear and without research," as one historian has put it, Fiske totally accepted the words of those who had been opposed to the Articles. The historian Merrill Jensen took the lead in exposing the myth of the so-called critical period. Attacking Fiske directly, Professor Jensen charged that

> The story told by Fiske and repeated by publicists and scholars who have not worked in the field . . . is based on the assumption that this was *the* "critical period" of American history during which unselfish patriots rescued the new nation from impending anarchy, if not from chaos itself. The picture is one of stagnation, ineptitude, bankruptcy, corruption, and disintegration. Such a picture is at worst false and at best grossly distorted.[14]

It must be conceded that depression and inflation hit the country very hard in the years after the war, that war with Spain over control of western lands was a real possibility, and that the newly united states were seriously debating the question of national versus state control of government. It must be added, however, that the nation's economy was well on its way to recovery by 1786, and that any new government would have had similar difficulties given a lack of power in foreign relations and the lack of prestige in the world community which every new nation must face. Even with these difficulties, however, the new American government did negotiate a highly successful treaty of peace with England in 1783. The Treaty of Paris "acknowledged the . . . United States . . . to be free, sovereign and independent States," allowed vital fishing rights off the eastern coast of North America, and granted the new nation land in the great interior regions of the continent from the Great Lakes to the Gulf of Mexico (exclusive of Florida and the port of New Orleans) and west to the Mississippi River. In addition, during the era of the Articles the newly acquired western lands were surveyed and sectioned for public sale under the Land Ordinance of 1785. Further, the Northwest Ordinance of 1787 established procedures allowing for the eventual organization of territories and states. Regarding these farsighted land management measures, one historian has said, "seldom has a legislative body acted more wisely."[15]

Considering the attitude of the American people at the time (i.e., that the states rather than the national government should control affairs) it distorts history to say that the Articles were woefully inadequate. In fact, quite the reverse seems to be true. The Articles were precisely what American society was demanding at the time. Rather than an unfortunate interlude in the nation's past, this period of American history was *critical* to the continued growth of American democracy. Without this era of trial-and-error, the Constitution which followed might never have succeeded in the way that it has. The Articles of Confederation, even with their weaknesses, served the cause of democracy well. Thomas Jefferson, writing from Paris in 1787, seemed to appreciate the key role which the Articles were playing as the governing principles of the nation. They were, he suggested, a "good, old, venerable, fabrick."

Serving in France on a diplomatic mission, Jefferson may have had a distorted view of the Articles of Confederation. Many fellow patriots closer to the scene apparently thought so. They were aware of the Articles' drawbacks. They could see the problems which resulted from states having the power to control commerce, foreign and domestic. They could see the economic difficulties created when each state, and some individuals, minted their own money. While Americans had been successful in achieving political independence, they were finding that the economic independence which accompanied it had its liabilities as well as its advantages. The war against England had barely concluded when economic problems brought on by independence led to the authority of the new government being challenged by rebellion from within.

Veterans from the Revolutionary War returned home to find staggering debts, non-payment of pensions and wages due them for war service, and their farms being confiscated for lack of mortgage payments. The grievances of these Regulators, as they came to be called, were as much directed at their state governments as they were at the new national government located in Philadelphia. In the state of Massachusetts, for example, veterans facing apathetic do-nothing legislators began to disrupt the tranquility of local communities. As early as February, 1782, protests were staged in Pittsfield. Over a five-year period rebels became organized behind the leadership of Daniel Shays and disturbed the peace in Northampton, Worcester, Springfield, and Petersham. Even though the insurgents were successfully dispersed by General Benjamin Lincoln, when the Constitutional Convention began its deliberations in Philadelphia in May, 1787 it was aware of these occurrences. The problems of debts and contracts, currency regulation, and internal insurrection all highlighted by Shays' Rebellion were clearly on the minds of the Founding Fathers. It was becoming apparent that the focus of attention had shifted considerably since 1776. American leadership was no longer interested in forging independence, but was directing its attention to the new problem of not allowing democracy to turn into anarchy. It could be expected, then, that the new constitution would attempt to conserve the fruits of revolution. The making of a constitution, as one historian has expressed it, was to be the "foremost and the noblest of all revolutionary deeds."[16] The designers would try to bring the Revolution to a successful conclusion and in their way build upon the work of earlier Founders.

The Constitution

The mixed success of the Confederation government in areas of foreign affairs and particularly trade, combined with such challenging rebellions as that of Daniel Shays, led to the suggestion that a modification of the Articles was in order. But since it was clearly the central government which was in crisis rather than state governments, it gradually became the view of some that change of an even more fundamental nature was necessary. For the changes which eventually came to pass—the writing, ratification, and implementation of a new constitution—also reflected a resurgence of American nationalism. Not only were the fifty-five men who gathered at Philadelphia concerned with specific problems which had surfaced in the previous years while the Articles had been in force, but they reflected the growing awareness of America as a nation and the consequent need for a strong central government. Simply put, many more people considered themselves Americans in 1787 than in 1776. This new sense of being an American would inspire the Founding Fathers to proceed in bold new directions. The nation was about to witness a revolution which would be somewhat less obvious but equally as profound as that of 1776. The founding period of the American nation had not yet been concluded.

The business of the Constitutional Convention was completed in four months—from late May to mid-September, 1787. And the actual writing of the final document was finished by the Committee on Style in two days. What was accomplished in such short order, however, has been the subject of unending debate ever since, and has enveloped both the Founding Fathers and their work in a haze of myth. For most citizens, of course, the Fathers and the Constitution hold a venerated place in American history. To the mind of the great mass of Americans even today the Founders are accepted as demigods and the document they produced is assumed by many to have been divinely inspired. In this sense the American Constitution has functioned as the "central myth" of our political culture. This elevation of the Founders to near-sainthood, and the Constitution to the level of sacred scripture, has led to the comment that

> Americans in the nineteenth century, whenever they reviewed the events of the founding, made reference to an Olympian gathering of wise and virtuous men who stood splendidly above all faction, ignored petty self-interest, and concerned themselves only with the freedom and well-being of their fellow-countrymen. This attitude toward the Fathers has actually never died out; it still tends to prevail in American history curricula right up through most of the secondary schools.[17]

Much recent research has concluded, however,

that such a view is too simplistic. Though this lofty vision of the inspired Founders fits well with the notion that America has been God's chosen nation and that the forces of democracy have always prevailed, it vastly oversimplifies the complex historical reality of the late 1780s.

Popular and scholarly veneration of the Founding Fathers and the Constitution first came under serious attack in 1913, with the publication of Charles A. Beard's sensational book, *An Economic Interpretation of the Constitution of the United States*. Writing in an age when wealth, monopoly, and economic privilege were widely viewed with great suspicion, Beard suggested that the Founders were not lovers of democracy at all. Rather, he insisted, they consciously represented the conservative segments of American society. They were the nation's lawyers, merchants, shippers, land speculators, and money lenders—not "the people." Their activities at Philadelphia represented a conspiracy to destroy the democratic legacy won by the Revolution. The Founders were not the enlightened leaders revered by American mythology, but traitors to the cause of the War for Independence. They were pocketbook patriots following their economic self-interest. Their contempt for democracy was well illustrated by the fact that they conducted their meetings in great secrecy behind closed doors. Given the authority only to amend and modify the Articles of Confederation, they illegally constructed an entirely new political document which was conservative, self-serving, and reactionary. Whereas before Beard the Founders had enjoyed the enviable reputation of sanctified heroes and the Constitution had been accepted as The Supreme Law, it was now fashionable to believe that both were somewhat un-American.

Charles Beard's myth-shattering yet myth-generating version of the founding of the nation naturally stimulated controversy. Professors and professional patriots alike challenged such an unpatriotic "lie" about this esteemed episode in American history. Over time, legitimate scholarship has largely cleared the Founding Fathers of many of Beard's allegations. While further research has come to emphasize the fact that the writing of the Constitution did reflect a growing conservative mentality in America, it has also shown that some 96 percent of the wealth represented at the Constitutional Convention was tied to land and could not therefore have been directly affected by the Founders' decisions. Also, according to Beard, convention members who held securities were supposed to have wanted a stronger central government to protect their investments; however, seven such individuals left the proceedings and did not sign the document. Elbridge Gerry of Massachusetts, who would have gained the most from such a conspiracy, not only failed to agree to the document in its final form but returned to his home state to work diligently against its passage.

While additional study into the events surrounding the Constitution has been as harsh on Charles Beard as Beard himself had once been on the Founding Fathers, his economic interpretation must be given credit for having reopened a subject which long had been considered too sacred to be debated. Even though Beard was wrong in many of his conclusions, he began the process of tearing away the mystique and myth which had surrounded the Founding Fathers and the Constitution. If nothing else, the Fathers of the Constitution were more human after 1913 than before. Further, since Beard had claimed that the Constitution had been forced on an unwilling people who in many cases could not vote, his study has also led scholars to see that other legends of the time had not been dealt with (i.e., those having to do with the Constitution's acceptance by the American people).

Before Beard, the Constitution and its architects were so blindly venerated that few persons appreciated the difficulty the document met in being accepted by the American people. The document is so accepted today that the assumption persists that it was always highly regarded and revered. Many staunch Americans in fact campaigned against its passage. Although Thomas Jefferson, serving on a diplomatic assignment in France, wrote that "As to the new Constitution, I find myself very nearly a neutral," Samuel Adams, one of the more radical leaders of the earlier Revolutionary cause, stated that he was opposed to the Constitution because it failed to offer a Bill of Rights protecting basic freedoms. And Patrick Henry, of "Give me liberty or give me death" fame, refused support, claiming that he "smelled a rat." Only after the famous *Federalist Papers* had forcefully argued for passage of the document, the promise that amendments to the Constitution would be made to protect fundamental rights, and a liberal dose of political shenanigans, were enough votes supporting the new federal structure found. Even at this point, however, the final votes within the state conventions— called specifically for the purpose of passing judgment on the Constitution—were very close. Reflecting the strength of the anti-Federalists who saw the document as a threat to the power of state governments and local control of the political process, most states endorsed it by slim margins. In Massachusetts the final vote totals were 187 to 168 in favor of passage, in New Hampshire 57 to 47, in Virginia 89 to 79, and in the critical state of New York, 30 to 27. Some states in fact resisted until it was clear that they were in a hopeless minority. Rhode Island, the last to reluctantly accept the Constitution, did not fall into line until thirteen months after George Washington had been inaugurated as the first president of the United States.

STUDY QUESTIONS

1. Analyze and discuss the many ways in which legendary misunderstandings concerning each of the following worked to create an elaborate mythology about the "tyranny" of the British government during the era of the American Revolution:
   a. The Navigation Acts
   b. Revolutionary rhetoric such as "No taxation without representation"
   c. Patrick Henry's "liberty or death" speech
   d. George III
   e. Thomas Paine's pamphlet *Common Sense*
   f. The Declaration of Independence

2. Concerning the American Revolution, what are the principle myths which have arisen concerning the Declaration of Independence, the Fourth of July, the Liberty Bell, Paul Revere, General George Washington, Betsy Ross, and General Francis Marion?

3. Analyze and discuss the major arguments which were offered by the Tories in support of their loyalty to king and empire. What were the principle motives which led many to take the viewpoint that a break with England in 1776 was ill-advised?

4. What are the principle misconceptions in American political history concerning the period from the end of the Revolution to the ratification of the Constitution?

REFERENCES

1. Carl Degler, "A New Kind of Revolution," in *Out of Our Past: The Forces That Shaped Modern America* (New York: Harper & Row, Publishers, 1970), p. 80.
2. Egbert Guernsey, *History of the United States Designed for Schools* (New York: Cady and Burgess, 1848), p. 192.
3. Robert Cecil, "Reflections on the American Revolution," in John A. Garraty, ed., *Historical Viewpoints*, I (New York: Harper & Row, Publishers, 1970), p. 127.
4. Degler, "New Kind," p. 75.
5. Bernard Bailyn, "The American Revolution," in John A. Garraty, ed., *Interpreting American History: Conversations with Historians*, I (New York: The Macmillan Company, 1970), p. 80.
6. Bernard Mayo, *Myths and Men: Patrick Henry, George Washington, Thomas Jefferson* (New York: Harper & Row, Publishers, 1959), p. 14.
7. Charles Warren, "Fourth of July Myths," *The William and Mary Quarterly* 2 (1945): 237.
8. Ibid., p. 247.
9. Ibid., p. 272.
10. Thomas Bailey, "The Mythmakers of American History," *Journal of American History* LV (June, 1968): 6.
11. Thomas Bailey, *Probing America's Past: A Critical Examination of Major Myths & Misconceptions*, I (Lexington, Mass.: D. C. Heath & Co., 1973), p. 88n.
12. Nicholas Cords, "Parson Weems, the Cherry Tree and the Patriotic Tradition," in Nicholas Cords and Patrick Gerster, eds., *Myth and the American Experience*, I (Beverly Hills: Glencoe Press, 1973), p. 157.
13. Wallace Brown, *The Good Americans: The Loyalists in the American Revolution* (New York: William Morrow and Co., 1969), p. 224.
14. Merrill Jensen, "The Myth of the Critical Period," in *The New Nation* (New York: Alfred A. Knopf, 1950), p. xiii.
15. John A. Garraty, *The American Nation: A History of the United States to 1877*, I (New York: Harper & Row, Publishers, 1975), p. 120.
16. Jack P. Greene, "Revolution, Confederation, and Constitution, 1763-1787," in William H.

Cartwright and Richard L. Watson, Jr., eds., *The Reinterpretation of American History and Culture* (Washington, D.C.: National Council for Social Studies, 1973), p. 291.
17. Stanley Elkins and Eric McKitrick, "The Founding Fathers: Young Men of the Revolution," *Political Science Quarterly* LXXVI (June, 1961): 181.

SOURCES FOR FURTHER STUDY

CAUSES OF THE WAR FOR INDEPENDENCE

BERKHOFER, ROBERT F. *The American Revolution: The Critical Issues.* Boston: Little, Brown and Co., 1971.

GREENE, JACK. "Revolution, Confederation, and Constitution, 1763-1787." In *The Reinterpretation of American History and Culture*, William H. Cartwright and Bichard L. Wilson, eds. Washington, D.C.: National Council for the Social Studies, 1973.

MAYO, BERNARD. *Myths and Men: Patrick Henry, George Washington, Thomas Jefferson.* New York: Harper & Row, Publishers, 1959.

PLUMB, J. H. "George III: Our Last King." In *Historical Viewpoints*, John A. Garraty, ed. New York: Harper & Row, Publishers, 1975.

RUTMAN, DARRETT B. *The Morning of America, 1603-1789.* Boston: Houghton Mifflin Co., 1971.

COLLECTED MYTHS OF THE WAR YEARS

BAILEY, THOMAS. "The Mythmakers of American History." *Journal of American History* 60 (1968): 5–21.

CHEW, PETER. "Black History, or Black Mythology." *American Heritage* 20 (August, 1969): 4–9, 104–106.

KETCHUM, RICHARD M. "England's Vietnam: The American Revolution." In John A. Garraty, ed. *Historical Viewpoints.* New York: Harper & Row, Publishers, 1975.

MORRIS, RICHARD B. "The Diplomats and the Mythmakers." In *The American Revolution Reconsidered*, New York: Harper & Row, Publishers, 1967.

WARREN, CHARLES. "Fourth of July Myths." *The William and Mary Quarterly* II (1945): 237–272.

THE ILLUSION OF UNITY

BORDEN, MORTON, AND BORDEN, PENN, eds. *The American Tory.* Englewood Cliffs, N.J.: Prentice-Hall, Inc., 1972.

BROWN, WALLACE. *The Good Americans: The Loyalists in the American Revolution.* New York: William Morrow and Co., Inc., 1969.

———. *The King's Friends: The Composition and Motives of the American Loyalist Claimants.* Providence: Brown University Press, 1965.

———. "The Loyalists and the American Revolution." *History Today* 12 (March 1962): 149–157.

LEGEND OF THE FOUNDING FATHERS

COMMAGER, HENRY STEELE. "The Constitution: Was It an Economic Document?" In John A. Garraty, ed. *Historical Viewpoints*. New York: Harper & Row, Publishers, 1975.

DEGLER, CARL. "A New Kind of Revolution." In *Out of Our Past: The Forces That Shaped Modern America*. New York: Harper & Row, Publishers, 1975.

ELKINS, STANLEY, AND McKITRICK, ERIC. "The Founding Fathers: Young Men of the Revolution." *Political Science Quarterly* 76 (1961): 181–216.

MORRIS, RICHARD B. "The Confederation and the Constitution." In John A. Garraty, ed. *Interpreting American History: Conversations with Historians*, I. New York: Macmillan Publishing Co., Inc., 1970.

VAUGHAN, ALDEN T. "Shays' Rebellion." In John A. Garraty, ed. *Historical Viewpoints*. New York: Harper & Row, Publishers, 1975.

3 Myths of the National Period

PREVIEW

George Washington and the Growth of National Mythology

Recent research in anthropology examining myth in so-called primitive societies indicates that "myth is the method men adopt to make coherent and therefore acceptable whatever is fundamentally self-contradictory in their beliefs or in their practical life."[1] But whereas scholars have claimed that myth works in this way among ancient peoples, the appropriateness of the same theory for American history seems to have escaped nearly everyone. Members of Western civilization today, and particularly Americans, seem unaware that they are capable of creating myths. Accordingly, such "advanced" humans are thought to be mythless and thus more rational than their ancient or medieval counterparts. Myth in both its primitive and modern setting, however, would seem to be humanity's most convenient means of explaining what it cannot readily understand. Primitive humans constructed myths about the creation of the world, the wonders of nature, and life after death. Given this pattern in less advanced societies, it would seem reasonable to suppose that Americans might find myth a convenient method of resolving the basic tensions in their historical traditions. How was it possible, for example, that the Founding Fathers could have created a political system based on both the "radical" Declaration of Independence and the law and order provisions of the "conservative" Constitution?

By the end of the Revolutionary era, Americans were seemingly committed to both rebellion and union. The country had been born in revolution yet had sought to save itself from the abuses of democracy by accepting a code of laws called the Constitution. Whether the American tradition was one endorsing the people's inalienable right to overthrow an unjust government or whether it was more committed to political order and stability remained in question. The tension between these two points of view—a kind of radical conservatism—presented a problem which would have to be faced during the early years of nation building. By far the easiest way to deal with this double tradition, of course, was to accept both. This resolution of paradox proved difficult in practice. One of the ways the nation learned to reconcile this contradictory tradition was through mythologizing its Founders.

Of the Founding Fathers, George Washington was the first to become enshrouded in myth. Like all folk heroes, Washington has become a blurred figure, a blend of fact and legend. He was for some a father figure, symbolizing the dignity and stability of the new republic. For others, he was a supreme revolutionary whose spirited leadership had brought America success in the War for Independence from England. The magic name of Washington would come to represent both the sword of revolution, and the rule of law. And he was acceptable to everyone because he personified many American folk-hero types rolled into one—frontiersman, soldier, statesman, politician, and farmer. In a way he was an early model for Davy Crockett, Robert E. Lee, Abraham Lincoln, and the legendary Happy Yeoman. George Washington became heroic and mythical precisely because his personality and career united nearly all of America's conflicting traditions. More than any man before or since he typified America.

The fact that George Washington became a universal symbol and nearly all things to all people is in many ways due to writers and historians who canonized him after his death. Even had they wanted to, Americans would not have been allowed to forget the father of their country. In a famous and bestselling biography of Washington published in 1800 and entitled *The Life of Washington the Great, Enriched with a Number of Very Curious Anecdotes, Perfectly in Character, and Equally Honorable to Himself, and Exemplary to his Young Countrymen*, the author, one Parson Weems, managed to single-handedly create much of the legendary Washington. The heroizing continued with Chief Justice John Marshall's five-volume biography of Washington (1804-1807) which John Adams compared to "a Mausoleum, 100 feet square at the base, and 200 feet high." And even in the hands of more professional historians such as Jared Sparks and George Bancroft the nation's first great hero remained a legend. By the time of the bicentennial celebration of Washington's birth in 1932, Harvard historians were claiming that "he was bolder than Alexander, more crafty than Hannibal, wiser than Caesar, more prudent than Gustavus Adolphus, more resourceful than Frederick, more sagacious than Napoleon, and more successful than Scipio." Apparently, by this time any uncertainties about Washington's character and the early history of America had disappeared. Myth was successfully burying the problem of paradox.

As historians and writers did much to end the confusion which Americans might have had about the origins of the nation and Washington by relying on myth, the public protested not a bit. Although Nathaniel Hawthorne wondered whether anyone had "ever see[n] Washington nude?" since it seemed to him that "he was born with his clothes on," the nation at large found the legendary George Washington perfectly acceptable.

The period from 1789 to the Civil War was in desperate need of heroes and a "usable past." In particular, one can see that "to be an American in the last decade of the eighteenth century was to be present at the crucial mythmaking time in the infancy of the Republic; it was comparable to being a Roman in the age of Romulus and Remus, or a Greek in the age of the Olympians."[2] With such a glorious period immediately behind them, Americans ransacked their history in search of the great and near-great who could provide even closer ties with their "antiquity." In Europe nation-states were based on a foundation of history and tradition, but in America—the first of the new nations created by modern nationalism—a sense of pride in the country and its destiny had to be invented for the most part. Even though Americans were somewhat uncomfortable with their lack of national history, they could use imagination and create one. The nation could not point to a regal court, a diplomatic service, manors, parsonages, or ivied cathedrals; but it did have the first Thanksgiving, Pocahantas, Indian Wars, the Minutemen, and Mount Vernon. And as the nation built its heritage, Francis Scott Key, Meriwether Lewis and William Clark, Monticello, the Buckskin hero, Billy Yank and Johnny Reb could be conveniently added to the

list. Taken together they would eventually give America a dynamic sense of unity and purpose. The quick creation of this "usable past" caused legend to be taken for history and fiction to pass for fact, and the paradox of it all could be brushed aside in favor of a brilliantly mythical past which quickly became one of the nation's most valued possessions.

Myths of Early American Foreign Policy

America's increasingly mythical past also proved to be highly "useful" in the nation's relations with foreign powers. In the popular mind, American foreign policy after the adoption of the Constitution is usually associated with the idea of isolationism. George Washington's warning words against permanent alliances, found in his Farewell Address; Jefferson's concerns about entangling relationships with foreign powers; and Monroe's statement in favor of keeping the Western Hemisphere free from European influence, enunciated in 1823, all seem to have moved American foreign relations in that direction. The new national government was in fact attempting to give America some kind of identity in the world; it was not trying to escape from its international responsibilities. Therefore, there are many ways in which the convenient label "isolationism" simply does not apply to the beginnings of American foreign policy. The Founders' concern with permanent and entangling alliances represented a sense of caution more than a commitment to isolationism. Despite the attempts of later legend-makers, particularly during debates over the nation's proper role in two world wars, to prove that isolationism was the essence of American foreign policy during its formative years, the record shows an interesting blend of international involvement as well as freedom from the affairs of the world to be the hallmark of early American foreign relations. Both economic realism and utopian idealism helped to shape American attitudes toward the Old World. Americans wanted to trade with Europe, yet they also wanted to steer clear of its many wars and petty politics. Attitudes supporting this dual policy in fact had begun to form even before Washington's presidency.

Adding considerably to this isolationist misunderstanding of early American diplomacy has been the mystique of Washington's Farewell Address. The "address," it should be remembered, was not an address at all. It first appeared in the *American Daily Advertiser*, a Philadelphia newspaper. In addition, it reflected not only Washington's point of view but also that of James Madison and, more important, Alexander Hamilton. Because of the numerous influences on it, historians have not at all agreed as to what motivated Washington's message. Some have argued that the "wisest and purest patriotism" prompted it. In this spirit, the diplomatic historian Samuel Flagg Bemis has claimed that it was a statement in favor of "a foreign policy of independence" consistent with the Revolutionary tradition. Others have insisted that Washington merely wished to announce his plan not to seek a third term. Still others have seen the message as a document designed to stimulate a counteroffensive against declining nationalism in America, a move to bring an end to the party passions of American politics, or as a call for economic expansion free from the competition of European nations. After consulting all shades of opinion on Washington's Farewell Address, however, it becomes clear that no reputable historian any longer accepts the legend that the nation's first president was endorsing anything like absolute isolationism, permanently binding on the nation. It is foolish to believe that Washington was attempting to establish long-enduring principles to guide future American foreign policy. To believe this, the historian Alexander DeConde concludes, "is to endow Washington with powers reserved for the gods of Olympus."[3] In any event, it can be said that Washington was not laying down a Great Rule for all generations to follow. Rather, he was speaking to the political leaders of his time.

Another persistent American legend, first apparent during the American Revolution, was that all patriotic Americans were unswervingly dedicated to victory over England at any cost. The myth reappeared following the War of 1812—the "Second War for Independence"—even though this was perhaps the most unpopular war America ever fought. Antiwar activity was rampant, comparable to that in evidence during the Vietnam conflict.

In Federalist New England such key figures as Harrison Gray Otis, John Lowell, and Caleb Strong (the governor of Massachusetts) proposed a "Reunion of the Original Thirteen States" in an attempt to separate them from the southern and new western states which were more "hawkish" on the war. Moves favoring the secession of the New England states, and nonpayment of taxes supporting the war, as well as antiwar resolutions from state legislatures, and even secret diplomatic missions seeking a separate peace treaty with England were all symptoms of the war's unpopularity. "The notion that only Yankee Federalists opposed the war is pure myth," adds one historian. The War of 1812 was hardly a united exercise in patriotism. Nearly every American generation, it seems, feels the need to embrace the illusion of unity about its wartime experiences.

Even as the War of 1812 concluded, there was a rather widely shared and growing sense of uneasiness over the possibility that European powers might begin to involve themselves once again in the affairs of North and South America. A formal reaction to the possibility of international crisis with European powers did not come, however, until 1823 when the Monroe Doctrine was issued. And no foreign policy statement in American history, with the possible exception of Washington's Farewell Address, has captured the American imagination so completely. Monroe's statement not only captured popular fancy, but it has served as a guiding light to many generations of American politicians and diplomats. Despite certain questions about the origin, authorship, and effect of Monroe's policy statement, its contents profoundly shaped the future direction of a nation whose people had already come to believe that it could be isolationist and nonisolationist at one and the same time. Its place in the halls of American diplomatic mythology, however, must be challenged. In the words of one historian familiar with the topic:

> The Monroe Doctrine was not a treaty, not an executive agreement, not an act of Congress, not a multilateral inter-American policy, and not international law. Its principles were not original with Monroe. It was not

56

effectively enforced by the United States for many years. And it was not even called the Monroe Doctrine until long after Monroe left the Presidency. It was simply a statement of policy included in the President's message to Congress on December 2, 1823.[4]

The Legendary Virginians: Jefferson and Madison

Even more than James Monroe, the political careers of his fellow Virginians—Thomas Jefferson and James Madison—have been the subject of myth and misconception. Jefferson in particular has been consecrated by legend, even though his place in the American pantheon of heroes was not established until well into the twentieth century. While Jefferson is today usually remembered as the cosmopolitan democrat who inspired public trust through his reasonable and humane leadership of the young nation, he has not always been seen thus. The so-called dark side of Jefferson's character has led some variously to criticize his leadership as governor of Virginia during the Revolutionary War, to question his record in the area of civil liberties, to claim that he was somewhat un-American because of his religious views, and to cast doubt as to his personal morals. To his fellow Republican supporters he was a man of integrity and virtue, but to those who opposed him—Federalists faithful to Alexander Hamilton—he was a hated radical. And ever since, the mood of the country and changing political fortunes have had much to do with Jefferson's shifting historical reputation. "As the pendulum of public favor swings from generation to generation," as one historian says, "he [Thomas Jefferson] and Alexander Hamilton exchange the roles of Saint Michael and Lucifer."[5] For these reasons, to achieve a balanced judgment of the nation's third president is difficult indeed. The American poet Walt Whitman insisted that he was "the Columbus of our political faith," even though Jefferson himself seems to have wanted to keep public popularity at arm's length and applause to a minimum. Meanwhile, his political rivals and those not inclined to his high-minded philosophy have insisted that the essence of Jefferson was his "intellectual sup-

erficiality and insincerity." Indeed, neither the myth nor the reality of Thomas Jefferson has as yet been finally determined.

Jefferson's fellow Virginian, James Madison, never enjoyed the personal magnetism which seemed to radiate so effortlessly from the Sage of Monticello. For this reason in particular he seems to have been lost in the shuffle of history. He has never quite made it into the revered inner circle of American historical heroes. Most people are content to see him in a supporting role, as the "errand boy" of Thomas Jefferson. While he enjoyed neither the splendid appeal of a warrior, such as Washington, nor the speaking skills of a gifted orator, such as Patrick Henry, Madison's political credentials were nearly impeccable. He helped to draft the Virginia Constitution (1776), sat in the Continental Congress, played a crucial role at the Constitutional Convention, served in the House of Representatives, acted as secretary of state to Jefferson, and was elected fourth president of the United States. Indeed, few leaders among the founding generation played such a key role in the affairs of the nation. Despite all of this, Madison is remembered for his supposed ineptness as president and his flight from Washington before the British attack during the War of 1812. Recent research, however, has called the legend of Madison's presidential incompetence into question. While Madison still is not at the point of challenging either Washington or Jefferson as an American folk hero, it can now be seen that developing political realities both at home and abroad, over which he had little control, helped shape his inglorious reputation. James Madison, it seems, deserves considerably more recognition than history has granted him.

The Mythology of the First Western Frontier

Unlike the case of Madison, legends about the frontier—the land to the west which was seemingly beyond the troubles of warfare and party politics—appear quite positive. And the problem is the opposite from that of Madison: history and myth have claimed more for the West than it deserves. To begin with, it is difficult to measure the impact of the West on the development of American institutions and traditions because the West cannot be clearly defined as a particular locale. Simply put, the West became the East as farmers and homesteaders moved in waves across the continent. The term "the West" loses some of its picturesque meaning, then, when it is understood that every portion of the country was a frontier at one time or another.

The problem of dealing with the history of the West is also complicated by the fact that the mere mention of the conquest of America's western frontier conjures up images of an almost endless cast of mythical characters. Judging from the typical response when the word "frontier" is mentioned, one would think that coonskinned trappers, Mountain Men, saddle-sore cowboys, and dance-hall girls held a monopoly on the high adventure of westward expansion. Fact and reason tell one that there were many Wests and that ordinary men and women tending their day-to-day affairs were the major characters of the frontier saga. Yet, not satisfied with the real story of the early frontier, which one would think was adventurous enough, "the American imagination seized upon the short period when the forest was indeed majestic and the tenant heroic, and wove the golden threads into a superlative tapestry which, like good whisky, improves with age."[6] America's first western frontier areas, such as Kentucky, Tennessee, and the Ohio Valley, and buckskin heroes like Daniel Boone and Davy Crockett, filled the need to find a glorious West and a *typical* frontiersman.

An additional pitfall with respect to mythologizing America's early frontier experience is that Americans have never quite been able to decide which image of the leatherstockinged pioneers they find most acceptable. Were they empire-builders bringing civilization to an untouched continent, or were they, rather, primitive fugitives from civilization happy only with the exhilarating freedom of the open spaces? Americans, it seems, have always wanted their western heroes both ways. As is often the case with American legendary characters who have been dipped in the waters of myth, the paradox of the stereotypes has been largely overlooked. Both the West and the pioneers who tamed it were destined to be all things to all people and become permanent fixtures of American mythology in the process.

SECTION I. GEORGE WASHINGTON AND THE GROWTH OF A NATIONAL MYTHOLOGY

While the Founding Fathers were busily at work creating a new nation, Thomas Jefferson, then in Europe, made the observation that they were behaving like "demi-gods." Struck with the importance of their destiny and mission, they were striking a pose which implied that they believed themselves such. Though obviously meant as an expression of his concern at the moment, Jefferson's comment has proven more astute than perhaps even he imagined. As a group, the Founders have continued to be viewed as men of uncommon and godly virtue. However, the president of the constitutional proceedings at Philadelphia has attained a more godlike stature than the others. By 1787, George Washington had already proven himself "first in war." He was now to add to his legendary reputation by being "first in peace" as well. About this man, Americans were beginning to construct one of the major mythical monuments. Already admired as the perfect soldier and savior of the nation's Revolutionary cause, Washington more than any other of the founding heroes was nearly perfect material for myth. The opportunity was quickly seized. Indeed, "although the word 'democracy' was foreign to his vocabulary," George Washington was about to "set the pattern for romantic democracy in the United States."[7]

Washington's Career

That George Washington should become "first in the hearts of his countrymen" and America's foremost mythical figure is a curiosity of sorts. Born into the cavalier traditions of Virginia, he was very much the country gentleman. In many ways an aristocratic squire, Washington also had a sense of public and civic responsibility. While such a class distinction might have disqualified others from potential sainthood in a democracy, with Washington it seemed not to matter. In fact, the aristocratic side to his character seems to have only added to his heroic appeal. It provided him just the right measure of chivalry, honor, and sense of duty to a noble cause. It may well have been these characteristics which brought him as a young man of twenty-two to side with the British in the last of their Great Wars for Empire against the French. While this early stage of his military career had its share of frustration and defeat—such as his surrender of Fort Necessity to the French—folklore and legend had begun to shape his destiny. According to Indian myth, for example, it was already believed that George Washington enjoyed the care and guidance of the Great Spirit.

General Washington's activities during the Revolution did little to diminish his potential

as a mythical personality. It is true that in some respects his prestige fluctuated sharply during the war years. So much had he become the symbol of colonial aspirations for independence from England that defeat or victory on the battlefield had an immediate effect on his reputation. Even though the Great Spirit was supposedly already on his side, Washington and his armies lost control of both New York and Philadelphia during the early years of the war. In the case of Philadelphia, Washington suffered defeats at Brandywine and Germantown which allowed the British general,

Washington Crossing the Delaware
Library of Congress

59

William Howe, to advance on the city unmolested. Despite Washington's lack of initial success, however, John Adams commented on "the superstitious veneration" which he still enjoyed. If these defeats had held any potential for detracting from Washington as a mythical and legendary figure, the opportunity was lost during the winter of 1777-1778.

Regrouping his forces after the battles of Brandywine and Germantown, Washington wintered at Valley Forge, some twenty miles from Philadelphia. While the experience there was anything but pleasant, the popular image of the ordeal has been greatly overromanticized. Pageant-makers, overly dramatic artists in particular, have emphasized hunger, death, and bloody footprints in the snow. Legend suggests as well that General Washington with all his dignity and humility prayed fervently in the snows for the Great Spirit to deliver him and his men from their sufferings. While these hardships were the price which had to be paid for independence, the historical record indicates that discomfort and hunger were not part of God's price for the eventual success of the Revolution. Rather, they were largely caused by congressional quibbling with the commissary department. The needs of the men in the field were lost in a shuffle of bureaucratic mismanagement. And as for General Washington's mythical behavior at Valley Forge, the historian Dixon Wector has concluded:

> That Washington apparently never knelt to pray even in church, but remained standing, did not affect the legend. It was carved in stone in a prominent place over the old Sub-Treasury building in New York City, and only a decade ago a Federal postage stamp showed Washington on his knees at Valley Forge. On the latter occasion Doctor Isaac R. Pennypacker, chairman of the Valley Forge Park Commission, made a public protest against this commemoration of a falsehood—but it did no good.[8]

Even though the general and his men had great difficulty living through the icy despair of Valley Forge, the mythical Washington survived intact.

As a peerless statesman both at the Constitutional Convention and later in the office of president, Washington discharged his duties with political skill and competence, adding to his mythical image in the process. Not only did he now qualify as a military idol, but as a profound statesman as well. He invited comparison with the mythical heroes of antiquity—Achilles, Julius Caesar, Alexander the Great, Charlemagne, and King Arthur. Like the legendary figures of old he was a patriot and a law-giver, a nation-builder and a maker of proud traditions. As the "Father of His Country" he not only shaped the nation's destiny through his work on the Constitution as did the other Founding Fathers, but with his decisive sense of presidential style he went well beyond what had been penned on parchment or what would later be chiseled in stone. As the first chief executive, Washington established precedents which had the effect of filling in the blank spaces of presidential authority. Under his leadership, an unwritten Constitution began to emerge from the written one. The Constitution specifically said, for example, that the president was to make treaties with the "advice and consent" of the Senate. After having called on them for advice and having failed to receive it, however, Washington established the practice of submitting treaties to that body for ratification. Washington increased the power of the presidential office by bringing together a cabinet, which also was designed to become a permanent feature of the unwritten Constitution. The growing prestige of the presidency, in short, both reflected and enhanced the imposing strength of the United States' first bonafide mythical hero.

After his Farewell Address warning against permanent entanglements with foreign powers, George Washington retired from public affairs and resumed the life of a gentleman farmer at Mount Vernon. Less than two years later, on December 14, 1799, he passed from this life and into history. Even though the distance of death in almost every circumstance has a way of removing blemishes and maximizing achievements, Washington scarcely needed the additional boost which the tranquility of memory often provides myth. For when he died the nation's capital had already been named in his honor, and his antique dignity had undergone the romantic distortions of artists like Charles Willson Peale and Gilbert Stuart. Folklore and rumor had already provided him the reputation of being a devoted son and faithful husband. Some ugly warts, it is true, still remained. For example, a malicious political pamphlet printed in London in 1776 claimed that the future Father of his Country had produced an illegitimate son whose initials were A(lexander) H(amilton). It was still being circulated at Washington's death. Those who believed this piece of gossip were probably the great-grandparents of those who in 1859 paid the circus master P. T. Barnum their hard-earned dollars to see the "Negro nurse of George Washington, 'aged 161 years'."[9] Indeed, the memory of the man who had once been a living legend dies hard.

Creating the Legendary Washington

While it is true that Washington himself played a considerable part in the creation of myths about him—mythical subjects usually do—the writings of one Mason Locke Weems were responsible in a major way for that portion of the mythic monument built after his death. Parson Weems was, if you will, the "father" of the Father of his Country. Weems was born in Anne Arundel County, Maryland, in 1759, and while little is known of his early life, legends abound. It is said that his younger years were spent in voyages on his brothers' ships, and that he studied medicine at Edinburgh or London. It is known that Weems studied for the Episcopal ministry and was ordained in 1784 by the Archbishop of Canterbury. In 1794, however, Weems left the permanent ministry in favor of a dual career as bookseller and writer of literary-historical works. His literary-historical works heavily emphasized patriotism, with liberal helpings of religion and morality. In the good parson's view, for example, the American Revolution had come about because "the king wanted money for his hungry relations and the ministers stakes for their gaming tables or diamond necklaces for their mistresses." In his biography of George Washington, Weems' patriotic historical writing—as well as his talent for myth-building—is best typified.

Upon Washington's death in 1799, the floodgates were opened to a tide of legend concerning him. Here was an opportunity for Mason L. Weems and many other authors to emphasize the traditions, values, and goals of the new nation in terms of the life and character of its most important citizen. Using a racy style, vivid description, and an ever-present sense of humor, Weems adorned his *Life of George Washington* with a glowing commentary on Washington's great virtues, religious principles, patriotism, and justice. The result of his effort, of course, was that Weems created a Washington whom research scholars have difficulty recognizing. Washington's character and accomplishments, as put forth by the parson, are exhausting just to contemplate. He had the old-fashioned virtues, loved his parents, loved and feared God, was a leader, a good student, and was born to be a soldier. The most famous of Washington's virtues as emphasized by Weems, however, was George's honesty. It was not until the fifth edition of his work in 1806, however, that Weems included the tale of Washington and the cherry tree. According to this famous yarn, George refused to flinch from the responsibilities of manhood and admitted to his inquiring father: "I can't tell a lie, Pa; you know I can't tell a lie. I did cut it [the cherry tree] with my hatchet." This story was contained in eighty-one editions of Weems' book up to 1927. Indeed, the story continues to this day.

Over the years some people have criticized Parson Weems' tinkering with the facts of Washington's life. With characteristic wit, for example, Mark Twain claimed moral superiority over Washington because George couldn't tell a lie, whereas he could, but wouldn't. For the most part, however, the Washington legend has survived with scarcely a blemish. In both folk culture and literature, testimonials to his appeal abound. Succeeding generations have supplemented the work of Weems by naming one state, eight streams, ten lakes, thirty-three counties, nine colleges and universities, and one hundred and twenty-one towns and villages in Washington's honor. American writers such as Washington Irving, William Cullen Bryant, Oliver Wendell Holmes, Walt Whitman, and Carl Sandburg have lent their assistance as well. As a testimony to his popularity outside of literary circles it can also be noted that "collectors of early American glass know that Washington topped all other favorites in the designs for whiskey bottles; a recent catalogue lists some forty-nine different specimens blown from about 1820 to 1825."[10] In the end, however, George Washington was not descended from a Norman baron of the time of William the Conqueror (as Washington Irving claimed), nor was he the inventor of ice cream (credited to him by the National Bicentennial Commission commemorating the second century of his birth in 1932). While one would think that the Father of his Country standing on his own merits and achievements would be admirable enough, Washington has become even more of a hero than he ever dreamed.

The elaborate mythology of George Washington which grew almost as quickly as the nation was not due only to the enterprising Parson Weems, folk traditions, and other twisters of historical facts. More important, the American people at large were co-authors of the Washington legend, for the people were psychologically prepared to create or manufacture a spirit and tradition to go along with the government which the Founders, including Washington, had produced. America was quite literally made, first by the statesmen of 1776 and 1787 and later by a people in need of roots, tradition, and a history.

Creating a "Usable Past"

The business of molding groups of people into a nation nearly always requires that they share such things as common territory, common religion, common government, common language, and a common body of history and traditions. Of these, however, early America had very few. Regionalism prevailed in early America. The principle of the separation of church and state, whether to keep religion out of politics or vice versa, was already widely respected. While it could be said that English was the common language, many ethnic groups did not speak it, preferring instead their native language. A common government for the thirteen states had been established by the Constitution, but the system was new and largely untested (Virginians still spoke of their state as "my country"). And as for history and tradition, the scant materials for history and tradition dated back only to 1607. The country was beginning without a common past to which all could relate, without well-established traditions, and almost without a history. The common triumphs, common de-

feats, common goals, and common outlook which held other nations like England or France together were missing. It was clear that Americans would have to creatively build with what they had on hand, meager though it seemed.

Seeking a greater feeling of national community, the nation invented a heritage. Aided by Yankee ingenuity and the pioneer spirit, Americans molded and shaped the past into what they wanted it to be. With spectacular speed and success they tried desperately to find a history which would be worthy of both America's utopian beginnings and the country's origins under the legendary Founding Fathers. There was, if one looked hard enough, an abundance of materials and conditions ripe for a people with imagination. Washington's popularity, and his death just at the point when the nation was about to turn from the eighteenth to the nineteenth century, greatly assisted the process, setting both him and the nation's history on the road to immortality. The temptation to mythologize was insurmountable. Displaying a tremendous urge to hurriedly create a "usable past," invention, exaggeration, falsehood, and romance concerning America's history were bound to occur. The results only contributed further to the American impulse for mythmaking.

Slowly, but most assuredly, a national consciousness was being created—myths included. Legend, combined with folklore, illusion, and fiction, was used by Americans to assure them that their history was as glorious and romantic as that of any other nation. The fabric of history, many facts and traditions, were altered and laundered in the tailoring process, but that—at least for the time—did not seem to matter. America could be proud of its past, its present, and its future greatness. While Americans could claim no lordly knights, no imposing castles, no princely palaces, they could revere the *Mayflower*, Plymouth Rock, Bunker Hill, and the Stars and Stripes. It was true that America had not produced a Hector, an Agamemnon, or a Joan of Arc; but Miles Standish, James Oglethorpe, and George Rogers Clark would substitute nicely. "We have not, like England and France, centuries of achievements and calamities to look back on," wrote the nineteenth-century diarist George T. Strong, but being without the eras that belong to older nationalities—Anglo-Saxon, Carolingian, Hohenstaufen, Ghibelline, and so forth—we dwell on the details of our little ... historic life and venerate every trivial fact about our first settlers and colonial governors and revolutionary heroes."[11] The American past could thus be decorated, adorned, and embroidered like a great tapestry if one were creative and not concerned with the mythical dimension it would give the nation's history.

With a heavy dose of imagination and myth, then, the new nation's history became associated with the noble deeds of ordinary people. History, legends, symbols, monuments, shrines, ballads, patriotic songs, and heroes were blended together in interesting confusion. It was the stuff from which a history with true pageantry could be fashioned. And as the years passed, the raw materials needed to continue the process never seemed to be exhausted. Eventually there would be the log cabin, the bald eagle, the Cumberland Gap, the southern plantation, the Santa Fe Trail, the Alamo, and Promontory Point. For personalities, the future would offer Daniel Boone, Captain Bonneville, John C. Fremont, Robert E. Lee, Sam Houston, and Brigham Young. The landscape itself provided an appropriate background against which such a lofty drama could take place—the Appalachian Mountains, Niagara Falls, the Ohio River, the Mississippi, the Great Plains, the Rockies, the Great Desert, and the golden coast of California. Artists would assist the making of myths by portraying the beauty of the Hudson River, an Old Kentucky Home, and the grandeur of the Tetons. Literary figures—whom the historian Henry Steele Commager has called the "Founding Fathers of American literary nationalism"—would weave the romance of history creatively through their tales of Rip Van Winkle, Leatherstocking, Hiawatha, Uncle Tom, and Huckleberry Finn. What resulted from all of this was a history both splendid and romantic. The American past would be built of a mixture of fact and fantasy; the story of the nation would emerge as a tightly woven blend of history and myth. It was a past that was in many ways factually false yet psychologically true for a nation which very much wanted a usable past in which to anchor its destiny.

SECTION II. MYTHS OF EARLY AMERICAN FOREIGN POLICY: REALISM AND IDEALISM

Among the distinct advantages which American colonists enjoyed and largely took for granted before independence was British administration of their foreign affairs. As a junior partner in the empire, the colonies could be assured that their dealings with foreign powers would be handled through the mechanisms of a highly respected English diplomatic system. This was, after all, one of their "rights as Englishmen." With independence, however, Americans had to fend for themselves in the international community of nations. It was clear that political freedom carried definite responsibilities with it.

Thomas Jefferson, in drafting the Declaration of Independence, had been among the first to recognize the importance of foreign relations to the new republic. While claiming that the "United Colonies are and of right ought to be Free and Independent States," Jefferson spoke to the "separate and equal station" which the thirteen United States desired "among the powers of the earth." To make his point clear, Jefferson concluded the Declaration by noting that the former colonies now claimed the right of "full Power to levy war, conclude Peace, contract Alliances, establish Commerce, and to do all other Acts and Things which Independent states may of right do." The Declaration of Independence, in short, was in many ways a foreign policy document. It was an attempt to mobilize the opinion of foreign nations in support of the American revolutionary cause. The impact of the Declaration within the United States is well remembered, but its role as an instrument of foreign policy has almost been forgotten.

Early Sources of Foreign Policy

Despite the belief that the patterns of American foreign policy were not established until the Constitution was ratified and George Washington became president, it is clear that the origins of the nation's foreign policy are traceable to the years before 1789. Some historians, in fact, have argued that the basic concepts of American foreign relations date even to the age of the discovery of America.

Felix Gilbert, a noted authority on the nation's early conduct of its international affairs, has found the fundamental patterns of American foreign policy tied to the different—almost contradictory—motives which in the very beginning had stimulated English settlement on American soil. "The promise of financial rewards and the belief in the possibility and necessity of constructing a more perfect social order," Gilbert says, "were the two motives which led people to embark on the dangerous voyage to the New World."[12] Realistically, exploiting the riches of the American continent also meant maintaining close relations with the community of states in Europe. Fortune and profit could be gained only if the wealth of American settlements was available to European consumers. Economic bonds with London merchants and the entire European economic establishment were needed for financial success to be realized. For those who had set themselves apart in the colonies in pursuit of a utopian life and society, however, there had to be a separation from the intrigues and affairs of Europe. Since those with utopian sentiments assumed that the Old World was corrupt and decadent, it was necessary that their new alternatives in America not be contaminated by the diseased societies they had left behind.

The very birth of America thus resulted in opposite views as to what the proper relationship of the New World should be to Europe. Conflicting desires for both luxury and liberty caused colonists uncertainty about which course of action toward Europe would best serve their ultimate needs. Both economic and utopian elements had combined to bring about the settlement of the colonies, and each colony in turn felt a sense of dependence *and* independence toward the world at large. Professor Gilbert writes:

> In all regions of the British settlements in North America, one could have found a strong feeling of material realism and a pervasive air of utopian idealism and, consequently, two different attitudes regarding the Old World: attraction and rejection.[13]

Each colony was at one and the same time an economic outpost of Europe and also committed to the idea of self-sufficiency in the Promised Land. While it is true that the colonies never considered themselves as a political unit in need of a unified policy in foreign affairs before 1776, the colonial psychology of realism and idealism was in many ways bound to determine the style and direction of foreign policy once the need arose.

When the Revolution came, colonial leaders relied on these traditional feelings of dependence and independence as well as European diplomatic procedures in giving form to their foreign relations. Thus, while Americans were in revolt against the English government, they could at the same time lay claim to defending their English heritage. The colonials, in short, depended on English ideas as a means of establishing political independence from the mother country. The basic framework of early American foreign policy would be both realistic and idealistic, convinced of the need for the new nation to be both involved and isolated from the affairs of the empire. The incompatibility of these two attitudes created a tension which became a persistent theme of American foreign relations during its formative years, and consequently the beginning stage of American foreign policy was rich in mythic possibilities. The conflicting views which Americans already had toward Europe—simultaneous involvement and noninvolvement—would largely be resolved through a reliance on myth and legend. This became more obvious when the American government confronted its first foreign policy problem—the French Revolution.

Foreign Policy of Washington's Presidency

Because of French assistance during the Revolutionary War, American enthusiasm for France found friendly expression in the nation's foreign policy during the postwar years. The military marriage of France and the United States in the struggle for American independence, itself the subject of considerable myth, was of strategic importance to Washington's first administration since the French Revolution began in the same year that he became the chief executive of the new nation. In July, 1789, a little more than ten weeks after Washington's inauguration, Paris was shaken by a wave of revolutionary activity. French citizens stormed the Bastille, the dreaded prison-fortress and symbol of tyranny, and shortly thereafter issued the Declaration of the Rights of Man and Citizen. Since the French Revolution had to some degree been brought about by the debts the French government had incurred while supporting the American war, and since the War for Independence had done so much to inspire the French revolt, it seemed likely that the United States would support the new political direction which France was taking. This crisis of Washington's first administration was complicated, however, by other forces and considerations.

The conflicting viewpoints of isolation and involvement made the new president's decision on American policy toward France much more difficult. Moreover, in formulating an American policy on the issue, friction developed between the two dominant personalities of Washington's cabinet—Thomas Jefferson, secretary of state, and Alexander Hamilton, secretary of the treasury. Jefferson was a great friend of France, no doubt because of his years of diplomatic service in Paris. Hamilton's loyalties to Britain were based on a warm admiration for English political institutions and practices. For these reasons passions ran high as supporters of the Jeffersonian point of view labeled Hamiltonian sympathizers "British bootlicks." Backers of Hamilton, in turn, were convinced that their opponents were "frog-eating, man-eating, blood-drinking baboons." These early clashes of opinion provided a partial basis for the eventual appearance of the first American political parties—Republicans and Federalists—but at the time they mostly confused matters for the important policy decision President Washington was destined to make.

Events became even more complex when France went to war with England in 1793. Despite the fact that the United States was still committed by an earlier treaty with France to defend the French West Indies "forever against all powers," Washington responded by issuing his famous Neutrality Proclamation. Contrary to legends about Washington's statement, however, the word "neutrality" does not appear in the document. Instead, Washington spoke of "conduct

friendly and impartial toward the belligerent powers." While myth has often implied that the idea of neutrality was born at the time of Washington's statement, or that the nation out of reverence for the Father of the Country must steer a neutral course in all matters of a similar nature which might ever arise, such a stance was obviously the best way to solve the problem of involvement versus noninvolvement for the time being.

Having survived the touchy issue of the French Revolution as well as additional diplomatic difficulties with both England and Spain, Washington, at the end of his second administration, was prepared to make his farewell to public life. His career was destined to end in much the same style as it had begun—in a cloud of myth and legend. There is in fact probably no document in the history of American foreign relations which has been as misused and misunderstood as Washington's Farewell Address. Legend holds that an aging Washington, exhausted after many years of heroic service to the nation, stepped before an attentive Congress to reaffirm his wise, timeless, and unbiased warning against the evils of foreign entanglements. Myth goes on to suggest that the nation took his sage advice to heart, and wherever possible thereafter tried to remain true to his stirring words in favor of splendid isolationism.

Almost every element of this elaborate mythology, however, does not fit the facts. In the first place, as noted above, Washington's last official statement was not an address at all but rather a position paper issued through the press. In addition, by this time Washington's reputation had lost much of its luster largely because of an unpopular diplomatic agreement he had signed with England in 1795 (Jay's Treaty). In fact, no president with the exception of Andrew Johnson after the Civil War (and more recently Richard Nixon) left office under more criticism. Finally, even though the Farewell Address has always been linked by legend to Washington's name, the principal ideas expressed in it were not only his but also those of Alexander Hamilton and the Federalist party. In his statement, Washington focused attention on the liabilities of the permanent alliance which the nation had agreed to with France at the time of the Revolution and the immediate political needs of the Federalist party to win the presidential election of 1796. As a result, Washington surely never intended that his message should be revered as timeless or binding on future generations of Americans.

Rather than an unbiased exercise in statesmanship, then, Washington's Farewell Address was a campaign document designed to help the Federalist candidate John Adams win election as second president of the United States. As a political manifesto it was issued to help prevent the election of Thomas Jefferson who, it was thought, if he became president, would immediately turn American foreign policy in favor of France. As the historian Alexander DeConde has said: "Under the banner of patriotism the Farewell spearheaded the attack on the opposition party and on French diplomacy."[14] While it is true that Washington warned against "a passionate attachment of one Nation with another," he in no way desired to set a precedent for isolationism. Even though the popular conception is that he wanted the nation to have no alliances with any nation at any time for any purpose, he was, rather, endorsing a policy of general noninvolvement and "temporary alliances for extraordinary emergencies." Washington seems to have wanted the best of all worlds—involvement and noninvolvement, on American terms. Since America's isolationist instincts dated all the way back to the nation's utopian beginnings, it is not surprising that the supposedly isolationist Farewell Address became a misunderstood cornerstone of American foreign policy. Again. Alexander DeConde's remarks are appropriate: "The Farewell Address . . . belonged to posterity and posterity has given it meanings to fit its own problems."[15] Indeed, the political mythology of later years has had a way of making Washington's final testament

American Frigate *Constellation* vs.
French Frigate *L'Insurgente* (1799)
Old Print Shop

to the nation a plea for isolationism—which it most definitely was not—and of encouraging the nation to forget the political circumstances within which it was written.

Foreign Policy of Jefferson's Presidency

The foreign policy of Thomas Jefferson, who became president in 1800, also has suffered from the misfortunes of historical mythmaking. In particular, the purchase of the Louisiana Territory from France in 1803 is misunderstood. Traditionally, the diplomatic dealings with Napoleon, which did much to assure continued western expansion by doubling the size of the United States at a cost of about three cents an acre, are seen as the crowning achievement of Jefferson's presidency. The nation's third president, however, had much less of a direct role in this success than is thought. In his instructions to the American ambassador to France, Robert Livingston, and later to his special envoy, James Monroe, Jefferson spoke only of the possible purchase of the port of New Orleans and West Florida. His most immediate concern was not the future destiny and glory of the United States, but rather his desire to meet the growing demands of western supporters in his own party who wanted convenient access to the sea in order to ship their agricultural goods to European markets. Because of his military and political intrigues in Europe and French military failures in the Western Hemisphere, Napoleon, it seems, was willing to sell not only New Orleans but also the vast piece of real estate to the north and west.

After diplomatic arrangements for the sale had been made, President Jefferson's first reaction was that the Constitution would not allow such a transaction and a constitutional amendment would be needed giving him the power to sign the agreement. In the end, Jefferson overcame his doubts about the constitutionality of the purchase, and America gained a territory equal in size to the combined areas of Britain, Germany, France, Spain, Portugal, and Italy. The historical myth has persisted, however, that the acquisition was attributable to the political and diplomatic genius of Thomas Jefferson.

The War of 1812

The War of 1812 also deserves closer scrutiny by those concerned with the element of myth in American history. Unlike topics such as the Revolution and the Founding Fathers, myths have developed around the "Second War for Independence" because it is among the least understood episodes in all of American history. Most people are content to think that the war came only because American honor had been challenged by English violations of international law on the high seas. In short, the war was caused by the British who were still poor sports over having lost the American Revolution. Myth and legend suggest that America heroically defeated the forces of English tyranny thanks to General Andrew Jackson's victory at the Battle of New Orleans.

Despite such a simplistic and mythical view of the conflict, the causes of the War of 1812 pose an immensely complex historical problem. While it is true that Americans were vitally concerned with the British policy of stopping and seizing American men and ships on the high seas, many historians have come to stress another important cause of the war. The writings of Louis Hacker and others have shown that frontiersmen in the expanding western regions favored war because they wanted to seize Canada. Economic depression in the West, as well as Indian problems which settlers felt were largely inspired by the English, were all part of an expanding American definition of national honor. Thus the notion that the war was fought to protect American shipping from British harrassment explains only part of the problem; it does not explain the fact that the war became exceedingly unpopular in many areas, especially in the seaboard states of New England. In addition, it can be said that while many of the issues with England did date back to the era of the Revolution, England was not pursuing "tyrannical" policies simply because it was a nation of evil-minded people still bitter over having lost the American colonies. Rather, England was engaged at that time in fighting a bitter war with Napoleonic France, and its government leaders believed that free trade by Americans with Napoleon's European allies was a threat to their nation's security. And as for General Jackson and the showdown at New

Orleans, it had absolutely no strategic military value since it was fought two weeks after the peace treaty was signed at Ghent, Belgium. Despite patriotic histories to the contrary, the United States never did defeat the British in the Second War for Independence; "but because of Jackson's victory at New Orleans, the American people came to believe that they had won it."[16]

The Monroe Doctrine

Popular histories have always given great emphasis to the Monroe Doctrine. Usually seen as an expression of the spirit of nationalism which grew out of the War of 1812, President Monroe's statement, issued on December 2, 1823, is often thought of as a cornerstone of American foreign policy. Because of its revered status, several myths have become associated with this doctrine. It is sometimes assumed, for example, that the statement was the result of delicate negotiations between Latin American countries and the United States who together agreed that European nations should stay out of the affairs of the Western Hemisphere—a statement of collective isolation, if you will. It is generally thought also that the Doctrine caused a stir of controversy in European capitals, and that it almost immediately had the status of a fundamental principle of international law.

Historical facts reveal, however, that quite the opposite is true; the Monroe Doctrine is not nearly what legend would suggest. The statement of policy which Monroe included in his message to Congress in 1823 was merely that—a statement. It was not the culmination of diplomatic negotiations with the nations of South America, but rather a declaration from the United States alone. As for its reception, Monroe's congressional message passed almost totally unnoticed in Europe. Far from being a law widely respected by the world community of nations, the impact of the doctrine was not felt for many decades; it was, in fact, often violated by European powers. The doctrine acquired its importance from later generations who named it after Monroe and elevated it to its present status. Furthermore, it is questionable whether the principles of the doctrine even originated with Monroe. It is clear, for example, that John Quincy Adams, Monroe's

secretary of state, was as responsible as the chief executive for its contents.

And finally, the doctrine had a quite unexpected result. Although designed to stem European colonialism in North and South America, the Monroe Doctrine had, according to historians, the long-range effect of opening the door for American commercial and territorial expansion. To the extent that it designated the Western Hemisphere as America's exclusive domain, it held vast potential to stimulate the nation's latent desire for territory and influence. Largely because of this, one must be particularly careful not to minimize the importance which the doctrine has had for American foreign relations. Even though our understanding of the Monroe Doctrine is distorted by misconceptions, it nonetheless has had a great impact on the course of America's relations with foreign powers. Surrounded by myth, the Monroe Doctrine grew in influence and stature in the American mind particularly after the Civil War. Even though the things that Americans would come to believe about it would be largely false, they have endured. Here, as with so many other cases in American history, myth has become more real than fact.

SECTION III. THE LEGENDARY VIRGINIANS: JEFFERSON AND MADISON

Even though Thomas Jefferson has not been as completely frozen in legend as George Washington, he is nonetheless a larger-than-life figure from the American past. Because he shared in the drama of nation-building, Jefferson has attained equal heroic stature with the other Founding Fathers. However, while Americans have usually felt a sense of spiritual kinship with Jefferson's political ideas, they have often had difficulty relating his democratic philosophy to his varied activities as revolutionary, diplomat, cabinet member, party spokesman, president, and country gentleman. Americans, it seems, have never quite been able to make up their minds about how deserving of their admiration the wise Virginian—the Sage of Monticello—really is. And no one has ever been completely neutral about Jefferson, which has tended to obscure if not obliterate the reality of his role in American history. Like Napoleon or Lenin, Jefferson is one of those mythical historical figures who inspires extremes of both love and hatred. Jefferson was a man of many talents and a wide range of interests, but his reputation has been built upon what the historian Merrill Peterson calls "the twin hysterias of exaltation and denunciation."[17] Thus, historians are likely to debate endlessly the question of what Thomas Jefferson was really like. For American society more generally, Jefferson's image also lives on amidst a battle of contending mythologies—one essentially positive, the other essentially negative.

Thomas Jefferson

It is not generally understood that Jefferson's halo has been made relatively secure only recently. In fact, the dark and negative side of his reputation predominated before the middle of the twentieth century. For many, Jefferson became a mythical historical figure not because of his many virtues, but allegedly because his abilities as an American leader were seemingly so inferior to those of George Washington or Abraham Lincoln. There was particular criticism, for example, of Jefferson's role as wartime governor of Virginia. Even most loyal Jeffersonians admit that the Old Dominion witnessed better leadership in earlier crises. Having succeeded Patrick Henry as the state's chief executive in 1779, Jefferson's wartime administration was stained by incidents of mistreatment of British prisoners of war, the bankruptcy of the Virginia treasury, and the inability of the state militia to stop the British Redcoats. By late spring, 1781, Jefferson was in fact thinking of resigning, but before he reached a decision, he was forced to flee his home at Monticello to escape the British advance. Even though a later inquiry by the state legislature acquitted him of charges of insufficient preparedness, "his prestige in Virginia was clouded by the disasters of his Governorship, and by his having given up the helm in a storm."[18] Unlike the state legislature of Virginia, however, Jefferson's later political opponents made much ado about his "cowardice" and lack of valor in the face of the enemy. The story of Jefferson, "coattails

flying in the wind," was quickly picked up by his enemies and led to the legendary belief that his commitment to the American cause was little more than a pose. Jefferson, it seemed, was a "sunshine patriot," who, according to the myth, was more a villain than a hero.

The cliché "the pen is mightier than the sword" did not hold true for Thomas Jefferson, at least not at first, because George Washington was far outdistancing him on the road to immortality. Jefferson's appeal, in contrast to Washington's, was not based on the glamour and heroics of military triumphs. As the historian Dixon Wecter says, "The drums and trumpets passed him by."[19] Myth often takes curious turns, and in this case Jefferson's image was lessened because he had not moved to the front ranks of military service once pens gave way to firearms. Convinced that his duty to America could best be served in Virginia, Jefferson had instead served a term as governor. After the conflict with England, supporters of Washington, Hamilton, and other future Federalists were quick to criticize him for having avoided the bloodletting, despair, and bitter hardship of the war years. Legendary stories, circulated by critics, told of cold, hungry soldiers at Valley Forge asking each other, "Where is Jefferson?"

Without having proven his revolutionary sentiments on the battlefield, Jefferson was thought by some to be at best inconsistent and at worst devious. To his enemies—and they were many—he was an intellectual Pollyanna too smitten by the romantic philosophy of the rights of man and republicanism. In taste and temperament he was a Virginia gentleman, but he was also a symbol of the spirit of democracy. He seemed much at home in the cosmopolitan atmosphere of Paris, but he also seemed to represent the rawboned confidence of young America. How was one to explain this bundle of conflicts and contradictions? The easiest way to explain him was to generalize and simplify his characteristics. But this is the very essence of stereotype and, eventually, myth. So he became the French sympathizer who blindly supported the brash demands of the mob no matter what the circumstances. In short, legend made Jefferson into a rigid supporter of radical democracy—called "republicanism" in those days. At a time when the growth of political parties was just beginning in Congress and the experiment with democracy was untried, Jefferson came to be caricatured as the country's resident radical. So long as the Federalist presidents Washington and Adams remained in power, political propagandists would not let the nation forget the unflattering images of Jefferson as inept wartime administrator, fair-weather friend, and dangerous left-winger. This was the same Thomas Jefferson who would be seen by later generations as more moderate than radical, and motivated more by what he saw as the public good than by any set of political ideas.

For a people convinced that their destiny was directed by God, Thomas Jefferson's most disturbing trait was his lack of religious conviction. His antireligious bias, it was said, had surfaced in 1779 when he initiated his famous statute on religious freedom in the state of Virginia. Though his reason for proposing this statute was to keep politics free from religious influence, prejudiced observers contended that he was at heart an atheist. He still might be considered harmless, however, so long as his ungodliness did not contaminate the country by his holding high political office. But as political fortunes changed and it became increasingly clear that the Virginia "atheist" (actually Jefferson was a Deist) was likely to become the nation's third president, critics with an eye toward creating instant legend came forward to predict dire consequences for the nation if he should be elected. Almost overnight Jefferson emerged as a threat not only to the nation's religious heritage, but to property, marriage, chastity, virtue, and decency. Dr. Timothy Dwight, president of Yale University, for example, warned that under a Jefferson administration all Bibles would be put to the torch and "we may see our wives and daughters the victims of legal prostitution." The day Jefferson took the oath of office it was reported that certain of the faithful buried their Bibles by the garden fence for safekeeping. Jefferson's failure to live up to Dr. Dwight's prediction, of course, soon forced many to forget what surely would have been America's darkest hour. Nonetheless, "even today a few conservative Virginia dames—born and bred in a socioeconomic stratum whose prejudices are well-nigh

immortal—think of Tom Jefferson as the freethinker and dangerous radical, who made the Episcopal Church of Virginia 'just like any other church.' "[20]

Even those who have been enchanted by Thomas Jefferson's liberal spirit have been troubled by the streak of antidemocratic behavior which seems to have also been part of his complex personality. Criticism, in fact, has gone beyond the occasional charge of political skulduggery which besets almost every successful politician. Though he will no doubt always be counted among those who vigorously defended the rights of the individual, Jefferson occasionally demonstrated that his commitment to those rights was not total. It is know, for example, that during his tenure as governor of Virginia, he heard rumors that American prisoners were being ill-treated by the British and retaliated by placing British captives under his control in irons. He was prepared to deal with them as common criminals, until a more compassionate George Washington intervened. At a later date, his handling of the Aaron Burr affair also demonstrated a less than total commitment to legal and civil rights. Burr, a fellow party member and Jefferson's vice president during his first administration, was thought to be involved in treasonous activities in the Louisiana Territory. The exact nature of Burr's activities are not clear even to this day, but since Jefferson had long distrusted his former colleague he pushed hard for Burr's conviction. He went so far as to demand that Burr be hung at once. Jefferson's potentially hostile temperament surfaced again at the time of the War of 1812 when he proposed that Americans burn the city of London if the British so much as touched on the nation's coastline. The most persistent question about Jefferson's humaneness, however, concerns his attitudes toward the institution of slavery.

Jefferson's reputation as America's venerated defender of civil liberties is well deserved. Yet his attitude toward blacks is puzzling at the very least. Jefferson asserted the conventional view of his time that "nature" had made a "distinction" between whites and blacks. While unsympathetic with the evolving racist mythology, Jefferson nonetheless prejudged the matter of black intelligence. As in episodes such as those mentioned above, Jefferson exhibited less than perfect democratic conviction. While capable of composing stirring maxims, he was at times undemocratic. In analyzing this complex personality, one historian has commented that it amounts to a question: "Which Jefferson do you quote?"

Historians have often wondered why Thomas Jefferson, the great enduring hero of American liberties, could have been master to some 180 slaves at the same time he was professing "that all men are created equal, that they are endowed by their Creator with certain unalienable Rights, that among these are Life, Liberty and the pursuit of Happiness." How could the man who was so obviously committed to freedom in so many other ways have written a slave code for the state of Virginia, opposed attempts in 1819 to limit the expansion of the peculiar institution, and discussed "the matter of slave breeding in much the same terms that one would use when speaking of the propagation of dogs and horses?"[21] The answer would seem to lie in the fact that Jefferson, even though he thought the institution of slavery morally wrong, was convinced that blacks were inferior to whites. In addition, he was a product of his time and thus reflected racial attitudes generally held in America.

Other facets of Jefferson's attitude toward slavery have provided fertile ground for the development of myth. It has been charged, for example, that the Great Democrat's difficulties with the institution of slavery can be traced to his sexual involvement with Sally Hemmings, one of his slaves.

Even during Jefferson's time, there were rumors that he was a southern gentleman of rather wide-ranging tastes. More specifically, it was said that he sought the sexual favors of black mistresses as well as good books and wine. It was said further that Sally Hemmings, one of Jefferson's mulatto slaves, was by far his favorite. *The Portfolio*, a Philadelphia publication issued in 1802, for example, sought to confirm the rumors by including in its pages a song allegedly written by Jefferson himself:

> Of all the damsels on the green,
> On mountain or in valley,
> A lass so luscious ne'er was seen
> As Monticellian Sally

Though this suggestive lyric was probably authored by northern Federalist party members trying to discredit Jefferson's administration, similar stories have persisted and given Jefferson a legendary reputation as a "secret swinger."

UCLA historian Fawn Brodie rekindled the controversy with her book *Thomas Jefferson: An Intimate History*. Jefferson's attitudes toward freedom for blacks, she argues, was clouded by his passion for Sally, who was mother to seven of his children. Convinced that her fellow historians—the "Jefferson Establishment"—out of reverence for his reputation have "canonized" him, Brodie finds much circumstantial evidence to imply that Jefferson could literally be called a father of his country. Trying to expose the great Jeffersonian coverup, she points out that as a young man he had attempted (by his own admission) to seduce his best friend's wife, that he had become a widower at the virile age of thirty-nine, and that he might have engaged in a Paris romance with an English woman, Maria Cosway. But all of this preceded his long-term affair with Sally Hemmings, which is supposed to have begun when she was but fourteen years of age. Miss Hemmings, described by a slave at Monticello as "very handsome" and by Jefferson's grandson, Thomas Jefferson Randolph, as "light colored and decidedly good looking," was conveniently at the same location as Jefferson nine months before the birth of each of her children. From this Brodie concludes that Jefferson was probably not the passionless austere figure historians have long claimed him to be. Her evidence, long known to historians, is at best circumstantial and speculative. Thomas Jefferson's involvement remains unproven. This darker side of Jefferson's image is still a legend in search of proof.

The most accepted evaluation of the Jefferson legacy, at least for the last few decades, is the belief that he was a complex man of many achievements. To most he is a towering figure of impeccable virtue. This viewpoint is based on the sophistication of his philosophical tastes and his enthusiasm for the political arena. He was the Virginia squire who became the people's friend. He had an originality and elegance of mind which was matched by a definite flair for writing. Jefferson himself suggested a woefully incomplete list of his achievements when he asked to be remembered for only three contributions: author of the Declaration of Independence, architect of the Virginia Statute for Religious Freedom, and father of the University of Virginia. However, he has come to be remembered for much more—minister to France, secretary of state, president, architect, inventor, and philosopher of democracy. While Jefferson's image as an American hero has been at times lost in the shadow of other legendary figures—Lincoln, for example—he is known today as one of the nation's more splendid figures from the past. His image has been revitalized through a series of national shrines at Mt. Rushmore, Monticello, and the Jefferson Memorial in Washington, D.C. He is the patron saint of the modern Democratic party. He has come to represent both the nation's heritage and its destiny. Every American school child knows, for example, that Thomas Jefferson died on the fiftieth anniversary of the nation's independence—July 4, 1826. Time has been on Jefferson's side. Today, he is remembered more for his achievements than for his quirks of personality. In balance, Jefferson seems worthy of the praise which has been cast in his direction.

James Madison

As the myth of Thomas Jefferson grows, some claim that it has overshadowed his fellow Virginian, James Madison, in the process. Though Madison's early career as the "Father of the Constitution" is well known, his succeeding activities, and particularly his role once he became president, have been scarcely noticed. Most often, Americans are inclined to see history from Jefferson's presidency to that of Andrew Jackson as an obscure interlude in American politics. James Madison, in short, has been little more than a shadow figure, largely obscured by the refurbished image of Thomas Jefferson. The major myth which surrounds James Madison and his times, then, is that he was always a lesser figure than his fellow Virginian. The radiance of Jefferson has in fact served to cast doubt on Madison's standing as an American hero. James Madison was an important shaper of American history, however. He was a significant governmental administrator in his own right. Rather than

the "errand boy" of Jefferson—as most are prone to see him—Madison was more often a positive force in the nation's affairs, well-attuned to developing political realities at both the state and national level.

While it seems certain that James Madison will never challenge the likes of Washington or Jefferson as an American folk-hero of the first rank, it is clear that he is more deserving of historical praise than legend would suggest. Curiously, in the instance of Madison, the historical record has been distorted not because his reputation has been inflated—as is usually the case—but rather because his genuine contributions never seem to have been fully appreciated.

Like Jefferson, Madison has a historical reputation at least somewhat determined by the passions of party politics. While students have long believed the myth that America's first political parties, the Federalists and the Republicans, were organized by Alexander Hamilton and Thomas Jefferson, the truth is that James Madison—not Jefferson—is principally responsible for creating the political opposition which arose in Congress during Washington's first administration against Hamilton's treasury policies. Convinced that Hamilton's desires to establish a national bank and support manufacturers would place entirely too much economic power in the hands of the central government, Madison and the clerk of the House of Representatives, John Beckley, quickly began to form an opposition. Before long, Jefferson did emerge as the symbolic leader of anti-Federalism, but Madison was most instrumental in laying the cornerstone of the Democratic-Republican party. Despite some well-entrenched political mythology, "the notion that Jefferson founded the opposition was an invention of the Hamiltonians, to suit their short-range vote-getting purposes."[22] Jefferson, in fact, was on a homeward voyage from diplomatic assignment in Paris to join Washington's cabinet when the first outlines of party politics were being established.

From these early episodes related to political control of the nation's affairs, James Madison gained the erroneous reputation as a leader of the second rank, destined to play second fiddle to the more decisive Thomas Jefferson. In no time, the idea that Madison was always a weak-kneed administrator developed. From the beginning of his career Madison seems to have lacked charisma and political glamour, and thus the idea was born that he was often overwhelmed by events and much less forceful as a political leader than many of the other founders. This misconception of Madison's talents plagued him throughout his political career, despite the fact that as secretary of state to President Jefferson, he seems to have played a key role in the diplomatic intrigues surrounding the purchase of Louisiana from France. Madison's instructions to Livingston, in fact, were instrumental in the eventual success of the negotiations, a success always credited to Jefferson.

The false picture of Madison as a hesitant leader ruled by stronger men was completed during the War of 1812. "Mr. Madison's War," with its military failures, the dissent which arose against it, and its inconclusive outcome, all worked to reinforce the stereotype of Madison as indecisive. Such a mythical caricature, however, fails to appreciate the very difficult circumstances with which he was confronted—lack of full support at home, incompetent military leaders, a raw militia, and an empty treasury. Against these liabilities, Madison's role can be viewed as much more vigorous than formerly imagined. After all, under Madison's wartime leadership, the nation weathered the conflict with strong feelings of national honor, optimism, and confidence still intact. By 1815 Americans had little doubt as to the path that their nation should follow. It now lay to the West, in the Valley of Democracy, in the regions beyond the Appalachian Mountains.

SECTION IV. THE MYTHOLOGY OF THE FIRST WESTERN FRONTIER

For Europeans, America had always been a western frontier. Dating from the era of discovery, they had seen areas in the western ocean as holding great potential for economic opportunity and as an ideal locale wherein their social and political goals might better be realized. The magnet which eventually drew American hunters, trappers, Mountain Men, yeoman farmers, and cowboys westward, then,

was part of a larger process which had lured Europeans to America centuries before. The sense of enchantment which Americans have always had for the West strongly resembles the utopian attitudes Europeans generally held for America in the very beginning. Being transplanted Europeans, Americans could easily envision their own utopias rising in a vacant continent just beyond the fringes of civilization. To those inspired by western utopian dreams, the Appalachian Mountains, the Mississippi Valley, the Great Plains, and the Rocky Mountains seemed more invitations than barriers to settlement. An optimistic belief in the future was the very essence of the American dream, but it had been created, at least in part, in Europe. In short to understand the mythology of the American West, one must first realize that the romantic appeal of the frontier was basically a European idea.

The Garden of the West

The enthusiastic westward movement of the mid-eighteenth century grew out of the extravagant myths about the frontiers of the New World which had existed for some time. Even though the brutal realities of America's wilderness were hardly a part of European expectations, the remote regions and magnificent forests of the great interior retained much of their magical appeal. The great open area to the west, however, also served another purpose. If ever Americans should feel the need for psychological or physical escape, such an escape could quickly be achieved in the "garden of the west"—the American Eden. The scholar William Goetzmann put it this way: "Old World dreams, myths and images constantly programmed the people's imaginations and kept them on the road to a wilderness utopia."[23]

Even before the Revolution the need for new utopias seemed urgent, and Kentucky came into the focus of myth just as the eastern shore of the New World had some two centuries before. Woodlands, evergreen foliage, fertile soil, meadows, and legendary bluegrass beckoned enterprising pathfinders who began to trickle into Kentucky territory beginning in the 1750s. Virginians making claims on western lands dispatched Thomas Walker and Christopher Gist into the eastern regions of

Kentucky in search of a wilderness utopia during this decade. What they found both stimulated and disturbed them. Both nature and game were flourishing, but so were Cherokee and Creek. Nonetheless, those who were "programmed" to see the new land in a romantic haze found their expectations rewarded. Gilbert Imlay, for example, combined an interesting mixture of fact and fancy when he wrote in 1792 that Kentucky surely rivaled paradise in its purity, fertility, and beauty:

> Everything here assumes a dignity and splendour I have never seen in any other part of the world. . . . Flowers full and perfect, as if they had been cultivated by the hand of a florist, with all their captivating odours, and with all the variegated charms that colour and nature can produce, here, in the lap of elegance and beauty, decorate the smiling groves. Soft zephyrs gently breathe on sweets, and the inhaled air gives a voluptuous glow of health and vigour, that seems to ravish the intoxicated senses.[24]

The trouble with such a first impression of America's new utopia was not only that it was exaggerated, but also that Imlay's words were intended to be and were accepted as the truth. Continuing the theme, poets such as Timothy Flint became intoxicated with the charms of Kentucky and began proclaiming it "the garden of the West."

By the 1850s the Kentucky myth was further nurtured by Judge James Hall. Guided by sentimentality, and relying heavily on his quite ample imagination, Hall wrote in *Legends of the West:*

> The beautiful forests of Kentucky, when first visited by the adventurous footsteps of the pioneers, presented a scene of native luxuriance, such as has seldom been witnessed by the human eye. So vast a body of fertile soil had never before been known to exist on this continent. The magnificent forest trees attained a gigantic height, and were adorned with a foliage of unrivalled splendour. The deep rich green of the leaves, and the brilliant tints of the flowers, nourished into full maturity of size and beauty by the extraordinary fertility of the soil, not

only attracted the admiration of the hunter, but warmed the fancy of the poet, and forcibly arrested the attention of the naturalist.[25]

Was this not the Kentucky of pioneer isolation, menacing wild animals, and threatening Indians? Was this not the same land where cold and heat, flood and drought were common? The likes of Imlay, Flint, and Hall saw it otherwise, and Americans believed them. Illusion never seemed to bother those who wanted to believe that "heaven is a Kentucky of a place."

The rosy hue through which people saw the Kentucky west began to attach itself to other western territories, and a succession of "Wests" continued to feed Americans' seemingly endless appetite for the heroic and the mythical. While the vast uncharted continent beyond the Appalachians and Alleghenies had held little sustained appeal for residents of the thirteen colonies, it came to have a profound impact on a people who by the time of the Revolution had increasingly come to see themselves as Americans. Having won independence, Americans could turn their attention away from the many Old World intrigues and redirect their energies toward the land that lay before them. "With the achievement of American independence," as Henry Nash Smith explains in *Virgin Land: The American West as Symbol and Myth*, "the belief in a continental destiny quickly became a principal ingredient in the developing American nationalism."[26] With new lands gained from the English from the Appalachian Mountains to the Mississippi River, America could now envision an "empire of liberty" across the continent. They could lavish their attention on Kentucky, Tennessee, the Ohio Valley, the banks of the Mississippi, and eventually, the prairies and mountains which lay beyond. The very thought was breathtaking. The empty fertile continent, bathed in a golden mist of myth, was coming to be seen as a "highway to the Pacific." The idea of the West fulfilled the people's need for a sense of purpose and destiny. Celebrated in song and story, the most stirring drama in the annals of America—the winning of the West—had begun.

Though the mainstream of American thought envisions the West only in terms of its later setting—cattle towns, Wyatt Earp, and Big Sky Country—America had many Wests which were developed long before the one celebrated by Western movies and local chambers of commerce. In turn, the interior regions of Virginia, and, later, of such states as Indiana, Minnesota, Alabama, and Arkansas all laid claim at various times to being the West. Obviously, historical experiences in these regions varied as much as the pioneers who settled the lands. America's western history was not a reality which the pen of an eastern writer, the brush of an inspired artist, or the lens of a Hollywood camera could capture easily. Rather, each new generation of Americans recreated and revitalized the myth of the West. The legend of the West— perpetuated by writers, the media, and the national appetite for romance—has exaggerated the influence of the frontier on the American experience. At no time did the frontier West, as understood by legend, account for as much as 10 percent of the nation's population. Thus, it is inappropriate for Americans to assume that the western experience is the most basically "American" portion of their history.

Still, the myth of the West did exert a very practical influence on American development. It must be remembered that Americans now firmly believe that the rugged adventure of settling the western lands is what made the country great. Whether this is true or not, the *idea* of the West has been a powerful force in making Americans believe that they *ought to be* individualistic, adventuresome, and democratic. In this sense, the West has done much to mold America. It can then be argued that a fundamental feature of the story of America is its western and frontier theme. This theme was one in which all regions of the country participated. From Jamestown to Juneau, and for places in between, rough and ready hands seemed always willing to extend the cutting edge of civilization. Though the process involved only a very few at any given time, one westerner after another—first in Massachusetts and Virginia, and then in such areas as Pennsylvania, Illinois, Nebraska, Utah, and California—was daring and ambitious enough to keep extending settlement. Stereotypes aside, there never was a typical Westerner—a westerner might as well have been a Mississippian as a Nevadan—but in

spirit, all Americans were and are Westerners. All those on the fringe of settlement played a part in the roll of frontier upon frontier—and on to the frontier beyond.

Adventure, escape, fast-talking land speculators, and personal motives such as the legendary nagging mother-in-law were all in varying degrees responsible for the winning of the West. Increasing population and the gradual improvement of internal transportation were of course also factors in the gathering momentum of expansion which caused American settlement to spill over the Appalachian Mountains by the mid-1700s. It had taken nearly a century after the first colonists had arrived for settlement to reach this geographic point. But by the eve of the Civil War many new Wests had been won, from Texas to California, from Wisconsin to Oregon. Some called the dynamic process Manifest Destiny, but "not many persons responded to the call.... Only about five thousand went to Oregon in the 1840s, about one thousand to California. Manifest Destiny as a moving force was not very important, but as a psychological force it had great significance."[27] The phrase "Manifest Destiny" itself seems not to have been coined until a New York journalist, John L. O'Sullivan, used it in attempting to justify the expanding country's claim to Oregon in 1845. But there was an earlier representative of Manifest Destiny—the Buckskin Hero of the late eighteenth and early nineteenth centuries. What had he been like, and what had motivated him to become a go-getter searching the horizons of the West for "free" land, a modest homestead, and ever-tantalizing new frontiers?

Heroes of the West: Boone and Crockett

To this earlier adventurer, the backwoods frontier beyond the Appalachian range seemed appealing. The British Proclamation of 1763 had forbidden settlement of this promising land to the west, but the fertile and uncrowded area was too tempting. And since this pioneer region was thought by many to be paradise itself, it was not surprising that the new frontier would turn out to be an incubator for western heroes. Legendary characters such as Daniel Boone and Davy Crockett were destined to become immortalized through the

Daniel Boone and the Opening of the West
Washington University Gallery of Art, St. Louis

popular imagination, folklore, and the fabrications of frontier literature.

Of the early western heroes Daniel Boone has proved to be the most irresistible to mythmakers. So great were his deeds supposed to have been that he seems plucked from some medieval romance from the time of King Arthur and Sir Lancelot. While it will probably never be known who the first white discoverers of Kentucky really were, legend has bestowed the honor on Daniel. It is known that more than a third of a century before Boone was even born the area had been explored and was known to the French and to a lesser degree the British. Such men of adventure as John Peter Salley, John Howard, Henry Scaggs, and John Finley had visited

Kentucky many years before Boone "discovered" it. Still, many Americans continue to believe that George C. Bingham's famous painting, "The Emigration of Daniel Boone" (1851), truthfully portrays the celebrated Kentuckian leading a hardy group of settlers into a dream-like wilderness. Boone indeed made his way to the Kentucky frontier, in 1769, well before the Revolution, but he was not an American Moses leading his flock into the Promised Land.

The real Daniel Boone (1734-1820) moved west during the frenzy stimulated by western land schemes. And eventually he was to leave Kentucky, not because he wanted elbowroom, but rather because incompetence in legal affairs forced him to vacate his land claims.

"Bankrupt in Kentucky, he moved on to Missouri," says the historian Dixon Wecter, "impelled by hope and restlessness, rather than by the legendary sense of claustrophobia."[28] The lore of Boone has also suggested that "Dan'l" was a man of imposing stature and strength, yet historical records based on the testimony of his son Nathan clearly show that in reality he was about five feet eight inches tall and weighed 170 pounds. What the Daniel Boone of Kentucky and Missouri frontiers had in common with Hollywood's Fess Parker—all of six feet four inches and 235 pounds—only movie scriptwriters know for sure. Myth has tampered so much with Boone and his historical reputation that the real Boone—minus the legend—is indeed difficult to know.

Also damaging, for those interested in accurate history, were the many biographies which popularized and sanitized the story of life on America's first frontiers. The schoolmaster John Filson, for example, wrote a supposedly authentic autobiography of Daniel Boone in 1784. Even though an autobiography is supposed to be written by a person about his or her own life, this one is essentially by Filson the mythmaker. Playing fast and loose with the facts, Filson's Boone emerges from the "autobiography" as a man of refined qualities and epic vision. Thanks to Filson, one learns that upon seeing Kentucky for the first time, Boone declared: "No populous city, with all the varieties of commerce and stately structures could afford so much pleasure to my mind, as the beauty of nature I found here." Expressions of this sort, one might guess, were hardly typical on the frontier, and Filson could have absolutely no way of knowing what Boone might have said. Nonetheless, it seemed only fitting that a man who was already a mixture of history, mythology, legend, and romance should be exceedingly elegant in both speech and grammar. Though not necessarily bad in itself—it made for entertaining reading—the result of this and other fabrications of language which Filson invented presented an inaccurate record of both Boone and the frontier life he came to symbolize.

Similarly, the hero's character as well as his language had to be altered to meet literary conventions and metropolitan preconceptions of what a bona-fide American frontier hero should be like. The hero must not smoke or drink. He must, of course, be a true believer in the Christian religion and extoll its virtues. He must have philosophical depth, and must above all be conscious of his historical role in settling the West. Again, in the words of Boone's biographer, one hears Daniel say in what must have been one of his few restful moments:

> I now live in peace and safety, enjoying the sweets of liberty, and the bountres [sic] of Providence, with my once fellowsufferers, in this delightful country, which I have seen purchased with a vast expense of blood and treasure, delighting in the prospect of its being, in a short time, one of the most opulent and powerful states on the continent of North-America; which, with the love and gratitude of my country-men, I esteem a sufficient reward for all my toil and dangers.[29]

Despite the fictitious conversations of such legend builders, one can safely assume that the frontier heroes of history were not philosophical types. Firsthand documents suggest that those who wore buckskin and coonskin caps were men of action who did not idle their time away pondering life's universal and philosophical problems. In short, Daniel Boone seems not to have been the American Socrates, John Filson notwithstanding.

The passion of Americans to romanticize their frontier experience through mythical heroes can also be seen in the legends of Davy Crockett, "The King of the Wild Frontier." Born in Tennessee in 1786, his exploits as hunter and woodsman made him nearly as much a "legend in his own time" as he is today. He was a local Tennessee politician for a time and served terms in Congress from 1827 to 1831 and again from 1833 to 1835. Crockett's legend, like that of Daniel Boone's, was greatly assisted by the tall tales of frontier literature. The first book on Crockett, which appeared three years before his death, in 1833, was politically inspired and was an early source of legendary material. Portrayed as "half-horse" and "half-alligator," it was said that Crockett could "ride upon a streak of lightening" and "whip his weight in wildcats."

Meanwhile, back in Washington, Crockett was not distinguishing himself politically though he seems not to have performed his political duties badly. He began his political career as a supporter of Andrew Jackson, but once in the nation's capital, he came to disagree with his fellow Tennessean over the question of land speculation in the West. Soon he began to side with the political enemies of "King Andrew," the newly developing Whig party. Seeing the need for a folk hero who might one day match the political popularity of Jackson, the Whigs got to the business of creating a mythical image for Davy to rival that of Andy.

Even though he may not have needed a fan club to engineer his mythical career, "it seems pretty clear that the Whigs, with the ready co-operation of Crockett and the folk imagination, built him into a legend."[30] Backers of the Whig cause wrote plays in his honor, "The Lion of the West" and "The Kentuckian," and a "Crockett March" was even composed to assist matters. Such efforts, while they had a way of preserving Crockett for posterity, seemed to have little immediate effect on his political constituents back in Tennessee. Frankly, they were not impressed. In the next election he was removed from office and "he wandered off to Texas—where celebrities were still sparse."[31] There he soon found himself involved in the Lone Star State's quest for independence from Mexico. And as was only fitting for an early American frontiersman, his life came to an end in a blaze of glory at the Alamo, thus firmly establishing him as a mythical hero.

Even with Crockett dead, however, legend would not allow him to pass benignly into history. It was soon reported that he had not been killed at all, but was roaming the high plains in search of more adventures. Some mythmakers went so far as to declare that he had miraculously escaped to California where he was passing his time hunting grizzly bears, or that he had made his way to the South Seas, seeking a fortune by diving for pearls. Thanks to oral tradition, almanacs, questionable biographies, and the continued fondness of Americans for tales of the lusty frontier, there were no less than six legendary Davy Crocketts by 1940. The gap between fact and fiction in the case of Crockett took a bit of time and a tragic death to accomplish. The age from which he came, however, seems to have been even more enchanted with that *other* man from the West—Andrew Jackson.

STUDY QUESTIONS

1. Analyze and discuss the many and varied ways in which Parson Weems, aided by the psychological needs of a youthful America, contributed to making George Washington the country's leading myth figure.

2. How and why did the dual forces of realism and idealism help to produce a mythical environment shaping early American foreign policy? More specifically, what are the principal legendary beliefs which have come to cloud Washington's Farewell Address, the Louisiana Purchase, the War of 1812, and the Monroe Doctrine?

3. Discuss the various features of Thomas Jefferson's and James Madison's personalities as they help explain the historical myths which have come to surround each.

4. In what ways did the psychology of the American people in the decades from the Revolution to the Civil War work to create an elaborate mythology of the first western frontier? How did Daniel Boone and Davy Crockett become the major beneficiaries of this enthusiasm for western myth and legend?

REFERENCES

1. Henry Tudor, *Political Myth* (New York: Praeger Publishers, 1972), p. 57.
2. Forrest McDonald, *The Presidency of George Washington* (Lawrence, Kans.: University of Kansas Press, 1974), p. xi.
3. Alexander DeConde, *Entangling Alliance: Politics and Diplomacy Under George Washington* (Durham, N. C.: Duke University Press, 1958), p. 503.
4. Wayne S. Cole, *An Interpretive History of American Foreign Relations* (Homewood, Ill.: The Dorsey Press, 1974), p. 108.
5. Marshall Smelser, "Mr. Jefferson in 1801," in *The Democratic Republic, 1801-1815* (New York: Harper & Row, Publishers, 1968), p. 5.
6. Arthur K. Moore, *The Frontier Mind: Cultural Forces That Shaped the West* (New York: McGraw-Hill Book Co., 1963), p. 43.

7. Dixon Wecter, *The Hero in America: A Chronicle of Hero-Worship* (Ann Arbor: The University of Michigan Press, 1966), p. 103.
8. Ibid., pp. 110-111.
9. Ibid., p. 120.
10. Ibid., p. 137.
11. Quoted in Henry Steele Commager, "The Search for a Usable Past," *American Heritage*, February, 1965, p. 90.
12. Felix Gilbert, *The Beginnings of American Foreign Policy: To the Farewell Address* (New York: Harper & Row, Publishers, 1961), p. 4.
13. Ibid., p. 6.
14. Alexander DeConde, "Washington's Farewell, the French Alliance, and the Election of 1796," *Mississippi Valley Historical Review*, March, 1957, p. 649.
15. Ibid., p. 169.
16. Samuel Eliot Morison, "Dissent in the War of 1812," in Samuel Eliot Morison, Frederick Merk, and Frank Freidel, *Dissent in Three American Wars* (Cambridge, Mass.: Harvard University Press, 1971), p. 31.
17. Merrill D. Peterson, ed., *Thomas Jefferson: A Profile* (New York: Hill & Wang, 1967), p. vii.
18. Wecter, *The Hero*, p. 153.
19. Ibid., p. 149.
20. Ibid., p. 165.
21. William Cohen, "Thomas Jefferson and the Problem of Slavery," *The Journal of American History* 56 (December, 1969): 525.
22. Smelser, "Mr. Jefferson," p. 175.
23. William Goetzmann, "The Frontier—From Jefferson to Turner," *In Search of the American Dream* Series, *St. Paul Dispatch* (November 25, 1974), p. 9C.
24. Quoted in Arthur K. Moore, *The Frontier Mind*, p. 21.
25. Ibid., p. 22.
26. Henry Nash Smith, *Virgin Land: The American West as Symbol and Myth* (New York: Random House, 1950), p. 10.
27. Ray A. Billington, "Westward Expansion and the Frontier Thesis," in John A. Garraty, ed., *Interpreting American History: Conversations with Historians*, I (New York: The Macmillan Company, 1970), p. 260.
28. Wecter, *The Hero*, p. 185.
29. Quoted in Kent L. Steckmesser, "The Frontier Hero in History and Legend," in Leonard Dinnerstein and Kenneth T. Jackson, eds., *American Vistas: 1877 to the Present* (New York: Oxford University Press, 1971), pp. 6-7.
30. Wecter, *The Hero*, p. 190.
31. Ibid., p. 191.

SOURCES FOR FURTHER STUDY

GEORGE WASHINGTON AND THE GROWTH OF A NATIONAL MYTHOLOGY

CUNLIFFE, MARCUS. *George Washington: Man and Monument*. Boston: Little, Brown and Co., 1958.

COMMAGER, HENRY STEELE. "The Search for a Usable Past," *American Heritage*, February, 1965.

———. "American Nationalism." In John A. Garraty, ed. *Interpreting American History: Conversations with Historians*, II. New York: The Macmillan Co., 1970.

CORDS, NICHOLAS. "Parson Weems, the Cherry Tree and the Patriotic Tradition." In Nicholas Cords and Patrick Gerster, eds., *Myth and the American Experience*, I. Beverly Hills: Glencoe Press, 1973.

WECTER, DIXON. *The Hero in America: A Chronicle of Hero-Worship*. Ann Arbor: The University of Michigan Press, 1966.

MYTHS OF EARLY AMERICAN FOREIGN POLICY

COLE, WAYNE, S. *An Interpretive History of American Foreign Relations*. Homewood, Ill.: The Dorsey Press, 1974.

DeCONDE, ALEXANDER. "Washington's Farewell, The French Alliance, and the Election of 1796." *Mississippi Valley Historical Review*, March, 1957.

GILBERT, FELIX. *The Beginnings of American Foreign Policy: To the Farewell Address*. New York: Harper & Row, Publishers, 1961.

MARKOWITZ, ARTHUR. "Washington's Farewell and the Historians." *Pennsylvania Magazine of History and Biography*, April, 1970.

MORISON, SAMUEL ELIOT. "Dissent in the War of 1812," in Samuel Eliot Morison, Frederick Merk, and Frank Freidel, *Dissent in Three American Wars*. Cambridge: Harvard University Press, 1971.

THE LEGENDARY VIRGINIANS: JEFFERSON AND MADISON

BRANT, IRVING. "James Madison and His Times," *American Historical Review*, July, 1952.

BRODIE, FAWN. *Thomas Jefferson: An Intimate History*. New York: W. W. Norton, 1974.

MAYO, BERNARD. "The Strange Case of Thomas Jefferson," in Bernard Mayo, *Myths and Men: Patrick Henry, George Washington, Thomas Jefferson*. New York: Harper & Row, Publishers, 1963.

PETERSON, MERRILL D., ed. *Thomas Jefferson: A Profile*. New York: Hill & Wang, 1967.

WECTER, DIXON. "Thomas Jefferson, The Gentle Radical," in Dixon Wecter, *The Hero in America: A Chronicle of Hero-Worship*. Ann Arbor: The University of Michigan Press, 1966.

THE MYTHOLOGY OF THE FIRST WESTERN FRONTIER

BILLINGTON, RAY A. "Westward Expansion and the Frontier Thesis." In John A. Garraty, ed. *Interpreting American History: Conversations with Historians*, I. New York: The Macmillan Company, 1970.

HINE, ROBERT V. *The American West: An Interpretive History*. Boston: Little, Brown and Co., 1973.

MOORE, ARTHUR K. *The Frontier Mind.* New York: McGraw-Hill Book Co., 1963.

SMITH, HENRY NASH. *Virgin Land: The American West as Symbol and Myth.* New York: Random House, 1950.

WECTER, DIXON. "Winning of the Frontier: Boone, Crockett, and Johnny Appleseed," in Dixon Wecter, *The Hero in America: A Chronicle of Hero-Worship.* Ann Arbor: The University of Michigan Press, 1966.

4 Myths from the "Age of the Common Man"

PREVIEW

Andrew Jackson: The Man and the Myth

The first decades of the nineteenth century witnessed a quickening of American expansion into the areas immediately beyond the Appalachian mountain chain. Moreover, these new regions eventually made themselves felt politically, and it seemed that American politics was destined to become more democratic as it became more western in character. As early as James Monroe's election to the presidency in 1816, excitement over the West was evident. Yet, although Monroe himself was from Westmoreland County in western Virginia, it was clear that the West had not yet become a political power, for Monroe's vice president was from New York State, and his secretary of state (John Quincy Adams) from Massachusetts. In other words the seaboard states retained their political power.

After Monroe's two terms as president, however, it became more evident that control of American political affairs was indeed shifting westward. John Quincy Adams won the presidential election of 1824, but a political upstart from the West—Andrew Jackson—had actually received more popular votes for the office (153,000 to 108,000). Since none of the candidates—a group which included William Crawford of Georgia and Henry Clay of Kentucky besides Adams and Jackson—had received a majority of the electoral votes, selection of the new president fell to the House of Representatives. Adams was duly elected. As a gesture toward the growing strength which the new West enjoyed, Adams appointed Clay his secretary of state. To supporters of Jackson the appointment confirmed their belief that a "corrupt bargain" had been negotiated between Adams and Clay—the "Judas of the West." Thus, it was no surprise to anyone when Jackson defeated Adams in 1828. And after four years of frustration he was apparently ready to open the doors of government to a new brand of upland democracy.

Legend holds that this set of circumstances —the rise of the West as a political force, the growing democracy of the frontier, and the new style of American politics—brought Andrew Jackson from Tennessee to Washington, from the backwoods to national leadership. Without a doubt Jackson was a remarkable individual, but much of his image and that of his time are based on sentimentalism, folklore, misinformation, and myth. The nation's attachment to Jackson is very much related to the mystique of the West. Here is a case of myth by association. Even in his own day, a popular song, called "The Hunters of Kentucky," which swept the nation in the 1820s, helped Jackson's move to the White House by associating him with the developing western myth of Daniel Boone. In the popular mind, both men seemed to be cut from the same cloth, and both were part of the democratic ritual of the time. Yet even though being a resident of the developing West was no assurance that one was either committed to the idea of democracy or sympathetic to the needs of the common man, Jackson rode his legend to fame and fortune.

Though a frontiersman by birth and upbringing, Andrew Jackson was also a Tennessee land speculator and a "sound money" man. Later in his career, as his democratic legend grew, he was fond of warning against a "moneyed aristocracy" as a potential danger to the country's liberties, but Jackson himself was a frontier conservative, a fact his political rhetoric obscured. The nation's enthusiasm for his sparkling image as an Indian fighter, frontiersman, and courageous general, pushed his years of economic and political conservatism into the background. As the country came to accept Jackson as a firebrand of democracy and the people's candidate, those who knew him better in his home state of Tennessee could only imagine that he must have undergone a miraculous conversion, even though they supported him as a favorite son. Despite some reservations, his appeal was nearly universal—to Easterners as well as Westerners he was the nation's invincible warrior. "On Inauguration Day," one historian has noted, "eager thousands stormed the Capitol to see their idol, erect, white-haired, sallow-faced, coming on foot from Gadsby's boardinghouse. 'It is beautiful, it is sublime!' exclaimed Francis Scott Key."[1]

Andrew Jackson's actual role in the events of his time, and of course whether he was responsible for adding a new democratic dimension to American political life or whether he was in essence a product of his image and a political opportunist, are exceedingly difficult to determine. While some historians applaud his masterful leadership of the democratic movement which they associate with his years in the presidency, others have criticized Jackson's brand of democracy for having opened the political system to loyal but incompetent political hacks. While most have come to accept the more pleasing image of Jackson as a "man of the forest," some refuse to overlook Jackson's high status as a member of the governing elite who used the people for selfish political ends. With Jackson, apparently, one must be content with paradox. A mythical hero who has become all things to all people must have many facets to his character. Certainly the people's admiration for Old Hickory has had as much to do with the myth as has the man, but the question as to which is more "real" remains elusive. Perhaps the easiest way to understand Jackson is to see him as did his first scholarly biographer, James Parton. Writing in the year before the onset of the American Civil War, Parton said that Jackson had to be viewed as both

> a patriot and a traitor. He was one of the greatest of generals, and wholly ignorant of the art of war. A writer brilliant, elegant, eloquent, without being able to compose a correct sentence, or spell words of four syllables. The first of statesmen, he never devised, he never framed a measure. He was the most candid of men, and was capable of the profoundest dissimulation. A most law-defying, law-obeying citizen. A stickler for discipline, he never hesitated to disobey his superior. A democratic autocrat. An urbane savage. An atrocious saint.[2]

Just as Andrew Jackson the man remains a curious mystery, a confusing mixture of motives and actions, so does the historical period which bears his name and the political movement which he led remain mysteries.

Jacksonian Democracy: Mirage or Movement?

Contrary to the thinking of most people, neither the West nor Andrew Jackson nor the Democratic party which he led held a monopoly on equality or democracy during the Age of the Common Man. Studies have shown that, in New York State at least, the use of the terms "equality" and "democracy" was indeed to be found among most political parties— including Jackson's major political opposition, the Whigs. Also, scholars have come to argue that the Jacksonian spirit was as much to be discovered among mechanics and expectant capitalists in the East as with pioneer farmers and hunters of the frontier upcountry. Jacksonian democracy, in short, was as much economic as political, and as eastern as western, in its appeal and direction. No one concept or label seems sufficient to capture adequately the essence of the era. Jacksonian politics became fashionable nationwide. Perhaps nowhere is the paradox and elusiveness of the period more apparent, however, than in the goals and values of one of the more legendary and least understood figures from the American past—the Mountain Man.

While it is true that the Westerner was not the only Jacksonian and the West not the only setting within which Jacksonian politics became fashionable, in the dichotomy of the Mountain Man one finds the two strongest elements that comprised the political movement known as Jacksonianism. The Mountain Man has two dominant stereotypes. As a romantic and mythical character, he is seen either as an American Robin Hood free from the suffocating limitations of civilization or as a rather pathetic primitive in greasy buckskins. Because he was a close cousin to such earlier frontier heroes as Daniel Boone, there is much about the Mountain Man's bandit-of-the-forest image which is appealing. In this light, he seems the supreme example of the Jacksonian Man—close to nature, contemptuous of civilized authority, and yet somehow committed to freedom and democracy. The other side of his character, however, that of a forlorn wanderer often seeking escape from his miseries through drunken debauchery, has also become a feature of his image. When thus portrayed, he seems somehow not quite acceptable even for those comfortable with the environment of the frontier. With the nation undecided as to which image best reflects truth, "the Mountain Man exists as a figure of American mythology rather than history."[3] Like all enduring myths, those surrounding the Mountain Man had enough validity to gain acceptance.

This "venturous conservative"—the Mountain Man—lived close to nature while pursuing the fur trade in the Rocky Mountain region. Given the chance at other occupations, few of them remained "free agents of nature, however." Most shared a strong desire to return to civilized comforts. Most sought, and many attained, the respectability and success so valued by the society they had left behind. They definitely valued the individualizing experience of the American frontier, yet their ultimate goal was to be assimilated in the economic and social mainstream of American life. They both looked back at a frontier America which was already beginning to vanish, and at the same time looked forward to the benefits which economic freedom in a civilized society might bring.

The Mountain Man, like so many others during the time of Jackson, was one who loved change and hated revolution. In sentiment and attitude he was like "the master mechanic who aspired to open his own shop, the planter, or farmer who speculated in land, the lawyer who hoped to be a judge, the local politician who wanted to go to Congress, the grocer who would be a merchant. . . ."4 Even though legend has made the fabled Rocky Mountain fur trade seem as though it were an adventurous and sporting life-style, the Mountain Man was very much economically oriented. He was an independent man in search of security. Most of his kind in fact were not the "free agents of nature" which myth suggests. Many worked for fur-trading companies such as Gantt and Blackwell; Bean and Sinclair; or Sublette, Fitzpatrick, Bridger, Gervais and Fraeb. Indeed, when given the opportunity, most left the adventure of fur trapping to devote their energies to more civilized careers: farmer, rancher, storekeeper, lumberman, or opera-house impresario. According to one study which sampled more than half of those in the mountain trade, "only five men out of the total [446] stayed with the great out-of-doors life of the free trapper that according to the myth they were all supposed to love."5 The melodramatic and highly romantic tales of Mountain Men on the far western frontier, though extremely popular to an increasingly urban reading public, bore only slight resemblance to their economic realities. Even such hardy characters as Jedediah S. Smith

and David E. Jackson sought respectability and success. As representatives of the Jacksonian period, the Mountain Man "looked to the future and the development of the West, not as a vast game preserve, but as a land like the one [they] had known back home. . . . The opera house went up almost simultaneously with the ranch, and the Bank of Missouri was secured before the land was properly put to hay."6 Like Andrew Jackson, they were free-spirited, committed to democracy in its economic sense, and destined to be ripe material in the developing mythology of the nation.

Religion, Reform, and Race Relations: Rhetoric or Reality

Even though most of the values and attitudes of the East found their way to the West as quickly as the settlers, it seemed to some that the religious spirit had been left behind. Reports from Kentucky, Tennessee, the western Carolinas, and Virginia spoke of the West being crowded with swearers, drinkers, and Sabbath-breakers. With corn liquor flowing freely, marriage celebrations coming long after children had arrived, and violence settling far too many legal disputes, it seemed that the West might be "lost" even before it was "won." Much of the frontier, in short, seemed in need of religious reform. Methodists soon took the lead in evangelizing the frontier. Through the use of circuit riders, camp meetings, and a call to fundamental "old-time religion," they were creating new forms of religious expression which harmonized with the changing times. As the old social and political order passed in a Jacksonian America concentrating its attentions on economics and politics, a Great Experiment was also taking place within American Protestantism. A commitment to a new style of utopianism—revitalized by a belief in progress and reform—convinced religious-conscious Americans that new Edens were still to be discovered. With optimistic confidence and a faith in human perfectability, the nation seemed anxious to commence the creation of a better tomorrow.

In this spirit, Joseph Smith set the Mormons on a trail which would eventually lead to a new religious utopia—a Zion in the Great Desert of the West. As is so often the case with many noble experiments, however, the history of the Church of Jesus Christ of Latter-day Saints was founded in and became an instrument for the development of myth. Mormonism was "mythical" in the sense that its basic doctrines reflected secular legends from the geographical area wherein it began, and also in the sense that its objectives and visions were utopian. Beyond this, Mormonism was not a frontier religion as is usually supposed. It began in the East, and its believers were for the most part New Englanders who only later became western pioneers.

In important respects, then, the Age of the Common Man was also the Age of the Great Experiment. It provided a climate not only for religious reform, but even for Amelia Bloomer to suggest new innovations in women's clothing. Most reformers took the business of changing American society very seriously. Well-entrenched ideas concerning the status of women and blacks, however, were extremely difficult to alter. Cultural myths in support of the idea that blacks were naturally inferior and women sacred vessels whose destiny bound them to the bedroom and the kitchen, and occupationally to "the little red schoolhouse," frustrated reform. In a society that proudly extolled individualism, personal and economic freedom, and an experimental approach to life, a majority of its members (blacks and women taken collectively) were systematically being excluded from participation in the legendary growth of democracy.

The ultimate concern of Jacksonian reform of course was the institution of slavery. Simply because it was the most obvious violation of the nation's democratic pretensions, it increasingly came to dominate the attention of the nation's reformers. Abolitionists seeking an end to black slavery could easily point to the absurdity of America's claim to being a true democracy. The myth of equality had to be challenged and the nation's self-delusion brought to light. In their humanitarian zeal to bring an end to the American tragedy of slavery, however, the abolitionists—in particular the most celebrated instrument of their protest, the Underground Railroad—became the subject of legend. The Underground Railroad involved far fewer participants, both black and white, than one would conclude from the publicity it has received, and myth has made white abolitionists the heroes rather than free blacks and black slaves who were the heroes.

Another important side effect of the myths surrounding the abolitionists has been the assumption that their sentiments were only to be found outside of the slaveholding South. Although the fact is largely unknown, numerous Southerners openly questioned the usefulness and justice of the slave system. Contrary to the mythical picture of the "solid South" staunchly defending black bondage, there was indeed another South opposed to slavery for ethical, economic, and political reasons. Cassius Marcellus Clay, a white Southerner and son of a wealthy slaveholder, was one of those who clearly espoused an antislavery position in Dixie. While Clay's motivations seem to have been more economic than humanitarian, he boldly suggested gradual emancipation for blacks with the provision that owners of slaves be reimbursed for their loss by state governments. What worried Clay most was the economic effect which "the unequal competition of unpaid labor" was having in his home state of Kentucky. His fear was that white workers in the South, in search of decent wages, would always be at a distinct disadvantage to the "free" labor offered through the slave system.

Hinton Rowan Helper was yet another Southerner who endorsed the abolition of slavery on the basis of economic arguments. Born in Rowan County, North Carolina, the son of a yeoman farmer, Helper later developed the literary skills which he used against slavery by describing his personal experiences in the California gold rush. His account, interestingly enough, was entitled *The Land of Gold: Reality Versus Fiction* (1855), and it revealed him to be deeply prejudiced against ethnic minorities. He then turned his talents to writing *The Impending Crisis of the South: How to Meet It* (1857), which contained his bristling attack on the institution of slavery. In line with Clay, Helper argued that slavery should be abolished not because it was morally unjust or because it exploited blacks, but rather because it threatened the economic prosperity of nonslaveholding whites. Even though Helper has been called an "abolitionist-racist," his writings and attitudes clearly underscore the fact that the South at no time was completely united in support of slavery. While it is impossible to determine accurately the actual number of Southerners who were abolitionists, and though it is true that antislavery activities were not nearly as widespread in the South as in the North, it is equally clear that important and influential Southerners spoke for the idea that slavery be abolished. Beyond this, important Southerners of an earlier era—Washington, Madison, Marshall, Henry, Jefferson, and Monroe—had all at various times remarked on the contradiction between the nation's stated ideals and the continued existence of black slavery. While the arguments against the peculiar institution shifted over time, it might well be said that it was Southerners themselves who were among the first to direct the nation's attention to the distorted relationship between American creed and conduct.

America as Peaceful Belligerent: Manifest Destiny and Mexico

The stresses between Americans' declared beliefs and their actual behavior also came to the forefront of political and military affairs in the decades before the Civil War. New circumstances and new conflicts arose which were rife with potential to mythologize. The circumstances initially involved political questions over Texas, and eventually much of what is today California, Nevada, New Mexico, Arizona, Utah, and Texas—lands gained as a result of the Mexican War. In line with the convenient belief that the nation's destiny was apparent, settlers, some with slaves, had moved into areas of northern Mexico during the 1820s and 1830s. After persistent conflicts with resident Mexicans and their government, the new immigrants formed the Republic of Texas. In the 1840s, the United States annexed Texas, invaded Mexico, and conquered California. Arguments condoning such high-handed and belligerent activities claimed that they represented America's Manifest Destiny at work. Natural right, geographical predestination, the need for land, and the extension of the area of freedom—all were offered as arguments to rationalize the growth of the American republic.

Contrary to recent claims that Vietnam was America's only unpopular war, it can be noted that many people dissented from this early period of expansionism. According to its critics the Mexican War was territorial piracy, pure and simple. Even Horace Greeley—who had helped inspire the mania of expansionism by his advice "Go West, young man, Go West!"—was appalled at the spectacle. Writing in his newspaper, the *New York Tribune*, Greeley urged the American people to be wary of the "abyss of crime and calamity" which lay before them. "Why sleep you thoughtless on its verge," he continued, "as though this was not your business?" Others, like Greeley, made it their business to take issue with expansionism and the myths that supported it. The state legislature of Massachusetts, for example, adopted a resolution in April, 1847, condemning the Mexican adventures as "a war of conquest, so hateful in its objectives, so wanton, unjust and unconstitutional in its origins." Moving from the tranquility of Walden Pond into the political arena, Henry David Thoreau echoed such feelings by writing his famous essay "On Civil Disobedience," urging passive resistance and asking that "all men become a majority of one" so as to end the war through "peaceful revolution." The war with Mexico did indeed end, but the myth of America as peaceful belligerent was not destroyed. It would survive the circumstances of events surrounding the Mexican conflict unscathed. In fact, Americans would respond to its appeal frequently in the future whenever expansionist policies were called into question. Again, during the period of imperialistic expansion in the 1890s and during the Vietnam war, the error-based belief that the nation was a peaceful belligerent served as a myth which Americans found well worth preserving.

SECTION I. ANDREW JACKSON: THE MYTH AND THE MAN

"This six-foot backwoodsman, angular, lantern-jawed, and thin, with blue eyes that blazed on occasion; this ... impetuous, Scotch-Irish leader of men; this expert duellist and ready fighter; this embodiment of the contentious, vehement, personal west, was in politics to stay." Thus did the frontier historian Frederick Jackson Turner describe the arrival of Andrew Jackson in Washington in his book *Rise of the New West* (1906).[7] Obviously charmed by what his namesake must have been like, Turner did much to sustain the nation's interest in the life of the frontier and Jackson's role in it. Turner's remarks, in short, are typical of the spectacular impact both have had on the American historical imagination.

Jackson the Leader

Some of the reasons for Andrew Jackson's popularity—and for his extravagant reputation as an American myth figure—are readily apparent. There were distinct qualities in his appearance, his style, his character, and his career which made him more appealing than most candidates laying claim to the historical affections of Americans. Andrew Jackson was very much a charismatic leader. Like other colorful figures of later ages—Abraham Lincoln, Theodore Roosevelt, and Martin Luther King—there was a look of leadership about him. Jackson's very physical presence—his ramrod frame and shock of white hair—seems of itself to have inspired confidence, allegiance, devotion, and hero worship. At the very least it affected people's perceptions of him in a positive direction. Both his military and political style complemented his powerful personal appeal. He was flamboyant and decisive, and left little doubt as to his willingness to stand and be counted. This character trait was evidenced in his subduing the British at the Battle of New Orleans, taking a firm position against secessionist sentiments in South Carolina, and assailing the Bank of the United States. Jackson did not always receive unanimous applause but he was always at center stage. Though no one has ever been known to have accused him of an overabundance of humility or tact, Americans were struck by his character nonetheless. Indeed, a man who legend claimed had rushed to the deathbed of his dear mother, and who in fact was the adoptive father of eleven children, could not be all bad. While definitely lacking the intellectual sophistication of a Jefferson or the fatherly image of a Washington or Lincoln, Jackson embodied the homespun qualities which Americans have always found rather fetching. As a member of the Tennessee state

constitutional convention, U.S. congressman, a judge on the Tennessee supreme court, U.S. senator, army general, military governor of Florida, senator for a second time, and president of the United States, Jackson's varied career did much to alter the normal flow of events. He was by almost any definition a spectacular personality.

For these reasons, and other less tangible ones, Andrew Jackson ranks among the greatest of America's political folk heroes. As a result, a substantial mythology necessarily surrounds the nation's historical understanding of him. Jackson was eminently successful at turning his personal assets to political advantage. He was, in the opinion of many, America's first popular president. Jackson's popularity stemmed not so much from the degree to which Americans came to admire him (for certainly George Washington before him was thus admired), but rather from the degree to which he was attuned to the pulse of the people. Indicative of the rapport which he supposedly had with the common man is the fact that he was the first outsider to become president. To many, Jackson personified the interests, the values, and the prejudices of newly emergent frontier America. And in addition to his identification with expansive "upland democracy," he was also viewed as a challenger of precedent, in that presidents before him had risen from the ranks of cabinet service—a national apprenticeship which Jackson never served. Finally, Andrew Jackson was the first chief executive close enough to the people to be widely known by a nickname—Old Hickory. When reference was made at the time to "Our Hero," no one paused to wonder for whom the complimentary title was intended. So close an association between heroic Old Hickory and the masses has been traditionally supposed, in fact, that the era surrounding his presidency became affectionately known as the Age of the Common Man.

Andrew Jackson's mythical reputation outlived him, and it has long been pampered by posterity. His commanding appearance, personal magnetism, self-made attributes, and flair for decision making had deeply impressed Americans before he passed from the scene in the summer of 1845. Consoling the nation, a funeral eulogist declared that America had just lost an "uneducated orphan boy of the

Our President, Old Hickory

Courtesy M. and M. Karolik Collection, Museum of Fine Arts, Boston

wilderness," and that he was worthy enough to be compared with Benjamin Franklin and George Washington. Jackson's public status as one of the patron saints of democracy caused future generations in both South and North Carolina to claim ownership of the sacred spot where he had been born. The Waxhaw borderland between the two states has seen many a feud over the question of Old Hickory's birthplace. Jackson Square in the city of New Orleans and the famous statue of America's seventh president in Lafayette Park facing the White House in Washington, D.C., are also testimonials to the durability of the Jackson mystique. The Hermitage, Jackson's estate near Nashville, Tennessee, is preeminent, however, as the hero's most sacred shrine. Though modern tourists to the area are usually inclined to see the Grand Ole Opry first, for history buffs the Hermitage "is the cradle of the Jackson cult."[8] Since the turn of the century members of the Ladies Hermitage Association, Nashville's counterpart of the Daughters of the American Revolution, have been the declared custodians of the general's memorabilia, manuscripts, and mementos. It seems that the popularity of tourist attractions such as this has always been a reliable barometer of pressures to inflate the reputations of legendary personalities from the past.

Jackson and Historians

Historians have also had a hand in making Andrew Jackson appear larger than life. For example, Claude Bowers in *Making Democracy a Reality* (1954) sees Jackson as a patriot of democracy, the very epitome of the American spirit. In an account which is more sentimental than reliable, in the opinion of one historian, "Bowers presented a magnificent hero worthy of a Homeric epic, a forest-born Sir Galahad leading the children of light to triumph over the children of darkness."[9] With more than a touch of hyperbole, Bowers portrays Jackson in dramatic detail. Andy, one is led to believe, was daring, brave, and the possessor of nearly every democratic and manly virtue. Bowers' treatment of Old Hickory presents a historical extravaganza and is for the most part an exercise in nostalgia.

Jackson emerged as a clear-cut champion of frontier democracy even earlier when he swaggered through the pages of Vernon Louis Parrington's *Main Currents in American Thought* (1927). For Parrington, Jackson was a giant in the service of the "plain people" who were organizing politically to "destroy the aristocratic principle in government."[10] The political aspirations of Westerners for liberalism and equality came to be focused, he said, on the nation's first great popular leader. As the "first man of the people" Jackson was labeled the spokesman for what Parrington calls the "coonskin voter"; the people needed him and he responded. It was Jackson's "innate chivalry and dignity" which saved the fragile flower of democracy from destruction.

Of course not all historians, nor all Americans, have been enthralled by Andrew Jackson. Even during his own age many fundamentally questioned his swiftly developing role as an American hero. It was in relation to his alleged associations with the "plain people," in fact, that criticism first arose. What was the essence of democracy to some was viewed by others as coarse, uncouth, and uncultured. To his detractors, Andy Jackson without a doubt was a political roughneck with few if any redeeming qualities. Addicted to horse racing, cock-fighting, and pistol duelling, he definitely lacked the polish that one would expect from a respected national leader. Rather than a representative of government of, by, and for the people, he was little more than a demagogue who catered to the riffraff of the country. Jackson, it was said, could barely write his own name, and some even became convinced that the Americanism "O.K." had originated with Old Hickory's blundering attempt to abbreviate "all correct." The nation's hero was in reality an illiterate barbarian. It was absurd, some concluded, to mention Andrew Jackson in the same breath with such eloquent and skillful men as Benjamin Franklin, George Washington, or Thomas Jefferson.

In ways somewhat similar to Jefferson, Andrew Jackson's morals created a flurry of discussion. It was reported that he frequently kept the company of mulatto mistresses and available prostitutes. The fact that Jackson had married Rachel Donelson of Nashville some two years before her divorce was legally settled also fed the imaginations of the nation's guardians of virtue. Charges of bigamy and adultery were frequently leveled at Jackson during the heat of political campaigning. The famous Peggy Eaton affair during his years in the White House also caused many a tongue to wag over the question of Jackson's moral fibre. Mrs. Eaton, the wife of Jackson's secretary of war, and by all reports a voluptuous brunette with striking blue eyes, was tempting material for gossip. Married quite young to a navy man, she was known to have been a frequent visitor to the chambers of widower Senator John H. Eaton of Tennessee while her husband was conveniently away at sea. When her husband died mysteriously early in 1829, possibly a suicide, she quickly married her not-too-secret lover. In Jackson's opinion she had finally become an "honest woman," but the wives of his other cabinet members could simply not accept this "hussy." The president was quick to come to her defense, proclaiming at one point before his assembled cabinet that she was "as chaste as a virgin." Jackson's marked support for this "scarlet woman" did little to lay to rest the spicy rumors which had often arisen to haunt his political career. In fact, in the years after his death "the youthful indiscretions of General Jackson between the ages of six and sixty" became increasingly legendary.

For those who have taken a more serious interest in Andrew Jackson as a major figure of American history, other more important and legitimate criticisms have been made. Perhaps the first twentieth-century scholar to challenge his traditional image, and thereby strike at the very heart of the Jackson legend, was Thomas P. Abernethy of the University of Virginia. Extremely wary of Jackson's heroic pose, Abernethy revised the knightly view of the general-president which Americans for the most part had always accepted as true. There was, he said, much more to the real Jackson than his military exploits and his role as a symbolic president. Abernethy pointed out that even before he became a general or occupied the White House, Jackson had been a Tennessee politician. And if one examined his early years, it could quickly be seen that Jackson's political attitudes and behavior bore little resemblance to the more famous Jackson of the national political arena. This phase of his career revealed a man something less than heroic—at least in terms of his democratic proclivities. Jackson's role at the Tennessee constitutional convention and his influence on that state's legislature had been that of a frontier aristocrat, land speculator, and political opportunist.

As a member of the committee which drafted the Tennessee constitution adopted in 1796, Jackson supported key proposals allowing the appointment of justices of the peace to life terms and the taxation of all land at the same rate no matter what its market value. The first provision went on to allow justices to personally select nearly all county officials, while the second flagrantly favored the holders of large tracts of valuable land—like Andrew Jackson himself. Far from being a spokesman for the "plain folk" of the frontier, Old Hickory was agreeable to these less than democratic provisions and was keeping a steady eye on his personal wealth and social position. Based on the record, one can only conclude that Jackson in his early career thought and behaved as a "frontier aristocrat." While conditions in Tennessee did not allow an aristocracy to develop in the classical sense, Jackson was obviously one of those to whom the thought of becoming a frontier gentleman was fetching. He was not at all embarrassed moving within the ranks of other aristocratic pretenders from Nashville and the surrounding countryside. In Aber-

nethy's opinion the real Andrew Jackson was at least as much a man-on-the-make as a man-of-the-people. Since Jackson's sympathies were secondarily with the common man, and since his closest ties were always with the conservative, moneyed members of the Nashville elite, he was not the great liberal democrat of legend. Though he was seldom given to snobbishness, it is nonetheless appropriate to ask whether Andrew Jackson himself was a Jacksonian. If Abernethy's views have captured the "real" Jackson, his legendary fame as a precocious democrat may well be mythical.

Beneath the glossy veneer of his legendary liberalism, Old Hickory's true grain begins to show, particularly in regard to blacks and Indians. Jackson's economic success and social standing rested solidly on the labor of black slaves at his Hermitage plantation. Cotton was, after all, his principal cash crop. In the national political scene he openly approved the extension of slavery, and the major wing of the Jacksonian Democratic party favored the status quo, including the continuation of the institution lest it disrupt the tranquility of the Union. While it should be remembered that on the slavery issue he was in tune with his time and region, Jackson was not in all respects the brash and innovative instrument of democracy of legend.

In a similar vein, no one has ever credited Andrew Jackson with being overly humane toward the American Indian. In fact, his lustrous legend rests solidly on his image as a colorful Indian fighter. Again, in this regard he reflected the biased attitudes of the nation at large; but in the face of recent attempts by historians to write more accurate accounts of the Indian experience in America, Jackson's Indian policies severely damage his democratic reputation. To many, he is the supreme example of the Indian-hating mentality which nineteenth-century Americans often found appealing in their political leaders. Indeed Jackson's military exploits against the Creeks in 1813-1814 provided the basis for his early national fame. He had additional skirmishes with the Cherokee and Chickasaw in 1815 and later with the Seminoles in Spanish Florida. The most famous case of Jackson's celebrated heavy-handed treatment of the Native Americans, however, concerns his removal of the Cherokee from Georgia to the dry plains of the

Oklahoma country in the 1830s. By ignoring a decision of the Supreme Court disallowing the state of Georgia to claim Cherokee land, Jackson personally sanctioned the callous removal of the Indians. Regarding these activities, historian Mary E. Young has revealed "the extent of frauds that accompanied the white man's land greed in the South and the Southwest." In short, she found little positive to say about Jacksonian justice.[11] There are some historians, however, who have argued that much of Jackson's anti-Indian reputation rests on mythical stereotype rather than solid fact.

Father Francis Prucha, a Jesuit historian from Marquette University, has recently challenged the caricature of Andrew Jackson as a wild-eyed destroyer of the Indian and his ways. While Jackson followed a "no-nonsense policy toward hostile Indians that endeared him to the frontiersmen," his anti-Indian stance was strongly influenced by his belief that the British were the real enemies. English agents, he thought, were the ones most responsible for frontier bloodshed. During his military career Jackson was instrumental in removing white squatters from Indian lands, believed in Indian self-government in the West, and supported the idea of establishing military forts in Indian country to protect tribal rights. Even Jackson's infamous removal policies while president, says Prucha, can be viewed as quite liberal for the time. Many were clamoring to destroy the Indians completely—through brute force, disease, or starvation. Jackson was not one of them. In fact, on numerous occasions he urged Congress to live up to the government's treaty obligations. Though usually cast in the role of a villain, Jackson does not completely deserve his widespread image as a bloodthirsty white devil. "To call Jackson an Indian-hater or to declare that he believed that 'the only good Indian is a dead Indian,'" Prucha concludes, "is to speak in terms that had little meaning to Jackson." It is true, of course, that "he did not consider the Indians to be noble savages. . . . Yet Jackson did not hold that Indians were inherently evil or inferior."[12]

Historians have obviously had great difficulty determining what Andrew Jackson was really like. He seems in some ways to have been a democrat and an aristocrat, to have been a political barbarian and an astute politician, and to have been both callous and kind to the Indians. Being such an elusive historical figure, it is possible that he was all of these simultaneously. Some interpretations of Jackson have suggested precisely this. In a landmark study by John William Ward, *Andrew Jackson: Symbol for an Age* (1955), the argument is made that there were in reality two Jacksons—one a historical figure, and the other a symbol of American mythology.

In many respects the Andrew Jackson of history was neither the natural frontiersman nor the self-made man of legend, Ward has argued, but what counted most was what the people thought he was. To them, or at least to many then and now, he was Nature's Nobleman, God's Right-Hand Man, and Self-Made Man of Iron. These were key features of Jackson's personality with which nearly all Americans could identify. Because he could dramatize the nation's destiny, the country made him a legendary figure and hero for his age. Even though the real Andrew Jackson and the policies he supported were a bundle of contradictions, nearly all Americans found something in him they could admire and support. As much as any president before or since, Old Hickory was a symbol of the republican virtues in which the country most fervently believed. He stood for the spirit of America in an age in which Americans were eager to test ideals and destiny against the future. He was the kind of man the majority of male Americans in his day wanted to be—or thought they already were. As one of his contemporaries, Washington McCartney, said upon Jackson's death: "Because his countrymen saw their image and spirit in Andrew Jackson, they bestowed their honor and admiration upon him." The Andrew Jackson that emerged from this national psychological drama was mysterious, charming, and mythical. In a way he was a very cosmetic figure but remained an authentic American hero nonetheless.

SECTION II. JACKSONIAN DEMOCRACY: MIRAGE OR MOVEMENT?

While debate among scholars has been spirited over the question of the "real" nature of Andrew Jackson, both admirers and detractors alike have tended to agree that he was a leader of great significance. Whether he was an aristocrat posing as a democrat or whether he was a true man of the people, or both, is in many ways less significant a point, however, than the fact that the period in which he lived bears his name and that the political changes of his time were of profound importance. In this regard, it is precisely the alleged political relationship between the Jackson movement and the "common man" that recent historical scholarship has sought to reexamine. Legitimate questions have arisen as to what degree democracy actually expanded during his term as president, and whether Jackson was a cause or a consequence of his age. Jacksonian democracy, then, eludes simple historical explanation not only because of Old Hickory's personal and symbolic importance, but also because of complex developments in American society which were contemporary with him.

The "New Democracy"

One of the more tenacious legends associated with Jacksonianism is that Andrew Jackson was swept to the presidency on a wave of popular voter support. The excitement of the time, as voters responded to the stimulus of Jackson's personal magic, is supposed to have opened up the political process to the point where most Americans began actively to participate. The political image of the Jackson years, which has long been accepted as real, is that of a "new democracy" and a "mighty democratic uprising" taking hold in America at the grass-roots. The popular conception that the Jacksonian era witnessed an orgy of democracy and that Jackson was its chief beneficiary has, however, been challenged.

A different perspective on Jacksonian politics, first offered by the historian Richard P. McCormick, has argued that voter participation during the Jackson years was uncommonly low in comparison to the periods immediately before and after Old Hickory's tenure in the White House. Jackson's term of office, from 1829 through 1837, did not in fact witness a burst of democratic energy. By simply comparing the number of eligible voters (almost exclusively adult white males) with the number who actually cast ballots, it is readily apparent that the American electorate became *less*, rather than more, involved in

political decision making during this span of time. Taking the presidential election of 1824 as a case in point—since this was Jackson's first attempt at the presidency—not one of the eighteen states then in the Union equalled the level of voter involvement achieved in earlier state contests for which election figures are available. Despite the notion that backwoodsmen, hunters, plain farmers, and other frontiersmen paraded to the polls to proclaim the new democracy, on the average only 26.5 percent of the nation's adult white males exercised their voting rights in 1824. This hardly suggests a "mighty democratic uprising," immortalized in legend.

Having lost the 1824 election due to the congressional selection of John Quincy Adams, one would think that frustrated Jacksonians would have mobilized their efforts to bring out the vote for their hero in 1828. While voter participation did increase with Andrew Jackson's second and successful attempt to capture the office of chief executive, in fact by more than double the rate four years earlier (26.5 to 56.3), it would still not be proper to see him as America's political pied piper. With twenty-two states keeping records at the time, only six established new highs in voter turnout. And even in those states where voter participation records were established, the increases were either quite small or due to recent changes in voting qualifications.

Jackson's election to a second term in 1832 actually saw a slight decline in voter participation. Even by this time, the supposed spectacular rise of democratic sentiment behind Jackson had not materialized. "Thus, after three Jackson elections," as McCormick has pointed out, "sixteen states had not achieved the proportions of voter participation that they had reached before 1824. The 'new democracy' had not yet made its appearance."[13] Studies have concluded, in short, that the voting behavior of Americans bore little special relationship to either Andrew Jackson or his political policies. While it is true that Jackson was elected to two terms and was indeed a spectacularly popular president, local issues such as the election of a state governor or a key legislative race were, at least in McCormick's view, far more important to the growth of democracy during the Age of Jackson. In fact, the real expansion of popular participation in national politics would not come until 1840.

The relatively modest involvement of voters in the various elections involving Andrew Jackson seems to have been caused by the demise of the Federalist party as a political force (Rufus King had been their last presidential candidate in 1816). As a result, the nation lacked a strong two-party system able to offer the electorate competitively equal political candidates. In many areas of the country, Jackson's campaigns against John Quincy Adams (1828) and Henry Clay (1832) were viewed as no contest. As such, conditions were not ripe for a spirited turnout by the voting public and should therefore not be construed as evidence of a lack of appeal on Andy's part. Nonetheless, all of this changed dramatically soon after Andrew Jackson decided to retire from public view and return to the life of a frontier gentleman at the Hermitage.

Martin Van Buren, the suave "little magician" from Kinderhook, New York, succeeded Jackson to the presidency in 1836, having been personally selected by Old Hickory as the heir apparent to the presidential throne. Even before the transfer of power had occurred, however, displeasure among some groups with Jackson's stand against the Second Bank of the United States and his veto of internal improvement bills had earned him the title of "King Andrew I." Thus, even before the election, charges were being heard that a Jacksonian form of "monarchy" would for all practical purposes still be in control. An anti-Jackson political party was thus formed by former members of the Federalist party, supporters of John Quincy Adams, and disgruntled Democrats. The new Whig party, which drew its name from the legendary patriots who had stood against King George III during the Revolution, failed to defeat the Jacksonian forces in the five-sided election of 1836, in which William Henry Harrison, Daniel Webster, Willie P. Mangum, and Hugh L. White ran against Van Buren. By 1840, however, the Whigs were united and ready to offer what they claimed was a true "man of the people" for the voter's sober consideration.

The Election of 1840

Even though Henry Clay took an early lead in the 1840 contest, William Henry Harrison finally emerged as his party's candidate and was selected to carry the Whigs' "anti-monarchy" banner. Harrison, the son of Benjamin Harrison, a signer of the Declaration of Independence, first delegate to Congress from the Northwest Territories, first governor of Indiana Territory, and military hero of the Battle of Tippecanoe against the Shawnee (1811), seemed a desirable candidate. Convinced that if they were going to win they must "go to the people," the Whigs concluded that the best strategy was to press their campaign against the image of Andy Jackson, even though he was by now four years removed from the scene. Thus, they would make their candidate as folksy as Jackson had ever been. What resulted was a political extravaganza, a perfect case study in the making of political myth.

The "Log Cabin Campaign" of 1840 would be the first during which a presidential candidate stumped the country in his own behalf. More important, however, it would also be the first great "image" campaign. It represented a concerted attempt by a political party to manufacture an "image"—to consciously construct a myth, if you will—for their candidate.

At first glance William Henry Harrison would not seem all that appropriate a subject for the strategy the Whigs were contemplating, since he was an aging general with only limited "exposure" and a minimum of political experience. He was nominated in the end, however, precisely because he was noncontroversial. Sensing an easy mark, his Jacksonian opponents quickly charged that Harrison was a dull-witted old farmer who would be much more at home in a log cabin with a barrel of hard cider than in the White House. Having started with a "clean" candidate, the Whigs skillfully made Harrison conform to the image which the Jacksonians had offered them. Almost overnight, the Harrisonites began to advertise their hero as the poor "Farmer of North Bend" who had been called by destiny from his plow to drive the corrupt followers of "King Andrew" from the "presidential palace." Harrison became the plainfolk's candidate and, for purposes of image at least, a substitute for the recently departed Andrew Jackson. The Whigs reasoned that since the electorate had fallen for Old Hickory, why not Old Tippecanoe? Harrison was soldierly in bearing, after all; the only things necessary were that proper emphasis be given his anti-Indian image and that "Old Tip" be associated with the expanding and colorful West. The log cabin and cider barrel became the campaign symbols of 1840, and Harrison and his vice presidential running mate were brought to the attention of the nation with the political jingle "Tippecanoe and Tyler Too."

The real William Henry Harrison was totally unknown during the campaign of 1840. Born into one of the first families of Virginia at Berkeley Plantation in 1773, he was not lowborn, not accustomed to poverty, and not familiar with the harsh realities of living in a log cabin. Nonetheless, the electorate accepted the image of Harrison as the spokesman for backwoods America.

Meanwhile, running for a second term, Martin Van Buren also found himself a subject of the developing campaign mythology. Even though he was a standard-bearer of the Democratic party, which had traditionally held more claim to the affections of the common man and the frontier west than the Whigs, Harrison and his image-making associates portrayed Van Buren as a rich, well-born eastern aristocrat. It was claimed that "Little Van" was fond of French food, ate from gold plates, wore silk underwear, and in general had lived off the labors of the common man during his first term in office. Since he was courteous, sophisticated, and fair of complexion, in the minds of many voters, Van Buren's image seemed to fit the man. The presidential campaign of 1840, consequently, was a contest between two images rather than two men. There was little discussion of real issues, and questions dealing with the United States Bank, internal improvements, and the tariff were responded to with slogans. Aided by voter discontent over a depressed economy resulting from the Panic of 1837, for which Van Buren was blamed, the result was a landslide victory for the "Farmer of North Bend"—234 electoral votes to 60, with more than 80 percent of the eligible voters participating. At last, the "mighty democratic uprising" had come to pass. Tragically, democracy's chosen man—William Henry Harrison—contracted pneumonia at his inauguration and died a month later. For better or worse, his greatest legacy would be the image-building and mythmaking tone which he and the first "modern" presidential campaign had given American politics. Unfortunately, the mythical tradition which

was created around Harrison, and the tendency of political parties to nominate electable rather than quality candidates, survived him by many years.

Jacksonian Democracy

The success of the Whigs' imaginative publicity on behalf of General Harrison had made it clear by 1840 that the American public had a glaring weakness for synthetic heroes and political poppycock. Even the aging Andrew Jackson, "forgetting that he had set the pattern for Harrison's campaign, called him 'the Mock hero,' and groaned in disbelief that the voters 'can be led by hard cider, coons, log cabins, and demagogues'."[14] Indeed, it had been Jackson himself who had drawn America's political attentions westward and directed its focus on the common man. Somehow this had been accomplished despite the fact that, contrary to long-standing political mythology, much of the support for Jacksonian democracy had come not from the West but from the East and from men who were anything but "common."

The political phenomenon known as Jacksonianism went well beyond Old Hickory's years in the White House and was a sprawling, diverse, and many-sided movement which appealed to varied segments of American society and all geographical regions. The notion that Jacksonian democracy was a monopoly of the western frontier was challenged more than thirty years ago in Arthur M. Schlesinger, Jr.'s Pulitzer Prize-winning book The Age of Jackson (1945). Questioning the myth of the fundamentally western orientation of Jacksonianism, Schlesinger points out that important support for Jacksonian democracy came from the urban centers of the East. There was quite solid support for Jackson and his policies, for example, in New England and New York City. Standing the Jacksonian legend on its head, Schlesinger was convinced that "the East rather than the West furnished the principal stage, and working men rather than the farmers the leading actors."[15] Some more recent scholars, on the other hand, have argued that there really was "western domination of the Democratic party during Andrew Jackson's presidency" given the great influence of his western advisors

Amos Kendall and Francis Blair of Kentucky. But even so, the fact remains that Jacksonianism was definitely not the product of one region.[16] Though Jacksonianism seems to have had intimate ties to the West, the East and indeed the South were as democratic and "Jacksonian" as the western frontier.

Lending credibility to the idea that the West was the nation's most democratic region during the Jackson years was the equally legendary idea that the South was simultaneously cultivating the growth of a political aristocracy. Supposedly, the Old South was different from the rest of the nation, and especially the West, in that it was consciously creating its own "way of life" as a land of aristocratic privilege. This romantic vision of the pre-Civil War South has been fostered by abolitionists, defenders of the South, Hollywood (e.g., *Gone with the Wind*), and historians. Despite the myth of "planter aristocrats" controlling southern politics, however, it now appears rather clear that the South was as much committed to democratic principles and practices as any other part of the country.

The South, in the decades before the Civil War, was not in any real sense an area of economic or social democracy; but in this respect it scarcely differed from the North. The ideas of liberty, equality, and democratic voting rights were as widely accepted in the South as in any other region of America, even though by no stretch of the imagination were Southerners committed to the doctrine of equality for all regardless of color or sex. But again, neither were Northerners, nor Westerners for that matter. In this regard it must be understood that no section of the country practiced democracy as we do today. In general, at least up to the time of the Civil War, democracy was taken to mean political or economic rather than social equality. Understanding that democracy has been defined differently by different generations of Americans, one can accept the fact that the degree of popular government in force in the South during the Jacksonian period was as broadly based and as open as in any area of the nation. In most every southern state, office holders were elected by the vote of all adult white males, and a spirit of democratic reform was widespread. While it is true that "John C. Calhoun . . . and other aristocratic leaders of the South openly denied the . . . ideal of equality of all men and bitterly condemned majority rule as the tyranny of king numbers," their views never in fact prevailed.[17] The hallmarks of Jacksonian democracy—the abolition of property qualifications for voting, the removal of religious restrictions for office holding, and the popular election of state legislatures and governors—were prominent in the South as elsewhere.

Jacksonian democracy, which according to the folklore of American politics has so often been taken as an obvious example of western influence on democratic theory and practice in America, thus found roots in nearly every portion of the country and among a wide variety of social and economic groups. The motives and beliefs which controlled the movement and gave it direction came from the West, the South, and the Northeast, and captured the loyalties of frontiersmen, farmers, middle-class workers, and businessmen. The common notion that only western pioneers served as the backbone of Jacksonianism is an oversimplification.

A balanced and nonmythical view of the Jackson era also requires that one see it not only as a "phase in the expansion of democracy," but in addition as part of the "expansion of liberated capitalism." Given the solid basis of the Jacksonian persuasion in the East, and among urban workers and small businessmen, the energetic capitalist—the man-on-the-make—was as much a typical Jacksonian as were the farmers of the American frontier. Economic as well as political freedom was a cardinal principle of Jacksonianism. Accordingly, it was a diverse group of interests which supported Jackson and made him an appealing symbol. Frequently in a subtle way, the political movement which attached itself to him was at least two-faced. It appealed simultaneously to those who wanted to preserve the republican virtues of the American frontier experience and to those who coveted economic freedom and the benefits of emerging capitalism. Jackson's supporters came to believe that, like him, they could be frontier farmers and speculators in a free-enterprise system at one and the same time. All Jacksonians, whether they were western frontiersmen or eastern businessmen, believed in freedom of opportunity—both political and economic. And if a choice ever had to be made between the two—as indeed proved to be the case for the Mountain Man—it was economic freedom which was chosen.

With the Jacksonian's attention focused so directly on freedom of opportunity, it is somewhat surprising that so few Americans made truly significant gains in their economic and political status during the Jackson era. In many respects, the Age of the Common Man gave little aid and comfort to those who were most common of all. The studies of the historian Edward Pessen, for example, show that very little upward social mobility took place during the Jackson period. Despite the comforting myth that substantial gains were made both politically and economically during these years, there were far fewer instances than myth implies where Jacksonian policies reached down to Americans of poor economic standing. "The extent of poverty and maldistribution of wealth of Jacksonian times," Pessen has concluded, has "punch[ed] wide holes in the Jacksonian man-on-the-make thesis."[18] The orgy-of-democracy approach to the Jackson years has led many to forget not only that the poor, blacks, and Indians were not part of this alleged democratic upswing, but has also made some blind to the fact that social privilege and economic elitism retained a solid hold in America. Pessen has well described the legend of economic equality during this period:

> According to the egalitarian [myth] the United States was a society dominated by the great mass of the people, who composed the middling orders. Unfortunate minorities aside, few men here were either very poor or very rich. For that matter the rich here were rich only by American standards, their wealth not comparing in magnitude to the great fortunes accumulated by wealthy European families. What rich men there were in America were typically self-made, born to poor or humble families.[19]

Even though this myth of economic equality was quick to become a part of Americana, the reality of Jacksonian democracy and the Age of the Common Man seems to have been that wealth was being concentrated in the hands of an ever *smaller* percentage of the nation's population. An illusion of equality was an important part of America's democratic window dressing in the years before the Civil War. At the very least, the economic opportunities of the period appear much more limited than legend has supposed. "Far from being an age of equality," concludes Pessen, "the antebellum decades were featured by an inequality that surpasses anything experienced by the United States in the twentieth century."[20] The conspicuous prosperity of those like David Sears, Harrison Gray Otis, and William B. Crosby—to say nothing of Andrew Jackson himself—indicates rather clearly that the phrase "age of the common man" was more rhetoric than reality.

SECTION III. RELIGION, REFORM, AND RACE RELATIONS: RHETORIC AND REALITY

The energy and vitality which was taking Americans westward and leading them to believe that they were on the verge of achieving something close to political perfection during the Age of the Common Man proved to be infectious. Despite the persistence of elitism and the limited scope of democracy in practice, the boisterous spirit of the age did much to revive optimism and revitalize the old idea that America was a utopia in the making. The notion spread that not only politics but humanity itself was perfectable. Accordingly, being persistent if not incurable romantics, Americans launched a series of reform movements. This reformist impulse would have a particularly important impact in the areas of religion, women's rights, and race relations.

The Mormons

The pioneers of early nineteenth-century America carried the idea of utopia with them in their western ventures. For many this enthusiasm and crusading spirit found expression not only in the physical conquest of the land, but in the creation of new spiritual horizons as well. In regions of western New York state, for example, numerous utopian forms of religious enthusiasm sprang up. From this area, a great revival in religious intensity and moral awareness was sparked, an impulse which would eventually spread throughout the nation. One movement which was to have a great impact on American history was Mormonism—the Church of Jesus Christ of Latter-day Saints. In the midst of this period of religious fervor, in 1826 at Mt. Cummorah, Vermont-born Joseph Smith experienced visions of the Angel Moroni. The angel's visitation provided Smith golden tablets bearing divine revelations which he was permitted to read with the aid of special eyeglasses. These revelations—the *Book of Mormon*—were first printed in 1830, and the Mormons embarked on becoming one of America's largest utopian religious communities.

Given its deep involvement with utopianism, Mormon history can be considered from the point of view of myth. Particularly for those not having been called to the faith, Mormonism has often seemed an excellent example of the workings of myth in human affairs. Mark Twain, for example, in commenting upon the *Book of Mormon* in his western travel narrative, *Roughing It,* declared that "the book seems to be merely a prosy detail of imaginary history, with the Old Testament for a model; followed by a tedious plagiarism of the New Testament."[21] Twain may have been quite witty in his remarks at the Mormon's expense, but by implying a mythmaking role for Joseph Smith he seems to have been right for the wrong reasons. While one might assume from Twain's statement that Mormonism could have appealed only to those who were intellectually naive, the historical record shows rather that many of its major converts—Brigham Young for example—had a superior education for their time. Joseph Smith, in short, was anything but an impostor and a victim of delusions. In the considered opinion of the religious historian, Whitney R. Cross, theories which in a negative way emphasize the "imaginary" dimension of the Mormon movement do little to help explain Mormonism as a historical reality:

This kind of hypothesis, like the one which claims that the *Book of Mormon* was copied from Solomon Spaulding's novel on the early Indian wars, is too transparently simple to explain the broad

appeal of the new church. Such myths not only distort Joseph's character but also breed serious misconceptions of how any religious novelty is likely to arise.[22]

A much more revealing analysis of Mormonism results, says Cross, from recognizing the historical context out of which it grew and the relationship it had to the religious revivalism of western New York during the Jacksonian period. The origins of Mormonism seem to have been directly tied to "the most prominent legend in the region's folklore."[23] Mormonism took many of its basic ideas from a local myth dealing with a great battle on the hill of Cummorah, in which a culturally advanced pre-Indian civilization was destroyed. It is from the vantage point of its utopian vision and its relationship to an existing myth, then, that Mormonism can most correctly be viewed as mythical. As Professor Cross has pointed out, in the 1830s "neither American society generally nor that of western New York in particular had passed the stage wherein common myth might reinforce Biblical sanction of doctrine."[24] In fact, the reliance of Mormon doctrine on believable and current mythology scarcely makes it different from many other forms of religious belief usually thought to be much less mythical.

Beyond the question of its "legendary" origins, additional forms of mythology have also attached themselves to Mormonism. It is often thought, for example, that the rise of the Church of Jesus Christ of Latter-day Saints is the supreme example of the frontier influence on American religious development. The sect's beginnings from within the longest-settled areas of western New York, and its successful recruitment of followers to the new Zion from within its original region long after the movement had relocated in the West, strongly implies, however, that Mormonism's basic appeal was not to pioneers at all. While it is obviously true that the church went on to develop substantially in a frontier setting, and that it kept moving westward with the wave of American settlement, "neither the organization of the church, nor its personnel, nor its doctrines were frontier products."[25] Unlike the case of the Baptists and Methodists in the frontier South, Mormonism seems not to have needed a frontier environment to grow and prosper. In a manner similar to the Jacksonian political movement which was developing during the same span of time, Mormonism drew as much of its inspiration, and as many of its adherents, from the East as from the West.

The most stirring era of Mormon history concerns the famous western migration to the Great Salt Lake Basin in 1846 under the inspired leadership of Brigham Young. The Saints, as Mormons called themselves, began their march from Nauvoo, Illinois, convinced that only by moving to a new Zion in the mountains could they escape the effects of religious prejudice. Mormons had come to this conclusion with good reason. After the founding period in western New York, "The Prophet," Joseph Smith, had led a Mormon migration to Kirtland, Ohio, to establish a community based on utopian concepts and build the first Mormon temple. Persecution and intolerance persisted, however, and new Zions had to be built in Missouri and Illinois, and finally in what became the state of Deseret in Utah Territory.

Unfortunately, it is most often only the Mormons' final trek to the desert land, then owned by Mexico, which is remembered. While by almost any criterion their migration to the West was an enterprise of epic proportions, the magnificence of their journey has led many to the false conclusion that it typified American frontier expansion. The misconception is of course that most settlers to the western frontier leaped the continent with giant strides from East to West, as did the followers of Brigham Young. Legend has burned the experience of a relatively few into the nation's memory—the Mormons, the famous five thousand who navigated the Oregon Trail in the 1840s, and the one thousand who responded to the lure of gold in California in the same decade. The harsh realities of the frontier, however, were quite otherwise.

Simple economics required a savings of the sum total of all earnings for one and one-half years by the average worker to allow a move in such grand style from one distant geographical point to another so as to begin life anew. Most western pioneers in fact were part of a much slower and less romantic process—the role of frontier upon frontier, and on to the frontier beyond. The frontier for most lay only beyond

the immediate horizon, in the next valley or over the nearest mountain. Once this basic truth of frontier expansion is understood it can be seen that only as regards their early experience—prior to their move from Illinois to Utah—were Mormons typical of the wider patterns of American frontier development. Like them, the typical American pioneer settler was one who at various points in time might have been able to call New York, Ohio, Missouri, *and* Illinois home.

Feminist Reform

As the spirit of political and religious change captured America during the Jacksonian period, there were also some who began to see the need to reshape America's social attitudes toward women. American women had long been the victims of sexual stereotypes and a social mythology which declared them second-class citizens. Before he wrote *Common Sense* and sparked Revolutionary America to declare that "all men are created equal," Thomas Paine had offered the opinion that women in America were "constrained in their desires, in the disposal of their goods, robbed of freedom and will by the laws, the slaves of opinions." Even during the Jacksonian years, American men believed that the extension of voting privileges only to adult white males was really "government by the people." It would, however, be inaccurate to report that all Americans blindly accepted this obvious evasion of democracy. Oberlin College in Ohio, for example, sought to offer educational opportunities on a broader scale by opening its doors to women in the 1830s. Also, in 1837, Mary Lyon founded Mount Holyoke Female Seminary as the first women's "college," in South Hadley, Massachusetts. But these were only limited victories on an ever-widening front. Women were still for the most part "slaves of opinions," and the opinions of most were strongly influenced by the "cult of true womanhood."

The image of women as guardians of virtue, morality, culture, and civilization was dear to the hearts of nearly all Jacksonians. Convinced that their "proper sphere" was in the home, social attitudes expressed in women's magazines such as *Ladies' Companion,* and religious literature of almost every denomination, joined to keep the myth of feminine delicacy and subservience alive. It was accepted by all—or at least those of established views—that religious piety was the greatest virtue a True Woman might have. Even Mount Holyoke was convinced that its progressive brand of education should correctly lead a woman to becoming "a handmaid to the Gospel and an efficient auxiliary in the great task of renovating the world." Apparently, a woman's major role in this life was to prepare herself and others for the next. The myth of the ideal woman, which seems to have taken solid hold in America in the years from 1820 to the eve of the Civil War, portrayed the "weaker sex" as the perfect combination of saintly beauty and practical usefulness. It seemed obvious that by being the devout and hardworking Christian woman in the home, she automatically qualified as the chief protector of the American Way.

While women's rights had generally come to mean the right to faithfully love and obey one's husband, the right to carry the burden of household chores with Christian humility, and the right to have most think she was a noble being of quiet heroism in the service of America, some began to object to this incompleteness of democracy. An early move to expand the definition of women's rights and lay to rest the myth of True Womanhood came to a climax in 1848 with the women's rights convention in Seneca Falls, New York. These organizing efforts of Lucretia Mott and Elizabeth Cady Stanton made some headway, but by then it was clear that the spirit of reform in America had come to focus most of its energies and attentions on another of American democracy's great evasions— slavery.

Slavery and the Abolitionists

The contradiction of the existence of slavery in a nation dedicated to the principles of democracy was one which some in the Age of the Common Man simply could not ignore. But this was a difficult problem to deal with, so deep-seated had the racist myth of the "innate inferiority" of blacks become. It was "common knowledge" and an assumed "fact" that blacks were by nature more childlike, less intelligent, and more savage than whites. It was this very

belief which continued to serve as the main justification for slavery. "In truth," said the black abolitionist leader Frederick Douglass, "this question [of the racist myth] is at the bottom of the whole [slavery] controversy."[26] If blacks were indeed something less than human, there seemed to be little need to include them in a system based on government by the people.

Abolitionist groups, calling for an immediate end to slavery, arose in American society during the 1830s and 1840s, directing attention to the intellectual and moral bankruptcy of such a convenient legend. Even though antislavery arguments based on humanitarian, moral, and religious grounds were being offered both in America and Europe, the nation generally refused to be converted to new ways of thinking. Americans seemed unable or unwilling to reject their racist mythology, which had infiltrated the "best" scientific thinking of the day. Highly respected professional scientists such as George Gliddon and Louis Agassiz were convinced that the world's various races were quite distinct in their achievement and potential, and that blacks by any measure were at the bottom of the scale. The American scientific community, in short, was overwhelmingly convinced of black inequality. Even though some abolitionists would argue that blacks' supposed natural inferiority was obviously a result of the restrictive environmental conditions of slavery and segregation, most people found it more convenient to believe the mythical findings of science. With science giving racist mythology respectability, the natural equality of blacks and whites was a reality which few Americans were forced to face. Even the abolitionists were not immune to the disease of the racist myth, for some abolitionist societies restricted their organizations to white members only.

Despite the solid footing which racist thinking enjoyed in the popular mind, the imaginings of scientists, and the abolitionist movement itself, a commitment to the idea of immediate freedom for slaves refused to die. The antislavery movement in fact found a firm basis in the long-standing American traditions of utopianism and national perfectability. Much the same kind of spirit which had awakened thoughts of utopia for Mormons in the religious sphere, and moved women to attempt a perfection of the social system, inspired the reform movement to seek to abolish the evils of American slavery. The abolitionists thought their moral crusade destined to succeed, for it had "applied the perfectionist formula to slavery."[27] Especially after 1840, abolitionist agitation focused its attacks on the transparent fictions of the peculiar institution, such as black inferiority and white superiority and thus the "naturalness" of the slaves to their condition, and sought to replace them with a higher morality based on the ideas of equality and the perfectability of man and society.

Underground Railroad

Ironically, just as the abolitionist reform movement did much to bring the racist myth of black inferiority into question, a well-developed mythology concerning the motives, tactics, and activities of the abolitionists themselves has flourished. Recent scholarship, for example, has done much to erode the romance which has long surrounded the legendary Underground Railroad—the most critical feature of the abolitionists' activities. Traditional stories of the Railroad, somewhat understandably, have degenerated into melodrama. Built on a complex combination of fact, fiction, and fantasy, the dramatic legend of the Railroad's activities departs from accurate history on many points. "Despite the mass of romantic and exciting underground railroad literature," says the historian Larry Gara who has studied its activities in great detail, "the secret organization loomed larger in reminiscence and propaganda than it was in reality."[28] In particular, the stereotype of the abolitionists who were involved in the Underground Railroad as moral heroes with bleeding hearts has undergone considerable revision. While it is true that many abolitionists were drawn to such activities for humanitarian reasons, it is equally clear that some blacks were indeed exploited by their saviors. As Professor Gara notes: "The institution was far more important as a propaganda device than as an aid to the fleeing slaves."[29] Cases abound where former slaves were exhibited and exploited either to keep the movement going or to assure abolitionists a profit for their

efforts. It seems the belief in black inferiority and white superiority was an affliction shared even by some bent on destroying it.

The most obvious outcome of portraying abolitionists as humanitarian heroes is that they invariably have been given top billing whenever the story of the Underground Railroad has been told. And since much of the historical understanding of the abolitionists is based on their own writings, the result has been an elitist emphasis on their role in underground activities. By electing themselves the heroes of the drama, abolitionists relegated the blacks to a subordinate position. The legendary image of trembling black fugitive slaves totally dependent upon courageous and noble whites is all too familiar. The end result of such tales, which made the benevolent abolitionist the star and gave runaway slaves only a supporting role, has been therefore to reinforce the mythical stereotype of blacks as "Uncle Toms." But given the geographical distances involved, to say nothing of the existence of strict fugitive slave laws, it seems reasonable to suppose that it was hardly submissive and cowering Uncle Toms who sought escape from the chains of slavery. It certainly must have taken courageous men and women to undertake such a rebellious move. Moreover, by the time that the abolitionists were in a position to help—when in fact the fugitive slave had already made his way north—the most difficult portion of the journey had already been completed.

Emphasizing the role of the abolitionist in the Underground Railroad led almost everyone to forget the critical role played by the northern free black in assisting his enslaved brothers. The latest research has concluded that the majority of those who escaped from the southern slave states in the years before the Civil War never did rely on the Underground Railroad. In the opinion of one who was familiar with the railroad's activities, James G. Birney, executive secretary of the American Anti-Slavery Society and vice president of the World's Anti-Slavery Convention, fugitive assistance was "almost uniformly managed by the colored people."[30] Indeed, to believe completely in the story of the Underground Railroad, as told by some publicity-seeking abolitionists, is to believe in a legend which treats blacks as invisible men.

The Underground Railroad: North Star Legend
Cincinnati Art Museum

Yet other failings of the legend-makers of the Underground Railroad are the gross misconceptions created by exaggeration. Biased memoirs, rumors, and colorful stories handed down from generation to generation—for the most part after the Civil War—have had the distinct effect of making the enterprise far more romantic than it ever was. Fed by the secret and conspiratorial nature of the affairs of the Underground Railroad, the full-blown myth is replete with tales of "floods" of fugitives being pursued by bloodhounds, blacks groping through dark underground tunnels with the help of numerous "conductors" who by "secret passwords" lead them to distant "depots" and out-of-the-way "hideouts." While all of this is a stirring tale of great adventure and almost unparalleled ex-

citement for the ten-year-old mentality, little of it is factual. There were relatively few blacks who escaped the slave states (fewer in fact than were freed by southern slave masters), and the activities of the abolitionists were neither as well organized nor as secret as the myth insists. Again, in the words of Professor Gara:

> Whether underground railroad writers told their tales to recall the days of heroic deeds, to lend aid to the political party of their preference, or merely to sell a book, all used material of an unreliable nature. The combination of dimmed memories, partial sources, and partisan motives mingled truth and fiction in these accounts.[31]

Indeed for these reasons, even historians who have gone to the "original sources" have often found their histories of the Underground Railroad to be testimonials to one of America's most enchanting and enduring legends.

Perhaps the most important, yet at the same time the least obvious, feature of the mythology surrounding the abolitionists and their reforming activities is what the legend of the Underground Railroad implies—that southern slaves could in fact find freedom in the North. The so-called North Star Legend, or the "Myth of the Mason-Dixon Line," mistakenly suggests that the commitment to white supremacy was a southern monopoly. But while the mythical assumption is that race prejudice occurred only south of the Mason-Dixon line and tolerance toward blacks was to be found only in the North, history records that in most important respects the northern states were not practicing what the abolitionists were preaching. One source has shown, for example, that "by 1840 about 93 percent of the free Negroes in the North were living in states that excluded them from the polls."[32] Even a quick analysis of the North's racial attitudes discloses that five states above the Mason-Dixon line prohibited black testimony against whites in court proceedings, that in Oregon blacks could not legally hold real estate, that they were admitted as jurors only in the state of Massachusetts, that their housing and job opportunities were strictly limited in Boston, and that five antiblack riots occurred in Philadelphia (the "City of Brotherly Love") between 1832 and 1849. Indeed, the North seems to have been as convinced as the South that the black should remain "in his place." Up to the very eve of the Civil War the North had devised as throughgoing a system of segregation as the South.

Thus, religion and reform had by the 1840s begun to expose many of the inconsistencies and inequalities of America's democratic society. The nation still seemed well able, however, to manage its mythology in such a way as to assure that for every myth destroyed a new one stood ready to take its place. American mythology emerged from this reform period somewhat altered but still intact and growing. And it stood ready to be of service other days and in other ways.

SECTION IV. AMERICA AS PEACEFUL BELLIGERENT: MANIFEST DESTINY AND MEXICO

American visions of a vast "Empire of Democracy" which might one day extend from the Atlantic Ocean to the western rim of the North American continent had been active at least since the Jefferson Administration's purchase of the Louisiana Territory in 1803. It was during the presidency of James K. Polk, however, some forty years later, that the expansionist ideas of the nation became most evident. At that time the annexation of Texas was completed, the Oregon country acquired, and vast areas formerly belonging to Mexico obtained. Statistically, American land holdings stood at some 1,788,000 square miles when Polk came into office in 1845 and ballooned to 2,992,000 by 1849—a total increase of 1,204,000 square miles in four years. Seldom in any country's history has territorial expansion exploded in such a fashion.

As with other historical examples of expansionism, America's move to the West was guided by a crusading spirit. As Arab expansionism had been motivated by Islam, Spanish expansionism by Catholicism, and at a later date Russian and Chinese expansionism by Marxist communism, so was that of the United States energized by political ideas at times reaching religious proportions. While this process of Manifest Destiny was not in a strict sense the sole "cause" of America's involvement in Texas, Oregon, California, and the Mexican War, it did provide the nation an overall justification for building an American empire to the Pacific.

Manifest Destiny

By the mid-1840s Manifest Destiny had become a cluster of ideas based on a complex mixture of ingredients—geographical predestination, natural growth, the white man's burden, world leadership, and others. These ideas were not true in any scientific or provable sense, but nonetheless they had become sacred American beliefs. They were, in short, national myths about the nation's past, present, and future which could support America's very practical behavior of expanding the orbit

The Frontier is the Future: American Manifest Destiny
Library of Congress

of its activity across the land. On the one hand Americans' sense of mission was admirable. In expanding the nation's boundaries they were attempting to spread the highest standards of political morality to an increasingly larger area. Republicanism, democracy, and freedom of religion were political ideals which Americans wanted to share with others. They saw their nation as a model republic having the potential to improve the world. Prompted by the belief that the nation's moral and political influence could be beneficial to humanity,

many Americans were shocked to see the nation's "mission" caught up in a flurry of military fame and false glory.

Expansionist Manifest Destiny had its aggressive side. In some cases the elbowing aside of others, false patriotism, and immoral conduct backed by brute force made the entire process one of the least glorious in American history. The nation never has seemed completely to understand its own, often conflicting motives. An idealistic spirit to redeem the world, coupled with a heavy-handed use of political and military power as a practical means to achieve it, has made Manifest Destiny both self-sacrificing and self-serving. Accordingly, there has always been a basic tension between America's image as a "redeemer nation" and the "rhetoric of peace" which has so often been used to explain its activities. A nation which has attempted to achieve noble ends by questionable means, America has frequently pretended that it was a peaceful belligerent. The myth of American innocence—from the period of nineteenth-century expansionism through the Vietnam war—has not always fit well with the nation's warlike conduct.

The illusion and self-deception involved in America's consistent claim that it has always been a nation of peace, when in fact its policies and practices have often been based on violence, is, then, very much due to the distorting legacy of nineteenth-century Manifest Destiny. As government leaders have often been forced to explain the nation's belligerent actions with a "rhetoric of peace" in the twentieth century, they have expanded on and borrowed from the major ideas surrounding this period of expansion in the previous century. Both then and now, for example, America has found it convenient to think of itself as having a natural right to engage in expansionist activities. The "rising glory of America," to use the phrase of the nineteenth-century poet Philip Freneau, was seemingly based on the nature of things. The dogma of America's mission became tied to the twin ideas that expansionism was not only *right* but *natural*, and in a sense part of the Creator's divine plan. Both nature and nature's God seemingly intended that the United States extend its influence westward to the Pacific.

For those not impressed by the natural right argument, the idea of geographical predestination served nicely. True believers in this appealing notion could argue that the land itself was drawing settlers west like a magnet. Since the land extended from "sea to shining sea" it seemed logical to assume that the crossing of the continent, and the acquisition of the land in between, was simply fulfilling what geographical realities had dictated in the first place. There were, it was said, no natural frontiers to interrupt the march to the West.

The Appalachians, the Great Plains, the Great American Desert, and the Rocky Mountains were only nature's way of making the land worth the taking. Since there seemed to be no insurmountable geographical barriers to expansion east of the Pacific Ocean, America's ultimate geographical limits seemed predestined to be the western rim of the North American continent. While the Frenchman Talleyrand had been convinced in 1789 that the Alleghenies were "the limits which nature seems to have traced" for America, and others at various times felt that the Mississippi River should serve as the western limit of the United States, the concept that America should have free passage to the western ocean finally carried the day. As the momentum of settlement continued, wider horizons were opened and Americans became convinced that the only real limit to their expanding nation was their own desire and imagination. The idea of geographical predestination, while obviously an exercise in rationalization, nonetheless readily provided a convenient way to justify expansion. America's claim to the continent, it seemed, came not from an ambitious lust for land, but merely from a recognition that its destiny was rooted in the earth. Though the geographically justified limit of one expansion movement became the point of departure for the next—first the Appalachians, then the Mississippi River, the Rockies, and on to Hawaii and beyond—the idea that the nation should seek its "natural boundaries" became a useful fiction which allowed territorial expansion to continue at a rapid rate.

In the emotion which surrounded the movement westward, the idea of a "destined use of the soil" was also put forward as an argument supporting national expansion. Often, the notion that white Americans through the intentions of the Creator held a superior right to the land was used as justification for the confiscation of Indian properties. Even though Thomas Jefferson had written in 1786 that "it may be taken for a certainty that not a foot of land will ever be taken from the Indians without their own consent," the nation consistently followed a policy of Indian removal based on the myth that the Native Americans, being an "inferior" race, were destined to be victims of the tide of white settlement flooding from East to West. Invariably, trespassing was justified in the name of economic progress. Obviously not convinced that "the meek shall inherit the earth," whites acquired and possessed Indian lands with a vengeance, comforted by the mythical belief that Indians were nomads who therefore possessed no legal claim to the soil. It seemed fitting that the Indian be restricted to reserved lands which he would actually cultivate. According to Benjamin Franklin in his *Autobiography*, it was "the design of Providence to extirpate [root out] these savages in order to make room for the cultivators of the earth."[33] Indeed, the advancement of American property rights into the virgin lands of the West rested heavily on the idea that the continent ought to be transformed from a vast game preserve into an agricultural empire.

During the 1840s a new argument arose in support of Manifest Destiny, particularly concerning expansionist activities in Texas and Oregon. No doubt reflecting the "democratic upheaval" evident in the presidential election of 1840, some now began to argue that American expansionism was right and proper in that it would bring about an "extension of the area of freedom." It was during this decade in fact that the phrase "Manifest Destiny" was coined and became an important part of the American vocabulary. While in earlier settings, philosophical, geographic, and economic arguments had been used to help explain American actions, now the idea that the political and economic freedom of the American states ought to be extended to the great interior of the continent became more pronounced. American nationalism was charged with excitement, an "Empire of Liberty" almost without bounds lay on the western horizon. It troubled some, however, that the new argument favoring expansion was being used primarily to support efforts toward the annexation of Texas. How could it be that the area of freedom would be extended when Texas was already a republic by virtue of its citizens' successful rebellion against Mexico? Aware of the distortion and meaningless rhetoric involved in the argument, U.S. Representative George P. Marsh of Vermont questioned the use of the phrase "extension of the area of freedom," seeing it as "an argument addressed to the ear and not the understanding—a mere jingle of words without meaning. . . ."[34]

Even though much of the expansionists' argument was apparently little more than an exercise in illusion, the cluster of ideas known as Manifest Destiny had a way of adding stars to the American flag. Future generations of expansionists would enshrine new and equally appealing arguments as to why the Americans should follow their destiny as a chosen people and make freedom ring from San Diego to Saigon. Some would claim to be on a "mission of regeneration," others would speak of America's "national interest," while still others would talk of the mortal dangers involved if America did not recognize the wide perimeter needed for her "self-defense" or accept the responsibility of "world leadership." Occasionally critics would submit such arguments to logical analysis, insisting the entire enterprise was an exercise in mythmaking, but for the most part Americans liked what they heard. They convinced themselves that the legal, philosophical, and diplomatic fantasies which had been created to excuse and justify expansion were based on facts rather than fictions. While many of the arguments supporting expansion were logically absurd and strewn with distortions, they were the very things which controlled and directed the nation's destiny. Myth, in this setting, proved itself as durable and useful as ever. It had once again served as a fundamental force in shaping the American experience.

Annexation of Texas and the Mexican War

Perhaps nowhere are the illusions, distortions, and myths which supported the notion of Manifest Destiny more evident than in the events surrounding Texas independence, its annexation to the United States, and the Mexican War which followed. The causes of war with Mexico (1846-1848) can be traced at least to the early 1820s. During the administration of James Monroe, in fact, settlers motivated by territorial ambitions, and under the leadership of Moses and Stephen Austin, moved into the northern sections of the Republic of Mexico. The Mexican government allowed the immigration of "Anglos" to the area with the understanding that they would convert to Mexico's national religion, Catholicism, and respect the existing system of Mexican law. American immigration, however, soon gave evidence of future difficulties between the two nations. Repeatedly during the presidential terms of Monroe, John Quincy Adams, and Andrew Jackson, the American government applied diplomatic pressures to bring about the sale of Texas to the United States. During the same period *empresarios* [contractors] such as Stephen Austin were carrying out colonization projects. Ultimately 1,540 land grants were issued to settlers, and by early 1831 some 5,665 people had made their way to the Austin colony alone. Basic cultural differences, however, tended to highlight tensions. Settlers were primarily Methodist or Baptist in religious background in a nation legally committed to upholding Catholicism and many Texas pioneers were slaveholders in an area where the institution was illegal. Culturally based hatreds between Texans and Mexicans ran deep. Blinded by cultural myths and ethnic stereotypes, most "Anglos" viewed Meixcans as lazy and superstitious "greasers," a "race of mongrels." To Mexicans, in turn, American colonists in Texas were seen as cold and arrogant, aggressive "gringos." Thus, when the Republic of Mexico passed a colonization law in 1830 prohibiting future emigration from the United States to Texas plantation lands along the Brazos, Colorado, and Bernard rivers, the stage was set for the movement toward Texas independence.

At this point Antonio López de Santa Anna, "The Napoleon of the West," actively entered the scene. Convinced that Texans of right ought to obey Mexican law, cease the importation of slaves, and pay taxes to the Mexican government, he dispatched troops to Anahuac to enforce his policies. Texans responded by occupying the garrisons at Anahuac and the Alamo, near San Antonio. According to legend, under a "great round southern moon" illuminating the Alamo, Texas frontiersmen gathered to make their stand against the certain invasion of Santa Anna's troops. In the myth of Texas history, "this encounter has been portrayed as that of a tyrannical Mexican dictator in opposition to freedom-loving, peaceful settlers. Such simplistic stereotyping [however] is far from the truth."[35] The Texas garrison was composed of many soldiers of fortune and a number of ordinary souls, among

them a house painter, a blacksmith, and a hatter. William Barret Travis, garrison commander, having recently read (according to his diary) Scott's *Ivanhoe*, was, in true romantic spirit, ready to die for a noble cause. James Bowie—knife fighter, Louisiana slave smuggler, seller of fraudulent Spanish land grants in Arkansas, and Texas land speculator—stood beside him. Not to be forgotten was Davy Crockett, the former "Coonskin Congressman" and a new arrival from Tennessee.

A fervent mythology bordering on the religious surrounds Santa Anna's assault on the Alamo, March 6, 1836. Though testimony as to what actually happened has often been contradictory, the Alamo epic has come to hold a special place in the hearts of myth-loving Texans and other Americans. Henry Arthur McArdle's heroic painting displayed in the Texas state capitol in Austin, and a comic book sold today at the Alamo souvenir shop, both capture the accepted picture of a tiny and gallant band of Texans standing to the last man against the assaults of hordes of Mexicans. Contrary to legend, however, Mexican superiority in arms and men did not parallel the classic matchup of a David and Goliath. The Texans, it is true, were badly outnumbered during the final seige, 183 to 1,800. They did, however, possess some distinct advantages. In artillery, they could count 21 guns; in the words of the historian Walter Lord, "perhaps the largest collection anywhere between New Orleans and Mexico City."[36] The Mexicans possessed only 8 to 10 artillery pieces and had to make the best of largely unseasoned troops, who in some cases did not even know how to aim their outdated muskets, which had a range of only seventy yards. The men of the Alamo, on the other hand, were for the most part skilled marksmen well able to handle their Kentucky long rifles with a range of 200 yards. What all this points to, of course, is the fact that Colonel Travis and his men were neither "resigned to martyrdom" nor convinced that theirs was a hopeless stand. Travis himself wrote shortly before the fall, "I believe this place can be maintained."

Even though the massacre outside San Antonio gave birth to more than its share of mythical heroes, historians have remembered the Alamo in slightly different form. While legend holds that the Texans fought to the last man, most recent unbiased records report otherwise. Also, while Travis may well have fallen to enemy gunfire, there is evidence to suggest that he committed suicide as Mexicans stormed the mission walls. In the case of Jim Bowie, all evidence agrees that he was out of action suffering from typhoid fever and pneumonia and was slain as he lay helpless on his cot in the mission's lower barracks—not in the sacred surroundings of the chapel, as fictionalized accounts would have it. The fate of Davy Crockett was supposed to have been sealed sometime in the early hours of the thirteen-day attack. The most recent findings, however, indicate that he was probably among the seven victims who surrendered during the hostilities only to be executed by Santa Anna. In the end, even though the loss of the Alamo momentarily dealt the Texans' cause a serious blow, its mythical value greatly boosted the morale of Sam Houston's remaining forces. Seeing parallels with the heroic stand of Spartan armies under Leonidas against Xerxes during the fifth century before Christ, newly inspired Texas patriots in Nacogdoches proclaimed that "Thermopylae is no longer without a parallel." Their cause given a spark of immortality by the Alamo episode, and with the aid of volunteers, arms, and money from the United States, Texans shortly thereafter defeated the forces of Santa Anna and wrested independence from him in eighteen minutes at the Battle of San Jacinto, near present-day Houston. The intense emotion generated by instant legend had done its work.

While Texas was now free from the political control of Mexico, a residue of deep hostility remained. The Texas rebellion had not ended in a clear victory, for Mexico refused to acknowledge the independence of the new Texas Republic. With settlers pouring in from the Old South and the Midwest, the annexation of Texas by the United States was probable. The inclusion of Texas in the union came closer to reality as Commodore Robert F. Stockton went to Texas, with President Polk's approval, to create an "incident" which might serve as the basis for war with Mexico and a pretext for annexation. With the failure of the Stockton conspiracy, Polk dispatched General Zachary Taylor to the disputed area of land between the Nueces and Rio Grande Rivers. The proper boundary between Texas and

Mexico was at the very least open to debate, but Polk, having eyes on California as well as on Texas, forged ahead. Feeling that their soil had indeed been invaded, Mexican troops retaliated by attacking Taylor's forces. Assuming the pose of a peaceful belligerent, President Polk went before Congress on May 11, 1846, to argue that "by the act of Mexico" American territory had been invaded and "American blood" had been "shed on American soil." In the war of conquest that followed, residents of Matamoros, Vera Cruz, and Mexico City all suffered from rape, plunder, and murder by American troops. Seeing through the patriotic rhetoric, and the highly fictitious arguments in support of American military efforts coming from Washington, one participant in the Mexican campaigns—Ulysses S. Grant—was forced to conclude: "I do not think there was ever a more wicked war than that waged by the United States on Mexico." Though the conflict brought on more than its share of criticism, most people quickly forgot that it had been a manufactured war and turned their attentions instead to the fact that the "glorious" victory over Mexico had done much to fulfill the mythical dreams of Manifest Destiny.

The nation, however, could not enjoy the luxury of savoring its victory for very long. In fact, even as the war had been in progress the dissent and debate against it had come to center less and less on the questionable constitutional origins of the conflict and had turned instead to the issue of the conflict's relationship to slavery. The controversy had come to dramatize for many a conflict between democracy and a slaveholding aristocracy. It seemed that America's expansion into new territories was being directed by a "slave power conspiracy." With existing areas suitable for cotton cultivation largely gone, was it not logical that the South supported the war with an eye to opening up the Southwest to slavery expansion? The argument seemed plausible enough, even though the belief was based more on fantasy than fact. John C. Calhoun of South Carolina gave convincing evidence against such a theory. By then a legendary leader of the southern cause, Calhoun had spoken decisively against the war, contending that it was draining the nation's resources to such a degree that urgent needs at home were not being met. Most illusory of all, the South was not the fabled land of cavalier slaveholders as many Northerners believed. The nation's romantic imagination had already fallen victim to the plantation legend.

STUDY QUESTIONS

1. How did Andrew Jackson's personal appearance, major traits of character, and reputation as a western frontiersman and Indian fighter combine to serve as the basis for his political and mythical appeal?

2. How have a good many of the basic images concerning Jacksonian democracy—its unleashing a "mighty democratic upheaval," its supposed basic western character, and its commitments to the economic opportunity of the common man—come to be significantly challenged by some historians?

3. Analyze and discuss the role which myth played in the history of the Mormons, the women's rights movement, and the issue of race relations from 1820 to 1850.

4. What were the major mythical ideas which served as a basis for Manifest Destiny? More specifically, how did the multiple illusions of Manifest Destiny serve as a solid basis for the nation's conduct during the annexation of Texas and the Mexican War?

REFERENCES

1. Dixon Wecter, *The Hero in America: A Chronicle of Hero-Worship* (Ann Arbor: The University of Michigan Press, 1966), pp. 211-212.
2. Quoted in James L. Bugg, Jr., ed., *Jacksonian Democracy: Myth or Reality?* (New York: Holt, Rinehart and Winston, 1962), p. 1.
3. William Goetzmann, "The Mountain Man as Jacksonian Man," *American Quarterly* 3 (Fall, 1963):402.
4. Richard Hofstadter, *The American Political Tradition and the Men Who Made it* (New York: Random House, 1948), p. 59.
5. Goetzmann, "Mountain Man," p. 409.
6. Ibid., p. 413.
7. Frederick Jackson Turner, *Rise of the New West* (New York: Collier Books, 1962), p. 138.
8. Wecter, *The Hero*, p. 219.
9. Bugg, *Jacksonian Democracy*, p. 3.
10. Vernon L. Parrington, *Main Currents in American Thought*, II (New York: Harcourt, Brace and World, 1926), p. 138.
11. Quoted in Frank Otto Gatell, "The Jacksonian Era, 1824-1828," in William H. Cartwright and Richard L. Watson, Jr., eds., *The Reinterpretation of American History and Culture* (Washington, D.C.: National Council for the Social Studies, 1973), p. 321.
12. Francis P. Prucha, "Andrew Jackson's Indian Policy: A Reassessment," *The Journal of American History* 56 (December, 1969): 531, 529.
13. Richard P. McCormick, "New Perspectives on Jacksonian Politics," *American Historical Review* (January, 1960):293.
14. Wecter, *The Hero*, p. 216.
15. Bugg, *Jacksonian Democracy*, p. 3.
16. Richard B. Latner, "A New Look at Jacksonian Politics," *The Journal of American History* 61 (March, 1975): 944.
17. Fletcher M. Green, "Democracy in the Old South," in Patrick Gerster and Nicholas Cords, eds., *Myth and Southern History* (Chicago: Rand McNally, 1974), p. 86.
18. Gatell, "The Jacksonian Era," p. 322.
19. Edward Pessen, "The Egalitarian Myth and the American Social Reality: Wealth, Mobility and Equality in the 'Era of the Common Man'," *American Historical Review* 72 (October, 1971): 990.
20. Ibid., p. 1027.
21. Mark Twain, *Roughing It* (New York: Holt, Rinehart and Winston, 1964), p. 83.
22. Whitney R. Cross, *The Burned-Over District: The Social and Intellectual History of Enthusiastic Religion in Western New York, 1800-1850* (New York: Harper & Row, Publishers, 1965), p. 144.
23. Ibid.
24. Ibid.
25. Ibid., p. 150.
26. Quoted in James M. McPherson, "A Brief for Equality: The Abolitionist Reply to the Racist Myth, 1850-1865," in Martin Duberman, ed., *The Antislavery Vanguard: New Essays on the Abolitionists* (Princeton, N. J.: Princeton University Press, 1965), p. 157.
27. John L. Thomas, "Antislavery and Utopia," in ibid., p. 248.
28. Larry Gara, "Propaganda Uses of the Underground Railroad," in Leonard Dinnerstein and Kenneth T. Jackson, eds., *American Vistas: 1607-1877* (New York: Oxford University Press, 1971), p. 157.
29. Ibid., p. 170.
30. Quoted in C. Vann Woodward, "The Antislavery Myth," *The American Scholar* XXXI (Spring, 1962):314.
31. Gara, "Propaganda Uses," p. 170.
32. Woodward, "The Antislavery Myth," p. 316.
33. Quoted in Albert K. Weinberg, *Manifest Destiny: A Study of National Expansionism in American History* (Chicago: Quadrangle Books, 1963), p. 77.

34. Ibid., p. 102.
35. Rudolfo Acuna, "Freedom in a Cage: The Subjugation of the Chicano in the United States," in Cartwright and Watson, *Reinterpretation*, p. 121.
36. Walter Lord, "Myths and Realities of the Alamo," *The American West* (May, 1968): 121.

SOURCES FOR FURTHER STUDY

ANDREW JACKSON: THE MYTH AND THE MAN

ABERNETHY, THOMAS P. "Andrew Jackson and the Rise of Southwestern Democracy," *American Historical Review*, October, 1927.

BUGG, JAMES L., JR., ed. *Jacksonian Democracy: Myth or Reality?* New York: Holt, Rinehart and Winston, 1962.

PRUCHA, FRANCIS P. "Andrew Jackson's Indian Policy: A Reassessment," *The Journal of American History*, December, 1969.

WARD, JOHN WILLIAM. *Andrew Jackson: Symbol for an Age*. New York: Oxford University Press, 1962.

WECTER, DIXON. "Old Hickory." In Dixon Wecter, *The Hero in America: A Chronicle of Hero-Worship*. Ann Arbor: The University of Michigan Press, 1966.

JACKSONIAN DEMOCRACY: MIRAGE OR MOVEMENT?

GATELL, FRANK OTTO. "The Jacksonian Era, 1824-1848." In William H. Cartwright and Richard L. Watson, Jr., eds., *The Reinterpretation of American History and Culture*. Washington, D.C.: The National Council for the Social Studies, 1973.

GOETZMANN, WILLIAM H. "The Mountain Man as Jacksonian Man," *American Quarterly*, Fall, 1963.

McCORMICK, RICHARD P. "New Perspectives on Jacksonian Politics," *American Historical Review*, January, 1960.

MEYERS, MARVIN. *The Jacksonian Persuasion: Politics and Belief*. New York: Vintage Books, 1957.

PESSEN, EDWARD. "The Equalitarian Myth and the American Social Reality: Wealth, Mobility and Equality in the 'Era of the Common Man'," *American Historical Review*, October, 1971.

RELIGION, REFORM, AND RACE RELATIONS: RHETORIC AND REALITY

CROSS, WHITNEY R. *The Burned-Over District: The Social and Intellectual History of Enthusiastic Religion in Western New York, 1800-1850*. New York: Harper & Row, Publishers, 1965.

GARA, LARRY. "Propaganda Uses of the Underground Railroad," *Mid-America*, July, 1952.

McPHERSON, JAMES M. "A Brief for Equality: The Abolitionist Reply to the Racist Myth, 1860-1865," in Martin Duberman, ed., *The Antislavery Vanguard: New Essays on the Abolitionists*, Princeton, New Jersey: Princeton University Press, 1965.

WELTER, BARBARA. "The Cult of True Womanhood, 1820-1860." *American Quarterly*, Summer, 1966.

WOODWARD, C. VANN. "The Antislavery Myth," *The American Scholar* XXXI (Spring, 1962).

MANIFEST DESTINY AND MEXICO

ACUNA, RODOLFO. "Freedom in a Cage: The Subjugation of the Chicano in the United States," in William H. Cartwright and Richard L. Watson, Jr., eds., *The Reinterpretation of American History and Culture*. Washington, D.C.: National Council for the Social Studies, 1973.

LORD, WALTER. "Myths and Realities of the Alamo," *The American West*, May, 1968.

MERK, FREDERICK. *Manifest Destiny and Mission in American History*. New York: Alfred A. Knopf, 1963.

STECKMESSER, KENT LADD. *The Westward Movement: A Short History*. New York: McGraw-Hill Book Company, 1969.

WEINBERG, ALBERT K. *Manifest Destiny: A Study of Nationalist Expansionism in American History*. Chicago: Quadrangle Books, 1963.

5 The Mythology of the South

PREVIEW

The Plantation Legend

The story is sometimes told that Dick Gregory—one of America's more successful black comedians, especially during the 1960s—while working for the Chicago Post Office, often filed mail destined for the state of Mississippi in the "foreign" mail bag. Apart from this being a brand of humor which one associates with the early years of the civil rights movement, Gregory's action also implies an interesting and generally held point of view toward the land of Dixie. Like many other Americans, Gregory seems to have been convinced that the South was and has been for some time a closed society, fundamentally different in mentality and temperament from the rest of the nation. While it is obviously true that Southerners have long thought themselves to be different in dialect, culture, and political style from "other Americans," the sense of difference between the North and the South is in large degree based on myth.

The belief that the southern way of life differed from that of the North may have taken hold as early as the American Revolution. Some historians have noted a move toward "southernism" even before 1789, which they claim as the basis for the eventual Southern Confederacy of the Civil War years. The general agreement among historians, however, is that the South became self-consciously aware of its distinct characteristics about 1830 and increasingly so as the North and the South moved ever closer to civil war during the succeeding decades. Further, according to legend, during the days of the Old South, the region south of the Mason-Dixon line is supposed to have achieved a model social order based on manners, formality, and a highly polished ceremonial style. The broad outlines of this Old South myth which served as the basis for the "two cultures" idea has been captured beautifully in the words of the southern journalist and historian Wilbur Cash:

> What the Old South of the legend in its classical form was like is more or less familiar to everyone. It was a sort of stage piece out of the eighteenth century, wherein gesturing gentlemen moved soft-spokenly against a background of rose gardens and dueling grounds, through always gallant deeds, and lovely ladies, in farthingales, never for a moment lost that exquisite remoteness which has been the dream of all men and the possession of none. Its social pattern was manorial, its ruling class an aristocracy coextensive with the planter group. . . . They dwelt in large stately mansions, preferably white with columns. . . . Their estates were feudal baronies, their slaves quite too numerous ever to be counted, and the social life a thing of Old World splendor and delicacy.[1]

One could easily assume that this ornamental quality of the southern way of life was but an outward sign of a perfect society which had at last erected a utopia. This supposed Eden of moonlight and magnolias, however, consisted neither in rescuing some romantic segment of the historic past nor in pursuing some fleeting mirage of future perfection, as is often the case with utopias, but rather in standing still so as to savor the benefits of a civilization which would one day, as it turned out, be "gone with the wind."

The basic historical problem with the legendary Old South is that its gesturing cavaliers and beauteous belles were not at all typical Southerners of that day or any other. Despite the historical fixation with the "aristocratic" planter, the independent small yeoman farmer working his "owned" plot of land was the average Southerner of antebellum days. There were of course some quite wealthy and leisured country gentlemen, but both their numbers and to an extent their influence have been seriously overestimated. The six to seven million nonslaveholders who made up the vast majority of Southerners prior to the Civil War were not, as myth would have it, "poor white trash," "crackers," or "rednecks" idling their time away in illiteracy, drunkenness, and a semisavage way of life. Rather, when one studies the more general economic and social structure of the South before 1861, one discovers that the common man was more often an unpretentious farmer caring for a small bit of acreage with his own hands. His energies were directed toward raising a wide variety of crops including significant amounts of tobacco, wheat, corn, and sorghum cane, as well as cotton. In the so-called sugar bowl parishes (counties) of Louisiana, for example, fully 80 percent of the farming population was not the stereotyped unproductive squatters sometimes portrayed in "historical" novels, but legal holders of property obviously involved in growing something other than cotton. From this it can be concluded that the economic and social affairs of the Old South did not rest completely on either King Cotton or the exclusive productivity of the large planters.

Another principal figure of fictionalized plantation life was the southern lady. Passive and properly innocent, the fabled "belle" assumed the role of indispensable helpmate to the mannered southern gentleman. Indeed, together they fashioned the distinct setting of plantation life so long associated with the South before the Civil War. The myth of southern womanhood, long a precious element of the South's historic past, survived the war and in fact continued to gain acceptance in the decades thereafter—even into the twentieth century. The misty view of the southern belle on her pedestal, however, has not withstood the scrutiny of historical scholarship, nor does it meet even minimal standards of reality. Though the image has been long pampered and exquisitely preserved in American mythology, the discrepancy between appearance and reality—in particular between the image of the southern lady and the facts of her daily life—is great indeed. Despite sentimental portraits of plantation mistresses drawn by such writers as John Pendleton Kennedy, John Esten Cooke, and Thomas Nelson Page, few southern women found their lives filled with an academy education, governesses, music, and polite manners. What life in the Old South really demanded from most of the "weaker sex" was a pioneer spirit sharpened by the personal experience of child-bearing, land clearing, and hard agricultural labor.

As opposed to the supposedly bright side of plantation life represented by the cavalier and his belle, the aristocratic country life of the antebellum South is also said to have had its darker features, one of which was the overseer.

If one were to believe the myth, he was the devil incarnate—the one "heavy" character in an otherwise lighthearted drama. In a backhanded way much of the plantation legend's glamour is related to the assumption that the "dirty work" of plantation management rested in the hands of overseers, freeing the planter to pursue a more leisured and cultured way of life. Aside from the fact that the actual number of plantation units was significantly smaller than the inflations of legend suggest, even on those that did exist the number of absentee planters has been much exaggerated. Evidence discloses that by far the majority of planters supervised their own slaves. While it is true that most of these made use of drivers or black foremen, the use of overseers was much less widespread than is usually supposed. Thus, the stereotype of the planters as economic parasites and "idlers" who entrusted the practical management of their holdings to dull-witted and monstrous overseers is largely without foundation. According to one recent authority:

> Among moderate-sized holdings (sixteen to fifty slaves) less than one out of every four owners used white overseers. Even on estates with more than one hundred slaves, the proportion with white overseers was just 30 percent, and on many of these the planters were usually in residence.[2]

Far from being a southern "colonel," with black shoestring tie, sitting in a rocking chair on a porch with imposing white pillars, calling, "Tom, you rascal, bring me another mint julep," the typical plantation owner was a man of energy, competence, and industry.

Even though historical research indicates that the planter's success was certainly as much related to his own efforts as to those of others, the ominous figure of the overseer continues to stalk the pages of history books. His darkly drawn stereotype as a sadistic dullard, however, scarcely acknowledges the skill and competence which he most often displayed. Many were drawn from the solid ranks of yeoman farmers while others were sons of planters who wished to learn the planting trade in a practical setting and in the process earn enough money to buy land and blacks themselves. Reflecting the fluid society of the Old South, some enterprising overseers, such as Ephraim Beanland, who served as an overseer to James K. Polk, became successful and respected planters in their own right. Thus, while the mythical image of the overseer as an immoral and uncouth tyrant no doubt has some basis in fact, it is a major historical disservice to suggest that the ranks of overseers as a whole were populated by the less desirable elements of society.

Any discussion of the plantation legend would be incomplete without mention of the slave—the so-called happy darkey. Allegedly, the average slave was lazy, easygoing, and quite childlike in character. The uniform description of the plantation slave, in short, has most always been that he was a meek victim of a system which produced a "Sambo" personality. As with all myths and stereotypes there is a measure of evidence to support such a view. Some historians have argued, for example, that the oppressive atmosphere of the plantation, built upon earlier traumatic experiences and intimidation, was calculated to make blacks respectful of authority, obedient, and humble. A "concentration camp" psychology, it is said, produced a rather distinct slavish personality. First examined by Stanley Elkins in his book *Slavery: A Problem in American Institutional and Intellectual Life* (1959), the validity of the Sambo argument continues to be strongly debated.

Even in light of the Elkins thesis, it is clear that the traditional myth of the typical slave must be revised considerably to be consistent with other findings of recent historical scholarship. The economic historians Robert Fogel and Stanley Engerman, for example, using newly developing techniques of historical research such as advanced statistics, applied mathematics, and computers in their study *Time on the Cross: The Economics of American Negro Slavery* (1974), have tried to show that southern slave agriculture was 35 percent more efficient than northern systems of family farming being used during the same period of time. Supporting their controversial view, they go on to argue that "the typical slave field hand was not lazy, inept, and unproductive. On average he was harder-working and more efficient than his white counterpart."[3] They contend as well that the

old belief that all slaves were menial workers is also false. Statistics reveal, they say, that more than 25 percent of all adult male slaves were craftsmen, managers, professionals, or semiskilled workers. Research results also prove, according to the Fogel and Engerman study, that the widespread view that slaves were victims of poor nutrition is "without foundation in fact." It is their conclusion as well that while slave housing was usually nothing more than the limited space of a rough log cabin, slave living quarters were very much similar to the housing available to the great majority of other Americans at that time.

Yet another possible major misconception related to slave life in a plantation setting which has engaged the attention of historical researchers is the alleged difference between house servants and field hands. Probate records and plantation registers disclose that there were no distinct cultural types within the peculiar institution but rather that there was considerable movement among blacks between the fields and the big house. House slaves tended to be either quite young—under fifteen—or relatively advanced in age, ranging from the late forties to well beyond. Hence, a slave's most productive working years—from the late teens through middle age—were usually spent as an agricultural laborer. It seems likely, then, that many blacks began their "careers" with domestic duties, then became field hands, and eventually moved to a modified form of retirement back to the big house.

Beyond this merging of roles and labor, and again according to the simplistic view of legend, the house slaves were also supposed to have been the Uncle Toms of the plantation system. According to historian Eugene Genovese, the house slaves were allegedly "a privileged caste apart, contemptuous of the field hands, jealous of their place in the affection or at least [the] eye of the white master and mistress, and generally speaking, finks, sellouts, and white man's niggers."[4] Beyond the fact that an acceptance of this stereotype ignores the mobility which existed between those who tilled the soil and those who labored at domestic chores, most slaves worked on agricultural units which were not of the large plantation type. Half the slaves in the Old South labored on farms with twenty or fewer hands, which indicates that few plantations were indeed large enough to allow a separate group, much less a caste, of house slaves to develop. Examples of Uncle Toms were more likely to have been found among house slaves in the South's larger cities, such as Richmond, Charleston, or New Orleans. Even for those who were house slaves in a plantation setting, however, as many examples can be found during the war years of those who joined hands in rebellion against their condition as those who dutifully stood by the missus and loyally hid the family heirlooms. The fundamental fact of the matter is that it was "townhouse slaves and a tiny group of privileged house slaves on huge plantations [who] could and sometimes did form a separate caste with the attributes described in the literature."[5] Uncle Toms there apparently were, but they were to be found more in the cities than on the few great landed estates of the wealthy.

In addition, Genovese's research has also concluded that, contrary to popular opinion, there is little evidence to support the view that slavery in the upper South was milder than allegedly harsher forms "down the river" in the Deep South.

Another of the major deficiencies of the plantation legend is the fact that it totally ignores the important dimension of slavery in the cities. It should not be forgotten that approximately 6 percent of all slaves worked in towns. In urban centers of the Old South, such as Savannah, Mobile, Montgomery, and Memphis, in fact, the slave population was expanding at least moderately between 1820 and 1860. There slaves were used as artisans and semiskilled craftsmen, as well as common laborers. At the Tredegar Iron Works in Richmond, Virginia, the South's largest iron manufacturer, for example, slaves usually made up as much as one half of the entire labor force. In other cases slaves functioned as blacksmiths, carpenters, and shoemakers. Indeed, if given a choice, and especially after having tasted city life, most slaves found an urban setting more to their liking. As the leading historian of slavery in the city has put the matter, "How could you keep them down on the plantation once they had seen Mobile?"[6] The isolation of the cane and cotton fields simply did not compare very favorably with the exhilarating and cosmopolitan atmosphere of city life.

Yet another misconception found in the plantation legend is its failure to acknowledge the quarter million free blacks who lived in the South in 1860. Those who had become free by means of purchasing their freedom through savings from extra work, or who had been granted liberty by their masters, usually were to be found in the city. Yet one would hardly suspect, given the attention which has been lavished on plantation life, that they even existed. But they did; for example, free blacks "outnumbered slaves ten to one in Baltimore and 9,209 to 1,774 in Washington. In the Deep South, too, their numbers grew with each census. New Orleans always had a considerable contingent; on the even of the Civil War it exceeded 10,000."[7]

Urban life for a free black in the antebellum South was of course not terribly different from that of a slave. As a New Orleans newspaper editor was quick to admit at the time, "We know full well that the pretense of any real freedom being designed or expected for these negroes is but a sham." Required to carry a pass, forever faced with the very real possibility that he might be judged a vagrant or a plantation escapee and sold back into slavery, the plight of the free black was at best uncertain. He was often viewed with considerable suspicion by white Southerners who saw him as a potential threat to the order and stability of the southern way of life. As a case in point they could always cite the example of Denmark Vesey, who after winning $1,500 in a lottery in 1800 and purchasing his freedom for $600, sought to lead a slave rebellion in Charleston in June, 1822. As a result, open discrimination and legal forms of segregation were soon developed in cities throughout the Deep South to deal with such problems, as well as with what was seen as the laziness, dishonesty, and drunkenness attributed to "free persons of color."

The Northern Origins of Southern Mythology

The cluster of myths known as the plantation legend was not, as it may first appear, entirely created by Southerners. People in regions to the north of the Mason-Dixon line had an important hand in these legendary creations as well. Northerners' passion for southern mythology, in the opinion of some, is mostly a result of their often hidden fascination with aristocratic societies. Beneath America's verbal commitment to democracy, a persistent elitism has sometimes shown through—recall the Jacksonian period for example—revealing Americans' deep-seated admiration for and fascination with the aristocratic way of life. As explained by the Swedish sociologist, Gunnar Myrdal, in his classic study of black-white relations, *An American Dilemma: The Negro Problem and Modern Democracy* (1944):

> The North has so few vestiges of feudalism and aristocracy of its own that, even though it dislikes them fundamentally and is happy not have them, Yankees are thrilled by them. Northerners apparently cherish the idea of having had an aristocracy and of still having a real class society—in the South. So it manufactures the myth of the 'Old South' or has it manufactured by Southern writers working for the Northern market.[8]

Not to misinterpret Myrdal's point it must be understood, however, that it was not only "Southern writers working for the Northern market" who portrayed an essentially legendary South, but northern writers joining forces with their artistic brethren who often allowed myth to masquerade as history. Nearly a decade before the Civil War, for example, Harriet Beecher Stowe allowed her antislavery feelings to get the best of her when creating a series of cardboard characters in *Uncle Tom's Cabin* (1852). Three years later, Daniel Christy of Ohio published his book *Cotton Is King*, which not only touched off a great deal of discussion in America and in Europe as to the industrialized world's dependence on the raw cotton of the South, but, in the process, created the impression that Dixie was an empire of plantations and slaveholders. Later generations of Americans often found a sympathetic treatment of the "aristocratic" culture of the Old South through the works of Yankee writers such as Herman Melville, Henry James, and Henry Adams. And even more recently Minnesota-born F. Scott

Fitzgerald drew the nation's attention to what he called the "strange courtliness and chivalry" of "the dead South" in such literary works as "The Ice Palace" (1920) and "The Last of the Belles" (1929). Indeed, it is important to notice that the legends of the Old South were cultivated by those who neither owned a slave nor planted an acre of cotton. The North has found southern mythology nearly as fetching as has Dixie itself.

Cavalier and Yankee

The credibility which the plantation legend has enjoyed nationally is matched by America's long acceptance of the stereotypes of Cavalier and Yankee. Long ago converted to the belief that before 1860 America was a culturally divided nation—a democratic and commercialized Yankee North pitted against an aristocratic and agrarian Cavalier South—Americans, and many historians specifically, have generally accepted the idea that the Civil War was a conflict which could not have been avoided because of the fundamental differences between the regions and their ways of life. Historian Charles Beard, for one, emphasized the essential disharmony of the sections and found its basis in the conflicting economic systems of the "capitalists, laborers, and farmers of the North and West" and the "planting aristocracy of the South." Many people of the time stressed differences too, and they translated their mythical ideas into practical action. The activities of abolitionists such as John Brown and the emotional defense of the South by fire-eaters such as William Lowndes Yancey and Edmund Ruffin succeeded in convincing many that the differences between the Yankee North and the Cavalier South could never be resolved through any means short of war.

Jefferson Davis, Robert E. Lee, and the Confederate Myth

The election of the "Black Republican," Abraham Lincoln, in 1860 was most instrumental in confirming Southerners' belief that the goal of the Yankee North was to destroy their way of life. And Confederate frustration, despair, and defeat during the war years only served to reinforce the South's already obvious tendency to allow fictions to serve in lieu of facts. As the North launched its crusade to subdue the Cotton Kingdom and its nation of slaveholding Cavaliers, Southerners played out their mythical fantasies by choosing Jefferson Davis to manage the home front and sending Robert E. Lee off to battle to preserve the Cavalier ideal and lead "the crusade of the planters" against sinister Yankees.

For many, the Confederate surrender at Appomattox, Virginia, was the great watershed of southern history. The Old South lay in ashes and in its place a New South would rise, committed to economic prosperity, progressive politics, and a new era of racial harmony for Dixie. For most Southerners, however, the widely heralded millenium of the New South never came to pass. Instead, guardians of the South's former glory began to offer warm praise for, and look nostalgically on, the supposedly picture-perfect age which had recently been obliterated in the smoke and blood of civil conflict. Through the writings of Joel Chandler Harris and Thomas Nelson Page, for example, a heavy "syrup of romanticism" poured from the presses to even further obscure in the nation's understanding what life in the Old South had really been like. The Plantation Legend, in short, was refurbished and revitalized as old memories consecrated the South's noble past.

Complementary to the rejuvenated Old South myth, moreover, was the rise during the post-Civil War period of what historians have come to call the Confederate Myth, or the Myth of the Lost Cause. Beyond dramatizing and sentimentalizing the grand civilization of the Old South, organizations such as the Confederate Survivors' Association, the United Daughters of the Confederacy, and the United Confederate Veterans lavished their emotions and attentions on the noble stand made by Southerners during the war years. In this highly charged atmosphere, the gray Confederate veteran became a mythical hero, and Jefferson Davis and, to a greater extent, Robert E. Lee began to emerge as champions of imagined southern magnificence who had taken their stand in defense of Dixie in the face of overwhelming odds. Journalists, educators, and clergy soon joined the chorus of romantic oratory in an attempt to replace the

feelings of humiliation, trauma, and bitter defeat with the more comforting throught that even though the cause of the Confederate States of America had been lost, it had nonetheless been valiantly defended.

SECTION I. THE PLANTATION LEGEND

The South is probably the most mythologized region in the country. Americans, both North and South, tend to view the history of the southern states, especially that of the period before the Civil War, from a distinctly romantic and mythical point of view. The Southern way of life during the Old South period allegedly centered on the personalities, the activities, and the affairs of plantation life. The antebellum or pre-Civil War South is made to appear a nearly perfect society. This southern utopia is supposed to have been one of luxuriant landscapes, occasionally graced by spacious white-columned mansions caressed by the intoxicating fragrance of magnolia blossoms. The legendary picture of when "things were different down there" reveals the principal inhabitant of this earthly paradise to be an aristocratic "colonel," either busily at the gentlemanly task of raising thoroughbred horses and cotton or, in courtly style, sipping mint juleps in the restful shade of a splendid portico. Close by his side sits a southern matron with auburn hair, delicate features, and a distinctly refined quality about her. She offers the perfect portrait of true womanhood—properly reserved, dressed in her ruffled hoop-skirt, and reading the latest novel then fashionable in polite society, most likely Sir Walter Scott's *Ivanhoe*. The scene also includes a self-effacing black butler who knows his place and is happy to be there. The conduct of the day-to-day affairs of the big house, of course, hinge on the loyalty and devotion of the black mammy who resembles Aunt Jemima and governs the "chilluns" while her own barefoot youngsters sit out behind the shanty in the black quarters eating watermelon and singing spirituals. The entire scene is one of serenity and security, and one can be assured that the singing darkey field hands are being kept hard to their task by the watchful eye and occasional whip of the overseer. Briefly here one has, in full bloom, the plantation legend.

The plantation myth—which the poet Stephen Vincent Benét called "the sick magnolias of the false romance"—was the product of many forces, northern as well as southern. Many white Southerners, even before the Civil War, had come to believe that they actually had created a perfect society, but it was after the war years, when reminiscence and romance were fused, that the plantation life of the early South was made into something it had never been. Southern writers such as James Lane Allen, Thomas Nelson Page, and John Esten Cooke were instrumental in eulogizing the splendid days "befo' the war." In the twentieth century, novelists such as Stark Young in *So Red the Rose* and Margaret Mitchell in *Gone with the Wind* succeeded in keeping the legend alive.

Historians also have done their part to maintain the image of idyllic life on the old plantation, demonstrating a tendency to write the elitist history of those who left the most durable records. According to one source, for example, "no single writer has been more influential in establishing patterns of belief about the plantation system of the Old South among scholars and teachers than ... Ulrich Bonnell Phillips."[9] During his years as a professor at Columbia University, Phillips gave slight attention to the nonslaveholding southern farmer, being preoccupied instead with the question of life and labor on the large "show" plantations. While it is certainly true that Phillips did not invent the plantation legend of the Old South, it can be said that he contributed heavily to its dimensions and perpetuation.

Plantation Life

The major difficulty with the Old South myth in the first instance is with the numerous misconceptions which surround the plantation itself. Most Southerners in pre-Civil War days in fact did not live on plantations. Indeed, historical evidence makes it perfectly clear that "large slaveholders were very few and that a great number of slaves lived on small

farms." Since small individually operated farming units far exceeded plantations in number, it is now obvious that the plantation was anything but the typical setting within which the average antebellum Southerner found himself. As one historian has explained:

> In 1850 ... the census reported 568,000 agricultural units in the South, of which only 101,335, or 18 percent of the total, could be classified as plantations—that is, a unit producing marketable quantities of one or more of the five basic staples of cotton, tobacco, sugar, rice, or hemp. If another definition of plantation is used, such as U. B. Phillips', of a farm with twenty or more slaves, then the proportion of plantations to farms shrinks still further, to less than one in ten.[10]

Given the fact that only 10 to 18 percent of the agricultural units in the South qualified as plantations, it is apparent that the greatest error of the plantation legend is its failure to acknowledge the yeoman farmer as the most numerous and therefore the most typical white Southerner before the Civil War. Rather than the great plantations of hundreds of slaves and thousands of acres, the Old South was for the most part a land of modest farms and plain folk toiling without the assistance of black slaves.

Despite the lingering illusion of the ease and abundance of plantation life, then, the vast majority of white Southerners were middle-class farmers clearing their land with the assistance of hardworking wives, unaware that picturesque estates such as Jefferson's Monticello, Madison's Montpelier, or Monroe's Farmington even existed. Indeed, while Margaret Mitchell may have captured the nation's fancy with her romantic description of Tara Hall and Twelve Oaks in *Gone with the Wind*, the writer Mark Twain, writing at an earlier time, seems to have had a much more realistic view of plantation life. In his classic novel *Huckleberry Finn*, Twain provides his version of what a one-horse plantation might have been like:

> A rail fence round a two-acre yard ... some sickly grass-patches in the big yard,

117

but mostly it was bare and smooth, like an old hat with the nap rubbed off; big double log house for the white folks—hewed logs, with the chinks stopped up with mud or mortar . . . one little hut all by itself away down against the back fence, and some outbuildings down a piece the other side.[11]

While Twain's portrait of the real South before the War Between the States has been less well remembered than that of Margaret Mitchell's and other popularizers of the legend, it is decidedly more accurate.

But what might still be said about the great planters, the country gentlemen of courtliness and stately hospitality who supposedly presided over southern society during the antebellum period? There were of course Southerners of economic wealth and social privilege who somewhat realistically could lay claim to a cavalier lineage and life-style. John A. Selden of Virginia, for example, owner of the famous Westover estate on the James River, was one who enjoyed the luxury of silver tea sets, private tutors for his children, vacations at White Sulphur Springs, and membership in the Richmond Whist Club. John Hampton Randolph of Louisiana, sugar planter at Forest Home plantation in Iberville Parish (county), was yet another who could rather easily afford to send his son to the University of Virginia, his daughter to study in the cultured atmosphere of a boarding school in Baltimore, and to purchase expensive books such as Audubon's *Birds of America* without being much concerned with its price ($166.67).

While the preoccupation with the aristocratic life-styles of landowners like Selden and Randolph encouraged the belief that all white male Southerners of the early South were "cotton snobs," the actual number of such individuals was infinitely small. To accept the idea of a European-style closed aristocracy as having existed in the South in the days before the war is in fact to ignore two of the most significant realities then at work in Dixie— the ever-present frontier environment and the element of time. Since the fundamental fact of life in the antebellum South was the frontier, conditions were not at all ripe for the growth of an aristocracy. Beyond this, the word "aristocrat" implies that one's position of economic

and social privilege has been acquired over time and that more than likely at least a portion of the wealth and prestige which goes with it has been inherited. When it is understood that prior to the American Revolution no cotton of any great quantity was even grown in America, the notion of a southern cotton aristocracy of long-standing wealth and prestige having emerged by the eve of the Civil War must be dismissed as a historical impossibility. Indeed, according to the figures of a highly reliable historian:

> The census of 1860 reported a surprisingly small number of "planters," only 46,274 persons, most of whom were heads of families, owning as many as 20 slaves. Out of this privileged group only 2,292 persons belonged to the large planter classification, that is, persons owning as many as 100 slaves. In the whole land of Dixie, the census officials of 1860 reported finding only 1 slaveholder, an individual in South Carolina, having as many as 1,000 slaves, and only 13 persons owning between 500 and 1,000 slaves. The large slaveholders, thus, were very few in number and comparable to the millionaires of modern America.[12]

Faced with statistics such as these, one is forced to conclude that the southern aristocracy of the Old Regime was for the most part one of imaginary rank rather than caste—a mythical creation of the mind of the South.

Of critical import to the imagined aristocracy of the southern planter was the role assigned to the fabled southern belle. While northern women were expected to be delicate, virtuous, and "Christian," the southern lady found her world not only being controlled by "the cult of true womanhood" but also by the unwritten codes of southern chivalry. Scarlett O'Hara, Margaret Mitchell's heroine in *Gone with the Wind,* is the supreme example in American literature of the mythical antebellum southern belle. In the cool shade on the porch of Tara Hall, her father's plantation, Scarlett plays the role of the southern lady flawlessly:

> she made a pretty picture. Her new green flowered-muslin dress spread its twelve

yards of billowing material over her hoops and exactly matched the flat-heeled green morocco slippers her father had recently brought her from Atlanta. The dress set off to perfection the seventeen-inch waist, the smallest in three counties, and the tightly fitting basque showed breasts well matured for her sixteen years.[13]

The romantic attitude of the age which Scarlett O'Hara was supposed to symbolize, however, also had its oppressive side for the ladies of the Old South.

Even those very few who may have experienced some of the leisured dignity of plantation life—such as Mrs. Charles Colcock Jones of Georgia or Mary Boykin Chesnut of Camden, South Carolina—came to understand the subtle forms of "slavery" which kept them "in their place," the pedestal upon which they had been set and then left. Despite the conspiracy of churches, schools, books, magazines, and parents to sustain the myth, and even though southern women made noble efforts to live up to their image as "queen of the home," some rebelled by seeking to expose the tyranny hidden behind their enforced, timid innocence. Mrs. Chesnut confided in her journal, for example, that a good many of the planters' wives were "abolitionists, and hot ones, too." They saw the need to liberate southern women as well as blacks. Few belles were able to savor the benefits of their exalted status. Southern ladies even in a plantation setting found that the demands of everyday life allowed precious little time for the enjoyment of the warm climate, semitropical flowers, and legendary southern hospitality. Despite the romantic tradition, the majority of southern women spent their days cooking, preserving fruits and vegetables, sewing, making soap, and rearing children. What activities there were in the way of riding horseback, attending teas on the lawn, and serving as gracious hostess to evening balls were reserved to but a privileged minority.

In addition to the myths surrounding the planter and the southern woman, and adding a dash of drama, has been the belief that every large cotton estate housed an evil, sinister overseer. From the unsympathetic portrait of the overseer Simon Legree, drawn by Harriet Beecher Stowe in her melodramatic novel *Uncle Tom's Cabin,* the entire class of plantation managers is thought to have been composed of heartless, cruel, and unscrupulous individuals. Mrs. Stowe, of course, was responsible for creating numerous stereotypes about plantation life in the Old South. With little first-hand knowledge of either slavery or the South, her portrayal of Uncle Tom appealed to the romantic tastes of the time while the northern-born Simon Legree served as a convenient villain. Through a succession of human crises, *Uncle Tom's Cabin* tells the stirring tale of a faithful old slave—Uncle Tom—being sold down the river from his "Old Kentucky Home" only to eventually die at the hands of the sadistic Simon Legree. Another character, Eliza, a mulatto slave girl, is forced to flee across the ice floe on the Ohio River with her infant child in a heartrending dash for freedom. Through a series of lurid episodes depicting bloodhounds chasing fugitive slaves, brutal whippings, and other atrocities, the novel attempts to expose the most gruesome features of plantation slavery. While all of this no doubt contributed to the effectiveness of the book, it also lent its share of myth to the understanding of slave conditions in the Deep South. In particular, it created a stereotyped picture of the overseer which was an exaggeration of historical truth.

Seemingly taking their cue from Mrs. Stowe, historians have also contributed heavily to the myth of the sinister overseer. While failing to speak to the key role which he had in the affairs of plantation management, historians whose opinions are highly regarded on other matters have claimed the overseers to have been "brutal and unscrupulous," "sometimes intolerable," and "at worst cruel, licentious tyrants." This image has some basis in fact. There were overseers who were brutal, intolerant, and cruel. The difficulty with such a view, however, is that it is too completely based on sources such as Mrs. Stowe, or, as is more often the case, on the prejudiced opinions of the plantation owners. "The myth of the general ineptness of the overseer class," maintains one historian, "was created by members of the planter community and has been perpetuated unwittingly by writers whose chief insight into the character of the overseer has been gained through the eyes of his employer."[14] Since the planter, to sustain the growing myth, was inclined to take full credit for his success, he not only seems to have downplayed the critical role of his black slaves, but also that of other supporting underlings such as the overseers. Journals and accounts reveal that cases of mismanagement were much more likely to be recorded than were examples of outstanding achievement. Since as a class the overseer was considered to be distinctly inferior to both the planter and the small independent farmer, it was his incompetence rather than his expertise in areas such as planting, cultivation, harvesting, and the care of land, stock, and farm implements which has received the greatest attention.

Another factor which has contributed significantly to the overseer's unsavory reputation is the fact that there was, particularly in the lower South, a fairly large number of "amateur overseers" whose performance and competence were not particularly admirable. "Many ... writers have equated the entire class of southern overseers with this group of ill-paid, inexperienced, unqualified wanderers," says the one historian who has done the most thorough study of them, "thereby producing a stereotyped image of the southern overseer which does not accord with the facts."[15] When one looks to the plantation overseers as a group and appreciates the superior ability of many as evidenced by the expansion and economic success of slavery preceding the Civil War, their distorted image as general incompetents becomes more apparent, if one can overlook their contributions to an immoral system. Given their many responsibilities, the great demand for their services, and the widespread protest of planters when attempts were made by Confederate officials to draft them for military duty at the time of the Civil War, it is reasonable to conclude that the overseer was considerably more talented and able than legend has been willing to grant.

Blacks in the Plantation South

The plantation legend obviously includes many inconsistencies, but perhaps the most inconsistent element of all is its most basic feature—the black slave. In the first place, it is odd that anyone could have thought the plantation system, based on inhumane slavery, the most nearly utopian system America had yet produced. But then again even Sir Thomas More had included slavery in his vision in *Utopia* (1516). In the second place, how could it be that allegedly insensitive, uncouth, and cold-blooded overseers were needed to manage the great landed estates of the Old South when the workers, the slaves, were supposedly so easygoing, docile, and happy? Indeed, despite the myth of black contentment immortalized by Stephen Foster's "Old Black Joe" and other songs, blacks were anything but satisfied with their lot as slaves. The familiar image of the average black slave as a "banjo-strumming darkey" or Sambo is usually based on the fact that there were relatively few slave rebellions before the Civil War, and the comparatively small number of blacks who escaped from the South by means of the Underground Railroad—at best some two thousand per year out of a black population of approximately four million. Measuring black discontent by the yardstick of militant rebellion, however, is inadequate.

Gauging slave unrest in terms of slave rebellions is a largely unsatisfactory method of analyzing the Sambo stereotype because it fails to take into account the psychological atmosphere which the plantation system created for many blacks. The paternalistic relationship between master and slave— within which the master considered himself a "father" to his slave "children"—most certainly did much to encourage some blacks to behave as if they were content with their existence. With most southern whites contending that blacks were theirs to care for, slaves in turn developed a childlike submission to the plantation system. According to the slavery historian Stanley Elkins, in fact, blacks were trained to be inferior since they were collectively "brainwashed." Having been taught to be submissive, docile, and happy over a long period of time, by their concentration camp-style environment, a good many slaves adjusted to their fate and were not at all inclined to engage in either isolated revolts or large scale revolution.

In analyzing the apparent black acceptance of the chains of slavery, it is also important to remember that the rural, often frontier character of the pre-Civil War South made any organized rebellion almost impossible. In addition, the statistics already cited as to the small numbers involved in underground railroad activities can just as easily be used as evidence to argue that the most aggressive and capable of black leaders left the South, leaving behind only the least capable and aggressive to organize a rebellion. Not to be forgotten as well is the fact that the legal system was then, as it is now, a tool for the maintenance of the status quo, working to control slave activities at every turn. With the laws in many southern states expressly forbidding the teaching of blacks to read and write, and with curfew laws being strictly enforced by night patrols, the chances of staging a rebellion were indeed slight. Finally, the overemphasis on slave rebellions as the only sign of black discontent presumes that slaves would find a more humane society in the North if escape or revolt were successful. The existence of national fugitive slave laws as well as much deep racial hatred toward blacks north of the Mason-Dixon line, however, suggests that slaves had very little to look forward to even if they could somehow free themselves from the bonds of the plantation.

Once one ceases to pose rebellion as the major test of black dissatisfaction under slavery, one can find important evidence of widespread discontent. Slave songs, for example, reveal a good deal about the attitude of blacks toward their condition. The lyrics of slave music reflect moods of discouragement, dissatisfaction, and melancholy. Additional evidence of black discontent is the fact that slaves did escape when the chance arose. Not only this, however, but the nearly religious reverence with which blacks viewed their emancipator—whether Union general or the president—is a clear indication of just how dearly they wished to break the suffocating limitations of slavery. After the war, blacks viewed both Abraham Lincoln and Republican party leaders as saviors. So strong was this attitude, in fact, that America, blacks voted almost exclusively Republican until the major shift in black political loyalties at the time of Franklin Roosevelt's New Deal. Most important of all, Southern slaveholders themselves

testified, and so did blacks, that freedom was the greatest gift a master could bestow upon a faithful servant. Finally, much evidence exists that slaves often gave vent to their frustrations by work slowdowns, the breaking of tools, feigning sickness, and various other forms of nonviolent protest and rebellion. When these less obvious expressions of black discontent are linked with the many documented instances of rebellion and individual acts of defiance, the picture of the happy darkey stands exposed as a less than complete portrait of the black slave. Indeed, almost every element of the plantation legend is based on falsehood and distortion. Nonetheless, the South—for that matter the nation at large—continues to prefer an illusory vision of what the Old South must have been like to a picture based on the facts of history.

SECTION II. THE NORTHERN ORIGINS OF SOUTHERN MYTHOLOGY

The South is more than a geographical expression; it is at one and the same time a way of life and a state of mind. Proud of their traditions and heritage, Southerners have often manipulated their past to make it into what they wanted to believe it had been.

The need for myth was apparent even among the fortunate few who successfully realized the full potential which the South had to offer. Freed from much of the drudgery common to middle-class yeoman-farmers, the well-to-do planter had ample opportunity to indulge romantic tendencies, and he was aided by novelists of the time. The romantic novelist Sir Walter Scott was indeed the "rage" during the antebellum period, and southern writers produced many a historical novel which reflected Scott's influence. William Gilmore Simms and the so-called Chronicler of the Cavaliers, William Alexander Caruthers, turned out historical romances which glamorized the southern way of life and helped make it legendary. In their hands the writing of history was a "romantic art," in which history and myth were blended to make them nearly indistinguishable. In many respects Southerners created a distinct and perhaps

Old Kentucky Home: Life in the South
Courtesy of The New York Historical Society, New York City.

unique mythology of their own. But they also had help from another region.

Song and Story

It must be emphasized, as the historian Henry Steele Commager has said, that "the most familiar of southern symbols came from the North: Harriet Beecher Stowe of New England gave us Uncle Tom and Little Eva and Topsy and Eliza, while it was Stephen Foster of Pittsburgh who sentimentalized the Old South, and even 'Dixie' had northern origins."[16] Connecticut Yankee Mrs. Stowe, basing her impressions of the South on extremely limited firsthand experience, is responsible for a good many of the erroneous stereotypes which most people assume are historically accurate portraits of Southerners before the war. She devised the faithful darkey—Sambo—image of blacks, graphically portrayed a villainous version of the plantation overseer, and indirectly gave vitality to the related ideas of cavalier and Southern belle.

Similarly, Stephen C. Foster composed "Old Suzanna" (1848) and "Swanee River" (1851) prior to a one-month excursion into the South; after which he published "Old Folks at Home" (1852), "Massa's in the Cold, Cold Ground" (1852), "My Old Kentucky Home" (1853), and "Old Black Joe" (1860). All these songs not only appealed to the emotions, but their lyrics voiced a strong sense of nostalgia for the old plantation. Immensely popular over the years, Foster's songs fed the American romantic imagination with a sentimentalized view of what life in the South is said to have been like before the Civil War. Undeniably, Foster's plantation songs have had a legend-creating impact on the popular mind, conveniently offering succeeding generations easily remembered versions of an idealized life in the sunny South.

With respect to myth-building, one of the tourist showplaces of Kentucky—Rowan Manor House, near Bardstown—where it is purported Foster wrote "My Old Kentucky Home," is of particular interest. The efforts of Kentuckians to satisfy nostalgic taste for the Old South notwithstanding, no records exist to prove that Foster ever visited the estate, much less that he wrote his famous song there. A historical record that does exist—the letters of

Stephen's brother, Morrison Foster—indicates that the lyrics and songs for which the composer is most famous—including "My Old Kentucky Home"—were actually composed at Foster's home in Allegheny County, Pennsylvania.

Further, it seems that Foster, as well as Bardstown's residents, was aware of the North's seemingly unquenchable thirst for the romance of the South. As a case in point, Foster's workbook shows that "My Old Kentucky Home" was originally entitled "Poor Uncle Tom, Good Night." This rather clearly implies that the song must have been inspired by that other, more famous northern mythmaker, Harriet Beecher Stowe. According to one source, "Foster later changed the title and refrain . . . so the song would have a wider appeal."[17] Seemingly, like northern artists before him, the "wider appeal" that Foster sought was to be found in the North's mythical imagination.

Since Civil War days perhaps no song has done more to capture the emotion and promote "southernism" than "Dixie." Symbolic of the southern way of life, it was written in New York City by an Ohioan, Daniel Decatur Emmett, in 1859. Though used as a marching tune by both Union and Confederate forces during the Civil War, it soon became the unofficial national anthem of the South and has remained the most important sentimental expression of southern regional feeling ever since. Together with *Uncle Tom's Cabin* and the works of Foster, "Dixie" helped unify national emotion and belief about the South.

The Grand Illusion

As early as 1924, the historian Francis Pendelton Gaines was attempting to explain the process whereby the South and the North became co-partners in the creation of southern mythology. Both the North and South, said Gaines, "agreed concerning certain picturesque elements of plantation life and joined hands to set the conception unforgettably in public consciousness."[18] In attempting to further explain this sectional compromise which allowed southern mythmakers to find counterparts in the North, Gaines cited America's love of feudalism, romantic hunger, and fascination for aristocratic societies. The

southern plantation, Gaines concluded, "alone among native institutions" satisfied "this craving for a system of caste."[19] While a titled aristocracy had long since been declared un-American and at odds with the nation's democratic creed, some people apparently continued to harbor longings for an aristocracy.

Yale historian C. Vann Woodward has suggested another explanation as to why the North conspired in southern mythmaking. Ironically enough, says Woodward, Northerners directly supported the plantation legend through their opposition to slavery. The abolitionists in particular made a contribution to misunderstanding between the regions by implying through their propaganda efforts that nearly everyone in Dixie was either a wealthy cavalier or a completely dehumanized black slave. By endorsing the traditional legendary picture of plantation life, many Northerners were able to hide their own mistreatment of the black man behind a facade of an antislavery myth. By creating the impression that all blacks would at last be free if only the institutions and traditions of the South were changed, the Northerners would not have to face up to their own forms of racially inspired inhumanity toward blacks. The antislavery myth did not, of course, square with the less obvious but still persistent northern commitment to keeping the black "in his place." But it appears that only to the degree to which Americans could be brought to believe that the South was morally inferior could Northerners validate their claim to moral superiority.

Yet another reason why the plantation legend enjoyed a sustained vitality in the North relates to the anxiety found in the decade of the 1830s. During the so-called Age of the Common Man ideas of democracy and equality, though not in any way completely realized, proved threatening to some who wished to maintain their status in economic, social, and political affairs. There were some Americans, in short, who viewed democracy as a threat to their elite positions. This crosscurrent of antidemocratic sentiment, as one historian sees it, produced a "hankering after aristocracy in the North [which] took the form of eulogizing the social system in the South."[20] The social structure of the South, which was imagined to be aristocratic, came to symbolize for these Northerners an enviable and undemocratic type of social order and stability. To them, this European-style aristocracy had apparently discovered a way of assuring stability and cultivating a sense of gentility and honor, yet at the same time had maintained a commitment to the public good under a republican form of government. Convinced that democracy could easily become mobocracy, Northerners inclined to the idea that it was the duty of the rich and the well-born to rule logically turned to the South for guidance and inspiration. If only the perfect society which Southerners supposedly had created could be duplicated in the North, America would surely be much the better for it.

Even after the Civil War the northern commitment to southern mythology continued. When finally faced with the question of what to do with the freed blacks, many middle-class Northerners came to better understand the position concerning blacks which white Southerners had taken a generation earlier. Northerners could find it both emotionally and practically convenient, even though the notion was at odds with America's declared belief that all men are created equal, to subscribe to the view that a distinct separation of the black and white races would be best for all concerned. Nowhere had such a separation of the races been achieved more successfully and with such style and grace, it seemed, than on the legendary plantations of the antebellum South. The mythical grandeur of plantation life thus became a fetching alternative to the immediate social problems which the North was facing.

The various myths of the Old South remained appealing in the North after the war even among those highly critical of American society during the period of scandal and corruption that Mark Twain labeled the "Gilded Age." Many northern writers argued that the political, social, and economic system of the Old South was preferable to the allegedly golden age they saw before them. In the process of criticizing the shortcomings of Yankee civilization in the 1870s and 1880s, such northern writers as Herman Melville, Henry James, and Henry Adams sought to compare the progress and optimism of the early South with the stagnation and despair of America's "age of excess." The antebellum South, it seemed, had been neither as hypocritical about human equality nor as materialistic as the America of Jay Gould, U.S. Grant, and "Boss" Tweed.

The shortcomings of American Yankee culture in the closing years of the nineteenth century seemed all the more obvious when measured against the seemingly vibrant and charming days of the Old South. Post-Civil War America seemed exceedingly vulgar and venal compared to the South of antebellum times. The South's long-standing commitments to family, leisured living, honorable conduct, and chivalry seemed to reflect precisely the values and virtues which America then lacked. In the words of the transplanted Southerner, Basil Ransom, the leading character of Henry James' novel *The Bostonians* (1886), the gilded age which the North had pasted together after the Civil War was "a nervous, hysterical, chattering, canting age, an age of hollow phrases and false delicacy...."[21] Though James later admitted to knowing "terribly little" about the kind of life he had attempted to describe, or of the supposed superiority of the South which he offered as an alternative, he nevertheless suggested that the South's heroic age had much to commend it. And the North's developing alliance with the South in the enterprise of creating southern mythology worked to unite the sections, for "to the North it offered a way in which to apologize without sacrificing the fruits of victory." Together with the forces already at work in Dixie supporting a legendary view of the southern past, the result could only be what one historian has called "a national love feast for the Old South."[22] The kinship which had eluded the sections through the Civil War period was to be more successfully achieved by means of mythology. On this level they could well communicate, for they were Americans all. They could join hands in a postwar setting for a mutual acceptance of a southern mythology which had been born decades before, had survived the war years, and was now at the point of maturing.

The conventional image of the South as a region of social grace and admirable gentility has never been erased from American consciousness. One might make a case, for example, that northern drama and northern-inspired minstrelsy, to say nothing of such northern artistic images of the South as Eastman Johnson's *My Old Kentucky Home* (1859) and Winslow Homer's *Sunday Morning in Virginia* (c. 1870), gave important consideration to mythical plantation materials and thereby did much to reinforce the Old South myth. The plantation legend was, in addition, to be rejuvenated in the late 1930s, when a Southerner (Margaret Mitchell) and non-Southerners (Hollywood producers) combined the mythical potential of literature and the cinema to create *Gone with the Wind* (1939). In that production Vivien Leigh and Clark Gable portrayed a South that was defunct, in fact a South that to a large extent had never been.

The mythology persists. Concerning the North's perennial interest in the mythical South, the region's most famous writer, William Faulkner, in the character of Gavin Stevens in *Intruder in the Dust* (1948), declared that the North has displayed a "gullibility: a volitionless, almost helpless capacity and eagerness to believe anything about the South not even provided it be derogatory but merely bizarre enough and strange enough."[23] A native Southerner, the historian David Potter, has noted one of the more obvious evidences of the South's success in capturing the imagination of its northern brethren when he observed: "Today, the predilection of Yankee children for caps, flags, and toys displaying the Rebel insignia bears further witness to the enduring truth that lost causes have a fascination even for those who did not lose them."[24] The nation's genuine fondness for both the South and its mythology remains as much alive today in Minneapolis as Montgomery.

SECTION III: CAVALIER AND YANKEE: SYNTHETIC STEREOTYPES

With the plantation legend enjoying such wide acceptance both North and South, it is not at all surprising that Americans have long believed that Dixie has been, and continues to be, quite different from the rest of the country. Whether one thinks of the Old South and its legendary leisurely plantation life, or of the stereotyped view of a newer South of one-party politics, "lynching bees," racist rednecks, sharecroppers, the poll tax, and "tobacco-road" bootleggers, the idea persists that southern civilization has developed differently from the rest of America. Seemingly, the habits of thought, the sentiments, prejudices, standards, and values of the South have worked to make the region below the Mason-Dixon line not quite a nation within a nation, but the next thing to it.

The general public, and scholars too, are accustomed to believing, as one historian has said, "that there is a place called the South and that it is inhabited by an identifiable people known as Southerners. We know that this is so, but many of those who most often tell us about it, including natives of the section, would have trouble defining their phrases if pressed for a formula."[25] And in fact many formulas have been offered to explain why things at least appear to be so different in the South. Some say it is the South's long-established ties to an agricultural economy, some claim that it is the rural heritage of the South or its distinct folk culture, while others insist that the region's unswerving commitment to white supremacy largely explains the difference between the southern and the northern ways of life. But while it is true that many common threads of experience have tied the region together, it is the diversity of the South certainly as much as its similarities which have made it the object of so much popular and scholarly attention.

Despite the continued emphasis on the habits, mannerisms, and qualities which seem to make the South so distinct—its dialect, climate, and religious patterns—the inner logic and essence of the South would seem to be the variety rather than the uniformity which its boundaries enclose. Even a minimum of thought reveals that the South during every period of its history has been a study in contrasts. The belief in an unchanging solid South is based more on hardened stereotype than solid substance. One glance at the South's landscape, for instance, quickly reveals a rather rich variety. It is a region which ranges from the pine country of Virginia, the Carolinas, and Georgia to the dry, nearly treeless plains of Texas, and from the relatively primitive mountain country of eastern Kentucky and Tennessee to cosmopolitan New Orleans. It is indeed only logical that an

Virginia Planter's Family
Kennedy Galleries, Inc.

environment different in so many respects should have produced values and attitudes, institutions and traditions, at variance with one another. Despite such geographical realities, however, a good many Americans, on the eve of the Civil War, shared the opinion that the civilizations of the North and the South, being uniformly the same within their respective regions, were classically at odds in the national arena. Supposedly by 1860, America had produced two cultures—one Cavalier, the other Yankee—which were destined to conflict and whose fundamental differences could be resolved only on the battlefield.

The Cavalier in Literature

The mistaken notion that the geographically diverse South had produced a singular "society of Cavaliers" in the decades before the Civil War grew logically out of the developing plantation legend. The concept of the flamboyant and heroic southern Cavalier as a

symbol of the prewar South became fixed after 1830, its development having begun during the early years of the century. The portrayal of Patrick Henry as a Virginia gentleman in the writings of the energetic mythmaker William Wirt seems to have been the first salvo in a barrage of southern literature which succeeded in making the planter into a natural aristocrat and a country squire. Even at the time, however, a select few realized where Wirt's brand of writing might lead. In the judgment of the truly aristocratic Thomas Jefferson, for example, who read the biography of Henry during his years of retirement at Monticello, Wirt had placed his hero in the unreal world of romance rather than history. And speaking of the heavily fictitious tone of Wirt's effort, the Virginian John Taylor of Caroline called it "a splendid novel." Former president John Adams responded to the work by noting that he found the narrative more delightful than the romances of Sir Walter Scott. With this nostalgic portrayal of Virginia's Revolutionary past, and in Wirt's words, "the giants such times produced," the tradition of the mythical southern gentleman had been born. At least to the imaginative mind of William Wirt, Patrick Henry had been the first of the South's "natural aristocrats."

The so-called plantation novels of succeeding years, such as George Tucker's *The Valley of Shenandoah* (1824), John Pendleton Kennedy's *Swallow Barn* (1832), and William Alexander Caruthers' *The Cavaliers of Virginia* (1834), also promoted the acceptance of the plantation legend. They had the effect as well of reinforcing the developing idea that the Cavalier society of the South was fundamentally different from Yankee civilization in the North. They achieved their mythmaking role, however, in a somewhat curious way. The effect of novels such as these was in fact less to portray plantation life as a sunny Shangri-la than to describe the economic decline of the planter class. "It is significant," says the historian William R. Taylor, "that not a single plantation novel was set in the bountiful heyday of plantation prosperity of the mid-eighteenth century."[26] Not having achieved the economic success evident in Yankee New England, Southerners—through their fiction—attempted to make their economic liabilities into assets. The South's growing sense of regionalism during the decades of the 1830s and 1840s fed on the belief that its true strength lay not in attempting to copy the profit-oriented capitalistic society of the North, but rather in cultivating the grace and social elegance which other regions of the country so obviously lacked. The southern Cavalier, while perhaps somewhat less successful in the economic marketplace than his northern counterpart, had a surer hand on immortality, it was thought, by virtue of his monopolistic hold on chivalry, natural dignity, refinement, and the ornamental qualities of life. The idea of a separate southern destiny governed by the Cavalier seemed infinitely more agreeable than a change of values and life-style which would simply duplicate those of the North. Predictably, the South moved from the point of trying to defend its differences to the idea that southern society was in fact more advanced than the North. The region, in short, reshaped its sense of inferiority into a sense of superiority.

The Cavalier spirit burned brightly in the South in the years before the Civil War. In fact, as the attitude of separatism and isolationism grew more widespread, it could be said that an inner civil war was being fought long before the actual war itself began at Fort Sumter. A psychology of conflict, built on a legendary sense of difference between North and South, came to be reinforced through debates over slavery, the tariff, and the role of the federal government in the affairs of the states. Even though recent scholars have been struck more by the essential similarity between the regions during the antebellum period than by the range of their differences, one cannot deny that Northerners and Southerners came to believe that irreconcilable differences existed. The image of a democratic, commercial, Yankee North pitted against an aristocratic, leisured, Cavalier South was based more on fantasy than fact, but it held firm. In succeeding years, activities of the so-called fire-eaters in the South, the raid of John Brown on Harper's Ferry, and the election of Abraham Lincoln in 1860, all took on a symbolic importance which reinforced the synthetic stereotypes of Cavalier and Yankee, to the point of helping bring on the Civil War. With the nation already convinced by the 1840s that America had succeeded in producing a divided culture, it became increasingly easy to let myth pass for reality and to play out fantasies in the arena of national political affairs.

The Cavalier Realized

Though the North and South in the 1840s were certainly much less different from one another in their racial views, economic systems, and political ideas than most had come to imagine, there were definite signs that residents of the two regions had come to believe in their alleged differences and were well on their way to separation. In 1844-1845, for example, the national organizations of the Methodist and Baptist churches formally split into hostile northern and southern factions. More important, the growing alienation of the South from the North could be seen in the changing values and attitudes of Southerners who came both to believe and live the Cavalier versus Yankee myth.

William Lowndes Yancey was one of these. Born in Atlanta, Georgia, reared in Abbeville, South Carolina, and Troy, New York, Yancey

127

eventually became a lawyer and politician in Alabama. Though liberally exposed to Yankee ways by virtue of his mother's second marriage to a northern schoolmaster, and three years of northern education at Williams College in Massachusetts, Yancey was a pronounced Southerner who assumed the role of the Cavalier and played it well. So pure was Yancey's belief in the southern way of life and the Cavalier ideal, in fact, that he resigned his position as congressman from Alabama in 1846 and pursued his secessionist activities thereafter without the slightest hint of a desire for personal political gain. Using rallies and barbecues as settings, he soon gained a reputation as "the orator of secession" through impassioned speeches warning Southerners that the hateful Yankee was bent on destroying the rights and privileges of the white South. Arguing that slavery ought to be protected by federal law and that the benefits of the peculiar institution should be extended to lower-class southern whites, Yancey organized the League of United Southerners in 1858 to assist his lobbying efforts to reopen the African slave trade. A colorful figure with a knack for engaging the emotions of his listeners, Yancey emerged for many as living evidence of the proud Cavalier whose principles and sense of honor demanded an unbending dedication to the southern way of life. Few men of the antebellum South lived the legend of the Cavalier more completely than did William Yancey—except, perhaps, Edmund Ruffin.

Born to fame and position through ties to the FFV (First Families of Virginia), Edmund Ruffin was also a man of great individual talent. Having inherited his father's plantation at the age of sixteen, he was, even with these advantages, very much a self-made man. Seemingly not satisfied with the small measure of historical fame which would have been granted him because of his early experiments with calcium carbonate (lime) fertilizers, Ruffin made his principal vocation that of a fanatical crusader for the South. Militant, even at times belligerent, in his defense of the moral superiority of the southern way of life, he spoke to his fellow Southerners with the enthusiasm and certitude of a true believer. In the style of an evangelical fundamentalist preacher, Ruffin warned the South that it was being contaminated by Yankeeism. Practicing

what he preached, he became a conspicuous figure and an authentic spokesman for the Cavalier ideal, clad as he was in homespun suits designed to symbolize his utter contempt for money-minded Yankee manufacturers upon whom most Southerners were forced to rely for the very clothes on their backs. Ruffin seems never to have doubted either the special virtues of southern society or the special fitness of the planter class to rule the region. Playing out his exaggerated Cavalier fantasies, his behavior reveals a man of extremist views who eventually lost touch with reality. As an honorary member of the South Carolina Palmetto Guard, Ruffin—in 1861 at age sixty-five—symbolically fired what many claim was the first shot against Fort Sumter. Ruffin apparently sought a measure of personal responsibility for committing the South to a war against the Yankee which he seems to have anticipated and in fact desired. He was obsessed by the idea that his beloved South had to be preserved, and the outcome of the Civil War not only destroyed his dreams of what the South might have been, but also in a very real way forced Ruffin to seek escape even further into the mythical world which he had created in the inner sanctuary of his mind.

Having personally witnessed the defeat of the "invincible" South, despondent over the death of his two best-loved children, taunted by obscene graffiti scribbled on the walls of his plantation home, Beechwood, by advancing northern soldiers, deserted even by his trusted black overseer, Ruffin felt he had nothing left but his sense of honor. In a style he thought became a southern gentleman of the "old school," and with a flair that only a "real" Cavalier could muster, Ruffin sat himself erectly in a chair, "propped the butt of his silver-mounted gun against a trunk at his feet, placed the muzzle in his mouth and . . . 'pulled the trigger with a forked stick'."[27]

Fire-eaters such as Edmund Ruffin did not, except in their own minds, represent the majority opinion of the South. The belief in states' rights, the virtues of slavery, the doctrine of nullification, and the legality of secession which he and Yancey supported were in fact not accepted without question by the typical Southerner. The doctrine of nullification—the idea that the various states enjoyed the right to declare federal laws unconstitutional at their own discretion—had been used as early as 1798 and again, in the North, during the War of 1812. The doctrine was not endorsed, however, by many staunch Southerners during the decades of debate between the sections before the Civil War. Virginian James Madison had moderately concluded that the American political system provided for a "mixed government" in which power had to be shared between state and national levels. Hugh S. Legare, a Charleston newspaper editor, was yet another who did not follow the southern pattern. Rather, he used the pages of his *Southern Review* to argue in favor of union and against secession. Beyond this, James Petigru and Joel Poinsett of South Carolina, Charles Galloway of Arkansas, Governor Sam Houston of Texas, and Henry S. Foote of Mississippi were strongly unionist in their points of view. No better testament to the strength of union sentiment within the South could be cited, however, than the fact that Alexander H. Stephens was chosen vice president of the Confederate States of America only weeks after having been Georgia's most articulate spokesman against secession. Until the final critical months before the South's secession from the Union, the possibility of a free and independent South appealed for the most part only to romantics and extremists— those who felt the greatest need to make the myth of the Cavalier South a reality.

Acceptance of the stereotypes of Cavalier and Yankee, and the haste with which these stereotypes encouraged movement toward conflict, gathered momentum when the legendary John Brown accelerated his private war against slavery in the summer of 1859. Born in Torrington, Connecticut, in 1800, Brown grew to be the North's most famous fire-eater. Driven by a crusading zeal to free the slaves, which was as militant as either Yancey's or Ruffin's zeal to keep them down on the plantation, Brown was personally active in a bloody local war over the slavery question in Kansas and responsible for what one foreign observer at the time called that "foolish affair at a place called Harper's Ferry." It was this second field of battle, of course, that assured John Brown a secure place in history.

Seeking to capture the U.S. arsenal at Harper's Ferry, where the river Shenandoah meets the Potomac, Brown nurtured the illusion that his bold stroke would be but the first stage in a great adventure which would even-

tually liberate the slaves of the southern states. Fancying himself a white Moses to the black, John Brown did not doubt that God was on his side. Brown's raid, however, was something less than a total success. With an assault force of twenty-one men (sixteen white and five black), Brown tasted almost immediate defeat, in the process losing ten men, including two sons. Even if this first battle of his private campaign against slavery had succeeded, only John Brown himself seemed quite able to understand how such a petty triumph could possibly lead to the destruction of the South's peculiar institution.

Historians would long ago have dismissed the Brown fiasco as but a minor footnote to the history of the pre-Civil War period were it not for the fact that the myth and legend which began to build almost immediately upon his capture had a devastating impact on the psychology of the nation and particularly on the South. The Brown affair, though of little practical significance in itself, quickly unleashed a flood of emotion in the country. The episode achieved its highest symbolic level, however, only after Brown's execution by hanging—one month and six days after the attack had occurred. Though he seems to have been given a scrupulously fair trial at the direction of Governor John Wise of Virginia on charges of conspiracy, murder, and treason, antislavery men saw to it that he received a martyr's halo and a hero's reputation. Even before his execution, the northern intellectual Henry David Thoreau declared that Brown had "a spark of divinity in him" and compared his noble deeds with those of Jesus Christ. Other writers and antislavery activists joined the growing chorus glorifying Brown—for Theodore Parker he was "not only a martyr . . . but also a SAINT," and Louisa May Alcott saw his gallows as "a stepping-stone to heaven." With such a glowing send-off the soul of John Brown could do little else but go marching on.

For Southerners, as one might suspect, the reaction to John Brown and Harper's Ferry was not nearly so positive. A crisis psychology surged through the cotton kingdom convincing multitudes that the Yankee North was infected with a bloody abolitionist spirit and that their suspicions of northern intentions were well founded. Southerners could now conveniently see the North as an army of John Browns plotting to strike a fatal blow against the South. Indeed the crisis had the effect of confirming the longstanding arguments of southern fire-eaters that the entire Yankee North was a hothouse of "John Brownism." Southern zealots such as Yancey and Ruffin were secretly pleased by Brown's theatrics which had accomplished more for their cause than they ever could have themselves. Even though Abraham Lincoln went on record stating that he could not "excuse violence, bloodshed, and treason," and even though Brown's activities were judged to be "insane" by a majority of Northerners, the South would not be convinced that he was anything other than a typical Yankee who through his actions spoke for the North. Most important, the John Brown affair heated emotions to the point where the stereotypes of Cavalier and Yankee began to pass for reality on the national stage. All that would now be needed to take the South out of the Union was the election of the "Black Republican" Abraham Lincoln as president of the United States in 1860. For in the mythical atmosphere which pervaded the country after 1859 "Republicans were all John Browns to the Southerners and slaveholders were all Simon Legrees to the Northerners."[28]

There is little doubt that this paranoid mentality took hold of Edmund Ruffin. He attended Brown's execution dressed in the uniform of a Virginia Military Institute cadet even though by this time he was sixty-three years of age. It was symbolic also that the institute's contingent should have been under the command of a man who up to this time had been known only as a professor of mathematics at the school, but who would shortly play a major role in the military affairs of the Civil War—Thomas "Stonewall" Jackson. But perhaps most interesting of all, the man who had been dispatched to suppress the rebellion in the first place was one whose career would also come to be haunted by myth and legend. His name was Robert E. Lee.

SECTION IV: JEFFERSON DAVIS, ROBERT E. LEE, AND THE CONFEDERATE MYTH

At the eve of the Civil War the flamboyant Southern politician Robert Toombs of Georgia advised the citizens of his state to take a stand for secession by declaring: "We are the gentlemen of this country." This appeal to the legendary Cavalier background of the South was primarily a call to something which bore only a remote resemblance to reality. The majority of Southern gentlemen were threadbare aristocrats at best. What the South seemed to need most by the early months of 1861 was a heroic leader who would symbolize the imaginary Cavalier ideal, stand in the front rank of the "crusade of the planters," and save the Old South from extinction.

When South Carolina seceded on December 20, 1860, no one had yet emerged as a clear-cut leader of the Southern cause. Indeed, despite the fact that the states of Georgia, Florida, Alabama, Mississippi, Louisiana, and Texas rather quickly followed South Carolina's lead, sentiment in favor of union—or at least the thought that the Southern states ought to move very cautiously in making their political decisions—remained quite strong. Since the South was neither a nation of slaveholders nor a region completely commited to states' rights, the cause of the South was at this point not as obvious as later generations accustomed to legend assume. Southern fire-eaters such as William Yancey and Robert Barnwell Rhett did not emerge as wartime leaders simply because of their extremist view that the Yankee North was out to destroy slavery and bring an end to the states' right to determine their own destinies. This was not held by the majority of Southerners. Most white Southerners were reluctant rebels who, in the end, felt much more comfortable selecting Jefferson Davis of Mississippi as their standard-bearer.

Jefferson Davis

Born in Todd County, Kentucky, in 1808, Jefferson Davis was a somewhat unlikely candidate either to lead a revolutionary movement or eventually to become a mythical hero. A graduate of West Point, he had served as an army officer in the Wisconsin Territory and in the Black Hawk War in 1832. Shortly thereafter he resigned his commission, having decided to retire to the life of a Southern planter. Over a decade later, in 1845, he stepped into the national limelight with his election to Congress from Mississippi. Davis soon resigned his congressional seat, however, to command the Mississippi Rifles during the Mexican War. Due to the somewhat legendary military reputation gained there, he returned to Washington after the war as a U.S. senator. Seemingly more interested in the affairs of his state than in national political intrigues, he ran for the governorship of Mississippi in 1851 but lost to his Unionist opponent Henry S. Foote by a margin of slightly over one thousand votes. He then returned to his Mississippi plantation, only to be called to national service again as secretary of war under President Franklin Pierce (1853-1857). In 1857 Davis was again serving the people of Mississippi as their U.S. senator, a position he held until twelve days after Mississippi seceded from the Union.

Though there is no doubt that Jefferson Davis' basic sympathies were with the ideas of a racially based class system and states' rights, he was neither a Southern radical nor a staunch secessionist. In fact, Davis was elected president of the Confederate States of America precisely because he was a moderate who might be successful in taking the newly organized Southern Confederacy gracefully out of the Union. Few men even in the Deep South thought at the time that the Northern states would resist the secessionist movement, much less go to war in the interest of preserving the federal Union. Thus, contrary to popular belief, Jefferson Davis was not at all blindly dedicated to the Southern cause, preferring to die rather than live a life of dishonor within the Union. As head of the Confederate government, Davis was not the supreme example of a Southern statesman fiercely loyal to states' rights and the racial integrity of the Southland.

The mythical image of Davis as a narrow-minded and bigoted Confederate defending the sacred soil of the South with grim zeal, then, simply does not square with the historical facts. History and legend have treated Davis badly primarily because both have been largely written by Northerners and because he did not share their nationalistic enthusiasms.

Davis proudly served as the only Confederate president, but it would be a major distortion to see him as a prolonged conspirator against the United States. As a staunch partisan defender of Davis has contended:

the facts show that as late as 1860 he, as a United States senator, was advocating appropriations for the army he was to fight in less than a year. A proper sympathy for the sectional values would perhaps lead to a condemnation of Davis because he did not become a conspirator against the Union soon enough. Unlike Caesar or Hitler, Davis was not one of the great revolutionaries of history; he was too honorable for that. Unlike William L. Yancey and R. Barnwell Rhett, he was slow in understanding that the North was in a revolutionary conspiracy against the Constitution as he interpreted it and could be answered effectively only by counterrevolution.[29]

As a man of aristocratic bearing and appearance, Jefferson Davis seemed to be a living example of the South's Cavalier sentimentalism, but he was scarcely the blind Southern patriot of legend. He was thus a poor candidate for hero worshippers of the South who have tried to make of him an image of the Confederacy's "Lost Cause." In one of his last public appearances, in fact, Davis advised his fellow Southerners to "let the past bury its dead, its hopes, and its aspirations . . . to lay aside all rancor, all bitter sectional feeling, and to take your places in the ranks of those who will bring about a reunited country." It was later generations who, as they twisted history by accepting the illusion that the Confederate South was solidly in favor of secession and the preservation of racial purity, have come to see Jefferson Davis personifying these regional sentiments.

Jefferson Davis was no hero to his contemporaries, and considering the tendency among nations to mythologize its founders, Jefferson Davis never enjoyed the abiding legendary respect which one might have predicted. When the War for Southern Independence ended it was already clear that Davis would never be "first in the hearts of his countrymen" as Washington had been in an earlier generation. Certainly, the fact that the South lost the Civil War had a good deal to do with this, for Southerners, like Northerners, apparently find winners easier to revere than losers. Moreover, he seems never to have actively cultivated a personal legend. Apparently sensitive to his role as a compromise president, Davis was almost always strangely detached from his constituents. He was neither a man of the people in the manner of an Andrew Jackson nor a strong enough advocate for the minority group of states' rights fire-eaters, such as Robert Toombs, who referred to him as "that scoundrel Jeff Davis." The Southern soldier also would not emerge after the war as a major spokesman for Davis' canonization, for he knew the Confederate president only as an armchair general who suffered the delusion of fancying himself a great military genius. Davis' conduct as the South's chief executive, particularly his bill to draft young men into the Confederate army, likewise insured that his popularity would not likely grow to mythical proportions once the war was over. The fact that at the close of the war he and his cabinet fled southward from Richmond when faced with the impending Yankee victory did not help his reputation, either. When captured near Irwinville, Georgia, Davis was disguised as a woman. Indeed, as the historian Dixon Wecter has pointedly suggested, "Nothing is so little heroic as transvestism."[30]

Despite these many handicaps, Jefferson Davis remains at least a semimythical figure if only by virtue of his unique role as the Confederacy's only president. A man chosen to construct a political state largely without an existing institutional framework to build on, and forced to defend his new nation against an enemy with ten times the industrial strength and four times the population, it is surprising that Davis was able to accomplish what he did. While his heroic stature is obviously somewhat less than other of America's legendary historical figures, the memory of Davis does live on. The state of Florida, for example, has continued to pay him special respects by having declared his birthday—June 3—a state holiday. In addition, an impressive monument dedicated to his "fortitude" in the face of "imprisonment and suffering" stands today in Richmond, Virginia. Even though there are now few who would agree with the assessment of Davis offered in 1864 by the South's most influential newspaper, De Bow's Review—that the leader of the Confederacy was as "brave as Ajax and as wise as Ulysses"—Jefferson Davis still ranks as a mythical hero whose reputation has suffered both cheap criticism and unadulterated praise.

Robert E. Lee

Since Jefferson Davis offered somewhat limited appeal as a heroic figure, the South, and ultimately the nation, eventually chose Robert E. Lee. "Commentators on Lee seem to have depicted every phase of his life," says one historian, "from his fourteenth century ancestors to the pet hen kept at his field headquarters."[31] Precisely because of this lavish attention, it is very difficult to separate the myth from the reality of Lee's personality and career. The outlines seem clear enough, but he remains a somewhat mystical and elusive historical figure nonetheless. There seems to be no negative side, as with Davis, to Lee's knightly reputation. Almost all agree that he was the unpretentious Cavalier gentleman gone to war. The image he projects is of the Confederate of commanding dignity—just, courageous, and self-controlled.

An illustrious lineage had much to do with the transition of Robert E. Lee from man to legend. Though it is doubtful that Lee's lineage can be traced to the crusaders and plumed knights of the Middle Ages (as some have claimed), he rose to a fame inspired by the glamour and pride which the name Lee had already come to symbolize. The general's father, "Light Horse Harry" Lee of Revolutionary War fame, was by all accounts a colorful and dashing soldier in his own right whose close associations with George Washington did nothing to detract from his, and subsequently his son's, notable prestige. And anything the younger Lee might have lacked in pedigree was amply provided by his marriage to the great-granddaughter of Martha Washington—Mary Anne Randolph Custis.

Certainly, Lee's own qualities must not be slighted in assessing the worth of his mythical reputation, but given his associations with Washington, some of the luster of that legendary figure rubbed off on the future hero of the Southern cause. Indeed, for Lee personally, George Washington was his major inspiration—legend and all. "To Lee," one historian of the Confederate general's career has concluded, "he [Washington] was as real as an ideal can ever be."[32] Like his historical ideal, Lee's commitment to duty was very real; but his many years in residence at Arlington, Virginia—a Washington shrine surpassed

General Robert E. Lee
National Archives

only by the venerable Mount Vernon—must have allowed the nation more easily to think that Lee was the obvious heir to Washington's personal glory. In short, Washington's mythology proved to be contagious. The public's association of Lee with Washington was

further assisted by his sincere attempts to make religion a crucial force in his everyday life, to say nothing of his legendary reputation for taking a keen interest in the religious well-being of his soldiers during military campaigns. For many, Lee's religious behavior bore a close resemblance to the religious emphasis that myth had long alleged for General Washington at Valley Forge. With his frequent display of inner quiet confidence, Lee could readily be accepted as the perfect Christian gentleman-soldier.

Given these circumstances, it is not surprising that the outlines of the legendary Lee should have been painted in by a man of the cloth. The Reverend J. William Jones, the so-called fighting parson of the Confederacy, was to Lee what Parson Weems had been to George Washington. Less than a decade after Lee's surrender at Appomattox Court House, the Reverend Jones published an adulatory biography of the Confederate hero entitled *Christ in the Camp; or, Religion in Lee's Army* (1874). In addition, as chaplain to the United Confederate Veterans for nineteen years, Jones enjoyed a captive audience as he broadcast the good tidings of Lee's Christian patriotism. And as if not satisfied with a Lee cult among the old Confederacy's elder citizens, Parson Jones sought to minister to the impressionable minds of youth by compiling a *School History of the United States* which became one of the more popular texts in the South following the war. Robert E. Lee's religious convictions were real enough, of course, but the parson's portraits had the effect of placing a halo over the head of one who was, after all, a mortal man.

Over and above Lee's ties with the Washington mystique and his elevation to sainthood by a pious clergyman, his mythical glory rests even more securely on his image as a military hero. Indeed, military leaders often assume a dazzling role in their nation's history and offer excellent raw material for mythmaking. The conquering Caesar, the crusading Richard the Lion-Hearted, and the swashbuckling Sir Francis Drake had all become legendary in earlier times; and Robert E. Lee was destined to be among America's major additions to this group. It can be argued that Lee's military achievements do in fact stand favorable comparison with such contemporary and later generals as U. S. Grant, "Black Jack"

Pershing, and George S. Patton. And Lee, it seems, graced the field of battle at a particularly opportune time. He was, in a sense, a soldier of the old school as well as a symbolic precursor of what was to come. Lee deftly maintained the chivalry of past military leaders while creatively commanding the Confederate army in line with developing modern tactics and strategies. Despite General Lee's legendary reputation as a military genius, however, there were some flaws in his military leadership. Military historians, for example, have seen fit to criticize Lee for never having developed an overall plan of Confederate strategy and for not being as aware as he perhaps should have been of the function of railroads in modern warfare. Also, contrary to myth, Lee displayed a basic flaw in his generalship by never developing an adequate staff. It is not entirely fair to fault Lee for this, however, for the major appointments and promotions of his supporting officers to high military positions was the prerogative of his commander-in-chief, Jefferson Davis. In spite of such criticism, historians have concluded that, on the whole, Lee deserves the military reputation he has gained. And the military defeat of the South and his service to a losing cause has not harmed his stature. Despite America's fascination with success, the nation's thirst for legend has allowed at least one of its heroes to be remembered for his graciousness in defeat.

Also, there was much about Lee's personal appearance which made it easier for an authentic hero image to develop. Even those who did not know him well saw him as the classic model of what one would expect a gentleman-soldier to look like. One British military officer, for example, with a trained eye for the symbolic value of looking the part of the professional soldier, thought Lee easily the most memorable fighting man of the Civil War era:

> General Lee is, almost without exception, the handsomest man of his age I ever saw [wrote Colonel A. S. L. Fremantle], . . . his manners are most courteous and full of dignity. He is a perfect gentleman in every respect. . . . He has none of the small vices, such as smoking, drinking,

chewing or swearing and his bitterest enemy never accused him of any of the greater ones.[33]

Though outshone in military style by the apparently reckless "Stonewall" Jackson, Lee was certainly not secretive, eccentric, and awkward, as Jackson most assuredly was. General Lee, as Jackson himself said, was a "fine-looking human creature" who inspired confidence and invited glowing admiration. His physical presence alone may have been basis enough for his magic appeal as one of American history's more memorable personalities.

Robert E. Lee was in many important respects a man of enviable achievement and true strength of character. The greatest of the Confederate generals, he was good enough in his own right not to need the forces of myth. As with most figures of legend, however, Lee became more of a hero after the fact than he had been during his active years of shaping the events of history. Indeed, as the War Between the States progressed, there were several Southern military figures who appeared more likely than Lee to emerge from the conflict with a greater claim to the affections of the South. At the time, Albert Sidney Johnston, P. T. G. Beauregard, Joseph E. Johnston, Jeb Stuart, and of course Thomas "Stonewall" Jackson, all seemed destined for lasting heroic fame. Jackson's death at the battle of Chancellorsville, however, and the bitter disputes after the war over questions of Confederate strategy and defeat concerning many of the other candidates for Southern sainthood, helped General Lee's supporters sweep the field.

The vitality of Robert E. Lee as the South's most enduring Confederate hero also owes much to a dedicated band of Lee admirers who gained control of the Southern Historical Society during the postwar period. While it might be an exaggeration to say that the society deliberately "managed" the South's history so as to portray Lee in an unblemished way after the war, it is nonetheless true that the group, dominated by Virginians, formed something very close to a fan club for the general. A Lee cult made up of relatives, former staff officers, and others dedicated to the preservation of his shining image, and having gained key positions within the society, sought to block the publication of any piece of writing in any way critical of their glorious warrior. Under the guidance of such men as Jubal Early, the society worked to sustain the illusion that Lee had never been defeated. The battles of Sharpsburg and Gettysburg, which Lee in fact technically lost, were explained away with interesting verbal gymnastics. In logic reminiscent of the modern Pentagon, it was argued that retirement from these battles was really "strategic withdrawals."

In succeeding years the romantic cult of Robert E. Lee spread to the point where he emerged as a semireligious figure—a "guardian angel," in the opinion of one historian. Some of his more enthusiastic biographers began to compare him to Jesus Christ, claiming to see some kind of magical comparison between Christ's agony in the Garden and Lee's decision to surrender. Others stressed Lee's Christlike qualities in overcoming the "three temptations" of fame, power, and material gain. Thus the image of Lee inevitably suffered from the exaggeration and distortion which befall most people of historical importance. Most unfortunately, Lee came to symbolize a dead past when he personally had staked his fame, his fortune, and his sacred honor on the future, as his postwar career as president of Washington College demonstrates. Within an already well-developed American tradition, the combined influence of history and myth molded Robert E. Lee into more than he ever was. He became what people wanted him to be. The forces which eventually brought him to this exalted status were varied, but most were a product of the recurrent human tendency to mythologize heroes. The time of troubles known to history as the American Civil War also ably assisted the process of Lee's, and the nation's, mythmaking.

STUDY QUESTIONS

1. Analyze and discuss the major historical deficiencies which have come to surround what historians now call the plantation legend. You might wish to organize your answer around a discussion of:
   a. The plantation
   b. The cavalier
   c. The southern belle
   d. The overseer
   e. The happy darkey

2. Identify some of the major figures and forces which might be offered as evidence in support of the argument that the North has contributed heavily to the creation, acceptance, and perpetuation of southern mythology.

3. How did novels about plantation life, the political crisis, the rhetoric of fire-eaters, John Brown's raid, and Abraham Lincoln's election all work to reinforce the cultural stereotypes of Cavalier and Yankee?

4. What were the qualities of appearance, background, personal style, and leadership which brought Jefferson Davis and Robert E. Lee to their respective positions as heroes of the Confederate cause?

REFERENCES

1. Wilbur Cash, *The Mind of the South* (New York: Vintage Books, 1941), p. ix.
2. Robert W. Fogel and Stanley L. Engerman, *Time on the Cross: The Economics of American Negro Slavery* (Boston: Little, Brown and Co., 1974), pp. 200–201.
3. Ibid., p. 5.
4. Eugene D. Genovese, *In Red and Black: Marxian Explorations in Southern and Afro-American History* (New York: Vintage Books, 1972), p. 115.
5. Ibid., p. 116.
6. Richard C. Wade, "Slavery in the Southern Cities," in Allen Weinstein and Frank Otto Gatell, eds., *American Negro Slavery: A Modern Reader* (New York: Oxford University Press, 1973), p. 330.
7. Ibid., p. 332.
8. Gunnar Myrdal, *An American Dilemma: The Negro Problem and Modern Democracy* (New York: Harper & Row, Publishers, 1962), p. 1376.
9. Richard Hofstadter, "U. B. Phillips and the Plantation Legend," *The Journal of Negro History* 29 (April, 1944): 109.
10. Carl Degler, *Out of Our Past: The Forces That Shaped Modern America* (New York: Harper and Row, Publishers, 1970), p. 163.
11. Quoted in Samuel Eliot Morison, Henry Steele Commager, and William E. Leuchtenburg, *The Growth of the American Republic*, I (New York: Oxford University Press, 1969), p. 470.

12. Clement Eaton, *A History of the Old South: The Emergence of a Reluctant Nation* (New York: Macmillan Publishing Co., 1975), p. 390.
13. Margaret Mitchell, *Gone with the Wind* (New York: Avon, 1973), p. 5.
14. William K. Scarborough, *The Overseer: Plantation Management in the Old South* (Baton Rouge: Louisiana State University Press, 1966), p. 195.
15. Ibid., p. 196.
16. Henry Steele Commager, "The Search for a Usable Past," in *American Heritage* (February, 1965): 96.
17. Harvey Einbinder, *The Myth of the Britannica* (New York: Grove Press, 1964), p. 362.
18. Francis Pendelton Gaines, *The Southern Plantation: A Study in the Development and Accuracy of a Tradition* (New York: Columbia University Press, 1924), p. 30.
19. Ibid., pp. 2-3.
20. William R. Taylor, *Cavalier and Yankee: The Old South and American National Character* (Garden City, N. Y.: Doubleday & Co., 1963), p. 73.
21. Henry James, *The Bostonians* (New York: The Modern Library, 1956), p. 343.
22. Paul M. Gaston, *The New South Creed: A Study in Southern Mythmaking* (New York: Alfred H. Knopf, 1970), pp. 170, 179.
23. William Faulkner, *Intruder in the Dust* (New York: The Modern Library, 1948), p. 153.
24. David M. Potter, "The Enigma of the South," *The Yale Review*, 1961, p. 142.
25. T. Harry Williams, "Romance and Realism in Southern Politics," in Patrick Gerster and Nicholas Cords, eds., *Myth and Southern History* (Chicago: Rand McNally, 1974), p. 110.
26. Taylor, *Cavalier and Yankee*, p. 133.
27. Ibid., p. 318.
28. C. Vann Woodward, "John Brown's Private War," in C. Vann Woodward, ed., *The Burden of Southern History* (New York: Random House, 1960) pp. 58-59.
29. Francis Butler Simkins, "Tolerating the South's Past," in Gerster and Cords, *Myth*, p. 312.
30. Dixon Wecter, *The Hero in America: A Chronicle of Hero-Worship* (Ann Arbor: The University of Michigan Press, 1966), p. 295.
31. Thomas L. Connelly, "The Image and the General: Robert E. Lee in American Historiography," *Civil War History* 19 (March, 1973): 50.
32. Wecter, *The Hero*, p. 276.
33. Quoted in ibid., p. 282.

SOURCES FOR FURTHER STUDY

THE PLANTATION LEGEND

EATON, CLEMENT. *History of the Old South: The Emergence of a Reluctant Nation*. New York: Macmillan Publishing Co., 1975.

ELKINS, STANLEY. *Slavery: A Problem in American Institutional and Intellectual Life*. Chicago: University of Chicago Press, 1959.

FOGEL, ROBERT W., AND ENGERMAN, STANLEY L. *Time on the Cross: The Economics of American Negro Slavery*. Boston: Little, Brown and Co., 1974.

SCARBOROUGH, WILLIAM K. *The Overseer: Plantation Management in the Old South*. Baton Rouge: Louisiana State University Press, 1966.

SCOTT, ANNE FIROR. *The Southern Lady: From Pedestal to Politics*. Chicago: University of Chicago Press, 1970.

THE NORTHERN ORIGINS OF SOUTHERN MYTHOLOGY

COMMAGER, HENRY STEELE. "The Search for a Usable Past," *American Heritage Magazine*, February, 1965.

GAINES, FRANCIS PENDLETON. *The Southern Plantation: A Study in the Development and Accuracy of a Tradition*. New York: Columbia University Press, 1924.

TAYLOR, WILLIAM R. *Cavalier and Yankee: The Old South and American National Character*. New York: Doubleday and Company, 1963.

WOODWARD, C. VANN. "A Southern Critique for the Gilded Age." In C. Vann Woodward, ed., *The Burden of Southern History*. New York: Random House, 1960.

———. "The Antislavery Myth," *The American Scholar*, Spring, 1962.

CAVALIER AND YANKEE/SYNTHETIC STEREOTYPES

DAVIS, MICHAEL. *The Image of Lincoln in the South*. Knoxville: The University of Tennessee Press, 1971.

DEGLER, CARL. "There Was Another South," *American Heritage*, August, 1960.

TAYLOR, WILLIAM R. *Cavalier and Yankee: The Old South and American National Character*. New York: Doubleday and Co., 1963.

WHITRIDGE, ARNOLD. "The John Brown Legend," *History Today*, April, 1957.

WOODWARD, C. VANN. "John Brown's Private War." In C. Vann Woodward, ed., *The Burden of Southern History*. New York: Random House, 1960.

JEFFERSON DAVIS, ROBERT E. LEE, AND THE CONFEDERATE MYTH

CONNELLY, THOMAS L. "The Image and the General: Robert E. Lee in American Historiography," *Civil War History*, March, 1973.

FISHWICK, MARSHALL. "Robert E. Lee: The Guardian Angel Myth," *Saturday Review*, March, 1961.

OSTERWEIS, ROLLIN G. *The Myth of the Lost Cause, 1865-1900*. Hamden, Conn.: Archon Books, 1973.

VANDIVER, FRANK E. "The Confederate Myth," *Southwest Review*, Summer, 1961.

WECTER, DIXON. "Lee: The Aristocrat as Hero." In Dixon Wecter, *The Hero in America: A Chronicle of Hero-Worship*. Ann Arbor: The University of Michigan Press, 1966.

6 Myths of the Civil War and Reconstruction

PREVIEW

Causes of the Civil War: Myths and Realities

Even today, the Civil War remains central to America's historical experience, the greatest single event in the nation's history. And from that epic struggle emerged a gallery of heroic figures and memorable episodes—Lincoln and Lee, Shiloh and Gettysburg, and many others. The American novelist and poet Robert Penn Warren has suggested that the Civil War marks America's "Homeric Age." Not unlike the Trojan War of the Achaean age, the War Between the States has become not only the critical episode in the nation's history but an inexhaustible reservoir of myth and legend as well. In the words of Warren:

> From the first, Americans had a strong tendency to think of their land as the Galahad among nations, and the Civil War, with its happy marriage of victory and virtue, has converted this tendency into an article of faith nearly as sacrosanct as the Declaration of Independence.[1]

Such events of the past, laden with emotion, frequently take on sacred qualities. Because of this, the detachment and objectivity which the passage of time is supposed to bring to one's historical understanding produces the opposite effect. Since the experience of that conflict has continued to stimulate the emotions of Americans, it is not at all surprising that the entire era of the Civil War—its causes, its major events, its personalities, its results—has been an exceptionally fertile breeding ground for additions to the nation's mythology.

The importance of recognizing what people thought, and think today, holds particular significance to one's historical judgments concerning the Civil War. Thus, a proper view of the "Homeric Age" of America requires that one keep in mind the American inclination to overemphasize the heroic qualities of its history. A proper understanding of this era of civil conflict must yield much more than a

knowledge of the pageantry and legend of the martyred Lincoln and the Christlike Lee.

One can begin to place the entire period in its proper historical perspective by noting the complex set of circumstances which caused the war. Perceived differences between North and South had multiplied to the point where irrational fears, sectional myths, and romantic dreams were combining with extraordinary, intense emotion. Southerners were attempting to act out their visions of an aristocratic society, while Northerners were going through both mental and political gymnastics in trying to sort out their attitudes toward the role of blacks in American white society. In such an emotional atmosphere a great deal of distortion and misunderstanding necessarily resulted. The decades preceding the Civil War, in short, were psychologically ripe for the development of both regional and national mythology. Thus, as historians have attempted to identify and weigh the causes of the war within the context of its mythical environment, some, reflecting on the emotionalism surrounding the event, have created legends, or at least exaggerations, of their own, thus clouding our understanding of why the war happened.

Sectional patriots monopolized early discussions among historians on the causes of the Civil War. They spoke in a biased way as scholarly defenders of either the North or the South. Southern writers labeled Northern aggression *the* cause of the war. Northern writers in turn claimed that their section was—in Robert Penn Warren's phrase—the "Treasury of Virtue." They insisted that the North had been forced to fight the war because of the illegal secession of the Southern states, and that those states seceded because Southerners were unwilling to share in the noble sympathy which Northerners felt toward the Union and the black slave. Both views, however, demonstrated a decided tendency to idealize figures and events.

The gradual cooling of the emotions which the war had created allowed historians in some ways to separate fact from fiction. But, as is frequently the case, their views reflected the period within which they wrote. A generation of writers around the turn of the century, for example, concluded that neither section of the country was wholly to blame for the war. This was an important historical insight, but it also reflected the spirit of regional harmony which had taken hold of the nation at the time, owing in part to American expansion and the Spanish-American War. Later, many historians endorsed an economic explanation as the key to the war. These writers, too, were influenced by their times.

Concluding that economic factors were the "real" causes of sectional differences, such historians as Charles A. Beard overemphasized the business versus agriculture theme of their own age, the 1920s. Though Beard was later to de-emphasize the "economics-explains-everything" approach to the Civil War, he had reinforced a point of view which many Americans still accept as the ultimate answer to the question of why the war happened. Economics did of course play a role in creating conditions for war, but the followers of a strictly economic explanation of the war's beginnings have seldom added the point—as future historians would—that the basic differences between the North's and the South's economic structures were as imaginary as real. When reading what historians have written about the causes of the Civil War, one must remember that history reflects the times in which it is composed and that even historians are not free from the influence of prejudice, distortion, and myth.

Historians since Beard have offered many different points of view on the causes of the Civil War—all by way of suggesting that the events were far more complex than tradition has usually suggested. Writers of history today have come to believe that no single force—except slavery perhaps—was at work in bringing about the clash of arms between North and South. Those who emphasize psychological factors in the coming of the war speak of sectional stereotypes and the detachment from reality which the political rhetoric of the time reflected. Some have labelled the politicians of the Civil War period as members of a "blundering generation." And even more recently historians have come to emphasize the critical role that the larger question of race adjustment, not just slavery, had in the development of an attitude which saw civil war as the only answer to the nation's difficulties. Each new generation has found a need to reexamine the meaning of the Civil War.

Collected Myths of the War Years

The war years themselves produced their share of national myths, as war experience always does. Particularly in the minds of later generations of Americans, to whom the years of the Civil War became a vanishing memory, the North-South conflict was a glorious and heroic age ripe with patriotic nationalism. That between 600,000 and 700,000 men were sacrificed in the prime of life seldom seems to cast a shadow over the glorification of what were truly tragic years. Instead of realistically recalling the hardships, anxieties, immorality, and atrocities which the war brought to both individuals and the nation, Americans are inclined to remember such myths as that perpetrated by the poet John Greenleaf Whittier in his sentimental celebration of Barbara Frietchie. This poem relates none of the war's violent impact on American life; instead it tells of the intense loyalty of a petticoat patriot to the Union cause. Though "bowed with her fourscore years and ten," Barbara Frietchie courageously shook her cane when Confederate General "Stonewall" Jackson passed through Frederick, Maryland, and proudly waved the "Flag of Freedom" when Union General Ambrose Burnside followed close behind. Even Whittier admitted that "the story was probably incorrect in some of its details," yet he persisted in contributing to the nation's legends concerning the war years with his romantic portrayal of "Dame Barbara" and the "rebel horde." The acceptance of this and other colorful improbabilities makes one wonder whether the American fixation with the Civil War reflects a proud regard for heritage or an abiding weakness for historical hearsay.

Americans' essentially romantic response to the Civil War has inhibited the formation of sound historical judgment in other ways as well; for example, with respect to the importance of the war in the development of the modern world. When viewed from a wider perspective, it can be seen that the American Civil War was an important benchmark in the development of liberalism and nationalism on the world stage. The war boosted the forces of liberalism by ending the evil institution of slavery in the United States. At the same time it contributed to the growth of national unity when similar movements were developing in

Italy and Germany. Further, many Americans, captivated by legends of the war's importance to union, have spoken of its contributions to the strength of democracy, forgetting that the Confederate States of America can be seen as a democracy destroyed. Others have emphasized the conflict's role in stimulating a spirit of national union, again failing to remember that the loyalty of Southerners to the Confederacy was every bit as nationalistic as that of the Yankees to the Union. In some ways, then, Americans have taken a much too narrow and limited view of the Civil War.

Abraham Lincoln and His Mythology

The legend, or myth, of Lincoln has had wide impact beyond American shores. Indeed, the memory of Lincoln has been a source of inspiration even for Europeans. To appreciate the Great Democrat's nearly universal mythical appeal, one need only visit his statue in Parliament Square in London or reflect on the words of Russian novelist Leo Tolstoy: "the greatness of Napoleon, Caesar, or Washington is moonlight by the sun of Lincoln." Historians, perpetrators of folklore, and the romantic imagination of mythologizers have all contributed to Lincoln's timeless quality. Not even the lives of those he touched have escaped the enveloping mist of Lincoln mythology.

Historical shrines in honor of Lincoln dot the American landscape—his birthplace at Hodgenville, Kentucky, the prairie towns of New Salem and Springfield, Illinois, and the Lincoln Memorial in the nation's capital. The very site of the cabin where Abraham Lincoln was born, for example, contributed to his legendary fame. In the years following Lincoln's death, fifteen different locations were touted as the sacred natal spot. And the states of Kentucky, North Carolina, and Tennessee put forth claims that he was a native son. But even though the debate among the states and localities subsided long ago—people now agree on a site three miles south of Hodgen's Mill, in what is now Larue County, Kentucky— Lincoln has not been freed from the mythmakers. Tourists to this day are pleased to discover in Hodgenville a Greek temple set in the wilderness. And engraved in its massive stone features one finds misinformation regarding the date of Lincoln's mother's birth,

the names of her parents, the date of her marriage to Thomas Lincoln, and the time of their move from Kentucky to the Indiana frontier. This casual attitude toward chronology compounds the difficulty of separating truth from fiction with respect to Lincoln.

Americans tend to have a special fondness for the mothers of heroes. But in the case of Nancy Hanks, Lincoln's mother, imagination has gotten a bit out of control. Though she died when Lincoln was but nine years of age, it is always emphasized that this "angel mother" was the primary source of her son's later greatness. To some robust romantics she emerges as a "Madonna of the Backwoods" whose virtuous qualities were unmistakable. It was she, it has been said, who inspired her son with gracious humility and who dutifully taught him to read and write. Actually, modern scholarship has established the fact that she was absolutely illiterate. And the depth of her influence otherwise—given the rigors of the frontier and her premature death—have no doubt been greatly overemphasized.

Abraham Lincoln's father, Thomas Lincoln, has undergone recreation at the hands of mythmakers, though he has often been treated as though he were a liability to the Lincoln legend. Probably it was normal to wonder how so unimpressive a backwoodsman could possibly have fathered the savior of the nation, since he appeared to possess few outstanding qualities of character. Accordingly, at various times after the president's death, rumor insisted that a political notable such as John C. Calhoun or Henry Clay was in fact Abraham Lincoln's real father. Perhaps the most amusing example of the lengths to which mythologizers have gone in attempting to find greatness in Lincoln's background was the fanciful tale that Patrick Henry had sired Nancy Hanks' brilliant son. Since Henry died in 1799, some ten years before Lincoln's birth in 1809, this seems unlikely.

The striking parallel of Abraham Lincoln's career to the public life of Jesus Christ has also been instrumental in influencing his legend. A number of years after Lincoln's death, American statesman John Hay spoke for many of his fellow countrymen when he declared that Lincoln had been "the greatest character since Christ." In trying to explain the appeal of Lincoln's elaborate political mythology, historian Richard Hofstadter has pointed out that:

Here is a drama in which a great man shoulders the torment and moral burdens of a blundering and sinful people, suffers for them and redeems them with hallowed Christian virtues—"malice toward none and charity for all"—and is destroyed at the pitch of his success.[2]

Lincoln died on Good Friday (April 14) in 1865, and this, plus other events which seemed to reflect parallels between Lincoln's and Christ's life, made it possible for many to compare him favorably to Christ. The sculptor of the Mt. Rushmore Memorial, Gutzon Borglum, was one of those who claimed to find great significance in the Lincoln-Christ relationship. "Lincoln's face," the creator of one of the nation's greatest national shrines is quoted as saying, "is infinitely nearer an expression of our Christ-character than all the conventional pictures of the Son of God." And if Lincoln was the American Christ figure, it was only logical that his assassin, John Wilkes Booth, would be seen as the American Judas. One biographer attempted to assist the mythology surrounding Booth's infamy by "proving" that he had given early signs of a traitorous spirit—at the age of ten he had sassed his mother.

If Lincoln was to be the American Christ, then, after his death, it was necessary to "convert" him to the Christian faith. Even though Honest Abe seemed to live the Christian virtues, he had seldom entered a Christian house of worship. Still, Quakers, Methodists, and Spiritualists, along with Freemasons, all submitted "records" which disclosed Lincoln's secret membership in their groups. Some Catholics believed that he had secretly been baptized by Jesuit missionaries on the frontier. The editor of the Springfield *Illinois State Register*, rejecting all previous claims, offered his own: " 'We are prepared to prove by indisputable evidence that he was a Mormon, and the boon companion of Joe Smith'."[3] And so it went. With mythmaking running full steam, Lincoln himself would eventually emerge as an American religion.

The Legends of Reconstruction

With Lincoln dead and the memory of the Civil War still fresh in their minds, Southerners and Northerners alike began the difficult task of reshaping the social and political affairs of the nation. The desire to "bind up the nation's wounds," and to redirect the energy of the war years into reconstructive channels, became a major concern of post-Civil War America. Indeed, the war had settled many issues, but had left even more unanswered. Given the difficult task and the emotions involved, it is understandable that this period of "reconstruction" should produce its share of myth and legend.

Today many Americans still see the postwar era as one of Southern corruption and graft, military despotism, black political control, and the subordination of Southern whites. As a consequence of the fresh attention given Reconstruction by historians in recent years, however, all of these conclusions have been qualified. For example, corruption can be seen as a national rather than simply a Southern phenomenon. Military rule in the South after the war was surprisingly benevolent under the circumstances. Most white Southerners were not in fact removed from positions of influence. Newly freed blacks did not carry out a wholesale takeover of the political system. Yet it is the first set of views—the major myths of Reconstruction—which Southerners, and later a good many Americans, have accepted as truth. Southerners, in search of comforting explanations, most desperately wanted to believe the myths. They fit well with Southerners' belief that the glory of the Old South was now "gone with the wind" and that with the Civil War chivalry had, in the words of Margaret Mitchell, "taken its final bow."

Many Southerners at the time of Reconstruction refused to face reality. The vision of a significant number remained firmly fixed on the past, influenced by the hypnotic spell still cast by the Old South of their dreams. For these people, the compulsion to mythologize proved overwhelming. They enshrined the cavalier in Southern memory, romantically recalled their "Lost Cause," and glamorized the "Knights" of the Confederacy. While the Civil War had saved the Union it had at the same time created a sense of unity among Southerners which caused many of them to resolve to maintain the past by keeping the black "in his place." This attitude gave rise to a number of groups, the most successful being the Ku Klux Klan. The Klan started in 1866 in Pulaski, Tennessee, not—as myth would have it—to organize Southern protests against blacks, carpetbaggers, and scalawags, but for the members' purpose of "masquerading before their girl friends, their mothers, and each other."[4] There were many other organizations similar to the Klan—the Knights of the White Camellia in Louisiana, the Red Shirts in South Carolina, and the White Line in Mississippi, for example, but none enjoyed the long-term success of the Klan whose members soon began to be referred to as the "ghosts of the Confederate dead." By surrounding their organization with the symbols of both romantic and folk myth drawn from Germany and Scotland, and boasting of Grand Wizards, Grand Dragons, Grand Titans, and cavalcades of hooded horsemen, many "true sons of Dixie" fashioned an invisible empire whose roots were deeply buried in the soil of mythology. Later generations, indoctrinated with the legendary belief that the happy darkey was a superstitious creature, invented the theory that the Klan's effectiveness was due to the ghostliness of the night riders. And the mythology surrounding the magic letters KKK continues to this day to be vivid in the minds of many.

The Reconstruction period also created a "New South" legend. Though some historians now question the idea that the Civil War greatly stimulated national economic expansion, a great many Southerners after the civil conflict became devout believers in a mythical "New South Creed." The creed was that Dixie was escaping its background of frustration and defeat and was on the verge of economic fulfillment. Southerners, it seemed, could now participate in the American Dream of upward economic mobility. But though such Southern prophets as Henry Grady, editor of the *Atlanta Constitution*, envisioned a bright future for the South based on manufacturing and industry, his dream proved to be only that. The situation is improved today, but bleak economic realities for a long time never allowed Southerners to fulfill their wish to become both the home of heroes *and* the land of plenty.

Neither did the Reconstruction period fundamentally alter the legacy of hatred and distrust between blacks and whites which spokesmen for the "New South" had also predicted would pass away. Instead, the era produced a kaleidoscope of stereotyped histori-

cal characters—villainous Union soldiers, vindictive congressmen, bungling blacks, conniving carpetbaggers, and traitorous scalawags—the equals to which any period in American history would be hard-pressed to create.

SECTION I. Causes of the Civil War: Myths and Realities

Humans find war endlessly fascinating. While warfare brings out the worst features of human nature, it also produces examples of heroism and self-sacrifice. And for Americans the Civil War, more than any other of the nation's conflicts, has drawn the greatest attention. The Civil War is *the* war as far as Americans are concerned and it seems to hold the key to the mysteries of the national experience. Why is this so? Because it was a conflict which pitted American against American. On the battlefields of Bull Run, Antietam, Vicksburg, and Chattanooga the future destiny of the nation was decided. The Civil War fundamentally tested both the American character and the strength of the nation's basic institutions. It sustained a national government and altered a developing national economy.

Having come to see that so much was at stake in the critical years from 1861 to 1865, both the American public and professional historians have never tired of studying, analyzing, and debating the meaning of the war. Books dealing with individual battles and the wartime exploits of such colorful individuals as Confederate General George Pickett and Union General John A. Logan roll from the presses each year. Magazines devoted to Civil War history continue to find popular appeal. Members of Civil War roundtables endlessly discuss the many engaging problems which the war offers both the trained professional and the history buff. Civil War battlefields still draw hundreds of thousands of vacationing Americans each year, many of whom have been said to feverishly purchase souvenirs inscribed "Made in Japan." The Civil War continues to have a deep effect both on the way that Americans behave and on their view of themselves as a people.

Yankee and Confederate Viewpoints

The process of myth development concerning the causes of the Civil War began shortly after the guns fell silent at Appomattox. And the first important expressions concerning causes were those written by men who thought they knew the situation well—they had either participated in the war directly or had solidly supported either the Union or the Confederate cause. But these were partisan points of view, and historical scholarship reinforced mythology. The Civil War seemed only to move from the battlefields to the pages of the history books. Professional historians in many cases became involved in a war of words as they allowed their regional loyalties to influence their histories.

Northern historians, reflecting what now appears to have been a political-geographical bias, were quick to label the recent hostilities "The War of the Rebellion." They seemed less interested in telling an unbiased story of the war years than in trying to pin war guilt on the South. Making their case on behalf of the Union, the North's most accomplished historians—Francis Parkman, George Bancroft, and John L. Motley—all concluded that the Southern states had illegally seceded and were thus solely responsible for the conflict. In a manner reminiscent of treatment later accorded Germany during and after the First World War, these Yankee historians lent their prestige to the arguments on the cause of the war which most Northerners already accepted; that is, the South had been the enemy of continuing union and democracy.

The belief that a Southern conspiracy to establish a "slave empire" had caused the war seems now to have been based more on emotion than on fact. One finds, for example, that the service of Francis Parkman's brother in the Union army and his detention for a time as a prisoner of war by Confederate forces may have had something to do with Parkman's prejudice against the South. In addition, the idea of the Union took on such a sacred quality after the Civil War that it proved easy for many Americans to believe that Southern activities against the Union had been close to sacrilegious. Thus, some Northern historians were responding more to what the war sym-

bolized than to what the evidence disclosed. They had a distinct picture of what the war should have meant to the nation before ever setting pen to paper. The pitched emotions of the war period were carried over into the histories. Historian Thomas Pressly has explained the psychology of these times particularly well:

> Just as the attack upon Pearl Harbor of December 7, 1941, served a later generation of Americans as a symbol of aggressive warfare, so did the Sumter episode serve the Unionists as a symbol of the belligerent confederacy in the very act of inaugurating unprovoked war . . . . In the wartime histories, as in the actuality of 1861, what gave meaning to Fort Sumter as symbol was the fact that the attack upon the fort was viewed as an assault upon the nation.[5]

The skirmish at Fort Sumter, which was the first military confrontation between the warring sections, was not in a strict sense of course an "assault upon the nation" at all. The point was, however, that the North elected to take it to be just that. Myth was doing its part to emphasize certain facts at the expense of others. Needless to say, the nation's historical understanding of what had caused the war was to this point imperfect at best.

Influenced by a curious blend of nationalism and sectionalism (nationalism and Northern sectionalism had come to mean essentially the same thing) Northern historians continued to produce prejudiced writing on the causes of the Civil War until well into the 1880s. The unshakeable conclusion that the secession of the Southern states was in reality rebellion and treason continued to be the key concept with which Unionist historians both began and ended their studies. The former Union General John A. Logan, for example, carried on the tradition of the North's historical bias against the South in his book *The Great Conspiracy* (1886), which held Dixie responsible for the war by having supported slavery and the destruction of the Union, and—as Logan said—the "un-American doctrine of Free Trade." Given the biased viewpoints of these so-called bloody-shirt interpretations of the Civil War, it is little wonder that one had to look long and far for a Northern history of the war and the preceding period which did not drip with anti-Southern emotion and which was not therefore crudely mythical.

Not to be outdone in mythmaking, Southern historians in the decades after the Civil War clearly viewed the political and military crisis as a "War Between the States." In the South from 1861 to the 1880s, Confederate views on what had caused the Civil War dominated historical writing. Southerners seemed both unwilling and unable to see it as anything other than the South's Lost Cause. Historians such as Richmond journalist Edward A. Pollard (during the immediate postwar years at least) told the tale of civil conflict with a rebel yell. Even the moderate former vice-president of the Confederacy, Alexander H. Stephens, in *A Constitutional View of the Late War Between the States* (1868–1870), wrote history with a distinctly Southern bias. Thus it appeared that what the South had lost in the political arena and on the battlefield could somehow be regained through the verdict of history. One finds, for example, that the formation of the Southern Historical Society in 1869 by such prominent Confederates as R. M. T. Hunter, Jubal A. Early, and Admiral Raphael Semmes was in the interest of "provid[ing] for the collection, preservation, and presentation to the world of materials which would vindicate Southern principles in the war."[6] To attempt to answer the charges directed against their region by Northern historians, some Southerners took the classic position of arguing that the secessionist movement had not been a revolution at all. It was neither treasonous nor illegal. Rather, what the South had attempted to accomplish in the war was to preserve the integrity of the original Constitution. By trampling on the rights of the states and by not allowing for the protection of the South's legitimate political and economic interests, according to this Southern position, the North had violated the spirit if not the letter of the political guidelines set down for the nation in the Constitution. The establishment of the Confederate States of America, the argument went, was not an attempt to destroy existing American institutions and traditions. On the contrary, the South had reluctantly found war necessary in order to save the American way of life from Yankee political and economic aggression. In this sense, the North and not the South was responsible for causing the War Between the States.

The Inevitable Conflict

In the last years of the nineteenth century and into the early years of the twentieth, the emphasis on what had caused the Civil War began to change. Historians came to the conclusion that earlier explanations were unsatisfactory or incomplete and had reflected biased opinions. The residue of hatred left from the war was eroding, and the times seemed to call for an era of greater friendship between the sections. The idea that the Republicans were the party of union, the Democrats that of "Southern treason," which had enjoyed favor right after the war, for example, gradually passed from the political scene. So completely were attitudes changing in fact that Democrat Grover Cleveland was elected to the presidency in 1884—the first from his party to achieve the office since James Buchanan in 1856. It had taken nearly thirty years for the emotions of the war to cool. The reunion of the sections seemed nearly complete when Cleveland followed his election with the appointment of an ex-Confederate as a key cabinet official—General Lucius Quintus Cincinnatus Lamar, C.S.A., secretary of the interior.

The warmer relations between North and South which developed during this later era helped foster a new conclusion regarding Civil War guilt and causes; neither section was to blame, though the existence of slavery had been the principal cause. Both sections were innocent because slavery was a factor over which neither the North nor the South had much control. Historians concluded that the peculiar institution—not mortal human beings—had made the war inevitable, for it would have been impossible for Southerners or Northerners to have successfully dealt with the irrepressible forces which history and circumstance had set in motion. Americans, the argument went, had simply been swallowed up in a tidal wave of historical determinism. "Destiny," rather than individual Yankees or Confederates, had moved the nation almost against its will to cruelty, violence, and mass destruction. Conveniently, questions of guilt, accountability, and responsibility could be set aside. An illusion of "blamelessness" carried the day.

Indeed, both the general public and professional historians found these new views on the Civil War thoroughly acceptable. Each of the seven volumes that historian James Ford Rhodes published between 1893 and 1906, whose general title was *History of the United States from the Compromise of 1850*, endorsed this point of view and the work was greeted with both popular and critical acclaim. As the nation's major historical spokesman for this new understanding of the Civil War's origins, Rhodes was perhaps the key figure in offering Americans what they had come to believe and wanted to hear. Rhodes, of course, reflected the spirit of his times, and with his and other academic assistance Americans accepted the fiction that the nation's Civil War could be explained as a case where people had been trapped by history. The myth prevailed that they had been innocent and therefore guiltless victims of history's irrepressible forces.

In the 1920s, a shift in emphasis occurred while historians continued to grapple with the problem of the "real" causes of the Civil War. Convinced, as earlier generations had been, that they were being completely impartial in their analysis, many now began to argue that the origins of the struggle between the Blue and the Gray could be explained in economic terms. This new "economic interpretation," set forth primarily by historian Charles Beard, became widely popular in its day as earlier views had been in theirs. Historians such as Beard could now explain the nation's past in terms of its economic development, having witnessed the great economic changes in America after Appomattox. America had moved from being a predominately rural and agricultural nation to one rapidly becoming urban and industrial. Publishing his views on the Civil War only two years before the beginning of the Great Depression of 1929, at the peak of 1920s "prosperity," it was logical that Beard would offer the explanation that the war had essentially been the capstone of a struggle between two conflicting economic systems—a capitalistic industrial North versus an aristocratic agricultural South. The

economic point of view was as deterministic as the Rhodes conclusion regarding slavery, and this interpretation was not to satisfy everyone for all time.

The Repressible Conflict

Judging from the avalanche of writing which historians have loosed since Charles Beard presented his economic interpretation, it is clear that historians' quest for the elusive reality of the war's true beginnings continues. Convinced that history told only from an economic point of view was something less than complete, many historians came to feel that a revision of all earlier points of view on the causes of the war was in order. Indeed, by the 1940s almost every earlier view was under challenge from a group called the "revisionists."

In particular, revisionist historians questioned the idea held by economic historians and others that the war had been unavoidable or inevitable. Led by James G. Randall of the University of Illinois and Avery Craven of the University of Chicago, they argued instead that the war really had been a "needless" conflict. Reflecting the strong antiwar feelings in America during the 1930s, both concluded that, in a sense, war had come precisely *because* it lacked any fundamental "causes." According to Craven, for example, not even the existence of slavery in the South had created enough of a difference between the sections to make the war necessary. The war resulted from the numerous images, stereotypes, and myths which each section had created about the other. The highly charged emotional atmosphere created by radical secessionists and belligerent abolitionists helped produce feelings and misunderstandings which were for the most part irrational and unrealistic. If one were forced to identify *the* cause of the Civil War, Craven concluded, the explanation lay in the irrational mythology extremists on both sides had manufactured. James Randall's conclusions on the Civil War were similar to Craven's in that he also believed that the crisis resulted from "artificial" and "unreal" issues.[7] His final emphasis was somewhat different from Craven's, however, in that he suggested that a "blundering generation" of politicians in union with a national psychology verging on the psychopathic were most responsible for the breakdown of what had been the United States.

Revisionism Revised

Predictably, the views of the revisionists have themselves been revised. Concerned that historians such as Craven and Randall had made too little of slavery as the institution and issue which had caused the Civil War, some historians have since come to argue the fundamental importance of the system of black bondage to the growth of hostile feelings between North and South. Whereas the revisionist historians had tended to focus their attention on the evil of war (writing as they did during the era of the 1930s and the Second World War), more recent historians, such as Arthur Schlesinger, Jr., in "The Causes of the Civil War: A Note on Historical Sentimentalism" (1949), have been inclined to emphasize the moral evils of slavery. Whereas earlier it seemed proper to condemn the nation for having allowed itself to degenerate into the immoral barbarism of war, historians now argued that the personal and economic exploitation of blacks was by far a greater corrupting influence on America. Questions of how the Civil War should have been avoided—which revisionists asked—completely miss the significant moral benefits which the war brought to the nation, according to this point of view. Only war could force the country to live up to its cherished ideals of human equality and freedom. Though war can seldom be condoned, in this instance it did have the effect of fulfilling America's faith. Despite such criticism, however, revisionism has had its positive effects in helping to clarify the nation's understanding of its Civil War. Revisionists did much to correct the errors, oversimplifications, and stereotypes created by earlier recorders of the historical record. In addition, they provided a solid platform upon which additional study into the causes of the Civil War could be built.

A final determination of the myth and the reality of the causes of the Civil War has, of course, still not been made. Each generation of historians must creatively select from the theories which previous scholars have offered, develop additional theories of their own, and attempt to move on to more complete and thorough explanations. The prejudiced views of early historians whose major efforts were essentially to justify the position of either the North or the South seem for the most part to have been rejected, but almost every other theory on the causes of the war appears to offer at least an element of truth. Beard's economic explanations of the war, for example, if viewed only by themselves offer at best an incomplete picture. It seems clear that humans are not driven to the point of war only by pocketbook considerations. Economic motives, however, do play a critical role in the affairs of nations. And even if it can be proven that the slave system of the South was as "capitalistic" as the industrial structure of the North—that the Yankee and the Cavalier were not distinct "types" economically—there is nonetheless much truth in the fact that the sections *believed* that they were different. In this way, most modern scholarship on the causes of the Civil War can accept the idea that both "the unrealities of passion" and "the failure of American leadership" were related in important ways to the myth that the North and the South had created conflicting cultures based on conflicting economies. Beard seemed to have fallen victim to the stereotypes of Cavalier and Yankee, yet the nation at large had also believed in them at the time of the Civil War and had at least to some degree based its conduct on a set of legendary beliefs similar to those with which Beard began his study.

In the final analysis, what historians have said about the causes of the Civil War vary widely. They have functioned as mythmakers in that they have too often offered far too simple explanations of a very complex era. Objectivity suffers and certain evidence is overlooked as historians read the predispositions and prejudices of their own generation into the past, and it is likely that similar charges will be lodged against scholars who today see slavery as the ultimate cause of the war—i.e., they reflect too much the civil rights consciousness of their age. All explanations of an event as historically important as the American Civil War are bound to be at least to some degree mythical. A total reconstruction of past reality is impossible, and it is equally impossible for a historian to divorce himself from his times. Keeping these caveats in mind it is understandable that, for the present generation at least, the significance of the Civil War lies not only with the political and economic problems created by slavery, but with the social problems of "race adjustment" as well. Thanks to the work of such historians as David Potter and Allan Nevins, one can see more clearly today than ever before that racial subordination of the black was the very root and essence of the American predicament of the mid-nineteenth century. Slavery, purely and simply, may not of itself have caused the Civil War, but slavery and the accompanying problem of the place of blacks in the affairs of the nation were the essential factors of American life upon which economic and political misunderstandings hinged. In attempting to explain these misunderstandings—both imagined and real—sometimes by overemphasis historians have created myths of their own. To emphasize one explanation of what caused the Civil War and to thereby exclude other explanations can only lead to the creation of myth. Understanding the many explanations offered by historians thus far would seem to offer the best hope of discriminating intelligently between myth and reality with respect to the coming of the Civil War.

SECTION II: COLLECTED MYTHS OF THE WAR YEARS

Reflecting on the American Civil War, General William Tecumseh Sherman was supposed to have said, "War is Hell." Yet it seems that few have truly taken his words to heart. War's pageantry and splendor, the fascination of its drama, have often resulted in the terrible features of war being ignored or quickly forgotten. The slaughter and destruction which all know to be the essence of warfare are buried as quickly as its casualties. And perhaps in no instance is this truer than with the classic confrontation between the Union and the Confederacy—the Blue and the Gray. The history of the Civil War is much too often slick and sweet. Indeed, a heavy layer of sugary Americana has come to coat the nation's understanding of the war years—particularly the death and tragedy which the conflict brought. Captivated by features of the war which exalt the spirit, commentators have tended to emphasize the pomp, circumstance,

and heroism with which nostalgia has enshrouded the events from 1861 to 1865.

"Patriotic Gore"

With the help of fading memories, Americans seem seldom to recall the despair, the butchery, and the poverty which were a major legacy of a time when Americans sought to kill their brothers. With an eye to what the literary critic Edmund Wilson has called "Patriotic Gore," historians as well as writers have been prone to picture the glorious panorama of military affairs and to see the entire spectacle as a "Glory Road." But even though there are facets of the war which were stirring and uplifting, the reality of the war for those who fought it was considerably less romantic. Unfortunately, the history of the war years has too often been told by those who somehow see the marching of troops to death on the battlefield, stately columns of black smoke, the flying of military banners, and the clash of arms as gallant and glamorous. It can be assumed that the typical fighting man—Billy Yank or Johnny Reb—would scarcely recognize his own experiences in the colorful histories written by contemporary and latter-day Pollyannas. With the history of the Civil War having been written in so many cases by those who have only seen the "rockets' red glare and bombs bursting in air," one begins to wonder whether at least this portion of American history has not been orchestrated by those to whom the world is always viewed through rose-colored glasses. Unable to see the carnage and agony of the war years in realistic terms, most Americans continue to participate in this patriotic sing-along.

While legend and myth has made it appear that the Civil War was an exercise in devotion and memorably romantic, its lustrous veneer must be stripped away for sound judgment to prevail. Historical integrity requires that the gore of the Civil War be considered as well as the patriotic hoopla. Setting aside for the moment the endless number of pictures, poems, novels, statues, and history books which celebrate the war as a heroic exercise in bravery and picturesque patriotism, one quickly is confronted with stark statistics which speak to the war's sober realities. The American Civil War was indeed one of the bloodiest in human history. Estimated fatality figures are a staggering 620,000 men. If that is true, the Civil War was not the greatest bloodbath in history to that point in time. The Taiping Rebellion which occurred in China about the same period (c. 1850–1864) was by far more gruesome, having taken the lives of some twenty million people. But even so, the raw statistics on those who died in America's great conflict only begin to tell the total tale of horror. For every Billy Yank or Johnny Reb who lost his life, many more suffered a lifetime of war-related injuries. Indeed, it is estimated that for every Civil War soldier who died in action two died of disease—usually pneumonia, typhoid, or dysentery. For an army to suffer fatal casualties of 25 percent in a major battle was not at all uncommon, and statistics for individual battles were in many cases even more staggering. At the battle of Gettysburg, for example, some regiments lost up to 80 percent of their fighting men. Percentages such as these of course owe much to individual instances of "valor" such as General Pickett's famous charge, which cost the lives of 3,000 men and left some 5,000 wounded.

It is understandable that Americans would have a decided preference for looking at the brighter rather than the darker side of the Civil War experience—people generally do the same regarding their own personal histories—but it simply leaves too much out of the historical equation. If one begins to examine the realities of the Civil War more honestly, not only do many obvious myths begin to fall by the wayside, but one can begin to replace the false and unimportant glories of the war with a greater sense of human and historical understanding. One then begins to discover reasons why the death toll, the suffering, and the agony of the war years were so very appalling. Indeed, unseasoned recruits may have been inclined to volunteer for military service secure in the belief that they were off on a road to high adventure. But the picnic atmosphere of the first days in camp—the new friends, the noble cause, the new life in white tents pitched in the countryside—soon gave way to the more sober details of military life.

Weaponry and Medical Care

The primary weapon used in the war was the .54 caliber Springfield rifle. Even though the

.54 Springfield was of the muzzle-loading type and could fire at best no more than two shots a minute, the weapon had an impressive "effective range" of 250 yards. Mass formation of regular troops was still the order of the day—at least in the early stages of the war—and many battles thus became exercises in mass homicide. Since one was not safe from the enemy unless more than one-half mile distant, and because of the use of trench warfare, frontal assaults were particularly hazardous. The Springfield rifle, though now a museum piece viewed by people coldly accustomed to the massive extermination capabilities of today's sophisticated weaponry, was for its time fiercely destructive of human life.

Concerning medical care, numerous victims of sickness, injury, and war wounds could not expect much assistance from the medical services which were crudely created to minister to their needs. As the hospital sketches of the poet Walt Whitman and the photographs of Matthew Brady (the Civil War's "historian with a camera") attest, medical *practice* was precisely that. Not the scientific craft it is today, medicine could offer precious little to sick, maimed, and dying men. As the historian Allan Nevins has explained:

> Armies the world over in 1860 were *worse* provided with medical and surgical facilities than in Napoleon's day. The United States, after its long peace, began the war with practically no medical service whatever. Surgical application of the ideas of Pasteur and Lister lay in the future. Almost every abdominal wound meant death. Any severe laceration of a limb entailed amputation, with a good chance of mortal gangrene or erysipelas.[8]

What medical service there was fell largely to the Sanitary Commission, a body which was both privately organized and supported. Since many men had enlisted without the benefit of medical examinations, and medical personnel such as stretcher bearers and hospital attendants were recruited—like cooks—from the less desirable element of those in the ranks, it was only logical that health care services, on the scale they were required, had but limited success at best. On the battlefield, it was not unusual for the wounded to lie for days and

Surgery in the Field
National Archives

often weeks without care of any kind. It was claimed not to be uncommon for a surgeon to whet his scalpel with a few quick strokes on the bottom of his shoe. Many who might have been saved died of hunger, thirst, shock, and exhaustion, wasting away in their own blood and excrement.

Southern Diplomacy

Much of the mythology concerning the glory of the war developed after the conflict ended. One Southern myth which developed during the war itself had to do with diplomacy, however.

In their eagerness to establish a political existence separate from the rest of the United States, leaders of the Confederate States of America seemed not to have given sufficient

thought to the international implications of their establishment of a new nation. Despite the eventual appointment by Jefferson Davis of an able secretary of state—an English-Jewish immigrant from the West Indies, Judah P. Benjamin—it early became evident that the wartime diplomacy of the Confederacy suffered from two distinct liabilities. One had to do with mythology of the South and the other with the South's failure to confront directly the realities of European politics. Skillful execution of a realistic Confederate foreign policy was crippled, for example, by the South's blind belief in its own invincibility. Southerners fell victim to the myth that any Confederate could lick ten Yankees. Having experienced some initial successes on the battlefield, for example, the first Battle of Bull

Run, which convinced them of the South's superior military abilities, Southern leadership failed to give top priority to realistic strategies needed to secure diplomatic recognition for the Confederacy from Europe's major nations. In turn, European powers saw no need to quickly commit themselves to the Southern cause either diplomatically or economically since the South itself seemed certain of its ability to handle the war effort on its own.

Because Confederate leaders were under the illusion that the South had the power to go it alone if it had to, the creation and pursuance of a well-conceived foreign policy simply was not given the attention it deserved. Instead, the South built a rather elaborate set of diplomatic myths which, as one historian has said, "reflected a strange combination of superficial assumptions and vague sentiments."[9] Specifically, the South assumed that the aristocratically controlled governments of Europe were sympathetically inclined to the "aristocratic" cavalier society in Dixie and therefore, without additional persuasion, would come forward with diplomatic recognition of the Confederacy as an independent nation. Aside from being an exaggerated view of the aristocracy's power in Europe, the South's attitude also implied that European states would gladly extend the foreign aid necessary for the new nation to survive, which was anything but a sure possibility. Even more erroneous, however, was the belief that the demand for raw cotton would influence attitudes in the capitals of Europe. The vast majority of Southern policymakers took it for granted that Europe's economic dependence upon raw cotton—"white gold" they called it—was enough in itself to assure friendly cooperation. Confederate leadership quickly concluded that in order to ensure the continued economic health of their textile industries, England and France, in particular, would do little else than follow their economic self-interest. King Cotton Diplomacy, as this theory and practice came to be called, expressed the South's confident belief that the modern world could not long survive without the continued exportation of Southern cotton to international markets. Time would quickly show, however, that these assumptions were to prove only partially true. While Southerners liked to delude themselves into thinking that Europe's social and economic attachments to the Confederacy guaranteed foreign assistance

to their cause, there were many additional factors which Europeans had to consider in trying to decide whether to provide support to the new Confederate nation.

Up to a point, close ties and dependencies had been established between the American South and the nations of Europe on the basis of the cotton trade. Statistics indicate that about four million Englishmen and one million Frenchmen held jobs dependent upon the importation of Southern cotton. Confederate leaders had calculated correctly; cotton was a keystone of the European economy. However, despite the wishful thinking of Southerners and a consistent exchange of diplomatic pleasantries which lulled Confederates into a false sense of security, no European nation ever went further than to grant recognition of the South's state of belligerency with the North.

The reasons for the failure of King Cotton Diplomacy are rather easily explained. For one thing, the English in particular enjoyed an excess supply of cotton. The bumper crop of 1859 was already in British hands, thus minimizing the economic-diplomatic leverage which the South was able to exert. The English Board of Trade reported in June, 1861, that its stock of cotton bales stood at 1,105,780—a surplus of some 450,000 bales over projected use. In addition, it was possible for European nations to supplement their cotton supplies with shipments from India, Algeria, and Russia. With such reserves the British could afford to move cautiously on the question of support for the Confederate States of America. And they did.

Up to the very end of the war the illusion persisted in the South that European recognition, intervention, or both, was on the immediate horizon. Vague sentiments became rumors which told of England engaging Union forces "on other fronts" and Louis Napoleon of France having "landed a large Army on the Texas Coast" so as to liberate the South from the Yankee invaders. But Southern hopes never materialized.

Southerners failed to realize another thing: a permanent division of America into North and South might damage the delicate balance of world power which Europeans had been working diligently to maintain ever since the system had been devised in the wake of Napoleon. Both Russia and Prussia, for example, had come to view the United States as an important counterbalance to the great power of the British on the high seas. Further, given the atmosphere of self-deception in Dixie, Confederate officials never realized that the intervention of France into the American Civil War would most likely have caused a flurry of dissent among many French citizens who had come to see America as a model republic. Southerners' romantic view of their international situation also blinded them to the fact that English investments in Northern land, mining, railroads, and banks exceeded the economic stake which the English had in the South's cotton industry. Also, liberal anti-slavery pressure from England's lower and middle classes would not allow the country's leadership to openly support the Confederacy. And finally, if Confederate policymakers had been able to free themselves from the tyranny of their own illusions, they might have predicted that Spain was most likely to follow the lead of Europe's major powers—Great Britain and France. Thus, a combination of illusion, myth, romance, and self-deception prevented Confederate leaders from realistically assessing their diplomatic relationship with foreign powers.

The Northern Blockade

Commerce with Europe was another matter. Trade between the Confederate States of America and nations abroad was so widespread, in fact, that the establishment of a blockade to intercept European ships making for such Southern ports as Wilmington, Charleston, Savannah, and Mobile was the North's major strategy for fighting the war on the high seas. Given the critical importance of the blockade to the Union's military plans for defeating the insurgent Southern states, it is not surprising that certain myths related to it developed.

The myths concerning the Union blockade must be understood in light of other wartime events—and in fact the conflict's outcome. It has always been understood that the Confederates lost the Civil War where its outcome had to be ultimately decided—on the battlefield. Outnumbered in men and industrial strength, the South appeared destined not to achieve final military victory. But as noted, a considerable measure of misunderstanding

and myth has developed around the supporting role which the U.S. Navy's blockade had in the South's eventual defeat as well as around another legend, that of Southern determination to persevere. The popular notion is that, despite the noble dedication of soldiers and those on the home front to the cause, the Confederacy was slowly strangled by the sea blockade into submission. While such a view might be appealing, it is untrue. Not only is this idealized version of the cause of Confederate collapse false, but it is false in two ways. The South in fact did not defend its Lost Cause to the last man and the last crust of bread. And the Northern blockade was not nearly as instrumental to Southern defeat as legend has often implied.

As to the matter of the South's supreme dedication to principle and the defense of its hallowed ground by heroes in gray and dedicated civilians, one need only consult the informed view of the Southern historian Frank E. Vandiver:

> There was probably more per capita desertion from Confederate ranks than from the ranks of the Union. Far more Rebel troops were absent from roll call at the end of the war than were with the colors. Much bravery, even shining, incredible heroism the southern men did display, but that they were all blind patriots is demonstrably untrue. . . . [And] while there were many magnificent examples of fate-defying loyalty by southern civilians, there were also many examples of petty speculation, wanton brigandage, Unionism, criminal selfishness, and treason. Defection behind the lines, open resistance to Confederate laws, became a matter of national scandal before the conflict ended.[10]

Indeed, it was later Southerners rather than the war generation itself who came to think of the war years as a time when all good citizens of the South were unswervingly dedicated to perish rather than survive under despised Yankee rule.

And as to the matter of the Confederacy's slow death at the hands of the Northern blockade, the fact is that the blockade was largely a failure until the Civil War was nearly over. Early in the war only one in ten blockade runners was destroyed or captured; in the last months of the conflict, it was one in three. The point is that the blockade became successful only after the fate of the Confederacy had already been sealed. The popular misconception of the blockade's success has taken hold because of the complementary myth of the South's noble dedication and because it is true that the South did suffer from a wholesale shortage of supplies during most phases of the war. These shortages, however, seem to have been due much more to distribution problems than to the fact that the North was successful in preventing supplies from reaching the Confederacy.

When the war began the U.S. Navy had but forty-two vessels commissioned for active service, and many of these were in foreign waters. Even later, when some 226 ships were equipped for blockade duty, it was necessary that each vessel be responsible for patrolling an average of 17 miles of the Atlantic coast. With 3,549 statute miles of coastline to patrol, including monitoring many dangerous areas along the Atlantic seaboard such as Cape Hatteras and Cape Fear, it was only logical that the North's attempts to close the doors of European trade to the Confederacy faced severe difficulties.

Most blockade runners, in addition to Southerners, were British, but there were some Portuguese, Danes, Mexicans, Spaniards, and an occasional New England Yankee. They sailed from the fabled ports of the Spanish Main and Havana, Bermuda, and Nassau. And it has been estimated that during the course of the war they made some eight thousand trips to Southern ports and in the process amassed legendary profits. As one historian relates:

> In all, they were as swashbuckling a crew of sailors of fortune as ever sailed the Golden Seas. The charred skeletons of some of their ships still stand today against the battering of the waves, caught fast in the shoals of the Carolina coast—etched forever against the sky in that graveyard of the Atlantic, beyond all salvage except by the historian or the spinner of sea yarns.[11]

The adventures of the blockade runners, in short, are themselves the material from which myths are made. In this instance, legend seems to have attached itself to both those who succeeded and those who failed.

SECTION III. ABRAHAM LINCOLN AND HIS MYTHOLOGY

The American imagination continues to cling tightly to the memory of the Civil War. Between the years 1862 and 1900, for instance, over 480 short stories and novels were published about the war and its effects on America. One scholar has counted 512 novels alone published on the subject between 1862 and 1948. Another measure of the war's impact over the years is the fact that the two bestselling novels in the entire history of American fiction are *Uncle Tom's Cabin* (1852) and *Gone with the Wind* (1936)—one concerning the great issues which brought on the war, the other dealing with its consequences. Though few statistics are available covering more recent times, the fact that over a hundred books dealing with the war were published in 1957 alone would seem to indicate that there is still considerable interest in measuring the conflict's meaning for America.

Perhaps more than anything else, Americans maintain high interest in the war's principal figure, Abraham Lincoln. And with Lincoln the problem of separating fact and myth is compounded, for it has been calculated that the man himself produced a body of printed work totaling 2,078,365 words. This is more wordage, we are told, than found in either the Bible or the works of Shakespeare. With so much having been said both by and about him, it seems inevitable that myth should soon obscure the man and his times. And indeed it has.

Lincoln's Legend

The real "Abe" of history is a compelling figure in his own right, but, in addition, a series of images about him live on in American memory—Self-made Man, Rail-splitter, Great Democrat, Honest Abe, the Great Emancipator, and Father Abraham, savior of the Union. With so many interesting facets to his character, Lincoln has remained the nation's greatest folk hero. His legendary reputation,

Abraham Lincoln: A Myth for the Ages
Time/Life

resting solidly on humility, integrity, and strength of character, remains unsurpassed in the folklore of the nation. Lincoln has become institutionalized nearly to the point of being the center of a national religion. He has served as an important resource for politicians, advertising agencies, booksellers, chambers of commerce, banks, clergy, and writers. Abraham Lincoln, both the man and the myth, has inspired America to what it has been, is today, and hopes to be in the future. Other historical heroes, Benjamin Franklin for example, have been put to somewhat similar use, but none have surpassed Lincoln as a precious object from America's usable past. And few seem to realize that it was Lincoln himself who instigated the enterprise of Lincoln mythology. As the historian Richard Hofstadter has forcefully argued, "The first author of the Lincoln legend and the greatest of the Lincoln dramatists was Lincoln himself."[12]

Very early in his political career, Abraham Lincoln seems to have been aware of the image he was projecting to the American people. In a creative fashion, he sought to capitalize on the magic appeal of his looks, character, and political style. Lincoln consciously developed a political personality for himself which would highlight and enhance qualities he actually possessed. His homespun nature was unmistakable, even in his own mind. Others, such as the American poet and essayist James Russell Lowell for example, were favorably struck by his "fireside plainness." The fact that he almost always looked as though he had slept in a hayloft seemed never to have been a political liability. Lincoln's angular features, wrinkled face, sober eyes, bony wrists, and six-foot-four frame combined to form the impression that he was a destined leader of men. One historian has commented thus on his political appeal: "Gestures that professional politicians attempted, before and after Lincoln's time, came as naturally to him as a reflex."[13] Lincoln's very appearance and manner, in short, were a potent suggestion of the well-honed political abilities which lay only slightly below the surface of the image he projected. With Lincoln, the individual and the image became very close to being inseparable. The man and the myth were in essence the same.

153

Lincoln's appeal as a self-made man, however, was his greatest political asset, both to him and to Americans generally. Born in obscurity, largely self-educated, appropriately ambitious, and possessed of good old American horse sense, he convinced both the voting public and party politicians that he was a force which could not be ignored. Lincoln himself was astutely aware of the flavor of his appeal, and with never the hint of being a political impostor, he could in good faith openly embrace the political symbolism which he and his colleagues created—that of the hardfisted rail-splitter. Indeed, here was a man of humble beginnings who would never lose touch with the common man, yet would grow to be one of the most accomplished politicians of his age. Here was a man of extreme simplicity who could still somehow capture the ideals of America by an artistic use of words. Born in the midst of the Kentucky forests, hardened by a youth spent on the Indiana-Illinois frontiers, Lincoln impressed one as able to engage in a spirited wrestling match with a son of middle America one day and still shape the inspiring phrases of a Gettysburg Address the next. Lincoln was one of the few men in American life who could satisfy his highly ambitious political aspirations yet never allow his compulsion for power to seem callous or immoral.

Life on the Illinois prairies offered opportunities to the ambitious sort, which Lincoln was, and he explored numerous roads which might eventually lead to success. But his work as surveyor, farmhand, ferryman, and storekeeper turned out to be both less satisfying and less successful than he had hoped. So it was that Lincoln "read law"—as the saying went at the time—to prepare himself for what was to be both his road to success and the means of satisfying a personal need to fulfill an ambitious spirit. In the political arena Abraham Lincoln's principal passions, to achieve success without losing his common touch, could merge. Before his fate had run its course the destiny of the entire nation would feel the effects of his career decision.

At the age of twenty-three, shortly after moving to the Illinois frontier community of New Salem, Lincoln launched his political career. The year was 1832 and Abe could already see himself a freshman member of the Illinois legislature. Though he failed to win election then, he experienced the exhilarating tempo of political life. By 1834 his fortunes changed and he won his first political election—a seat in the lower house of the Illinois legislature which had eluded him two years earlier. Though he did not permanently enter the national political limelight until 1858—the year of his famous debates with Stephen A. Douglas—his years from 1834 until his death in 1865 were exclusively devoted to political activity. As a persistent officeholder or officeseeker he succeeded in making a deep impression on his constituents by always presenting himself as a self-made man. Lincoln early recognized the importance of an appealing political personality, knowing that his image as a commoner who had pulled himself up by his bootstraps was a highly salable political commodity and one which Americans had prized at least since the Jacksonian era. As the principal architect of his own mythology, Lincoln did not indulge in political fraud, but it is equally clear that he recognized the benefits which myth could render in political affairs. He knew the charm which his political style would have on a people who were already deeply attached to the concept of the self-made man. How could people help but respond positively and affectionately to one who said, "God must love the common people, he has made so many of them."

As a symbol of self-help, hard work, and thrift, Abraham Lincoln was thoroughly middle class in his thinking. Even though he has long enjoyed a legendary reputation as a political maverick, he was ever and always decidedly middle-of-the-road, both in his ideas and his stand on political issues. First as a Whig and then as a Republican, Lincoln was consistently a spokesman for the party line. Only later generations would see him at the cutting edge of political reform and an early supporter of their favorite cause. Communists, for example, sought to claim him as one of theirs simply because Karl Marx had written him a letter. The real Lincoln, however, found it both more comfortable and politically safe to follow the mainstream of public opinion. Lincoln, in reality, was hardly an outspoken democrat during his political career; he was mainly interested in and successful at achieving political office. On the question of the banking system, on the issue of the tariff, on the problem of internal improvements—political issues which meant a lot to early nineteenth-century America—he was almost always firmly in line with "acceptable" views. For the majority of his political career Lincoln was neither a "boat-rocker" nor a political crusader. As one student of his career has written, "Lincoln had a passion for the great average."[14] One as interested as he in political success could not have been otherwise.

Lincoln and the Issue of Slavery

Since his position on issues was always consistent with his ideals and convictions, it is no surprise to learn that Abraham Lincoln was openly middle-of-the-road on the slavery issue. It is here of course that facts are often ignored and myths abound, for the world has come to know and love Lincoln's heroic role as the Great Emancipator. Americans have become so accustomed to thinking of Lincoln as the predestined white savior of blacks in America that the truth concerning Lincoln's attitudes has been obscured. The Lincoln legend has made it appear that Lincoln at a tender age was appalled by the South's peculiar institution, as a consequence of witnessing the selling of slaves at auction during a trip to New Orleans. Then and there, it is said, Lincoln vowed that if ever given the chance he would strike out at slavery and "hit it hard." Though the tale of Lincoln as a youthful abolitionist has been a subject for story time in grade school classrooms, its authenticity is at least questionable. Based only on the testimony of John Hanks some thirty-five years after the fact, it is doubtful on this count alone. Further, Lincoln himself volunteered that Hanks had failed to accompany him on the journey in question beyond St. Louis. Still, the romantic legend persists that Abraham Lincoln's presidency was the fulfillment of the young rail-splitter's dream to free the blacks from the chains of slavery.

An examination of Lincoln's record on the slavery issue quickly reveals the hollowness of his image as the Great Emancipator. Far from being an abolitionist—that is, one passionately interested in slavery's immediate removal from the American scene—Lincoln, during his early political years, consistently displayed a public indifference to the entire question. As a member of the Illinois legislature, speaker of the Illinois House of Representatives, and U.S. congressman, Lincoln had many occasions on which to speak out and did not. Being of Southern heritage—his parents native Virginians, and he a Kentuckian by birth—he was not predisposed to question the merits of something which to him was already a solidly established part of the American way of life. While compassionate, kind, and moral in his personal affairs, he was too cautious a politician to spearhead a reform movement of such importance and magnitude as abolition.

If any clear position on slavery is apparent in Lincoln's words prior to 1854, it was that the institution would die a "natural death" if not allowed to expand. Such sentiments, however, had always been expressed in private so as not to alienate any considerable group of voters. But by 1854, Lincoln found that he could no longer ignore an issue that had muscled its way into the political arena and as a consequence would have to be included on his political agenda. Thus it was that Lincoln, by now forty-five years of age, spoke against "the monstrous injustice of slavery itself." He felt it necessary to convince his audience, however, that he meant no special disrespect toward the people of the South. "My first impulse," he added, "would be to free all the slaves and send them to Liberia, to their own native land." The thought of such a massive undertaking seemed unfeasible even to Lincoln, and so he temporarily concluded that the best approach might be to free the slaves and keep them "as underlings." By going on to say that slavery ought to be restricted to those states where it existed at the time, Lincoln made it clear that he was bending with the winds of public opinion. As with the great majority, Lincoln had come to the point of concluding that slavery was "a great moral wrong." But he was just as convinced that the nation's blacks ought not be granted social and political equality.

The core of Lincoln's "antislavery" attitude, however, only gradually began to emerge as he became an increasingly important political personality in the rising Republican party. By their own admission, members of a "white man's party," the Republicans through Lincoln found that they could satisfy both the antislavery and black-fearing factions in their midst by appealing for a limitation on slavery with the argument that it threatened the future freedom of Northern white laborers. If slavery were allowed to spread, the argument went, one day all forms of labor—in both North and South—might be reduced to such a condition. Thus the extension of slavery might well engulf the free labor of workers in the North. While reminding Americans that Chief Justice Roger Taney of the Supreme Court, in the Dred Scott Case of 1857, had declared Congress powerless to exclude slavery from the territories, Lincoln warned:

> We shall lie down pleasantly, dreaming that the people of Missouri are on the verge of making their State free; and we shall awake to the reality instead, that the Supreme Court has made Illinois a slave state.[15]

The growing fear that white society in the North might be enslaved, rather than a humanitarian impulse to see to it that blacks were freed, brought Lincoln to the point of believing that slavery ought to be restricted to the Southern states. It was clear that Lincoln's overriding interest was to preserve the freedom of whites, not to assure the emancipation of blacks. In this Lincoln was the complete politician.

Lincoln sought to remain consistent with his earlier views on slavery when he assumed the presidency in 1861. In an open letter to Horace Greeley just prior to issuing the Emancipation Proclamation, for example, he made his position clear: "My paramount object in this struggle is to save the Union, and it is *not* to save or destroy Slavery." Indeed, the historian Dixon Wecter made a telling point when he observed how strange it is "that the Civil War should have found its two great heroes in Lincoln, who was no abolitionist, and Lee, who was no secessionist. Both had higher loyalties—Lincoln to the Union, Lee to his native Virginia—which plunged them into the conflict."[16] Consequently, it is somewhat curious that Lincoln should be known as the Great Emancipator. The Proclamation upon which his legendary reputation most solidly rests, of course, was issued in September, 1862, but it as much reflected Lincoln's political expertise

as it did a moral concern on his part for the status of blacks in American white society. Seeking to gain both moral and diplomatic advantage from the Union victory at Antietam five days before, Lincoln issued the Emancipation Proclamation in an attempt to quiet abolitionists, to help influence world opinion in support of the Northern cause, and to stem the possibility of European intervention in the war—which he thought a real possibility—on the side of the South. Its major values were psychological and symbolic, for it failed to free a single slave directly. The Proclamation spoke to the emancipation of the slaves—but specifically applied only to those behind Confederate lines and ignored the border states. Liberation from the chains of slavery for black people would not of course become a constitutional reality until after Lincoln was gone from the scene and the Thirteenth Amendment was passed (1865). While it is definitely invalid to conclude that Lincoln was proslavery in his outlook, two facts about the Great Emancipator seem inescapable—his attitudes were shaped by the atmosphere that surrounded him and, because of this, he was never able to shake the tyranny of America's racist tradition.

Lincoln's Death

The forces of myth which propelled Lincoln into American political life, his behavior during the war, and the coincidence of his death on Good Friday, 1865, have combined so that the legendary image of the Great Democrat and Great Emancipator often bears only superficial resemblance to historical reality. The veneration of Lincoln has indeed produced its share of romantic Americana—ranging from myth disguised as history to sheer fabrication. The mythical process which he began started to accelerate even before his body was cold in the grave. His death at the hands of the assassin John Wilkes Booth produced an outpouring of feeling which was at once touching and distasteful. The poet Walt Whitman sought to capture the mass sorrow and grief of the nation and spoke for many Americans when he wrote:

> O how shall I warble myself for the dead one there I loved?

And how shall I deck my song for the
large sweet soul that has gone?
And what shall my perfume be for the
grave of him I love?[17]

As the funeral train of eight black coaches,
bearing the body for burial, wound its way
from Washington, D.C., to the heartland of
America, approximately seven million people
paid their final respects to the greatest of the
nation's heroes. And when the train reached
his home state of Illinois, thousands stood
ready to participate in what they knew would
later be seen as one of history's great moments:

As soon as the hearse was empty,
souvenir-hunters fell upon it and had to
be scattered by soldiers with bayonets.
The people, for whom Lincoln had toiled,
displayed their heartbreak, their callous
curiosity, their vulgarity. Even in
Springfield, after the funeral, the red,
white and blue blanket on "Old Bob,"
Lincoln's horse, was torn to pieces by
relic fans.[18]

For others, Lincoln's death prompted familiar
exercises in vulgar hero-worship. The American martyr's features soon began to appear on
souvenir handkerchiefs, paper weights, and
dinner plates.

Given his colorful career, his success as a
self-made man, the leadership he had provided
his people in time of war, and the dramatic
circumstances of his death, it was already
clear, as his secretary of war, Edwin Stanton,
was supposed to have said, that Lincoln "be-
longs to the ages." The historical Lincoln had
died, but his myth was destined to live on.

SECTION IV: THE LEGENDS OF RECONSTRUCTION

In writing about America's past, historians
have most often used the term "Reconstruction" to refer to the period in the nation's
history after the Civil War when the attempt
was made, in Lincoln's words, "to bind up the
nation's wounds." This era of readjustment
and rebuilding supposedly spanned the years

from 1865 to 1877, from the war's end to the
removal of Union troops from Southern soil.
But contrary to conventional thinking, Reconstruction was much more than an important
page in the history of the South—it was
national in scope. To reunite a nation which
had been so separated by emotion would be a
difficult enterprise, since for a considerable
period of time Americans had been neither
talking nor acting like citizens of a single
nation. Since the problem of "race adjustment," which had done so much to bring on the
war in the first place, was a problem of the
North as well as the South, the addition of the
Thirteenth, Fourteenth, and Fifteenth
Amendments to the Constitution was bound to
send shock waves through the nation at large.
The law of the land now held that black slaves
were free, were citizens, and enjoyed the right
to vote. It seemed that all Americans—black
and white, Northerners and Southerners—had
to face up to new responsibilities. When it is
understood as well that Reconstruction helped
further the rise of big business, the first trusts,
and the consolidation of the railroads, and saw
the emergence of the Republican party as a
long-term power in national politics, it becomes obvious that during these years more
than just the South was being "reconstructed."

As historians have attempted realistically to
examine the Reconstruction era, they have
faced a task ripe with mythic potential. The
dates of the period itself, the years 1865 to
1877, are more convenient than meaningful.
Despite the impression often drawn from
textbooks, it was not as though the curtain
went down on one stage of American development in 1865 and up on another. Nor did such
an overnight transformation recur in 1877.
Rather, the era of Reconstruction blended with
both the preceding and succeeding periods.

Prior to the official conclusion of the war at
Appomattox Court House on April 9, 1865,
when General Lee surrendered the Army of
Northern Virginia to General Grant, the nation had already gone through a rehearsal for
reconstruction. The atmosphere within which
the reconstruction of the nation would be
conducted had been established perhaps as
early as the Emancipation Proclamation of
1862. In addition, under a plan developed by
President Lincoln, attempts had been made in
1864 to establish rehabilitated governments in

the Southern states of Arkansas, Louisiana, Tennessee, North Carolina, and Florida. Beyond this, a wartime division of lands between blacks and whites foreshadowing what was to come had been carried forth in Port Royal, South Carolina. And finally, patterns typical of Reconstruction had been inaugurated during the war years in Washington, D.C., where many of the social, political, and economic problems later to be confronted on a larger scale pressed for settlement as refugee slaves in search of freedom flooded the city.

Similarly, the use of 1877 as the terminal date of Reconstruction is unsatisfactory and misleading if only because by that time all of the original Confederate states but three—Florida, South Carolina, and Louisiana—had been formally "reconstructed." More important, Reconstruction continued long after 1877 in that its major issue—the question of how to carve out a place for the black in a white society—remained unsolved. Understood in this sense, it can be said that the process of reconstruction continues today in the minds and hearts of both Southerners and Northerners—in the streets of Birmingham and Boston, Dallas and Detroit.

"Radical" Reconstruction

In attempting to see beyond the old set of beliefs which prevailed concerning Reconstruction, historians have not only questioned the continued usefulness of considering it as having taken place within a well-defined period of a dozen years, but have wondered at the term "radical" which has often been used to further describe it. It has been said that the term "radical" used in connection with Reconstruction validly describes the motives, styles, and success of those members of Congress who imposed harsh retributive measures on the conquered South. But in asking the question, How *radical* was Radical Reconstruction? historians have increasingly answered: not very.

To begin with, those in search of villains lurking in the halls of Congress who failed to live up to Lincoln's ideal of "malice toward none and charity for all" are destined to come up nearly empty-handed. Benjamin Wade, Charles Sumner, and Thaddeus Stevens urged prompt emancipation of slaves without payment to former owners, but once one moves

beyond these three individuals, the group of Radical Republicans that historians used to refer to as "Vindictives" quickly disappears. Given the realities of the American political system, specifically that the membership of the House of Representatives can change considerably every two years, it is mistaken to think that a highly disciplined group of congressmen completely controlled the policies of the nation from 1865 to 1877 in a vindictive way—or any other for that matter. The script makes for an exciting novel or motion picture but it is actually a scenario for historical fiction. As a case in point, and contrary to the widely held view which helps support the myth of Reconstruction's radical nature, there was in fact no significant breakup of the plantation system in the South. While it lends drama to think that a conspiratorial group of strong-willed and self-interested men rode roughshod over fallen Southerners under the pretense of reconstructing the nation, such a theory cannot be proven. "Territorial Piracy" was almost unknown.

Despite the thick haze of legend, the striking fact is that in legislative matters the radicals seem seldom to have gotten their way. For example, they wanted the Fifteenth Amendment to specifically declare that all blacks should vote. As finally adopted, however, the amendment contained the more moderate language that "the right of citizens to vote shall not be denied or abridged by the United States or by any State on account of race, color, or previous condition of servitude." This, of course, left loopholes. It was still possible constitutionally to restrict voting rights on the basis of literacy or education, as the South would later do during the decade of the 1890s. Upon reconsideration, the alleged radicalism of Reconstruction appears quite moderate, especially by today's standards. Beyond this, it may be unrealistic to envision Congress ever passing much in the way of *radical* legislation.

Furthermore, to help support the idea of the era's radical character and to fulfill the needs of those in search of historical entertainment, it has been fashionable to believe that the South after the Civil War had to endure the outrage of "military despotism" as an instrument of "federal tyranny." According to legend, bayonet rule was the typical approach of the national government to solving the postwar problems of Dixie. It was, myth contends, Washington's Southern strategy. While this Reconstruction myth had, as most myths do, a shadowy basis in fact, it has been much overemphasized. The truth is there were no mass arrests, no indictments for treason or conspiracy. There was very little in the way of war-related trials, convictions, or imprisonments. Especially when considered against the background of civil wars which have gripped other countries in the twentieth century, the nearly complete absence of such activities suggest that Reconstruction was characterized more by its tone of sympathy and generosity than by its alleged oppressiveness.

It was clear from the outset that brutality and revenge would not be official policy. When the Confederate army surrendered, the officers in gray were paroled and allowed to return home with their men. In like manner, General Lee bid farewell to his fighting men and spent his remaining years unmolested in Virginia. There was, in short, no exile of Confederate leaders. Not a single military figure of the Rebel cause was tried for treason. Only one, Jefferson Davis, was imprisoned for any length of time, and he was released after two years. There was, if you will, no "enemies list" or candidates "marked for execution." The only Southern leader to die for war-related activities was Captain Henry Wirtz, commandant of the infamous Andersonville prison camp in Georgia. But even in his case, the arrest, trial, conviction, and execution were based on evidence of his "war crimes" rather than on treason or conspiracy. By 1872 Congress had pardoned nearly all Confederate leaders, though it is interesting to note that General Lee was not restored to full citizenship until July, 1975—110 years after he had applied.

To draw a balanced picture of Reconstruction it is necessary to understand that even though "bayonet rule" in the South has been much overemphasized, the military did play a crucial role in the affairs of Dixie during the period. Under plans enacted by Congress in 1867, the South was divided into five military districts. It was the duty of district commanders to oversee the registration of voters and the establishment of new governments in the respective states within their region. Civilian governments based on newly written state constitutions, however, soon replaced the rule of the generals. Military control came to an end in 1868 in all the Southern states except Mississippi, Virginia, and Texas. In addition, the actual number of troops dispatched to the South was quite small (twenty thousand), especially when compared to the number of Northern soldiers who were at arms when the war ended (nearly a million). It can be noted as well that during the period of occupation over one third of the federal troops were stationed in two states—Louisiana and Texas. But even so, the presence of troops had much to do with factors other than monitoring the South's obedience to Reconstruction policies. In the case of Louisiana, for example, protection of the port of New Orleans was seen as critical to postwar security, and in Texas troubles with Mexico required the presence of military garrisons. While it is true that for varying periods of time military law was supreme in the Southern states, and that the twenty thousand troops in question represented nearly the entire force of the U.S. Army after demobilization, military oppression was not synonymous with Reconstruction in the South. Though military brutality is often heard of in relation to this era, it was more imagined than real. Even in the estimation of its severest critics, military rule of the South after the war of the rebellion was for the most part just and efficient.

"Black Reconstruction"

Few features of Reconstruction history have come to be more colored with myth than the supposed domination of the newly freed blacks—aided and abetted by infamous carpetbaggers and scalawags—over the political affairs of the South. Supposedly, in attempting to secure a place for former slaves in American life, the policies of Reconstruction allowed blacks to control Southern politics. It is primarily this feature of Reconstruction which has prompted some to call the period "Black Reconstruction," "The Age of Hate," and the "Dreadful Decade." To North Carolinian novelist and Baptist minister Thomas Dixon, who wrote a series of bestselling books on what he saw as the tragic consequences of Reconstruction, the results were catastrophic.

"Radical" Reconstruction:
A Conventional View
The Granger Collection, New York

In his novel *The Traitor* (1907), Dixon portrayed the supposed depths to which the administration of the South had plunged. Choosing his words carefully so as to arouse the emotions of his readers, Dixon described the trial of the aristocratic John Graham before a Reconstruction court:

> The jury corruptly chosen for this case marked the lowest tide mud to which the administration of justice ever sank in our history. A white freeman, a man of culture and heroic mould, whose fathers created the American Republic, was arraigned to plead for his life before a jury composed of one dirty, ignorant white scalawag and eleven coal-black Negroes! The white man was not made its foreman, a Negro teamster was chosen.[19]

While it is profitable to consult the work of Thomas Dixon to appreciate what passed as the reality of Reconstruction for many years, recent scholarship has judged views like Dixon's to be no more than melodramatic racist nonsense.

Obviously, the passage during Reconstruction of the Thirteenth, Fourteenth, and Fifteenth Amendments granting blacks freedom, citizenship, and the vote allowed a great number of blacks to enter the political process for the first time. And given the novelty of black participation in politics and related activities, it is inevitable that considerable attention be directed toward the black's new status. It would be a disservice, both to those involved and to historical accuracy, however, to believe either that former slaves consistently directed political affairs or that they were generally inept in the performance of their new civic duties. The term "Africanization" which has been used to describe the postwar South is erroneous, and justification for its use is simply not found in the record. During all of Reconstruction only two blacks were elected to the U.S. Senate—Hiram Revels and Blanche K. Bruce of Mississippi—and they discharged their duties well. In the national House of Representatives, only fifteen blacks ever served. No Southern state during this span of years was ever controlled by black officeholders. Since there were no black governors, and only in the states of South Carolina and Louisiana did blacks temporarily hold a majority in the legislature, one wonders how the view that former slaves mismanaged Southern affairs has continued to find acceptance. Certainly one answer lies in the fact that, historically, a legend of black-controlled political incompetence helped support the racist idea that blacks ought to be excluded from the mainstream of American life. It is a misuse of history and a none-too-subtle way of suggesting that blacks once had their chance and "blew it."

Carpetbaggers, Scalawags, and Corruption

Important supporting characters in the myth of "Radical-Black Reconstruction," of course, are the carpetbaggers and scalawags. When, in Margaret Mitchell's phrase, the "tattered Cavaliers" returned to their Southern homelands after the war, they were supposedly accompanied by a host of profit-minded Northerners who were destined to become economic and political parasites and cripple the South's recovery from the ravages of war. Legend holds that these ambitious Northern carpetbaggers—named for the suitcase that travelers typically carried at the time—took advantage of the removal of the South's "natural leaders" and were responsible for the destruction of the honesty and virtue which had characterized Southern life. They were, allegedly, the grand masters of the sinister plot to "Africanize" and plunder Dixie. The South's continuing paranoia over "outside agitators" no doubt partially dates from these supposedly shabby years. Firm believers in the myth of "the carpetbagger-as-disgraceful-brute" may well be those who have blindly accepted the dramatic words of Thomas Dixon at face value. For in his novel *The Traitor* he created a false picture not only of politically inept blacks but also of carpetbaggers by claiming that "from the sewers of the North, jailbirds and exconvicts had poured into the stricken South as vultures follow the wake of a victorious army."[20] While it would be patently false to claim that all carpetbaggers were humanitarian crusaders for black rights, they were not as a group jailbirds or adventurous vagrants intent upon fleecing and degrading the South. Most important, the mythical stereotype of the carpetbagger shows little understanding of the variety of personalities and motives involved. Northerners moving south after the Civil War were from very different backgrounds and came for very different reasons. They were teachers, preachers, farmers, merchants, discharged Union soldiers, mechanics, and laborers. They traveled south for economic, educational, political, and religious reasons. Many in fact sustained their new relationships to the South by remaining and establishing permanent roots.

In addition to the idea that the South labored under offenses of Northern intruders, public fancy has always reserved a special place for those Southerners who became accomplices to supposedly depraved and dishonest activities. The scalawags—as the title of Thomas Dixon's fiery novel pointedly declares—were "traitors" to the South. Southerners who were too cozy with Yankee soldiers during the war, or with "radical" carpetbaggers and blacks thereafter, were claimed to be the most degenerate individuals of all, for they collaborated with the enemy. But here again, such a view does not take into consideration the complexity of either their motives or behavior. Interestingly enough, the term "scalawag" came from the North—having been used before the Civil War in western New York State to describe a "mean

fellow." In the mouths of Southerners after the war, however, the word came to be used indiscriminately to describe any Southerner who differed with those who opposed Reconstruction. Scalawags thus became yet another convenient and particularly despicable enemy—along with carpetbaggers and blacks—to whom those wanting to "redeem" the South as a white man's country could point as tyrants deserving of destruction. Many of these Southern turncoats, however, were personally convinced that they had the best long-term interests of the South at heart. Some saw their acceptance of Reconstruction as the best means of rehabilitating the economy of the old Confederacy. Others viewed their activities as the surest way for the South to regain power in the national political arena. Still others could envision the future destiny of the South as best assured by allowing the black freedman to take his place beside whites in shaping a New South based on racial understanding. In short, the scalawags were in many instances people of vision and idealism.

Another mythical thread which serves to tie the legends of Reconstruction together is the overall view that the South reeked with corruption. Military commanders, blacks, carpetbaggers, and scalawags are all supposedly at fault on this count. But while the charge of "corruption" has been headline-catching even for historians, it does not account for many notable exceptions and a larger view of things. The Reconstruction history of states such as Florida, Louisiana, South Carolina, and Alabama offer many examples of fraud and political dishonesty. There indeed were those who by their behavior *did* degrade Southern democracy. The Pennsylvania carpetbag governor of South Carolina is but one example. But to make corruption the central theme of one's understanding of the Reconstruction era is again to be guilty of distortion by exaggeration. Such an attitude overlooks the energy, idealism, and humanitarianism displayed by both Southerners and Northerners toward training the blacks for citizenship, rebuilding the South's economy, legislating for education, and generally reconstructing the society of the South with "malice toward none." As important, it must also be recognized that the entire country—not just the South—suffered a decline in political morality after the Civil War. The years of Reconstruction were contemporary to the swindles of the Tweed Ring in New York City, to say nothing of the rampant corruption which characterized the nation's capital during the administration of President Ulysses S. Grant. Further, it is most profitable to see that many in the South after the Civil War were in search of opportunity. Though they may have defined it differently at times, blacks, carpetbaggers, and scalawags were all men of enterprise. In this sense, they were not so very different from those who were in search of opportunity and adventure on other American frontiers at approximately the same period of time. For the period of Reconstruction quickly began to blend into a new era in which Americans saw fortunes and adventure to be gained on agricultural and cattle frontiers, in the growth of the nation's cities, and ultimately even on foreign shores.

STUDY QUESTIONS

1. Analyze and discuss the major schools of thought which have arisen among historians as they have debated the causes of the Civil War. How has each, including those currently being proposed, strongly reflected the biases of the time in which they were written?

2. Concerning the Civil War, what are the various forms of myth which have come to surround the experiences of the fighting men, the South's King Cotton Diplomacy, and the North's wartime naval blockade?

3. How did Abraham Lincoln's homespun appearance, character, and political style, as well as the tragic circumstances of his death, work to create an elaborate Lincoln legend for the nation? Also, to what degree and in what ways was Abraham Lincoln himself the first author of the Lincoln legend?

4. Analyze and discuss the major myths of the Reconstruction period. You might wish to organize your discussion around a treatment of its dates, radicalism, military despotism, black political control, carpetbaggers, scalawags, and corruption.

REFERENCES

1. Robert Penn Warren, *The Legacy of the Civil War: Meditations on the Centennial* (New York: Random House, 1964), pp. 70-71.

2. Richard Hofstadter, "Abraham Lincoln and the Self-Made Myth," in *The American Political Tradition* (New York: Alfred A. Knopf, Inc., 1959), p. 92.
3. David Donald, "The Folklore Lincoln," in *Lincoln Reconsidered* (New York: Vintage Books, 1961), p. 153.
4. Grady McWhiney, "The Ghostly Legend of the Ku Klux Klan," in Grady McWhiney, ed., *Southerners and Other Americans* (New York: Basic Books, 1973), p. 148.
5. Thomas J. Pressly, *Americans Interpret Their Civil War* (New York: The Free Press, 1965), pp. 39-40.
6. Ibid., p. 105.
7. Ibid., p. 314.
8. Allan Nevins, "The Glorious and the Terrible," *Saturday Review* (September 2, 1961), p. 10.
9. Henry Blumenthal, "Confederate Diplomacy: Popular Notions and International Realities," *Journal of Southern History* 32 (1966): 152.
10. Frank E. Vandiver, "The Confederate Myth," *Southwest Review* XLVI (Summer, 1961): 201.
11. Daniel O'Flaherty, "The Blockade That Failed," *American Heritage* 6 (1955): 105.
12. Hofstadter, "Abraham Lincoln," p. 93.
13. Dixon Wecter, *The Hero in America: A Chronicle of Hero-Worship* (Ann Arbor: The University of Michigan Press, 1966), p. 235.
14. Hofstadter, "Abraham Lincoln," p. 102.
15. Ibid., p. 114.
16. Wecter, *Hero*, pp. 250-251.
17. Walt Whitman, "When Lilacs Last in the Dooryard Bloom'd," in Harold W. Blodgett, ed., *The Best of Whitman* (New York: The Ronald Press Company, 1953), p. 232.
18. Ibid., p. 264.
19. Thomas Dixon, Jr., *The Traitor: A Story of the Fall of the Invisible Empire* (New York: Grosset and Dunlap, 1907), p. 305.
20. Ibid., p. 80.

SOURCES FOR FURTHER STUDY

CAUSES OF THE CIVIL WAR: MYTHS AND REALITIES

BEALE, HOWARD K., "What Historians Have Said About the Causes of the Civil War." In *Social Science Research Council Bulletin* 54 (1946): 55–102.
NICHOLS, ROY F. "The Causes of the Civil War." In John A. Garraty, ed., *Interpreting American History: Conversations with Historians*, I. New York: The Macmillan Co., 1970.
POTTER, DAVID M. "Civil War." In *The South and the Sectional Conflict.* Baton Rouge: Louisiana State University Press, 1968.
PRESSLY, THOMAS J. *Americans Interpret Their Civil War.* New York: The Free Press, 1962.
WARREN, ROBERT PENN. *The Legacy of the Civil War: Meditations on the Centennial.* New York: Vintage Books, 1964.

COLLECTED MYTHS OF THE WAR YEARS

BLUMENTHAL, HENRY. "Confederate Diplomacy: Popular Notions and International Realities." *Journal of Southern History* 32 (1966).

CATTON, BRUCE. "Soldiering in the Civil War." In John A. Garraty, ed., *Historical Viewpoints*. New York: Harper & Row, Publishers, 1975.

NEVINS, ALLAN. "The Glorious and the Terrible." In *Saturday Review*, September 2, 1961.

O'FLAHERTY, DANIEL. "The Blockade That Failed." *American Heritage* 6 (1955).

POTTER, DAVID M. "Civil War." In C. Vann Woodward, ed., *The Comparative Approach to American History*. New York: Basic Books, 1968.

ABRAHAM LINCOLN AND HIS MYTHOLOGY

DONALD, DAVID. "The Folklore Lincoln." In *Lincoln Reconsidered*. New York: Vintage Books, 1961.

HOFSTADTER, RICHARD. "Abraham Lincoln and the Self-Made Myth." In *The American Political Tradition and the Men Who Made It*. New York: Alfred A. Knopf, 1948.

JOHANNSEN, ROBERT. "In Search of the Real Lincoln, or Lincoln at the Crossroads." *Journal of the Illinois Historical Society* 61 (1968).

LEWIS, LLOYD. *Myths After Lincoln*. New York: Grosset & Dunlap, 1957.

WECTER, DIXON. "Lincoln: The Democrat as Hero." In *The Hero in America: A Chronicle of Hero-Worship*. Ann Arbor: The University of Michigan Press, 1966.

THE LEGENDS OF RECONSTRUCTION

COCHRAN, THOMAS C. "Did the Civil War Retard Industrialization?" In *Mississippi Valley Historical Review* 48 (1961).

DEGLER, CARL. "Dawn Without Noon." In *Out of Our Past: The Forces That Shaped Modern America*. New York: Harper & Row, Publishers, 1970.

DONALD, DAVID. "Reconstruction." In John A. Garraty, ed., *Interpreting American History: Conversations with Historians*, I. New York: The Macmillan Co., 1970.

GASTON, PAUL M. *The New South Creed: A Study in Southern Mythmaking*. New York: Vintage Books, 1970.

STAMPP, KENNETH. *The Era of Reconstruction*. New York: Alfred A. Knopf, 1965.

7 American Myths at Century's End

PREVIEW

Hero of the "Last Frontier": The American Cowboy

The end of the nineteenth century was a transitional period for America. Industrialization and urbanization were steadily increasing, and agriculture as a dominant characteristic of the nation was surely fading. Americans looked to the future with confidence but also to the past with nostalgia. Thus, the myths that appear in the late nineteenth century clearly reflect not only America's experience with new economic and social realities, but also a desire to secure that which the nation seemed about to lose. As the frontier faded, Americans began to picture it as something it had rarely been, and made the frontiersman a candidate for national hero worship. The cowboy in particular symbolized the golden past of a preindustrial age, and the West came to rival the South as a major source of American mythology.

Even today, far from receding into the mist of lost memories, the cowboy continues to stimulate the nation's imagination. In fact, he may be more active today, in an imaginative sense, than he ever was in the past. And the durability of the cowboy as an American folk hero is not difficult to explain. Among the colorful figures from America's western frontier experience—the buffalo hunter, the Mountain Man, and the prospector, among others—who might have challenged the cowboy for mythical prominence, none has succeeded in displacing him. His bravery, staunch individualism, and swaggering confidence are virtues which many of those who conquered the Great Plains, the Rocky Mountains, and the arid spaces of the Great American Desert shared. But unlike the others, the cowboy was the most conspicuous fixture of the frontier precisely at the time when Americans concluded that the nation's frontier experience was ending and its experience as an urban-industrial society was accelerating.

The origin of the word "cowboy" is somewhat uncertain. It is known that as early as the American Revolution the term was applied in parts of New York State to Loyalists who stole cattle and various other property from Patriots. Later, the name was used to refer to Texan bandits engaged in stealing cattle from Mexicans. Only after the Civil War did the term assume its modern sense and become forever associated with the American West. Long before the cowboy era began, in the postwar years when cattle ranching developed on the Texan frontier, a breed of professional Mexican horsemen calling themselves *vaqueros* had already set the style, perfected the equipment and techniques, and developed much of the vocabulary that later generations would believe the American cowboy had invented. In a real sense, then, Mexicans were the earliest "American" cowboys, for they first rode the open range and developed the use of saddles, spurs, lariats, wide-rimmed hats, bandannas, and chaps.

Though the mythical image of America's western cowboy has been greatly exaggerated in literature, movies, radio, and television, his legendary reputation does have some marginal claim to authenticity. The American cowboy is supposed to have been a superb horseman, and in fact he was by all accounts; he is reputed to have been an expert user of the Colt revolver, though few cowboys in fact were gunfighters; and he is said to have cherished the days on the open range, which historical research suggests most cowboys did not. In reality, the life of the American cowboy was a good deal less romantic than myth might suggest. For one thing many cowboys were just that—boys, most of them between the ages of eighteen and twenty-five. The real American cowboy was a dirty, overworked laborer earning about $30 a month, who seldom owned his own horse, rode endless miles in heat, wind, rain, and snow, and seldom rose above his humble station. So monotonous was life on the western frontier that many were driven to memorizing labels on discarded tin cans in a vain attempt to relieve the boredom. Yet when true accounts of cowboy life appeared they were usually ignored. Andy Adam's classic and realistic portrayal of the essentially dull life of the cowpuncher, *The Log of a Cowboy* (1903), was declared "too true to be good" by one critic. Such is the American attachment to mythology.

Even as the cowboy was still meeting the

challenge of the frontier, he had already begun to become the stuff of legend. A British traveler to the United States in 1887, for example, could already see that Americans were beginning to mythologize the cowboy.

> The cowboy has at the present time become a personage; nay more, he is rapidly becoming a mythical one. Distance is doing for him what lapse of time did for the heroes of antiquity.... The true character of the cowboy has been obscured, his genuine qualities are lost in fantastic tales of impossible daring and skill.... Every member of his class is pictured as a kind of Buffalo Bill, as a long-haired ruffian who, decked out in gaudy colors, and tawdry ornaments, booted like a cavalier, chivalrous as a Paladin, his belt stuck full of knives and pistols, makes the world to resound with bluster and braggadocio.[1]

William Cody—Buffalo Bill—was in the forefront of the quickly developing cowboy myth. He had already become the model of what the idealized western man on horseback was supposed to have been like.

Born in Scott County, Iowa, early in 1846, William Frederick Cody provided excellent material for his own mythology. At the age of eleven he took leave of his family (which had moved to Kansas) and worked as a wagoner and messenger for the freighting firm of Russell, Majors, and Waddell. At fourteen he was a rider for the Pony Express. In the Civil War Cody served the Union cause. Contrary to a legend largely of his own making, however, he was never "chief of scouts in the U.S. Army." As Buffalo Bill himself told the story in one of his more sober moments, he awoke one morning in 1863 "after having been under the influence of bad whiskey . . . to find myself a soldier in the Seventh Kansas."[2] At the conclusion of the war Cody began the portion of his career which was to serve as the major basis for his later legendary fame. Under contract to the Kansas Pacific Railroad he earned the nickname "Buffalo Bill" by providing buffalo meat for the railroad's construction camps, and shortly began capitalizing on his developing legendary reputation.

With the help of his friend Edward Z. C. Judson, better known as Ned Buntline, Buffalo Bill Cody made his theatrical debut in Chicago in the 1872 production, *Scouts of the Prairie*. In succeeding years, the West's greatest hero placed the destiny of his extraordinary career in the hands of "Arizona John" Burke—a native of Washington, D.C. With the help of Burke as press agent, and the business know-how of promoters like Nate Salsbury, "Buffalo Bill's Wild West Show" was formed and succeeded in bringing the color, nostalgia, and sense of adventure of the frontier West into nearly every major exhibition hall and arena in America. So successful was this combination carnival, sideshow, circus, and all-around extravaganza that the troop, with the later addition of "Little Sure Shot" Annie Oakley and Sitting Bull, toured the capitals of Europe on four separate occasions. Cody's fame reached its high point in the mid-1890s when it was suggested that Buffalo Bill would make a fine president.

According to historians, Buffalo Bill Cody was neither the greatest scout nor the greatest gunfighter of the Great Plains era. He could make as much of a claim as any man, however, to being a major architect of cowboy mythology. Though in his declining years he was forced to resort to a white toupee in order to sustain his long-haired image as the plainsman, Buffalo Bill supremely symbolized a historic time and place which will probably always romantically be seen as an era when pioneer Americans encountered numerous dangers and lived a life solidly based on a breathtaking freedom of action. Nearing the end of his illustrious make-believe career, William F. Cody was reported to have said that he was "growing very tired of this sort of sham hero-worship sometimes." Apparently, Americans have never come to share his sentiments.

Myths of the Yeoman Farmer and the Self-Made Man

The cowboy of course was but one of several types of Westerners. For every hired man on horseback there were thousands of small independent farmers who in a less glamorous way did their part to win the West. The agricultural frontier would in the end more than match the cattle frontier in economic significance. Corn and wheat much more than the steer caused American civilization to expand. Indeed, one of the basic appeals of the western myth in general was its pastoral setting, an arena of nature's impressive landscape. The seemingly simple rustic life of the remote western frontier—the little house on the prairie—added a long-standing and appealing dimension to all who possessed the pioneer spirit. It provided a rich atmosphere within which additional myths could develop. Consequently, as agricultural America was fading and rural life was becoming increasingly subject to many of the same complex forces which appeared to be bringing the golden era of the cowboy to a close, the simple heritage of the farmer became an inexhaustible resource to stimulate the American romantic imagination. The novelist of the "middle border," Hamlin Garland, reflected this state of mind in recalling an element of his own rural experience:

> It all lies in the unchanging realm of the past—this land of my childhood. Its charm, its strange domination cannot return save in the poet's reminiscent dream. No money, no railway train can take us back to it. It did not in truth exist—it was a magical world, born of the vibrant union of youth and firelight, of music and the voice of the moaning winds.

In such fashion did America react spontaneously to the myth of the happy yeoman. Americans repressed the tragic and cruel elements of their rural past in favor of an idealized version of what life in the country was like.

And even as the realities of country life came to be clouded in a romantic haze of myth, a good many more Americans were finding the nation's cities a frontier of sorts, where a certain mythology prevailed. Immigrants and native American farmers alike flooded the nation's largest cities, convinced that they could become self-made men and find the wealth and happiness which had eluded them either in Europe or in rural America. But

while the big cities did offer numerous opportunities for success, they offered equally as many for failure. Some, like the Scottish immigrant Andrew Carnegie, did become giants of American transportation, manufacturing, and finance. Native-born Americans like Jay Cooke, moving from the rural background of a village school and a clerkship in a general store, did rise to become one of America's leading investment bankers. Carnegie and Cooke served as models, but probably the nation's leading symbols of the self-made man during the industrial age were the heroes created by Horatio Alger, Jr.

Born in Revere, Massachusetts, in 1834 and a graduate of Harvard, Horatio Alger wrote more than a hundred novels concerning city boys who struggled upward in search of middle-class respectability. Famous for his colorful tales of "Ragged Dick" and "Tattered Tom," Alger also wrote several biographies of bright young Americans who had conquered poverty to become national leaders, such as *From Canal Boy to President* (1881), the story of James A. Garfield. It is with such novels as *Robert Coverdale's Struggle*, *Timothy Crump's Ward*, and *Adrift in New York*, however, that Alger achieved his greatest fame.

In each of these books a hardworking, virtuous young hero triumphs over a series of perils and hardships and by "pluck and luck" achieves a measure of fame and fortune. By embodying the American Dream, Alger's books were popular reading fare for the likes of Carl Sandburg, Ernest Hemingway, the baseball hero Christy Mathewson, and Notre Dame's legendary Knute Rockne. The most conservative estimate places the total sales of Alger's works at better than seventeen million copies. Some estimates have run closer to 400 million. Appropriate to the Alger myth, a few book collectors have gained a modest fortune and a bit of fame by collecting rare editions of Alger's books which today demand prices of over a thousand dollars each for some titles.

Like the value of his books Horatio Alger's popularity continues to escalate. Recent disciples of the Alger message, for example, have formed a national organization known as the Horatio Alger Society—HAS. Scholars meanwhile have questioned the uses to which Alger has been put—his heroes were never "alone and unaided," never "rose to the top of the economic heap," were not "common men," and seldom relied on organized religion to achieve success. His melodramatic portrayals in novels such as *Silas Snobden's Office Boy*, however, had a way of supplying flesh and blood to the American Dream. Though his treatment of economic life in America was overly sentimentalized and his novels have been misinterpreted by people who never bothered to read them, the name Horatio Alger, Jr. will probably continue as a symbol of values and aspirations which "made America great."

The Gay Nineties

Americans have long been favorably disposed to think of the twilight years of the nineteenth century—the so-called Gay Nineties—as the "good old days." As a decade in which the cowboy, the yeoman, and the self-made man were coming to be viewed as heroic symbols of democracy and the American spirit, the age in general spawned a false sense of well-being, increased national optimism, and public confidence. Railroads were expanding rapidly in every region of the country. Finance capitalism was in control of the nation's economic growth, and at first glance at least all seemed well in the land of the free. Viewed in closer perspective, however, the latter years of what Mark Twain sarcastically labeled the "Gilded Age" were considerably less buoyant and gay than they would appear. On further inspection the period loses much of its golden luster and reveals instead considerable self-deception and make-believe on the part of those who lived at the time and those who came to fondly remember it later, after the trauma of the First World War.

The decade of the 1890s was not a golden age except to the upper crust—the privileged classes. The seeming confidence, innocence, stability, comfort, and security of the time was in fact a mask hiding a good deal of doubt, ferment, protest, violence, and hate. America's industrial statesmen were indeed masterminding the development of an economy which would provide the nation the world's highest standard of living, eventually contribute much to the people's health, education, and welfare, and build an industrial establishment capable of great contributions to winning world wars

in the twentieth century. At the same time, however, they were contributing heavily to a state of affairs which included poverty, miserable working conditions, inadequate housing for most, and a continuation of elitist and racist attitudes which took their inevitable toll on many racial and ethnic minorities.

As a case in point, for Native Americans, the 1890s proved anything but gay. Over the decades they had been in retreat from the land expansion, military superiority, and cultural arrogance of whites. Some refused to accept their "destined" extermination. The Sioux under Little Crow, for example, staged a short-lived counteroffensive against white encroachment and broken treaties on the Minnesota frontier even as the Civil War raged. And between 1869 and 1874 more than two hundred battles were fought in various regions of the West as the resolution of the "Indian problem" became the U.S. Army's major postwar activity. In the early summer of 1876, ten days prior to the nation's celebration of its centennial, Colonel George Armstrong Custer, who though graduated last in his class at West Point had been a general during the Civil War, led a charge against a large group of Sioux encamped on the banks of the Little Big Horn River in present-day Montana. Several hours later Custer and all his men lay dead. The Sioux, however, had gained only temporary advantage. For the ghost of Custer lived on and helped to energize a spirit of revenge among whites.

A book, *Story of the Wild West and Campfire Chats*, issued by the Historical Publishing Company of Philadelphia in 1888 and attributed to Buffalo Bill Cody, helped to keep the Custer legend alive by reminding Americans of "Custer and his squad of noble heroes." Shortly thereafter, anticipating their own great leader who would direct them to final triumph over the arrogant and racist whites, two hundred Hunkpapa Sioux gathered at Wounded Knee, South Dakota, in late December, 1890. They planned to stage a Ghost Dance designed to recapture the spirit of dead warriors and bring forth the appearance of a savior who would destroy the whites and bring back the buffalo herds. Fearful of such "pagan superstition," the cavalry that Custer had commanded, the Seventh Cavalry, proceeded to massacre some 200 men, women, and children. Their frozen bodies were dumped into a snowy common grave.

The decade of the 1890s was one of incredible discrimination for the nation's almost nine million blacks. By 1900 they comprised over 11 percent of the population but were in the process of losing ground in their battle to move up from slavery and find an accepted place in American life. For a time it had appeared that genuine efforts were being made by both blacks and whites to accomplish this goal. Constitutional reforms during Reconstruction and political alliances attempted later between blacks and poor whites, such as that led by Tom Watson in Georgia, offered hope for the future. The foremost reality which blacks had to face by the 1890s, however, was not the formidable task of melting into the American Way, but the task of adjusting to so-called Jim Crow laws which sharply restricted the social and economic mobility of blacks in America.

While there were many glowing reports of the openness of American society, and the illusion was fostered that all elements of the nation were being assimilated into the mainstream of national life, blacks were faced with a legal code forbidding interracial marriage and upholding separation of the races in schools, restaurants, restrooms, trains, depots, hotels, barbershops, and theaters. In the political arena the Gay Nineties for blacks was an age of literacy tests, so-called grandfather clauses which prevented one from voting unless one's forefathers had been free, poll taxes collected during planting periods when few had money, and other devices for keeping them once again "in their place" and out of politics. Indeed, the highest tribunal in the land, the Supreme Court, made its own contribution to this period of national self-deception by declaring in the famous case of *Plessy* v. *Ferguson* (1896) that the "separate but equal" standing of blacks in American life was constitutional. This legal fiction went unchallenged for more than fifty years as black Americans increasingly found their legacy of the 1890s to be one much more of separation than equality. In the South discrimination took the form of legal segregation (*de jure*) whereas in the North it was more often a case of subtle segregation in fact (*de facto*). In either case, however, it amounted to a significant retreat by the country from the

American creed of equality and opportunity. In itself this was bad enough, but the process occurred in an age that often prided itself on its creative fulfillment of the American Dream.

For immigrants the situation was scarcely better. Lured by promises of boundless opportunity, they were often forced to view the American scene from the vantage point of ethnic ghettoes in the poorest sections of the nation's cities. Yet, the idea of social and economic opportunity was not entirely mythical. There were many immigrants—John Peter Altgeld in business and politics, Jacob Riis in social reform, Joseph Pulitzer in journalism, Louis Aggassiz in science—who found the American system sufficiently open to allow them greatly to enrich the nation's heritage. America, especially in comparison with other countries at that time or since, was an open society with an unusual rate of assimilation for foreigners. The fact remains, however, that for every Altgeld, Riis, Pulitzer, or Aggassiz who found America the Promised Land, there were thousands who found themselves strangers in the land during the supposedly gay years at century's end.

America's Rise to World Power

The atmosphere of myth which still clings to the 1890s has also worked to create a series of misunderstandings about the nation's rise to world leadership which allegedly occurred during that decade. It is usually assumed that two major events—the Spanish-American War of 1898 and the Open Door Notes of 1899-1900 dealing with the China trade—were of major significance in bringing America out of an isolationist shell hardened by the Civil War, its aftermath, and the attentions being lavished on the country's industrial growth. While both of these international developments may well have contributed greatly to the nation's self-image of finally becoming a world power, it is important to note that the United States had been following expansionistic policies for some time, and that it did not burst onto the stage of international politics with "new" policies in the late 1890s. The myth of American isolationism from the Civil War to century's end simply does not tally with the fact that secretaries of state from William

Seward to John Hay (from 1861 until the turn of the century) had aggressively served as architects of American expansion.

On another point, it is clear that the United States did not initiate a Far Eastern policy with designs on the fabled commercial trade of China through its Open Door notes in 1899. Later generations of Americans looking for evidence with which to support the legend of America's meteoric rise to world power in the final years of the nineteenth century would assume that the Open Door policy in China was an "American idea" which demonstrated "energy and shrewd skill in negotiation." Such a view, however, is far from accurate. While it is true that American Secretary of State John Hay dispatched an initial memorandum to the world's leading powers—England, Russia, Germany, France, Italy, and Japan—in late 1899, asking them to leave the door of trade in China open to all nations, like the Monroe Doctrine seventy-five years earlier the notes did not amount to much in their time. The idea was simply a restatement of existing British policy and in fact is thought to have been inspired by a British subject (A. E. Hippisley of the Chinese Imperial Customs Service) who offered his advice through a friend of John Hay (William W. Rockhill) that there would be strategic advantage in the United States reestablishing its claim to China's trade. The government attempted to do this even though America had enjoyed equal trading opportunities in the area since the Wanghia Agreement in 1844. In lieu of facing facts, however, "the myth was established that 'in this episode of the Open Door notes, a tremendous blow had been struck for the triumph of American principles in international society—an American blow for an American idea.' "[3] Ironically, the notion of China's fabled wealth, upon which these expansionist policies were based, proved to be mythical too. Despite the persistent legend, dating from the Age of Discovery, that there would be huge economic benefits in trade with the Chinese, the China trade, at its peak, amounted to only about 3 percent of American exports.

In matters of foreign affairs the nineteenth century ended as it had begun for America—in a proliferation of new myths. The victory over Spain was achieved at the expense of a second-rate power, and policies in support of

trading privileges in China merely confirmed long-standing practice. Neither activity, in hindsight, was much of a break with the past—either in goals, accomplishments, or mythmaking character. Armed with the illusion that it had come of age because of its victory in the war with Spain and through its brilliant diplomacy in the Far East, America was set to enter the twentieth century with a sense of destined world leadership based on fact thoroughly colored with fiction.

SECTION I: HERO OF THE "LAST FRONTIER": THE AMERICAN COWBOY

Because of growing complexities at home and abroad, America was particularly ripe for the creation of myth and legend at century's end. An increase in the literacy rate of Americans in the decades after the Civil War did much to help create a vast new reading public which readily consumed the thousands of dime novels produced—the paperbacks of their time. In great demand were the yarns and tales which were being told about life on the vanishing frontier. The national thirst for adventure, escapism, and the glorification of self-reliance came to be satisfied directly through the publication of ten-cent thrillers which brought the action and romance of pioneer western life into the parlor. The first of the dime novels—creations of Erasmus and Irwin Beadle—had appeared just before the Civil War, but during the postwar period they reached their greatest level of success with the American reading public.

Nineteenth-century versions of today's Westerns, the dime novels told of the adventure and great deeds taking place on the panoramic stage of the American West. They related tales of bloodshed and stirring heroism against a background of nature's glorious landscape. They implied that the frontier was truly *the* proving ground of Americanism. Their cardboard characters were hunters, plainsmen, outlaws, badmen, "desperadoes," gamblers, dance-hall girls, cattle thieves, and of course cowboys and Indians. The novels' romanticized and stereotyped plots dealt with holdups, cattle drives, vengeance, violence,

170

and murder. Scarcely a page could be turned without the bloody death of a dozen "Injuns," and the smell of gunsmoke seeped from every volume. They were semihistorical tales based in an indirect way on the exploits of real characters of the frontier such as Jim Bridger, Kit Carson, and Buffalo Bill Cody. These salmon-colored paperback books became standard reading matter for countless Americans, young and old, and the American News Company had a standing order for 60,000 copies of each new issue published. Country stores and local newsstands quickly sold out, so anxious were Americans to immerse themselves in the galloping mythology of the Wild West. Enthusiasm for the dime novels continues even today. First editions of the Beadle classics draw hundreds of dollars from collectors still interested in this vital piece of Americana.

The Cult of the Western

Gradually, the vast audience of Western enthusiasts which the dime novels had created was taken over by a new class of Western writers. While the cowboy had been forced to share center stage in the dime-novel sagas with other frontiersmen like the fur trapper, the gold miner, and the western scout, by the turn of the century he came to stand alone as the greatest of America's Western heroes. In the early years of the twentieth century a Philadelphia lawyer, Owen Wister, succeeded in liberating the cowboy from the dime novels and giving him a new synthetic stature all his own. Wister first achieved success with a novel, *The Virginian* (1902), which has come to serve as a model for hundreds of Western books, movies, and television productions for more than seventy-five years. This novel, dedicated to Wister's close personal friend, Theodore Roosevelt, who shared his enthusiasm for the West, became an immediate best-seller, and has sold over 1.6 million copies in hard cover alone. Like Roosevelt, Wister grew alarmed at the modernization of American life—its sprawling cities, booming industry, the rise of organized labor, and the complexities of finance capitalism—and thus sought an imaginative escape to a simpler time through his literary portraits of the "real men" of the American West. The Virginian, riding the ranges of Wyoming, undisturbed by the complexities of civilization, was the embodiment of grace, honesty, bravery, and chivalry—virtues that seemed to be disappearing.

Owen Wister was a cultured Easterner, a graduate of Harvard, and for a time a student of Ernest Guiraud at the Paris Conservatory of Music. His writings, however, spoke in "plain talk" to the nation at large. They allowed both him and his readers to enjoy romantic images of virgin prairies and gallant cowboys which acted as models for alternative life-styles to an America caught in the midst of urban-industrial growth. The energy, initiative, freshness, and innocence of the West which Wister's work portrayed was more imaginary than real, but through his efforts the ghosts of the past continued to live on for an America already convinced that modern society was somehow superficial and unnatural. Some critics found his novel, which contained a veritable encyclopedia of Western plots, "too melodramatic." Americans ever since, however, have accepted Wister's mythical Virginian as an admirable period piece from a bygone era worth preserving. *The Virginian* was the first and most popular of the new Western novels. Since publication it has been highly influential, inspiring the television program of the same name, and leading the citizens of Wyoming to name a peak in the Teton mountain range for its author. Its greatest legacy, however, was the spirit and structure it provided writers of Western novels throughout the twentieth century.

The popularization of the myth and cult of the cowboy no doubt got underway with the writings of Owen Wister, but the body and substance of the Western myth was developed at the hands of twentieth-century authors such as Ernest Haycox, Max Brand, Luke Short, and Zane Grey. Ernest Haycox (1899-1950), though less widely known than many other of his colleagues, displayed a unique gift for recreating vivid, colorful images of the West.

> This was one of those years in the Territory [he once wrote] when Apache smoke signals spiraled up from the stony mountain summits and many a ranch cabin lay as a square of blackened ashes on the ground and the departure of a

stage from Tonto was the beginning of an adventure that had no certain happy ending. . . . Out below in the desert's distance stood the relay stations they hoped to reach and pass. Between lay a country swept empty by the quick raids of Geronimo's men.

Indeed, given his concise, evocative style, his professional peers considered him the most accomplished writer in this genre. His short story, "Stage to Lordsburg," from which the passage above is quoted, was the source of John Ford's classic Western film, *Stagecoach*.

Max Brand (1900-1944), the pen name of Frederick Faust, was among the most widely read of Western writers, having published more than eighty-five novels, most of which were Westerns. Perhaps better known as the creator of Dr. Kildare, Brand, in stories such as "Wine on the Desert," contributed much to the legendary appeal of the cowboy through his rich mixture of history and nostalgia. Of equal stature was Frederick Glidden (1909-1975), better known by the pen name Luke Short, who was born in Illinois and authored more than fifty hell-bent-for-leather Westerns. Glidden was a master at portraying swift action and suspense, and many of his works were later adapted into successful movies, such as *Ramrod* and *Vengeance Valley*. Neither Haycox, Brand, nor Short, however, attained the popularity or success of Zane Grey.

The "most beloved Western story teller of all time" (if one is to believe the advertising claims of his publisher), Zane Grey (1875-1939) was born in Ohio, attended the University of Pennsylvania on a baseball scholarship, and tried his hand at both minor league baseball and dentistry before turning to the writing of Western fiction. A peerless recorder of the distant days of the Old West, Grey can be credited with ninety-five published books—seventeen of which were issued after his death. After nearly a half century such works as *Riders of the Purple Sage*, *The Lone Star Ranger*, *The Vanishing American*, *The Thundering Herd*, and *The Light of Western Stars* are still very much in popular demand. His works have sold an estimated twenty-seven million copies, and it has been estimated that some fifty-four million Americans have

read one or more of his novels. As well as any other writer in the Western tradition, Grey's works contain the common misconceptions which Americans hold about the seemingly glorious days of the frontier West. Critics, of course, have charged that Grey's work lacks artistic responsibility and historical accuracy, but to a nation constantly in need of the escapism which historical romance provides, Zane Grey and the American West have become nearly synonymous.

The romantic images of the West portrayed in the works of frontier artists Frederic Remington and Charles Russell also helped mythologize the region and its cowboys. Frederic Remington (1861-1909), of Canton, New York, and Yale University, was, according to the postage stamp issued in his honor in 1961, America's "Artist of the Old West." Remington's paintings are endlessly reproduced on postcards and prints, and reproductions of his work are sold as souvenirs in museums, national parks, and nearly every drugstore west of the Mississippi River, not to mention those east of the Mississippi. Believing that masculine strength came from conflict with nature, Remington translated his love for the great outdoors into artistic portrayals of the personal encounters of rugged individuals with the savage wilderness of the West. In such works as "The Scout," "Stampeded by Lightning," and "The Outlying Camp," this confrontation is strikingly realized. He helped the American public romantically savor the color of the great West by providing convenient, ready-made images of the robust frontier.

Charles M. Russell (1864-1926) held a more legitimate claim to being a Westerner and student of cowboy life than Remington. Born in St. Louis, Missouri, Russell was exposed at an early age to the rich memories of such heroes of the West as Lewis and Clark, Zebulon Pike, and Kit Carson. Having spent his boyhood on the Mississippi River waterfront, he was familiar with the stirring tales of the role that St. Louis had played in the westward migration. At age sixteen he had his first taste of what was coming to be thought of as "the real West" when he visited the Montana ranch of a family friend. So taken was he with this new environment that he spent most of his life thereafter in Cascade and Great Falls, Montana. Depicting the land and individuals he saw around him, Russell's paintings and sketches soon became an important part of the romantic conception that was being formed about the frontier. In 1903 he signed a contract with the firm of Brown and Bigelow of St. Paul, Minnesota, and for many years they printed his Western paintings on calendars. In his painting, "When Guns Speak, Death Settles Disputes," Russell foreshadowed the later efforts of radio, movies, and television to exploit the sentimental attachment which Americans had already developed for the Western hero and his locale.

In the 1930s and 1940s, radio gave a new boost to the myth of the cowboy and Western hero. The Lone Ranger series, created by James Jewell (also the creator of Jack Armstrong, the "All-American Boy"), was first presented over station WXYZ in Detroit. The Lone Ranger program lent the Western myth a dimension of reality which it had never before enjoyed. Having developed a taste for Jewell's version of the West, generations of Americans might find it disappointing to discover that "Kee-Mo-Sah-Bee," Tonto's greeting to the masked Ranger, was not derived from some exotic bit of Western Americana, but rather from the name of a boys' camp owned by Jewell's father-in-law.

The Lone Ranger, according to legend the last gallant survivor of a group of Texas Rangers caught in an ambush, has allowed Americans to return to "those thrilling days of yesteryear" without realizing that the guardians of virtue, law, and order on the high plains were something less than giants in their time. That many modern scholars have a much less romantic view of the Texas Rangers—some insisting that they were little more than paid assassins of Texas ranchers—seems not to matter.

The longevity of the cowboy myth is indebted also to the continuing efforts of Hollywood in assisting in the image-making process. Its contribution has been to project the sights, sounds, and colors of the saga of the West on a silver screen. Since the movie mogul Edwin S. Porter produced *The Great Train Robbery* in 1903, the nation has continued to be enthralled by the legendary heroics of such stars as William S. Hart, Tom Mix, Gene Autrey, Roy Rogers, Hopalong Cassidy, Gary Cooper, John Wayne, and Clint Eastwood. Films and box office receipts have demonstrated anew—if anyone ever doubted the point—that mythology can and often does translate itself into very profitable consequences. With the help of Hollywood studios, Americans can relive the Winning of the West. That a good many of those Hollywood productions are produced in the San Fernando Valley, back lots of Universal City, or "on location" just beyond the fringes of Palm Springs has seldom caused anyone to question their authenticity.

The Cowboy and American Values

The survival of the cowboy as the most durable of America's myth-figures has become the subject of scholarly criticism. Some academicians find it inappropriate that a group of men totaling no more than forty thousand, whose presence on history's stage lasted for little more than a quarter of a century, should be the subject of such lavish and error-based attention. Indeed, many of those who have come to be legends in their own time and beyond—Wyatt Earp and Bat Masterson for example—in real life turn out to have been little more than brawling, boozing men of very dubious reputation. Without the mythic garb, the cowboy emerges as an essentially dull character who knew little about and seldom used a six-shooter, and more likely than not was a nearly helpless pawn of a ruthless cattle economy which left little room indeed for his allegedly free spirit. Eleanor Aveling, the daughter of Karl Marx, described the cowboys as victims of the economic forces of capitalism, but erred in claiming them potential revolutionaries of the class struggle in her book, *The Working-Class Movement in America* (1891).

What troubles one most about cowboy mythology, however, is the expression it gives to a good many of the nation's more questionable values—racism, sexism, and violent lawlessness. It is an indisputable fact that approximately one cowboy in four was either Mexican, Indian, or black. Only a few of these, however, have shared in the benefits of the matinee-idol image of the Western hero. Nate Love, for example, was born into slavery in Tennessee in 1854, moved to Dodge City at the age of fifteen, and by all reports rode the trails of the West in truly expert fashion until 1890,

Nate Love ("Deadwood Dick"):
Authentic Westerner
Library of Congress

after which he gained fame on the rodeo circuit. For the most part, however, blacks have been invisible men of the epic of the West. Similarly, Mexicans, if portrayed at all, emerge as treacherous, cowardly, ignorant, and uncouth persons. Reflecting Texas-based racism developed decades earlier, the actions of both white cowboys and Americans since has been in agreement with the attitude of Larry McMurtrie, a cowboy himself and a participant in the activities of the open range: "The way to handle Mexicans is to kick 'em in the ribs."

More visible than either Mexicans or blacks, Indians became the most direct object of the West's racist mythic code. At its best, the myth of the West portrayed Native Americans in a

"Tonto" image—the faithful companion who in wooden fashion held the cowboy hero's horse or ministered to his wounds. At its worst, the myth openly declared that "the only good Indian is a dead Indian." To some degree it is true that in the folklore of today the Indian is replacing the cowboy as a symbol of self-sufficiency and vigor. But by far the principal thrust of the West's mythology has been to show clearly that the Indian was an inferior being to the godlike cowboys of the frontier's vanished golden age.

The appeal of the myth of the cowboy-hero is generally found in its openly sexist overtones. While it is true that life on the range had a decidedly masculine flavor to it, like most other supporting characters in the myth, women's only usefulness apparently was to highlight the virtues of the chivalrous ranger or to willingly satisfy his sexual needs. As the myth has found expression in ballads, movies, and literature, the heroine is invariably characterized as either a delicate Easterner of refined tastes somehow smitten by the clean good looks and dashing manner of the hero, or a whore with a "heart of gold" who gladly offers the men of the plains a few blessed moments of relief from their arduous task of settling the frontier. Intent upon emphasizing the cowboy's immunity from "feminine weakness," the myth and legend of Western history has violated fact by rarely allowing a real woman to complicate the hero's image of simplicity and innocence. In this way the myth has become a vivid statement of American values. The magnetic attachment of Americans to the cowboy has reflected the nation's mythology—western, racist, and sexist.

Despite the many negative features of the Western myth, however, it seems not likely to ride away into the setting sun. Local chambers of commerce, seeking to parlay the mythology of the West into hard dollars, vie with one another in claiming their town more "Western" than the one at the next exit on the Interstate. State departments of tourism have also come to realize the potentially positive economic consequences of the Western myth. The state of North Dakota lays claim to being the site of the "real West," while college students in Nebraska find summer employment corraling Easterners at freeway oases, urging them to take the time to see the restored home of Buffalo Bill Cody near North Platte. "Colorful Colorado" and the "Big Sky Country" of Montana have long reaped benefits from the summer tourist who, camera in hand, seeks to relive one of American history's supposedly grandest eras. The state of South Dakota, moreover, has launched one of the more recent and successful campaigns to capitalize on the strength of the West's often synthetic historical heritage. Urged to "roam free in South Dakota," and "capture on film the remains of homesteaders' cabins, and ghost towns before the claws of time finally succeed in wearing them away," one is easily enticed by advertising of the South Dakota Division of Tourism:

> It costs nothing to re-live the West. Become part of it in Deadwood where Wild Bill Hickok was gunned down, holding a poker hand of aces and eights. Experience cattle kingdoms with their barbed wire boundaries. And rub shoulders with real cowboys who ride in real rodeos. It costs little or nothing to camp within a flicker of 1876 and arise to the scents and sights that captivated Jim Bridger, Crazy Horse, Lewis and Clark, Sitting Bull, and General Custer.[4]

Indeed, given the Madison Avenue techniques, the production capacity of toy manufacturers, the activities of the Cowboy Hall of Fame in Oklahoma City, and the cleverly packaged illusion of Frontierland in the "wonderful world of Disney," the West is likely to remain as the American poet Archibald MacLeish described it some time ago—"a country in the mind, and so eternal."

SECTION II: MYTHS OF THE YEOMAN-FARMER AND THE SELF-MADE MAN

At least since the third century B.C., highly educated and urbane people have written nostalgically of country life as though it were serenely free of the pressures and problems of "civilized" society. Far from the madding crowd, the Greek poet Theocritus, for example, wrote rhapsodically of goatherds in Sicily, and in Imperial Rome the poet Virgil dreamed that he might be with shepherds in far-off Arcadia. Many writers since, in emotional and enthusiastic response to what they imagined to be the pure and innocent existence found in a small village or rural environment, have sought to transport their readers on a romantic journey through the country away from the chaos of social, political, and economic problems which seem to center in the city. Simplicity, innocence, and freedom for the spirit, in short, have long been associated with rural life. The romantic idea of hardworking, independent yeoman farmers patiently tilling their fields, their quaint cottages in the background, has endeared itself to both poets and public alike.

The notion that humans enjoy the greatest happiness of spirit only in a rural setting found perhaps its most classic statement in the writings of the English poet Oliver Goldsmith who wrote just before the American Revolution. His "The Deserted Village" (1774) was written in outrage against the Enclosure Acts which were forcing many small tenant-farmers, who up to that time had operated under a system of open-field agriculture, off the land. With graceful style, and sincere effort to describe the good old days of country living in England which the Enclosure Acts threatened to end forever, Goldsmith wrote:

> Sweet Auburn, loveliest village of the plain,
> Where health and plenty cheered the laboring swain [rural laborer]
> Where smiling spring its earliest visit paid,
> And parting summer's lingering blooms delayed,
> Dear lovely bowers of innocence and ease,
> Seats of my youth, when every sport could please,
> How often have I loitered o'er thy green,
> Where humble happiness endeared each scene;
> How often have I paused on every charm,
> The sheltered cot[tage], the cultivated farm,
> The never-failing brook, the busy mill,
> The decent church that topped the neighboring hill. . . .

Oliver Goldsmith, of course, has not been the only one to praise the "ease" and "charm" of the rural life or to suggest the fundamental virtue which village and farm provide. Across the English Channel, during the same century, a group of French philosophers, called Physiocrats, believed that the land was the source of all wealth. For them, agriculture was the only productive economic activity; it followed the "rules of nature." Commerce and industry, for the Physiocrats, were sterile, nonproductive, unessential, false, and corrupt. Emphasis on the beauty, simplicity, and economic importance of nature and the peasant life, they concluded, was essential for bringing human affairs into alignment with the "natural law" and the "natural order of things."

From such a viewpoint it is but a short distance intellectually to what historians have come to call the agrarian myth—the essentially romantic and persistent view of rural life as ideal and the farmer as a folk hero. Indeed, over time, the notion that rural districts were sites of virtue, and cities correspondingly dens of vice, moved from an idea common only to poets and philosophers to a popular and political ideal. By the late eighteenth century the agrarian myth found expression in such bizarre happenings as Marie Antoinette playing a shepherdess on the grounds of the royal palace at Versailles. And in a more serious vein, Thomas Jefferson, in the new United States, was stating his belief that "those who labor in the earth are the chosen people of God."

The Agrarian Myth in America

Though the basic features of the agrarian myth—or the myth of the happy yeoman, as it is sometimes called—were established in Europe, they came to have increasing appeal in America throughout the nineteenth century. Here, the countryside with its values and virtues became the focus of much of the nation's imaginative attention largely because of an "abundance of nature." The American frontier, particularly after the Louisiana Purchase of 1803, seemed to be a limitless expanse of virgin land. Heroes were needed to match the qualities of the land. As a result, the buckskin frontiersman and later the cowboy

emerged as candidates for myth-making, but in many ways the frontier farmer was the most obvious candidate of all. His honest industry, his ability to produce abundant goods for the expanding nation, and his straightforward spirit of equality and independence made him appear as both an ideal man and ideal citizen.

Indeed, the growing nationwide importance of the yeoman-farmer in both economic and political affairs led many to picture him as the ideal American. Benjamin Franklin, expressing the attitude of many generations, unqualifiedly praised agriculture as "the only honest way for a nation to acquire wealth . . . and the yeoman farmer receives from God a reward for his honesty, his innocent life and his virtuous industry." Some years later, Ralph Waldo Emerson, the American essayist, reinforced the same point when he spoke of "the advantage which the country-life possesses, for a powerful mind, over the artificial and curtailed life of cities." Early American politicians, writers, and country editors had reason enough to court the "tillers of the soil," for the majority of citizens were farmers. But while early America had been an agrarian society very much tied to the land, and out of habit looked favorably upon the family farm and its way of life, the cherished notion that agriculture was the most basic of industries and the yeoman-farmer the most virtuous of men became even more precious with the passage of time.

Once it appeared that such a healthy and happy way of life might be losing out to the forces of urbanization and industrialism, the yeoman-farmer became even more the object of sympathy, admiration, and sentimentalism. The process whereby the myth of the happy yeoman gained currency and vitality in the face of America's urban-industrial development during the late nineteenth century has been explained particularly well by the historian Richard Hofstadter:

> The more commercial this society became . . . the more reason it found to cling in imagination to the noncommercial agrarian values. The more farming as a self-sufficient way of life was abandoned for farming as a business, the more merit men found in what was being left behind. And the more rapidly the farmer's sons

moved into the towns, the more nostalgic the whole culture became about its rural past. Throughout the nineteenth and even the twentieth century, the American was taught that rural life and farming as a vocation were something sacred.[5]

This nostalgic attitude toward the farmer and the rural life quickly became part of the nation's standard political vocabulary. For example, William Jennings Bryan, as a candidate for the presidency in 1896, never tired of reciting the litany of agriculture's virtues to the nation. In the 1920s Calvin Coolidge found it useful to have himself photographed on his Vermont farm, for he sought to project himself as a man of the soil. And later politicians in much the same style have been quick to discover the advantages of "shirt-sleeve" campaigning and a "down home" approach to electioneering. Only occasionally have politicians been aware of the false romance which so often surrounds the nation's understanding of life in rural America, as when Dwight Eisenhower pointedly noted that "farming looks mighty easy when your plow is a pencil and you're a thousand miles from a cornfield."

Life on the country meadows and rolling plains of America's agricultural frontier did in some ways offer the kind of simple pleasures which myth claimed for it. It afforded a less hurried life-style, created the sense of being close to nature, and in general offered a sanctuary from the multiple problems of an increasingly urban-industrial society. In important respects, however, the myth of the happy yeoman failed to live up to its promise. Many people found the "crusade to the West," symbolized by the covered wagon, the log cabin, and the plow, a good deal less idyllic than the legend purveyed by poets, philosophers, artists, and politicians. For many pioneer "sodbusters" the reality of the frontier was its heat, sweat, flies, mosquitos, drudgery, and dirt. The conquest of the soil often left the scars of isolation, tragic futility, loneliness, and desperation upon the conquerors. For many, the agricultural frontier was not a "land of milk and honey" but rather a region plagued by grasshoppers, blizzards, drought, cholera, and high infant mortality. The rigors of tilling soil and just sustaining

The Yeoman Farmer: Ideal Man and Ideal Citizen
Library of Congress

one's life usually left little energy for barnraisings, square dances, husking and quilting bees, quiet sleigh rides through snow-covered forests, and the leisured exchange of rural gossip over the cracker barrel at the country store.

Physical, mental, and spiritual hardships made pioneer life on the frontiers of Iowa, Minnesota, Kansas, Nebraska, and the Dakotas not a romantic epic but a constant race to escape early death. Dirt-floored houses smelled more of the barnyard and the dried buffalo dung being used for fuel than of Aunt Polly's biscuits and home-baked bread. The legendary country kitchen was more often a primitive combination dining room, living room, and washroom rather than a sun-filled area of gingham curtains, starched ruffled aprons, and the aroma of fresh blueberry pie. Waving fields of grain at harvest time and old oaken buckets to this day remain romantic folksy images of the rural way of life, but they scarcely reflect the natural and economic hardships with which the yeoman-farmer had to contend. Novelists such as Hamlin Garland in *The Son of the Middle Border* (1917) and, particularly, O. E. Rolvaag in *Giants in the Earth* (1924) have dealt realistically with the humble life of the agricultural pioneer. Perhaps American poet Edwin Markham has captured best the grim reality of the peasant yeoman-farmer. In "The Man with a Hoe" (1899), he describes a happy yeoman quite at odds with Goldsmith's mythical view of more than a century before:

> Bowed by the weight of centuries he
>   leans
> Upon his hoe and gazes at the ground,
> The emptiness of ages in his face,
> And on his back the burden of the world.
> Who made him dead to rapture and
>   despair,
> A thing that grieves not and that never
>   hopes,
> Stolid and stunned, a brother to the ox?
> Who loosened and let down this brutal
>   jaw?
> Whose was the hand that slanted back
>   his brow?
> Whose breath blew out the light within
>   his brain?

Agrarians Challenge the Legend

To alleviate their economic plight, the nation's farmers during the last decades of the nineteenth century launched a series of political efforts designed to bring rural America into the mainstream of the competitive capitalistic system. Victims of agrarian mythology, and bypassed in the struggle for political power, yeomen-farmers formed the People's party. Populism, as the movement came to be called, demanded a flexible currency, a graduated income tax, public owner-ship and operation of railroads, and reclamation of railroad lands illegally held, as well as other reforms designed to ease the plight of rural America. Specifically, they sought to deal with the farmers' eroding income, exorbitant railroad rates, and excessive interest rates ranging from 8 to 40 percent. Mary Lease of Kansas urged farmers to "raise less corn and more Hell," and Davis H. Waite, governor of Colorado and the so-called Abraham Lincoln of the Rockies, joined the camp-meeting atmosphere of the Populists' National Political Convention in Omaha, July 4, 1892. Even though the Populist party made a respectable showing in the national election of 1892, it did not become a force in national politics. As one of their number, Ignatius Donnelly of Minnesota, remarked after the defeat: "Our followers scattered like dew before the rising sun." Apparently, the nation's continued fascination with the agrarian myth, combined with the "radical" proposals of the party's platform, worked to seal the Populists' defeat. Indeed, even among Populist orators themselves Oliver Goldsmith's "The Deserted Village" continued to be quoted with great approval even as Grover Cleveland soundly trounced the Populist candidate, James B. Weaver.

The Self-Made Man

With farming life on the frontier turning out to be less idyllic and lucrative than Americans nostalgically thought it was, it seemed increasingly evident that the promise of American life could more easily be found in the city. As census figures bear out, many yeomen left the farm and its demoralizing monotony to find their fortune in the opportunities offered by America's great cities. For every urban worker who followed the beacon of the agrarian myth by moving to the country, twenty farm youths left for the city with tantalizing thoughts of moving from rags to riches. Lured by the romance, the activity, and the excitement which such great urban centers as New York, Philadelphia, and Chicago seemed to offer, restless souls left what they saw as the "slavery" of farming and small-town life to seek their fortune amidst the glitter of urban America. How to keep them down on the farm was already a recurring question.

Like the agrarian myth, the myth of the

self-made man is not of American origin. The story of worthy types who rose from poverty and obscurity to honor, glory, and respectability is indeed as old as recorded history. In legend and literature stories of those who rose from the ranks date at least as far back as Charles Perrault's classic written version of the fairy tale, "Cinderella," published in 1697. At least in folklore, however, success most often fell to the self-made man rather than his female counterpart. Historical periods of rapid change in ancient Greece and Rome and throughout the Renaissance period all witnessed an emphasis on upwardly mobile heroes. But while many societies have endorsed the ideas of self-help and individual initiative, Americans have accepted them religiously. In America, the sacred cult of the self-made man has consistently been expressed in the durable but questionable thought that through hard work, luck, and a life modeled after the Christian virtues any man can become president of the United States. The idea of "rugged individualism" is one of the sacred dogmas of the American creed.

The myth of rags to riches is of course a reflection of truth. Upward mobility—the rise of men and women to higher social and economic station—is possible in America. What makes the idea mythical, however, is the fact that the openness of American society is more imaginary than real, and the rise of Americans from rags to riches has occurred neither with the frequency nor in the manner generally presumed. The myth of the self-made man —or the Horatio Alger myth—has failed to depict the many features of American life which frustrate social mobility. Instead, it has sketched the ideal.

The sources of America's mythological love affair with the self-made man are varied indeed. They seem to be related, first, to the nation's emphasis on the so-called Protestant ethic. Believers in this ethic—from the Puritan minister Cotton Mather through Dr. Norman Vincent Peale—have consistently emphasized the importance of piety, diligence, and frugality for one's worldly success. Second, they reflect the more secular emphasis on success apparent during the nineteenth century—represented by Abraham Lincoln in politics, Samuel Clemens in literature, and

P. T. Barnum in the business world—that self-improvement and economic opportunity were the inevitable rewards of initiative, competitiveness, and self-discipline. Third, the self-made man has continued to survive as a popular hero and as a central symbol of the American way of life because of the political efforts of such Americans as Benjamin Franklin and Thomas Jefferson who furthered the idea that the self-improvement of the individual assured a healthy state of affairs for the nation and American society generally. To most Americans, however, the Gospel of Success will always be most closely linked to the name Horatio Alger, Jr.

One of the true publishing sensations of all time, Horatio Alger has indeed become synonymous in the public mind with the self-made man. Alger has in fact become a patron saint for those who see the great strength of America in individualistic free enterprise. The enthusiasm of groups like the American Schools and Colleges Association, which annually present a bronze desk plaque—The Horatio Alger Award—to eight Americans who have reached positions of great economic success from humble beginnings, however, is greatly misguided. For contrary to popular belief, Alger's writings never fully advocated the kinds of values which later generations of Americans have attributed to them.

It is a popular misconception, for example, to believe that Alger's fictional heroes were "alone and unaided." In fact, the leading characters in Alger's novels, such as Ragged Dick and Mark, the Match Boy, do not find the key to success entirely through individual enterprise and achievement. In nearly every story Alger wrote the successful lad was one who received considerable assistance. Useful friends and kindly patrons always seemed to appear at the right moment to advance the hero's "individual" success.

It must be emphasized as well that the Alger hero never "rose to the top of the economic heap." By story's end, Alger's self-made man is firmly at the threshold of "respectability," but in few instances does he rise to high social status or economic position. Recent winners of the Horatio Alger Award—James H. Carmichael, chairman of the board of Capital Airlines, and Benjamin F. Fairless, past chairman of United States Steel Corporation—seem rather curious Alger heroes indeed. Also, Horatio Alger never glorified the virtues of the Common Man as most are prone to believe. Rather, in terms of ability and personal character, his heroes are exceptional and anything but "common." Finally, a reading of Alger's novels shows that religion plays a very minor role in the hero's "rise," despite the misconception that Alger emphasized the critical importance of religion to the success of one's climb to fame and fortune.

Alger's formula for success, or at least what the nation has taken it to be, is indeed highly sentimentalized. And the folklore of the self-made man—whereby it is believed that the poor boy (either a farmer's son or an immigrant) could through self-help, pluck, and luck rise to economic, social, or political prominence in the "land of the free"—represents a mishmash of ideas. It is based on the few instances in which true success did occur, a misreading of the writings of Alger, the rhetoric of politicians and the clergy, and the wishful thinking of the many Americans who devotedly believed the myth. In late nineteenth-century America, historical forces such as the industrial revolution and immigration did have the effect of increasing mobility and the chance to get ahead. To some extent America was a fluid society, but this point has been greatly exaggerated. In real life, the saga of "little tyke to big tycoon" was rare indeed. For while it is often thought that nearly all the so-called captains of industry—John D. Rockefeller, Cornelius Vanderbilt, David Guggenheim, Collis P. Huntington, J. Pierpont Morgan, and others—rose from the lower strata of society, were often poorly educated farmers' sons, and were in many instances foreign-born, the facts simply do not support such a view.

Intrigued by the persistence of the Horatio Alger mystique in America, a number of economic historians and sociologists have studied the backgrounds of America's leading businessmen and industrialists during the alleged heyday of the self-made man—the 1890s. Their findings lead inescapably to the conclusion that by far the majority of men who made it to the top in that era were not poor farm boys or uneducated immigrant lads starting from the bottom. Instead, they were those who had been given rather exceptional oppor-

tunities to make the race to the top of the social and economic ladder. The studies of the economic historian Thomas Cochran and the sociologist C. Wright Mills, for example, find that more than 50 percent of the industrial leaders born between 1820 and 1879 attended college, in an age when the average American was lucky to have completed high school. In a later study by the historian William Miller, it was found that 70 percent of the nation's leading businessmen born between 1850 and 1879 came from the upper class or upper middle class. The Miller study, which concentrated on leading corporation executives who rose to fame and fortune in the first decade of the twentieth century, also found that only 12 percent came from farming backgrounds and a mere 5 percent were men who started as poor boys. In addition, 48 percent had fathers who had been businessmen, and close to 90 percent had been native-born. Indeed, it seems clear that the best way to have become a self-made man in America was to have been a native-born WASP—white, Anglo-Saxon, Protestant—of well-established background.

SECTION III: THE GAY NINETIES: A MISCONCEPTION

Few stereotyped visions of the "good old days" are more out of line with fact than those related to the so-called Gay Nineties. The very mention of the phrase conjures up a series of mythical images—the corner ice cream parlor, the penny arcade, Victorian brownstone houses, the bicycle-built-for-two, Gibson Girls with full blouses and wasplike waists, and the colorful sights and sounds of vaudeville and Tin Pan Alley. One need only throw in spectacular scenes such as six thousand miners dashing to the Klondike and references to the formative years of baseball as America's national pastime, orchestrate it all with a few choruses of "There'll be a Hot Time in the Old Town Tonight" or "Tra ra ra Boom De Aye," and there is the complete picture. Indeed, to most people the decade of the 1890s is thought to have been a fun-loving and charming era from America's golden past. Once one looks beneath the cover of musical gaiety which became the hallmark of the age, however, the color and excitement begin to fade. For the great mass of Americans who experienced the decade directly, the enthusiastic "razzmatazz" of the era was simply a brittle veneer which hid many sober realities of American life.

The mythical notion that the 1890s bubbled with frivolity and excitement fails, for example, to take into account the frustration and despair which had already been evident for some time in rural America. Despite the efforts of Populism to give voice to the despairing American farmer, matters got worse rather than better. Farmers in the Northeast abandoned their homesteads to seek a better life in the West, while the tillers of virgin land on the vast prairies and plains between the Appalachian and Rocky Mountains were faced with the harsh reality of mounting debts and pitifully low prices for the few crops they could coax from the soil. Planters in the South fared even worse. Despite earlier dreams of becoming a bountiful utopia, Dixie was a region of widespread poverty. Tired of cliches about the simplicity and blessed advantages of being a farmer in the "valley of democracy," many yeomen with good cause complained of "14 cent corn, 5 cent cotton, and 12 percent interest."

Life in the small towns and cities of America could be equally depressing. There, people were increasingly forced to deal with alcoholism, wandering vagrants, rural crime, poverty, and insanity. A cozy community nestled on the Wisconsin banks of the rolling Mississippi River, for example, reported one such tale of rural "gaiety":

> A young woman, 20 years old, who gave her name as Edith Eberhardt, occupied a cell at the LaCrosse police station Friday night [December 17, 1896]. She came from Winona and wanted to go to St. Louis, but was without money. She was evidently suffering from some form of dementia, for she persisted in sitting on the floor of her cell, refusing food, and [talking] strangely. She claimed something terrible had befallen her, but she refused to say what it was. She was sent on.[6]

But even when times were fairly good, life on the farms and in the small cities and towns taxed one's physical and psychological stamina. One faced a nearly hopeless future which would likely never bring freedom from a rural life too often spent in wretched frame or sod housing and a diet consisting of cooked pigweed, sowbelly, and corn flapjacks that often tasted like "disks of red flannel."

Life in the nation's large cities during the "good old days" was equally grim. There, the leisured life was enjoyed by only the privileged few. A basic root of the problem, in many ways, was wages. Statistics of the U.S. Bureau of Census reveal, for example, that the average annual wage of the nation's workers in 1890 stood at $438. A decade later, in 1900, the figure had declined to $428—an earning's loss of $10, or $1 per year in an era of capitalistic expansion. While freight handlers in New York City were being paid 17 cents an hour—$10 for a seven-day work week—Chicago merchandising tycoon Marshall Field enjoyed an income calculated to have been $600 per hour. In short, it took more than one year working seven days a week for the New York worker to match the wealth which one of America's "self-made men" was able to muster in a matter of 60 minutes. Incredibly, a good many others fared even worse—blacks received 50 cents a day, women $3 to $5 a week, and factory workers in the South less than $250 a year.

During the 1890s, of course, the days of the coffee break, sick leave, paid vacations, pensions, company-paid life and health insurance, cost-of-living adjustments, and overtime pay still lay far in the future. By comparison to today's standards, the fringe benefits and working conditions of laboring men and women during the Gay Nineties were skimpy and brutal. To say that many laborers worked under hazardous, unsanitary, and generally miserable conditions would be a gross understatement. Industrial accidents claimed 20,000 lives per year of which approximately 7,500 involved railroad workers. Miners also became fatalities of America's industrial growth with 45 men killed for every 10,000 employed. Even for those who did not become such statistics the ordeal of making a "living" had a way of considerably shortening one's life. Ironworkers suffered the consequences of suffocating smoke and gas, while tannery employees wallowed in stench, miners inhaled massive quantities of coal dust, and laborers in chemical plants exposed eyes, lungs, and skin to constant danger. Nausea, premature aging, maimed fingers, and severed limbs were often the inevitable result of inhuman working conditions and lack of safety practices. Never have so many given so much to American industrial development.

A special feature of the world of work during the Gay Nineties was child labor. The National Child Labor Committee, formed in 1904, and the book *The Bitter Cry of the Children* (1906) by the humanitarian reformer John Spargo, eventually exposed the callous attitude of many employers, summed up by a southern factory manager: "We take them as soon as they can stand up." Many youngsters of the 1890s had to accept wages of from $1.50 to $2.50 per week, work a torturous twelve- to fourteen-hour day that might begin or end at 2 o'clock in the morning, and risk the chance of permanent injury while filling the labor needs of canneries, mines, and glass factories. Some viewed the youthful working force as a protective measure against children's "idleness." Parents reluctantly agreed to the practice in order to keep their meager house and home together—they needed even the pitiful income a child produced. Only a few observers condemned the grisly practice of treating the younger generation as industrial commodities. Child laborers made up one third of all employees at many textile mills, but there were substantial numbers as well who spent their childhood in tobacco fields, meatpacking houses, and as garment workers. Government statistics in 1900 placed the number of working children at 1,752,187. Out of a national population of some 76,094,000 such a figure was staggering enough, but it failed to include the literally thousands of little "Shabby Nels," "Ragged Dicks," and "Tattered Toms" who wandered city streets as vendors, messengers, and bootblacks. Unlike their counterparts in the picturesque stories of Horatio Alger, Jr. and others, the youthful proletariat of the 1890s found the nation's cities a place of vicious exploitation rather than one of prosperity.

As might be expected, life for the urban poor was spent almost totally either working or sleeping. The good life and chances for leisure—which might have renewed the spirit and made such conditions somewhat more bearable—were seldom even within the expec-

tation, much less the reach, of most. What diversions there were ran to the rough and vulgar. Gambling, for example, became a favorite pastime of the urban masses—not at Las Vegas-style pleasure palaces or the racetrack, but more often at the corner tavern. Prey to confidence men or a fellow worker with a streak of luck, pitifully scarce "bread money" was often lost over tables of poker or dice. For many, the wheels of fortune kept the cycle of poverty spinning at a dizzying rate. For the more adventuresome, bets could be placed at local animal-baiting arenas where hungry rats from city waterfronts were pitted in bloody combat, with the tattered survivor paying his "owner" handsomely, thanks to the volume of customers.

Leisure-time activities also included spectator sports—when they could be afforded. The violence and despair which was so commonplace in nearly every other facet of people's lives was reflected in the popularity of such sports as boxing and football. There, barbarism and savagery matched the brutality of the workaday world. As in the game of life the rules were casual, and contestants viewed their activities as a case of survival of the fittest. Such professional boxers as the "Boston Strong Boy," John L. Sullivan, kicked, clawed, and punched their opponents senseless as they fought their way into the hearts of a people desperately in need of a hero who might for a time take their minds off their own mindless existence.

Social conditions being what they were, it was predictable that a good many men, women, and children would seek an escape from their lives of work, drudgery, and despair through drunkenness. The local tavern, saloon, or "beer joint" became the most convenient gathering place where one could spend the little leisure time that existed in the company of friends and fellow sufferers. Since beer often had an unusually high alcoholic content in order to keep it fresh for as long as possible, its effects on the consumer were usually swift and telling. While some slid comfortably into a mellow haze of drunken oblivion, others of more violent temperament soon found themselves in jails, insane asylums, or the nearest gutter. Meanwhile, others took their place in the great race to escape reality. And bartenders willingly obliged, selling their wares to anyone tall enough to hook his chin over the counter. In the view of one commentator, the social reformer Jacob Riis, author of *How the Other Half Lives* (1890), conditions in the worst of the old-time taverns were such that dogs were forced to flee the pungent atmosphere. These "institutes of vice" outnumbered churches ten to one and schools twenty to one. According to Riis's personal calculations compiled in New York City, between 13th Street in lower Manhattan and New York Bay there were 111 Protestant churches and 4,065 saloons.

Despite the Victorian male's pose of cold detachment from the ways of the flesh, prostitution flourished. "Temples of Lust," as they were called at the time, operated with surprising openness. Laws against the "world's oldest profession" remained on the books as a feeble gesture toward public decorum, but the trade in sex-for-pay ranged from prostitutes "caked with dirt" in city slums to sophisticated "ladies of the night" catering to an upper-class clientele. In all, according to the police commissioner, there were an estimated forty thousand prostitutes in New York City alone in 1890. In an age of spirited free enterprise perhaps it was only proper that all sectors of the economy be on the make.

The tone and style of the 1890s, then, was a good deal less joyful than the merchants of nostalgia have often suggested. Conspicuous consumption could be seen in Jay Gould's $500,000 yacht, in Cornelius Vanderbilt's two-million-dollar home with its $50,000 art collection and $20,000 bronze doors, and the financier J. P. Morgan's new $100,000 automobile. The sight of this led a religious magazine, the *Methodist Quarterly Review*, to assert that if Adam and Eve themselves had been able to save $500 per day since the creation they would still be $200,000 poorer than John D. Rockefeller. Meanwhile, the masses spent their scanty incomes on butter made of gelatin fat mixed with mashed potatoes, "fresh" chickens which had hung in outdoor markets for days in the hot sun, and milk cosmetically colored with chalk or plaster of paris. As industrial statesmen established giant corporations, monopolies, and trusts, streetcar drivers demanding a twelve-hour

workday were branded as "communistic" by New York State Assemblyman Theodore Roosevelt. While business tycoons spent summers in Europe and Newport, Rhode Island, and built palatial homes on New York's Fifth Avenue and in places like Asheville, North Carolina, the lower classes lived in tar-paper shanties or decaying tenements. As some enjoyed a world of carriages, the theatre, private clubs, and gentlemanly hunting in the Catskills, the majority found their lives filled with the noise of elevated trains, the smells of garbage, urine, and horse manure rotting in the streets, and the sights of young street hoodlums amusing themselves by harrassing police. Of course, every society has had its difference of life-style between the elite and the masses. In the America of the 1890s, however, the distribution of wealth and the social system that it supported was more than mildly at odds with stated American goals and beliefs.

Other "Features" of the Gay Nineties

The temptation to oversimplify and mythologize the nation's past, and particularly the decade of the 1890s, is perhaps nowhere more evident than in regard to the subject of immigration. Uprooted from their native lands, inspired by the thought that the promise of American life might be theirs, some thirty-eight million Europeans came from the Old World to the New in the century between 1820 and 1920. At first they came primarily from western and northern Europe—the British Isles, Germany, and the Scandinavian countries. Later in the nineteenth century and into the twentieth, during the period of the "New Immigration," their numbers were drawn principally from the areas of southern and eastern Europe—Italy, Greece, Rumania, Poland, Austria-Hungary, and Russia. At the time of the Civil War it had been widely believed that the acceptance of Europe's "huddled masses" was essential to the continued growth of the nation, even though there had been some earlier attempts by such groups as the American party to severely limit the immigrant's political activity. As the flow of immigrants continued and its complexion began to change toward century's end, however, the American faith in the concept of the melting pot began to wane. Wage earners became concerned that a continued flood of immigrant labor would help to keep wages down and make unionization difficult. Other pessimists began to argue that such foreign influences might undermine the racial and political "superiority" of America by introducing alien blood and radical ideas. Congress responded to the growing fears by passing a series of laws between 1868 and 1903 denying admission to certain "undesirables"—prostitutes, the insane, paupers, contract laborers, Chinese, and anarchists. In 1897 attempts were made to control immigration even further through the administration of literacy tests, but such a bill, though passed by Congress, was vetoed by President Grover Cleveland. In theory America was a country of freedom, democracy, and golden opportunity where people of every race, color, and creed were accepted as equals. In practice, however, the ideal of America as a "nation of nations" in many ways turned out to be an illusion.

The myth of the melting pot, part of which contends that America has willingly accepted foreigners and minority groups in a spirit of harmony and friendship when in fact it has not, was clearly evident during the Gay Nineties. Racism, discrimination, and the ugly features of nativism (the practice of favoring native-born citizens over aliens) were all too evident in both the teeming cities and the impoverished countryside. Indians, blacks, and the more than 400,000 immigrants who came to the nation's shores each year during that decade knew all too well that the American creed was having little direct influence on American conduct. Yet, it is important to add that foreigners themselves helped create this mythical vision of brotherhood. They did so through numerous so-called American letters written throughout the nineteenth century which romantically portrayed the wonders of the United States to kinfolk left behind in Europe. "The ease of making a living here and the increasing prosperity of the farmers," wrote the Swedish immigrant Peter Cassel from Jefferson County, Iowa, "exceeds anything we anticipated. If only half of the work expended on the soil in the fatherland were

utilized here, the yield would reach the wildest imagination. . . ." The magic promise of America which made those like Cassel feel that they were involved in an adventure rivaling that of Marco Polo centuries before, however, was not shared by all and cannot be passed off as typical. J. N. Bjorndalen, writing from the state of Wisconsin, for example, warned his parents in the old country against blindly believing in the legendary beauty and lush conditions of the New World:

> almost all reports and letters received in Norway from America are good. But this is very wrong; only about a third part of these letters are true. People only write down accounts of the good, although they themselves have had no experience of it. . . . I do not advise any of my relatives to come to America. If you could see the conditions of the Norwegians in America at present, you would certainly be frightened; illness and misery are so prevalent that many have died.[7]

The image of America as the hope of the oppressed, the land of opportunity, and the home of the free indeed had its share of flaws and distortions.

Despite the obvious discrepancies between the myth and the reality of the immigrant's assimilation into American society, the cherished idea prevailed that most if not all had sampled the American Dream. According to legend, the Little Red Schoolhouse made equal opportunity available to children of every social and economic class and was truly America's greatest instrument for assuring the children of immigrants entry to the American way of life. Public schooling, according to the myth, was the nation's surest gauge that the melting pot process in America was a great success. Even as victory for democracy was being proclaimed, however, the state of the nation's educational system was in disarray. Teaching was an occupation of low prestige, poor pay, low standards, and a high turnover rate. It was proving very difficult for those in "semislavery" to be teachers of a free people. School buildings were often dilapidated structures (painted with red ocher, the very cheapest paint available), or crowded and filthy basements with little light and ventilation.

In 1890 Senator Henry W. Blair of New Hampshire produced census data for Congress which showed that one out of every three American children was without schooling. The statistics painted a grim picture, one hardly in keeping with the illusion that the public schools were competently performing the task of helping the nation fulfill the dream of the melting pot. Six million American youths were not even enrolled in school, and among adults an equal number could neither read nor write. By comparison, the generation of the nation's Founding Fathers had been twice as literate as that of 1890. In San Francisco, 29 percent of all the city's children were growing up without the benefits of formal education. In Chicago, the figure stood at 43 percent, and in Milwaukee 55 percent. Further, many of those attending classes were doing none too well. A study conducted by educators in the city of Chicago in 1898, for example, demonstrated that schooling was doing very little to instill the skills and necessary competencies for social and economic mobility. Only 60 percent of the pupils studied were found to be at their normal grade level in overall achievement. The function of schools, it appears, was simply to certify the lower position, rather than improve the standing, of those outside the mainstream of American life. Rather than lead the nation in a quest to fulfill its ideals, the schools were primarily a force for the status quo. In a setting which witnessed a general lack of immigrant interest in education because of the need to put children to work, many sons and daughters of minority groups and the immigrant poor were destined for unskilled occupations.

As the decade of the 1890s drew to a close, some Americans attempted to move beyond the stereotypes, the myths, and the democratic slogans to a realistic assessment of the problems which still flawed America's claim to perfection. Reformers, for example, pointed to the false claims and low standing of the nation's educational system but were met by charges that government aid to improve its condition would "kill initiative" and "destroy character" thus crippling the free-enterprise system. Efforts on behalf of the working poor were labeled socialistic, communistic, and destructive of the Constitution. As women moved in the direction of seeking voting rights, guardians of tradition rose to the challenge.

One obviously nearsighted clergyman responded that since all women looked alike such a move would only lead to multiple voting and thus the destruction of democracy.

SECTION IV: AMERICA'S RISE TO WORLD POWER: REALITY AND FICTION

A nation that permitted the enslavement of one race of people, conquered another, and persistently refused to grant full citizenship rights to females would not seem to be in a good position to declare itself a model republic. Yet many Americans viewed their nation as such at the turn of the century as government leaders began to recognize the power the United States could assert in world affairs. Motivated at least in part by feelings of political and cultural superiority, America gained entry to the "great power club"—that is, began to see itself as a world power and be widely accepted as such—with the victory of Commodore Dewey at Manila Bay in the Philippine Islands on May 1, 1898. Commander of the U.S. Navy's Asiatic Squadron, Dewey had sailed from Hong Kong on orders from then Assistant Secretary of the Navy Theodore Roosevelt, in accord with plans developed in the Navy Department as early as 1896, and defeated the entire Spanish fleet in the Philippines without the loss of a single man or ship. The background for this deed was the Spanish-American War. But what had preceded this episode was as important as what was to follow. "The conviction that we were God's chosen people, and that we had a divine mandate to spread our ennobling democratic institutions over the rest of the benighted [darkened] globe," says the diplomatic historian Thomas Bailey, "encouraged us to shoulder the White Man's Burden in the Philippines and elsewhere at the turn of the century."[8] Yet what Bailey goes on to call the "myth of American righteousness" was anything but new to the national scene in 1898. It was a myth revisited.

Patterns of Expansionism at Home and Abroad

While many history textbooks, and certainly the majority of Americans, have long accepted the cherished belief that the nation burst onto

**The March of the Flag: Marines
Land at Guantanamo Bay (1898)**
The Bettmann Archive

the stage of world affairs with the flash of Dewey's guns in 1898, such a view is in many ways inaccurate. For when the imperialistic activities of the late 1890s are viewed in the light of the decades which came immediately before these fateful steps into the grand arena of world affairs, it becomes clear that the nation was not striking out in completely new directions but simply once again unleashing its expansionist energies. The "May Day myth" concerning expansion, as one historian has called it, fails to recognize both that the United States had been a world power before 1898 and that an energetic expansion had already been demonstrated in the conquest of the North American continent.

Viewed against the background of the nation's history up to 1898 it can be argued that the United States had been a world power

since its birth in 1776. In more ways than generally realized America had been playing a key role in world politics for some time. The Declaration of Independence itself stated the desire of the new nation "to assume among the Powers of the earth the separate and equal station to which the Laws of Nature and of Nature's God entitled them." America's success in securing assistance from France to support the Revolution, as well as the generally favorable treaty with England which concluded the hostilities, implied that the new nation was even at this early date capable of profoundly influencing the direction of world affairs. In addition, American activities throughout the nineteenth century in Europe (during the Civil War diplomatic efforts helped prevent European intervention), in Africa (for example, the various naval campaigns against

Tripoli and other North African states between 1801 and 1815), and in the Far East (Commodore Matthew Perry's missions to Japan in 1853-54), all suggest a fairly active involvement with international trade and politics.

The emergence of America as one of the world's powers, like most every type of historical change, did not occur overnight. America was doing much more than simply tending its own garden in the years from the end of the Civil War to the end of the century. Throughout the decades before 1898 the nation was moving gradually—sometimes strenuously—in the direction of world leadership. Blessed with a growing population, an abundance of natural resources, a developing economy, and an expanse of territory well along in the process of settlement, the country naturally assumed a high profile in world politics.

Part of the myth of America's quick rise to world power in 1898 involves the idea that foreign affairs can somehow be viewed freely and clearly from developments within the nation. As the history of the United States during the nineteenth century so clearly demonstrates, the foreign policy of a nation is often a direct reflection of forces, values, and attitudes which are at work in domestic affairs. Thus, in many ways American attitudes toward the world abroad were molded by expansionist forces at home.

While America may not have been as aggressively expansionistic before 1898 as the expanding powers of Europe were—that is, in acquiring overseas colonies—it was nonetheless imperialistic in other, less obvious ways. If national expansion is a reliable index to world power, and indeed it seems to have been in the nineteenth century, the United States was very much a member of the great power club. While the nations of Europe could point to colonial expansion in Africa and the Far East as a solid basis for their prestige and influence in the world, America could claim itself an authentic world power by virtue of its settlement of the continent under the banner of Manifest Destiny. "The point is often missed," one historian has noted, "that during the nineteenth century the United States practiced internal colonialism and imperialism on a continental scale. When the Western European nations expanded, they had to go over-

seas; when we expanded we had to go west."[9] Because America gave the appearance of being a "power of the future" and a "youthful nation," the sacred belief that it was the nation's destiny to expand eventually matured to the point where expansion included both the land to the west, and colonies beyond.

During the period 1850 to 1898 England's continued supremacy on the high seas, Europe's general preoccupation with internal affairs due to unsettled conditions caused by growing feelings of nationalism, and a general desire to sustain a balance of power on the continent allowed the United States a measure of immunity from world problems. Even so, however, it should not be assumed that either the will or the means for American involvement in the world community were absent. The expansionist idea was already part of the American creed because of the successes of Manifest Destiny. In a relatively short span of time the vast Louisiana Territory, portions of Florida and New Mexico, as well as Texas, California, Oregon, and much of what would become Arizona had already been acquired through military conquest or diplomatic negotiations. As to the world at large, the nation's exports had increased from an average of $116 million annually during the period 1838 to 1849 to a considerably more impressive annual rate of $274 million between 1850 and 1873.

Long before 1898 some political leaders began to speak of overseas expansion in terms of the economic advantages which would accrue to the nation should it be undertaken. Before this could be accomplished, however, it was necessary to redirect the energies of America's Manifest Destiny into foreign channels, and eventually, when the limits of America's western frontier had been reached, the Philippines, Guam, Hawaii, and Puerto Rico became new sites for the nation's expansionist spirit. Even before the Civil War, in fact, an expansionist movement was already evident as Americans began to think in terms of commercial rather than landed frontiers.

When one examines the situation in the light of the nation's developing trade with foreign powers and its expansionist ideas which supported such a move, it becomes clear that the United States was deeply involved with the rest of the world during the latter part of the nineteenth century. Despite the greater attention which is often and justifiably given the topics of the slavery controversy, the Civil War, the continuing settlement of the West, and the period of Reconstruction, to think of this era as a period of American isolationism is to misread history. In light of Manifest Destiny and world trade, as one of the leading scholars of this period has concluded, "the familiar story of American isolation becomes a myth."[10]

A Policy of Expansion

"We have a record of conquest, colonization, and expansion unequaled by any people in the nineteenth century. We are not to be curbed now." When Massachusetts Senator Henry Cabot Lodge uttered these words in 1895, it had been long clear to him, though not necessarily to all Americans, that key power brokers in Washington for some time had wanted an increasingly greater role for the nation in world affairs. Although there were but sixty employees in the State Department in 1885, policymakers had rather consistently displayed an enthusiasm for national expansion and a greater role by the United States in international politics. As early as William Seward's tenure as Abraham Lincoln's secretary of state, it was already recognized that America's farming, cattle, and mining frontiers were well on the way to being conquered. It would be necessary, then, to move more vigorously beyond the continent to find suitable foreign markets for agricultural and industrial goods—at least such was the belief.

In addition to being a secretary of state of notable achievement by virtue of his successful efforts at keeping European powers officially neutral during the Civil War, William H. Seward was in a major way responsible for charting an early course for the nation's expansion overseas. While opposing American involvement in international alliance systems and any form of direct intervention in European affairs, Seward in both theory and practice gave great attention to America's imperial ambitions. He seemed continually motivated by a belief that American security, commerce, and destiny could all favorably be served by expanding westward across the continent and then the Pacific. At Seward's instruction, for example, State Department officials began to explore the possibility of annexing Hawaii. In addition, Seward initiated diplomatic moves designed to bring Cuba, the Danish West Indies (Virgin Islands), Haiti, and Santo Domingo into the American orbit. In all of these efforts, however, he was unable to convey to Congress his vision of the nation's future lying in the arena of world affairs and world markets. But whereas Seward's ambitions often exceeded his accomplishments, he proved successful in achieving his goals with respect to both the Midway Islands and Alaska. Seeing the fabled markets of China as the nation's ultimate commercial goal, he accomplished the purchase of both in 1867. In obvious ways the Midway Islands, 1,200 miles west of Hawaii, would serve as important outposts for America's eventual economic expansion into the Far East. In similar ways, as one of Seward's supporters in the House of Representatives saw it, the Aleutian Islands which spread from Alaska nearly to Russia were the "drawbridge between America and Asia." Though Seward was unsuccessful in some of his expansionistic moves, he set a tone and direction for American foreign policy which others would eventually fulfill. Even though some criticized his efforts—Alaska, for example, being jokingly labeled "Seward's icebox"—he was very much in harmony with things to come.

In succeeding presidential administrations additional moves were made to bring the United States even more squarely into international politics. The administration of Ulysses S. Grant, for example, showed clear signs of a desire to expand American interests beyond the mainland of the continent. Though many at the time expressed a passionate desire to annex Cuba, the area which claimed Grant's most strenuous efforts was Santo Domingo. Since his administration displayed a hand-in-glove working relationship with the military and the business community, Grant based his arguments in favor of colonizing the Caribbean islands on national security and the growing need for foreign markets. Unconvinced, the Senate rejected his proposed treaty, but in the process Grant succeeded in giving continued life to the idea that only by rising to the status of a world power both militarily and economically could the United

States achieve the full measure of its destiny.

The pattern of American expansionism continued during the presidency of Rutherford B. Hayes. Giving priority to trade expansion, Hayes' secretary of state, William M. Evarts, sought to enlarge America's commercial activities in the Far East, Samoa, and Madagascar, as well as in Canada. Through his consistent efforts to settle new investment frontiers, Evarts hastened the progress of America's rise to world leadership and kept the nation moving along a path which would eventually lead to the era of imperialism in the late 1890s. His successors in the State Department, James G. Blaine and Frederick T. Frelinghuysen, channeled the nation's energies in the same direction. Centering his attention on Latin America, Blaine vigorously pursued a policy of Pan-Americanism through which he hoped to build peaceful relations with the countries of Central and South America, relations which would serve as a basis for increased commerce and trade. For much the same reasons, Frelinghuysen negotiated trading agreements with Mexico, Cuba, Puerto Rico, the British West Indies, Santo Domingo, El Salvador, and Colombia during the presidency of Chester A. Arthur.

Grover Cleveland's first term as president, beginning in 1885, again focused attention on trading possibilities with the Far East and saw renewed attempts, particularly by Secretary of State Thomas Bayard, to make both Hawaii and Samoa American way stations on the route to Asia. Indeed by this time the direction of American empire was becoming clear. Nothing less than an equal share of China's legendary wealth would do.

Chinese Trade and War with Spain

Americans turning once again to the trading frontiers of China were handicapped by accumulated layers of misunderstanding and myth concerning that land. Most Americans—policymakers and the public alike—held distorted images of China which bore only a faint resemblance to fact. For centuries China had remained almost entirely secluded from the outside world, comfortable in the belief that the world at large was inhabited by "barbarians." As a result, China remained for

most Westerners a strange land known only through folklore and myth, an exotic region of medieval warlords and the teachings of Confucius. This view, based for the most part on legends which had been built around Marco Polo's journeys to "Cathay" in the thirteenth century, perceived China to be a land of ancient wisdom and rich economic potential. Had it not been China, in fact, which had been the goal of European trading vessels at least since the Age of Discovery? Had not the fabled East been the ultimate destination of Old World explorers as they sailed West?

By the second half of the nineteenth century, however, attitudes had changed considerably. These attitudes were based on rumor, a measure of fact, and second-hand information fed by the encounter in the early 1840s between China and the West known as the Opium War. Some had come to believe the Chinese to be a nation of barbarians. For many, the picture of China as a backward region strangely out of step with the modern world replaced that of a land rich in learning and wealth. In describing America's new perception of China, one Far Eastern scholar has explained:

> Merchants and missionaries soon began to see China as a "backward" nation. The exotic now acquired a tinge of the inferior. In almost all of these early American travelogues there are stories about pigtails, bound feet, ancestor worship, female infanticide, and a host of other sinister practices. Life in China was no longer described as superior but as upside down. The people read from right to left, wrote their surnames ahead of their given names, made soup the last course of a meal, and made a gesture of "come here" when they meant "good-by." The respected Chinese became "Chinamen"; the bearers of a superior civilization became "teeming faceless millions"; and the originators of a profound ethical system became godless heathens.[11]

Both views served American purposes. For those who still saw China through the mists of ancient legend it was a tantalizing storehouse ready to fulfill the dreams of American merchants. To those convinced of Chinese superstitious backwardness, China seemed greatly in need of the enlightened ideas of democracy and Christianity. In important respects, then, America's lust for empire in China was based on an elaborate mythology which bore only a superficial relationship to reality. For China was neither a mythical country of exotic economic treasures nor the land of barbaric superstition American expansionists envisioned.

Despite Americans' fascination with China toward century's end, however, it would be a misconception to believe that the United States had developed a China policy prior to 1898. According to John K. Fairbank of Harvard's East Asian Research Center, "most studies of American China policy have been pursued as national history. They comb American sources and seek to define American interests, aims, and achievements. This is what Confucius called 'climbing a tree to seek for fish,' acting on a false assumption and using erroneous means."[12] As America expanded its trading activities into China it was in fact following on the coattails of European powers—principally England—which had opened the door to the China trade many decades before. Accordingly, America's trading privileges in the area must be understood within the framework of a general invasion of China by many powers—England, France, Germany, Russia, Japan, and finally the United States. Contrary to America's national mythology, the idea of the Open Door—the concept of equal trading opportunities in China—marked no special or unique American contribution to Far Eastern diplomacy.

While the development of colonies in the European style seems never to have been foremost in the minds of expansionists in America, a consistent desire to increase commercial relations was always at the forefront of the nation's foreign policy after the middle of the nineteenth century. Policymakers in Washington, and particularly in the State Department, had taken many decades to plant and nurture the roots of empire. In the course of time commercial ambitions and America's "informal empire" became more formalized as forces throughout the country—presidents, the business community, the military establish-

ment, and public opinion—converted to the faith and began to support the idea of a new empire in the Pacific.

Even though America throughout the last half of the nineteenth century often gave the appearance of noninvolvement, isolation, and an overriding concern for internal affairs, it did not become a world power in a sudden, spur-of-the-moment fashion with the Spanish-American War of 1898. In fact, Commodore Dewey's victory in the Philippines was a rendezvous with destiny—a logical result of all that America had wanted and tried to be for the better part of its history. The episode at Manila Bay was symbolic of numerous decisions made in the past. More important, the events of May 1, 1898, pointed to the complex fate which America faced in the future. As the nation entered the twentieth century, it would be the beneficiary and victim of a past which had both encouraged and witnessed its rise to world power.

STUDY QUESTIONS

1. How did basic changes in American society at the end of the nineteenth century, the collective impact of the dime novels, the work of Western writers and artists, Hollywood, radio, and the general commercialization of Western mythology combine to make the cowboy the hero of America's "last frontier"?

2. How did the efforts of poets, politicians, and philosophers, both in Europe and America, create what historians have come to call the agrarian myth?

3. What are the religious, political, and literary sources for the myth of the self-made man?

4. In what ways, and to what degree, is the historical term "The Gay Nineties" mythical, especially as applied to the historical experience of Indians, blacks, immigrants, children, farmers, and the urban poor during that decade?

5. How did the dynamics of Manifest Destiny and the pattern of decision making by foreign policy makers such as William Seward, Ulysses Grant, William Evarts, James G. Blaine, and Thomas Bayard demonstrate an American commitment to world leadership long before the Spanish-American War of 1898?

6. How did conflicting images of China during the period from the Civil War to the turn of the century help to stimulate America's rise to world power?

REFERENCES

1. Quoted in Joe B. Frantz and Julian Ernest Choate, Jr., *The American Cowboy: The Myth and the Reality* (Norman: University of Oklahoma Press, 1955), pp. 69-70.
2. Dixon Wecter, *The Hero in America: A Chronicle of Hero-Worship* (Ann Arbor: University of Michigan Press, 1966), pp. 344-345.
3. John G. Stoessinger, *Nations in Darkness: China, Russia and America* (New York: Random House, 1975), p. 26.
4. "Roam Free in South Dakota," *St. Paul Sunday Pioneer Press*, April 20, 1975, p. 17.
5. Richard Hofstadter, "The Myth of the Happy Yeoman," *American Heritage*, April, 1956, pp. 43.
6. Quoted in Michael Lesy, *Wisconsin Death Trip* (New York: Pantheon Books, 1973), section "1896." Unnumbered book.
7. Quoted in Carl Degler, *Out of Our Past: Forces That Shaped Modern America* (New York: Harper & Row, Publishers, 1970), p. 276.
8. Thomas Bailey, "The Mythmakers of American History," *Journal of American History* LV (June, 1968): 18–19.
9. Thomas Bailey, "America's Emergence as a World Power: The Myth and Verity," *Pacific Historical Review* 30 (February 1961), 9.
10. Walter LaFeber, *The New Empire: An Interpretation of American Expansion, 1860-1898* (Ithaca, N.Y.: Cornell University Press, 1963), p. 2.
11. Stoessinger, *Nations*, pp. 15-16.
12. John K. Fairbank, *China Perceived: Images and Policies in Chinese-American Relations* (New York: Alfred A. Knopf, 1974), p. 87.

SOURCES FOR FURTHER STUDY

HERO OF THE "LAST FRONTIER": THE AMERICAN COWBOY

ADAMS, ANDY. *The Log of a Cowboy: A Narrative of the Old Trail Days*. Lincoln: University of Nebraska Press, 1964.

DAVIS, DAVID BRION. "Ten-Gallon Hero," *American Quarterly* 6 (1954).

DURHAM, PHILIP, and JONES, EVERETT L., eds. *The Western Story: Fact, Fiction, and Myth*. New York: Harcourt Brace Jovanovich, 1975.

FRANTZ JOE B. and CHOATE, JULIAN ERNEST, JR. *The American Cowboy: The Myth and the Reality*. Norman: University of Oklahoma Press, 1955.

WILBUR, W. ALLAN. *The Western Hero: A Study in Myth and American Values*. Menlo Park, Ca.: Addison-Wesley Publishing Co., 1973.

MYTHS OF THE YEOMAN-FARMER AND THE SELF-MADE MAN

CAWELTI, JOHN G. *Apostles of the Self-Made Man: Changing Concepts of Success in America* Chicago: The University of Chicago Press, 1965.

HOFSTADTER, RICHARD. "The Myth of the Happy Yeoman," *American Heritage* (1956).

LESY, MICHAEL. *Wisconsin Death Trip*. New York: Pantheon Books, 1973.

SCHMIDT, PETER J. *Back to Nature: The Arcadian Myth in Urban America*. New York: Oxford University Press, 1969.

WYLLIE, IRVIN G. *The Self-Made Man in America: The Myth of Rags to Riches*. New York: The Free Press, 1954.

THE GAY NINETIES: A MISCONCEPTION

BETTMANN, OTTO L. *The Good Old Days–They Were Terrible!* New York: Random House, 1974.

GLAZER, NATHAN, and MOYNIHAN, DANIEL P. *Beyond the Melting Pot*. Cambridge, Mass.: M.I.T. Press, 1954.

GREER, COLIN. "Public Schools: The Myth of the Melting Pot," *Saturday Review* 52 (1969).

WIK, REYNOLD M. "The Gay Nineties—Reconsidered," *Mid-America* 44 (1962).

WOODWARD, C. VANN. *The Strange Career of Jim Crow*. New York: Oxford University Press, 1966.

AMERICA'S RISE TO WORLD POWER: REALITY AND FICTION

BAILEY, THOMAS A. "America's Emergence as a World Power: The Myth and the Verity," *Pacific Historical Review* 30 (1961).

FAIRBANK, JOHN K. *China Perceived: Images and Policies in Chinese-American Relations*. New York: Alfred A. Knopf, 1974.

LaFEBER, WALTER. *The New Empire: An Interpretation of American Expansion, 1860–1898*. Ithaca, N.Y.: Cornell University Press, 1963.

STOESSINGER, JOHN G. *Nations in Darkness: China, Russia & America*. New York: Random House, 1975.

VARG, PAUL A. *The Making of a Myth: The United States and China, 1897–1912*. East Lansing: Michigan State University Press, 1968.

8 Myths of Progressivism and the 1920s

PREVIEW

Progressivism: Movement or Mirage?

Despite the fact that some people were calling the social and political change which swirled around them "progressive," the majority of Americans living at the beginning of the present century had not the slightest thought that the entire era would one day be known as the "Progressive Period." The average American was born, grew up, married, reared children, and died. Most passed into history without the advantage—or disadvantage—of having their successes and failures recorded for posterity. But as in every age, of course, there were memorable events and personalities that historians would write about. Theodore Roosevelt, William Howard Taft, Woodrow Wilson, Warren G. Harding, Calvin Coolidge, and Herbert Hoover served as presidents during the period. Four new amendments to the Constitution were enacted, adding the income tax, the direct election of senators, prohibition of alcoholic beverages, and women's suffrage. The real importance of the progressive era was its spirit and enthusiasm for reform. Though never a political movement with a set of unified goals, progressivism nonetheless succeeded in making its mark on American history. Ever since, there has been disagreement over when and why it began, what its significance was for America, and when, or indeed if, it ever ended.

Progressivism was once considered rather easy to define. Accordingly, the myth prevailed for nearly a quarter-century that "progressives" were simply all those who, in one way or another, sought reform during the early part of the twentieth century. Within the past twenty-five years, however, historians have realized that this definition was insufficient. They have concluded that the earlier definition was too simplistic, too all-inclusive, for not all progressives supported every reform. A Midwest progressive, for example, might lack a burning impulse to become involved in ghetto reform on New York's Lower East Side. As a result of a total reexamination of the period, then, a good

many "facts" about progressivism have been exposed as at least partially mythical.

The "typical" progressive came from diverse occupations and backgrounds. There were business executives of old American stock (George W. Perkins) and immigrant writers with a zest for social reform (Jacob Riis). They came from the ranks of both major political parties (Theodore Roosevelt and Woodrow Wilson). In religion they were Quakers (A. Mitchell Palmer), Jews (Henry Morgenthau), Catholics (Father John A. Ryan), and Baptists (Walter Rauschenbusch). They lived in the East (Charles Evans Hughes of New York), the Midwest (Albert Cummins of Iowa), the South (Hoke Smith of Georgia), and the Far West (Hiram Johnson of California). The great majority of progressive reformers were solidly middle class. Most were economically secure. Most were college graduates. Most came from the professions—lawyers, editors, publishers, independent manufacturers, doctors, and bankers and many of the women reformers were Quakers. Wealthy progressives were most often of the Jewish faith. As a whole, however, progressives were Congregationalist, Unitarian, or Presbyterian.

Though progressivism was long considered a revival of such earlier expressions of American reform as abolitionism and Populism, most historians now contend that it was more urban, more middle-class, and more optimistic than its alleged forebears. Progressivism also was earlier thought to be a classic form of American liberalism, but some historians now argue that the movement was naive, ineffective, and profoundly conservative in its motivations and results. For example, since progressivism was a reform movement which almost completely ignored the problems of black Americans and strongly supported imperialism, immigration restriction, and prohibition, one must wonder just how "progressive" the movement was. In addition, since most people believed that the East, North, and West monopolized the progressive spirit, the South was often overlooked—even by such national progressive leaders as Robert M. LaFollette—as having contributed little to the movement. In an attempt to combat the myth that Dixie was and always has been conservative politically, however, historians have shown how southern educators, clergy, and editors took up the cause. Indeed, in the reform of party machinery, railroad regulation, and corrupt practices legislation, the South made a significant contribution to national progressive achievements. Progressivism, in short, has been found to be more unique, less progressive, and more broadly based geographically than originally thought.

Similarly, many other notions about progressivism have been discarded. For example, recent studies have brought into question the legendary reputation that Wisconsin holds as the "laboratory" of state progressive reform. One twentieth-century historian studying progressivism at the state level has shown that Massachusetts, though not a vigorous participant in the reform movement, had already achieved most progressive goals even before these reforms were legislated in other states like Wisconsin. Further, another recent study of Wisconsin has exposed the myth of a progressive reform through an analysis of railroad regulation in that state from 1903 to 1910. Its findings indicate that despite the claim of the state's progressive leaders that "the people" had triumphed over the "selfish interests" of railroads, the Wisconsin Railroad Commission was less an advocate for the public interest than an ally of railroad management. At least in this area of reform Wisconsin progressivism enjoyed limited success.

The Progressive Personality

More than anything, progressivism was a spirit which moved women and men of goodwill into reform activities. It was less a political movement with agreed upon objectives than an enthusiasm which sparked the vital energies of individuals. Progressive personalities such as Wisconsin's Robert M. LaFollette and Chicago's social reformer Jane Addams came to symbolize the genuine desire to improve the quality of American life.

Born in a log cabin at Primrose, Wisconsin, in 1855, Robert Marion LaFollette was one of the few men in American political life whose heroic standing rivaled that usually reserved for presidents. In his career as congressman, governor of Wisconsin, U.S. senator, and lastly unsuccessful candidate for the presidency, LaFollette came personally to symbolize the progressive spirit. His piercing eyes, thick mane of hair, strong jaw, and reputation for honesty and courage marked him as a man logically destined for political fame. Using his personal assets to the best advantage, "Fighting Bob," as he came to be known, quickly emerged as a crusader for progressive reform. His early career brought him into conflict with Wisconsin Senator Philetus Sawyer, a powerful lumber king, and boss of the state Republican organization. After conquering Sawyer's political machine, and being elected governor in 1900, LaFollette's administration established laws limiting campaign expenditures, passed a corrupt practices act, and launched what came to be called the "Wisconsin Idea." More a practical program than a theory, the Wisconsin Idea was the label attached to LaFollette's attempts to combine the political talents of those in state government with the technical knowledge of state university professors. Through an alliance between his administration and academic experts at the University of Wisconsin at Madison, he sought to reshape Wisconsin politics through the establishment of a series of commissions and agencies. Primarily because of these efforts, Wisconsin gained its reputation as the great "laboratory" of state progressive reform.

At this point, however, Robert LaFollette's political career had just begun. A gifted orator, he conducted a "county fair crusade" and achieved a seat in the U.S. Senate in 1906. In the Senate, LaFollette became the idol and darling of early twentieth-century national reformers. Consistently pressing for reform measures, he ultimately became the presidential candidate of the League for Progressive Political Action in 1924.

Despite his legendary reputation as the champion of liberal reform at both the state and national levels of American life, "Fighting Bob" LaFollette was in some ways less liberal, less reformist, and less progressive than his mythical reputation suggests. While it would be grossly unfair to charge, as some at the time did, that he was a hypocrite posing as a friend of "good government," he nonetheless did much to establish a political machine in his own right. Even sympathetic scholars have had to admit that LaFollette made effective—even ruthless—use of patronage. He demanded obedience from his henchmen, and rewarded faithfulness with appointments to public office. . . . Furthermore, if his speeches were effective and filled with facts, they were also often oversimplified and sometimes distorted the information he was presenting to the electorate. In his powerful attacks on the "interests," he never tried to understand the motives, methods, or accomplishments of the "villains" he assaulted. His was the hardhanded farmer's unreasoning suspicion of men who won wealth by manipulating symbols.[1]

One must not conclude from all of this, however, that LaFollette lacked a genuine zeal for reform. The point is that, like the progressive movement of which he was a part, his mythical image as a shining knight must be tempered.

Just as Robert LaFollette's glowing reputation as "Mr. Progressive" has been reevaluated, so also has the image of one of the heroines of the cause, Jane Addams. Born in small-town America—Cedarville, Illinois—in 1860, she typified the progressive personality in the sense that she enjoyed the background of a prosperous middle-class upbringing and a college education. Miss Addams became interested in social reform at an early age, having traveled widely in Europe where she was impressed with the accomplishments of Toynbee Hall, a settlement house in London. Working from this English model, and with the assistance of a college friend, Ellen Gates Starr, she established the famous Hull House in 1889 on Halsted Street in Chicago's near West Side. Offering a sanctuary to the immigrant poor, Jane Addams soon became renowned for her humanitarian activities. Her personal awareness of the limitations of both the Horatio Alger and melting pot mythologies in America seem to have been instrumental in her involvement in social welfare activities. In sympathy with the antiwar philosophy of Leo Tolstoy, the Russian novelist and writer, she became an ardent pacifist in her later life. In recognition of her dedication to social reform and humanitarianism, she received the Nobel Peace Prize in 1931.

A legend in her own time, Jane Addams became the recipient of public praise and the subject of children's books which showed her as a model of self-sacrifice and noble dedication. It was said that as a precocious child she had made a youthful commitment to "help the poor." Other tales told of her being "converted" to the idea of humanitarian reform while watching a Spanish bullfight on a grand tour of Europe. Some admirers compared her to Joan of Arc or the Virgin Mary. To one British visitor she was surely "the only saint America had produced." Until the eve of the First World War, her public image was that of a selfless madonna and friend of the underprivileged. While much that was being claimed for Jane Addams was true, she was at times less than humble and hardly the complete model of self-sacrifice her myth portrayed. The "real" Jane Addams, according to her most recent scholarly biographer, was "proud," "ambitious," and "gloried in publicity." While she most certainly enjoyed less of the "good life" than she could have experienced had she wanted to use her father's wealth for personal advantage, she frequented the best hotels and restaurants in her travels and was often lavishly entertained by wealthy friends. Moreover, Hull House (historically the most important, but not the first settlement house in America), while not providing her and its residents a life of luxury, was genteel and quite comfortable by the standards of the day.

The mythical image of Jane Addams became even more clouded during the First World War. Following her pacifist philosophy, she opposed American entry into the conflict. Given her view that the American cause in Europe was not particularly heroic, she quickly began to lose her stature and became, instead, a symbol of treason and disloyalty. In the words of her biographer, "even after the war she remained a special symbol of Bolshevism and betrayal for groups such as the Daughters of the American Revolution and the American Legion. Late in the twenties she was still denounced as 'the most dangerous woman in America,' and accused of 'strengthening the hands of the Communists'."[2] Until her death in 1935, she remained, for the public, a bewildering blend of heroine and villain. As with many progressive personalities the real Jane Addams, of history rather than mythology, has proven difficult to discover. But as is also the case with others of legendary reputation, Jane Addams' mythology may well be a sure sign of her fundamental importance to the American experience.

America and the Era of the First World War

Like other progressives, Jane Addams was of complex character, but her pacifism sets her markedly apart from the progressive movement itself. For though one might logically assume, as historians often have, that the progressives' humanitarianism at home would cause them to oppose the nation's imperialistic adventures abroad, quite the opposite seems to have been true. Most progressives supported American involvement overseas, motivated by the belief that the American way of life should be exported. Thus, legends created by historians obscured the progressives' activities in support of America's expanding role as a world power by emphasizing the effects of their energies at reshaping the nation's democratic systems at home. Yet, such key progressive leaders as the conservationist Gifford Pinchot (chief of the U.S. Forest Service under Theodore Roosevelt), Idaho Senator William Borah, and trust-busting Philander C. Knox (Roosevelt's attorney general who prosecuted the famous Northern Securities Case against J. P. Morgan) endorsed the nation's imperialistic activities from 1898 to 1916.

Even expansionist-minded progressives, however, were reluctant to quickly involve the United States in war in Europe in 1914. Nearly all Americans felt that the conflict was not America's concern. There appeared at first to be no national interest involved. In addition, the historical tradition of detachment from the quarrels and controversies of Europe was strong. Based on these considerations, the official policy of the United States from 1914 to 1917 was one of neutrality—an attempt to remain detached from the war in both thought and action. But with the illusion of noninvolvement finally proving difficult even for Americans to maintain, the United States eventually abandoned neutrality in favor of intervention. And instead of clinging to the myth that America entered the war only as a reaction to what it saw as Germany's international criminal conduct, historians have concluded that the reasons for America's entry into the First World War were far more complex than that. Even before the period of official neutrality came to an end in 1917, America had given clear signs that its psychological, ideological, and economic sympathies lay with the foes of Germany— England, France, and Russia. In addition, administration officials, including President Woodrow Wilson, had realistically concluded that a world order sensitive to the principles of democracy and freedom was being directly threatened. Beyond this, some, also including Wilson, realized that the United States would be excluded from any role in postwar diplomatic settlements if it failed to actively intervene with military force.

Contrary to many overly patriotic histories of the United States, military intervention, with the appearance of "Yanks" on the Western Front, did not of a sudden bring on the defeat of Germany and the other Central Powers. American "doughboys" in fact did not see action on any considerable scale until May, 1918, only six months before the German surrender at Compiegne, France. American intervention and the critical victories of American troops in battles such as Chateau Thierry and the Second Battle of the Marne must not be minimized of course, but it appears that the role of American forces in the First World War receives more significance in legend than in history. The boost in morale which the appearance of American troops gave the Allied cause was of incalculable significance, but it was the British who first broke through the defensive Hindenburg line. And by war's end British casualties stood at twenty times those suffered by the Americans; the death toll for the French and Russians was even higher.

As the world attempted to recover its sanity after the trauma of world war, President Woodrow Wilson emerged as a savior in whose hands the fate of the world seemed to rest. A symbol of democracy and hope, Wilson proved physically unable, however, to meet the challenge that lay before him. Having suffered a major stroke in 1906, even before he became president, Wilson suffered another in 1919 which made his behavior stubborn, irritable, rigid, and unyielding. Accordingly, the postwar Treaty of Versailles, and the idea of the League of Nations which was specifically called for by its provisions, failed to receive senatorial support. This was largely due to Wilson's unwillingness to compromise with key members of the Senate Foreign Relations Committee such as Henry Cabot Lodge. For these reasons it can be seen that the nation's move toward limited responsibility in world affairs after the conclusion of the First World War was not a move toward isolationism, as is often said. More accurately, it reflected the legitimate differences of opinion which developed as to what kind of role the nation should play in world affairs. Indeed, even though America chose a course of political noninvolvement in Europe after the war, the nation was still involved in diplomatic questions such as postwar recovery in Germany and the limitation of naval armaments. When one recognizes as well that the decade after the war also saw a period of government-supported business expansion throughout the world—what one historian has called "the internationalization of business"—the myth of American isolationism in the 1920s can be recognized as just that.

The Roaring Twenties

The most persistent myths of the 1920s, however, are not concerned with the nation's activities abroad but rather with its supposedly gaudy life at home. As in the case of the Gay Nineties, a haze of romantic nostalgia has led many to falsely conclude that the twenties was the Jazz Age—a decade of "booze, bobbed hair, and the blues." Securely housed in the nation's collective memory, the Roaring Twenties remain an era which, in a phrase often used in an attempt to recapture it, seems "only yesterday." One would think, on the basis of the attention such matters have received, that Americans had little on their minds during the decade other than Babe Ruth, hip flasks, roadsters, the ring battles of Gene Tunney and Jack Dempsey, and the movie heroics of Tom Mix and Hoot Gibson. Yet, the period certainly amounted to more than the desert epics of the pimp-turned-movie hero Rudolph Valentino, the golfing triumphs

of the boy wonder Bobby Jones, and such musical achievements as "Carolina in the Morning," "Singing in the Rain," and "Honeysuckle Rose." All of these things of course have given the 1920s the distinctive character which makes the decade all the more memorable. But to concentrate only on the period's colorful panorama of images, as if one were paging through a *Life* picture history of the decade, presents a much too limited view of the era. No doubt such visions are entertaining, but they remain mythical in that they capture only a small portion of the age, and imperfectly at that.

The mythical twenties are also filled with misunderstandings about Warren G. Harding, Calvin Coolidge, Herbert Hoover, the Ku Klux Klan, religious fundamentalism, Prohibition, and the so-called Lost Generation of American writers whose disenchantment with the period has become legendary. But the most popular notion about the 1920s, and in some ways the most mythical, is its supposed general prosperity. It is the principal legend which supports the larger mythology of the decade's freewheeling image.

As with most myths, the myth of the "prosperous twenties" has some basis in fact. There was a ripening of capitalism during the period, as witnessed by sharp increases in the gross national product. Significant production increases in the automobile industry (by 1929, 16 million Americans relied on the automobile for their livelihood), oil, chemicals, machine tools, and retail trade were all in evidence. But as is most always the case, prosperity was a commodity enjoyed only by the upper classes. While a few experienced the mellow world of martinis, lawn parties at Newport, European holidays, and the company of debutantes and Ivy League fraternity gentlemen, most people were struggling to meet life's basic needs. Even before the Great Depression, 40 percent of the American people were not indulging in the good life as portrayed in the F. Scott Fitzgerald novel *The Great Gatsby* (1925), but were earning less than $1,500 per year; 20 percent earned less than $1,000 annually. Corporate affluence simply had not trickled down to the masses. The controlled calm between labor and management during the decade helped to sustain the image of prosperity. Few observers since have noticed that "the combined incomes of 0.1 percent of the families at the top of the [economic] scale were as great as those of the 42 percent at the bottom."[3] The soft spots in the American economy—the evidence of poverty in the midst of apparent abundance, the buying of stock "on margin," and the unhealthy condition of American agriculture—were ignored by a society which even at the time was falling in love with the myth of success. Prosperity during the 1920s turned out to be only a superficial sampling of the American Dream. This would be a fact made only too clear by the national nightmare of the Great Depression and the slow period of recovery during the era of the New Deal which followed.

SECTION I: PROGRESSIVISM: MOVEMENT OR MIRAGE?

Despite the many troublesome features of national life during the decade of the 1890s, the twentieth century dawned on an optimistic America. Surprisingly, the belief in progress and the mood of expectancy which was already a hallmark of American life had been little eroded by the hard times of recent years. The harsh realities of the Civil War, Reconstruction, and economic crisis were already fading before memories of the "good old days" which had just drawn to a close. Prosperity was returning to America's agricultural heartland. Job opportunities for industrial laborers were improving if not plentiful. Still, the many social and economic problems which continued to beset immigrants, ethnic minorities, the urban poor, women, and labor, remained obvious. Despite improved conditions there was a widespread recognition that the fruits of American life had not been evenly distributed, and that the situation was getting worse. Between one third and one half of the nation still lived in poverty while the most favored one percent of the population owned 40 percent of the nation's property and monopolized 15 percent of the country's gross income. The atmosphere of optimism and concern—a combination of confidence and a commitment to smoothing the rough edges of the American system—produced a spirit in the early decades of the twentieth century which both contem-

poraries and historians have come to call progressivism.

Progressivism and the Historians

As with every important era of American history, the progressive period has generated a good deal of debate among historians as to its origins, its meaning, and the time and circumstances of its "death." The usual amount of exaggeration, distortion, and myth was bound to attach itself to the various views offered to explain the reality of progressivism by historians wanting to make their explanations convincing. The mythical nature of the period has been compounded, however, by the fact that professional scholars themselves took a personal hand in shaping the movement. As one recent writer has suggested, many of the early attempts to explain progressivism were written by those who were "its partisans in life as well as in print."[4] The nation's first generation of professional historical scholars—the so-called new historians—were active progressives themselves and thus were predisposed to see the thrust toward reform in a positive way. Important beginnings toward understanding the meaning and directions of progressivism were undertaken by several participating historians—Frederick Jackson Turner, Vernon Louis Parrington, and Charles Beard—but it seems now that at times they allowed their activities as citizens to clash with their scholarly responsibilities. Some found it difficult to engage actively in the shaping of history one week and then to give the movement an objective treatment in their classrooms or writings the next. Indeed, a review of their writings on progressivism reveals that their involvement in the age of reform somewhat affected their abilities to be completely reliable spokesmen for scholarship. Given their direct participation in the movement itself and the ensuing history that described it, it was inevitable that the creation of scholarly myths would result. And it is not surprising that in their hands progressivism emerged as a significant expression of democratic-liberal reform.

In a real sense, what textbooks have long called the Progressive Movement was never a coherent force. Reformers pursuing many different ends all laid claim to being progres-

New York's Lower East Side:
A Progressive Challenge
Brown Brothers

sives. But what passed for "progress" in the eyes of one may well not have been viewed as progressive by others. Thus a rural southern progressive might not get excited over urban reform legislation; an urban northeastern progressive might well lack a deep interest in Midwest agricultural reform. Yet, despite the many different fronts on which campaigns in the name of progress were being launched, and the widely varying personal visions which gave the reforming spirit energy, the "progressive historians" who came first to explain the movement were prone to see it as a rather easily defined moral drama of exceptional excitement. Progressivism was a fairly simple case of the "good guys" versus the "bad guys," a triumph of "the people" over the "special interests," but another stirring episode in the developing saga of American democracy. It was, they concluded, the latest example of America's age-old commitment to liberalism, one which updated the nation's continuing effort to have its conduct reflect its lofty ideals.

They pointed with pride to the successes of the period—government moves against monopolies and trusts in the business sector; the direct election of senators; legislation instituting the initiative, referendum, and recall; and the establishment of the income tax, among others. For many years their deceptively simple historical explanation of progressivism remained convincing.

Even during the generally enthusiastic days of the progressive age itself, however, there were those who saw such an optimistic assessment as an exercise in illusion. The Baltimore journalist, Henry L. Mencken, was one such critic. To him, Theodore Roosevelt—the fair-haired boy of many progressives—was little more than a pseudo-liberal. Teddy was, Mencken insisted, an American kaiser pretending to be a man of the people. Woodrow Wilson, too, failed Mencken's self-styled tests of leadership miserably. He could be dismissed, Mencken sneered, as a moralizing fanatic with a second-rate mind. Both were

199

masters of what Mencken called "the quasi-religious monkeyshines" which passed for serious politics in America. They were, in the end, pathetic national heroes whose key to success lay with their talent as entertainers. Theodore Roosevelt in particular possessed a special knack for "bamboozling" the nation into believing that his zest for reform was genuine.

Another journalist, John Chamberlain, also fundamentally questioned the intellectual wisdom and near-blind faith of the progressive historians who had become academic cheerleaders for the movement. His book *Farewell to Reform* (1931) was the first widely read scholarly study which did not characterize progressivism as an exercise in goodness and farsighted change. For Chamberlain, the progressives failed spectacularly to right the wrongs of capitalism. Amused by their "Little Golden Day" during the years from Roosevelt to Wilson, Chamberlain claimed that progressives built a political mirage on the empty rhetoric of people who were wasting their time trying to "patch up" the "unpatchable." From his leftist point of view, the feeble gestures which the progressives made in the direction of reform were in the end counterproductive—"paralyz[ing] the will to radical action" which might have brought meaningful change to America. As a case in point, Chamberlain argued that the popular election of senators—provided by the addition of the Seventeenth Amendment to the Constitution in 1913—had simply replaced the stuffy members of the government's "rich man's club," formerly elected by state legislatures, with demagogues selected on the basis of their image and impressive ways of saying nothing. The U.S. Senate, if you will, had simply moved from being a country club of corruption to a myth factory fueled by the energy of colorful windbags. To be sure, Chamberlain granted, some gains were achieved—the Adamson Law imposed eight-hour working days on the nation's railroads and the Federal Reserve Act made the national banking system a more flexible instrument for meeting the country's economic needs. Even at this, however, progressivism was a vast disappointment. It was hardly the kind of reform movement destined to send shock waves through an American system in which citizens were for the most part

quite satisfied with what a later historian writing in the Chamberlain tradition would call "the politics of make-believe."

The views of John Chamberlain, however, were perhaps as overly critical as earlier views had been sympathetic. While an important corrective, historians have since come to see the Chamberlain interpretation as biased. Most later historians have assumed, by reviewing the record, that whatever its shortcomings, its lack of unified purpose, and its quite different expressions at the national, state, and local levels, progressivism was, after all, a true reform movement of major importance to the nation. Accordingly, many recent historians who have made progressivism the focus of their study have sought to discover the forces in American life which gave it birth. Convinced that progressivism was never intended to be a radical movement destined to alter fundamentally either capitalism or the operations of American democracy, some have sought to connect it to other periods of national reform. John D. Hicks, for example, saw progressivism to be an offspring of the rural Populist movement which had climaxed in the bitter years of the 1890s. Both movements, Hicks suggested, shared a belief that government must restrain the selfish tendencies of those who would take advantage of the free-enterprise system, and both had a conviction that "the people" rather than the moneyed interests should hold ultimate control over the affairs of government. Pointing to the fact that most of the important proposals for reform which had been emphasized by the Populists were eventually passed into law during the progressive period (for example, the graduated income tax, primary elections for making party nominations, and regulation of railroad rates), Hicks saw a cause and effect relationship between the two reform eras.

Though this "Populism-to-progressivism" theory continues to find its way into many textbooks, numerous historians have come to question its accuracy. Early in this century most historians agreed with the journalist-reformer William Allen White of Kansas that progressivism was Populism with the "hayseeds removed," but a majority of historians of late have pointed to the fact that Populists were for the most part rural and agrarian while progressives were more often those from the city and of business and professional backgrounds. Beyond this, Populism was very much the result of the period of agricultural depression at century's end, while progressivism sprang to life during an age of relative national prosperity. Finally, the movements differed fundamentally in their leadership. Populist leaders tended to be those like James H. "Cyclone" Davis of Texas, Tom Watson of Georgia, and "Sockless Jerry" Simpson of Kansas—homespun individuals of little formal education with a utopian vision of returning to some golden moment in the past when the yeoman-farmer had been lord of the land. Progressives, on the other hand, were usually from more sophisticated backgrounds—well-educated urban leaders drawn from the ranks of journalism (Lincoln Steffens), education (Richard Ely), law (Oliver Wendell Holmes, Jr.), or the ministry (Walter Rauschenbusch). Thus, the ties between Populism and progressivism have come to be de-emphasized and attempts made instead to see why progressive reform became the predisposition of so many relatively successful Americans.

Seeking to discover the origins of the progressive spirit through a case study of the movement in California, George Mowry in 1951 suggested that progressives had been middle-class reformers disturbed by the growing power of large corporations, newly organized labor unions, and political bosses. They had sought reform not so much because of economic grievances (for they were for the most part already reasonably well-to-do), but because they thought their social class was being replaced in influence by a new elite. Much the same theory was updated and expanded four years later by Richard Hofstadter in his book, *The Age of Reform: From Bryan to F.D.R.* (1955). Here, the argument was made that progressivism could best be explained in psychological terms. Progressives sought to regulate capitalism, spoke for clean government, and urged social justice, Hofstadter argues, largely because their status, prestige, and power were being threatened. During most of the nineteenth century, before the rise of industrialism and big business, the progressives' occupational forebears had been the "decision-makers" and "power-brokers" in

America. Anxious about their fading status, their support of the progressive movement represented a "status revolution" based largely on a nostalgia for the "good old days" when the opinions of their class had been valued and their influence significant. They became convinced that corporate capitalism was destroying the economic individualism which had been most responsible for their success. This could only be restored by restoring an older, more competitive, more individualistic small-enterprise economy. A victim of its own mythical vision of a vanished era which may never have existed in the first place, said Hofstadter, progressivism failed to be as much of a force for progress as traditionally supposed. Agreeing with Hofstadter's analysis of the progressives, one historian has said: "Since their goals were more psychological than economic . . . they accepted weak legislation like the Sherman and Clayton Antitrust Acts as 'ceremonial' solutions to problems that warranted more [than] toothsome responses."[5] Because of their romantic feelings for the supposed glory of yesteryear, progressivism was built on a mirage. As such, it was destined to be much more conservative than liberal in its results.

The conservative nature of the movement has also been emphasized in a number of recent studies. Cultivating a wider view, for example, some historians have suggested that reform in America during the early twentieth century was not progressive, or at least nothing new, because many countries in Europe had instituted reforms of a similar nature long before. While new to America during the progressive period, the municipal ownership of utilities had been in operation in England and Germany for some time. Similarly, progressive ideas on conservation seem to have come from France and Germany, workmen's compensation dated back to the era of Otto von Bismarck in Germany during the 1880s, and the use of the initiative, referendum, and recall (designed to place more control of government in the public's hands) was already part of political practice in Switzerland. Indeed, when viewed from the perspective of Western history, the movement seems less progressive, less radical and even less American than usually portrayed.

In a somewhat similar vein, tying in with

the urban features of the movement, the argument has also been offered that the progressives were more often than not upper-class businessmen. Rather than a replay of the ancient struggle between democracy and privilege, progressivism was the privileged segments of society leading a reform movement. Rather than marking a glorious victory for democratic principles, progressivism resulted in even further control of government by the business community. Civic groups led by doctors, lawyers, engineers, bankers, architects, and industrial executives saw to it that progressive reforms such as the move toward the commission and city manager forms of government actually had the effect of placing the control of "democracy" further from the people. Now, political decisions were being made by a small group of experts sympathetic to the "free enterprise" needs of the business community and free from bothersome electoral politics. According to such historians as Samuel P. Hays and Robert Wiebe, the progressive movement consisted mainly of the introduction of business techniques—centralization, administrative control, bureaucracy—into the American political system. Furthermore, it was more involved in a "search for order" than in an attempt to carry the banner of American democratic reform on to new liberal horizons.

Perhaps the most deliberate and forceful challenge to the legend of progressivism as democratic can be found in the work of the so-called New Left historians, for example, Gabriel Kolko. Progressive reform such as it was, says Kolko, was not only conservative in its results, and undemocratic in some of its features, but was purposefully designed to be so by the business community:

> I contend [Kolko declares] that the period from approximately 1900 until the United States' intervention in the war [First World War], labeled the "progressive" era by virtually all historians, was really an era of conservatism. . . . Progressivism was . . . a movement that operated on the assumption that the general welfare of the community could be best served by satisfying the concrete needs of business.[6]

According to the Kolko thesis, the so-called progressive period was in reality an age of "political capitalism" which shows conclusively the American idea of "free" enterprise to be a myth. In Kolko's account, *The Triumph of Conservatism* (1963), it is argued that the supposedly progressive Pure Food and Drug Act of 1906, for example, was promoted by large meat-packing companies in an attempt to destroy competition from small firms. Federal regulation allowed the larger businesses greater efficiency by cutting the costs of both legal fees and lobbying efforts. Costs were less because prior to that time the wide variety of state standards governing the industry's activities had made it necessary to duplicate such efforts endlessly. In addition, the cost to the small producers of complying with the new federal law was prohibitively expensive. In the end, small firms were forced out of business and only the giant monopolies survived. The regulation of railroads and insurance companies, says Kolko, had much the same effect. It made the business of big business more economical and guaranteed that only the largest of corporations would enjoy the benefits of free enterprise. Progressivism, despite its glowing democratic rhetoric, was little more than a cover for the developing detente between government and business. Neither radical nor progressive, the movement was mythical window dressing which helped preserve the wealth, power, and privilege of the corporate rich.

What Happened to the Progressive Movement?

Just as historians disagree as to what forces brought progressivism to the center stage of American life, and whether its reforms worked to expand the frontiers of democratic liberalism or secured the place of conservative capitalism, they also disagree as to what happened to the movement. Traditionally, they have accepted the myth that it ended on the eve of the First World War. Indeed, by that time two of those who thought of themselves as progressives—President Woodrow Wilson and Governor Hiram Johnson of California—declared that their reform programs had been largely accomplished. Beyond this, it is argued, by 1918 a good many of those who had labored on behalf of reform had become weary—they were "tired radicals." Not unlike much of the reforming spirit dealing with race relations and the Vietnam War, which gripped the country in the decade of the 1960s, progressivism is said to have simply faded into new concerns and day-to-day tasks.

Since progressivism was a "spirit" or an "enthusiasm" rather than an easily definable force with common goals, it seems more accurate to argue that it produced a climate for reform which lasted well into the 1920s, if not beyond. Definite traces of the progressive spirit can be seen at the national level, for example, in the McNary-Haugen Bill of 1924 which sought to establish "fair exchange" or "parity" prices for America's farmers. They can be found as well in the efforts of those like Senator George Norris of Nebraska, who involved the federal government in the development of what would become the Tennessee Valley Authority. The TVA brought the benefits of electricity and economic development to remote and rural areas of the western Appalachian region beginning in 1933. In the area of social justice it seems clear as well that progressivism had not died by the advent of the twenties. Indeed, a sensitivity among those still committed to reform seems to have carried the desire for social action on into the period of Franklin Roosevelt's New Deal during the 1930s. Since progressivism continued to express itself in aggressive ways well beyond the First World War in cities such as Cincinnati in its attack on bossism and through the efforts of those like Governor Huey Long in the state of Louisiana, it seems clear that an epitaph for progressivism cannot carry the date 1917 or any of the years of the 1920s.

Until recently, historians have been prone to rely on sweeping generalizations and easily remembered clichés to explain progressivism. But the customary quest for easy answers certainly must be abandoned when considering the progressive period. While one might wish to simply say that progressivism was a political reform movement in America, lasting from 1900 until the First World War and which made the country more democratic, the facts suggest that to do so would be to mythologize a significant portion of the nation's history in the twentieth century. As the case of the progressive movement demonstrates, no group of historical beliefs concerning the past ever have complete immunity to alteration. In the end, the reality of progressivism seems to have been the spirit, energy, commitment, and imaginative enthusiasm which it held for the "men of good hope" who shaped its destiny and shared its achievements. Whether the nation ultimately decides that the progressive movement was visionary or naive, democratic or antidemocratic, liberal or conservative, it must eventually make such judgments in terms of the men and women who tried in good faith to improve the society in which they lived as a consequence of a belief in the American Dream.

SECTION II: THE "PROGRESSIVE" PERSONALITY: ROOSEVELT AND WILSON

Because of the powerful office they hold, presidents of the United States always have been prime targets for the distortions of myth and legend. A chief executive with a pleasing personality and some political skills can with proper energy spark his own rise to immortality. Perhaps because Americans emotionally feel that the office symbolizes the nation, or feel some psychological participation in the power that resides there, the presidency has become one of the most fertile sources for mythologizing in America. The election of a president on many occasions has meant the birth of a mythological hero.

The process whereby the prestige of the presidential office carried with it the fringe benefit of mythical fame was, of course, already well established by the early years of the twentieth century. It would therefore have been disappointing were the nation's presidents during the progressive period not the subject of legend. Of the first three who served—Theodore Roosevelt, William Howard Taft, and Woodrow Wilson—at least two were excellent candidates for myths. Both Roosevelt and Wilson, though different in temperament, style, and performance, had a quality which the majority of Americans found usable material for myth.

Theodore Roosevelt

The case of Theodore Roosevelt as America's most colorful and mythical progressive personality is in some ways curious. He was born into economic comfort and social prominence whereas the majority of the nation's presidents since the time of Jackson had come from humble or middle-class origins. One might not have predicted that the country would one day accept him as a genuine man of the people. But in Roosevelt's case his blue-blood background seems never to have been held against him. And with slight effort one could see him as another in a long line of classic Americans—a self-made individual. Sensing this, Edward S. Ellis, a pulp novelist, published *From Ranch to White House: The Life of Theodore Roosevelt* in 1906 as part of a "Log Cabin to White House" series designed to inspire young Americans. Despite Roosevelt's wealth, Harvard education, and close associations with the political and economic elite, Ellis made him a sort of barefoot character out of a Mark Twain novel romping in the White House. "The life of Theodore Roosevelt," as the historian Dixon Wecter has said, "was the dream of every typical American boy: he fought in a war, became President, killed lions, and quarreled with the Pope."[7] Most found the youthful flair which he gave American politics refreshing. By comparison, American presidents at the end of the nineteenth century—Hayes, Garfield, Cleveland, Harrison, and McKinley— were a good deal less colorful and exciting. In fact, Mark Twain himself remarked on this facet of Roosevelt's character, seeing him as his own best press agent. In conversation with the industrialist Andrew Carnegie, Twain described Roosevelt as "the Tom Sawyer of the political world of the twentieth century; always showing off; always hunting for a chance to show off; in his frenzied imagination the Great Republic is a vast Barnum circus with him for a clown and the whole world for an audience." Given T. R.'s vibrant style of speechmaking, prominent teeth, flashing eyes behind rounded spectacles, and personal energy, one could easily enough imagine him a boy scout-turned-cowboy who had grown to be a self-made man.

An important element of Theodore Roosevelt's youthful and vigorous image was his association with the frontier West and the cattle kingdom of the cowboy. Asthmatic and nearsighted as a child, at an early age he determined to live the masculine life of a cowboy and invested 20 percent of his fortune in a cattle ranch near the North Dakota Badlands. At his Elk Horn Ranch he found tranquil escape from the pressures of urban life and the hurly-burly of political affairs. To Roosevelt, the cowboy was the most thoroughly "American" of all the nation's heroes. Seen as independent, bold, fearless, and free, the cowboy served as a model or symbol of the values that Roosevelt—and of course much of the nation—held most dear. Completely at home in the congenial atmosphere of cowboy mythology, Roosevelt convinced himself that his personal experience with the West strengthened him body and soul. Engaged in hunting elk, buffalo, and grizzly bear, and riding the range, he could feel himself a part of an older, more stable, and "true" America. Though his boyish face and "greenhorn" vocabulary have led some to see him as the nation's "original dude rancher," for Roosevelt personally and for much of the nation he became a living symbol of the cowboy myth. Fittingly, Owen Wister, a friend and former classmate at Harvard, dedicated his classic Western novel, *The Virginian* (1902), to him in recognition of his importance in popularizing the legendary and strenuous life of the western frontier. For his own part, an inspired Roosevelt took time from his busy schedule to write a four-volume history on the *Winning of the West* (1889-1896).

The mythical appeal of Theodore Roosevelt, however, was not only due to his image as a Dakota cowpuncher. He combined the cult of the cowboy with a dash of romantic militarism to give the nation another kind of hero to worship. Roosevelt the cowboy took to the battlefield in defense of Americanism when he became a Rough Rider during the Spanish-American War. Though Roosevelt did not coin the term "Rough Rider"—it had been used at an earlier date to refer to the Pony Express and had been part of the vocabulary of the dime novelists—he popularized it and gave it mythical appeal. Certainly, Roosevelt himself was the principal mythmaker of his own Rough Rider image. As war with Spain was brewing in 1898 he is reported to have exclaimed: "We will have a jim-dandy regiment if we go." And in fact he wrote a boastful book of his adventures, *The Rough Riders*, soon after the war was over. Beyond this, Richard Harding Davis, a journalist for the Hearst newspaper chain on assignment in Cuba,

T.R.: Cowboy, Rough Rider, Politician
Library of Congress

wrote colorful commentary on the hostilities from the front, and became an accomplice in Roosevelt's mythmaking effort. As "The Prose Bard of the Rough Riders" and as a promoter of "Theodore the Conquerer," Davis wrote of Roosevelt's military accomplishments with more of an eye to romantic drama than journalistic objectivity. It mattered little, for example that the fabled Rough Riders rode no horses into battle. This contingent of ex-cowboys and ex-polo players no doubt displayed considerable valor in their charge up Kettle Hill (which Roosevelt later romantically renamed San Juan Hill), but stories of their heroics seldom bothered to mention the invaluable assistance they received from the crack 10th Negro Cavalry. Believing himself personally responsible for victory, Roosevelt later vainly sought to have himself decorated with the Congressional Medal of Honor for his dashing deeds. He became an ardent believer in his own press clippings. But even though his efforts to obtain a citation failed, Americans seldom paused to question Teddy's rash and transparent red-blooded patriotism. To a nation in need of a swashbuckling hero he filled the bill admirably. The citizens of Medora, North Dakota, site of his cattle ranch, have done their best to promote the dual image of Roosevelt as cowboy and idol of the Spanish-American War. To the present day they invite those of adventurous spirit to "Rough Rider Country" where supposedly the glorious days of America's earliest twentieth-century myth figures live on.

Roosevelt's well-publicized flair for the dramatic, however, led some to see him as something less than a hero. Just as there were those much impressed by his vim and vigor, others saw him as little more than a high-class phoney. Even though conceding Roosevelt a place as one of the commanding personalities of American history, Richard Hofstadter, looking beyond the hero image, claimed his flurries of activity were due to a "nervous tick." Seeing him as "the master therapist of the middle class," for Hofstadter, Roosevelt simply told Americans what they wanted to hear. And while accepting the opinion of one of Roosevelt's contemporaries that he was "the most interesting man of our times," Ray Ginger notes that he "quickly made the White House into the chief flapdoodle factory in the nation." Even for those willing to accept

205

Senator Nelson Aldrich's estimation of Roosevelt as "the greatest politician of his time," the question of his ultimate importance to America and the progressive movement remains. Again, in the estimation of Ginger:

> His concern was not with justice but with the retention and expansion of office. He came to high power due to his birth, due to his courage in warfare, due to his frenetic energy, due to his speechifying loquacity. He never understood that huge numbers of Americans were being treated wrongly by the federal government. . . .
> His analytic mind might have been as dense and amorphous as potato chowder, but he had cunning; he gave to voters a few dreams in which they could get lost.[8]

Thus while some have emphasized Roosevelt's colorful yet "responsible conservatism" others have called his rhetoric "full of platitudes" and criticized his "false leadership."

In the crosswinds of opinion which have swirled around Theodore Roosevelt, myths have disguised both sides of his personality and character. Remembered for his championing of the Pure Food and Drug Act and his strenuous efforts on behalf of conservation, he also agreed with the idea that "the only good Indian is a dead Indian." Awarded the Nobel Peace Prize for his critical role in settling a major war between Japan and Russia in 1905, he also conducted a foreign policy based on the West African proverb, "Speak softly and carry a big stick." Known in his time as a trustbuster because of his legal action while president to dismantle the Northern Securities Company controlled by J. P. Morgan and E. H. Harriman, he was nonetheless often an ally of business interests. Theodore Roosevelt who was the nation's first president to sympathize with workers in the conflict between labor and management at the time of the Anthracite Coal Strike in 1902 was the same Roosevelt who, after inviting the black leader Booker T. Washington to lunch at the White House, announced in private that it had been "a mistake."

Roosevelt was many things to many people—bird-watcher, historian, cowboy, amateur prizefighter, language expert, legislator, police commissioner, naval expert, Rough Rider, governor, vice president, president, and all-around character. A cartoonist's delight, he was tempting material for mythmakers. In fact, Roosevelt's major political programs, first the Square Deal and later the New Nationalism, cast him neither as a complete champion of the common people nor as a pawn of business-minded conservatives. Though Roosevelt has held the reputation as the nation's most dashing progressive personality, it now seems clear that his belief in nationalism, both domestic and foreign, ran much deeper than his so-called progressivism. Further, legend has insisted that Theodore Roosevelt was the most "typical American" of his time even though it now appears that in mind, in background, and in character he was no more so than William Jennings Bryan, Robert LaFollette, or for that matter Woodrow Wilson. Still, it is the progressive Rough Rider that the nation remembers as well or better than any of these others.

Woodrow Wilson

The progressive movement's other great leader was Woodrow Wilson. Wilson's background of study at Princeton, the University of Virginia, and Johns Hopkins University, from which he received his Ph.D. in 1886, served to mark the differences between the two men. Roosevelt, it appeared, was the man of action; Wilson, the man of intellect. Roosevelt was a doer and Wilson a thinker. The popular image of Roosevelt as the man of practical affairs and Wilson the scholarly idealist, however, is largely mythical. Historians agree that the sum total of Roosevelt's practical accomplishments was slight. Despite his flurry of activity which did much to create the illusion that things were moving forward, he did little to alter the basic structure of either the American government or economy. His contributions in the area of foreign affairs—tainted as they were by authoritarianism and romantic militarism—also did not represent a move away from well-established patterns. Wilson, despite his image as scholarly idealist, accomplished much more. Roosevelt "shouted and waved his arms, but his feet never moved." Wilson, on the other hand, significantly altered the course of American life in practical ways. Indeed, according to his most authoritative biographer, Arthur Link, he must be "judged from the point of view of success and effectiveness. His proper place cannot be understood apart from his concrete achievements."[9] The legend of Wilson as only an impractical idealist, in short, needs to be considerably revised.

The question of Wilson's idealism—the topic which has had a way of dominating studies of Wilson, and has been the essence of the Wilson mythology—must be approached cautiously. Wilson's brand of idealism was not that of a dreamy-eyed visionary, but rather that of one seeking to use ideals to inspire action. He was an idealist in the sense that he consistently gave voice to noble ideals, thereby prompting both himself and Americans generally to strive for even higher achievements. For example, his reluctance to quickly involve the United States in fighting the First World War, though immediately branded by some as lacking in realism and labeled "pussyfooting" by Theodore Roosevelt, may well have been more a case of what historians have come to call Wilson's "higher realism." Wilson apparently understood that the warrior is but one type of hero, that it could be as commendable to avoid crisis as to court it. Thus, Wilson's idealism had a way of spawning rational policies. In fact, viewing the long span of his public career one is immediately struck by the success which he enjoyed in translating idealistic impulses into realistic results.

To say that Woodrow Wilson was "only an idealist," then, is wrong. In his career as teacher and scholar (at Bryn Mawr, Wesleyan, and Princeton), as an educational administrator (president of Princeton University from 1902 to 1910), and as a politician-diplomat (as both governor of New Jersey and president of the United States) Wilson achieved a measure of practical success enjoyed by few other Americans.

In the political arena, Wilson was one who got things done. In New Jersey he established a standard of executive leadership which has seldom been rivaled. In national affairs, as president, he greatly increased the power of that office through his appeals to public opinion. His "New Freedom" reform program reshaped governmental policies related to tariff, banking, antitrust measures, labor, and welfare issues. As the foremost Wilson scholar, Arthur Link, has stated: "Even more than Theodore Roosevelt, who began the process,

Woodrow Wilson was the architect of modern American economic policies."[10] Though less colorful in style than T. R., Woodrow Wilson succeeded in making his ideals and actions more heroic than himself. He was much less his own mythmaker than the Rough Rider.

Wilson's Mythmakers

Woodrow Wilson like other great American presidents has attracted his share of biographers, many of whom have contributed myths in reconstructing his life and times. The Wilson mystique, the image of the nation's twenty-eighth president as a "liberal-idealist," has drawn a wider range of biographers than most other chief executives have. In the first scholarly biography of Wilson, *Woodrow Wilson and His Work* (1920), the author, William E. Dodd, initiated the mythmaking process. Favorably disposed to the progressive movement, Dodd fell victim to what one historian has called "academic homosexuality"—falling in love with one's historical hero. The objectivity one might expect from one of America's distinguished historians was lacking. Dodd's study of Wilson clothed the president in shining armor.

Though longer, more detailed, and based upon what was thought to be the complete body of Wilson's personal papers, Ray Stannard Baker's eight-volume biography, *Woodrow Wilson: Life and Letters* (1927-1939), was disappointingly similar in tone to Dodd's earlier effort. Also influenced by an intense admiration for Wilson's eminence in American affairs, Baker's *Wilson* as much reflected the author's progressive personality as it did the former president's. The Wilson that emerged from Baker's monumental study became, in the words of a more recent scholar who has come to understand Wilson much better, "a caricature" and "too good to be true—or human." Indeed, the result of both the Dodd and Baker efforts to uncover the "true" Wilson was distortion, and a very imperfect understanding of his historical importance. Again, despite apparently honest efforts, historians had functioned as mythmakers.

The biased phrases which echoed from the pages of these early sympathetic studies of Wilson were, however, no more distorted in their conclusions than a number of other sources published at about the same time which claimed to offer a better understanding of the "darker sides" of the progressive president's personality. The papers of Robert Lansing, for example, Wilson's secretary of state from 1915 to 1920, were an indispensable primary source of information about the Wilson administration but suffered severely from the bitterness which Lansing felt toward his former boss. Dismissed from his cabinet post by Wilson in 1920, Lansing's prejudiced testimony against him cannot be accepted as completely accurate. (This dismissal supposedly occurred because Lansing had called an "unauthorized" cabinet meeting during the president's illness, but some have argued that the chief executive came to see Lansing as "disloyal" to his foreign policies.) In a somewhat similar way, the diary of the president's close advisor, Colonel Edward M. House, though in many ways indispensable to understanding the Wilson years in the White House, suffers from the fact that it displays an intense effort on the author's part to prove that the wisdom of his views in the area of foreign affairs was superior to Wilson's. While both the Lansing and House papers might seem a clear record of what actually happened in the inner chambers of national power, by themselves they unfortunately offer documentary evidence tainted by myth. Their effect has been to structure a legendary facade for Wilson built on half-truths. In them, Wilson emerges as petty, vindictive, and less than open to advice. While no doubt strong-willed and given to the belief that his own views were right on most occasions, Wilson was much less the fanatic tyrant than such sources portray.

The grossest example of the newest form of Wilson mythology has only recently been published, in 1967. Entitled *Thomas Woodrow Wilson: Twenty-eighth President of the United States, A Psychological Study*, it represents an attempt in the name of "science" to remove the mysterious veil of myth from one of America's most commanding personalities. Coauthored by the American millionaire-diplomat William C. Bullitt (the nation's first ambassador to the Soviet Union) and the renowned Viennese psychoanalyst Sigmund Freud, the work claimed to find Woodrow Wilson living in a world of illusion and fantasy. After the death of his father, Dr. Joseph Ruggles Wilson, a Presbyterian minister, the president-to-be is alleged to have lived in his own mythical

universe. "Distortion of fact thereafter became a pronounced trait of Wilson's character," Bullitt and Freud contend, and "thousands of distorted, ignored or forgotten facts mark the remainder of his life."[11] Wilson's inability to escape his own delusions, his consistent failures to distinguish fact from fancy, they conclude, ably explain his lack of success both as president, and as a diplomat on the world stage after the Great War.

Posing as a "masterly, professional, and scientifically objective" study of major significance, the Bullitt-Freud analysis of Wilson (withheld from publication until the death of Mrs. Wilson) has since been exposed as an intellectual fraud based upon extremely shaky evidence, questionable logic, and what one highly informed critic of the study has called "a solid foundation of nonfact." With little fear and scant research Bullitt and Freud attempted to persuade readers that Wilson suffered from a father fixation, psychosomatic illnesses, homosexual tendencies, a warped sexual libido, a craving for little-brother substitutes as male friends, and inevitably "left fact and reality behind for the land in which facts are the mere embodiment of wishes."[12] As with no American president before or since, the forces of myth disguised as science have sought to distort and obscure Wilson's progressive personality in a cloud of cheap gossip, character assassination, and pure fiction. Again, as is often the case with myths, those surrounding Woodrow Wilson have sought to strip a major historical figure of his humanity. Once exposed, they reveal the compulsive need Americans have so often expressed, even to the point of accepting the bizarre, to accept gossip about America's historical past.

SECTION III: AMERICA AND THE ERA OF THE FIRST WORLD WAR: MYTHS AND REALITIES

Progressivism and Imperialism

An important aspect of progressivism was its influence in the field of world affairs. Though the flurry of progressive activity was most obvious at home, it also had some bearing on what the nation did abroad. Despite the progressives' vital concerns over the direction of American foreign relations, however, the legend has developed that their interest in matters of this type was peripheral at best. The myth that progressives were concerned solely with the American domestic scene misses the attention they gave international matters as early as the age of imperialism at century's end. Further, when attention *has* been focused on the role of progressives in American foreign affairs, the domestic "liberalism" of the typical progressive has led many to assume that they must have acted as sensitive humanitarians when dealing with questions of foreign policy.

It has usually been assumed, then, that progressive leaders were anti-imperialists who favored limited international activity on the part of the United States because their first priority was overhauling democracy at home. Theodore Roosevelt, who preached the benefits of an aggressive and at times bellicose foreign policy, is thought not to have been representative of progressive attitudes. Research has clearly shown, however, that his perceiving a relationship between democratic and humanitarian values at home and nationalistic aspirations abroad made Theodore Roosevelt very much a typical progressive. Finally realizing that many things which occurred at the time might well not be defined as progressive by today's standards—immigration restriction, the prohibition of alcoholic beverages, and legal limitations on black rights for example—scholars have also come to question the legendary notion of progressivism as anti-imperialistic. In his study of progressivism and its relation to imperialism, William Leuchtenburg comes to the conclusion that

> the Progressives, contrary to the orthodox accounts, did not oppose imperialism but, with few exceptions, ardently supported the imperialist surge or, at the very least, proved agreeably acquiescent. The majority of the Progressive members of Congress voted for increased naval expenditures and for Caribbean adventures in imperialism.[13]

It appears that the national goals of imperialistic expansion were thought not to be at odds with progressive goals at home. And no better individual example of the ties between imperialism and progressivism can be found than Senator Beveridge of Indiana.

Born in Ohio during the Civil War (1862), Albert Jeremiah Beveridge came upon the national political scene in the 1890s with a vigor and assurance befitting the biblical character who was the source of his middle name. A fiery speaker for the Republican party, matched in spirit and eloquence only by the Democrats' William Jennings Bryan, he soon emerged as an ardent spokesman for imperialism. Believing that "the Philippines are ours forever," and that the United States should hold firm to "the mission of our race, trustees under God, of the civilization of the world," Beveridge was totally convinced that the "march of the flag" to foreign soil represented a progressive step. Thus, at the same time that he nursed key progressive legislation through Congress—the Pure Food and Drug Act, Child Labor Laws, trust regulation, and codes governing the eight-hour-day—he also carried on the fight for a national policy in favor of America's expanding role in world affairs. A congressional ally of President Theodore Roosevelt, Beveridge could with equal enthusiasm lobby for passage of laws calling for the regulation of big business and for legislative support of "Big Stick" diplomatic policies. So close did his relationship with T. R. become, in fact, that he delivered the keynote address to the national Progressive party convention in 1912 which endorsed Roosevelt's return to the political wars. To Beveridge, it seemed not inconsistent that one who passionately sought to improve the workings of democracy at home should want to extend the benefits of these reforms to the world at large—whether or not others wished to accept them. The aim of the progressives' foreign policy was to extend the influence of democracy—however that elusive term might be defined.

Progressives of all kinds supported imperialism. William Allen White, reforming journalist of the *Emporia* (Kansas) *Gazette*, and Elizabeth Cady Stanton, advocate of women's rights, for example, found common cause in imperialistic goals. A good many progressives endorsed Admiral Alfred T. Mahan's idea of a strong navy to protect and extend Americanism. They never protested America's imperialistic adventures in such places as

Panama or the Dominican Republic. The racism progressives displayed toward blacks at home helped make them receptive to the appeal that democracy ought to concern itself with the "little brown brothers" in distant lands who, like black Americans, were thought to be too inept and politically naive to plot their own destiny. Thus, the condescending attitude which some progressives displayed toward the disadvantaged elements in American society was reflected in arrogance abroad. Just as they labored to extend the blessings of democracy to those Americans who had been overlooked—the urban poor for example—they wished to reform the world in line with their newly designed vision of democracy. Indeed progressives' support for imperialism reveals a good deal about both the strengths and weaknesses of the total progressive movement, particularly the connection between its humanistic values and nationalistic aspirations. The progressives could delight in the rise of America to the status of a world power because then the model republic they were in the process of creating would be more influential. Predictably, the tone and direction set by progressivism's sympathies for imperialism also were destined to lead the nation to a more pronounced role in the affairs of the world's other expanding powers. This was a lesson learned only too quickly. Those who were aware of international realities could see that conflicting imperial ambitions among European nation-states were already causing storm clouds of war to form.

America and the First World War

The Great War which engulfed Europe in 1914 was the result of many factors. While it has become traditional to think that German militarism alone was responsible for bringing on the world conflict, it can now be seen that growing nationalism, the interlocking system of alliances, and imperialistic competition for colonies involving various powers were all to blame for causing the war. In addition, the war guilt of 1914 must include Austria—as well as Russia, France, and England—for its issuance of a war-provoking ultimatum to Serbia after Archduke Francis Ferdinand of the Austro-Hungarian Empire had been assassinated by a Serbian student. Russia responded to the

growing sense of crisis developing in Europe by swiftly mobilizing troops along its frontiers with both Austria and Germany. France, in turn, was eager to atone for its military defeat at the hands of Germany during the Franco-Prussian War of 1870-71, and thus belligerently affirmed its support of its ally Russia if war should come. For its part, England attempted to cling to its nineteenth-century image of "splendid isolation" from the petty affairs of Europe. In doing so, it contributed to the eventual hostilities by refusing to indicate clearly what its policy would be if either of its allies, France or Russia, were invaded. For its part, the United States was nearly as nationalistic and imperialistic as the world's other major nations. The affairs of Europe which brought the world to global war from 1914 to 1918, then, were infinitely more complex than the legend of unique German militarism which has so often been used to explain it allows.

The emotion of war shapes an environment receptive to mythmaking. Images of allies and enemies, scurrying diplomats, crusading generals, and marching soldiers, all add to the distorted psychological atmosphere which war produces. Given these circumstances surrounding what was viewed as the first *world* war, it is little surprise that American historians have had a difficult time reconstructing the reality of the nation's intervention and participation in the affair. Initially and officially, America's response to the guns of August, 1914, was neutrality. While there were some like ex-president Theodore Roosevelt who questioned Woodrow Wilson's policy, the majority of Americans were watching European developments with interest but little desire to become directly involved. Roosevelt, for example, caused little more than an amused reaction when he criticized the pacifist song "I Didn't Raise My Boy to Be a Soldier" as making about as much sense as one entitled "I Didn't Raise My Girl to Be a Mother." But even though most Americans agreed in theory with Wilson's plea that the nation remain neutral in both thought and action, insulating America from the European war proved impossible.

The resolution marking the official intervention of America into the First World War passed the Congress in April, 1917. This was nearly three years after the war began in Europe. Thus, the key question that has intrigued historians, and the matter over which considerable myth and legend has developed, is what happened in the United States between August, 1914, and April, 1917, which prompted the move from neutrality to intervention. What eventually led America into the "war to end all wars?"

The traditional answer to the question of America's involvement in the war can be expressed in a word—submarine. In accord with the belief that Germany was principally responsible for having caused the war to begin with, the theory is that the United States was forced to enter the conflict because of Germany's consistent violation of American neutral rights and its callous disregard for international law. The sinking of British ships carrying American passengers, such as the *Lusitania*, and Germany's declaration of unrestricted submarine warfare on January 31, 1917, the argument continues, were intolerable affronts to national honor which could be met only by American intervention. It seemed clear that America's commitment to neutrality was gradually eroded due to forces outside the country, and this is a view endorsed by such historians as Charles Seymour. Immoral, ruthless, and illegal activities on the part of Germany caused the breakdown of American neutrality and provided the motive for the United States' eventual decision to intervene.

While never fundamentally questioning the truth of the theory that German submarine warfare helped to shape American policies toward intervention, a number of "revisionist" historians—Charles Tansill, Harry Elmer Barnes, and Paul Birdsall, in particular—have emphasized the nation's essentially *unneutral* role in the months and years before intervention as the real cause of America's entry into World War I. Characterizing the United States as a "benevolent neutral," a supporter of England, France, and Russia, with no desire to engage in the fighting, these historians have presented a quite different picture of how America became involved in the war. They note, for example, that disputes over neutrality rights first arose with England. Thus, if America went to war to preserve its neutrality rights, the enemy could as well have been England as Germany. They also point out that

the *Lusitania* and other destroyed vessels were not American ships and therefore could not serve as valid legal excuses for America's eventual intervention. Beyond this, there might have been some justification for Germany's sinking the *Lusitania*. Salvaged documents clearly show that the passenger ship was carrying 4,200 cases of small arms ammunition and was therefore not the innocent, neutral vessel as was claimed. The *Lusitania* incident, revisionists say, illustrates that very complex issues of international law were involved. Thus, the loss of 128 American lives due to the sinking should not hide the fact that the celebrated *Lusitania* affair was not simply the legendary case of good versus evil that most assume.

The revisionists have also pointed to the distinct cultural and economic ties which lay behind America's illusion of neutrality. Most Americans reflected their cultural relationship to England, based on common ethnic background, common language, and a common political tradition. President Wilson in particular, note the revisionists, was personally an admirer of the British system of government, having studied it with enthusiasm while a student and teacher. Also, with only one fifth of the American people of German or Austrian extraction as compared to about one half possessing an English or French background, it should have been clear from the outset that America's basic sympathies lay not with neutrality but with an eye to intervention should the Allies be threatened with defeat. This favoritism toward cultural friends, they continue, was most evident in economic affairs. While America from 1914 to 1917 wore the mask of a neutral it had made loans to its eventual allies totaling nearly $2.5 billion whereas only some $27 million had found its way to Germany, Austria, and their allies to finance the war. With better than $92 going to support the cause of England, France, and Russia for every one dollar to their enemies, simple economics would seem to suggest that American neutralism was a sham. In addition, according to Document No. 9433 of the War Materials Division, the War Department had defensive war plans drawn before the conflict, with Germany as the theoretical opponent. When one discovers as well that President Wilson's key foreign policy advisor, Colonel

Edward M. House, had signed a diplomatic memorandum with British Foreign Secretary Sir Edward Grey as early as 1916 stating America's moral commitment to the Allied cause, the suggestion that the neutrality of the United States was a myth became compelling to the revisionists.

Clearly, there is much to be said for the arsenal of evidence which has been compiled questioning the sincerity of American neutrality in the critical years from 1914 to 1917. It is now fairly certain that America was probably more inclined to support the cause of its eventual allies than the nation ever imagined at the time. But even while there are important indicators that the United States was not as neutral in thought and action as it claimed, it does not follow that America entered the First World War because of the evil designs of conspiratorial men or the desire of business capitalists to force the nation into the European conflict for the sake of corporate profits. Thus, even though the views of the revisionists have been twisted by some persons intent on proving a massive conspiracy of aggressive capitalistic imperialists forcing America into war, such a theory is little more than a leftist legend. The economic advantage which munitions makers, businessmen, and large lending institutions would gain if the United States joined the conflict was little more than they already enjoyed by supplying the needs of a warring Europe. Indeed, the best assurance the business community had of continued profits—with the least amount of risk—was an investment in neutrality which allowed them to trade with and supply all of the belligerent powers. In short, there is little evidence that the efforts of big business prompted America's entry into the war. And even if some such pressure was applied, President Wilson was unmoved by it.

The most likely answer to the question of what caused American intervention in the First World War, then, seems to be neither that the United States was attempting to remain innocently neutral and was finally forced to join battle against the "Huns," nor the dramatic notion that weapons manufacturers were anxious to get American doughboys into the trenches of the Western Front so as to fatten corporate profits. Both explanations are heavily encrusted with legend. In recent years historians have come to argue

instead that American neutrality began to break down as the nation became increasingly aware that the defeat of England and France in the European campaigns would result in a direct threat to American security. Americans became convinced that a triumph by the combined forces of Germany and Austria-Hungary would pose a menacing set of circumstances to democracy and freedom throughout the world. National honor, vital economic interests, as well as military and political security were all deemed to be in jeopardy. What was fundamentally at stake was the international balance of power. This larger view of America's entry into the war also fits with the other explanations which have been offered to explain intervention. For in appreciating such realistic considerations one need not reject the argument that the emotion-charged *Lusitania* incident and the nation's uneven neutrality also figured in bringing America into the European conflict.

Wilson and American Involvement

Despite the general agreement among historians that concern for American security was the important reason why America intervened in the war, only recently have historians appreciated the degree to which President Wilson shared these views. For decades the legend persisted that only the president's foreign policy advisors—Colonel Edward M. House, Secretary of State Robert Lansing, and Ambassador (to Great Britain) Walter Hines Page—understood the threat which Germany and her allies presented to America's national interests. But recent studies by noted authorities have concluded that Wilson's decision to bring America to war was based solidly on his awareness that German victory would upset the world balance of power and threaten the long-range interests of the United States. While holding solidly to his sense of morality and idealism, Wilson nevertheless was greatly influenced by practical considerations confronting the nation. Despite the force of strong antiwar sentiment, a reluctant Congress and people, and no immediate act of war against America, Wilson realistically foresaw the consequences of the European war for America and committed the country to the conflict. All this considered, it now seems clear that simplistic and mythically based explanations of American involvement in the European war will no longer suffice. Neither the simple notion of the kaiser's use of submarines nor the argument of America's essentially non-neutral economic ties to the allied powers, by themselves, grasp the reality of one of the more complex eras in American history. Realistic considerations, shared by President Wilson, involving national interest and national security also played their role in prompting the fateful move to "save the world for democracy."

Once the decision to enter the war had been made, Woodrow Wilson emerged as a superb war leader. Creatively combining his unique capacity for both idealism and realism he gave the impression of being an invincible prophet. "Holding aloft the torch of idealism in one hand and the flaming sword of righteousness in the other," as the diplomatic historian Thomas Bailey has expressed it, "he aroused the masses to a holy crusade."[14] Indeed, once the tangled events of the war years came to a close he stood nearly alone as the savior and hero of democracy in the world's imagination. Seemingly chosen by fate, as in the myths of old, to lead humanity back from the brink of disaster, Wilson accepted the heroic mantle which events had offered him, and at war's end journeyed to Europe on the ship *George Washington* to minister to the business of a postwar diplomatic settlement. An air of anticipation greeted him upon his arrival in Europe.

> Hundreds of thousands thronged the streets of Paris, while banners and transparencies proclaimed "Vive Wilson" and "Honor to Wilson the Just." A boulevard was christened after him— perhaps a more impressive honor than that bestowed by an American mother who had lately named her triplets Wood, Row, and Wilson—and Warsaw prepared to erect his statue in her central square. To the peasants and shopkeepers and weary soldiers of Europe, his advent, as William E. Dodd observed, was like the Second Coming of Christ.[15]

Armed with his famous Fourteen Points which called for an end to secret diplomacy, a review of all colonial claims, freedom of the seas, and, most important, an international organization to prevent war (the League of Nations), among other things, Wilson soon discovered that his personal heroic prestige was matched in intensity by the nationalistic designs of the other peacemakers. Clemenceau of France, for example, stated privately: "Mr. Wilson bores me with his Fourteen Points; why, God Almighty has only ten!" With France still fearful of German "warlords," and England unwilling to accept Wilson's concept of "freedom of the seas," the treaty in final form, aside from Wilson's cherished League, contained few of his original Fourteen Points. It called for heavy payment of war debts (reparations) by Germany, reflecting the Allied belief that the "Hun" had been totally responsible for causing the war, created or recreated many new nation-states in East-Central Europe (such as Yugoslavia and Poland), divided Germany into two parts (Germany proper and East Prussia), stripped Germany of its former colonies (Southeast Africa for example), and called for the creation of a League of Nations. For the Versailles agreement to succeed, given its harsh treatment of a defeated Germany, and its failure to involve Russia in the proceedings, it was imperative that the United States maintain a high level of involvement in world affairs for some time to come. It was soon clear that the treaty itself would do little to assure a world made "safe for democracy."

For his part, Woodrow Wilson was willing to accept the many aspects of the new treaty with which he did not particularly agree. Once the new League of Nations was operational, he felt, the new international agency for peace could settle outstanding issues in a more deliberate way. Despite the president's attempts to sell the idea of the League to the American people, however, a reluctant Senate refused to provide the necessary votes for acceptance.

Postwar Isolationism

This apparent rejection of world responsibilities, together with such later actions as the refusal of the United States to join the World Court, has led many to the incorrect conclusion that during the decade of the 1920s America largely withdrew from international affairs. According to legend, the nation was content to tend its own garden, again cultivat-

Flaming Youth: The Roaring
Twenties in Film
Museum of Modern Art

ing a policy of isolationism. While it is reasonably accurate to say that America followed a policy of limited diplomatic responsibility during the 1920s, it is equally necessary to understand that the nation's allegedly isolationist stance toward the world at large during this span of time is in large part a myth. In his article "The Legend of Isolationism in the 1920s," William Appleman Williams argued a nonisolationist interpretation of that era. Historians have increasingly come to agree with Williams' conclusion that equating the 1920s with isolationism is an idea drawn from "the folklore of American foreign relations." Believing that isolationism was never more than a myth commonly agreed upon, Williams finds expansionism the central theme of the nation's foreign relations during that decade. America's consistent support for international economic measures and

agreements, as well as the hosting of its first international diplomatic meeting (the Washington Naval Conference of 1921-22), added to its intimate involvement with postwar Germany in helping it manage its reparations payments through the Dawes Plan of 1924 and the Young Plan of 1929, all suggest that the State Department had not retired completely. Indeed, America's urge for world power which had been building for decades did not suddenly pass from the scene like a mirage during the decade of the 1920s.

SECTION IV: THE ROARING TWENTIES: FACT OR FICTION?

Historians have recently come to appreciate the importance of nostalgia as a historical force. They have gradually realized that the combination of memory and emotion, the stuff of which a sentimentalized past and myths are made, help to create a fond though not always accurate portrait of bygone ages. In the light of this growing recognition, then, historians have begun to reexamine the so-called Roaring Twenties. Sandwiched between the period of progressivism and the New Deal, the twenties give the impression of having been a time when Americans retreated from their efforts as a world power and their crusade for reform simply to enjoy themselves.

The twenties, it is thought, was an age of wonderful nonsense when the nation indulged itself in bathtub gin, raccoon coats, flappers, the Barrymores, Will Rogers, a youthful Rudy Vallee, a scar-faced Al Capone, and passed its leisure moments at cocktail parties discussing the theories of Sigmund Freud. In hindsight, it almost seems as if the typical American of the twenties, caught between war years and the Great Depression to come, was enjoying one last glorious fling. The tastes, sights, and sounds of America ran to Lucky Strike cigarettes, dancing marathons, Jack Dempsey, petting parties, Douglas Fairbanks, Man O'War, Amos and Andy, Mary Pickford, and the strains of Paul Whiteman's orchestra. It was also the age of the execution of Sacco and Vanzetti, the Scopes "Monkey" Trial, a revitalized Ku Klux Klan, and the "Lost Generation" of American writers. The nickelodeon gave way to the silver screen and a new media, radio, made it possible to hear history in the making—Rogers Hornsby leading the National League in hitting, Charles Lindbergh flying the Atlantic, Gertrude Ederle as the first woman to swim the English Channel, and new musical hits like "Sweet Georgia Brown," "Alexander's Rag-Time Band," and "When the Red-Red-Robin Comes a Bob-Bob-Bobbin Along." But the gaudy era of Cecil B. DeMille's movie extravaganzas, Aimee Semple McPherson's religious revivalism on behalf of her International Church of the Four Square Gospel, and speakeasies with their stale air, bad murals, and poor booze was in many ways a facade. Beneath its superficial adolescent style, the age had prime historical significance.

Politically, the 1920s were the final years of Woodrow Wilson's presidential administration. Defeated in his efforts on behalf of the League of Nations, and in ill health, Wilson continued in office until March, 1921. If he had died earlier perhaps his legend as a progressive idealist might have developed more quickly, but his final years in the White House were soured by his staunch refusal to either compromise with the Senate over the League or step down from office because of his physical condition. Since Wilson was unable to fulfill his presidential duties, much power in Washington fell to his attorney general, A. Mitchell Palmer, an old-line progressive and former backer of child-labor legislation and women's suffrage. Palmer, however, helped launch the decade of the twenties by feeding America the fantasy that it was on the brink of subversion by Bolsheviks. The period of the "Red Scare," which lasted from 1919 through 1920, was indeed, as one historian has said, a "study in national hysteria." Wartime hatred of the German "Huns" was transferred to American "radicals," and the nation followed Palmer's lead in discovering plots and conspiracies behind nearly every organization whose ideas or actions seemed to be anything less than "100 percent American." Even the Boston police force in striking for higher wages, for example, found itself identified as a subversive element, and became a victim of the growing myth that "Commies" and "Reds" had infiltrated the country to a perilous degree. Palmer's prediction that radicals would attempt to take over the United States on May 1, 1920, failed to materialize, however, and the nation soon regained some of its perspective. But even though the country appeared to be returning to normal it had had its first glimpse of what would prove to be an unusually fertile decade for mythmaking.

Warren Harding

The nation had barely recovered its composure after shadowboxing with the myth of an impending Communist revolution when it entered the almost equally mythical world of Warren Gamaliel Harding. Harding had easily disposed of his Democratic opponent James M. Cox of Ohio in 1920 on the strength of a "front porch campaign" and vague promises of a return to "normalcy," and was swept to the presidency with 61 percent of the popular vote. Endowed with a conservative mind more suited to the nineteenth century than the twentieth, and distinguished in looks, Harding was a symbol of stability to many people. He seemed to personify perfectly the mood of the country. However, in the judgment of one leading historian, "Harding was a handsome, semieducated political hack with a modest talent for golf; a larger taste for women, liquor, and poker; a complaisant disposition; an utterly empty mind; and an enduring loyalty to the Republican creed of 1890. He was probably the least qualified candidate ever nominated by a major party."[16] Indeed his image as an honest small-town newspaper editor straight from Main Street, U.S.A., was in many ways a mythical front which hid a man whose true character ran to vulgar habits, cronyism, and poor judgment. After his presidency had run its course, it would be discovered that he had used the White House for extramarital affairs. And beyond this, he had looked the other way as his attorney general, Harry Daugherty, became involved in improprieties and probable corruption; his head of the Veteran's Bureau, Charles R. Forbes, embezzled public funds; and his secretary of the interior, Albert B. Fall, accepted gifts and payments in return for leasing governmental oil reserves to private interests at Teapot Dome, Wyoming, and Elk Hills, California. The voting public, however, saw through the mirage too late, having already opened its arms to the man who in a homey way claimed to be "just folks."

No amount of fresh research will ever completely free Warren G. Harding from charges that have been leveled against him and his administration. Nonetheless, there have been some attempts of late to reconstruct the reality of the Harding years in a way more sympathetic to the nation's twenty-ninth president. Largely as a consequence of the efforts of Robert K. Murray, the popular image of Harding as a complete failure is being challenged. Insisting that an objective and unbiased assessment of Harding has not been made because historians have never bothered to look beyond the immorality and corruption of his administration, Murray has attempted to sweep away at least the more obvious myths of the Harding era. He was, Murray claims, neither the inefficient nor the ineffective chief executive usually imagined. Harding was not, as it may seem, propelled to the presidency by a fluke or by a "gang" of Ohio politicians. He

took his political career seriously and had a shrewd way with compromise and public opinion. "Contrary to myth," Murray concludes, "Harding was an extremely hardworking president and grew in the job as time passed."[17] Though his appointments of Daugherty, Forbes, and Fall clearly display questionable judgment, he must be credited with having also surrounded himself with such highly competent individuals as Secretary of Agriculture Henry C. Wallace, Secretary of State Charles Evans Hughes, and Secretary of Commerce Herbert Hoover. In the area of foreign policy he displayed moral courage in supporting the World Court, and better than average diplomatic skill in repairing deteriorated relations with Mexico. In short, it seems that Harding was a president of some political skill but was also a man of limited insight and ability. In the end, perhaps the man who knew his strengths and weaknesses best was Harding himself. He seemed seldom to harbor personal illusions. He knew his failing of putting friendship and loyalty above ideals and ethics and could openly admit, "I know how far removed from greatness I am." In a moment of self-analysis he once confessed that if he had been born a woman he would almost always have been in a "family way." It seems he could never say "No."

Fate allowed Warren Harding little chance to personally clarify differences between the myth and reality of his administration. After approximately two-and-one-half years in office, returning from a political junket to Alaska, he died of a heart attack in San Francisco on August 2, 1923. At the time of death his extracurricular activities were still at the stage of rumor and the full measure of corruption with which his administration would later be so intimately associated had not yet been exposed. Consequently, his public image in late 1923 was still relatively uncontaminated and news of his passing was met with a genuine outpouring of national grief.

Calvin Coolidge

Harding's vice president, Calvin Coolidge, who had come to national prominence as a result of his actions during the Boston Police Strike of 1919 while still governor of Massachusetts, was awakened at his family farmhouse in

Plymouth, Vermont, at 2:30 A.M. to take the oath of office on the family Bible, fittingly, by the light of a flickering kerosene lamp. The wave of emotion following Harding's sudden death, and the quaint image of Mr. Coolidge being sworn in by his aged father in such a picturesque setting, caused almost everyone to look favorably upon their new president. The emotional atmosphere led some to immediately clothe Coolidge in heroic garb, reflecting the decade's obsession with heroes. Ignoring Coolidge's mediocrity, journalists such as William Allen White were moved to say that they found Calvin "marvelous." Again in the words of Robert K. Murray, "Coolidge thus became an innocent victim as newspapers created a Coolidge myth."[18] A nation being fed a steady diet of stories in the press detailing gangland slayings and the antics of people like "Shipwreck" Kelly, the flag-pole sitter, found it comforting to know that a steady and stable hand was once again in firm control of the country's affairs on Pennsylvania Avenue. Preferring to ignore his rural New England background and a worsening economic depression in American agriculture, Coolidge became the darling of big business. Reflecting the views of finance capitalism, and the advice of his secretary of the treasury, Andrew Mellon, he at one point took precious time away from his daily nap to declare: "The chief business of the American people is business." A genius, as he himself said, at "avoiding trouble," and never saying anything that might cause controversy, Coolidge has never been accused of being one of America's most colorful chief executives. In fact, his glum manner, stinginess with words, and particularly his laziness have become legendary. The story is told, for example, that on one occasion he was approached by a dinner guest obviously aware of his reputation as a man of few words. "Mr. Coolidge," the visitor is supposed to have said, "I've made a rather sizeable bet with my friends that I can get you to speak three words this evening." Coolidge replied simply, "You lose." Even the thirtieth president's first biographer could not overcome the temptation to say something about "Silent Cal's" most obvious trait. Whenever Calvin opened his mouth, the writer claimed, a moth flew out. Indeed, his quiet image haunted him beyond his death. Upon hearing of his demise in 1933 at the age

of 60, the New York literary wit Dorothy Parker asked, "How can you tell?" President Coolidge was at the very least a curious representative of the supposedly *Roaring* Twenties.

In defense of Calvin Coolidge, and despite the myth of his total incompetence, it can be said that he had a sincere commitment to public service, and certainly displayed a more commendable form of integrity than his immediate predecessor. Under his unspectacular but steady administration, continued attempts were made to improve the nation's foreign relations with Latin America, and the Kellogg-Briand Pact, an attempt to "outlaw war as an instrument of national policy," was signed. Thus while the nation subsequently has failed to see as much in Coolidge as the many who voted for him in 1924, he was not as completely lacking in redeeming qualities as is usually supposed. "Despite his definite limitations," as one informed scholar of the 1920s has concluded, "Coolidge was in many ways a man of perseverance, ability, and complexity, and any history of the twenties should not, as is often done, merely dismiss him with a joke."[19] To judge the Coolidge years as nothing but frivolous and unimportant only supports the mythology which is so often mistakenly adopted about the decade of the 1920s in general.

Herbert Hoover

"Silent Cal's" successor to the presidency, Herbert Clark Hoover, is frequently dismissed as little more than a fat Coolidge. In terms of innate talent, however, few presidents have surpassed the man whose name has become synonymous with the Great Crash and the Great Depression. Born in the heart of Middle America at West Branch, Iowa, in 1874, Herbert Hoover soon gave evidence of the drive and brilliance which would eventually carry him to the presidency. Graduating from Stanford University in 1895, he became a highly successful and wealthy mining engineer in Australia and China. During the First World War, he performed admirably as chairman of the Commission for Relief in Belgium, and was rewarded by President Wilson with the chairmanship of the Food Administration Board. At the conclusion of the war he headed economic relief operations in Europe, and served as secretary of commerce in both the Harding and Coolidge administrations. In that capacity he demonstrated qualities of administrative and managerial ability which made him the Republican party's logical candidate for president against the Democrats' "Happy Warrior," Alfred E. Smith, in the election of 1928.

Hoover's decisive victory over Smith, by 444 electoral votes to 87, has often been credited in American political folklore to Smith's Roman Catholicism. Supposedly, Hoover came to the presidency on a wave of anti-Catholic sentiment. In reality, however, Hoover's triumph seems to have been connected to other issues. The nation was riding the tide of the "Coolidge boom" and seemed to believe that another Republican should be elected to assure continued economic growth. Also, Smith's close associations with big-city politics in New York and his call for the repeal of Prohibition caused many to see Hoover as the better candidate. In the end, Smith's image as the "Abe Lincoln of the tenement people" simply did not have enough national appeal to successfully challenge an entrenched Republican party viewed as responsible for American prosperity and Herbert Hoover's honest image as a resourceful and competent leader.

It is important to emphasize Herbert Hoover's worthiness for the presidency because in national mythology he has often been seen as personally responsible for the Great Depression which soon engulfed his administration, and his image has suffered accordingly. The historical burden of twelve million Americans unemployed, breadlines, soup kitchens, apple sellers, and shanty towns called "Hoovervilles" housing the impoverished masses of the depression years indeed has fallen most heavily upon Hoover. On the eve of his election defeat by Franklin Roosevelt in 1932, there were those who were enthusiastically chanting the refrain, "They're Cannin' 'Erbie 'Oover in the Mornin'."

Contrary to popular thinking, however, Hoover worked hard to deal with the swiftly declining economy. He seemed to recognize, for example, the complex and international character of the nation's depressed economic situation. His greatest downfall, however, was his inability to see beyond the limits of his personal mythology. The principles of free enterprise, self-help, a balanced budget, and the limited role which he thought the government should play in the economic market place had served him well in his preceding career. They failed badly, however, when applied to the unique set of circumstances which faced the nation in 1929 and the early thirties. A staunch believer in rugged individualism and in private relief programs as the only way for Americans to deal with the economic crisis, Hoover seems never to have fully appreciated the degree to which all of these sacred ideas were more mythical than real. One result was his use of a traditional American double standard. He could support the creation of the Reconstruction Finance Corporation to make loans to banks, railroads, and insurance companies, but argued that it would violate American economic tradition to give any form of direct aid to individuals in need. In response to the pressures of tradition, Hoover's support for the myth of American free enterprise forced most to "rough it out" by themselves.

The Twenties in America

The real substance of the 1920s, however, included much more than "politics as usual." The decade also witnessed, for example, the resurgence of the Ku Klux Klan. The newly resurgent Klan, it must be noted, was different in many important respects from the Klan of Reconstruction days. The Klan of the twenties was a national, rather than a southern phenomenon, with its greatest strength in the state of Indiana. Also, considering the organization's membership of from three to five million, it would be simplistic to think of the citizens of the "Invisible Empire" as only "crackpots," "psychotics," and "moral monsters." In reality, the Klan served as a focal point for men and women of varying anxieties. It provided a sense of stability not only for those who were fearful of blacks, but also those who felt threatened by Catholics, Jews, Darwin's theory of evolution, and the city. Found in both rural and urban America (there were approximately two hundred thousand Klansmen in the Chicago area alone during the twenties), the strength of the movement seems to have rested on the force of nostalgia and a growing fear of what could generally be called "modernism." Unwilling or unable to accept a new America of sprawling cities, industrial development, Model Ts, lipstick, *True Confessions* magazine, and jazz, Klansmen became spokesmen for a simpler time and an older form of morality. In their quest to recapture the lost golden days from the nation's past which existed only in their minds, and seeking an acceptable set of explanations for their ideas, they placed their greatest emphasis on the nebulous concept of "100 percent Americanism." As with so much else during the 1920s, the rise of the KKK was brought on by a clash, between the idea of progress and the emotion of nostalgia.

Given its basic appeal to those who longed for a simpler America, the Klan was bound to find acceptance chiefly among those who were white, Anglo-Saxon, and Protestant, especially those of a fundamentalist point of view. While it would be an oversimplification to say that all religious fundamentalists were Klansmen, in most cases the reverse was true. In both rural and urban settings defenders of the Rock of Ages and believers in the "old-time religion" sought to challenge the new technology, the new morality, and in general the ideas of a new America. Their efforts were based on appeals to the "eternal truths" expressed literally in the Good Book. In both folklore and television melodramas the fundamentalists of the 1920s appear as suspender-snapping, tobacco-chewing, Bible-clutching, simple-minded bigots. They stood as vitally concerned spectators at the trial of John Thomas Scopes, a young high school biology teacher who was brought before a local court at Dayton, Tennessee, in 1925 for violating an act which made it "unlawful for any teacher in any of the . . . public schools of the state, to teach any theory that denies the story of the divine creation of man as taught in the Bible." The real John Scopes was not the persecuted soul of folklore, but was one who taught Charles Darwin's theories of evolution so as to challenge directly the state statute in a test case. The famous "monkey trial," with its confrontation between William Jennings Bryan (for the prosecution) and Clarence Darrow (for the defense), has often been cited as the classic case of rural-fundamentalist ignorance. But the old form of morality and Bible interpreta-

tion for which Bryan spoke so eloquently in the hot summer of 1925 was not the monopoly of rural America. It was found not only in the Cumberland Mountains but elsewhere in the nation. In national mythology the Scopes trial is thought to have marked the death of fundamentalism. In reality, however, this is not true. "Assemblies of God, Soul-Saving Stations, and Billy Graham," as one student of the twenties has concluded, "bear witness to the endurance of that old rural morality that supposedly died in the twenties."[20]

Another manifestation of the enduring fundamentalist spirit, and a subject also drenched with myth, is the "noble experiment" of Prohibition. Despite folklore and Hollywood's portrayal to the contrary, Prohibition was not nearly the exercise in futility commonly supposed. In proof of this, statistics show that the national consumption of alcoholic beverages was cut by close to one half. The decline was most apparent, of course, among those who could not afford "bootlegged hooch" spirited into the country from places such as Cuba and Canada. Thus, while the wealthier classes continued to enjoy illegal "hard stuff," the beer-drinking public cut its consumption rate considerably. After the repeal of Prohibition by the Twenty-first Amendment in 1933—and again contrary to popular legend—the drinking of alcohol did not increase to any great degree. Rather, a long-term period of moderation developed.

The mythology of the 1920s has not only come to obscure matters such as fundamentalism and Prohibition, however; it has also obstructed a clear understanding of cultural affairs. According to popular myth, for example, the literary scene of the twenties was one of struggling writers and alienated artists rejecting the crass and artificial character of American culture in favor of the more sophisticated atmosphere of European capitals—particularly Paris. Of course, there was much in America during the 1920s which intellectuals found less than stimulating. Evidence of an emerging mass culture was everywhere. The "talkies" had come to Hollywood in the form of such "arty" films as *Women Who Give* and *Rouged Lips*, and the general public was coming to believe itself cultured through its reading of the latest Book-of-the-Month Club selection (established in 1926) or the *Reader's*

Digest (first published in 1922). To believe that all or even most of those who left America in favor of the European cultural scene were "angry young men" of what Gertrude Stein called the "Lost Generation," however, is for the most part to accept a precious, yet erroneous, bit of folklore. While such individuals as Ernest Hemingway and F. Scott Fitzgerald have traditionally been viewed as "protest figures" who left the country as a gesture of revolt against the American system of values and culture, it has been estimated "that among all the Americans settled in Paris at any one time in the twenties, no more than one tenth to one fifth of them were those celebrated figures commonly called expatriates."[21] Beyond this, many who later came to be romantically viewed as cultural exiles left the United States not because of any profound disillusionment, but simply because Paris was the world's cultural center during the era. It was more a case, it seems, of intellectuals being "turned on" by Paris than being "turned off" by America. In addition, an exaggerated emphasis on the Lost Generation writers causes one to overlook the black or Harlem Renaissance in writing during the same decade led by Claude McKay, Langston Hughes, and Jean Toomer. Finally, many of the small minority who did reject American culture during the twenties still found their artistic inspiration in writing about the American scene. But while some intellectuals such as T. S. Eliot became convinced that America was a cultural "wasteland," others like Carl Sandburg and Stephen Vincent Benét took occasion during the same decade to applaud the genius of America, both past and present. Most writers of the period, in short, were not particularly "lost" in the sense of being alienated, but rather, like the culture as a whole, seemed to be reflecting a growing deep concern with both the history and future of America.

The meaning of America during the 1920s was also reflected in the heroes which the decade created. Thomas A. Edison's inventive genius led many to view him as a classic case of the Horatio Alger dream come true. Henry Ford captured much of the same spirit, seemingly a twentieth-century edition of Benjamin Franklin. However, Charles A. Lindbergh most fully symbolized the spirit of his age. The first aviator to fly solo across the Atlantic Ocean, with his famous flight from Roosevelt Field, New York, to Le Bourget airport near Paris in 1927, Lindbergh became an instant legend. For some he was but the latest example of the American pioneer tradition. "Captain Lindbergh personifies the daring of youth. Daniel Boone, David Crockett, and men of that type played a lone hand and made America. Lindbergh is their lineal descendant," [22] commented the son of former president Theodore Roosevelt. Indeed what the nation saw in this farm boy from rural Little Falls, Minnesota, was a trailblazer of a new frontier who had found inspiration for his deeds in the legendary frontiersmen of old. He represented the strength America might draw from its glorious past. For others, however, he emerged as the new hero of the machine age. His exploits represented a triumph of technology over nature. At one and the same time, then, Charles Lindbergh symbolized America's continuing love affair with its mythical past and its utopian visions of the future. But Americans were soon to discover that the American Dream was on the verge of being severely challenged by the crisis of the Great Depression. In a new setting America would feel the need to search for new national heroes, and they were destined to find one in the person of Franklin Delano Roosevelt.

STUDY QUESTIONS

1. Discuss the principal myths concerning progressivism. In your discussion refer to the varying and conflicting views of scholars such as Vernon L. Parrington, H. L. Mencken, John Chamberlain, John D. Hicks, Richard Hofstadter, Robert Wiebe, and Gabriel Kolko as explained in this chapter.

2. Compare and contrast Theodore Roosevelt and Woodrow Wilson as American political heroes. In what ways were the sources of their mythologies fundamentally different?

3. Concerning the era of the First World War, what are the principal myths that have developed concerning the progressives' foreign policy before the conflict, American "neutrality" from 1914 to 1917, Woodrow Wilson at the

Versailles Peace Conference, and American isolationism during the postwar period?

4. What is the continuing mythical image of the 1920s? Also, what are the major myths which have come to surround the presidencies of Warren Harding, Calvin Coolidge, and Herbert Hoover? Finally, what are some of the more important myths about America during this decade?

REFERENCES

1. John A. Garraty, "Robert M. LaFollette: The Promise Unfulfilled," in John A. Garraty, ed., *Historical Viewpoints*, II (New York: Harper & Row, Publishers), p. 146.
2. Allen F. Davis, "Jane Addams," in John A. Garraty, ed., *Encyclopedia of American Biography* (New York: Harper & Row, Publishers, 1974), p. 19.
3. Burl Noggle, "Configurations of the Twenties," in William H. Cartwright and Richard L. Watson, Jr., eds., *The Reinterpretation of American History and Culture* (Washington, D.C.: National Council for the Social Studies, 1973), p. 476.
4. David M. Kennedy, ed., *Progressivism: The Critical Issues* (Boston: Little, Brown and Co., 1971), p. viii.
5. Ibid., p. x.
6. Gabriel Kolko, *The Triumph of Conservatism* (New York: The Free Press, 1963), pp. 2-3.
7. Dixon Wecter, *The Hero in America: A Chronicle of Hero-Worship* (Ann Arbor: The University of Michigan Press, 1966), p. 374.
8. Ray Ginger, *People on the Move: A United States History Since 1860*, II (Boston: Allyn and Bacon, 1975), p. 511.
9. Arthur S. Link, "World War I," in John A. Garraty, ed., *Interpreting American History: Conversations with Historians* (New York: The Macmillan Company, 1970), p. 142.
10. Ibid.
11. Quoted in Arthur S. Link, "The Case for Woodrow Wilson," *Harper's* 234 (April, 1967):86.
12. Quoted in ibid., p. 93.
13. William E. Leuchtenburg, "Progressivism and Imperialism: The Progressive Movement and American Foreign Policy, 1898-1916," *Mississippi Valley Historical Review*, December, 1952, p. 483.
14. Thomas A. Bailey, "Woodrow Wilson and the League of Nations," in Garraty, ed., p. 225.
15. Wecter, *The Hero*, p. 402.
16. John M. Blum, "War and Its Sequel," in John M. Blum et al., *The National Experience: A History of the United States* (New York: Harcourt Brace Jovanovich, 1973), p. 579.
17. Robert K. Murray, "Warren Gamaliel Harding," in Garraty, ed., *Encyclopedia of American Biography*, p. 484.
18. Robert K. Murray, "The Twenties," in Garraty, ed., *Conversations with Historians*, II, p. 162.
19. Noggle, "Configurations," p. 466.
20. Ibid., p. 474.
21. Ibid., p. 480.
22. Quoted in John William Ward, "The Meaning of Lindbergh's Flight," *American Quarterly* 10 (Spring, 1958): 9.

SOURCES FOR FURTHER STUDY

PROGRESSIVISM: MOVEMENT OR MIRAGE?

KENNEDY, DAVID M., ed. *Progressivism: The Critical Issues*. Boston: Little, Brown and Co., 1971.

KOLKO, GABRIEL. *The Triumph of Conservatism*. New York: The Free Press, 1963.

LEUCHTENBURG, WILLIAM E. *The Perils of Prosperity, 1914-1932*. Chicago: University of Chicago Press, 1958.

LINK, ARTHUR S. "What Happened to the Progressive Movement in the 1920's?" *American Historical Review* 64 (1959).

MOWRY, GEORGE E. "The Progressive Profile." In *The Era of Theodore Roosevelt, 1900-1912*. New York: Harper & Row, Publishers, 1958.

THE PROGRESSIVE PERSONALITY: ROOSEVELT AND WILSON

DAVIS, ALLEN F. *American Heroine: The Life and Legend of Jane Addams*. New York: Oxford University Press, 1973.

GARRATY, JOHN A. "Robert M. LaFollette: The Promise Unfulfilled." In John A. Garraty, ed., *Historical Viewpoints*, II. New York: Harper & Row, Publishers, 1975.

KELLER, MORTON, ed. *Theodore Roosevelt: A Profile*. New York: Hill & Wang, 1967.

LINK, ARTHUR S. *Woodrow Wilson: A Profile*. New York: Hill & Wang, 1968.

———. "The Case for Woodrow Wilson." *Harper's* 234 (April, 1967).

AMERICA AND THE ERA OF THE FIRST WORLD WAR: MYTHS AND REALITIES

BAILEY, THOMAS A. "Woodrow Wilson and the League of Nations." In John A. Garraty, ed., *Historical Viewpoints*, II. New York: Harper & Row, Publishers, 1975.

BASS, HERBERT J., ed. *America's Entry into World War I: Submarines, Sentiment or Security*. New York: Holt, Rinehart and Winston, 1964.

LEUCHTENBURG, WILLIAM E. "Progressivism and Imperialism: The Progressive Movement and American Foreign Policy, 1898-1916," *Mississippi Valley Historical Review* 49 (1962).

SMITH, DANIEL M. "National Interest and American Intervention, 1917: A Historiographical Appraisal," *The Journal of American History* 52 (1965).

WILLIAMS, WILLIAM APPLEMAN. "The Legend of Isolationism in the 1920s," *Science and Society* 18 (1954).

THE ROARING TWENTIES: FACT OR FICTION?

LEVINE, LAWRENCE W. "Progress and Nostalgia: The Self-Image of the 1920's." In Malcolm Bradbury, ed., *The American Novel and the 1920's.* London: Arnold, 1971.

MAY, HENRY F. "Shifting Perspectives on the 1920's." *The Mississippi Valley Historical Review* 43 (1956).

MURRAY, ROBERT K. "The Twenties." In John A. Garraty, ed., *Interpreting American History:* *Conversations with Historians.* New York: The Macmillan Company, 1970.

NOGGLE, BURL. "Configurations of the Twenties." In William H. Cartright and Richard L. Watson, Jr., eds., *The Reinterpretation of American History and Culture.* Washington, D.C.: National Council for the Social Studies, 1973.

WILSON, JOAN HOFF, ed. *The Twenties.* Boston: Little, Brown and Co., 1972.

F.D.R., Wide World

9 Mythology of Roosevelt, the New Deal, and Beyond

PREVIEW

Legacy and Legend: FDR and the New Deal

The decade of the Roaring Twenties came to a close not with a whimper but a bang. For in late October of 1929 the apparent prosperity of the previous years, which had dazzled Americans with visions of easy riches, collided with economic realities to produce the Great Crash. The long-range impact of the market crash would be a new chapter in American mythology. As one historian has observed:

> Like the Battle of Marathon, the assassination of Julius Caesar, the voyage of Columbus, and the storming of the Bastille, it has entered the realm of mythology and semitruth, no longer studied as an historical event, but more as a symbol of greater forces and new beginnings.[1]

Such "new beginnings" were indeed evident even to those at the time. Americans quite literally began to hum a different tune. Songs such as "You're the Cream in My Coffee," which might well have been sung with enthusiasm at King Oliver's Dreamland Cafe in Chicago during the twenties, soon gave way to more sober efforts such as "Brother, Can You Spare a Dime?" Indeed, on "Black Thursday," October 24, 1929, the debts of "prosperity at any cost" came due. A tremor of fear swept through Wall Street as sixteen million shares of stock were sold in a single day. On Monday, October 28, the paper value of stocks slid a staggering $14 billion. By the end of 1931, securities losses were an estimated $50 billion. Paper millionaires became paupers overnight in a country which had recently heard its president declare the real possibility that poverty would be "banished from the land." As the decade of the thirties opened it was difficult to find many who were still "bullish on America."

What had happened to the American utopia? Economists and historians tend to agree that its failure owed much to the nation's blind belief during the 1920s in the myth of capitalism's invincibility. Corporate insanity had passed for "normalcy" in a nation already well accustomed to self-delusion. Hypnotized by the glittering and immediate rewards which economic individualism and free enterprise seemed to offer, few people were willing or able to examine some of the system's obvious faults. Income distribution, for example, was conspicuously unequal, as anyone who cared to take notice could observe. Under the guidance of the secretary of the treasury, Andrew Mellon, who served in that capacity from 1921 to 1932 for Presidents Harding, Coolidge, and Hoover, the well-being of the well-to-do was carefully protected through a series of measures which reduced income taxes in the higher brackets and repealed inheritance and gift taxes. The overall effect of such legislation was to encourage further consolidation of wealth. This inevitably led to a national economy which increasingly came to depend on the consumption of luxury goods and services by the rich for its continued vitality. Correspondingly, the lower classes were left less and less of the economic "pie," and severe limitations were placed on their buying power. The economic gap between the upper and lower classes was expanding, the Horatio Alger mythology notwithstanding. Few people, least of all Andrew Mellon, paid much attention to the fact that the average annual "real" income—what their money would actually buy—of construction workers, farmers, and miners declined during the 1920s. But then again, as the economist John Kenneth Galbraith has observed, "income distribution in the United States had long been unequal. The inequality of these years [therefore] did not seem exceptional."[2] Americans who had been raised on a steady diet of clichés praising work and economic self-reliance therefore had little reason to feel that the system was in need of reform. It would take the experience of the Great Depression itself to force Americans to question the mythology that poverty could be due only to a lack of "pluck, luck, and hard work" and that failure was always the consequence of personal shortcomings rather than social circumstances.

Another basic flaw in the American economic system contributing to the Great Crash was underhanded and monopolistic business practices. Even Al Capone was prompted to declare that Wall Street was "too crooked." Despite a flood of rhetoric which continued to speak glowingly of free enterprise and economic individualism, the fact of the matter was that the nation's largest corporations had consistently attempted to frustrate competition by controlling various industries at all levels. Corporate profits soared as large conglomorates came to dominate the production of goods from the raw materials stage to the marketplace. More important, most corporations held stock in related firms to the point where many of the nation's leading business concerns were largely dependent upon supporting business establishments for their continued success. This interlocking nature of the American business structure helped create an economic pyramid in which a firm's basic strength was directly related to the earnings of the company below. Also, the American banking system had invested heavily in the future growth and prosperity of these interdependent business enterprises. A major shock to any part of the system would send much of the structure tumbling like a house of cards. Though some seem to have been aware of the precarious foundation upon which the prosperity of the 1920s rested, most preferred to trust that business "confidence" and the continued dreams of investors would be sufficient cement to patch any cracks which might appear on America's road to fame and fortune. It would require the depression itself to show that such beliefs were mostly mythical daydreams and "airy castle buildings."

In important respects the Great Depression was caused not only by serious weaknesses in American business establishment but by the pressures in the world economy as well. This was so because during the First World War the United States became a creditor nation—that is, it reached the point where foreign nations owed the country more in principal and interest on loans than America owed abroad. As a result, the United States became more intimately tied to the world economy and thus increasingly subject to its ups and downs. Complicating matters was the fact that large American lending institutions became involved in arranging risky loans, often accompanied by bribes, to various foreign powers, such as one for $50 million to Peru in 1927. Investment houses also became deeply in-

volved in the economic recovery of postwar Germany through the processing of loans to various German municipalities. Given these numerous international monetary obligations, the cycle of depression which was also being felt in foreign capitals predictably caused grave effects in the United States. When one of Vienna's leading banks, the Kreditanstalt, defaulted, a wave of bankruptcies and business calamities followed throughout the world. The ripple effect eventually reached American shores.

Numerous additional explanations have been offered by various scholars attempting to sift through the myth and the reality of what caused the Great Depression. Some have emphasized the failure of the American economy during the 1920s to assure an adequate level of purchasing power among farmers and workers. Others have pointed to the heavy burden of debt against both farms and homes in the form of mortgages and the sharp decline of both business and residential construction during the immediate pre-Depression period. Still others insist that all of these were merely symptoms of a general failure of national leadership during the decade. The noted conservative economist Milton Friedman, for example, has argued that the Great Depression need not have been anything more than a mild business recession had it not been for catastrophic errors in economic management committed by officials of the Federal Reserve Board. The equally famous liberal economist John Kenneth Galbraith has criticized, instead, incompetent individuals dating as far back as President Harding's comptroller of the currency, Daniel R. Crissinger, a crony from Marion, Ohio, and a man of extremely limited experience. It is claimed by Galbraith that "Jack Dempsey, Paul Whiteman, or F. Scott Fitzgerald would have been at least equally qualified" as he to act as comptroller.[3] The ultimate reality of the Great Depression which followed, however, was the searing experiences of hunger and frustration brought to millions of average Americans outside of the power structures of either Washington, D.C., or Wall Street.

The Great Depression affected the poor most directly. For many millions it meant despair, joblessness, hunger, starvation, and even death. The glassy-eyed stares of unemployed workers, thirtyish housewives looking twenty years older than their age, and emaciated children all reflected the suffering caused by unheated tenement houses, foreclosures on their homes and farms, and the effects of malnutrition. An unemployed Polish artist from New York City committed suicide by leaping from the George Washington Bridge leaving this note to posterity: "To All: If you cannot hear the cry of starving millions, listen to the dead, brothers. Your economic system is dead."[4] Indeed, by 1932 wages had fallen by as much as 35 percent in some occupations, new construction had almost ceased, and for millions, jobs were nonexistent. In the same year, more than three times as many people left the United States as entered it through immigration. In rather abrupt fashion America no longer seemed to be the Promised Land.

Despair and suffering were not the only social realities of Depression America, however. While the dominant image of the depression-wracked thirties as a time of public and private misfortune is basically accurate, the period also had a lighter side. Most people found the day-to-day business of life more difficult than it had been in the recent past, but they were also witness to some rather exciting changes in the American scene despite the sad state of the economy. Hollywood, for example, enjoyed an era which the American public now considers classic. Edward G. Robinson starred in *Little Caesar* in 1931 and James Cagney immortalized the movie gangster in *Public Enemy*, released during the same year. In some ways the artificial glamour of the film capital seemed to be giving way to "realism," but Hollywood's romantic and fictitious escapism was merely assuming a different form. The gangster as folk hero was no more real to life than other synthetic Hollywood characters.

However, it was radio which captured the attention of most Americans. The 1930s was an age of "Ma Perkins" and "Just Plain Bill," who shared their trials and tribulations in radio fiction with millions of Americans eager to believe that they were not alone in their problems. But while it is obvious that these early radio programs, along with movies, offered new and unique opportunities for Americans to escape the reality of their social and economic environment, it is less widely

recognized that they also became a primary force for the updating and dissemination of American values, sacred beliefs, and myths. Radio became an instrument in the service of American mythology by creating a new sense of common experience for the nation. Speaking of radio's mythic role in American life during the 1930s, the historian Warren Susman has explained how radio, and particularly soap operas, molded a set of national beliefs and images which brought the people even more into agreement as to what America supposedly was "all about":

> Timeless and consistent in portraying patterns of crisis and recovery, they provided a sense of continuity, assuring the triumph of generally shared values and beliefs, no matter what "reality" in the form of social and economic conditions might suggest.
>
> It is possible to see in the notorious "soaps" the operation of what might be called the force and power of myth. . . . [They] helped create a unity of response and action not previously possible; it made us more susceptible than ever to those who would mold culture and thought.[5]

Radio indeed made the sense of being an American much more immediate. By breaking down barriers between city and country, rich and poor, it added an important dimension to the mental picture Americans had of where the nation had been in the past and where it was going in the future.

The growing consciousness of "Americanism" which radio helped to create during the 1930s through the soap operas as well as through such new public personalities as Fred Waring and the Pennsylvanians, Kate Smith, and the Lone Ranger, reflected an idealization of America also found in other areas of national activity. Such historical romantic novels as Margaret Mitchell's *Gone with the Wind* (1936), for example, found great popularity by offering Americans yet another chance to participate in a growing sentimental mythology. In somewhat similar ways, the nation was giving expression to its idealization of the country's past and future and emphasizing the legendary worth and glory of

America through the use of a phrase first coined during the thirties—"The American Dream." With a patriotic flourish, motivated both by a desire to escape the effects of the depression and a resurgent interest in the myths of America, the nation entered a new era which would both preserve old values and sustain the long-held utopian belief in the possibility of a better future. Indeed, the 1930s found a creative combination of old myths and new utopias in the political programs of FDR and the New Deal. Given the national experience of the Great Depression, America was in a mood to question some of its legendary ideas in the areas of both economics and politics.

Masterfully sensing the temper of the times, Franklin Delano Roosevelt came to the presidency in 1933 with ideas, slogans, and myths uniquely tailored to the needs of Depression America. "Let it be symbolic," he had advised the Democratic party's nominating convention which presented him to the American people, "that I broke tradition. Let it be from now on the task of our Party to break foolish traditions." Indeed, with the New Deal's emphasis on federal action as a method of dealing with the slumping economy, Roosevelt broke with the traditional American adherence to laissez-faire. Under FDR's guidance Americans came more openly to concede that a hands-off policy on the part of the government in the face of economic crisis was an idea whose time had passed. Before his New Deal had run its course many "foolish traditions," whose consistent acceptance up to that time had been based for the most part on the tyranny of political and social mythology, had been cast aside. The revered tradition of severe peacetime limitations on the powers of government was broken. The legendary belief that the nation must always resign its fate to the "inevitable" business cycle was swept into the dustheap of discarded mythologies. In many ways the period of the New Deal seems to have been an era of significant change in America.

Despite generally wide acceptance, both FDR and the New Deal drew a wide range of criticism, much of which continues to be reflected in historians' accounts of Roosevelt and his times. Conservative critics have been alarmed at what they consider the obvious "socialistic" tendencies of the era. Liberal critics, on the other hand, including many of the social planners from within the Roosevelt Administration itself, argue that the government did not take sufficient advantage of the economic crisis to move the country more in line with its stated ideals of equality, opportunity, and freedom from want. To them, the New Deal was not sound, innovative, and far-reaching but merely an attempt to repair the tattered traditions of capitalistic democracy. There were too many barriers against radicalism in America, they said, for the New Deal to have been truly "new." In important ways, according to this point of view, the New Deal did little more than rescue and revitalize the old mythologies of the nation, despite its rhetoric to the contrary. Indeed, today's liberal critics of the New Deal find the legend of FDR as a communist or socialist laughable. For when the supposedly reform-minded hero-president and his New Deal programs are analyzed in close detail, they insist, it becomes increasingly apparent that little or nothing had been accomplished on behalf of the nation's minorities, and at times seems to reveal only "a-basket-for-the-poor-folks-down-the-street" attitude toward the problems of poverty. Roosevelt's mythically based instincts to safeguard property rights over human rights, to preserve the structure of capitalism, and to rule by the power of rhetoric rather than performance have all been cited as evidence against his supposed liberalism. For many, the "Roosevelt Revolution" was in reality superficial window dressing and the New Deal a symbol of national failure.

America and the Second World War

While the myth and reality of FDR and the New Deal continue to be unresolved, nearly all agree that the nation's full economic recovery from the depths of the depression did not come until America's entry into the Second World War. As the country moved to a war-based economy to meet the threats of fascism, it finally began to achieve recovery. At least at the outset of international crisis, President Roosevelt went through the motions of pretending to maintain traditional, old-style neutrality. The threat of Hitler's war machine which had conquered France and stood on the

The Election of 1948: A Victorious
Harry Truman
UPI-Compix

verge of destroying England, however, soon led Roosevelt to violate repeatedly the country's neutral stance. The transfer of destroyers to England in late 1940 and the government's pledge in 1941 to make American resources available to defeat the aggressive powers of Italy and Germany, in the end left little doubt that American "neutrality" was more rhetoric than reality.

In the Far East, diplomatic and military difficulties between the United States and Japan climaxed with the attack on Pearl Harbor, Hawaii, on December 7, 1941. Contrary to popular legend, however, the attack on Pearl Harbor was not a total surprise, the Japanese were not completely to blame for the Pacific war, and the origins of the conflict between the two powers were to be found in a series of incidents dating back to the early years of the twentieth century.

The Second World War was to end with the atomic blasts over Hiroshima and Nagasaki in early August of 1945. In the view of most Americans at the time and since, President Harry Truman's policy decision to drop the A-Bomb was based on the sound counsel of military advisors who calculated that a military invasion of Japan (which seemed the only plausible alternative) would likely bring a million casualties to American forces and perhaps three to four times as many to the

Japanese. The approximately 120,000 people who died in or as a result of the blasts thus supposedly represented but a small portion of those who might have died had the bomb not been used. In the years since the atomic bomb, however, critics have argued that the decision to use the weapon was not based on such concerns at all. In the opinion of this vocal minority, humanitarian arguments in favor of Truman's decision reflect a biased, amoral, and romantic view of American conduct and most important, the myth of American righteousness. They point to the fact that the president knew that the Japanese had little fuel remaining with which to carry on the war and thus he must have had other motives in using the deadly weapon. They argue that Truman was an instrument of American racism and amoral attitudes in that the bomb supposedly would never have been used against white people. Still others linked the use of the atomic weapon to the beginning of the cold war between the United States and the Soviet Union. To them, the Japanese seemed the bloody sacrificial victims of a highly questionable and largely mythically based American fear of the threat of communism in the postwar world. President Truman, it is said, made use of the atomic bomb to impress Russia with American power in an attempt to prevent Soviet entry into the

Pacific war against Japan as had been agreed upon at Yalta, and to gain political leverage in international politics once the war was over. Here, the myth of American righteousness and innocence has once again been challenged.

Postwar America

In his first presidential term, Harry Truman faced two immediate problems: how to bring the fighting to a successful conclusion and how to live with what one historian has called the "myth of the empty chair." The impact of FDR's years in the White House had been so profound both upon the American people in general and the Democratic party in particular that Truman found it extremely difficult to escape a constant comparison of his performance with that of his predecessor. Truman in fact did not free himself from the shadows of the "empty chair" until his surprise triumph over Thomas E. Dewey in the presidential election of 1948. By that time Truman and the nation were already deeply involved in a bout of international shadowboxing with world communism which would come to be known as the cold war. Reinforced by imaginary fears and illusions held by both the Soviet Union and the United States, the cold war continued to plague the affairs of the nation for many years both at home and abroad.

In international relations an elaborate vocabulary of make-believe succeeded in convincing the American people that all Communists were the same and that they were constantly plotting to destroy the precious American ideals of popular government and free enterprise. "The master myth of the cold war," in the words of former Arkansas Senator J. William Fulbright, "[was] that the Communist bloc [was] a monolith composed of governments which [were] not really governments at all, but organized conspiracies, divided among themselves perhaps in certain matters of tactics, but all equally resolute and implacable in their determination to destroy the free world."[6] In America, the cold war politics based largely on imaginary fears found its champion in Senator Joseph R. McCarthy of Wisconsin, who succeeded in building an image for himself as an anti-Communist crusader not only on the basis of the elaborate mythology of the cold war, but on the strength of a personal myth which claimed him to be a

noble and patriotic Marine hero. Indeed, the twin pillars supporting the mythical facade of McCarthyism did not begin to crumble until well into the presidency of Dwight D. Eisenhower.

President Eisenhower gained the White House in 1952 largely on the strength of his legendary fame as a military hero who had been principally responsible for the Allied victory over Nazi Germany in the Second World War. Projecting an image of quiet confidence, he led the nation until 1961 without great fanfare, but never fulfilled the predictions of those who felt he would do little more in office than give flesh and blood to the stereotype of a general-turned-politician. Rather than assuming a stiff-necked, authoritarian, and militaristic pose, he brought an end to the Korean War, worked to keep a lid on the arms race, and left office alerting the American people to the dangers of a developing military-industrial complex.

Eisenhower's successor, John F. Kennedy, stepped up the tempo as the nation continued marching to the pied piper tunes of the cold war, and in the process created a mythical political style all his own as a man of destiny, vision, and youthful yet intelligent vigor. His death in Dallas by an assassin's bullet in November, 1963, seemed to rob the nation of a heroic leader who might have pointed the nation toward the path of a golden kingdom—a political Camelot—had he lived. As a consequence, an almost instant legend grew around him at his death, claiming for him a place in American mythology formerly reserved only for leaders such as Abraham Lincoln. Even though the reins of power had now been taken up by Lyndon Baines Johnson, the memory and myth of JFK burned on as brightly as the "eternal flame" at his grave in Arlington, Virginia, always ready to rekindle the spirit of the Kennedy years.

The afterglow of John Kennedy's instant legend did much to help inspire the utopian flavor of Lyndon Johnson's early years as president. A master politician from Stonewall, Texas, LBJ pressed Americans to live up to their legendary ideals. His liberalizing of the nation's immigration laws, and especially his moral and practical support for civil rights, stand as progressive monuments to his term in office. His quest for the Great Society dramatized the many shortcomings of the nation in fulfilling the promise of the American Dream. In this sense he forced America to accept the political and social reality that blacks, the elderly, and minorities generally had to become part of the mainstream of national life. His appointment of Robert C. Weaver as the nation's first black cabinet member, his support of Medicare, and his pursuit of other social legislation were heroic efforts toward achieving a just and humane society. Like so many heroes, however, Lyndon Johnson had a tragic flaw. It would become most obvious as the nation's attention became drawn away from the creation of the Great Society and toward the great and tragic circumstances of Vietnam.

Vietnam and Watergate

Vietnam was not Lyndon Johnson's war. This was true in the sense that its origins were to be found in the practices and policies of administrations as early as Franklin Roosevelt's. Yet, it was Johnson who was swept from office in the backlash of the American people against involvement. The conflict had been brought on in the first instance by American excursions into the fantasy world of the cold war. For decades every international move by Communist powers instantaneously became a "Communist conspiracy" which could only be met by the use of American power. The nation seemed to enjoy its self-ordained image as the savior of the "free world." Similarly, Asian policies of the United States were simple-mindedly interpreted by Communist powers as examples of "capitalistic aggression."

American understanding of political and social realities in Asia had been less than satisfactory at least since the days early in the twentieth century when Nebraska Senator Kenneth Wherry announced to a cheering audience that, "With God's help, we will lift Shanghai up, ever up, until it is just like Kansas City." The application of such international misunderstanding to Vietnam, however, was catastrophic. In the end, it would be evident that the United States largely fought the war in Vietnam over mythical abstractions—"democracy for the Vietnamese," "Communist aggression," and finally "peace with honor." All parties to the conflict suffered from a less than realistic understanding of the character, intentions, and capabilities of the

"enemy." In hindsight, the war seems neither to have been a case of evil-minded Communists attempting to enslave the Vietnamese by pulling them into the orbit of Russia and China, nor completely a case of the United States attempting to hide imperialistic goals behind democratic rhetoric. The passage of time would show, for example, that Ho Chi Minh was as much a nationalist as a Communist. And while America might once again have suffered from its inflated mythical sense of destiny and righteousness, it did so partially out of its continuing commitment to the dream of sharing democracy with any nation.

The events lumped under the heading "Watergate" also reflect the tendency of Americans to believe too strongly in mythology. Just as the country was attempting to play the role of "redeemer nation" in Vietnam, Richard M. Nixon came to view himself as the self-ordained "savior" of a threatened America. Hypnotized by the myth of national security, and after appearing to perform reasonably well during his first term as president, Nixon attempted to hide the corrosive activities of his administration through a series of diversionary tactics calculated to deceive the American people. As the public estimation of Richard Nixon began to shrivel in the heat of the Watergate spotlight, he inflated the tradition of executive privilege to mythical proportions and even attempted to clothe himself in the venerable mythology of Abraham Lincoln. Standing symbolically before the Lincoln Memorial, Nixon declared that like America's Civil War president his integrity and statesmanship were being cheaply brought into question. His fall from power, however, eventually revealed the arid emptiness of his mythical world. Both Vietnam and Watergate pointed to the extreme danger in store for a nation which allows distortions of the truth to pass too long for reality.

SECTION I: LEGACY AND LEGEND: FDR AND THE NEW DEAL

Roosevelt as Political Hero

In fact as well as legend, Franklin Delano Roosevelt surely ranks among the nation's greatest presidents. Supporters and detractors alike agree that he was more central to his age than either Theodore Roosevelt or Woodrow Wilson had been to theirs. Accordingly, in assessing the New Deal, the public as well as scholars have been compelled to deal with FDR's rather elusive personal style; indeed, for many this is the key to understanding the man and his times. Roosevelt himself was acutely aware of his crucial place in history. He left a total of more than fifty million items—letters, speeches, documents, books, pamphlets, photographs, and assorted materials—to the Roosevelt Presidential Library in Hyde Park, New York. Since historians possess such a vast body of materials with which to work, one might think that they would be in a good position to rebuild the reality of the Age of Roosevelt with few flaws or faulty conclusions. Unfortunately, quite the opposite seems to be true.

As in the case of Thomas Jefferson, the massive body of available evidence on the Roosevelt years has made the task of determining the true significance of FDR's administration all the more difficult. Similarly as with Jefferson, no one seemed to be neutral about Roosevelt. A man who inspired extremes of love and hatred, and thus extremes of praise and criticism, he has necessarily come to be obscured both by the myths which accompany hero-worship and those created by enemies. A recent scholar writes:

> One Congressman compared him to Jesus Christ and in a poll of New York schoolchildren God ran him a poor second. Yet he was just as strongly detested by others who ... depicted him "as a liar, a thief, a madman, a syphilitic, and a communist."[7]

Given all this, what can be said about the "real" FDR who served the nation as president from March 4, 1933, until April 12, 1945?

Admirers of Franklin Roosevelt legitimately point to a man of superior accomplishments, a creative leader who guided the nation through the crisis of the Great Depression and the perils of the Second World War. Indeed, no earlier president held office for so long or exercised so much power in critical circumstances. The unusually severe situations which faced him, together with his forceful

personal energy, created a combustible combination which brought major changes to American life. Not surprisingly, the powers of the presidency expanded enormously; the role of the federal government in the day-to-day lives of average Americans became much more visible. Also, the Democrats replaced the Republicans as the nation's majority party. Indeed, since FDR, Republicans have been able to elect a controlling majority in Congress only twice. Other important legacies of the Roosevelt years included the placing of poverty on the national agenda for action, assistance in improving the status of organized labor, expansion of the role of intellectuals in government operations, and the noticeable shift in control of the nation's financial affairs from Wall Street to Washington, D.C.

While some have argued, wrongly, that all or some of these changes placed America on the road to national disaster, it cannot be denied that they profoundly affected modern American life. For this reason and others, Franklin Roosevelt stands solidly in the ranks of the nation's "hero-presidents." As is the case with Washington, Jefferson, Jackson, Lincoln, his fifth cousin Theodore, and Wilson, time has done little to tarnish FDR's reputation as one of the nation's most stirring leaders. He was not a conquering "man on horseback" as was Washington. He did not enjoy the subtle intellect of Jefferson. He was without the commanding appearance of Jackson. He lacked the delicate common touch of Lincoln. He never quite matched the flamboyant character of T. R. He was not as eloquent as Wilson. Franklin Roosevelt nonetheless had a sufficient amount of all of these qualities in combination to assure him a secure position in the nation's historical memory.

Born to the established wealth of the Roosevelt and Delano families, Franklin's early life was filled with quality education, trips to Europe, and the full life of an enterprising young country gentleman. His undergraduate years at Harvard did little to alter his aristocratic view of the world or to injure his chances for success. A term as Democratic state senator in New York, a seven-year apprenticeship as assistant secretary of the navy in the Wilson administration, and an unsuccessful Democratic vice-presidential candidacy in 1920, gradually brought his personal charm and political artistry to national attention. It was at this point, however, that fate dealt Roosevelt what at first appeared to be a blow fatal to his career. He was stricken with infantile paralysis, or polio.

Though at the outset he nourished false hopes of complete recovery, Roosevelt soon was forced to live with partial paralysis, and he determined to continue his political career in spite of his infirmity. For its part, the voting public responded to his affliction by coming to view his handicap as an asset. In the national imagination the aristocratically born Roosevelt became an underdog who would presumably have deep sympathy for the less fortunate or those in distress. As some observers have suggested, Roosevelt's experience with infantile paralysis came to be a worthy substitute for the log cabin in the public mind. The folklore of American politics could easily allow for such a thing. From here, on the basis of both political talent and his courageous image, his path to prominence would lead to two terms as governor of New York and eventually election as president of the United States in 1932.

Roosevelt as a "Hero-President"

Americans were ready for a new deal in 1932. With the stock market crash already behind them, and with the depression deepening, they responded forcefully to Franklin Roosevelt's contagious optimism—472 electoral votes to 59 for Herbert Hoover. Whether FDR came into the White House on the strength of an anti-Hoover vote or whether he was primarily responsible for creating a new Democratic political coalition composed of labor, urban voters, and black Americans that swept him to victory remains a point of continued debate among historians. Some contend that the real beginnings of large city identification with the Democratic party may well have begun under Al Smith and that blacks did not fully move into the Democratic column until 1936. There seems to be no disagreement, however, that Roosevelt ran a campaign attuned to the mood of the people and that he most definitely captured their imagination. So desperate was their need to find answers to the dilemma of the Great Depression, that Americans sought a leader who would measure up to the mythical heroes of the past. In Roosevelt they were

convinced they had found him.

Although the myth of Herbert Hoover as a do-nothing president in the face of the depression has been challenged, Americans in the fall of 1932 believed he had been. They craved new directions and a new personality on Pennsylvania Avenue, and Franklin Roosevelt stood ready to rekindle utopian beliefs in his fellow Americans. The spirit of the times was not lost on Roosevelt as he spoke in his inaugural address of the "false leadership" which had failed in its vision of what needed to be done to meet the depression crisis, and his "firm belief that the only thing we have to fear is fear itself." Even in the words of one of his scholarly critics,

> Roosevelt, as President, gave millions of Americans a transfusion of courage. They still remember. From his confidence, his optimism, they gleaned bits of hope in times of trouble and confusion. . . . It was a pervasive part of the New Deal, yet tied to no policies and no programs. It was the magic of a man, based as much on illusion as on reality. There was much fear in 1933, as there is today. Only fools or gods believed otherwise.[8]

It is now rather clear that Roosevelt's solution to the crisis at hand was to preserve the American Dream by reforming the means of achieving it. Whether he did so in the fashion of a "fool" or a "god," however, has remained open to debate.

Upon assuming office, Roosevelt immediately called a bank holiday, invited the nation's leading money managers to a Sunday conference at the White House to discuss the dismal state of the economy, and called Congress into special session. The famous "100 days" which followed witnessed a series of changes in governmental policy which reflected the vitality and self-confidence of what appeared to be a new hero at the reins. An Emergency Banking Act was passed, as was an Agricultural Adjustment Act designed to raise depressed farm prices by controlling production, and a National Industrial Recovery Act seeking business stabilization. An important provision of this last measure— Section 7a—granted labor the right to organize and bargain collectively. The flurry of legislation during the first portion of FDR's first term also produced the Tennessee Valley Authority for purposes of flood control, soil conservation and the building of power plants in one of America's most depressed areas. The problem of unemployment was also attacked through a number of public management measures. The Civilian Conservation Corps was created to employ working men between the ages of eighteen and twenty-five in conservation projects and road construction. A Public Works Administration was established to aid in the construction of civic buildings, dams, and bridges. Later, the Civil Works Administration, though temporary in nature, employed four million people in winter jobs during 1933-34. A Home Owners Loan Corporation Act for refinancing mortgages threatened with foreclosure, a Security and Exchange Commission Act to regulate the stock market, and the Social Security Act providing for old-age pensions and unemployment insurance were enacted. A Works Progress Administration was also created in 1935 to provide jobs for unskilled construction workers as well as artists, writers, actors, and musicians. The idea of national leadership in economic recovery had by now been established.

During his first term as president Franklin D. Roosevelt had moved from being a somewhat hazy figure at the time of his election to a full-fledged hero four years later. His policies had not produced full recovery, but they had done much to conquer fear and despair. Apparently recognizing that one's image was as powerful a force for political success in modern America as military glory had been to earlier ages, Roosevelt made liberal use of lively press conferences and "fireside chats" over radio, both to draw the people into the inner circle of national affairs and to capitalize on his pleasing radio personality.

Radiating energy, confidence, and decisiveness, Franklin Roosevelt was riding a crest of great popularity by 1936. If anyone still doubted that America had discovered a new "hero president," Roosevelt's landslide victory over the "Kansas Coolidge," Alfred M. Landon, in 1936 proved them wrong—523 electoral votes to 8. Landon, hindsight suggests, seems to have had more to offer the country than was apparent at the time, and he was certainly more progressive than legend has been willing to admit. His speeches, however, which have been described as being "flat as a Midwest plain," simply failed to inspire the nation nearly as much as those of the giant of a man entrenched in the White House.

The Tarnished Hero

Despite the great expectations created by the national Democratic landslide victory of 1936, the myth of FDR's knightly invincibility began to crack during his second term. Though such additional New Deal legislation as the Fair Labor Standards Act of 1938 would be passed—establishing a minimum wage, an end to child labor, and a standard work week of forty hours—the Roosevelt mythology began to lose some of its force in the face of new challenges. The first involved the Supreme Court and the second resulted from the effects of a renewed economic recession during 1937-38.

In 1936 the Supreme Court of the United States was much more conservative than either the president or the majority of the members of Congress, and it had therefore ruled major pieces of New Deal legislation unconstitutional. By narrow margins the Court had struck down both the National Industrial Recovery Act and the Agricultural Adjustment Act as unconstitutional. The fate of the already imposing legacy of the New Deal seemed to be at best uncertain, for in addition the Court's calendar called for a review of such other important items as social security. Perhaps believing that his place in history was threatened, Roosevelt sent a message to Congress in February, 1937, urging a reorganization of the Supreme Court. Charging that the Supreme Court had not kept pace with its work load, and that a more efficient form of administration was therefore in order, the president respectfully suggested that an additional justice be added to the nation's highest tribunal for each one already on the Court who refused to retire on reaching the age of seventy. Soon exposed for what it was—a political move on Roosevelt's part to allow him to appoint sympathetic justices to the Court and save the New Deal—the proposal was met with a chorus of criticism and eventually defeated. FDR's attempt to pack the Supreme

Court benefited those who had already begun to charge that his Boy Scout image was little more than a mask behind which lurked a dangerous figure bent on manipulating or even destroying the American system.

Also harmful to the future destiny of the Roosevelt legend was the return of economic crisis to the country in 1937, after most had come to believe that the depression had bottomed out. Indeed the slow but steady period of economic recovery which had blessed the late years of Roosevelt's first term in office began to erode because of the collection of social security taxes and the attempts of the president to cut back government spending and thus return to a balanced budget. Recalling the earlier economic shock waves of 1929-30, national income fell 13 percent and the problems of unemployment, the evaporation of business confidence, and general economic jitters came back to haunt the country. Government spending programs were quickly reinstated to reverse the slide, but it was already clear that full economic recovery was as yet far away. The Court fight and the return of economic problems, then, concerned even those who had become cheerleaders for FDR and his New Deal. Indeed by 1938 the New Deal was losing much of its energy. The Roosevelt magic seemed much less appealing and reassuring. Before the full impact of these new developments could be completely digested, however, the attention of both the nation and the Roosevelt Administration was drawn to Europe, where signs pointed to the possibility of another world war.

With the creative portion of the New Deal drawing to a close, and with the remaining years of Franklin Roosevelt's tenure in the White House destined to be focused on the strategies and policies of the Second World War, the nation's assessment of the New Deal was already underway. Predictably, opinions and interpretations differed rather widely, especially among scholars. The man and the movement have been viewed as both wildly radical and disappointingly conservative.

The Hero and the Historians

Until the decade of the 1950s it was generally agreed among both the public and scholars, that the New Deal had been of fundamental

importance to American history because it represented an important break with the nation's established traditions. Praise was heard from New Deal supporters for its having made important changes in the nation's economic structure, its success at placing the federal government in a position to administer the welfare of the country, and its attempts to force America finally to live up to its democratic ideals. For these reasons Roosevelt and the New Deal were said to stand in the proud tradition of American liberalism dating from Jefferson through Jackson, Lincoln, Theodore Roosevelt, and Wilson. A true hero of democracy, Roosevelt was credited with leading the nation through the crisis of the Great Depression, creatively expanding the positive role of the national government in the day-to-day lives of the people, and forcefully achieving social justice in America. Emphasizing the importance of how people have perceived the New Deal and its continuing effects on American life, one historian has argued that it was "the third American Revolution," ranking in importance with the Revolution and the Civil War.

Even during the Roosevelt Administration, however, critics had already argued that the image of FDR as liberal and democrat was little more than a myth. While agreeing that the New Deal had been revolutionary in its results, they emphasized the essentially "un-American" activities of the Roosevelt presidency. Newspaper critic Henry L. Mencken of the *Baltimore Sun*, for example, emphasized what he saw as the phoney superficiality of FDR's democratic pose. "If he became convinced tomorrow that coming out for cannibalism would get him the votes he so sorely needs," Mencken charged, "he would begin fattening a missionary in the White House backyard come Wednesday." For Mencken, the Roosevelt revolution consisted of a self-conscious manipulation of the American people in Roosevelt's own self-interest. For others, Roosevelt's heroic image was little more than a front for a presidential reign which weakened the country's revered constitutional system, destroyed America's political morality, and injected the poisonous influence of socialism into the nation's political bloodstream. Indeed, for those most suspicious of the Roosevelt legacy, the charge has been made that it overturned venerated American traditions to such a degree that it deserves to be classified as a "Communist conspiracy." According to this point of view, New Deal legislation helped destroy such cherished American ideas as free enterprise, individual initiative, and laissez-faire capitalism. By tampering with the American system in alien ways, the argument runs, Franklin Roosevelt and the New Deal are guilty of having unforgivably tarnished the American Way by introducing the Welfare State.

More recent attempts to gauge the significance of the Age of Roosevelt and the New Deal, however, have come to emphasize its essentially conservative impact on American life. Claiming that Roosevelt's radicalism was mostly legendary, numerous historians have insisted that the New Deal did more to preserve "traditional America" than the Sears catalogue, Coca-Cola, the American Legion, and the Daughters of the American Revolution combined. Looking in vain for evidence of the legendary Roosevelt revolution which has so disturbed some, historians Barton Bernstein, Howard Zinn, and Paul Conkin note that the New Deal failed to bring economic recovery to the nation, did little indeed to end poverty in America, did next to nothing to redistribute the nation's wealth, nearly completely ignored the plight of minorities, never caused a new progressive spirit to take hold at the state or local levels of government, ran hot and cold in its relationships with labor, and in general brought little significant change to American society. The New Deal, they say, was conservative in its intent, its programs, and its outcome. Its basic objective was not socialism at all; its goal was to save capitalism. America in 1939, they continue, was not fundamentally different from what it had been at the beginning of the decade. In *The New Deal and the Problem of Monopoly* (1966), Ellis Hawley argues that the conservative tone of the Roosevelt years was strikingly similar to that of the earlier progressive period. Reflecting this point of view, Otis Graham has commented that

one learns how much of the regulatory activity entered into by the government in the 1930s was done at the urgent request of the affected industry which

often preferred the haven of regulated status to the rigors of competition in a slack market. . . . The New Deal's vigorous expansion of the regulatory functions of government appears at best a forlorn experiment and at worst the premeditated capture of governmental power by capitalistic interests to shore up crumbling monopoly structures. . . . The story of regulation . . . during the 1930s . . . seems often to have been reform by, of, and for the regulated industries themselves.[9]

Though widely claimed in national mythology as the supreme triumph of American liberalism, it seems increasingly clear that while the New Deal brought a measure of change to America, it scarcely ushered in an era of social revolution.

In the end, the reality of FDR's New Deal would seem to lie somewhere between its having been either an "insurance policy" for big business or an "un-American" effort to establish secretly the ideas and practices of socialism in the United States. In turn, it would seem proper to portray Franklin D. Roosevelt as somewhere between the white knight of American liberalism and a "syphilitic Communist." His revolutionary or conservative character aside, it is still possible to grant that Roosevelt was one of the major figures of American history. As has been true with all of America's legendary heroes, it can be said of Roosevelt that he enjoys a stature and greatness enhanced by mythology. His personal commitment to social improvement was no doubt genuine, and perhaps more than any president before or since he sincerely tried to make the American government responsive to the needs of the people. And if indeed his response was a conservative one, it may simply have been so because this was precisely what the many millions who voted for him wanted at the time. Few men so dominated their times as he. Yet any balanced account of the Roosevelt presidency must concede that he was somewhat less the superman than Americans and perhaps even he imagined. FDR was, as most humans are, a complex combination of admirable traits and human failings. The extreme forms of mythology which have come to surround him have frequently obscured this point. And further, distorting emotions of hatred and affection have combined in such a way as to make the Roosevelt legacy an enduring legend.

SECTION II: AMERICA AND THE ERA OF THE SECOND WORLD WAR: REALITIES AND MYTHS

Whether the New Deal was to be temporary or permanent was of less concern to Americans by the late 1930s than it had been earlier. The major focus of America by then was increasingly being drawn away from economic and social problems at home and toward a new set of international realities growing out of developments in Europe and the Far East: the rise of Adolph Hitler's Third Reich (a modern successor to earlier "reichs," or empires—the Holy Roman Empire and that of Otto von Bismarck) and the expansionistic policies of Japan in the South Pacific.

American Neutrality: Pose or Policy?

Whether internationalist or isolationist, what all regions of America were responding to by the mid 1930s were the forms of dictatorship developing in different areas of the world. In 1922 in Italy, Benito Mussolini became Europe's first fascist dictator, preaching a doctrine of romantic nationalism. In Russia, Joseph Stalin had come to power in 1924 and urged his nation to establish "socialism in one country" before attempting to achieve a world-wide Communist revolution based on the Marxian myth of the classless society. In Germany, Adolph Hitler became chancellor in 1933, developing his theories of Nazism, or National Socialism, based on the myths of German racial and cultural superiority. In Japan, the heavily mythical traditions of the *samurai* warrior class and the divinity of the emperor were also contributing to aggressive policies and practices. In response to all of this, the official policy of the U.S. government was neutrality. Aware that the fight against the depression had not yet been won, conscious of the fact that many of America's First World War allies still had not paid their outstanding

war debts, and wary that bankers and munitions makers might accumulate vast profits as some apparently had during the earlier European conflict, American leaders were reluctant indeed to launch the nation into another war. Reflecting such isolationist sentiments, Congress passed various Neutrality Acts between 1935 and 1937 to help assure the nation's continued nonparticipation in any war which might develop.

Shifting realities in Europe, however, made America's neutral position difficult to maintain. President Roosevelt himself was not particularly sympathetic to complete neutrality, believing instead that the United States could best remain at peace by working to prevent the outbreak of war in Europe. However, Italy's imperialist attack on Ethiopia and the Japanese invasion of China forced the president to rethink his position. Comparing the growing world lawlessness to a bodily disease, in his famous "Quarantine Speech" in Chicago in 1937, he suggested that the free world attempt to economically isolate aggressive nations in the interest of preserving peace. The unfavorable reaction on the part of both the public and Congress to the president's message, however, convinced him that different strategies were necessary. It is at this point, in the opinion of some historians, that FDR made neutrality an illusion and in some instances deliberately deceived the American people. Believing that America must be ready if and when Europe cascaded into war, President Roosevelt moved cautiously to adjust American preparedness through methods short of war. In 1938 he asked Congress to honor his request for a billion dollar naval building program. And after Germany attacked Poland on September 1, 1939, he moved further toward support of England and France, arguing that "even a neutral has a right to take account of the facts."

As neutrality became more a pose than a policy, $13 billion was spent to strengthen national defense, and a Selective Service Act was passed (September, 1940) drafting 800,000 men into the armed services. Attempting to support Europe's democratic powers, yet trying to do so without directly involving the United States in the conflict, Roosevelt continued his quest to make America the "arsenal of democracy" by trading fifty "overage" destroyers to England in exchange for naval bases in Newfoundland, Bermuda, and six additional sites in the Caribbean. This was followed by the Lend-Lease Act (1941) which placed military supplies into the hands of all countries opposing the Rome-Berlin Axis of Mussolini and Hitler. With the myth of American neutrality becoming more transparent, Roosevelt sensed that the still isolationist attitudes of congressional and public opinion would be unwilling to accept the transport of lend-lease materials to England by ship convoy. What followed was a set of events destined to reveal President Roosevelt to later generations as a master mythmaker. In the words of the diplomatic historian Robert Ferrell:

> [Roosevelt] didn't know how to get public support for convoying without lying about it. So he lied. He invented something which he called a "patrol," which was, he told the American people, something quite different from convoying. . . . This particular example of press-conference pleasantry or joshing, at which he was a master, was a piece of misrepresentation, to put it mildly. He followed this up with a series of other deceptions, the most notable of which was his description of the attack by German submarines on the destroyer *Greer* in the early autumn of 1941. The *Greer* had been pursuing a submarine and broadcasting the submarine's position. It was only in desperation that the submarine launched a torpedo or two at the destroyer. Nonetheless, Roosevelt then went on the radio. In this broadcast . . . he said that the *Greer* was carrying mail to Iceland.[10]

The issue of how far American preparedness could go before the nation found itself involved in the war was irreversibly settled by the Japanese attack on Pearl Harbor at 7:50 a.m., December 7, 1941, a day, in President Roosevelt's words, that would "live in infamy." Events proceeded swiftly from that point. Congress speedily passed a declaration of war the following day—82 to 0 in the Senate and 388 to 1 in the House, with Congresswoman Jeannette Rankin of Montana casting the only

dissenting vote. Three days later, both Germany and Italy saved the country the trouble of determining what its policy would now be toward the conflict in Europe by declaring war on the United States. The national debate between interventionists and isolationists was now over, but the scholarly debate among historians as to what had truly caused American entry into the war had only just begun. As in past wars, the potential for myth was enhanced by the emotion and bias which historians brought to their work.

The Historians Hold Court

Histories of American intervention in the Second World War which appeared during the war years were nearly unanimous in their support of the Roosevelt Administration's prewar policies. The emotional atmosphere of the war itself, the need for a united front at home, and the limited availability of documents from all the warring countries, made the pattern of American involvement seem rather clear. Warlords in Germany, Italy, and Japan had obviously become serious threats to America's interests and security. Germany had already used its *blitzkrieg* (lightning war) tactics to smash Poland, Denmark, Norway, the Netherlands, Belgium, and France long before the United States was drawn into the conflict. Posing direct threats to England, Russia, and the Middle East, it appeared possible that Hitler's war machine would not stop at anything short of world conquest. Japan, having formed a ten-year alliance with Germany and Italy in September, 1939—the Rome-Berlin-Tokyo Axis—was almost equally dangerous. The vital interests and democratic principles of the United States, these early histories concluded, made the policies of the Roosevelt Administration appropriate to the threatening circumstances. Preparedness, the sale of war materials to England, the destroyer-bases deal, Atlantic patrol systems, and convoying were all designed to meet Fascist aggression through means short of war. The essential cause of America's actual intervention, then, was to be found outside the country. International realities finally determined the role which the United States would play in Europe and the South Pacific. Japan's "unprovoked and dastardly attack," in Roosevelt's phrase, and the declaration of war by Germany and Italy left the United States no other alternative than active participation in the war.

Though most histories of the war years have been favorable to Franklin Roosevelt's policies and leadership, a small but vocal group of historians has arisen to challenge the accepted causes of American involvement. In attempting to reexamine traditional explanations, these revisionists have sought to clear away what they see as the principal myths obscuring numerous flaws in motive, judgment, and policy by the Roosevelt Administration. Reflected primarily in the writings of Charles A. Beard, Charles Tansill, and Harry Elmer Barnes, the argument is that the Axis powers were not as imposing a threat to American security as most have come to believe, that Roosevelt developed policies calculated to involve the United States in the world conflict, that the president consistently tried to conceal this fact by deceiving the American people, and that his policies and conduct of the war did much to bring on a more serious threat to the nation from Communist Russia once the war was over.

The revisionists note first that Nazi Germany never had developed any concrete plans for the invasion of the United States, thus the militaristic expansion of Germany was not a threat to America's security. While it is true that no documentary evidence exists showing a plan by Hitler to occupy territory in the Western Hemisphere, this does not "prove" a neutral stance toward the United States by the Third Reich. The revisionists have created their own brand of mythology, then, by claiming that the expansion of German Fascism was no direct menace to the United States and New World security. Also, even though American security may have been less threatened than many believed, the possible defeat of such democratic powers as England directly involved American interests. Further, Hitler was accustomed to acting upon the basis of quick personal decisions and could well have decided to direct military action against the United States without the benefit of long-range plans, as in fact he did in the case of the Nazi invasion of Russia in June, 1941. The additional revisionist arguments that American neutrality was in many ways a sham, that Roosevelt's deceptions were very real, and their suggestions that the policies of the United States helped provoke the Japanese attack on Pearl Harbor, however, seem to have a more solid basis in fact.

In the light of hindsight it seems undeniable that the neutrality of the United States during the period preceding American involvement in the war often involved diplomatic fantasy and political make-believe. Even supporters of Franklin Roosevelt's prewar leadership have been forced to admit that at times he was inclined to camouflage his true intentions, as in the handling of the already mentioned *Greer* affair. All of this, along with many scholarly challenges to the myth that Japanese imperialism was inspired only by saber-rattling militarists and their mad-dog supporters, has led some revisionist historians to the conclusion that Roosevelt led the United States into the Second World War through the "back door" by knowingly following policies which he should have understood could only lead to a conflict.

Ever since the Russo-Japanese war in 1904-05 relations between the United States and Japan had been less than cordial, and some historians have claimed to find a pattern of American anti-Japanese policy which virtually guaranteed a Pearl Harbor-style reaction by Japan eventually. At that time, President Theodore Roosevelt had helped work out a peace settlement between the two warring nations which the Japanese felt had been concluded much less favorably for themselves than they had hoped. The so-called Gentlemen's Agreement in 1907 which excluded Japanese laborers from the United States was additionally viewed as an insult. The Japanese were also inclined to blame the United States for attempting to limit its navy to second class status at the Washington Naval Conference in 1921. An immigration act passed in 1924 in part to deny Orientals entrance to the United States was also justly seen as an American slap at Japanese national pride. Military action by Japan in Chinese Manchuria in 1931, during which the United States labeled Japan the aggressor, was yet another incident leading to a deterioration of Japanese-American relations. And after an incident at the Marco Polo bridge near Peiping, in July, 1937, hostilities ensued between Japan and China which prompted additional anti-Japanese sentiment in America. The Japanese bombing of the American gunship, *Panay*, on the Yangtze River in China in December, 1937, heightened tensions even further. During 1938 the State Department continued to criticize Japanese military actions in China with arguments that American rights and interests in the area were being violated. All of these incidents were a reflection of increased Japanese imperialism, but with some justification Japan was on solid ground in arguing that its interests in the Far East were more legitimate than those of the United States, and that "consistent American meddling" was a potential threat to its national security.

By early 1941, then, diplomatic relations between the United States and Japan were cool to say the least. In fact, Secretary of the Navy Frank Knox was already warning accurately that "if war eventuates with Japan, it is believed easily possible that hostilities would be initiated by a surprise attack upon the Fleet or Naval base [at] Pearl Harbor." When Japanese expansion continued into Indochina (Vietnam, Cambodia, Laos), President Roosevelt responded by freezing all Japanese assets in the United States. Understandably, this action, along with cutting off Japan from essential oil supplies, strained Japanese-American relations to the breaking point by sharply restricting trade between the two nations. When the President, through Secretary of State Cordell Hull, coldly rejected a Japanese proposal that he meet personally with Premier Fumimaro Konoye to resolve outstanding differences, the Japanese concluded that they were faced with the alternative of backing down or going to war. Rather than "lose face," they chose to fight.

Clearly, the postwar legend that the Pearl Harbor attack came as a complete surprise, then, is quite at odds with the facts of history. One need not accept the revisionist historians' contention that Franklin Roosevelt manipulated the country into war through the "back door" to see that many opportunities presented themselves before December 7, 1941, to try to settle misunderstandings short of open war. In ways that few Americans have realized the United States must be said to bear at least some responsibility for "causing" the outbreak of hostilities in the Pacific. The myth of American righteousness and virtue, the idea that the nation has always been on the side of goodness and honor, has not allowed the

country a totally realistic assessment of this important episode in its history.

It has been unfortunate that since the end of the Second World War most histories which have been written about the conflict and America's role in it have had a pronounced tendency to praise or to damn Franklin Roosevelt's policies and strategies, creating myths in the process. The so-called internationalist historians, who have been inclined to a pro-Roosevelt interpretation of the war, have in almost every instance been those who supported American intervention prior to the war. Having personally had a hand in the nation's foreign policy debates before Pearl Harbor, and having seen their point of view result in military victory, they have spent little time examining the warts and blemishes of the Roosevelt Administration. Similarly, the revisionist historians of the postwar period just happen to be those who were isolationists and Roosevelt-haters before the war began. Convinced that Roosevelt was wrong, some have forced the argument that the president was the leader of a sinister conspiracy specifically designed to get the United States into the war at any price, including the destruction of much of the nation's Pacific fleet at Pearl Harbor. Because of both hero worship and the effects of sensationalism, then, FDR has been portrayed as either a savior or a devil. He has seldom been seen simply as a man of good will with human failings. With the flair and emotion of evangelists, historians have carried the passion and prejudice of the war years well into the postwar period.

Yalta

Considering subsequent events, however, perhaps the single most important element of the anti-Roosevelt mythology and the misunderstandings involving the Second World War was the diplomatic conference at Yalta. One of the summit meetings held during the course of the war between the Big Three (Franklin Roosevelt, Winston Churchill, and Joseph Stalin), the conference of February 1945, at the Russian resort city on the Black Sea, has become a symbol of America's "sellout" to the Soviet Union and the beginning of cold war. According to the myth, President Roosevelt "betrayed" the interests of the United States by relying on "personal diplomacy" in his relations with Stalin and gave away too much. The story goes that he "appeased" the Russian leader by agreeing to significant Communist influence in both Eastern Europe and the Far East after the war was over. A popular political topic during the postwar period even to the present day, the so-called failure and treason of Yalta serve as a convenient explanation for those who maintain that Soviet promises can never be trusted and the years of Roosevelt leadership were a disaster both at home and abroad. A close examination of such Yalta mythology, however, clearly reveals its many distortions of historical facts.

While it is undoubtedly true that Franklin Roosevelt relied on personal relationships in his diplomatic dealings with both Churchill and Stalin, the American delegation to the Yalta Conference included an expert support staff which had much to do with both the proceedings and decisions. It included, among others, Secretary of State Edward Stetinius; Fleet Admiral William Leahy; the ambassador to the Soviet Union, Averell Harriman; Army Chief of Staff George C. Marshall; the naval aide to the President, Vice Admiral Wilson Brown; and Department of State Deputy Director Alger Hiss. This would seem to suggest that rather than Yalta being a classic case of arrogant presidential diplomacy, it reflected instead an effort on Roosevelt's part to surround himself with a highly competent and nonpartisan group of advisors.

The charge that President Roosevelt "appeased" the Russians by submitting to their demands also can be exposed as lacking a solid understanding of the complete evidence. To begin with, Yalta mythmakers have either ignored or forgotten the fact that Stalin came to the conference table holding almost all the diplomatic aces. He was negotiating from a position of strength. The Red Army had been a major force in overcoming Hitler to that point in the war. It was in military control of the areas of Eastern Europe, Poland for example, over which Stalin was demanding control once the war came to a successful conclusion. Beyond this, anti-German national resistance movements in countries like Yugoslavia, Poland, and Albania had been led by Communists who could justly lay greatest claim to postwar political power. In addition, this area of East–Central Europe, which Russia was to

dominate after the war, was legitimately within the Soviet Union's sphere of national security since German armies had invaded Russia through that corridor in both the First and Second World Wars. Finally, American agreement to rights and privileges for Russia in the Far East—for example, the return by the Japanese of the Kurile Islands—was viewed as absolutely essential by Roosevelt in the interest of securing Russia's guarantee that it would enter the war against Japan in the Pacific three months after the conclusion of the war in Europe. It was only later understood, after the Yalta agreements, that American forces and the development of the atomic bomb were sufficient to defeat the Japanese without Soviet assistance. At the time of the signing of the Yalta agreement, Roosevelt's best diplomatic and military advice was that the friendship and military support of the Soviet Union was critical to victory over the forces of General Hideki Tojo in the home islands of Japan.

It is also essential to note that the Yalta myths developed quite some time after the agreements had been signed. After the summit, Franklin Roosevelt's Yalta diplomacy was hailed as a triumph of considerable importance. Only later, in 1948, in a more hostile atmosphere, when all facets of the Yalta decisions became known, did the myths of betrayal, personal diplomacy, and failure begin to find acceptance. "Several political developments contributed to the evolution of this mythology," says the diplomatic historian Athan Theoharis. Specifically, "the postwar international crisis between the United States and the Soviet Union, the impact of the cold war on domestic politics, and the shift after 1948 in Republican campaign strategy had changed popular perceptions about Yalta."[11]

SECTION III: POSTWAR AMERICA: DISTORTED REALITIES

The Changing of the Guard

A wave of shock and dismay spread across the country only two months after Yalta, in the late afternoon of April 12, 1945, as the nation heard the sobering news that after twelve years, one month, and eight days in office, President Franklin Roosevelt was dead of a cerebral hemorrhage in Warm Springs, Georgia. Americans huddled close to their radios that day to hear details of his passing, intermixed with reports that the 2nd Armored division had successfully crossed the Elbe River in Germany and was advancing toward Berlin. General Douglas MacArthur announced that American troops had made a successful landing at Zulu in the Philippines even as the transfer of presidential power was taking place with the swearing in of Harry S. Truman as the thirty-third president of the United States. For Truman, who had spent his early years managing the family farm near Kansas City, serving as an artillery captain on the Western Front during the First World War, managing a haberdashery shop, and coming up through the ranks of the Democratic party, it seemed that "the moon and all the planets had fallen" on him. The problem was not that he was unprepared to assume the responsibilities of the presidency, but that he had to deal with the effects of FDR's political mythology.

The memory of Franklin Roosevelt's accomplishments was perhaps the most significant difficulty which President Truman had to face during the first years of his presidency. Roosevelt had been a hero-president, very nearly the patron saint of most American liberals, and had provided both his party and the nation inspiration with his New Deal and wartime leadership. As a consequence Democrats consistently used the liberal legacy of the recently departed Roosevelt as a yardstick with which to measure the performance of the new president in the White House. Truman, it was being said, was a "nice man, but no superman." What was implied by such remarks of course was that Roosevelt *had* been a superman.

FDR, in the romantic memories of the liberals, had been a forceful and independent reformer, whereas Truman was little more than a party regular who had come to prominence within the Democratic party with the help of the notorious Pendergast political machine in Missouri. Truman, it seemed, would never match the performance of the departed Roosevelt. In quite rapid succession,

old-style New Dealers who had been architects of American affairs during the Roosevelt years, and who were now disenchanted, departed the new Truman Administration either through dismissal or personal choice. William H. Davis was fired as head of the Office of Economic Stabilization, for example, while Secretary of the Interior Harold Ickes and former Roosevelt advisor Chester Bowles both resigned their posts. And when the new president fired Secretary of Commerce Henry Wallace, most Democrats saw little reason to doubt that one of America's golden eras had ended. "There was . . . more to liberal politics in the early postwar years than the memory of FDR," one historian has observed, "but liberal rhetoric and political perceptions were dominated to a remarkable extent by symbol and myth. . . . If Truman's style was unlike Roosevelt's then Truman could not be a liberal leader. Truman's policies might be discussed rationally; the FDR mythology, however, added an emotional and subjective element to the liberal attitude."[12] As had happened so often, Americans were disappointed with current leaders because they suffered from inflated and mythical notions as to how great their previous leaders had been. A nation whose history seemed to contain nothing but heroes, victories, and achievements was finding it difficult to live with the thought that its latest president might be an ordinary human, and yet capable of inspired leadership. In a predictable way, however, the forces of nostalgia and myth would one day also come to cloud the record of Harry S. Truman as well.

Truman Stands Alone

Harry Truman established his independence from the Roosevelt legacy and began the development of a mythology of his own in 1948. In that year, he scored one of the most stunning upsets in American political history by defeating the "sure winner," Republican candidate Thomas E. Dewey. Early in the campaign, pollsters George Gallup and Elmo Roper predicted a Dewey victory, and even on the morning after the election the *Chicago Daily Tribune* prematurely announced, "Dewey Defeats Truman." Dewey's abilities to make such profound observations as "Our future lies before us," however, failed to

Nuclear Fission as Weapon: During the post-Second World War period, a series of atomic tests were conducted at the Bikini atoll in the Marshall Islands. The force of this blast totally destroyed the atoll as well as many of the obsolete warships moored in the harbor.
Stockmarket, Los Angeles

inspire the majority of voters, and Truman's flair for old-fashioned whistlestop campaigning and his pleasing image as a common man from the Midwest captured the imagination of the country and gave him a political personality of his own at last free from the Roosevelt mystique. Because of his upset victory, as well as his forceful efforts in the area of foreign affairs and his leadership in desegregating the armed forces, contemporary professional historians have been inclined to include Truman as one of America's "near-great" presidents. Future historians may give him an even better rating.

It has been Harry Truman's image as a common man who identified with ordinary Americans which has become particularly dominant in the years since his death in 1972. Stage plays, television specials, books, and movies have been responsible for a wave of

Truman nostalgia, marking an important stage in the development of a full-fledged Truman mythology. To this new legion of admirers he has emerged as a feisty and colorful president—"The Man from Independence"—who moved from the local political wars of Missouri to the arena of national affairs without ever losing his solid small-town qualities. A man who could "raise hell" with both big labor and big business, a president who sat in the Oval Office behind a desk plaque which read "The Buck Stops Here," and a humble leader who according to legend used his own postage stamps as a way of showing that the "hifalutin" privileges of his office had not corrupted him, seems refreshingly from a bygone era. Most every facet of Truman's career not in keeping with the public image of a man who spent his final years walking the streets of Independence with cane in hand and flashing a broad smile which seemed to reflect the spirit and flavor of Middle America has been put aside.

The reality of the Truman presidency has been difficult to measure, first, because of the Roosevelt legacy which dominated Truman's early years in the White House and, second, because of the Truman nostalgia which has arisen since his death. Any balanced picture of Harry S. Truman must take into account his scrappy political style as well as his successes in preserving the liberal traditions of the New Deal through his own Fair Deal proposals calling for national medical insurance, federal aid to education, civil rights legislation, and public housing. Relatively new attempts to inflate Truman's legendary fame by emphasizing his supposed defiance of the Ku Klux Klan early in his political career and his work as an early champion of civil rights, however, would seem to be somewhat misguided. The new image of Truman suggests that in 1924 he personally attacked the Klan while still in Missouri politics, supposedly only because of a courageous sense of duty to freedom and democracy. The historical record indicates, however, that Truman's repudiation of the Klan had much more to do with his desire to keep the political support of Missouri Catholics than with any profound commitment to independence, openness, and honesty. In a similar way, Truman was not among the supporters of the famous civil rights plank in the Democratic party platform of 1948, and in fact some have insisted that he worked vigorously to kill it. The most direct challenge to the image of President Truman as a homespun and small-town politician of liberal sentiments, however, has had to do with the charge that he was instrumental in creating the atmosphere of diplomatic and political fantasy which led to the cold war abroad and McCarthyism at home.

The Cold War and McCarthyism

The American people have always accepted the illusion that Russia was totally responsible for causing the cold war confrontation. The myths of American righteousness and virtue have led the country to assume that the essence of the cold war was repeated instances of Soviet aggression countered by pure-

hearted attempts by the United States to defend the so-called free world. Actually, the origins of the cold war might be traced to the First World War. After that conflict, Russia was excluded from the diplomatic deliberations at the Versailles Peace Conference because of a Western fear of Bolshevism. In 1919-20 the United States went through a period known as the "Red Scare," during which the nation believed firmly in the existence of a Communist conspiracy. Indeed it was largely because of this fear that Russia was not accorded diplomatic recognition by the United States until 1933. And it took the rising threat of fascism in Europe and the Far East to force a Soviet-American alliance during the Second World War. Thus, the myth that the cold war came unexpectedly after the defeat of Germany and Japan ignores the long course of strained relations between Russia and the United States throughout earlier portions of the twentieth century. It was precisely this longstanding tradition of anticommunism in fact that Truman helped rekindle during the post-Second World War period, at least according to his critics.

The renewal of icy relationships between Soviet communism and American democracy shortly after 1945 owes much to the wartime diplomatic agreements signed by Roosevelt at Yalta, and Truman at Potsdam. Collectively, these conferences provided for the postwar partition of Germany and the city of Berlin into American, British, French, and Russian zones. It soon became evident to the Western powers, however, that contrary to the Potsdam Agreements of 1945, the Soviets were eager to turn Germany into a satellite state. And even though the Soviets had agreed at Potsdam to treat Germany as a whole as an economic unit, they flatly refused to send food from their predominantly agricultural eastern zone to other areas of Germany. Reflecting on the situation at the time, General Lucius Clay, American military governor of Germany, remarked: "Concerning the division of Germany the Russians got the agriculture, the British the industry, and the Americans the scenery."

What followed was a series of steps by both Russia and the United States which fed the suspicions of both parties that the other was intent upon engaging in "naked aggression" and threatening the "national security" and "national interest" of the respective countries. Communist governments were established in Poland, Czechoslovakia, Hungary, Rumania, Yugoslavia, Bulgaria, and Albania. A nine-nation Communist Information Bureau was formed in 1947 for purposes of disseminating Soviet propaganda explaining the position of the Communist nations to the world community. Shortly thereafter, Russia formulated what was called the Molotov Plan to assist the economic recovery of Eastern European Communist nations and organized the Warsaw Pact as a military defense system in response to the North Atlantic Treaty Organization and programs of military cooperation in Western Europe.

Under the leadership of President Truman the United States was responding to, and at the same time helping precipitate, these developments out of a fear that Communist "stooges" and "tools of the Kremlin" sought to spread their influence throughout Europe. Declaring that he was "tired of babying the Soviets," and that he favored a policy which would "get tough with Russia," Truman came before Congress in March, 1947, to announce his famous Truman Doctrine, designed to "contain" Communism. In fairly rapid succession, this doctrine was followed by the Marshall Plan, which sought to provide economic assistance for the economic recovery of war-torn Europe, and the establishment of the North Atlantic Treaty Organization (NATO) for purposes of providing military protection for Western Europe from "Russian imperialism." Thus in the eyes of the United States, the new reality of the postwar world was that the Soviet Union was guilty of aggression through its establishment of "puppet" governments. To the mind of the Russians, equally convinced of the reality of their view of the postwar world, it was only proper, and certainly in its national interest, that it control the political, military, and economic affairs of Eastern Europe since during the two world wars it had been invaded by Germany through this corridor. In addition, and given its perception of the situation, Russia could quite easily believe that the Truman Doctrine was a form of political aggression by the United States, the Marshall Plan motivated by Truman's desire to bring Western Europe into the American orbit, and NATO a blatant example of military belligerence on the part of the United States. A combination of emotion, political and diplomatic rhetoric, and a mythical impulse to see the world in shades of good and evil, could lead only to mass distortion and mythmaking in world affairs during the postwar era by both the superpowers.

The fantasy, illusion, and mass deception of the cold war environment in the world at large inevitably influenced the direction of American politics at home. Indeed, as tensions increased between the "Communist world" and the "free world" in such areas as Korea, and against the background of Winston Churchill's earlier observation in a speech at Fulton, Missouri, that an iron curtain had rung down to separate the two, a relatively obscure U.S. senator from Appleton, Wisconsin, began a crusade designed to combat an imagined Communist conspiracy in America. In a famous Lincoln Day speech in Wheeling, West Virginia, in February of 1950, Senator Joseph R. McCarthy began his campaign to save America from Communist "bogeymen" by declaring that the State Department was "infested" with disloyal conspirators. Before he was eventually condemned by the U.S. Senate in December 1954, for conduct "contrary to senatorial traditions," McCarthy succeeded in casting suspicion on the character and patriotism of numerous Americans through a series of unsubstantiated charges, through the use of what one historian has called "multiple untruths."

It would be to misjudge the situation, however, to see McCarthyism only as the product of a disturbed mind. The basis for McCarthy's rise to fame as an anti-Communist crusader was the mythical cold war atmosphere which Americans, including President Truman, had done so much to create and perpetuate. For this reason he was not the lone disturbed figure which liberal legends have often suggested; he was, rather, a symbol of a disorder national in scope. What is perhaps most disturbing about the senator's attitudes and style, based as they were on the myth that all Communists were the same and that all were a massive threat to liberty and freedom, was the fact that they grew out of the normal channels of American politics and were widely accepted by many Americans of all political persuasions. The meaning of McCarthyism, with its futile witch-hunting attempts to find "Communist conspirators" within the State Department and the U.S. Army, is most likely to be found in the normal symbolic and mythmaking aspects of the human mind. Further, McCarthy was not the first nor would he be the last political leader to find a receptive audience for the fanciful and mythical idea that Americanism could best be preserved through a destruction of the principles of free speech and freedom of the mind.

The phenomenon of McCarthyism spanned the last years of the Truman Administration and the early years of the Eisenhower presidency. Anticommunism was further brought to the center of attention for Americans by the probings of the House Un-American Activities Committee (HUAC), which began its work in the 1930s. This congressional committee came to focus on Hollywood, with the result that a large number of movie personalities thought to have Communist sympathies were blacklisted in the industry. On the basis of testimony of several well-known personalities, performers and writers such as José Ferrer, Elia Kazan, Lloyd Bridges, Sterling Hayden, Zero Mostel, Ring Lardner, Jr., and Arthur Miller were identified as "dangerous Communist dupes." One of HUAC's members, Republican Congressman Richard Nixon of California, also carried the issue to the nation in the presidential campaign of 1952 as Dwight Eisenhower's running mate. Riding the wave of anti-Communist sentiment, Nixon declared that "Mr. Truman, Dean Acheson [Truman's secretary of state], and other administration officials covered up this Communist conspiracy for political reasons." It was the personal popularity of the leading man on the Republican ticket, however, rather than the Communist issue, which carried the Eisenhower-Nixon team into the White House. According to public opinion polls, no president—not even Franklin Roosevelt—was more popular in his time than "Ike."

The Eisenhower Presidency: A General in the White House

A living example of the American success story, Dwight David Eisenhower was born in Denison, Texas, in 1890 to humble circumstances. After living the greater portion of his youth in one of the historically famous cow towns of the frontier West—Abilene, Kansas—he spent his adult life in governmental service, first as an illustrious military officer, and later as a Republican president. Combining a shining reputation as Supreme Commander of the Allied Expeditionary Force in Western Europe during the Second World War with a pleasing image as a man above party battles and a father to his people, Ike decisively defeated Adlai Stevenson of Illinois in the presidential race of 1952. He did so with the good wishes of those who wanted to halt the "creeping socialism" of Truman's Fair Deal, and those who saw in Eisenhower a leader who would bring a measure of moderation, security, and tranquility to America after the many years of depression, liberal politics, world war, and cold war international tensions. Interestingly enough, though never openly embracing the legacy of the New Deal, Eisenhower nonetheless was destined to carry it forward and continue the dominant role of the federal government in the day-to-day affairs of the nation.

In many ways, the Eisenhower years revitalized old brands of American mythology. There was a renewed commitment, for example, to the economic legend that an unbalanced budget would bring financial ruin to America, even though Eisenhower succeeded in balancing the budget in only three of his eight years as president. Ike's years in office also witnessed a reemphasis on the sacred American belief that the affairs of the nation could be best handled by those of business background and predisposition. Conservatism reigned within Eisenhower's cabinet of millionaires, which included such men as Charles E. Wilson, Douglas McKay, and Sinclair Weeks (all recruited from General Motors), and Ezra Taft Benson, an elder of the Mormon Church. Believers all in the mythology of the self-made man, their presence in Washington as architects of Eisenhower Republicanism led one historian to describe their cautious leadership as a case of "the bland leading the bland." The expectations of the American people during Ike's presidency were modest and their hopes were rewarded. One writer on the subject has said: "They expected Eisenhower not to solve problems but to serve as a good-luck amulet to charm them away."[13] Indeed it is clear that

America's national political scene from 1953 through 1961 will never be viewed as vibrant, colorful, or free from the tyranny of old forms of American mythology. With the assistance of historical hindsight, however, there are elements of the Eisenhower years which deserve at least a certain amount of praise. The stereotyped image of the general-president as a conservative leader with few redeeming qualities is already on its way toward being revised.

There are portions of the Eisenhower record which fit badly with Ike's conventional image as a purposeless party leader of little creative leadership ability. It is worth recalling, for example, that he was in important ways responsible for ending the Korean War, that he appointed Earl Warren chief justice of the Supreme Court, and that he refused to give direct military assistance to the French as they attempted to reestablish colonial control over Vietnam. Unlike both his predecessor and successors, he did much to control the nation's participation in a spiraling arms race with Soviet Russia despite the persistent rhetoric by both Republicans and Democrats that the United States was in a "death struggle" with world communism. Instead, Eisenhower cautioned the nation on the dangers of creating a military-industrial complex while at the same time he reduced the size of the armed forces and held a ceiling on the number of intercontinental ballistic missiles (ICBMs) in the nation's defense arsenal. Shortly after he turned over his office to John F. Kennedy in 1961, the nation was back on the track of the arms race, with a thousand ICBMs aimed against all manner of "enemies," both real and imagined. Finally, and especially for an America which now looks back to the Eisenhower presidency through the haze of the Watergate experiences, Ike's years in the White House—despite the Dixon-Yates syndicate contract scandal and questionable conduct involving Sherman Adams, assistant to the President—appear open, temperate, and moral. Eisenhower's personal qualities of honesty and integrity, enhanced by his famous grin and relaxed manner, inspired a measure of public confidence which perhaps no occupant of the Oval Office has since matched. It may have been, of course, that Dwight Eisenhower was simply living the major myth of the presidency—that the nation's chief executive should be pure of heart, friendly, and a man of sober virtue.

Kennedy's Political Camelot

The myths of the Eisenhower years have been outshone by the grand mythology which has come to enshroud the man who replaced him in the presidency—John Fitzgerald Kennedy. He was blessed with youth, magnetic personal appeal, an image of excellence, and a wife of noted beauty. It is interesting to note that JFK privately thought himself an "idealist without illusions," in light of the fact that his few years in the White House provoked a rejuvenation of American mythology perhaps unparalleled in the twentieth century. The legendary "Kennedy style" of grace, commitment, and vigor, combined with a political program which has been variously described as the politics of "promise" and "expectation," brought a warm response from the American people. Americans could readily relate to Kennedy's leadership as though he were a valiant warrior of old, directing them to a New Frontier. Helping Americans to hear echoes of their legendary past, John Kennedy built upon the elaborate mythology of the frontier and American destiny to create a delightful dream of fulfillment for the nation. For many, JFK was Sir Galahad or Prince Valiant leading America out of the doldrums of the Eisenhower era toward the bright promise of a political Camelot. It appeared that he would give new substance to the old belief that America was promises and limitless opportunity.

The dramatic "one thousand days" of the Kennedy presidency began with gusto and convinced the nation that it had elected a president who could creatively combine a sense of cherished American traditions with a flair for action. Intellectuals, academicians, and "bright young men" flocked to the nation's capital as they had not done since the early days of FDR's administration nearly thirty years before. Some of Kennedy's programs—the Alliance for Progress and the Peace Corps for example—enjoyed early success. When it became known that Kennedy had approved a CIA-organized invasion of Cuba in 1961, however, his fortunes began a decline. Partially as a consequence, the president's plans for federal aid to education, new civil rights legislation, medical care for the aged, and a tax cut to stimulate economic growth met with only mixed success in Congress. An enlargement of American involvement in Vietnam and discontent in the South stemming from forced desegregation of the University of Mississippi in October, 1962, were also problems which even one of JFK's seemingly knightly abilities was finding difficult to solve. By mid-November, 1963, a good many Americans were reading with approval Victor Lasky's best-selling book, *J.F.K.: The Man and the Myth,* which claimed that the Kennedy mystique was a facade which hid a man who was in truth "immature, slick, intellectually shallow," and deserving of the nickname "Jack the Knife." All of this was soon to be forgotten, however, after November 22, 1963.

The assassination of John Kennedy by Lee Harvey Oswald carried the Kennedy mythology to a new height by providing it a quality it had formerly lacked—a dimension of tragedy. The grief of the nation was instantaneous. Americans remembered a fallen hero who had tried to highlight the promise of American life and lead them to the political promised land. It was soon apparent that JFK, a prophet of his people and a martyr, was destined for sainthood. It took little time for the nation to equate the recent Kennedy tragedy with that of an earlier hero, Abraham Lincoln. In fact, the alleged similarities between the two men went to bizarre extremes—for example, that the names John Wilkes Booth and Lee Harvey Oswald both contained fifteen letters. And Jacqueline Kennedy helped to enhance the mythology of her late husband by consciously associating him with the Lincoln legend. In the words of one historian:

> At her direction, Kennedy's coffin, like Lincoln's, stood in the candlelit East Room of the White House beneath chandeliers draped in black, and then in the great rotunda of the Capitol on the same catafalque, covered in black velvet, that had held Lincoln's coffin. Following the ninety-eight-year-old scenario, six gray horses drew it down Pennsylvania

Avenue to the same ruffled roll of drums. Behind the wooden caisson walked, as in 1865, a riderless gelding with boots reversed in the stirrups, the military symbol of a fallen warrior.[14]

Given such fanfare, it was little wonder that many former Kennedy men, such as his press secretary Pierre Salinger, soon felt the compelling need to leave government service because "the memory of JFK was too overpowering." The sustained fascination of Americans with the Kennedy years, and in particular with the circumstances of his death, would seem to show that little of the energy and power of the Kennedy mythology has been lost with the passage of time.

Johnson as President: A Rancher in the White House

The mythical and utopian qualities of the Kennedy presidency did not escape his successor, Lyndon Baines Johnson. A son of the Texas hill country, LBJ had earned his political spurs during the pioneering days of the New Deal. Moving from the rough-and-tumble arena of Texas politics to Washington with his election to Congress in 1937, and eventually to the U.S. Senate with a scant eighty-seven vote majority in 1948, "Landslide Lyndon" soon emerged as a talented party leader. Having been Democratic minority leader (1953-55) and then majority leader (1955-61), Johnson brought more political savvy to the White House than most other presidents. In tune with the Kennedy legacy, LBJ sought to revive the age-old spirit of American utopianism through his War on Poverty and the creation of a Great Society. The result of these programs was an impressive array of legislation in the areas of civil rights, medical assistance for the aged, and federal aid to education. But though he could point with pride to the fact that as a Southerner he would be remembered as "the Civil Rights President," and though his support for education reflected the idealistic belief that self-improvement was the surest way for the poor and the young to rise through the ranks to fame and fortune, he seemed never able to arouse the enthusiasm nor receive the affection that the American people continued to bestow on the memory of JFK. The Johnson Administration was persistently haunted by the popularity of the Kennedy mystique.

Lyndon B. Johnson in a sense never escaped the mythology of his early years. For, more than any president since Theodore Roosevelt, he was a cowboy riding the range of American politics. While it would probably be too simplistic to say that LBJ thought himself a Texas Ranger in the twentieth century, it seems nonetheless true that he had a distinct tendency to see the world as divided between "good guys" and "bad guys"—Ranger-style. With characteristic western confidence he was consistently earthy, shrewd, and blunt in manner. For LBJ, his "quick draw" intervention in the Dominican Republic in 1965 was, as he phrased it, "just like the Alamo." Indeed, for one so much in step with America's legendary past, it is little surprise that Lyndon Johnson would ultimately become the victim of both personal and national mythology. The long and costly conflict in Vietnam, that he would not avoid, could not win, and failed to end, never seemed to jibe with the view of the world LBJ had from the rocking chair on the front porch of his Texas ranch. He persisted in seeing the war in Vietnam "as a hunt which must end, in Davy Crockett fashion, 'with that coonskin on the wall'."[15] In time, the American public dissented from such myth-dominated logic to the point of forcing the president not to seek reelection. As the Johnson years in the White House began to suggest, however, the essential tragedy in Southeast Asia, both for Lyndon Baines Johnson personally and for the nation at large, would be the manipulation and misuse of American mythology.

SECTION IV: VIETNAM AND WATERGATE: A MARRIAGE OF MYTHS

Perhaps no episode in the American experience has been more associated with myth than the war in Vietnam. Consistently, until the American withdrawal in April, 1975, all the major parties to Vietnamese affairs—the United States, the North and South Vietnamese, China, and Russia—engaged in a freewheeling manipulation of international reality based on myths concerning the intentions, policies, and objectives of each other and themselves. As one close observer of American involvement over the years commented in 1971:

> One is struck constantly by the curious mirages, the discordance between image and reality which seem to persist not only in American perceptions of Indochina but in the evaluations by other great powers and the Indochinese themselves of the actual nature and goals of U.S. policy.[16]

A spiral of myth, deception, and illusion based on preconceived notions drawn from the cold war, rumors, diplomatic fantasies, and political and military make-believe over the years all produced a pattern of escalated involvement by the United States. Indeed, it was changing political and military realities in Vietnam, along with the gradual recognition that the United States was behaving toward the Vietnamese as the British had behaved toward America in 1776, that a measure of international realism eventually appeared.

The pattern of American involvement in the affairs of Southeast Asia can be found as early as the years before the Second World War. Though not practically involved in a military sense at that time, President Franklin D. Roosevelt went on record in July, 1941, suggesting that French colonial aggression in Indochina (which dated from as far back as the seventeenth century) had much to do with the deterioration of American-Japanese relations in that portion of the world. In conversation with Admiral William D. Leahy, American ambassador to occupied France early in the Second World War, Roosevelt stated that "if Japan wins [the war] Japan gets Indochina—if the Allies win we would" take it over. Later, in 1944, Roosevelt proposed that China might wish to exercise a "trusteeship" over Indochina after the war, based on his misinformed view that the Indochinese and the Chinese were obviously "the same kind of people." While not plotting a strategy of American postwar control of the area, it is clear even at these early dates that national leaders had begun to focus their attention on the fate of Vietnam and its role in America's future. Contrary to the widely held opinion that American interest in

Vietnam was not expressed until the Korean War, then, a period of psychological involvement seems to have predated the period of diplomatic, economic, and military engagement which would become so obvious later on. Beyond this, President Roosevelt's dubious idea that French colonialism in Indochina had a direct relationship to Japanese-American hostilities in the South Pacific during the war, and his erroneous assumption that China and its neighbors to the south were strong historical allies, offered a forewarning of the distortion and misunderstanding which was to plague American activities there for the next thirty years.

During the course of the Second World War, the American Office of Strategic Services forces, as part of the policy of the Pacific military campaign against the Japanese, came to share a friendly relationship with Ho Chi Minh and the nationalist Vietnamese movement, or Vietminh. In the words of one OSS officer, for example, Ho was an "awfully sweet guy." Indeed, during this period, America's perception of Ho and his followers was rather uniformly favorable. It seemed fitting that the Vietnamese should be free from the control of France, which had held the area in colonial bondage for decades, and from the Japanese, who were now in military control of the area. It seemed not at all odd, then, that Ho Chi Minh's proclamation of September, 1945, announcing the new Republic of Vietnam, served as a reminder that his Vietnamese revolution was a historical grandchild of the American war for independence from British rule in 1776. Ho's declaration in fact began: "All men are created equal. They are endowed by their Creator with certain inalienable rights, among these are Life, Liberty and the Pursuit of Happiness. . . ." For many, it seemed appropriate to compare Ho Chi Minh to the legendary George Washington, as the Father of his Country. In the opinion of the *Christian Science Monitor* in late 1946, Ho's heroic activities were a "part of the struggle of colonial peoples for liberation from foreign influence or control. The peoples of Indochina [were] join-[ing] the forward march toward independence."

The postwar American experience of confrontation with communism in Europe and cold war influences at home, however, strongly began to discolor and finally fundamentally alter the American view of Ho Chi Minh's revolutionary activities in Southeast Asia. In this regard the year 1949 seems to have been the most critical, for it marked the triumph of Mao Tse-tung's Communist revolution in China over the forces of Generalissimo Chiang Kai-shek. Shortly thereafter, in February, 1950, the new Chinese regime signed a mutual defense agreement with the Soviet Union, which created the impression that a move was afoot to unite the forces of Asian communism behind a common front. An invasion by North Korean Communists into South Korea in June of the same year also gave credibility to the growing theory that a disciplined and expansionistic Communist move was under way in Asia, similar to that which had engulfed East and Central Europe in the years after the Second World War. It was at this point that the Truman Administration ceased to see Ho Chi Minh's efforts as a spirited fight for national independence and began instead to offer economic support to assist the French against the "rebellious" Vietminh. This would indeed prove to be a momentous initial step toward the nation's entanglement in Vietnam.

A combination of circumstances both in Europe and in areas of Asia other than Vietnam, then, began to shape a new perception for Americans as to the "reality" of the Indochina situation. Ho Chi Minh had not changed, the objectives of the Vietminh had not changed, but the image of them in the American mind had. Where shortly before he had been accepted as the George Washington of Vietnam, the American image of Ho was now as an "agent of Communism." The Vietminh was no longer a gallant band of freedom fighters but rather, in the words of *Atlantic* magazine in June, 1951, "a rebellious horde." Out of the general American fear of a mythical Communist "monolith"—the assumption that all Communists were like-minded in their political objectives—the suspicion arose that Vietnam was likely the next target for the cancerous spread of world communism. The theory also began to take hold that the strings of worldwide Communist revolution were being pulled in Moscow. A vast network of sinister intrigue supposedly was stretching from the Russian capital into Eastern Europe, China, Korea, and now Vietnam. Given this altered view of reality, Ho Chi Minh became a "puppet" of international communism and the French emerged, in the vocabulary of the time, as "defenders of the West."

Perhaps the most dramatic change in American outlook, however, involved Bao Dai, who had come forward to help the French subdue Ho's hordes. As one who spoke fluent French, clumsy Vietnamese, wore sharkskin suits, and whose tastes ran to French cooking, expensive prostitutes, and political corruption, Dai had been mockingly referred to as the "nightclub emperor" ever since his installation by the French in 1949 to help support the fiction of an "independent Vietnam." In the face of these new developments, the same *Christian Science Monitor* which had earlier applauded Ho Chi Minh's "march to independence" could declare in September, 1951, that Bao Dai offered "more opportunity to the Vietnamese people to develop their own national life than a leader who . . . must obey the orders of international Communism." Indeed, the phantom of communism was already beginning to have profound practical effects. The imposing mythical image of international communism, personified by a view of Chairman Mao and Uncle Ho as twin devils in disguise, helped give life to the continued policy of American support for a series of corrupt regimes beginning with Bao Dai which the United States would long try to delude itself into thinking were democratic.

With American leaders defining any and all conflicts throughout the world as but different theatres of the holy war against communism, the nation began the gradual process of escalation in Southeast Asia. In May, 1950, a month prior to the beginning of the Korean War, President Truman authorized the first direct American aid of major consequence to Vietnam. On June 27, 1950, two days after the Korean conflict began, administration officials announced the assignment of a thirty-five-member Military Assistance Advisory Group to Southeast Asia to instruct anti-Communist Vietnamese in the use of American military hardware. While holding firm in his decision not to bail out the French who were losing their grip on Vietnam, President Eisenhower followed Truman's lead by committing both military and economic assistance to the futile effort to prop up both France and its puppet,

Bao Dai. Indeed, by the time of the French defeat in the spring of 1954 at the legendary battle of Dienbienphu, the American stake in Vietnam had risen to 700 military advisors and one billion dollars in support funds. In October, 1957, the first report of injuries to American advisors was received. In July, 1959, these advisory units had suffered their first fatalities. By the time of John F. Kennedy's death in 1963, the American presence in Vietnam had swelled to some sixteen thousand people. And it was during the years of Lyndon Johnson's presidency that American involvement peaked with more than a half million people and untold billions of dollars being poured into the attempt to contain communism.

Finding a military solution to the problem in Southeast Asia consistently elusive, the United States eventually found it necessary to change its policies toward de-escalation and what came to be called "Vietnamization"—the phased takeover of the war effort by the South Vietnamese themselves. Before such would happen, however, the nation and particularly the troops who fought in the Highlands, the rice paddies, hamlets, and the coastal plains of Vietnam would be forced to suffer through the war experiences of Pleiku, Khe Sann, the Tet offensive, and My Lai. South Vietnamese leaders such as Ngo Dinh Diem, Nguyen Cao Ky, and Nguyen Van Thieu succeeded one another to power as a consequence of a series of efforts calculated to stem the tide of what turned out to be an eventual Communist victory. The stark ending to America's Vietnam experience was built on an international game of make-believe which continued to insist that the Vietnamese Communists (now called Vietcong) and their allies in the South (the National Liberation Front) were instruments of a worldwide and centrally controlled Communist menace, an idea which was more alive in the American imagination than in fact. Ho Chi Minh was a Communist to be sure. He had, after all, been one of the founders of the French Communist party during his years in Paris early in the century. It was always clear to close observers of the Vietnam scene, however, that Ho was as much or more a Vietnamese nationalist as he was a believer in Communist ideology. Far from being on orders from the forces of international communism, Ho had explained his relationship to the twin forces of communism and nationalism when he told one Western observer, "My party is my country, my program is independence." Obviously, America never took Ho Chi Minh at his word. As any visitor to the Museum of the Revolution in Hanoi could have discovered—given its recording of Vietnam's heroic and longstanding efforts against China—the Vietcong insurgents were quite aware of the long history of conflict which their Vietnamese ancestors had been engaged in against the hated Chinese. Traditional antagonists of the country of Mao, the North Vietnamese ultimately formed an alliance of convenience with China in the interest of securing needed military assistance during much of the Vietnam conflict, but their major objective was first and always the independence of their fellow Vietnamese.

The American image of Ho Chi Minh and his movement changed focus, then, in line with what Americans wanted to believe. Moreover, the mythical American view which saw a unified Communist effort against its national interests was solidifying precisely at the time when Russia and China, beginning in the early 1960s, began to drift into opposing camps. In the words of one informed source, America was "blinded ... to the reality that the world is full of natural, locally produced chaos which arises and runs its course quite independent of deliberate policy by the Soviet Union or any great power."[17] In hindsight it appears clear that the American imagination became far more enslaved by the myth of a universal Communist threat than the Vietnamese ever were by the supposed evil designs of Hanoi, Peking, and Moscow.

Watergate

The era of national self-deception in Vietnam was not yet ended when Richard M. Nixon was inaugurated president of the United States in January, 1969. Given an extended political career, much of which was based on his persistent warnings about the "Communist menace," it was not logical to think that he would be successful in freeing himself from the multiple myths which bound America to its Vietnam commitments. Yet during his first term in the White House, Nixon rejected a past

built on largely fanciful suspicions of communism to achieve important new breakthroughs in detente with the Soviet Union and a de-escalation of the crusade against communism in Southeast Asia. In the place of calls for Americans to respond to another heroic effort against the evil forces of Hanoi, Peking, and Moscow, by the middle of 1972 Nixon had reduced the level of American troops in Vietnam to 39,000 and considerably lessened former cold war tensions through visits to both the People's Republic of China and the Soviet Union. There was still a good deal of talk about "peace with honor" and the desire that Vietnam must not turn out to be "the first defeat in [the nation's] proud 190-year history," but the gradual movement away from the old mythology of Communist containment was refreshing for the majority of Americans. So much was this true, in fact, that it contributed to the "new" Nixon's victory over his Democratic rival, Senator George McGovern, in the presidential campaign of 1972 by better than 12 million votes. Even as the reelected president was scaling the heights of public popularity, however, the nation was becoming increasingly aware of another pattern of deception, mythmaking, and government-by-lying, which would finally be exposed as an ongoing presidential disease.

In June 1971, the *New York Times* published the now famous *Pentagon Papers* which had been leaked to them by Daniel Ellsberg, former employee of a government-funded "think tank," the Rand Corporation. The secret *Papers* disclosed a series of communiques, memos, recommendations, and decisions, dating back to the Kennedy Administration, which were specifically designed to mislead the American people by distorting the reality of the war in Vietnam. One year later, in June, 1972, the apparently unrelated episode of a burglary attempt at the Democratic National Committee headquarters in Washington's Watergate Hotel was destined to lay bare the Nixon Administration's talent for evasion, misrepresentation, and mythmaking. As the facts of both Vietnam and Watergate became known, it began to be more clear that the pageantry of the presidency had been consistently used as a cover for unethical and often illegal activities. The mirage of honesty, credibility, and sincerity which through history

The Oval Room: Symbol of
the Imperial Presidency
UPI-Compix

had come to surround the Oval Office—what president-watcher Theodore H. White has since called the "myth of the presidency"— gradually began to evaporate. With trappings removed, what finally lay exposed was "the imperial presidency."

The clash for political power between Congress and president has been a rather consistent theme in American history. At various times the pendulum of power has swung first to one and then the other. Congress has enjoyed its star figures—Daniel Webster, Henry Clay, Thaddeus Stevens, Joseph Cannon, Henry Cabot Lodge, Sam Rayburn, and Lyndon Johnson—who were instrumental in tipping the balance of American political power at given times more toward Capitol Hill than the White House. And of course the

presidential office has also witnessed its share of powerful men—Washington, Jefferson, Jackson, Lincoln, Wilson, and the two Roosevelts. Indeed, in the give-and-take of a democracy, it is expected that the contest for power will be spirited, played according to the rules, but always with the ideal in mind that the best interests of the people be served. But while the acquisition and use of political power is not new to America, the events of Vietnam and Watergate together demonstrated the essential truth contained in Lord Acton's famous remark that "power tends to corrupt and absolute power corrupts absolutely." Throughout the twentieth century, and particularly since the Government Reorganization Act of 1939 created a White House staff, the office of president of the United States has offered to its occupants opportunities to use power in an arrogant way. This, combined with the legendary prestige which the office already carried, has led in particular to the use of what has been called the "myth of national security" as a screen to hide misdeeds. The abuse of "imperial" power has run to adventures in foreign wars, systematic violation of the civil liberties of American citizens, and foreign assassination plots. Using their sacred presidential image to the utmost advantage, and making use of such institutional power sources available to a chief executive as the Pentagon, the CIA, and the FBI, recent presidents have too often mythologized both their executive role and their relationship to the American people. Thinking themselves a world apart from those they served, American presidents of recent memory have cultivated a self-image strangely like those of kings of old—above the law. Richard Nixon in particular seems to have lived in just such a mythical world, especially during his last years as president.

The image of Richard Nixon during his first presidential administration as a fair-minded, mature politician surprised a good many political analysts who for many years had found the "real" nature of his mind, character, style, and personality to be evasive. In their eyes he was "Tricky Dick." In their judgment, his early political victories had been due for the most part to questionable use of the issue of communism as a scare tactic upon which to build voter support. Indeed, in 1946 against Congressman Jerry Voorhis and again in 1950 against Senator Helen Gahagan Douglas, he used a strategy of innuendo, half-truths, and unsupported charges to win the acclaim of Californians as a warrior against Communist subversion. Since he followed much the same style and technique in his successful campaigns as Dwight Eisenhower's running mate in the national elections of 1952 and 1956, it now seemed clear to his political enemies, at least, that he was, in the words of Adlai Stevenson, "McCarthy in a white collar." The later emergence of a new Nixon image which conveyed the impression that he was at last a politician of more mature stature—based both on his efficient performance as a molder of national affairs during President Eisen-

hower's heart attack recovery in 1955, and the foreign policy successes of his first administration as chief executive—suggested that the real Nixon had finally emerged. The serenity of the mythical world which Richard Nixon had succeeded in building around himself, however, began finally to crumble as a result of Watergate. The episode would finally expose him as a liar and pretender, and drive him from office.

The dismantling of the new Nixon mythology began innocently enough. In the early morning hours of June 17, 1972, police arrested five men carrying an array of cameras and bugging devices at the Democratic Party's National Committee offices at the Watergate. One of the figures apprehended was James McCord, in charge of security for the Republican party's Committee to Reelect the President, known thereafter as CREEP. Subsequent events disclosed over the following two years gradually revealed the major flaws of the Nixon Administration. Though he attempted to hide behind a myth of executive privilege as well as the myth of the presidency, and becoming increasingly remote, secretive, and inaccessible in the conduct of his office, Richard Nixon saw the walls of the imperial presidency brought down by the Watergate affair. As one historian has expressed it:

the Watergate scandals terrifyingly revealed the inner state of his administration. Nixon, it appeared, for all his industriousness, shrewdness, cleverness, and combative courage, was essentially a hollow, empty man. . . .[18]

As the nation watched, a series of fresh disclosures, hearings, subpoenas, and trials finally made it "perfectly clear" that Nixon associates such as former Attorney General John Mitchell, Secretary of Commerce Maurice Stans, and White House aides H. R. "Bob" Haldeman and John Erlichman, perhaps the president himself, had all participated in complicated illegalities. In the process, Sam Ervin, John Dean, Donald Segretti, and Rose Mary Woods became household names, and such words as "plumbers," "tapes," "dirty tricks," and "cover-up" became part of the nation's political vocabulary. To the end,

Nixon desperately sought to sustain an illusion of personal noninvolvement. As White House tapes would reveal, however, he had instructed his associates to maintain the mythical facade at any price: "Let them plead the Fifth Amendment, cover-up or anything else if it'll save it—save the plan."

As the Watergate affair unfolded, an increasingly defensive Richard Nixon seemed to retreat even further from political reality. The imperial president was now protected only by a new palace guard directed by former General Alexander Haig and one-time Disneyland public relations man turned presidential news secretary, Ronald Ziegler. In ways strangely reminiscent of Vietnam, a distortion of language gave a strong hint that facts were being covered up by an elaborate smoke screen of lies. During the Vietnam experience, the American public was told by Pentagon mythmakers that bombing was really "air support" or "protective reaction exercises." And the classic example of verbal fantasy to emerge from the Vietnam war, of course, was the statement from the American officer who explained: "It was necessary to destroy the village in order to save it." The attempts at self-deception, and the creation of myth through the manipulation of language, became even more obvious in the words surrounding Watergate. "Intelligence-gathering operations" became a tidy phrase which really meant "breaking and entering." "Containment" became a word substitute for "perjury" and the illegal withholding of evidence. Americans were asked to believe that lying could be passed off as "misspeaking oneself." In the end, it was inevitable that the process of government-by-lying, supported by rhetoric specifically designed to deceive, would finally be exposed for what it was—an elaborate mythology specifically created to place the reality of Watergate, like Vietnam, out of focus and beyond the scrutiny of the American people.

In the case of both Vietnam and Watergate, new myths had been manufactured in an attempt to cover up old ones. Both episodes used the myth of national security and the myth of the presidency to excuse an abuse of power. Together Vietnam and Watergate courted disaster by a marriage of myths. Both reflected the hollowness of the American legends of invincibility, innocence, righteousness, and perfection. Attempts to rescue these sacred ideas through a barrage of mythical language failed in each instance. In the case of Vietnam, the nation emerged from the experience with a healthier, and one might say more realistic, awareness of the limits of national power. In the case of Watergate, one finds it easy to agree with the assessment of Theodore H. White, that "the true crime of Richard Nixon was simple; he destroyed the myth that binds America together"—a profound faith in the office of the president as a place of honesty and integrity.[19] For this he was driven from power. Little wonder that American society has since sought rightly or wrongly to leave the mythology of Vietnam and Watergate behind, and to divorce itself from both.

STUDY QUESTIONS

1. What were the major elements of background, character, and personal style which worked to create Franklin Roosevelt's heroic stature in the minds of the American people? In what ways did the New Deal, and some of its specific programs, assist this process? How has FDR's historical reputation as a "hero-president" survived the scrutiny of scholars?

2. Analyze and discuss the involvement of the United States in the Second World War. Specifically, in what ways and to what degree have revisionist historians claimed that Franklin Roosevelt's neutrality policies and Japan's attack on Pearl Harbor deserve to be reexamined? Also, what are the Yalta myths?

3. In what ways were the early years of the Truman presidency a period dominated by a lingering Roosevelt mythology? What was Truman's relationship to the mythologies of the cold war and McCarthyism? Finally, compare and contrast the presidential mythologies of Dwight Eisenhower, John F. Kennedy, and Lyndon Johnson.

4. How and to what degree was American policy toward Vietnam, beginning as early as the presidency of Franklin Roosevelt, a policy consistently influenced by American mythology? Also, how did the Watergate experience

eventually expose basic flaws in both national and presidential mythologies?

REFERENCES

1. Robert Sobel, *The Great Bull Market: Wall Street in the 1920s* (New York: W. W. Norton, 1968), pp. 9-10.
2. John Kenneth Galbraith, "The Causes of the Great Crash," in John Garraty, ed., *Historical Viewpoints*, II (New York: Harper & Row, Publishers, 1975), p. 275.
3. Ibid., p. 280.
4. Quoted in Edward Robb Ellis, "What the Depression Did to People," in Thomas R. Frazier, ed., *The Underside of American History: Readings in Everyday History*, II (New York: Harcourt Brace Jovanovich, 1975), p. 200.
5. Warren I. Susman, "The Thirties," in Stanley Coben and Lorman Ratner, eds., *The Development of an American Culture* (Englewood Cliffs, N. J.: Prentice-Hall, 1970), pp. 192-193.
6. J. William Fulbright, *Old Myths and New Realities* (New York: Vintage Books, 1964), p. 8.
7. William E. Leuchtenburg, ed., *Franklin D. Roosevelt: A Profile* (New York: Hill & Wang, 1967), p. ix.
8. Paul Conkin, *The New Deal* (New York: Thomas Y. Crowell Co., 1975), p. 2.
9. Otis L. Graham, "The Age of the Great Depression, 1929-1940," in William H. Cartwright and Richard Watson, Jr., eds. *The Reinterpretation of American History and Culture* (Washington, D.C.: The National Council for the Social Studies, 1973), p. 499.
10. Robert H. Ferrell, "The United States in World Affairs: 1918-1941," in John A. Garraty, ed., *Interpreting American History: Conversations with Historians*, II (New York: The Macmillan Company, 1970), pp. 212-213.
11. Athan G. Theoharis, *The Yalta Myths: An Issue in U.S. Politics, 1945-1955* (Columbia: University of Missouri Press, 1970), pp. 18-19.
12. Alonzo L. Hamby, "The Liberals, Truman, and FDR as Symbol and Myth," *Journal of American History*, March, 1970, p. 866.
13. Samuel Eliot Morison, Henry Steele Commager, and William E. Leuchtenburg, *The Growth of the American Republic*, II (New York: Oxford University Press, 1969), p. 675.
14. Andy Logan, "J.F.K.: The Stained-Glass Image," *American Heritage*, August, 1967, p. 78.
15. Thomas A. Bailey, "The Mythmakers of American History," *Journal of American History* LV (June, 1968): 10.
16. Harrison E. Salisbury, "Image and Reality in Indochina," *Foreign Affairs*, (April, 1971), p. 381.
17. Gaddis Smith, "The United States in World Affairs Since 1945," in Cartwright and Watson, *Reinterpretation*, p. 550.
18. Kenneth S. Davis, "Richard Milhous Nixon," in John A. Garraty, ed., *Encyclopedia of American Biography* (New York: Harper & Row, Publishers, 1974), p. 815.
19. Theodore H. White, *Breach of Faith: The Fall of Richard Nixon* (New York: Dell Publishing Co., 1976), p. 409.

SOURCES FOR FURTHER STUDY

LEGACY AND LEGEND: FDR AND THE NEW DEAL
CONKIN, PAUL. *The New Deal*. New York: Thomas Y. Crowell Co., 1975.
GRAHAM, OTIS L. "The Age of the Great Depression, 1929-1940." In William H. Cartwright and Richard L. Watson, Jr., eds., *The Reinterpretation of American History and Culture*. Washington, D.C.: National Council for the Social Studies, 1973.
LEUCHTENBURG, WILLIAM E., ed. *Franklin D. Roosevelt: A Profile*. New York: Hill & Wang, 1967.
———. "The Great Depression and the New Deal." In John A. Garraty, ed., *Interpreting American History: Conversations with Historians*, II. New York: The Macmillan Company, 1970.
SUSMAN, WARREN I. "The Thirties." In Stanley Coben and Lorman Ratner, eds., *The Development of an American Culture*. Englewood Cliffs, N. J.: Prentice-Hall, 1970.

AMERICA AND THE ERA OF THE SECOND WORLD WAR: REALITIES AND MYTHS
BILLINGTON, RAY ALLEN. "The Origins of Middle Western Isolationism." In *Political Science Quarterly* 60 (1945).
COLE, WAYNE S. "American Entry into World War II: A Historiographical Appraisal." *The Mississippi Valley Historical Review* 43 (1957).
FERRELL, ROBERT H. "The United States in World Affairs: 1918-1941." In John A. Garraty, ed., *Interpreting American History: Conversations with Historians*, II. New York: The Macmillan Company, 1970.
LERCHE, CHARLES O., JR., "Southern Internationalism—Myth and Reality." In *The Uncertain South: Its Changing Patterns of Politics and Foreign Policy*. New York: Quadrangle Books, 1964.
THEOHARIS, ATHAN G. *The Yalta Myths: An Issue in U.S. Politics, 1945-1955*. Columbia: University of Missouri Press, 1970.

POSTWAR AMERICA: DISTORTED REALITIES
FULBRIGHT, J. WILLIAM. *Old Myths and New Realities*. New York: Vintage Books, 1964.
HALLE, LOUIS J. *Dream and Reality: Aspects of American Foreign Policy*. New York: Harper & Row, Publishers, 1959.
HAMBY, ALONZO L. "The Liberals, Truman, and FDR

as Symbol and Myth." In *Journal of American History*, March, 1970.

KEARNS, DORIS. *Lyndon Johnson and the American Dream*. New York: Harper & Row, Publishers, 1976.

LOGAN, ANDY. "J.F.K.: The Stained-Glass Image." In *American Heritage*, August, 1967.

VIETNAM AND WATERGATE: A MARRIAGE OF MYTHS

COX, ARTHUR M. *Myths of National Security: The Peril of Secret Government*. Boston: Beacon Press, 1975.

MCGARVEY, PATRICK. *C.I.A.: The Myth and the Madness*. Baltimore: Penguin Press, 1972.

SALISBURY, HARRISON. "Image and Reality in Indochina." In *Foreign Affairs*, April, 1971.

SCHLESINGER, ARTHUR M., JR. "Watergate and the Corruption of Language." In *Today's Education* 63 (1974).

WHITE, THEODORE H. *Breach of Faith: The Fall of Richard Nixon*. New York: Dell Publishing Co., 1976.

SURE THE WORLD'S A MESS NOW... ..BUT LOOK AT THE BRIGHT SIDE.. THINGS WILL PROBABLY GET WORSE !!...

©1976 Universal Press Syndicate

...THEN THESE WILL SEEM LIKE THE GOOD OLD DAYS !!!

TomWilson

10 And the Myths Continue . . .

PREVIEW

Problems in Paradise: Ecology and Energy

To anyone with an awareness that myth is an important ingredient of America's past, it should be evident that affairs of the present are also distorted by the forces of mythology. The present, after all, is an extension of the past, even though, as the historian Carl Becker noted some time ago, "We are apt to think of the past as dead, the future as nonexistent, [and] the present alone as real." Of course such an easy distinction cannot be made. The past is prologue; it underscores the present and conditions the future. Since myth has so often provided the inner logic of American history, it would be illogical to think that myths do not continue. Today perhaps the most significant long-term issues based in American mythology are ecology and energy, the American middle class, women, and the false yet believed notions which still obscure a clear understanding of blacks and Indians in contemporary America.

There are today but precious few wilderness areas where one can still view the beauty of the American landscape as it must first have appeared to the Native Americans more than 30,000 years ago. Long ago Americans seem to have lost touch with their respect for the land. Some historians have argued in fact that the conquering Europeans themselves brought with them a set of values and attitudes destined to bring on the desecration of that wilderness masterpiece known as the New World. Though they stood in awe of the New Land as a natural utopia, their Christian view that humans ought to subdue and have dominion over nature held the seeds of an arrogance which eventually grew beyond control in the fertile environment of the American paradise. Europeans brought with them also a commitment to the new scientific spirit which would one day ripen into what one observer has called the "myth of scientific supremacy"—the mistaken idea that science will always be able to rescue the nation from any impending crisis or disaster.

The mythical ideas which accompanied Europeans to the American continent contrasted sharply with those which had been long cultivated by the Indians who pioneered the land. As would be true not only in America but in other areas of the world at later times, European discovery, exploration, and colonization lacked the land-wisdom of the natives who were mastered. The cultural myths of the advancing Europeans were often considerably less sensitive to ecological matters than those of the so-called primitives they vanquished. Drawing on other examples, but nonetheless demonstrating the point, one scholar has noted: "It is interesting to discover that the impact on environments as fragile as the Eskimo's arctic habitat or the desert of the Kalahari bushmen in Africa is minimal until an introduced culture displaces the original mythological [beliefs]."[1] As the white frontier moved across the green landscape and engulfed the Indians in America, much the same process of "an introduced culture" replacing "the original mythological beliefs" took place. From the beginning, the new Americans ignored much that they might have learned from the Native Americans. In the end, both land and people were the victims of their error.

Later generations of Americans would have great difficulty keeping their utopian dreams within reason. Following the impulses which Europeans had passed on as a cultural inheritance, they set out across the inviting continent with energy to spare. Ironically, their utopian visions of the virgin land caused them eventually to abuse the very landscape they loved:

> It was the intoxicating profusion of the American continent which induced a state of mind that made waste and plunder inevitable. A temperate continent, rich in soils and minerals and forests and wildlife, enticed men to think in terms of infinity rather than facts, and produced an overriding fallacy that was nearly our undoing—the Myth of Superabundance. According to the myth, our resources were inexhaustible. It was an assumption that made wise management of the land and provident husbandry superfluous.[2]

Pioneers, Mountain Men, circuit riders, trappers, missionaries, cowboys, miners, cattlemen, and farmers—all inhaled the invigorating atmosphere of the new land while at the same time holding to an American mythology which would prove destructive of nature. The winning of the many Wests that America had to offer would in the end mean an environmental loss for the nation. In place of the many Indian myths and legends which affirmed humanity's ties to the sacred earth by telling of the original creation of humans out of earth, clay, or wood, white America developed the folklore of Paul Bunyan who

> swung his acre of hand and slapped the impudent river sprawlin'. He knocked a dozen twists out of it that he did. Then what did he do but grab a mountain in both fists, tear it up by the roots, and heave it down so it covered Big Auger Valley, and damned the rebellious river's course.[3]

Though the mythology of Paul Bunyan, like that of the cowboy, did not develop until the frontier was disappearing, it nonetheless symbolized already developed attitudes toward nature.

America's fanciful, Paul Bunyan-style approach to the continent's abundance of nature came gradually to be reinforced by its embracement of science and technology in the latter part of the nineteenth century. Predictably, a tension between love of comfort which advancing civilization would bring and love of the land consistently offered the nation difficult choices between what one observer has called the "machine" and the "garden." Expanding technology and the quest to maintain a green republic have long been on a collision course. Yet, determining whether the nation should stake its future on industrial progress or preservation of nature has consistently been a decision which Americans have avoided. Instead, they have contended that the two might be creatively combined. America's late nineteenth-century attempt to somewhat mythically portray the nation's cities as new frontiers is a particularly apt case in point.

In the years between the Civil War and the First World War America's urban population expanded sevenfold as the nation's Horatio Algers took to the city in search of fame and respectability. As early as 1870, in the opinion of one contemporary observer, "city folks" were becoming the "heroes and heroines" of an increasingly urbanized America. Indeed, a little more than a century later the nation's cities had become an "urban wilderness," but not in the frontier sense that those who had first envisioned the urban centers of the nation had anticipated. The vast expanse of city upon city, stretching from Boston to Washington, D.C., which the French scholar Jean Gottman called "megalopolis"—in memory of the utopian city which the Greeks centuries before had dreamed would be the envy of the world—had become the scene of blight, crime, the collective effects of smoke and fog (smog), and in general, a sore on the body of the nation. Extravagant industrial progress had brought urban sprawl, city freeway systems which monopolized close to one third of urban real estate, ghetto conditions in the inner cities, and an assortment of evils ranging from inefficient public services to the bankruptcy of city treasuries. But even while becoming more and more sensitive to such urban decay, the nation has also had to face the realities of an energy crisis which threatens the old myths of both scientific supremacy and superabundance. During the early 1970s, for example, the nation became concerned for the sea around it (Rachel Carson had urged this concern as early as 1950), and to the possibilities of "ecocatastrophe" for planet earth (which Stanford biology professor Paul Ehrlich was predicting). At the same time, however, President Gerald Ford vetoed a bill which would have severely limited the continued use of strip-mining techniques. Obviously, the old tensions remained between long-range human needs and economic "progress." Indeed the nation is still faced with decisive choices as to just what kind of utopia America ought to become.

The Myths of the Middle Class

As an alternative to the deteriorating conditions of megalopolis—overpopulation, a corruption of individual and social values, and environmental decay—Americans have sought the creation of a new utopia in the nation's suburbs. Statistically, in fact, the suburbanite is today the typical American. The latest expression of the time-honored traditions of grassroots America, the suburbs are nonetheless usually seen as symbols of a new set of directions and values for the nation. To its supporters, suburbia projects an image of solid, Christian, American virtues. It is a green oasis populated by the silent majority. To its detractors, however, it is the epitome of the crass middle class—America through the looking glass. Thus, whether the new suburban America is the nation's best hope for the future, or a center of confusion, conformity, and a preoccupation with conspicuous consumption remains open to debate. The current folklore of suburbia, of course, usually suggests that salvation is not likely to be found in the miniature metropolis. Slowly coming to be plagued by the same variety of problems which haunt the larger cities, and being an artificial attempt to recapture what used to be small-town life in America, the suburbs have in many respects forfeited individuality and allowed a sense of community to disappear—both supposedly detrimental to democracy.

If these traditional views of suburbia are carried to extremes, however, they rather quickly become mythical. As many recent studies have shown, America's suburban communities are not middle-class ghettoes of rootlessness, escapist promiscuity, and creaking conservative dullness. Indeed, despite the legendary veneer of conformity—both among the communities themselves and those who live there—on closer examination the suburbs of America offer striking differences in class structures, political ideology, life-styles, and racial composition. In the words of sociologist Bennett M. Berger, "the myth of a homogeneous 'suburbia' . . . for a long time obscured, and to some extent still obscures, the actual variety of suburban life."[4]

Perhaps the most interesting feature about the myth of suburban uniformity, however, is the appeal it has found among a wide variety of Americans—supporters and detractors alike. Those of a chamber-of-commerce–realtor point of view, for example, have gushed over the image of suburbia as truly reflecting the American way of life. Pointing to the image

with civic pride, they imply that their status in the new utopia is deserved since they are the heirs to the American tradition of free enterprise. Many local business people, CPAs, bankers, doctors, and dentists like the mythical idea of suburbia, in short, because it is that which supports their status and privileged condition in contemporary society. Unsympathetic to this view, "city planners, architects, urban design people and so on could use the myth of suburbia," says Bennett Berger, "to warn that those agglomerations of standardized, vulgarized, mass-produced cheerfulness which masqueraded as homes would be the slums of tomorrow. Liberal and left-wing culture-critics could (and did) use the myth of suburbia to launch an attack on complacency, conformity, and mass culture."[5] In the end, suburban mythology has grown both because of supporters who love it and want to believe in its existence for purposes of maintaining the status quo, and critics who have allowed it to serve as an object of scorn, wishing that it would pass away.

While defenders and critics have carried on their debate about the merits and demerits of the alleged conformity of suburbia, they have seldom been at all challenged in their views by the people who actually live there. Debate has been somewhat silenced because for Americans generally the tendency has been to believe strongly in the myth of suburbia as a means of confirming the mythical notion of the melting pot in a modern setting. In the nation's suburbs, it seems, a unified American culture at last has been created. In a society offering so much variety in religion, class, race, and ethnic composition, the idea that there are after all "typical Americans," and that they can be found in the suburbs, has had wide-ranging appeal. The conflict which Americans see around them every day—rich versus poor, white versus black, management versus labor—seems to dissolve when one's thoughts turn to the mellow, comfortable conformity of the suburbs. There, supposedly, conflict is absent and everyone is preciously American. All can pretend that they have stepped inside the cover of the *Saturday Evening Post*. Again Bennett Berger writes:

> The myth of suburbia fosters an image of a homogeneous and classless America

without a trace of ethnicity but fully equipped for happiness by the marvelous productivity of American industry: the ranch house with the occupied two-car garage, the refrigerator and freezer, the washer and dryer, the garbage disposal and the built-in range and dishwasher, the color TV and the hi-fi stereo. Suburbia: its lawns firm, its driveways clean, its children happy on its curving streets and in its pastel schools. Suburbia, California style, is America.[6]

America has always been less a *United* States than believers in the myth of the melting pot have usually been willing to grant. And the myth of the suburbs is simply the latest attempt, by a nation increasingly beset with complex political, economic, and social differences, to convince itself that America is just one big happy family. The myth of suburbia has found wide acceptance simply because it has rekindled a belief in other elements of American mythology. Suburban mythology offers the impression that America is a land unified under the banner of progress and perfectability. The myth suggests that America has found a magic formula whereby achievement has always been rewarded yet equality faithfully preserved—women, blacks, and Indians notwithstanding.

The American Woman

There is an interesting relationship between the forces of myth which have helped to shape suburbia and those which today work to keep women "in their place." Increasingly aware that an elaborate social mythology has long worked to keep women out of the mainstream of American life, social critics are only beginning to discover how "the move to the suburbs . . . was a moved based on a view of women's role as being pretty well nonexistent outside the family. It accepted a picture of the world as divided between man, the breadwinner, and woman, the homemaker."[7] As America began its move to the suburbs, then, it did so secure in the knowledge that women's place was in the home. A clear separation of women from the world of work—secure in their suburban oasis—seldom allowed for the possibility that

a woman's career could be anything other than that of mother and housewife. The mythical suburb, in short, became the perfect setting for the mythical woman. But the mythologizing of women, though expressed more recently in the myths of suburbia, has long been a major enterprise in America.

It is revealing that American mythology itself has usually portrayed women as second-class citizens. Indeed, despite their numerical majority in American society, women have seldom been credited with contributing much to the legendary development of the nation. In America's historical folklore, for example, heroes have by quite a margin outnumbered heroines. Legend tells of Molly Pitcher of Revolutionary War fame, who at the Battle of Monmouth (June 28, 1778) is said to have carried water to patriotic fighting men and inspired them to greater efforts. It tells as well of Betsy Ross, who upon orders from General Washington obediently plied her talents as a seamstress to sew the nation's first flag. In both cases, of course, Americans have seen fit only to heroize women who fit society's preconceived notions of what a "true" woman ought to be like. Chaste, submissive, and relegated to the fringe of historical importance, Molly Pitcher and Betsy Ross can be safely designated heroines because their heroics were cast as secondary to those of dominant males. Only to the degree that they display a noble dedication to their social role as "homey" types—providing the nation in time of great need the assistance of "womanly skills"—have women ever been allowed anywhere near the inner sanctum of the American hall of fame.

Much the same kind of polarization of the sexes can be seen in contemporary American popular culture. Here, male characters—whether in movies, television, comic books, or the funnies—are almost always self-sufficiently engaged in a solitary journey of adventure. What modern feminists have come to call the "macho mystique," the overemphasis on manliness, demands that the male hero always stand alone in his rendezvous with crisis and adventure. Commenting on this male-centered hero worship, Jules Feiffer, in *The Great Comic Book Heroes*, has noted the fundamental difference in American folklore between the "sissy" and the "man" and the role of women with respect to both:

A sissy wanted girls who scorned him, a man scorned girls who wanted him. Our cultural opposite of the man who didn't make out with women has never been the man who did—but rather, the man who could if he wanted to, but still didn't. The ideal of masculine strength, whether Gary Cooper's, Li'l Abner's, or Superman's, was for one to be so virile and handsome, to be in such a position of strength that he need never go near girls except to help them. And then get the hell out. Real rapport was not for women.[8]

To the degree that the expressions of such popular culture reflect American social attitudes at large, one can legitimately conclude that the nation harbors antifeminine sentiments. And in the stereotyped figures of popular fiction, as a further example, women usually emerge not as unique human beings but rather as pathetic figures. As a specific case in point, in traditional Westerns, such as Owen Wister's *The Virginian*, the cowboy is a dashing, hardy soul of admirable virtue and strength while "the Eastern belle's role is that of a glorified horse. A woman in the Western drama is somebody to rescue, somebody to protect."[9] Calm and straightforward dignity is, apparently, a male monopoly. Whether it be semiserious literature such as Wister's or the antics of Superman, a real rapport between men and women has usually been lacking. Superstar status invariably has been reserved for men, with female characters little more than satellites. Indeed, American mythology reflects many of the same kind of social attitudes found in the so-called real world— the complementary myths of male superiority and female inferiority.

Blacks and Indians

The plight of black Americans in American society has been that of the "invisible man." Kept "down on the plantation" early in the history of the republic, and until recently segregated socially, politically, and educationally from the mainstream of American life, the black has at best been a shadowy and hazy figure not allowed to play a significant role in the nation's history. Appearances of blacks

were most often limited to the obscurity of poverty-stricken rural homesteads, or among fellow blacks in the country's ghettoes, or as caricatures. The Sambo-like movie personality Stepin Fetchit symbolized the image of blacks Hollywood projected in the early years of the twentieth century. And through the days of radio's popularity the white middle class was allowed to visualize the black American only as a faint figure in the style of Rochester, a favorite of "The Jack Benny Show," or Kingfish and Sapphire on "Amos 'n' Andy." The political awareness and ethnic pride expressed in "Black is Beautiful," which took hold in the 1960s, has had the effect of sketching in at least a bit more of the diversity and complexity of the black experience in America. But while the civil rights efforts of Julian Bond, Rev. Jesse Jackson, Dr. Martin Luther King, Jr., and others forced White America to recognize the black American as something other than an invisible man, a spin-off from this movement has been the rise of a new black mythology at times as fradulent as the one it replaced.

With a sizeable share of American white society feeling pangs of guilt over the multitude of injustices committed against blacks in the past, and with blacks themselves experiencing a vigorous new sense of worth about their race, a frenzy of activity has occurred. During the 1960s and 1970s attempts were made at all levels of the nation's educational establishment, for example, to incorporate relevant materials into curriculums through the addition of "Black History," "Black Culture," and "Black Studies" programs. But while the study of the black experience was long overdue, and while such ventures recognized a legitimate and urgent academic need, the tendency has been toward overcompensation and myth-building. Mythology, apparently, knows no color line. For a new historical tale is being told of the black in America, one often mixed with romance, distortion, legend, inflated claims, and the making of instant heroes out of men and women of meager accomplishment. Afro-American history, to meet the fashions of the day, has created a highly questionable situation where as one scholar says "a great many philosophical descendants of Parson Weems are abroad in the land, hard at work on separate but equal black fables to match such stories as the one about George Washington and the cherry tree."[10] Though presented with the relatively unique situation of being offered the opportunity to write a "myth-free" history, since so little of significance has been written on the topic in the past, recent scholars, both black and white, have instead on many occasions served anyone who might read or listen a liberal helping of historical fabrication. There have of course been blacks of remarkable achievement in the nation's past—the black rights advocate Richard Allen, the political activist Frederick Douglass, the scholar-journalist William E. B. DuBois, and the scholar-diplomat Ralph Bunche to name only a few—but simply to supplant the mythical "inferior-Negro" with an equally mythical "super-Negro" can serve no good end. Among those possessing intellectual honesty, such extravagance cannot be condoned. And even those of a radical point of view should see that to follow the primrose paths of legend would be to repeat the mistakes of earlier, "honky history." To lionize the obscure and the questionable in the black experience—as has been the case with Crispus Attucks for example—does little but compromise historical accuracy, and point once again to the element of myth in American history.

As with blacks, the historical myths and legends which have always fogged the nation's understanding of the American Indians continue to be factors at work in contemporary society. The stereotypes of the Indian as Bloodthirsty Savage or Noble Red Man have lost little of their basic appeal. Even though America has changed, and the Indian has changed with it over the decades, the images of the First Americans remain in many ways the same. If any change has occurred, it would be that the original stereotypes have become scrambled, to the point where the nation feels more comfortable in believing both at the same time. Americans do not find it inconsistent to view the Indian as simultaneously appealing and menacing. One historian has expressed this continued tension toward the Indian particularly well:

To many people, the typical Indian was the Plains Indian, a painted brave in full regalia, trailing a war bonnet, astride a horse which he rode bareback, sweeping down upon a wagon train, in glorious technicolor.[11]

In actuality, this picturesque portrait of the Indian distorts history for many reasons. Aside from the fact that the Plains Indian was neither completely a fierce warrior nor a Noble Red Man, the era was but one of the many stages of Indian experience during the nation's historical development. While it is accurate to say that after the Civil War two thirds of the Indians who survived the onslaught of white settlement belonged to the Great Plains civilization, one must not after all forget about the other one third nor that even among those of the Great Plains cultural development was enormously varied. In addition, while it is true that the introduction of the horse by the Spaniards caused a veritable revolution in the Indians' style of living, it must be remembered that the horse was not always used as an instrument of warfare. The use of the horse did allow the Indian to better transport his culture westward just one step ahead of the tide of white settlement—though often, of course, his movement was not fast enough to suit white Americans. It allowed him as well to better hunt the buffalo and thus meet his need for shelter, food, and clothing.

America's ability to live with two images of the Indians in the twentieth century has of course been ably assisted by Hollywood. Early attempts by the cinema to depict the saga of the American West were limp attempts, at best, to tell the truth about the Indian in white society. Movies such as *Stagecoach* were exercises in the reinforcement of a mythology about the first Americans. "Classics" such as this must bear much of the responsibility for making a mockery of Indian character for modern America. The motion picture industry has, to be sure, attempted to make amends for its past errors. It has tried to go back to the historical sources rather than continue to rely any longer on the old bankrupt Hollywood myths. Films began to show the Indian in a more sympathetic light as early as 1950 in the film *Broken Arrow*. In 1964, John Ford, who earlier had directed *Stagecoach*, somewhat redeemed himself with *Cheyenne Autumn* which offered much more of an Indian point of view than Ford's earlier work. Yet, even in its attempts to compensate for past wrongs, Hollywood tends merely to revitalize the quaint nobility of the original Americans. In other words, one well-known stereotype is replaced by another.

Even as one becomes aware that the old mythical Indian remains alive and well, it is necessary to note that new attitudes have developed concerning the Native Americans both among themselves and with what the writer D. H. Lawrence called their "mystic enemy"—White America. An Indian occupation of Alcatraz Island in November, 1969, "by the right of discovery," for example, strongly reflected an awareness of myths about themselves, both old and new. They had come to Alcatraz, they said, because it "already had all the necessary features of a reservation: dangerously uninhabitable buildings; no fresh water; inadequate sanitation; and the certainty of total unemployment. They said they were planning to make the five full-time caretakers wards of a Bureau of Caucasian Affairs, and offered to take this troublesome real estate off the white man's hands for $24, payment to be made in glass beads."[12] But as contemporary Indians have tried to persuade America to reject the fantasy that they belong only to the past century, and suggest that they are a reality of today, they are confronted with new stereotypes complementary to the old ones. What the nineteenth-century social critic, Helen Hunt Jackson, long ago called "centuries of dishonor" toward the Indian continues. Their historical legacy has been further buried beneath the image of the Indians collectively as a "vanishing race" and the individual Indian as a "lazy, good-for-nothing"—convenient stereotypes indeed for a society which has never been willing fully to confront its mythology. The American Indian continues to be the victim of white stereotyping and misunderstanding.

SECTION I: PROBLEMS IN PARADISE: ECOLOGY AND ENERGY

A nation's collective mythology contains its fundamental traditions, values, and sacred ideas. An analysis of a society's cultural myths, as anthropologists discovered long ago,

offers the sensitive observer insights into both the history and current attitudes of its social groups. As one scholar recently put the matter:

> Universally, both historic and current cultures have used mythology, ritual and folklore to record, reinforce and pass on to succeeding generations the ethics, values and morality deemed necessary for a practical way of life.[13]

Like all national myths, an examination of the myths of America not only help one understand the nation's past, but also to comprehend the meaning of America today. And perhaps no better example of the influence of mythology as both shaping and reflecting the intellectual and practical habits of contemporary America exists than in the areas of ecology and energy. Dominant forces in American life, including the mythology of Christianity, the nation's longstanding love affair with science and technology, and the frontier experience, have all combined to create the country's contemporary environmental predicament.

Christian Mythology and "Arrogance Toward Nature"

Understandably, one might think Christianity a somewhat curious contributor to the present ecologic and energy crises. In the opinion of Lynn White, Jr., a distinguished professor of history at UCLA, however, it has come to profoundly influence both. A scholar of the Middle Ages and the European Renaissance, White has concluded that the insensitivities displayed by Americans toward the problems of ecology are deeply rooted in the historical traditions of Western civilization. Striking at one of the most subtle and sophisticated sources of the ecologic crisis, White has claimed that it is the religious attitudes of American and all Western society which are most to blame for the critical state of the nation's environment. The religious mythology of Christianity, specifically the idea of "arrogance toward nature," lies at the core of modern America's ecology problems. It seems to White that America's unnatural treatment of nature is in some measure due to the biblical grant to humans of domination over the earth. In the Judeo-Christian myth of the creation, found in the opening chapter of Genesis, the relationship of human to nature is made clear. It states that after God created "every living creature," "winged fowl," and "the beast of the earth after his kind," He then turned to His most creative act:

> And God said, Let us make man in our image, after our likeness: and let them have dominion over the fish of the sea, and over the fowl of the air, and over the cattle, and over all the earth, and over every creeping thing that creepeth upon the earth. . . . And God blessed them, and God said unto them, Be fruitful, and multiply, and replenish the earth, and subdue it: and have dominion over the fish of the sea, and over the fowl of the air, and over every living thing that moveth upon the earth.[14]

Like Christians everywhere, Americans have taken the word of the Bible as God's command. America has embraced the world's most human-centered religion and has remained proud of its Christian tradition. By accepting the notion that humanity is the height of creation, the nation developed an arrogance toward nature. "While many of the world's mythologies provide stories of creation," White has concluded, "Christianity . . . not only established a dualism of man and nature but also insisted that it is God's will that man exploit nature for his proper ends."[15] As heirs to Christian mythology, Americans were destined to remain in harmony with one of the dominant ideas in the Western world, however out of step they might be with the physical realities around them.

With the growth and acceptance of the Christian myth that God's plan explicitly called for the control of nature by humanity, then, the assumption prevailed, first in Western Europe and later in America, that ruthlessness toward the physical world was in keeping with religious doctrine. The so-called pagan belief that plants and animals enjoyed a spirit or soul gave way to the appealing belief that only humans were so blessed. Again in the words of White: "The spirits *in* natural objects, which formerly had protected nature from man, evaporated. Man's effective monopoly on spirit in this world was con-

firmed, and the old inhibitions to the exploitation of nature crumbled."[16] Despoliation began in the Middle Ages. By 1285 it was reported that the city of London was already suffering from a smog problem caused by the burning of soft coal. The case cannot be made of course that the Bible caused the environmental problems of thirteenth-century London, but it is possible nonetheless that the mythically based attitudes of Christianity helped shape the point of view that the land and its resources existed only for human exploitation.

The Myth of Scientific Supremacy

From the tradition that humanity was superior to its natural surroundings, yet another of the notions critical to an insensitive and arrogant attitude toward nature developed. A faith in science and technology also contributed to the modern world's ecologic crisis. During one of the high points of Christianity—the Middle Ages—technology began to flower. In about the eleventh century, subsistence farming, which was based on a precarious cycle of agricultural production and consumption, gave way to technological progress. Beginning with the development of such new agricultural methods and implements as the moldboard plow, people eventually were able to produce more than they could consume. While these early scientifically inspired improvements helped immeasurably to increase productivity and caused a revolution in nutrition, they had the negative effect of alienating northern European peasants from their former close and intimate associations with nature. "Distribution of land was based no longer on the needs of a family, but, rather, on the capacity of a power machine to till the earth," says Lynn White. "Man's relation to the soil was profoundly changed. Formerly man had been part of nature; now he was the exploiter of nature."[17] Over the course of centuries the sensational successes of science in the service of technology would eventually lead to a social attitude that one twentieth-century observer has called the "myth of scientific supremacy"—the comforting but false belief that science has the potential to correct all the errors of the past at some golden moment in the future. An intellectual pattern which allowed the Christian-technological attitude to flourish—that ruthlessness toward nature could be both religiously and practically condoned—was thus established early.

The European attitude of humanity's inherent right to subdue the natural environment was firmly entrenched by the time Europeans conquered the "fresh, green breast" of the New World. The spread of Christian ideas was in fact one of the driving motives behind the age of discovery, exploration, and settlement. And science and technology, which had already become sacred words in the European vocabulary, played a critical role in expanding the influence of the Old World to the New. Not surprisingly, the New World Indian culture which the Europeans encountered, being both non-Christian and nonscientific, was immediately labeled "primitive." Despite the fact that Native Americans had for centuries lived by a mystical awareness of the interrelationship between humans and the Great Spirit of the physical world, they struck Europeans as "savages." Ironically, then, the Indian's reverence toward nature helped not only to create the Noble Red Man stereotype, but helped as well to reinforce the image held by early Christian explorers and discoverers that the Indian was a pagan devil. The European mythologies of Christianity and science helped sustain the idea that, like nature itself, the Indian should be arrogantly exploited by white Christian conquerors. Indeed, wherever white civilization expanded across the American continent, white arrogance toward nature would eventually destroy the great variety of Indian cultures which through centuries of ritual, folklore, and mythology had built the idea that an awareness of nature's sacredness was normal. It is only recently that many white Americans have come to see that few have surpassed the Native Americans' wisdom concerning relationships between humans and nature.

Frontier Mythology and Ecological Values

Imported ideas from Europe, however, only partially explain the historical sources for America's present environmental problems. As Americans pushed westward the frontier experience itself contributed in important ways to an already insensitive attitude toward the land. In the early years of the republic, Americans accepted the idea that the region stretching from the Mississippi River to the Rocky Mountains was the Great American Desert. The nation was saddled with the mythical belief that the trans-Mississippi area was one of vast desolation, a desert barrier, whose landscape should scarcely be crossed, much less settled and preserved. Based on the reports of early government explorations, such as that of Zebulon Pike in 1810, and periodically reinforced by hardy pioneers who had crossed the plains in the deadly heat of summer, the image of the West as a forbidding wilderness prevailed for decades. In the course of time, however, the myth of the Great American Desert gradually gave way to the idea that the Great Plains were, in reality, an agricultural utopia. As explained by Henry Nash Smith in *Virgin Land: The American West as Symbol and Myth:*

> As settlement moved up the valleys of the Platte and the Kansas rivers, the myth of the desert was destroyed and in its stead the myth of the garden of the world was projected out across the plains. . . . The myth had behind it the momentum of fifteen hundred miles of frontier advance across the Mississippi Valley. In addition, it coincided with the economic interest of every landowner in Kansas and Nebraska, and of every business enterprise in these new states.[18]

With dreams of an agricultural paradise now stimulating them, and further encouraged to move into the unsettled land by the Homestead Act of 1862, Americans moved into the virgin plains area with new enthusiasm.

Filled with a new utopian optimism, and blessed at the outset with a series of wet years which seemed to confirm their vision of the West as a land of milk and honey, western frontiersmen soon trampled the barriers of nature in search of "free land," adventure, and an economic fulfillment of the American Dream. Thereafter believing that the open land offered unlimited chances for opportunity, Americans conquered a series of trans-Mississippi frontiers with seldom a thought as to the damage their conquest was bringing to the national landscape. Frontier legend soon made it appear that the Garden of the West was a horn of plenty whose resources would somehow always replenish themselves. The West became a national symbol for the "second chance," continued renewal, and endless opportunity for personal success. Natural abundance, it seemed, had made Americans a people of plenty. As a consequence, the western frontier exerted a telling impact on the nation's folklore, national character, and traditions. Conveniently, Americans found religious, intellectual, political, economic, and geographical reasons for their exploitation and destruction of the natural environment of the frontier. It seemed the destiny of an expanding Christian republic to subdue the land in the name of God, science, and country.

"After we won our independence, the making of land-myths became a national pastime," according to John F. Kennedy's secretary of the interior, Stewart L. Udall. "The mythmakers infected our politics and produced the Go West and Manifest Destiny movements. As long as men were convinced that our continent was a succession of pastures of plenty, they would attempt great and foolhardy deeds, and their forward thrust would ultimately move beyond Jefferson's Louisiana Purchase."[19] Enticed by the openness, beauty, and lavish richness of the continent, Americans ignored the elementary laws of nature. No matter how many buffalo were shot, there seemed to "always be more where those came from." The assault on the land was being carried out by pioneers who had convinced themselves that they were patriotic instruments of civilization. The consequences of the misuse of the land and of the destruction of the wildlife which for centuries had roamed its seemingly endless panoramic vastness was seldom to be understood in realistic terms.

The great American compaign to subdue the land and plunder its resources was further carried out in order to starve the Plains Indians, to assure an open range for the free-enterprise activities of the cattlemen, to provide safe routes for railroad development, and to provide the growing nation a steady diet of adventure and entertainment. All of this, however, had come at great expense. General Philip Sheridan of Civil War fame gave voice to the illusions of the nation as he stood before the Texas state legislature during the 1870s. His remarks concerned attempts to make the buffalo an extinct species, and thus bring starvation to Indians, but his words reflected the American attitude toward nature in general: "Let them kill, skin and sell until the buffalo is exterminated, as it is the only way to bring about lasting peace and allow civilization to advance." To Americans who today face the last quarter of the twentieth century, the words of Philip Sheridan ring hollow indeed. For the generations who settled the land in the nineteenth century, however, they conveniently served as a romantic sugarcoating over the bitter heritage they would leave behind.

Challenges to the Myths

The rapid growth of the national economy in the post-Civil War period stimulated such intoxicating illusions of prosperity that unthinking and ruthless exploitation of the West's natural resources was only occasionally seriously questioned. Only a few issued warnings that arrogance toward nature could only result in waste and a diminished quality for the available land. One such individual was John Wesley Powell, director of the federal Survey of the Rocky Mountain Region. After leading a party of naturalists and surveyors to the mountains, mesas, and canyons of the Colorado Plateau country after the Civil War, Powell hoped to replace the myths of the frontier with a more realistic attitude toward the true nature and limitations of land in the West. Supported by funds provided by Congress and the Smithsonian Institution, Powell sought to instruct Americans in the proper use of the environment, but it was only much later that they came to appreciate his pioneer efforts to save the land. He lived only to see the myth of the Great American Desert give way to the myth of the West as the Garden of the World. As one historian has explained:

> Men who had never been west of the Mississippi—dime novelists, artists, eastern politicians, and others—aided the creation of this romanticized picture of the West. Few and far between were men like Major Powell, dedicated to spreading knowledge based on scientific field investigation. Instead, Americans quickly

forgot one false idea in favor of another; the concept of an implacable western desert gave way to the concept of a West waiting to fulfill the American dream of free land developed by free individuals for the betterment of all.[20]

Powell's expeditions to the West led him to the conclusion that the nation's natural resources were not inexhaustible, but few responded to the alarm he sounded. Through such official publications of the U.S. Geographical Survey as his *Report on the Lands of the Arid Region of the United States* (1878), Powell advised that the semiarid West lacked sufficient rainfall to become a paradise, but most people ignored his words. Instead, the Garden of the West became the scene of untold waste, wanton destruction, and insensitive land mismanagement. "Because of his knowledge of the essentials of Western living," one observer has said, "Powell was an instinctive enemy of the myths and the mythmakers. In a harsh and inhospitable land men would court disaster, unless they came to terms with nature."[21] Though his vision would one day serve as an important basis for the conservation movement, it was not until the twentieth century that Americans came to understand the full import of Powell's warnings of a vanishing frontier.

By the time of John Wesley Powell's death at Haven, Maine, in 1902, and despite his strenuous efforts to counteract the myths of old, the nation was already thoroughly indoctrinated with what Stewart Udall would later call the "myth of superabundance." The reckless era of Manifest Destiny, fed by the false pride of both individuals and the nation, had made many areas of America a wasteland and had caused mass plunder of the nation's physical and animal resources. The cherished yet shortsighted notion that progress was inevitable had prompted tobacco and cotton farmers to wear out their farmsteads, loggers to strip many a forest, and fishermen to believe that salmon would always come leaping up the rivers of the Pacific Northwest. The orgy of waste found perhaps its most insane expression, however, in the oil boom which gripped the country beginning in the 1860s. Aside from the fact that oil technology was crude—causing oil producers, for example, to allow natural gas deposits which they had discovered to escape untapped in the open air—the myth was almost universally held that oil was continually and rather rapidly being formed beneath the earth's surface and was thus inexhaustible. Oil capitals such as Titusville, Pennsylvania, Tulsa, Oklahoma, and Kilgore, Texas, became outposts for the sacred American belief that each individual had the right to follow his own economic self-interest even to the point of raping the land. While the myth of economic individualism remained alive and well, however, natural resources were slowly being depleted.

A few other conservationists in addition to John Wesley Powell punched holes in the myth of superabundance even though they failed to destroy it. As early as the age of Thomas Jefferson, for example, the southern crusader Edmund Ruffin—the self-styled cavalier of the antebellum South—had taken his stand in support of the idea that something had to be done immediately to change the land misuse habits of his fellow Virginia planters. Greatly concerned over the already evident patterns of land waste, soil erosion, and senseless farming practices, Ruffin became a forceful spokesman for contour plowing, better drainage systems, crop rotation, and soil restoration through the use of lime fertilizers.

Other nineteenth-century Americans, both in theory and practice, offered alternative choices to growing ecological insanity and the myth of superabundance. There was the famous naturalist John James Audubon, for example, who through his collected paintings of birds, published in 1839, sought to create a greater feeling of respect toward this form of American wildlife while at the same time furthering the idea that nature might more properly be the object of study than conquest. Mormon settlers in the Salt Lake Basin during the late 1840s also must be credited with displaying an admirable sensitivity toward the land. Believing that the land was the Lord's, not man's to subdue but to use, they transformed their desert environment, by copying ancient Indian irrigation techniques, into a bountiful landscape through sensible land-management practices.

Scientist, diplomat, and naturalist George Perkins Marsh was another of America's early spokesmen for greater wisdom in managing the land. While serving as President Zachary

Taylor's minister to Turkey in the late 1840s, and Abraham Lincoln's envoy to Italy beginning in 1861, Marsh became acutely aware of what careless exploitation of the land had done to reduce formerly great nations to impoverished status. Part of the reason Rome and other empires fell, he concluded, was because they had blindly exhausted the environment which had served as a basis for their early greatness. Having personally witnessed the grim cycle of drought, flood, and erosion at work in the area of the Mediterranean, Marsh published his famous *Man and Nature* in 1864, which questioned man's "treacherous warfare on his natural allies." Marsh warned that "the earth is fast becoming an unfit home for its noblest inhabitant, and another era of equal human crime and human improvidence . . . would reduce it to such a condition of impoverished productiveness, of shattered surface, of climatic excess, as to threaten the depravation, barbarism, and perhaps even extinction of the species." Though Perkins was a prophet of conservation and ecological sanity, his *Man and Nature* would only later have a profound impact on his native land. For Gifford Pinchot, who read his book while a college student during the 1880s, however, the effect was more immediate.

Of urban background and considerable wealth, Pinchot might at first glance appear a curious challenger to the myth of superabundance. Reared in the environment of New York City, his family's country estate, Phillips Exeter Academy, and Yale University, Pinchot seems to have gained his first taste for the need to protect the natural environment from his father, James Pinchot, who during family trips abroad had been much impressed by forest-management practices in Europe. Urged by his father to pursue the study of forestry after graduation from Yale, the younger Pinchot responded by returning to Europe where through the influence of the German forester, Sir Deitrich Brandis, he enrolled at the French Forest School in Nancy, France. Drawing on his European education, Pinchot could see that the use of forest resources in the United States was governed by a set of old myths and misconceptions:

> He [Pinchot] questioned the idea generally accepted in the United States

that a forest had either to be cut and destroyed or preserved. Instead he believed that proper methods would permit commercially profitable logging and the preservation of the forests at the same time. In addition, he thought that good forestry depended on government control of private cutting.[22]

Pinchot would by historical chance find a practical outlet for his new found ideas. For just as he came upon his new knowledge, men of his social background and education were beginning to speak out for closer national governmental supervision over natural resources. Within the progressive movement Gifford Pinchot found a means of achieving his vision, and in his fellow New Yorker, Theodore Roosevelt, he found an ally for his cause.

Together, Gifford Pinchot and Theodore Roosevelt carried the message of conservation to the American people in a dramatic way. The progressive Roosevelt "dealt a decisive blow to the Myth of Superabundance," according to Stewart Udall, by giving the nation "new attitudes toward the land and a new appreciation of the nature of democratic government."[23] Roosevelt began by appointing Pinchot the nation's chief forester, and soon progressive conservation reached full stride. As a team they sought the scientific management of the nation's natural resources and environment. A White House Conservation Conference was held in 1908 to promote both individual and governmental conservation practices. Before the Roosevelt-Pinchot alliance came to an end with Roosevelt's retirement from the White House, the country witnessed a host of new national conservation policies governing the reclassification of public lands, reforestation programs, a substantial increase in National Forest acreage, soil-erosion abatement, and a vast expansion in the activities of the Forest Service. Pinchot is in fact credited with coining the term "conservation" to describe scientifically planned management of the total environment in the long-term interest of the American people. Pinchot and Roosevelt accomplished a great deal toward protecting and preserving the country's natural beauty, but in the process Congress, partially influenced by lumber interests, came to resent the president's con-

269

Nuclear Fission as Energy:
An expensive and controversial source of power
Los Angeles Times

sistent failure to seek its authorization for a good many of his actions. In addition, Roosevelt's leadership had become so forceful that it encouraged the public to adopt a "let-Teddy-do-it" attitude toward the nation's ongoing ecological problems. As a result, Americans tended to lapse back into old habits of land abuse once the Rough Rider rode from the scene. The hypnotic myth of superabundance staged a comeback not counteracted until the return of another Roosevelt to the White House.

The twenty-odd years between the presidencies of Theodore and Franklin Roosevelt was a period of gradual erosion of national awareness toward conservation problems. There were those, however, who continued the effort to dramatize the need for land revitalization. Senator George Norris of Nebraska, for example, authored federal development bills designed to initiate conservation measures at

Muscle Shoals on the lower Tennessee River. Norris' efforts in 1928 and 1931, however, were greeted by the presidential vetoes of both Calvin Coolidge and Herbert Hoover. Reviving the tired myths of rugged individualism and free enterprise, Hoover criticized the Norris bill on the grounds that it would "break down the initiative and enterprise of the American people." But even as Hoover was reciting the litany from the holy book of American mythology, the economic bankruptcy of the depression was accompanied by bankruptcy of the land as well. Rural poverty was not only eroding the spirit of the American people, but ecological disaster was spreading with each dust cloud that rose from the now drought-stricken Great Plains.

In the tradition of his distant cousin, Franklin D. Roosevelt attempted to make conservation, sound land-management practices, and the rehabilitation of the environment an integral part of his New Deal. Attempting to stem the nation's economic decline while at the same time arresting myth-inspired land abuse, his first "one hundred days in office" saw the establishment of the Tennessee Valley Authority and the Civilian Conservation Corps. The first measure authorized the development of flood-control and soil conservation projects, and the second supplied the labor force to attack erosion problems, plant two billion trees, assist in wildlife restoration, and build national park facilities. Later, a Soil Erosion Act (1935) and a Soil Conservation Act (1936) provided payments to farmers who maintained and restored the fertility of the soil. Through tree planting, land terracing, contour plowing, and the cultivation of soil-conserving crops such as soybeans in place of soil-depleting crops such as cotton, tobacco, and corn, two thirds of the nation's 16.8 million farmers participated in the country's first nationwide conservation effort. As had been the case in the past, however, America's new-found enthusiasm for a wise use of its natural environment largely evaporated once the crisis was thought to have passed. Franklin Roosevelt had tried to draw America's attention to its outdoor heritage, but conservation was neither a colorful campaign issue nor a glamorous theme upon which either politicians or the public seemed willing to focus its attention for long. Such organizations as the Sierra Club and the Izaak Walton League continued to keep their lonely vigil, and Secretary of the Interior Stewart Udall spoke out during the Kennedy Administration. It was not until the ecology consciousness and energy crisis of the 1970s, however, that Americans perhaps for the first time were forced to consider the difficult choices they would have to make between conservation and civilization.

The present energy crisis is but the latest in the areas of conservation and ecology. It is surely only the most recent chapter in a continuing story of the interaction of man and land in the New World. It is a chapter which is in the process of being written by the needs and habits of the American people. The energy crisis is indeed real. Once again, as in the past, the country is being asked to make a choice between human needs and those of the land. Unfortunately, the historical pattern to this point has surely been that when given such an option Americans have too often sided with the satisfaction of immediate over long-term human needs.

For the original settlers, both red and white, who experienced it, the new land of America was a utopia. And perhaps the day has already passed when America can any longer lay just claim to being, as Michael Drayton said centuries ago, "Earth's onely Paradise." Perhaps the mythical idea of America as nature's paradise would be a myth worth revitalizing. At least it would be a point from which to build a saner attitude toward the nation's wilderness resources.

SECTION II: THE MYTHS OF MIDDLE-CLASS AMERICA: MASS-MEN AND MAKE-BELIEVE

The great attraction of America has always been individual freedom. In turn, to most Americans individualism is the key factor assuring freedom as well as the fundamental concept binding their national identity. It is with this concept, in fact, that Americans appear to define their national consciousness; it serves as their central symbol of identification. Historians and sociologists have noted that America is a "land where individualism is the national faith," and that "of all peoples it was we who have led in the public worship of individualism."

The Myth of Individualism

Some Americans, however, have of late come to question the depth of the American commitment to individualism. But even for those willing to admit that mass conformity of contemporary society makes it increasingly difficult to practice individualism in modern America, the argument often still prevails that in some fabled portion of the nation's historic past men and women were able to achieve a great measure of personal freedom. This golden moment is usually thought to have been the period of America's nineteenth-century frontier development. It was supposedly the kind of exhilarating personal freedom, for example, that Mark Twain wrote about in *Huckleberry Finn* (1884). It was the kind of social and political individualism the historian Frederick Jackson Turner described in his famous paper, "The Significance of the Frontier in American History" (1893). Writers since Twain, however, have often remarked on the reluctance of Americans to follow Huck's lead "to light out for the territory," and historians since Turner have demonstrated that the overriding tendency of frontiersmen was to imitate older and time-tested political models. Walter Prescott Webb, combining good literature and history, for example, argued decades ago that the men, women, and children of the Great Plains frontier seized certain technological innovations to improve their lot, but showed little capacity for independence. "The status of the frontiersman as an independent thinker is questionable indeed," says Webb.[24] Perhaps it is unfair even to expect that the frontiersman should have been an independent thinker. Nonconformity implies the possibility of varied reactions to the same situation, and "the frontier with its rigorous conditions of life, was too exacting in its demands to allow of such choice for the frontiersman in the mode of his reaction."[25] In recent years, then, the alleged individualism of America's frontier past has been judged to be largely mythical. Scholars increasingly have come to see that the supposed individualism of the "out country" was more a condition of hardiness and stamina than of intellectual independence and personal self-expression. Contrary to its mythology, and judging from the experience of its hardy pioneers, the American heritage seems as much one of conformity as freedom. At the same time, and to an increasing number of observers, the equation of individualism with Americanism—whether past or present—is more myth than reality. Despite the preciously mythical notion that America has been a breeding ground for individualism, it seems more certain that conformity and a lack of real variety in American life has often been the case in the land of the free.

The idea that America is a nation of individualists is not only false when applied to mythologized Puritans, frontiersmen, and legendary Huckleberry Finns and Horatio Algers, but also certainly lacks justification in its application to the average contemporary middle-class American. The nation of "individualists"—today represented by the pseudo-America of *TV Guide*, Monday Night Football, shopping malls, Dial-a-Prayer, "Let's Make a Deal," TV dinners, and Miss America Pageants—seems rather a country of mass conformity. Indeed, at various times social critics have warned of the dangers of mass culture and the "sphere of public opinion" while others have fundamentally questioned the tastes of mass society and what has been called "the herd mentality." All of this, however, has seemingly had little effect on a contemporary America which continues strenuously to proclaim its individualism. It seemingly continues to believe fervently in what the novelist Henry Miller has pointedly called the "air-conditioned nightmare"—the often plastic world of conformity that somehow passes for freedom.

True to their history, modern Americans continue to mouth the rhetoric of individualism while at the same time practicing mass consumption and receiving their values from the mass media. But even though it is proper to sharply criticize American society for its pretensions about individualism, it seems equally clear that undue emphasis has at times been given the by-now familiar picture of American middle-class uniformity. A particularly well-etched mythology, related to the questions of individualism and conformity, for example, has arisen concerning American suburbia.

The Myth of Suburbia

As with so many of America's myths, those of suburbia perhaps first found expression in literature. Sloan Wilson's *The Man in the Gray Flannel Suit* gave fictional substance to the myth, while Peter De Vries in *The Mackerel Plaza*, Max Shulman in *Rally Round the Flag, Boys*, and John Updike in *Couples* caricatured mindless middle-class and suburban life. Academicians quickly followed in the tradition of De Vries, Shulman, and Updike, observing depressing images of Suburban Man—as if he or she were an archeological artifact—and noting the negative effects of suburban living on American values and attitudes:

> In the late 1950s, social critics began to find in suburbia the source of many of the ills they saw plaguing American society.

272

**Middle America: Suburban Blight
or Suburban Paradise?**
Thomas Airviews

And what one sociologist [Bennett M. Berger] called the myth of suburbia emerged. The fault, the myth ran, lay in the homogeneity of both the population and the lifestyle in the typical suburb. This sameness led to a mass culture and the apparent ethic of conformity that so concerned the critics.[26]

Studies such as William H. Whyte's *The Organization Man* (1956) criticized the way in which America's "utopian faith" in individualism was being slowly smothered by shallow suburbanites who revered individualism in theory but failed miserably to practice it. More recent scholarly studies of middle-class suburban communities, however, have been most notable for their rejection of this suburban myth. Columbia University's Herbert J. Gans, for example, author of the famous book, *The Levittowners* (1967), has

found the stereotypes of suburban communities lacking in many important respects. Based on findings compiled while living in the "bedroom community" of Levittown, near Philadelphia, Gans' sociological data clearly suggests that the American suburbs are not the "rootless" and "dull" outposts of middle-class conformity celebrated in mid-twentieth century literary and academic folklore.

There are a number of notions about suburban living that are more imaginary than real. First, suburban living is not a totally new phenomenon in American life. As early as the 1920s the growth rate of the suburbs began to outdistance that of the cities. In fact, during the 1880s, when the horsedrawn streetcar offered the first breakthrough in mass transit, many of the urban well-to-do began to abandon their former homesteads in fashionable city neighborhoods in favor of newly developing outlying areas where they could escape both the real and imagined problems of urban life. Not until after the Second World War, however, did the move to the suburbs began to receive serious attention from writers, sociologists, city planners, and historians; and with this increased attention a new form of American mythology was born.

Second, a crucial element of the suburban stereotype which lacks much solid basis in fact is its alleged rootlessness. Supposedly, the turnover among families in suburban communities is at such a rapid rate that little identification among the local citizens and their civic activities ever results. It is said that community involvement, civic pride, and eventually the process of democracy itself suffer because suburban Americans without local ties wander the countryside from one locale to another without ever staying long enough to sustain a commitment to the well-being of the community and the country at large. Suburbanites, statistically the typical Americans, supposedly have become a people of incurable wanderlust, and the nation in turn a country of transients.

Aside from the unproven assumptions in the rootless suburbia myth that strong and lasting ties to an area are in and of themselves good and population turnover is bad, the rootlessness of Americans is hardly a new phenomenon. History tells of the "roll of frontier, upon frontier, and on to the frontier beyond" as being a notable pattern of American population development during at least most of the nineteenth century. The American frontier, if you will, was continually settled by rootless individuals willing to cut ties with their former communities and move on. One is forced to wonder when the golden age of *rootedness*, for which critics of modern suburban mobility pine, was supposed to have occurred. Indeed, the United States may well be much better off today precisely because citizens of an earlier era refused to stay put. And in a related way, one would have a difficult time making convincing the argument that those in the past who were tied to specific areas and communities were by that fact alone better off for the experience. As much as rootedness in an older America may have contributed to a stirring sense of community consciousness, it also had the effect at times of frustrating the economic and social

mobility of those who found it impossible to leave the past behind and start anew. The rootedness which Sinclair Lewis described in such novels as *Main Street* and *Babbitt* is testimony to the psychological destructiveness and conformity which commitment to the local community can produce. The "village virus," as Lewis called small-town mindedness and boosterism, can be fatal. Roots can strangle individual and community growth as well as encourage it.

Third, the myth of rootless suburbia suffers from an overemphasis on how different the suburbs supposedly are in this regard compared to the population generally. National estimates of mobility suggest that approximately 20 percent of the American population moves annually—a figure which compares favorably with "normal" turnover figures in the nation's suburbs. Herbert Gans' study of Levittown, for example, notes that 27 percent of the first 1,800 families to move into that community were still in residence ten years later. A good many of the original Levittowners had moved on after a decade, but a significant number remained, and those who moved did so in most instances (65 percent of the cases) either because of job transfers or a change in occupation. Levittowners who left, in short, did so not because they were rootless when they came or bored with their existence, but rather because they realized a chance for greater opportunity and a personal fulfillment of the American Dream. Most who live there seem to enjoy life in what Lewis Mumford once mockingly called the "green ghetto." While of course there are many instances in which suburban living and the rat race has caused psychological decay, a decline in the nation's quality of life, and the spread of truly mediocre cultural tastes, most Americans who call the suburbs home are quite happy with their lot. Yet, it is precisely with the notion that these grassy, tree-shaded suburban Edens are securely middle-class, however, that another and perhaps the greatest myth resides.

The Myth of the New Affluence

It is only during periods of economic recession or inflation that Americans are made aware of the sobering fact that the nation's allegedly middle-class affluence—symbolized by the suburbs—is very precarious. Americans are prone to forget the extent of poverty in the world, in the nation's urban and rural wastelands, and even in their own backyards, says the social critic Richard Parker, because of the "myth of the New Affluence." Continually impressed with the upward curve of the gross national product, and nurtured on Horatio Alger mythology, Americans have participated in an orgy of consumption since the Second World War, secure in the belief that prosperity was here to stay. But the supposed economic well-being of the middle class is in many ways an illusion. In fact, in an important sense there is no American middle class.

The myth of the New Affluence rests on the gullibility of Americans continually willing to follow the mirage of affluence—the comforting but precarious fantasy that most Americans enjoy middle-class security. This myth has been given strategic reinforcement by the mistaken belief that national taxes have a leveling effect on income, when in fact since 1952 "the effective federal tax rate on the upper one percent of the population has dropped from 33 to 26 percent."[27] The myth has been fed as well by the dissemination of unrealistic governmental statistics which persist in pegging the poverty line at somewhere near $4,000 of income a year—a mythical amount on which, as one critic has noted, "Betty Crocker herself would starve." But even among those who see themselves as enjoying a "comfortable living," the case usually is that they hover at the threshold of prosperity and poverty at one and the same time without ever finding the security they thought was within their grasp. Among those who insist on calling themselves "middle class," perhaps the majority have and always will lack the income to be what they say they are. Living little more than two weeks away from poverty, the vast American middle class hides its steep mortgage payments, its week-to-week race to meet the grocery bill, and its unending indebtedness behind a mask of fabricated optimism. The American Dream, which in other areas of national activity has allowed imperialism to parade as Manifest Destiny, genocide toward Native Americans to pass for "resettlement," defeat to be called victory, segregation of blacks to cover up social injustice, and discrimination toward women to

be accepted as "equality," has also nurtured a brand of self-deceiving economic logic which greatly limits equitable income distribution to all Americans. Crucial to the maintenance of economic inequality in America, Parker concludes, is the sacred myth that "we are people of the *middle* class, bourgeois, home folks, people who still like Norman Rockwell and live decent, unextravagant lives."[28] Surely it will take more than wars on poverty and a continued belief in the promise of American life to dislodge the middle class from its own mythology.

Contemporary middle-class America, it would seem, is a confusing array of mythical contradictions. Hopelessly conformist in their utopian mentality, custodians of the American Dream, members of the middle class remain nonetheless tyrannized by an economic mythology which is a major force frustrating the accomplishment of that which it promises. Secure in its illusions of individualism and the creation of personal utopias, the middle class remains the victim of a capricious national economy which persistently threatens to erode the very security Middle America has worked so o desperately to attain. The middle class, in short, reflects some of the best—and worst—features of American life. It would appear deserving of both praise and criticism. Therein perhaps lies its fascination as well as its continued usefulness to a nation with an ever-expanding mythology.

SECTION III: ROMANCE AND REALISM: THE AMERICAN WOMAN

From the beginnings of Western civilization there has been a tendency to hold women in low esteem. There seems never to have been an era when women directed affairs and were leaders. Social practice, literature, mythology, and folklore attested that women were inferior creatures—the second sex. The history of Western civilization is in important respects, then, the history of interrelated myths—male superiority and female inferiority.

The Greek philosopher Aristotle, who was also a defender of slavery, spoke for an already developing Western tradition when he defined femininity as "a certain lack of qualities; we shall regard the female nature as afflicted with a natural defectiveness." A woman, he continued, "may be said to be an inferior man." The Greek attitude in general toward women was something less than enlightened and democratic. The use of concubines, courtesans, and prostitutes was common Greek practice. And while history records that the Greek prostitute was the most highly educated of her kind in history and esteemed by Greek society, it also reports that the Greek wife was afforded no formal education whatsoever. As the orator Demosthenes put the matter at the time: "We have hetairae [prostitutes] for the pleasure of the spirit, concubines for sensual pleasure, and wives to bear us sons." Indeed, women in Greek society were purchasable, available, and conveniently usable, and "woman's role" was already defined as inferior in the ancient "cradle of democracy."

Succeeding generations of Western Europeans followed the Greek way, their attitude toward women also influenced by the statement in Genesis, II: 20-23:

> but for Adam there was not found a help meet for him. And the Lord God caused a deep sleep to fall upon Adam, and he slept; and he took one of his ribs, and closed up the flesh instead thereof. And the rib, which the Lord God had taken from man, made he a woman, and brought her unto the man. And Adam said, this *is* now bone of my bones, and flesh of my flesh: she shall be called Woman, because she was taken out of man.

In line with such biblical teachings, Europeans assumed it part of God's and nature's plan that women be obedient and passive creatures. Accordingly, the early Fathers of the Christian Church in their studies of the Bible apparently thought it logical to translate the Greek word *diakonos*, when applied to men such as Saint Paul, to mean "minister" or "deacon," while translating it as "servant" when the same word was used to describe the churchly duties of women. Gradually, the dual myth—male superiority and female inferiority—gathered momentum as it continued to enjoy a sacred dimension. No Christian would dispute Saint Thomas Acquinas,

for example, who in the thirteenth century expressed the view that "a female is something deficient and by chance."

The fantasy of women as lesser beings became even more widely established through the ages as a number of Europe's great men—legendary figures in the area of religion, politics, and science—cast the weight of their prestige behind the myth. The venerable Martin Luther, for example, may have been forward-looking in his religious reforms, but was decidedly "medieval" in his view of women. Said Luther:

> Men have broad and large chests and small narrow hips, and are more understanding than women, who have but small and narrow chests, and broad hips, to the end they should remain at home, sit still, keep house, and bear and bring up children.

The famous political philosopher Jean-Jacques Rousseau who declared "Man is born free; and everywhere he is in chains" was also of the opinion that "woman was made to yield to man and put up with his injustice." Science also supported the myth of male superiority and female inferiority. For the best scientific thinking over a number of centuries persistently saw the male as dominant in the processes of reproduction. Still in its infancy, the science of genetics continued to assume well into the eighteenth century that the entire "preformed" body of a human being was contained in the male sperm. Until recently, in fact, the *Homunculus*—"little man in a sperm cell"—theory prevailed. As one historian of science has explained:

> By the 17th century sperm and egg had been discovered, and the Dutch scientist [Jan] Swammerdam theorized that sex cells contained miniatures of the adult. Literature of that time contains drawings of models or manikins within sperm heads which imaginative workers reported seeing. Such theories of preformation persisted well into the 18th century, by which time the German investigator [Caspar] Wolff offered experimental evidence that no preformed embryo existed in the egg of the chicken.

But [Pierre] Maupertuis in France, recognizing that preformation could not easily account for transmission of traits to the offspring from both parents, had proposed in the early 1800s that minute particles, one from each body part, united in sexual reproduction to form a new individual. . . . Maupertuis was actually closer to the truth, in general terms, than anyone realized for more than a century.[29]

By the time of America's discovery and settlement, then, leaders of religious, political, and scientific thought in Europe were convinced that women rightfully ought to assume a passive role in this "man's world."

Woman's Place Is in the "Home"

Contrary to another pervasive myth concerning the role of women, it was not until well into early modern times that family life, as the term is now understood, developed. The historian Philippe Aries in his study of the social history of childhood and the family in France, *Centuries of Childhood* (1967), has concluded that the concept of the family, the idea of a closely knit household of parents and children, did not arise until the sixteenth and seventeenth centuries. Indeed, Aries' findings strongly suggest that, contrary to a good deal of popular mythology, home and family are not at all the ancient European institutions they are usually thought to be. Correspondingly, the "home" with its modern focus on child-rearing, and what is supposed to be "woman's place" by nature, was not "invented" until rather late. The traditional picture of women as mistresses of the hearth, dutifully preparing bread in the oven, busily sweeping timbered floors, and serving as spiritual and moral guardians to their offspring, is quaint, but is drawn more from fairy tales than history. Indeed, not so very long ago, the hearth, the home, and children gathered about the woman's knee were much more the exception than the rule.

Before 1700, with but few exceptions, there were scarcely any "homes" in the modern sense for women to be tied to. Children, persistently seen up to that time as miniature adults, were expected to assume an adult-like role at about the age of seven, and thus the woman's role as custodian of domestic affairs was sharply limited. The private world of homemaking and child-rearing was therefore the creation of modern times. The harsh life of both city and country prevented women from being fixtures of the home. All members of a household—parents, children, relatives, visitors, and, if any, servants—had to contribute to the continual task of meeting life's basic needs. The family, in short, was not designed as a unit separate from society enjoying a privacy all its own, and the modern *concept* of the family had not yet been formed. With family life absent, the house had not yet become a home. As Elizabeth Janeway, a student of the social mythology of women reflecting Aries' findings has suggested, history simply does not support the myth that woman's place is in the home:

> Our ideas of the old-fashioned home may be derived from memories of our grandparents' style of living, or from 19th century novels. We cherish the cozy warmth of such images. But the sort of home we "know" seems to have come into being as an ideal and an invention of the rising middle class, the people who ended the Middle Ages and ushered in modern times. Much of their mythology still surrounds us, and the home they created, as the middle-class revolution spread across Europe, is the home we imagine to be the eternal, unchanging locus of women's activities. Note how this assumption strengthens the idea that, in moving away from home, [woman] is acting to overthrow an eternal image and abandon relationships that have existed since time began.[30]

Recognizing family-centered life as an invention of the middle class—and a rather late one at that—one can begin to see that much of what has passed for reality about women is based neither on time-honored traditions nor the nature of things. The family had organized itself around the child only by the eighteenth century. It was then that the house became the home and a wall enforcing privacy was raised between the family and society. In the process, women became like prisoners. Their social and economic options came to be severely limited,

277

and a mythology defining their new place joined hands with traditional attitudes of feminine inferiority to assure women a second-class status in the modern world. As Aries has explained:

> The old society concentrated the maximum number of ways of life into the minimum of space and accepted, if it did not impose, the bizarre juxtaposition of the most widely different classes. The new society on the contrary, provided each way of life with a confined space in which it was understood that the dominant features should be respected, and that each person had to resemble a conventional model, and ideal type, and never depart from it under pain of excommunication.[31]

A product of Europe's "new society," America would follow these earlier historical developments by providing both conventional and idealized models within which the "fairer" or "weaker" sex would be expected to function. The old mythology of Europeans would grow to maturity in the virgin and enchanted forests of the New World.

The "New" Woman in the New World

From the very beginning of American national development, assumptions about women sharply limited their social, economic, and political role. The early United States was destined to reflect not only Europe's political traditions, but its social mythology concerning women as well. Predictably, history would remember America's great nation-builders as Founding Fathers. This was a point which did not go unnoticed by the early feminist advocate Abigail Adams, wife of John Adams, one of the Founding Fathers and second president of the United States. While her husband was in Philadelphia from 1774 to 1778 serving with the Continental Congress, and she remained at home in Braintree, Massachusetts, with the children, Abigail was prompted to write: "I can not say I think you very generous to the Ladies, for whilst you are proclaiming peace and good will to Men, Emancipating all Nations, you insist upon retaining an absolute

power over Wives." Apparently speaking also for his fellow Founders, the absentee husband replied: "As to your extraordinary Code of Laws, I cannot but laugh. . . . Depend on it, we know better than to repeal our Masculine systems." And indeed, the words of John Adams *could* be depended upon.

The course of events in nineteenth-century America gave evidence that the nation was continuing to work vigorously to shape the kind of country the Founding Fathers had envisioned. By the age of Jackson, a cult of true womanhood reflected a national consensus that women belonged in the home. The few working wives were by generally accepted practice not allowed to keep their wages but instead required to turn them over to the "head of the house." In legal matters things were no better. Having little if any legal status, women were unable to bring suit, give court testimony, inherit property, or make a will. Barred from holding public office, and rather systematically excluded from public life generally, women simply were unable to better their impoverished status. And during much the same period in the South, the plantation legend flowered, with the southern belle being imaginatively portrayed as delicate, Christian, and coy mistress to the fabled southern cavalier gentleman. In truth the life-style of the southern lady was quite different from that portrayed by legend, but in the social sphere she was still prisoner of the European traditions of courtly love and family life which had been transplanted to the land of moonlight and magnolias. Abetting the process, and true to their national tradition, most American novelists of the nineteenth century reinforced the hardening stereotypes by portraying American girls and women as "a gallery of nincompoops, self-righteous prudes, and naive innocents."[32]

The nineteenth-century American woman was taught to believe that she was at heart a fragile homebody. Occasional attempts to break the stereotyped mold through political action generally met with failure and the pat arguments that women were not to be stained by the rough-and-tumble affairs of public life or were too uninformed in public affairs to vote intelligently. Hemmed in by the sweetness-and-light chivalric nonsense of the South and the enforced national mythical traditions of the cult of true womanhood, few women seemed at all willing or able to achieve emancipation or liberation. By about 1900, however, historical forces were already at work to disrupt the entrenched patterns of prejudice which had already been questioned by such famous women as Dorothea Dix, Frances Wright, and Susan B. Anthony. Toward the close of the century, in fact, foreign travelers such as the Englishman Lord Bryce were commenting that in America "it is easier for women to find a career, to obtain work of an intellectual as of a commercial kind, than in any part of Europe." While certainly not a "paradise for woman" as an earlier German commentator had optimistically labeled it, America seems truly to have been—by comparison to Europe at least—a land of opportunity for women. The settlement of the frontier which had consumed much of the energy of nineteenth-century America had, for example, forced a measure of equality between the sexes. As the "old society" of Europeans described by Philippe Aries had found it necessary to share the "world of work," so also did the rigors of frontier America tend to shuffle social and economic roles in the interest of survival. The western territories of Wyoming and Utah came to reflect such realities by granting the vote to women earlier than the rest of the nation, in 1869 and 1870, respectively. Frontier conditions had helped create what the historian Carl Degler has called "a vague feminine bias." And even though such a bias for the most part continued to remain veiled, breakthroughs for women to more equal opportunities were being realized in areas such as education. Colleges on the fringes of the frontier, most notably the universities of Iowa and Michigan, began opening their doors to female students after the Civil War. And by 1900, in contrast to Europe, more girls than boys were enjoying the status of being high school graduates.

During the formative years of American industrialism, the labor of the nation's more independent women had done a great deal to make America's self-made men possible. But the industrial revolution, like the frontier, while isolating some women even more within the home, also had somewhat of a liberating effect in that it helped lift a number of legal barriers which formerly had prevented women full participation in the American way of life. For just as the development of industry had the effect of cutting a great many men loose from the land and the home—where they had until then been coworkers with women—so also to a lesser degree did at least a portion of women in America so benefit. Despite the multiple drawbacks of low wages, dismal working conditions, and other sweatshop forms of exploitation, advancements in industrial technology did much to free the average woman from the traditional toils of domestic affairs. The chores of the home surely continued, and in most instances required that the lady of the house assume the double role of bread-maker *and* bread-winner, but over time the movement of working women away from the home brought them into contact with a new world of urban sophistication, unionism, and politics. The Victorian stereotype of women as weak and timid incompetents slowly began to dissolve. Gradually becoming more wordly as she expanded the orbit of her activities and experience, by the eve of the First World War the American woman stood ready to directly challenge the social mythology which had for so long worked to keep her in her place. With the coming of war the old dual mythology of male superiority-female inferiority came under relentless attack.

The movement of American doughboys to the trenches of France beginning in 1917 caused a labor shortage at home. Their removal from the working force in turn brought a good many more women than ever before out of the home and into the economic marketplace. As had been true in the past, historical forces, rather than a collective free decision on the part of American males trying to right the wrongs of women's unequal status in a supposed democracy, brought change to society. Having tasted the exhilarating atmosphere of life outside the home, women capitalized on their new-found freedom to secure the vote through the Nineteenth Amendment in 1920 and openly challenge a wide range of social taboos. Women stepped from their pedestals in increasingly large numbers and began to sample more freely the formerly forbidden worlds of decision making, smoking, drinking, and illicit sex. Meanwhile, even in the home, women were coming to be seen more as partners in marriage than strictly as mothers, sexual companions, and housekeepers. "By the close of the '20s," says Carl Degler, "the ordinary woman in America was closer to a man in the social behavior expected of her, in the economic opportunities open to her and in the intellectual freedom enjoyed by her than at any time in history. To be sure there was still a double standard, but now its existence was neither taken for granted nor confidently asserted by men."[33] With such women as Jane Addams and Eleanor Roosevelt coming more and more to public attention, the nation as a whole could no longer in good faith continue to hold quite as strongly as it had in the past to the myths of feminine inferiority and incompetence.

The faltering image of women as little other than guardians of the home and baby-makers, then, was fading in the twenties, but the First World War and its aftermath also witnessed an unleashing of various forces whose effect would be to somewhat revitalize traditional mythology regarding women. War had interrupted the steady flow of business-as-usual and, in the words of Carl Degler, broken "the cake of custom," forcing many people to take another look at old habits of thought; but the movement of women into the mainstream of American life was hardly unopposed. The war period and after, for example, also saw a resurgence of sexual stereotypes in line with the popular psychoanalytic theories of Sigmund Freud. In its vastly simplified and distorted form, Freudianism supported the idea that "anatomy was destiny." Theoretically, physical differences between the sexes destined women to a status inferior to men. In the hands of some, Freud's doctrines seemed scientifically to condone the stereotype of male superiority and female inferiority, gave new significance to sexual physical differences, and thus reinforced the associated notion that woman's place was in the home. The Viennese psychiatrist of course did little himself to deter such thinking. His work was rife with what has been called "unconscious masculinity," and a good many critics ever since have pointed particularly to his theory of "penis envy"—women secretly wanting to be men—as little more than Freudian folklore parading as a scientific principle.

The 1920s also experienced a revitalization of sexual mythology thanks to the fiction of such American writers as Ernest Hemingway

and F. Scott Fitzgerald. A firm believer in the machismo, or macho, mystique of virility, Hemingway spoke favorably in his work of the masculine ideal of aggressive and "manly" self-reliance. The Spanish Civil War, the plains of Africa, and the forests of the north country served as settings for his books. While allowing Hemingway to deal imaginatively with decidedly masculine themes, his chosen locales also suggested that such territory was alien terrain for a person possessing feminine qualities. Using an almost equally narrow focus, Fitzgerald portrayed a fictional covey of dazzling female characters with soft voices and coy manners who were superficially enticing but lacked a solid human dimension. The Fitzgerald hero, in short, often falls victim to the charms of a Daisy or Sally who is long on glitter and short on substance. The Fitzgerald heroine, in turn, emerges as a pampered belle with few redeeming qualities. Particularly in such stories as "The Last of the Belles," Fitzgerald helped resurrect traditional ideas concerning American women precisely at the time when women were seeking new images and life-styles.

Given the counter-forces unleashed by Freud, Hemingway, and Fitzgerald, in important respects the changing status of the American woman between 1918 and 1930— symbolized by bobbed hair, short skirts, and public smoking and drinking—turned out to be more cosmetic than substantive. Socially and politically, women could indeed point to their expanding orbit of activity outside the home and to the Nineteenth Amendment, but economically feminist gains were more limited. While it was true that many thousands of women were finding their way into the nation's working force, and some even finding permanent places in new job categories formerly reserved for men, the vast majority of women continued to be tied to nonskilled or semiskilled, low-paying positions. The professional occupation categories were welcoming women at double and triple the rate of the late nineteenth century, but such statistical data in areas such as library and social work and college teaching become considerably less impressive when one remembers the pitifully small number upon which the data were based. The much greater percentage of women in professional positions after 1930, in short, is largely explained by the fact that the number of women who had "made it" had been so miserably low before that time.

The Second World War, much like the First, had a liberating effect upon women in American society. Nearly four million women became new entries to the work force. But here again, job openings were most often to be found in the most menial, least prestigious, and lowest paying sectors of the economy. The tendency still was to have women fill occupations which they traditionally and historically had held. Even by 1950 most women were still servants, clerks, teachers, nurses, telephone operators, typists, secretaries, or stenographers. Again in the words of Carl Degler:

> Two thirds of all professional women [were] either nurses or teachers. . . . Women [were] notoriously underrepresented in the top professions like law, medicine, engineering and scientific research. No more than 7 percent of all professional women in 1950 were in the four of these categories together. Only 6 percent of medical doctors and 4 percent of lawyers and judges were women. In contrast, almost three quarters of medical doctors are women in the Soviet Union; in England the figure is 16 percent. In both France and Sweden women make up a high proportion of pharmacists and dentists; neither of those professions attracts many women in the United States.[34]

The postwar period also saw a deterioration of the position of women in education. Greater numbers of women than ever could be found on the campuses of the nation's colleges and universities, but the *proportion* of women to men had actually declined. Perhaps even more disturbing, especially in light of the American woman's limited success at achieving professional occupational status, was the fact that only 10 percent of the doctorates awarded by the nation's universities in 1950 were to women, whereas in the decade of the 1920s it had stood at 15 percent. Indeed, statistics such as these were destined to prompt renewed efforts by women to once again move beyond the stereotypes and challenge the mythology underlying their subordinate role in American society.

The Myth and Women's Liberation

It was fitting that the latest round of the American woman's continuing bout with stubbornly persistent social mythology should have begun where it all started and where the myths themselves had first been created—in Europe. For in 1953, Simone de Beauvoir's *The Second Sex* was published in France and the new move toward woman's liberation began. Questioning the false sanctity which had for so long attached itself to the rigid conventional sex roles of both women and men, de Beauvoir examined what she called the Myth of Woman and found

> the myth . . . so various, so contradictory, that at first its unity is not discerned: . . . Pandora and Athena—woman at once Eve and the Virgin Mary. She is an idol, a servant, the source of life, a power of darkness; she is the elemental silence of truth, she is artifice, gossip, and falsehood; she is healing presence and sorceress; she is man's prey, his downfall, she is everything that he is not and that he longs for, his negation and his reason for being.[35]

Perpetuated for centuries by social custom, literature, and ignorance, the Myth of Woman, de Beauvoir said, had given birth to the related myths of the family, maternity, and the maternal instinct. The substitution of "reality" for "myth," she argued, was the only way for modern women to escape their oppression and move to the elevated plane of acceptance as full human beings. A move had to be made, she concluded, to "dethrone the myth of femininity."

Greatly impressed by Simone de Beauvoir's *The Second Sex*, Betty Friedan of Peoria, Illinois, Smith College, the University of California at Berkeley, and New York City, brought the new women's liberation to America, arguing also that myth lay at the bottom of woman's social inferiority. Through her enormously popular book, *The Feminine Mystique* (1963), she was instrumental in launching a spirited campaign for women's rights which continues in the latter years of the 1970s. In America, she insisted, it had been women's magazines, the mass media, and outdated notions of Freudian psychology which created a mythical image of women's proper role as being housewives and mothers. The effect of this "feminine mystique" was the erosion of the American woman's creativity, freedom, and happiness. The ultimate core of "the problem which has no name," as Ms. Friedan says, was the "strange discrepancy between the reality of our lives as women and the image to which we are trying to conform." In attempting to live according to mythical standards established by others, women had been robbed of self-identity. They had become "Bob's wife" or "Sally's mother," not significant self-sufficient human beings in their own right. To challenge this mythology, Friedan founded the National Organization of Women (NOW) in 1966, and "Bob's wife" and "Sally's mother" mobilized to free their "sisters" from the multiple forms of mythology which had kept women down.

Based on what Women's Liberation had accomplished by way of replacing the fiction and fantasy of old with more clear-headed thinking, some women in recent years discovered that Women's Liberation was losing a measure of its magic precisely because in certain quarters new brands of mythology were replacing the ancient aura of legend which most thought had been left behind. A vocal and militant minority within the movement, sloganeers and headline-seekers, wanted it believed that all men were "male chauvinists" interested only in using the "little woman" to their own advantage even though in reality there were many men supporting feminist objectives. As much enslaved by notions of "sisterhood" as they had been by the older mythology of male supremacy, the radical fringe of the women's movement had difficulty convincing the nation that most men were animals who kept women in semislavery. On other fronts, and as with blacks, the academic and commercial worlds did their part to aid and abet the new mythology by scurrying to cash in on the new interest in women. An avalanche of books, television productions, college courses, and woman's studies programs of varying quality offered a confused mixture of myth and reality for national consumption. As a result, some persons were creating myths by rewriting history, producing exaggerated heroines such as Phyllis "Soul Sister" Wheatley, Harriet "Moses to Her People" Tubman, and a romanticized Dolly Madison to stand

beside such important women from the past as the antislavery activists Sarah and Angelina Grimké, the writer Margaret Fuller, and Elizabeth Blackwell, the nation's first woman doctor (1849). And the "truth" about women has been additionally mythologized by a small but vocal number of men, such as the machismo-conscious novelist Norman Mailer, who have represented the "uppity libber" as "typical" of the movement and not to be trusted as spokeswomen for their American sisters. In the midst of such confusion, and with fantasy once again posing as fact in many quarters, it seems clear that a good many supporters and detractors of the movement have not as yet succeeded in discovering the "real woman." The women's rights crusade is still being fought within a world of mythology. The Women's Movement has not yet come upon the utopian world free from myth where, in the words of Betty Friedan, there are "no Gods, and no Goddesses" and both men and women are free from their male and female stereotypes.

SECTION IV: BLACKS AND INDIANS: "INVISIBLE MEN" AND "VANISHING RACE"

Most right-thinking people have little trouble recognizing the gross and ugly face of racism when it openly appears. Racism, however, is not always, or even most often, straightforward and obvious in its expressions. On many occasions it lies hidden in the myth-laden value systems and social structures that people design to organize their existence. The force of what Mark Twain once called "petrified opinion," the subtle taken-for-granted assumptions which lay at the bottom of how a society conducts its legal business, can perhaps be seen nowhere more clearly than in the mythical manipulations of black Americans by their white brethren. For it was the nation's segregationist legal codes which for the better portion of the twentieth century conveniently allowed American society to keep the black "in his place" by pretending he was a nonperson. Unwilling to count blacks as Americans, whites allowed the legal system to serve as their agent of discrimination. This cycle of legal mythology, of course, began with the slave codes which defined the black as property, insisting that his destiny lay completely in the hands of the supposedly superior white race. For modern America, however, the development of such legal fantasy began in earnest with the segregationist legal codes—the so-called Jim Crow laws—of the 1890s and later.

The Legal Fiction of "Separate But Equal"

The flickering promise of freedom and equality which ignited thoughts in freedmen that they could sample the American Dream was extinguished but a quarter-century after the "war to free the slaves." Political and civil rights, supposedly assured by the passage of the Fourteenth and Fifteenth Amendments to the Constitution turned out to be temporary. Rather quickly eroded by a combination of unsympathetic public opinion, a cooling of congressional fervor, and backsliding by the nation's courts, black rights were less than apparent by 1890. The glowing promise of full equality for blacks in fact was snuffed out during that decade as Northerners increasingly began to look at the black as Southerners did. Former crusaders for the rights of freedmen grew weary in their efforts at about the same time as many were beginning to argue that the nation was being threatened by new waves of alien immigrants. As a result, Northerners looked with new understanding upon the racial fears of Southerners. While dusting off the banner of white supremacy, and rejuvenating the old American practice of lynching, the southern states by 1900 had enacted a series of laws specifically designed to assure blacks second-class status. Reflecting the prejudice and persuasiveness of such redneck, black-hating demagogue politicians as "Pitchfork Ben" Tillman of South Carolina and James K. "White Chief" Vardaman of Mississippi, the color line became more clearly drawn. A separation of the races was carried out through state and local laws making it illegal for the races to mix on beaches and playgrounds, and in prisons, parks, libraries, hotels, and indeed in most every sphere of activity. But the racial hatred, fear, and discrimination which these new Jim Crow

laws represented was not only to be found in the South. The North was equally willing to accept the legal mythology which condoned segregation.

The avalanche of antiblack legislation in the South during the 1890s was in many instances inspired by similar laws already in force in the North. The supreme court of the state of Pennsylvania, for example, had upheld state statutes allowing the segregation of railroad passengers on the basis of color as early as 1867. And during the 1870s the supreme courts of both Ohio and Indiana had condoned school segregation. Over the question of a Louisiana law calling for segregation of the races in railroad passenger cars, that august tribunal—the Supreme Court of the United States—was asked to rule on the constitutionality of such legislation in the famous case of *Plessy* v. *Ferguson* (1896). Arguing in support of the new segregation laws, attorneys prepared a case which claimed to expose the mythical arguments of those who were seeking to challenge the new racial practices. In mock innocence they said:

> We consider the underlying fallacy of the plaintiff's argument to consist in the assumption that the enforced separation of the two races stamps the colored race with a badge of inferiority. If this be so, it is not by reason of anything found in the act, but solely because the colored race chooses to put that construction upon it. . . . The argument also assumes that social prejudices may be overcome by legislation, and that equal rights cannot be secured to the negro except by an enforced commingling of the two races. We cannot accept this proposition. . . . Legislation is powerless to eradicate racial instincts or to abolish distinctions based upon physical differences, and the attempt to do so can only result in accentuating the differences of the present situation.

Finding this exercise in self-deception "realistic," the Court found the "separate but equal" provisions of the new laws an acceptable legal justification for segregation with but one dissenting vote.

One of only two Southerners on the Court, Justice John Marshall Harlan of Kentucky, saw through the legal fiction of "separate but equal" and challenged his colleagues on the Court to face up to their betrayal of the nation's stated ideals. The equality envisioned by the Founding Fathers, Harlan pointed out, was not at all the type of "equality" condoned by the majority opinion of the Court. It was clear that the ringing phrase from Jefferson's Declaration of Independence—"all men are created equal"—was again becoming an embarrassment rather than a reality for the nation. Harlan's address to the Court spoke clearly to the illusion of equality in America:

> The white race deems itself to be the dominant race in this country. . . . But in view of the Constitution, in the eye of the law, there is in this country no superior, dominant, ruling class of citizens. There is no caste here. Our Constitution is color-blind, and neither knows nor tolerates classes among citizens. In respect of civil rights, all citizens are equal before the law. The humblest is the peer of the most powerful. The law regards man as man. . . . It is, therefore, to be regretted that this high tribunal, the final expositor of the fundamental law of the land, has reached the conclusion that it is competent for a State to regulate the enjoyment by citizens of their civil rights solely on the basis of race.

Despite the words of this former Kentucky slaveowner, the mind of the Court—as that of the nation—was firmly in support of the idea that inequality could be allowed to pass for equality, and the social, economic, and political privileges of the white majority were the inevitable result of "racial instincts" and "physical differences" over which the Court had no control. Armed with the freshly legalized mythology of *Plessy* v. *Ferguson*, American white society quickly pushed the black from view—relegated him to the status of an invisible man.

Despite this attempted mythical whitewash of the "Negro problem," and the nearly effortless ease with which the nation retired from its democratic commitments after 1896, America continued to be haunted by the idea of equality into the twentieth century. The unequal impact of the "separate but equal" decision, and the mythical legalities which served as its basis, were simply too glaring for all Americans to ignore. Some gradually became aware that here was a classic case where myth was serving as the basis for the cultural attitudes, the laws, and certainly the prejudices of the nation. The discrepancy between the country's social and political rhetoric, and the norms and principles it was in fact living by, needed correction. The United States would have to overhaul both its attitudes and laws so as to get practices back into alignment with democratic theory. But before such changes could come to pass, the status of segregation as "a cosmic law" would have to be altered dramatically. An early sign that American segregationist attitudes and racist values were beginning to change was the reception accorded the black writer Ralph Waldo Ellison's book, *Invisible Man*, in 1952.

The Invisible Man Made Visible

A participant in the New Deal's Federal Writers Project, Ralph Ellison received the National Book Award and a National American Academy Arts and Letters Fellowship on the basis of his study of the intricate blend of fact and fantasy which was passing for reality in American society. Intended as a commentary on the ways in which a twentieth-century person in general tends to lose his or her identity in a mass, complex society, Ellison's invisible man was the black person in particular. Repressed in the nation's consciousness, the American black had become even more of an invisible man than his white counterpart, since the cosmic laws of segregation had come to allow the nation at large to pretend that the black American and his problems did not in fact exist. The meaning of Ellison's book lay with its exploration of white mythology in conflict with black reality. In the words of one critic:

> *Invisible Man* is about a central character (who remains nameless) whose odyssey leads him from the rural South to New York and through a succession of experiences which ultimately results in withdrawal from the world. . . . The central character learns that things are not as they seem, that institutions may

The Invisible Man/Woman Gains Visibility
Lejeune/Stockmarket, Los Angeles

mask the operation of quite arbitrary forces, and that the apparent orderliness of the society about him only thinly veils impinging chaos. The more he becomes convinced of the irrationality of the society, the more he retreats into himself, becoming, finally, totally dependent upon his own instincts and intelligence in order to define himself and reality.[36]

White society, blinded by its mythology, Ellison implied, had never clearly "seen" the black American in human terms. Race relations in the United States, in short, offered a classic case of mass deception, where the nation continually played a deceitful game of out of sight, out of mind. In Ellison's perceptive vision the segregated black, pushed and shoved to the fringes of American society, had become a nameless, invisible phantom at once abused and ignored by a nation of "free men." Shortly after the appearance of Ellison's work, however, the invisible man began a move to overcome his status as a nonperson. For the mythology which served as the platform upon which racism had been built in the twentieth century—the deceptive concept of separate but equal—was finally unmasked by the U.S. Supreme Court in 1954, the same institution which had done so much to construct it in the first place. By its landmark decision in *Brown v. Board of Education of Topeka, Kansas*, the Court struck down the separate-but-equal

viewpoint, and a new era in race relations began.

On May 17, 1954, Chief Justice Earl Warren read the unanimous and historic Brown decision, thereby destroying the legal basis for the practice of racial segregation in America's public schools which had been established fifty-eight years earlier. The case made its way to the Court's docket on behalf of Linda Brown, an eleven year old fourth-grade student from Topeka, and through the early efforts of her father the Reverend Oliver Brown. Forced to attend a separate and supposedly equal black elementary school in her hometown, and having been rejected in attempts to attend a closer all-white school by a special three-judge panel, the Browns appealed their cause to the nation's highest legal authorities. Examining the case with extraordinary care (for example, spending seven months simply discussing the matter of whether they would hear the case at all), the Court studied its features from historical, political, social, and legal points of view. And upon hearing testimony from both parties to the case—the legal staff of the NAACP headed by future Justice Thurgood Marshall for Brown, and the 1924 Democratic presidential candidate John W. Davis for an array of forces arguing that existing legal practice be sustained—the Court issued its momentous decision that the principle of separate but equal was unconstitutional by virtue of its violation of the due process of law provision of the Fourteenth Amendment. A year later the desegregation of the nation's public schools was ordered to proceed "with all deliberate speed." It was fitting that the final Justice to read his supporting opinion to the second phase of the Brown decision, concerning its implementation, was John Marshall Harlan, Jr., whose grandfather had written the famous dissenting opinion in the *Plessy* v. *Ferguson* case of 1896. Whereas the elder Justice Harlan had been an unwilling witness to the birth of the grand illusion of separate but equal, his grandson willingly wrote its epitaph.

In the years since 1954, the nation has lived in the sunshine and shadow of the Brown decision. For in its aftermath, America has witnessed both the solid gains justly earned by the civil rights movement and a white backlash of racial hatred. Schools in Little Rock, Arkansas, and Tuscaloosa, Alabama, were desegregated over the protests of governors Orville Faubus and George Wallace. Yet the movement has also witnessed the deaths of Medgar Evers, Viola Liuzzo, and Dr. Martin Luther King, Jr. The crusade for black civil rights has done much to successfully expose the darkest features of America's racial mythology and has at the same time availed itself of the nation's other mythical traditions. For example, it has tapped much of its energy from the nation's most dependable resource—the American Dream. And its leadership has largely come from a figure destined to be counted as one of America's great mythic heroes—Martin Luther King, Jr. Dr. King worked strenuously to provide the nation's blacks with a usable myth of their own—a black version of the American Dream. "I've been to the mountaintop and I've looked over, and I've seen the Promised Land," King declared the evening before his assassination, giving modern voice to the Bible's legendary story of Moses on Mount Sinai. In the end, Martin Luther King's mythical vision of equality for blacks may well hold a key to the fulfillment of the American Dream which the nation collectively has to this point found so elusive.

Native Americans: The Myth of the "Vanishing Race"

While the problem for blacks in American society most often has been that of whites

treating them as invisible men, the plight of the American Indian has been more that of escaping the tenacious hold of mythically created and sharply etched stereotypes. For through "centuries of dishonor" the American Indian has persistently been misunderstood, misrepresented, and obscured by the stereotypes of Noble Red Man and Bloodthirsty Savage. But in the twentieth century, white America's understanding of the Indian has become even further clouded. Even as the old images continue to live on, new myths portraying the Indians as a "vanishing race" and "lazy, good-for-nothings" have arisen to join them. As for the first of these new myths, unlike the buffalo and the antelope, the modern Indian cannot be so easily dismissed and is not on the road to extinction.

The myth of the vanishing race contains enough elements of truth to be believable. Confronting the advancing white civilization over centuries, the Indian *was* an endangered human species for nearly four hundred years. Of the approximately one million natives who inhabited the land at the time of Columbus' arrival, only about 340,000 remained by 1865. And by 1910 their numbers had been reduced to 220,000. In 1925, Zane Grey wrote a novel about the Indian which he called *The Vanishing American*. Embarrassed by their treatment of the Native Americans, whites believed that Indians were disappearing because that belief allowed them to conveniently forget and cover up past injustices. The idea was a convenience also because, if the Indians remained only a historical artifact, it absolved the nation from feeling any great need to deal with their current and changing problems. It suggested as well that the Indian may have played a historical role of some importance in the past but no longer did. The phrase itself also implied an old notion—that the Indian was like a feature of the land, more like the trees and the animals than a flesh-and-blood human being. As modern America came to witness the near extinction of the bison (from some 13 million in 1600 to 34 in 1903) and the vanishing wilderness of the frontier, so could it too believe that the Indian had fallen victim to the same process. Finally, the idea of the Indian as a vanishing American was a quaint but grim image much in keeping with the often expressed idea that "the only good Indian is a dead Indian." The notion that the Native

Americans were fast becoming a vanishing race was, therefore, appealing both for those who saw the Indians as savages and those who had found them to be noble. If it was true that the Bloodthirsty Savage was at last passing on, it could be believed that a major "obstacle" to American progress no longer posed a threat. While for those still believing in the image of the Noble Red Man it meant that at least the "antique" value of the natives as a curiosity was likely to soar.

Even though the myth of the Indian as a vanishing race continued to be presented to Americans through novels, movies, cowboy ballads, and Wild West shows, the truth of the matter was that the Indian population had merely leveled off. The population figure for Indians in 1865 (340,000) remained relatively unchanged for approximately eighty years. Beginning in 1950, however, anyone aware of population statistics could begin to see the vanishing American idea for what it was—a myth. By that year Indian population had grown slightly, to some 357,000. By 1960 the native population had reached 524,000. With the advent of the seventies the figure stood at 793,000. In select cases, moreover, the growth was even more apparent. Due to declining death rates, increases in the birth rate, and the benefits of modern medicine, the Navajo population, for example, has increased sixfold in the past century. No longer vanishing, the Indians are now the nation's fastest growing minority.

The Myth of the Indolent Drunk

The modern equivalent of the Indian as a barbarian is the idea that he is a lazy good-for-nothing. Today's widely held view that the Indian is basically a renegade, in need of both help and policing, finds its roots deep in America's past. The good-for-nothing image was evident when Dartmouth College was established in 1769 partly "for civilizing Children of Pagans." The college apparently was bent on "making something" of the Native American. Later policies of the national government toward the Indian reflect this attitude even more clearly. Ever since Congress first authorized the War Department to handle Indian affairs in August, 1789, the dominant attitude has been that the Indian had to be constantly under the view and supervision of

his "betters." And since the War Department monitored the Indian's activity, the assumption surely was that somehow the Indian should be regarded as an "enemy." As whites began to spread across the continent in the nineteenth century, the need for surveillance seemed even more acute. Accordingly, a Bureau of Indian Affairs was created in 1824 within the War Department of Secretary John C. Calhoun even though it enjoyed only the status of a "desk in the corner." The Bureau's orbit of control was expanded when it was more firmly established in 1834, with army officers serving as Indian agents. The principle attitude toward the Indian thereafter would clearly be that the ignorant savage had to be both cared for and supervised.

A change of symbolic importance somewhat altered governmental policy beginning in 1849. Consistent with the established American view that the natives were more or less simply features of the landscape, Indian affairs fell under the jurisdiction of the Department of the Interior. The same agency whose job it became to oversee land management and the national park system also was made responsible for managing the affairs of Indians who, it was said, could do little for themselves other than harass white settlers on the Great Plains and consume liquor. It was under the banner of the Interior Department that policies offering removal, bogus treaties, and reservations for the "redskins" were established. Since the first reservation was established in 1853, the system has expanded to the point where today 284 exist, principally in the western states. More than half of the Indian people still live in a reservation setting, where suicide rates among teenagers run three times the national average, where one's life expectancy is 27 years shorter than that enjoyed by white America (44 years compared to 71 years), where the average income is approximately $1,500 per year, and where the average length of schooling is five and a half years. Indians, of course, are not statistics, but through the use of statistics the alien white system has almost convinced some of them that they are good-for-nothing, as American society has long believed.

The notion of the Native American as a lazy good-for-nothing has gained in popularity since the Second World War. For over the past three decades there has been an increased movement of Indians from the rural reservations to the urban centers of the nation where they are more under the eye of a White America quick to judge their faults. Today more than 39 percent of Indians live in what the Bureau of Census calls "standard metropolitan statistical areas." The presence of the urban Indian is a current American reality in Los Angeles (60,000), San Francisco (20,000), Chicago (15,000), Phoenix (12,000), and Minneapolis-St. Paul (12,000). Contrary to the prejudiced and simplistic belief held by many in non-Indian America that they have an "inherited" weakness for liquor, or "fire water," Indians have often turned to drink as an alternative to a life of despair. Today, then, America embraces the myth of the Indian not simply as a lazy good-for-nothing, but as a drunken, lazy good-for-nothing. Confirmed in their belief that the Indian still requires policing, White America has noted that Indians have over twelve times the chance of alcohol-related arrests as the average non-Indian. One must wonder, however, how much this statistic reflects the Indian's very real problems in the areas of housing, health, education, and employment. How much does it also merely reflect the built-in biases and prejudices of White America's law enforcement systems? If indeed there are more drunken Indians than drunken whites, it is no doubt much more related to prevalent social problems than it is to any basic weakness the Indian allegedly has for fire water. Obviously all Indians do not conform to the myth of their supposed love for cheap wine and governmental handouts.

Tragically, the celebrated case of the Pima Indian, Ira Hayes, who became a Marine hero by helping to raise the American flag over Mt. Suribachi on Iwo Jima in the Second World War, has only served to reinforce the drunken Indian stereotype. The widely circulated photograph of his achievement and his many personal appearances made him an instant legend in the period after the war. His equally publicized death in a watery ditch in Arizona in January, 1955—a victim of drunkenness—had the undesirable effect of confirming that which whites viewed in movies and wanted to believe about the Indians' supposed need for liquor. In fact, the very essence of the Indians' most recent stereotype—that according to

common folklore they are less able than whites to hold their liquor because of an inherited intolerance for alcohol—was not systematically examined by medical science until 1975. Then, as a consequence of the work of two medical researchers (Drs. Lynn J. Bennion and Ting-Kai Li), who conducted a controlled study at the National Institute of Health in Phoenix and the Indiana University School of Medicine, the stereotype was directly challenged. Their findings, reported in the *New England Journal of Medicine*, stated that there was indeed no significant difference between the absorption rate of alcohol into the bloodstream of the Indian and white volunteers. Alleged physical differences between the races as a cause of drunkenness among Indians, in short, has no solid basis. The depressed social situation in which Indians often find themselves would seem to much better explain the higher incidence of socially recognizable drunkenness among Indians.

Despite such recent scholarly studies, however, it seems doubtful that the Native Americans will be successful in escaping the shadows of myth in the future. One can expect that the myths will continue, since whites still find melodramatic stereotypes about the Indian very fetching. According to one leading newsmagazine, in fact, new myths about the Indian—or at least variations of old ones—are in the process of developing. The image of the Indian as tourist attraction, for example, may be but the latest addition to Indian-white misunderstanding:

> there is a recent image, often seen through air-conditioned automobile windows. Grinning shyly, the fat squaw hawks her woven baskets along the reservation highway, the dusty landscape littered with rusting cars, crumbling wickiups [huts] and bony cattle. In the bleak villages, the only signs of cheer are romping, round-faced children and the invariably dirty, crowded bar, noisy with the shouts and laughter of drunkenness.[37]

In the opinion of yet another observer of Indian affairs, any list of contemporary stereotypes of the Native American must also include "that of the sophisticated, intellectual tribal leader who wears tailor-made suits and carries an attaché case." And of course one's list would be incomplete without "that of the militant Indian; the Red Power publicity seeker, burning buildings, taking hostages, and desperately seeking identification with Crazy Horse and Sitting Bull—the Wounded Knee image."[38] But superficial knowledge of this sort, which makes generalizations based on fragmentary fact, can only result in more deeply imbedded myths. Blending myths about Indians from the past and the present, America continues to allow fantasy to pass for reality. And no one knows this fact better than many of the Indians themselves. A Crow Indian, looking at both the past and the present, once captured the meaning of myth for the Indian particularly well: "We are people," he said, "who are better known for what we were not than what we were, for what we are not than for what we are." Indeed, much can be said to support this idea not only for the Indians, but for all Americans. This is at least one heritage which Americans of every race have come to share.

As in the ages before Columbus, there are the Native Americans. Only now, the opportunity presents itself to Americans collectively to relate to their past in the kind of creative way that Indians have for centuries—aware of the historical significance of their mythology.

STUDY QUESTIONS

1. How did the mythology of Christianity, the myth of scientific supremacy, and the mythology of the frontier combine to form a historical legacy destined to provide a set of attitudes and values making Americans insensitive to the natural environment? List and discuss significant individual challenges to the myth of superabundance.

2. In what ways are the major elements of the popular myth of suburbia more stereotype than substance? Also, what is the "myth of the new affluence"?

3. How has the myth of male superiority and female inferiority been perpetuated by religious and scientific thinking, misconceptions concerning the historical development of family life, the American "cult of true womanhood," and the plantation legend? Con-

versely, how have the American frontier experience, the industrial revolution, and the First and Second World Wars had a liberating influence on the role of women in American society?

4. How did the U.S. Supreme Court in *Plessy* v. *Ferguson* help sustain the legal mythology of "separate but equal" for black Americans for more than half a century? How have such forces as the writings of Ralph Ellison, the *Brown* decision, and the activities of Dr. Martin Luther King altered such mythology in the last quarter century? Also, how have new stereotypes concerning Native Americans been added to earlier stereotypes to further cloud white understanding of the Native Americans?

REFERENCES

1. Jon Isaacs, *Environmental Education Report* (Washington, D.C.: Environmental Educators, November, 1974), p. 3.
2. Stewart L. Udall, *The Quiet Crisis* (New York: Holt, Rinehart and Winston, 1963), p. 54.
3. Quoted in Isaacs, *Environmental Education*, p. 4.
4. Bennett M. Berger, "Suburbia and the American Dream," in Joe R. Feagin, ed., *The Urban Scene: Myths and Realities* (New York: Random House, 1973), p. 108.
5. Ibid., p. 110.
6. Ibid., p. 113.
7. Elizabeth Janeway, *Man's World Woman's Place: A Study in Social Mythology* (New York: William Morrow and Co., 1971), p. 302.
8. Jules Feiffer, *The Great Comic Book Heroes* (New York: The Dial Press, 1965), p. 21.
9. David Brion Davis, "Ten-Gallon Hero," *American Quarterly* VI (Summer, 1954): 117-118.
10. Peter Chew, "Black History, or Black Mythology?" *American Heritage*, August, 1969, p. 4.
11. Peter Farb, "The Birth and Death of the Plains Indians," in Thomas R. Frazier, ed., *The Underside of American History*, I (New York: Harcourt Brace Jovanovich, 1971), p. 334.
12. John Collier, "The Red Man's Burden," in Thomas R. Frazier, ed., *The Underside*, II (New York: Harcourt Brace Jovanovich, 1974), p. 296-297.
13. Isaacs, *Environmental Education*, p. 3.
14. Genesis I: 26, 28.
15. Lynn White, Jr., "The Historical Roots of Our Ecologic Crisis," *Science* 155 (March 10, 1967): 1205.
16. Ibid.
17. Ibid.
18. Henry Nash Smith, *Virgin Land: The American West as Symbol and Myth* (New York: Random House, 1950), pp. 208, 211.

19. Udall, *Quiet Crisis*, pp. 28-29.
20. Douglas H. Strong, *The Conservationists* (Menlo Park, Ca.: Addison-Wesley Publishing Co., 1971), p. 48.
21. Udall, *Quiet Crisis*, p. 89.
22. Strong, *Conservationists*, p. 68.
23. Udall, *Quiet Crisis*, p. 136.
24. Quoted in David M. Potter, "American Individualism in the Twentieth Century," in Gordon Mills, ed., *Innocence and Power: Individualism in Twentieth Century America* (Austin: University of Texas Press, 1965), p. 99.
25. Ibid., pp. 99-100.
26. Thomas R. Frazier, ed., *The Underside of American History*, II (New York: Harcourt Brace Jovanovich, 1975) pp. 278-279.
27. Richard Parker, "The Myth of Middle America," *The Center Magazine*, March, 1970, p. 64.
28. Ibid., p. 67.
29. George W. Burns, *The Science of Genetics: An Introduction to Heredity* (New York: The Macmillan Company, 1969), p. 3.
30. Janeway, *Man's World*, p. 15.
31. Philippe Aries, *Centuries of Childhood: A Social History of Family Life*, trans., Robert Baldick. (New York: Alfred A. Knopf. 1962), p. 415.
32. Ernest Earnest, *The American Eve in Fact and Fiction*, 1775-1914 (Urbana: University of Illinois Press, 1974), p. 10.
33. Carl Degler, "Revolution Without Ideology: The Changing Place of Women in America," *Daedalus*, Spring, 1964, p. 659.
34. Ibid., p. 661.
35. Simone de Beauvoir, *The Second Sex* (New York: Alfred A. Knopf, 1964), p. 143.
36. Donald B. Gibson, "Ralph Waldo Ellison," in John A. Garraty, ed., *Encyclopedia of American Biography* (New York: Harper & Row, Publishers, 1974), p. 332.
37. "The Angry American Indian: Starting Down the Protest Trail," *Time*, February 9, 1970, p. 14.
38. Franklin Ducheneaux, "The American Indian: Beyond the Stereotypes," in *Today's Education* 62 (May, 1973): 22-23.

SOURCES FOR FURTHER STUDY

PROBLEMS IN PARADISE: ECOLOGY AND ENERGY
LAWRENCE, ROBERT M., and WENGERT, NORMAN I., eds. "The Energy Crisis: Reality or Myth," *The Annals of the American Academy of Political and Social Science* 410 (November, 1973).
STRONG, DOUGLAS H. *The Conservationists*. Menlo Park, Ca.: Addison-Wesley Publishing Co., 1971.
UDALL, STEWART L. *The Quiet Crisis*. New York: Holt, Rinehart and Winston, 1963.
WHITE, LYNN, JR. "The Historical Roots of Our Ecologic Crisis," *Science* 155 (March, 1967).
WINKS, ROBIN W. *The Myth of the American Frontier: Its Relevance to America, Canada and Australia*. Atlantic Highlands, N.J.: Humanities, 1971.

MYTHS OF MIDDLE-CLASS AMERICA
BERGER, BENNETT M. "Suburbia and the American Dream." In Joe R. Feagin, ed., *The Urban Scene: Myths and Realities*. New York: Random House, 1973.
GANS, HERBERT J. "The Quality of Suburban Life." In Thomas R. Frazier, ed., *The Private Side of American History: Readings in Everday Life*, II. New York: Harcourt Brace Jovanovich, 1975.
PARKER, RICHARD. "The Myth of Middle America," *The Center Magazine*, March, 1970.

ROMANCE AND REALISM: THE AMERICAN WOMAN
DE BEAUVOIR, SIMONE. *The Second Sex*. New York: Alfred A. Knopf, 1964.
CHAFE, WILLIAM H. *The American Woman: Her Changing Social, Economic, and Political Roles, 1920-1970*. New York: Oxford University Press, 1972.
COFFIN, TRISTRAM POTTER. *The Female Hero in Folklore and Legend*. New York: The Seabury Press, 1975.
DEGLER, CARL N. "Revolution Without Ideology: The Changing Place of Women in America," *Daedalus*, Spring, 1964.
JANEWAY, ELIZABETH. *Man's World, Woman's Place: A Study in Social Mythology*. New York: William Morrow and Co., 1971.

BLACKS AND INDIANS: "INVISIBLE MEN" AND "VANISHING RACE"
CHEW, PETER. "Black History, or Black Mythology?" *American Heritage*, August, 1969.
COLLIER, JOHN. "The Red Man's Burden." In Thomas R. Frazier, ed. *The Underside of American History*, II. New York: Harcourt Brace Jovanovich, 1974.
FARB, PETER. "The Birth and Death of the Plains Indians." In Thomas R. Frazier, ed., *The Underside of American History*, I. New York: Harcourt Brace Jovanovich, 1971.
McWHINEY, GRADY. "Black History or Propaganda?" In *Southerners and Other Americans*. New York: Basic Books, 1973.
NADER, RALPH. "American Indians: People Without a Future," *Harvard Law Record*, April 5, 1956.

INDEX